Sports Analytics

World Scientific Series in Finance
(ISSN: 2010-1082)

Published:*

Vol. 18 *Sports Analytics*
by Leonard C. Maclean (Dalhousie University, Canada) &
William T. Ziemba (University of British Columbia, Canada)

Vol. 17 *Investment in Startups and Small Business Financing*
edited by Farhad Taghizadeh-Hesary (Tokai University, Japan),
Naoyuki Yoshino (Keio University, Japan),
Chul Ju Kim (Asian Development Bank Institute, Japan),
Peter J. Morgan (Asian Development Bank Institute, Japan) &
Daehee Yoon (Korea Credit Guarantee Fund, South Korea)

Vol. 16 *Cultural Finance: A World Map of Risk, Time and Money*
by Thorsten Hens (University of Zurich, Switzerland),
Marc Oliver Rieger (University of Trier, Germany) &
Mei Wang (WHU – Otto Beisheim School of Management, Germany)

Vol. 15 *Exotic Betting at the Racetrack*
by William T. Ziemba (University of British Columbia, Canada)

Vol. 14 *Dr Z's NFL Guidebook*
by William T. Ziemba (University of British Columbia, Canada) &
Leonard C. MacLean (Dalhousie University, Canada)

*To view the complete list of the published volumes in the series, please visit:
www.worldscientific.com/series/wssf

World Scientific Series
in FINANCE vol. 18

Sports Analytics

Leonard C. MacLean
Dalhousie University, Canada

William T. Ziemba
University of British Columbia, Canada
London School of Economics, UK

World Scientific

NEW JERSEY • LONDON • SINGAPORE • BEIJING • SHANGHAI • HONG KONG • TAIPEI • CHENNAI • TOKYO

Published by

World Scientific Publishing Co. Pte. Ltd.
5 Toh Tuck Link, Singapore 596224
USA office: 27 Warren Street, Suite 401-402, Hackensack, NJ 07601
UK office: 57 Shelton Street, Covent Garden, London WC2H 9HE

Library of Congress Cataloging-in-Publication Data
Names: MacLean, L. C. (Leonard C.), author. | Ziemba, W. T., author.
Title: Sports analytics / Leonard C. MacLean, Dalhousie University, Canada, William T. Ziemba, University of British Columbia, Canada, London School of Economics, UK.
Description: Hackensack, NJ : World Scientific Publishing Co. Pte. Ltd, [2022] | Series: World Scientific Series in Finance, 2010-1082 ; volume 18 | Includes bibliographical references and index.
Identifiers: LCCN 2021047914 | ISBN 9789811247514 (Hardcover) | ISBN 9789811247521 (Paperback) | ISBN 9789811250217 (eBook) | ISBN 9789811250224 (eBook Other)
Subjects: LCSH: Sports--Statistical methods. | Sports--Statistics.
Classification: LCC GV741 ,M33 2022 | DDC 796.02/1--dc23/eng/20211105
LC record available at https://lccn.loc.gov/2021047914

British Library Cataloguing-in-Publication Data
A catalogue record for this book is available from the British Library.

For any available supplementary material, please visit
https://www.worldscienti ic.com/worldscibooks/10.1142/12566#t=suppl

Desk Editors: Soundararajan Raghuraman/Pui Yee Lum

Typeset by Stallion Press
Email: enquiries@stallionpress.com

Dedication

This book is dedicated to the memory of Stanford Professor Tom Cover who helped us get started with this sports analytics book and contributed some good analyses that we have included here.

Tom was a legend in many ways and we greatly miss him as a friend and brilliant scholar.

Leonard MacLean acknowledges the support and patience of his spouse Gwendolyn.

Bill also wants to thank the many co-authors he was fortunate to work with including Donald B Hausch and the late Professor Mark Rubinstein who suggested to me to view racing as a financial market and then Don worked with me to make this a reality.

Preface

Sports games and events have much data so they are a fruitful area to study and do betting. There is massive mean reversion in NFL games with scores and prices trending, then reversing and bouncing up and down. Moreover, little errors like a penalty to a player or an error in a call by a referee can change the score of a game and corresponding betting prices. These events frequently happen. In 1982, Bill Ziemba designed sports lotteries for the Singapore Pools and the Canadian Sports Pool. The idea there, being on the management side, was to design games such that the lottery players think they can determine a trading advantage but, in fact, the game is random. For the sports bettor a trading advantage can arise from a variety of game factors. Some games are those with three outcomes which can be a home win, an away win, or a tie. Even in games like baseball that cannot end in a tie, for the purpose of betting a tie can be a one run game. One edge a bettor can have is to exploit home advantage which is present in many sporting events. The reasons for this include: a favorable crowd, building a team consistent with the arena/stadium, travel (visiting opponents that may be tired from traveling to the game), judging bias. This book on sports analytics documents our ideas and studies the results of many events, players, games, etc. We focus on both the statistics of the sporting events and the betting on the events. The subject is fascinating with many twists and subtle complicated questions.

Sports analytics involves the application of mathematical and statistical methods to important questions in the structure and performance of sporting activities. Sports analysts use the same basic methods and approaches as data analysts in other disciplines. Through the collection and analysis of in-game data, analytics can inform players, coaches and staff on effective decision making during sporting events. As technology has advanced in recent years, data collection has become more in-depth and can be conducted with relative ease. This has led to the development of advanced statistics and machine learning approaches.

Another impact of sports analytics is on sport gambling. Analysis has taken sports gambling to new levels. In fantasy sports leagues or nightly wagers, bettors now have more information at their disposal to help aid decision making. A number of companies and web pages have been developed to help provide fans with up to the minute information for their betting needs.

This book is not a comprehensive treatment of sports analytics. Rather it is a collection of applications of analytic techniques to popular sports. The flow of the book is as follows: Part 1 introduces some fundamentals. This section discusses utility theory, the formal approach to determining preferences, which we use to define what criteria to use in the analysis of games and betting. Then we discuss optimal betting using the Kelly criteria and its variants.

Kelly betting is risky short term so has critics, but it maximizes long run wealth almost surely and has been used by many great investors such as Warren Buffett, George Soros, and John Maynard Keynes. The strategies are not well diversified but focus on a small number of the very best investments leading to high volatility but usually the highest final wealth.

In subsequent parts we discuss various sports: baseball, basketball, hockey, Jai Alai, NFL football and horseracing.

In the baseball section, Chapter 4 we investigate who were the greatest batters. This is done various ways including calculating who would be best if they could bat in all nine positions using stochastic dominance and by evaluating their production measured by on base percentage and by batting impact on game outcomes. We investigate the batting performance of three legendary hitters in their best seasons: Babe Ruth, Ted Williams and Barry Bonds.

In Parts III and IV we consider basketball and ice hockey, respectively. Using the linear weights approach, we evaluate the performance of NBA and NHL teams. The contribution of individual players to team performance is also considered. A niche sport for gambling is studied in Part V.

Chapter 5 on Jai Alai discusses arbitrage and risk arbitrage using data from the Mexico City fronton. The prices change as the score changes so one can construct mean reversion risk arbitrage investments with good gains. The same idea is used in the stock market, NFL football and other speculative sports investments. Jai Alai is a sport played in Spain and Latin

America. Like in horseracing, gambling is an important part of the game of Jai Alai. It provides a setting for discussing arbitrage and risk arbitrage in sports betting.

Chapter 6 uses game box scores to evaluate the actual contribution to team success of specific players. Those who contribute the most are not necessarily the best players. We found that defensive players like the famous Bill Russell who won 11 championships in 13 years with the Boston Celtics, and Wilt Chamberlin who only won two despite being the all time scoring leader in the NBA with 100 points in one game and was the all time rebound leader. In the two years 1967 and 1972, when his team won the NBA Championship, he was not the scoring champ. In 1972, he was on the all defensive first team and had legendary stars Jerry West, Elgin Bayler and Gail Goodrich as well as future star coach Pat Riley on the team plus former Celtics great Bill Sharman as coach. So Wilt got a lot of help to win the championship. In 1989–1990, Dennis Rodman, Bill Lambier, A. C. Green and Vlade Divac standout in the playoffs above the great NBA player Magic Johnson. Los Angeles, led by Magic Johnson, was the regular season top NBA team but Detroit beat them in the playoffs.

The NBA playoffs and finals are ideal games to watch and they have many lead changes, mean reversion, risk arbitrage is an ideal way to bet and watch these games. Chapter 7 on risk arbitrage in the 2021 NBA championship discusses the general risk arbitrage principles and its application to various sports betting, political and stock market mean reverting situations. Then this is applied to the NBA playoffs and finals.

In the hockey section, Chapter 8, we discuss player and team impact and determine which players actually contribute the most to team success and, again like basketball and the NFL, the best players are not necessarily those who contribute the most. This is analyzed using the box scores for players and teams with a logistic regression to link outcome to team variables and the player analysis was multiple regressions to identify player variables which impact team variables. The analysis is applied to the 2021 season featuring the Canadian division. Ziemba (1982) set the line for the BC Lottery commission sports lotto for the 1982 NHL playoffs.

In the section on NFL Football, we discuss several topics. In Chapter 9, we show various formulas to compute NFL statistics to estimate the expected value of various field positions, using posted spreads to calculate probabilities of winning, combining odds, ratios, aggregation of performance measures and quarterback ratings. In Chapter 10, we discuss the famous Belichick decision to go for a 4th down with three yards against

Peyton Manning's Indianapolis Colts. We also discuss making optimal decisions on home field advantage, the jet lag effect, two point versus one point conversions, and fourth down decisions with short yardage needed.

In Chapter 11, Peter Cotton shows that on first, second and third down with short yardage, it is optimal not to go for the first down unless the runner can gain two or more additional yards. It is actually optimal to stop short of the first down marker and go for a larger first down later.

In Chapter 12, we show that the odds posted by Las Vegas and other rating agencies are more or less correct so the NFL market is weak form efficient. Hence to obtain winning strategies one needs superior handicapping of player injuries and other factors and/ or superior betting. We focus on superior betting in 12 showing that a strategy of mean reversion in the scores leads to successful risk arbitrage most of the time. This is shown for 2018–2019, 2019–2020 and 2020–2021 seasons in Chapters 13–15. Further demonstration for the previous ten years is in our book Ziemba and MacLean (2018). In Chapter 16, we investigate whether or not the best players are on the best teams. This leads to the conclusion that having many good players is more important that one great player in terms of success and top linemen are important for winning games.

In the horse racing section of this book we cover several topics. Breeding is important so Chapter 17 is a primer on the dosage theory which has been useful for betting and analyzing the Kentucky Derby, the Belmont Stakes and other races. In the Derby and Belmont, the ideas are very useful since the horses have never run so far. In Chapter 18, we apply the dosage theory merged with the track odds to study the 1981–2005 Kentucky Derbies.

Racetrack betting is an application of portfolio theory which we discuss in Chapter 19. There we discuss topics such as rebates, various wagers and their analysis and professional betting syndicate teams. We also discuss betting strategies that use prices to evaluate the worth of bets and handicapping ideas combined with the pricing.

Then in Chapter 20, we visit Northern Italy to go to the farms of arguably the world's best trainer Frederico Tesio who had many champions and undefeated horses. In Chapter 21, we discuss buying top quality horses such as my co-owned Honor Code who was Older Dirt Champion in 2015 after winning The Met Mile and the Whitney and was third to Triple Crown winner American Pharoah in the Breeders' Cup Classic.

In Chapter 22, we discuss the popular Pick 6 and Rainbow Pick 6 and how to wager on them. Chapter 23 discusses some interesting Pick 6's and Rainbow Pick 6's. In all cases shown, the parlay is well below the Pick 6 payoff because the bettors in the Pick 6 focus more on longshots rather than the top horses. So this is a new favorite-longshot bias because its thought that bettors would go for the favorites to have a better chance at winning with a limited budget but they don't bet this way.

Then we move on to major races such as the Triple Crown, Pegasus, Saudi Cup, Dubai World Cup and the Breeders' Cup in Chapters 24–27. Then in Chapter 28, we discuss using our place and show betting system with Ed Thorp at the first Breeders Cup.

Many thanks to Paul Wilmott for inviting Ziemba to do a regular column in his *Wilmott* publication. Most of the papers in this book were revised and updated from columns that appeared in different form in the London based journal *Wilmott*.

Leonard C. MacLean
Halifax
William T. Ziemba
Vancouver
July 2021

Contents

Chapter 1

Utility Theory and Preferences

Leonard C. MacLean and William T. Ziemba

Utility theory allows us to have a way to make good normative decisions that should improve performance. We present axioms that lead to expected utility theory. In reality people might make decisions based on other precepts so we discuss the prospect theory of Kahneman and Tversky which has good points and critics. Finally we discuss various good utility function and their Arrow-Pratt risk aversion characteristics.

1.1. Introduction

Decision makers under uncertainty are faced with a variety of opportunities and must decide how much resource to allocate to the various assets in the opportunity set at points in time. Allocation to assets produces returns (gains/losses), resulting from the changes in states of the system. The returns on a unit of resource invested in assets are uncertain, that is, the return vector is a random variable. The basic information input to the decision on how much to allocate to each asset is the distribution for the return vector. Assuming that the return distribution is known, the allocation decisions are based on preferences for changes in returns or accumulated returns. To structure the decision process, a theory of preferences is required. The theory of preferences concerns the ability to represent a preference structure with a real-valued function. This has been achieved by mapping it to the mathematical index called utility. To put the preference relation for an individual into a theory of utility the following axioms were proposed by Von Neumann and Morgenstern (1944) and Savage (1954).

Let S be the set (possibly infinite) of alternatives for a system each having a monetary payoff with a known probability. There are four axioms of the expected utility theory that define a rational decision maker. They are completeness, transitivity, independence and continuity.

Completeness: For any two alternatives A and B in S, either A is preferred to B or B is preferred to A or there is indifference between the alternatives.

Transitivity: For alternatives A, B, and C, if A is preferred to B and B is preferred to C, then A is preferred to C.

Continuity: For alternatives A, B, and C, if A is preferred to B is preferred to C, then there exists a probability π such that B is as good as (indifferent to) $\pi A + (1 - \pi)C$.

Independence: For alternatives A, B, and C, with A preferred to B, for $\alpha \in (0, 1], \alpha A + (1 - \alpha) C$ is preferred to $\alpha B + (1 - \alpha) C$.

If the four preference axioms are satisfied then the preference relationship can be expressed in terms of a utility function $u(X(A))$, where $X(A)$ is the random monetary payoff from an alternative A and $F_{X(A)}$ is the distribution for $X(A)$.

Expected Utility Theorem: For any two alternatives A and B in S, A is preferred to B if and only if $Eu\left(X\left(A\right)\right) > Eu(X\left(B\right))$ and there is indifference iff $Eu\left(X\left(A\right)\right) = Eu(X\left(B\right))$.

A general proof of the expected utility theorem is provided in the article by Fishburn (1969). The fact that preferences can be defined by a utility function is very useful for the analysis of preferences and the decision problem of choosing the best alternative. In following this approach it is important to keep in mind that it is assumed that decision makers satisfy the axioms in stating their preferences. This is referred to as rational decision making (Savage, 1954).

Expected utility theory implies that rational individuals act as though they were maximizing expected utility, and that allows for the fact that many individuals are risk averse, meaning that the individual would refuse a fair gamble (a fair gamble has an expected value of zero). If $X(A)$ is a random outcome and $X(B)$ is a random outcome with distribution equal to that of $X(A) + \varepsilon$, where ε is uncorrelated noise, then $X(A)$ is preferred to $X(B)$ by any risk averter. With the inverse cumulative distributions $F_{X(A)}^{-1}$ and $F_{X(B)}^{-1}$, let

$$T\left(\alpha\right) = \int_0^{\alpha} \left[F_{X(A)}^{-1}\left(p\right) - F_{X(B)}^{-1}\left(p\right)\right] dp$$

the area between the distributions in the α tail.

Then $T(\alpha) \geq 0, 0 \leq \alpha \leq 1, T(1) = 0$, which follows from the greater variability of $X(B)$ around the same mean as $X(A)$. So there is a class of decision makers who are averse to risk as characterized by greater uncertainty. Going back to the expected utility theorem, this class has a particular type of utility function. A utility function u for which:

$$\int_0^\alpha \left[F_{X(A)}^{-1}(p) - F_{X(B)}^{-1}(p)\right] d \geq 0, 0 \leq \alpha \leq 1$$

implies $Eu(X(A)) \geq Eu(X(B))$ is a concave function (Rothschild and Stiglitz,1970). The area/integration condition implies that the utility has decreasing first derivatives (negative second derivatives). So the risk averter has a concave utility. In fact the degree of aversion at an outcome level is defined by the size of the second derivative relative to the first derivative (Pratt, 1964; Arrow, 1965). The risk aversion implied by expected utility theory has a shortcoming in that it does not provide a realistic description of risk attitudes to modest stakes. To have realistic risk aversion for large stakes produces virtual risk neutrality for moderate ones. Rabin (2000) presents a theorem that calibrates a relationship between risk attitudes over small and large stakes. The theorem shows that, within the expected-utility model, anything but virtual risk neutrality over modest stakes implies manifestly unrealistic risk aversion over large stakes. For example, A person who would for any initial wealth turn down 50-50 lose \$1,000/gain \$1,050 bets would always turn down 50-50 bets of losing \$20,000 or gaining any sum. With utility function u and initial wealth of \$20,000, the first bet implies on a wager of \$1,000 that $0.5u(19{,}000) + 0.5u(21{,}050) < u(20{,}000)$, and therefore on a wager of \$20,000, it follows that $0.5u(0) + 0.5u(220{,}000) < u(20{,}000)$. In this sense, expected utility theory can be misleading when analyzing situations involving modest stakes.

A decision that maximizes expected utility also maximizes the probability of the decision's consequences being preferable to some uncertain threshold (Castagnoli and LiCalzi, 1996; Bordley and LiCalzi, 2000; Bordley and Kirkwood, 2004). In the absence of uncertainty about the threshold, expected utility maximization simplifies to maximizing the probability of achieving some fixed target. If the uncertainty is uniformly distributed, then expected utility maximization becomes expected value maximization. Intermediate cases lead to increasing risk-aversion above some fixed threshold and increasing risk-seeking below a fixed threshold.

There are examples of choice problems where preferences do not satisfy the axioms. The Allias paradox (Allias, 1952), the Ellsberg paradox (Ellsberg, 1961), and the Bergen paradox (Allias and Hagen, 1979) provide well known contradictions to the expected utility theorem. The Allias paradox has received particular attention. From the independence axiom, for alternatives A, B, and C, with A preferred to B, for $\alpha \in (0,1]$, it follows that $\alpha A + (1-\alpha) C$ is preferred to $\alpha B + (1-\alpha) C$. However, it has been experimentally demonstrated that the preference for $\alpha A + (1-\alpha) C$ can be reversed depending on the value of α. The independence axiom is the key to the linearity in probabilities of the expected utility and that property is violated in the Allias paradox. In expected utility theory, the utilities of outcomes are weighted by their probabilities. It has been shown that people overweight outcomes that are considered certain relative to outcomes which are merely probable, a phenomenon which is labelled the *certainty effect.*

There have been a variety of proposals for dealing with the violation of the independence axiom and the linearity in probabilities. One approach is Prospect Theory (PT) proposed by Kahneman and Tversky (1979). The bilinear form of expected utility is retained, but probabilities and outcomes are transformed. The value of a prospect, denoted V, is expressed in terms of two scales, π and v. The first scale, π, associates with each probability p a subjective decision weight, which reflects the impact of p on the overall value of the prospect. The second scale, v, assigns to each outcome x a number, $v(x)$, which reflects the subjective value of that outcome. The outcomes are defined relative to a reference point, which serves as the zero point of the value scale. Hence, v measures the value of deviations or changes from that reference point. The value function is S-shaped, being convex for losses ($x < 0$) and concave for gains ($x > 0$). This idea dates to Markowitz (1952) who commented on the Friedman–Savage (1948) utility functions leading to the S-shape.

The basic equation of the theory describes the manner in which π and v are combined to determine the over-all value of regular prospects. In a simple case, if $(x, p; y, q)$ is a prospect then the value of the prospect is $V(x, p; y, q) = \pi(p) v(x) + \pi(q) v(y)$, where $v(0) = 0, \pi(0) = 0$, and $\pi(1) = 1$ This equation generalizes expected utility theory by relaxing the expectation principle. An axiomatic analysis of this representation is provided in Kahneman and Tversky (1979).

Prospect Theory has its critics. Levy and Levy (2002, 2004) cast doubt on the S-shaped value function, based on experimental results. The class of all prospect theory value functions are S-shaped with an inflection point at

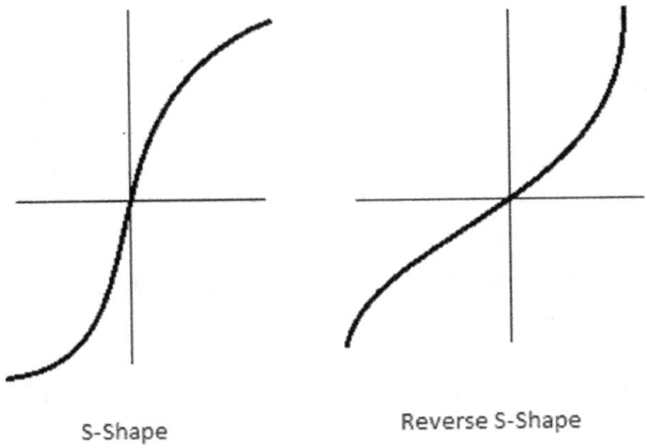

Figure 1.1. Non-concave utilities.

$x = 0$. Thus, $v' > 0,\ v'' > 0$ for $x < 0$, and $v' > 0,\ v'' < 0$ for $x > 0$. This is contrasted with the class of all Markowitz (1952) value functions which are reverse S-shaped with an inflection point at $x = 0$. Thus, $v' > 0,\ v'' < 0$ for $x < 0$, and $v' > 0,\ v'' > 0$ for $x > 0$. Markowitz's function, like the prospect theory value function, depends on change of wealth (see Figure 1.1).

Levy and Levy (2002) define Prospect Stochastic Dominance (PSD) and the Markowitz Stochastic Dominance (MSD). If Prospect F dominates Prospect G by PSD, then F is preferred over G by any prospect theory S-shaped value function. MSD rule corresponds to all reverse S-shaped value functions. PSD and MSD are opposite if the two distributions have the same mean: Let F and G have the same mean. Then F dominates G by PSD if and only if G dominates F by MSD.

Levy and Levy (2002) conducted a set of decision making experiments to determine if the decision behavior of subjects conforms to prospect theory. The focus of their analysis is the S-shape of the value function in prospect theory and contrasted that function with the Markowitz reverse S-shape. With the stochastic dominance approach they take the weighting function as $\pi(p) = p$, so the probabilities are not transformed. In each of the Levy and Levy experiments the subjects decision behavior supported the reverse S-shape value function and they considered that as evidence against prospect theory, or at least the S-shape value function.

By defining stochastic dominance (PSD, MSD) based on the value function while retaining the original probability distribution, the weighting function of prospect theory is not a factor. In Kahneman and Tversky the bi-criteria (value, probability) are both transformed. That is, the decision maker distorts both dimensions. To illustrate this affect, Wakker (2003) analyzes the Levy and Levy experiments using decision weights to transform probabilities based on assumptions of Tversky and Kahneman. The result is that the observed decision behavior in the experiments is consistent with the S-shape of prospect theory.

In the experiments conducted by Levy and Levy neither of the competing gambles were preferred by second order stochastic dominance (SSD). Baltussen *et al.* (2006) augmented the LL tasks with a third gamble which by SSD is preferred to either original gamble, with all gambles having the same expectation. The empirical evidence supports SSD as opposed to either PT or MSD.

The support for the S-shaped function as obtained by Kahneman and Tversky (1979) is actually due to the certainty effect. Obviously, different individuals have different preferences. Classes of functions: concave, S-shaped, reverse S-shaped, represent contrasting perspectives on risk. There is evidence to support different utilities for gains and losses, which are defined with respect to a reference point. When considering gains and losses separately the utility is concave for gains and convex for losses (Abdellaoui, 2000, 2007) as implied by prospect theory. However, evidence indicates individuals are less sensitive to probability differences when choosing among mixed gambles than when choosing among either gain or loss gambles (Wu and Markle, 2008).

An interesting perspective on risk assessment comes from the "risk matrix" used in reliability engineering, where value and probability are on a log scale, see Figure 1.2.

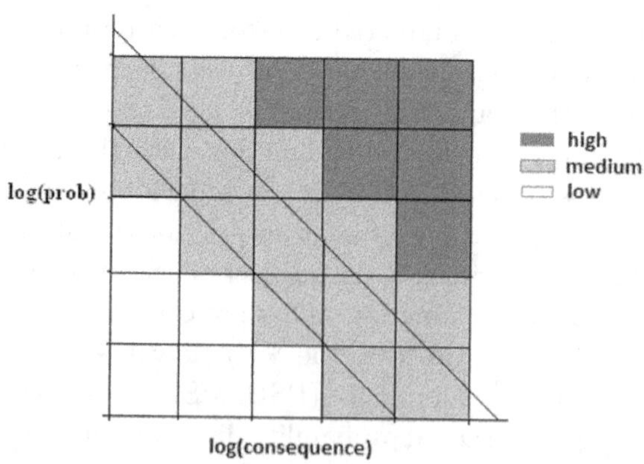

Figure 1.2. Risk matrix.

The classification of risk is based on the combination of outcome and probability. There are criteria for a consistent classification defined in Cox (2008).

The stochastic dominance definitions provide a way to characterize consistent preferences for risk. A standard technique for defining risk preferences is mean–variance analysis (Markowitz, 1952). Assuming a normal distribution for outcome returns, the mean–variance (MV) rule is consistent with expected utility and second order stochastic dominance (concave utility). So MV and PT are not compatible when considering the preferences between two alternatives. However, Levy and Levy (2004) establish that the efficient sets (un-dominated) from second order dominance (MV) and prospect stochastic dominance are almost identical when dealing with a mixture of sets of alternatives (diversified portfolios).

The value and utility functions to this point have been a temporal, being concerned with preferences between alternatives. In financial decision making the system is dynamic and the alternatives consist of outcomes such as consumption at points in time. For example, in discrete time the outcome could be the consumption stream $= (c_1, \ldots, c_t, \ldots, c_T)$. The standard approach to valuing C is to have $V(C) = \sum_{t=1}^{T} \rho^{t-1} u(c_t)$, for the discount factor ρ. With this form of inter-temporal additive and homogeneous utility, the expected utility theory translates readily. However, the problems giving rise to non-expected utility apply to this inter-temporal format. An additional problem is that the two distinct aspects of preference, inter-temporal substitutability and relative risk aversion, are intertwined; indeed the elasticity of substitution and the risk aversion parameter are reciprocals of one another.

Epstein and Zin (1989) consider the inter-temporal utility issues. They define a general class of preferences which is sufficiently flexible to permit those two aspects of preference to be separated. The utility V is recursive, so that V satisfies the following equation:

$$V(c_1, \ldots, c_T) = W(c_1, \mu(c_2, \ldots, c_T)),$$

where W is an increasing aggregator function and μ is a certainty equivalent. They require that the aggregator function have a constant elasticity of substitution. The certainty equivalent can be any member of a broad class of mean value functionals. A form of continuity is required of the functional. Epstein and Zin (1989) establish the existence of the inter-temporal utility V following from the aggregator W and functional μ.

Appendix: Technical Fundamentals for Utility Theory

Utility Function. Consider a set of objects $\mathcal{X}$ and the real line $\mathcal{R}$. If there is a preference relation $\succcurlyeq$ which orders pairs of elements in $\mathcal{X}$, i.e. for $X_1, X_2 \in \mathcal{X}$ either $X_1 \succcurlyeq X_2$ or $X_2 \succcurlyeq X_1$, and the relation is complete, transitive, and continuous, then there exists a function $U : \mathcal{X} \to \mathcal{R}$, which gives the corresponding order:

$$X_1 \succcurlyeq X_2 \Leftrightarrow U(X_1) \geq U(X_2).$$

Probability. The elements of $\mathcal{X}$ are often random variables or lotteries. With the probability space (Ω, B, P), then $X \in \mathcal{X}$ is a function $X : \Omega \to \mathcal{R}$, which generates a distribution function F_X. So $F_X(x) = P[B_x]$, where $B_x = \{\omega | X(\omega) \leq x\}$.

Stochastic Order. A real random variable X is less than a random variable Y in the "usual stochastic order" if $F_X(z) \geq F_Y(z)$, for all $z \in (-\infty, \infty)$.

Alternatively, $F_X^{-1}(\alpha) \leq F_Y^{-1}(\alpha)$, for all $\alpha \in [0,1]$.

The usual order is first degree or first order stochastic dominance, written as $\preccurlyeq_1$ It is a partial order, but the class of ordered random variables can be increased by integration of lower orders. So second order stochastic dominance of X and Y is $X \preccurlyeq_2 Y$, where

$$\int_0^1 F_X^{-1}(\alpha)\, d\alpha \leq \int_0^1 F_Y^{-1}(\alpha)\, d\alpha, \text{ for all } \alpha \in [0,1].$$

The nth degree ordering of X and Y is $X \preccurlyeq_n Y$ where

$$\underbrace{\int_0^1 \cdots \int_0^1 F_X^{-1}(\alpha) d^{n-1}(\alpha)}_{(n-1)\ integrations} \leq \underbrace{\int_0^1 \cdots \int_0^1 F_Y^{-1}(\alpha) d^{n-1}(\alpha)}_{(n-1)\ integrations},$$

for all $\alpha \in [0,1]$.

A lower order implies all subsequent orders, but the reverse is not true.

Expected Utility. The order based on inverse distribution functions also has an alternative formulation in terms of expected utility. If we have a function u of the random variable X, with distribution F_X, the expected value is

$$E[u(X)] = \int_{-\infty}^{\infty} u(x)\, dF(x).$$

Then $X \preccurlyeq_1 Y$ iff $E[u(X)] \leq E[u(Y)]$, for all non-decreasing functions of u. So $u^{(1)}(x) = \frac{d}{dx}u(x) \geq 0$.

Also $X \preccurlyeq_2 Y$ iff $E[u(X)] \leq E[u(Y)]$ for all non-decreasing, concave functions u. So $u^{(1)}(x) = \frac{d}{dx}u(x) \geq 0$ and $u^{(2)}(x) = \frac{d}{dx}u^{(1)}(x) \leq 0$.

In general, $X \preccurlyeq_n Y$ iff $E[u(X)] \leq E[u(Y)]$ for all u such that $(-1)^c u^{(c)}(x) \leq 0,\quad \text{for } c = 1, \ldots, n$.

Utility functions with alternating signs on derivatives, $(-1)^c u^{(c)}(x) \leq 0,\quad \text{for } c = 1, \ldots, n$, characterize types of preference functions. For example $u^{(1)}(x) \geq 0 \; and \; u^{(2)}(x) \leq 0$ defines concave utilities, where marginal utility is decreasing.

Common Utility Functions

Logarithmic: $u(x) = log_e(x)$.

Power: $u(x) = \frac{1}{1-\gamma}x^{1-\gamma}, \gamma < 1$.

Exponential: $u(x) = -e^{-\beta x}$.

Quadratic: $u(x) = ax - bx^2$.

Prospect: $u(x) = (x-k)^\alpha, x \geq k > 0, 0 < \alpha < 1$
$\qquad\qquad = -\lambda(k-x)^\beta, x \leq k, \alpha < \beta < 1, \lambda > 1$.

Certainty Equivalent. For wealth w the certainty equivalent of the uncertain return X is the deterministic value $\hat{x}$, where

$$E[u(w+X)] = u(w+\hat{x}).$$

Risk Aversion and Concavity

Concave Utility:

$$u^{(1)}(x) > 0,\; u^{(2)}(x) < 0.$$

Absolute Risk Aversion:

$$\rho(x) = -\frac{u^{(2)}(x)}{u^{(1)}(x)}.$$

Relative Risk Aversion:

$$\rho^*(x) = x\rho(x) = -\frac{xu^{(2)}(x)}{u^{(1)}(x)}.$$

Global Risk Aversion:

$$\Upsilon(x_0) = \frac{-x_0 E\; u^{(2)}(x)}{Eu^{(1)}(x)}.$$

Chapter 2

Fortune's Formula: How the Pros Wager Using the Kelly Capital Growth Investment Criterion?

William T. Ziemba

Daniel Bernoulli, 1700-1782

Claude Shannon, 1916-2001

John Kelly, 1923-1965

Many top investors in the futures market and in sports betting use Kelly investing since it maximizes long run growth almost surely. The idea goes back to Daniel Bernoulli in 1738 who postulated that there was declining marginal utility in wealth and it might be equal to the reciprocal of current wealth. Thus expected log was the chosen utility function. Kelly in 1956 showed its use in investments. For many applications it results in not diversifying investments but instead focusing on a small number of best opportunities. It is a risky but wise strategy. But is very risky short term since it has essentially zero Arrow-Pratt absolute risk aversion. So in some cases fractional Kelly, which blends full Kelly with cash, might be better. That gives more security but less wealth long term. Fractional Kelly is associated with negative power utility when the assets are log normal and approximate otherwise for non lognormal assets. We discuss lottery applications and good versus bad properties of the strategies.

2.1. Introduction

The use of log utility dates to the letters of Daniel Bernoulli in 1738. The idea that additional wealth is worth less and less as it increases and thus utility tails off proportional to the level of wealth is very reasonable. This utility function seems safe for investing. However, I argue that log is the most risky utility function one should ever consider using and it is most dangerous. However, if used properly in situations where it is appropriate, it has wonderful properties. For long term investors who make many short term decisions, it usually yields the highest long run levels of wealth. This is called Kelly betting in honor of Kelly's 1956 paper that introduced this type of betting. In finance, it is called the Capital Growth Theory or *Fortune's Formula.*[1]

Shannon playing chess with M. Botvinnik

Kelly was working at Bell Labs and was greatly influenced by Claude Shannon, the father of information theory.[2] Thorp, who worked with Shannon at MIT around 1960 on various gambling gadgets, told me that he suspected that Shannon actually did the work Kelly is famous for but since Shannon was the top Bell Labs scientist, management did not want him writing a gambling paper. I know that Shannon liked Kelly investing because he did it with Thorp and was a full Kelly investor in his personal

[1]For those who would like a technical survey of capital growth theory with the key methodological papers, see *The Handbook of the Kelly Investment Criterion*, MacLean, Thorp and Ziemba (2010, 2011).

[2]Photo of Shannon and Botvinnik from Fay Zadeh (1998) *My Life and Travels with the Father of Fuzzy Logic*

portfolio. His portfolio had only three stocks, a typical full Kelly strategy, and made a geometric mean of 28%.

Two great investors who behave like full Kelly bettors are Warren Buffett and George Soros. Evidence of this is in their wealth paths which are very violent with many monthly losses but even bigger monthly gains and the most final wealth. Full Kelly investors have large positions in a few of the very best investments. Their September 30, 2008 equity portfolios were very concentrated. Soros had a 50.53% position in Petroleo Brasileiro plus 11.58% in the Potash Corporation of Saskatchewan, 5.95% in Walmart, 4.49% in Hess Corporation and 3.28% in Conoco Phillips. Buffett has many close to 10% positions such as 8.17% in Conoco Phillips, 8.00% in Proctor and Gamble, 5.62% in Kraft Foods and 3.55% in Wells Fargo. Both of them, especially Soros, trade futures, options and other derivative positions as well.

The famous economist John Maynard Keynes was another Kelly type bettor. He ran King's College Cambridge's Chest Fund from 1927 to his death in 1945. Keynes lost a lot of money, over 50% in the first two years, as did the market index in that depression era. Obviously his academic brilliance and the recognition that he was facing a rather tough market kept him in this job. His geometric mean[3] return over the whole period beat the index by 10.01%. Keynes was an aggressive investor with a capital asset pricing model beta of 1.78 versus the benchmark United Kingdom market return, a Sharpe ratio of 0.385, geometric mean returns of 9.12% per year versus −0.89% for the benchmark. Keynes had a yearly standard deviation of 29.28% versus 12.55% for the benchmark. These returns do not include Keynes' (or the benchmark's) dividends and interest, which he used to pay the college expenses. These were about 3% per year. Kelly cowboys have their great returns and losses and embarrassments. Not covering a grain contract in time led to Keynes taking delivery and filling up the famous chapel. Fortunately it was big enough to fit in the grain and store it safely until it could be sold.[4]

Keynes emphasized three principles of successful investments in his 1933 report:

[3]To measure returns over more than one period, the geometric mean is more accurate than the always at least as high arithmetic mean. Suppose I win 50% and then lose 50%, that turns 100 into 75 which at −13.7% is the geometric mean. The zero arithmetic mean is not correct here.

[4]Keynes' investment behavior, according to Ziemba (2003) was equivalent to 80% Kelly and 20% cash so he would use the negative power utility function $-w^{-0.25}$

1. a careful selection of a few investments (or a few types of investment) having regard to their cheapness in relation to their probable actual and potential intrinsic value over a period of years ahead and in relation to alternative investments at the time;
2. a steadfast holding of these in fairly large units through thick and thin, perhaps for several years until either they have fulfilled their promise or it is evident that they were purchased on a mistake; and
3. a balanced investment position, i.e., a variety of risks in spite of individual holdings being large, and if possible, opposed risks.

He really was a lot like Buffett with an emphasis on value, large holdings and patience.

In November 1919, Keynes was appointed second bursar. Up to this time King's College investments were only in fixed income trustee securities plus their own land and buildings. By June 1920 Keynes convinced the college to start a separate fund containing stocks, currency and commodity futures. Keynes became first bursar in 1924 and held this post which had final authority on investment decisions until his death in 1945.

And Keynes did not believe in market timing as he said:

> We have not proved able to take much advantage of a general systematic movement out of and into ordinary shares as a whole at different phases of the trade cycle. As a result of these experiences I am clear that the idea of wholesale shifts is for various reasons impracticable and indeed undesirable. Most of those who attempt to sell too late and buy too late, and do both too often, incurring heavy expenses and developing too unsettled and speculative a state of mind, which, if it is widespread, has besides the grave social disadvantage of aggravating the scale of the fluctuations.

This chapter discusses three topics: investing using unpopular numbers in lotto games with very low probabilities of success but where the expected returns are very large (this illustrates how bets can be very tiny); good and bad properties of the Kelly log strategy and why this led me to work with Len MacLean on a thorough study of fractional Kelly strategies and futures.[5]

[5]The UMASS *Alternative Investment Analyst Review* published my paper trying to explain why Kelly strategies should be used more, that is titled "Understanding and using the Kelly capital growth investment strategy". This paper is half of the two part explanation of the Kelly criteria for institutional investors. The other paper, "A response to Professor Paul A Samuelson's objections to Kelly capital growth investing" in the

2.2. Unpopular Numbers

Betting on unpopular lotto numbers using the Kelly criterion

Using the Kelly criterion for betting on favorable (unpopular) numbers in lotto games - even with a substantial edge and very large payoffs if we win - the bets are extremely tiny because the chance of losing most or all of our money is high.

Lotteries predate the birth of Jesus. They have been used by various organizations, governments and individuals to make enormous profits because of the greed and hopes of the players who wish to turn dollars into millions. The Sistine Chapel in the Vatican, including Michelangelo's ceiling, was partially funded from lotteries. So was the British Museum. Major Ivy League universities in the US such as Harvard used lotteries to fund themselves in their early years. Former US president Thomas Jefferson used a lottery to pay off his debts when he was 83. Abuses occur from time to time and government control is typically the norm. Lotteries were banned in the US for over a hundred years from the early 1800s and resurfaced in 1964. In the UK, the dark period was 1826–1994. Since then there has been enormous growth in lottery games in the US, Canada, the UK and other countries. Current lottery sales in the UK are about five billion pounds per year. Sales of the main 6/49 lotto game average about 80 million pounds a week. The lottery operator takes about 5% of lotto sales for its remuneration, 5% goes to retailers, 12% goes to the government in taxes, and another 28% goes to various good causes, as do unclaimed prizes.

One might conclude that the expected payback to the Lotto player is 50% of his or her stake. However, the regulations allow a further 5% of regular sales to be diverted to a Super Draw fund. Furthermore we must allow for the probability that the jackpot is not won which is about 15% of the time. This means that the expected payback in a regular draw is not much more than 40%. This is still enough to get people to play. With such low paybacks it is very difficult to win at these games and the chances of winning any prize at all, even the small ones, is low.

Journal of Portfolio Management, 2015, which is reprinted in *Great investment ideas*, Ziemba (2016), responds to Professor Paul A Samuelson's critique of Kelly investing articulated in three letters to me. It lays out the four basic critiques and argues that they are correct and sharpen the theory but do not affect much the good applications. Samuelson points relate a lot to not overbetting and the fact that Kelly investing provides the most final wealth most but not all of the time.

There are various types of lottery games in terms of the chance of winning and the payoff if you win. Lottery organizations have machines to pick the numbers that yield random number draws. Those who claim that they can predict the numbers that will occur cannot really do so. There are no such things as hot and cold numbers or numbers that are friends. Schemes to combine numbers to increase your chance of winning are mathematically fallacious.[6] One possible way to beat pari-mutuel lotto games is to wager on unpopular numbers or, more precisely, unpopular combinations.

Another is to look for lottery design errors. As a consultant on lottery design for the past thirty years, I have seen plenty of these. My work has been largely to get these bugs out before the games go to market and to minimize the damage when one escapes the lottery commissions' analysis. Design errors are often associated with departures from the pure parimutuel method, for example guaranteeing the value of smaller prizes at too high a level and not having the games checked by an expert. In lotto games players select a small set of numbers from a given list. The prizes are shared by those with the same numbers as those selected in the random drawing. The lottery organization bears no risk in a pure pari-mutuel system and takes its profits before the prizes are shared. I have studied the 6/49 game played in Canada and several other countries.

Combinations like 1, 2, 3, 4, 5, 6 tend to be extraordinarily popular: in most lotto games, there would be thousands of jackpot winners if this combination were drawn. Numbers ending in eight and especially nine and zero as well as high numbers (32+, the non-birthday choices) tend to be unpopular. Harvard Professor Herman Chernoff found that similar numbers were unpopular in a different lotto game in Massachusetts. The game Chernoff studied had four digit numbers from 0000 to 9999. He found advantages from many of those with 8, 9, 0 in them. Random numbers have an expected loss of about 55%. However, six-tuples of unpopular numbers have an edge with expected returns exceeding their cost by about 65%. For example, the combination 10, 29, 30, 32, 39, 40 is worth about $1.507 while the combination 3, 5, 13, 15, 28, 33 of popular numbers is worth only about $0.154. Hence there is a factor of about ten between the best and worst combinations. The expected value rises and approaches $2.25 per dollar wagered when there are carryovers (that is when the jackpot is accumulating because

---

[6]Ziemba *et al.* (1986), *Dr Z≪s Lotto 6/49 Guidebook.* shows how these schemes are fallacious. While parts of the guidebook are dated, the concepts, conclusions, and most of the text provide a good treatment of such games. For those who want more theory, see MacLean, Ziemba and Blazanko (1992) and MacLean and Ziemba (1999, 2006)

it has not been won.). Most sets of unpopular numbers are worth \$2 per dollar or more when there is a large carryover. Random numbers, such as those from lucky dip and quick pick, and popular numbers are worth more with carryovers but never have an advantage. However, investors (such as Chernoff's students) may still lose because of mean reversion (the unpopular numbers tend to become less unpopular over time) and gamblers' ruin (the investor has used up his available resources before winning). These same two phenomena show up in the financial markets repeatedly.

The most unpopular numbers in Canada in 1984 were 39, 40, 30, 20, 41, 10, 42, 38, 46, 48, 45, 49 and 1. These were 34.3 down to 8.4% more unpopular than average. In 1986 the advantages were 26.7–8.2%, somewhat lower but the numbers were very similar; they were: 40, 39, 29, 30 and 41 for the top five, the same top five as in 1984. The remaining numbers were 38, 42, 46, 29, 49, 48, 32, 10, 47 and 1. Ten years later in 1996, the top three numbers are the only ones that were 10% or more unpopular than average. The best numbers in 1996 were 40, 39, 48, 20, 45, 41, 46, 38, 42, 37, 29 and 30, which is 6.2% more unpopular than average. Similarly, as some stock market anomalies like the January effect or weekend effects have lessened over time. However, the advantages are still good enough to create a mathematical advantage in the Canadian and UK lottos.[7]

Strategy Hint #1: When a new lotto game is offered, the best advantage is usually right at the start. This point applies to any type of bet or financial market.

[7]In Dr Z's 6/49 Lotto Guidebook (1986), the question is asked "how good are the unpopular numbers?" There are six numbers chosen so the expected return is $\$0.45F_1F_2F_3F_4F_5F_6$ where 0.45 is the payback and the F_is are the individual unpopularity factors. These factors are not the individual unpopularity indices but rather how people pick these numbers in combinations of six numbers. Then the best numbers are 32, 29, 10 and 30. They are not the most unpopular by themselves but in combinations they are better than numbers like 39, 40, 20 and 41 which, although they are more unpopular by themselves are over bet in combinations largely because the lottery organization published the marginal distributions, but, as a consultant, I had access to the six-tuples. Using these factors yields some good combinations with edges despite a 55% take. The most unpopular six-tuples are worth about \$1.50 per dollar wagered with no carryover. A table with many such positive edges is in the guidebook, page 49. Also some popular combinations are worth only 15 cent, about a tenth of the best combinations. With carryover the best combinations are worth \$2–2.25 per dollar invested. McLean, Ziemba and Blazenko (1992) discuss the chance of actually winning and how long that might take. The experiments in the text, with cases A and B uses this research to compute the statistics stated.

Strategy Hint #2: Games with more separate events, on each of which you can have an advantage, are more easily beatable. The total advantage is the product of individual advantages. Lotto 6/49 has 6; a game with 9 is easier to beat and one with 3 harder to beat.

But can an investor really win with high confidence by playing these unpopular numbers? And if so, how long will it take? To investigate this, consider the following experiment:

Case A assumes unpopular number six-tuples are chosen and there is a medium sized carryover. Case B assumes that there is a large carryover and that the numbers played are the most unpopular combinations. Carryovers (called rollovers in the UK) build up the jackpot until it is won. In Canada, carryovers build until the jackpot is won. In the UK 6/49 game, rollovers are capped at three. If there are no jackpot winners then, the jackpot funds not paid out are added to the existing fund for the second tier prize (bonus) and then shared by the various winners. In all the draws so far, the rollover has never reached this fourth rollover. Betting increases as the carryover builds since the potential jackpot rises.[8] These cases are favorable to the unpopular numbers hypothesis; among other things they correspond to the Canadian and UK games in which the winnings are paid up front (not over twenty or more years as in the US) and tax free (unlike in the US). The combination of tax free winnings plus being paid in cash makes the Canadian and UK prizes worth about three times those in the US. The optimal Kelly wagers are extremely small. The reason for this is that the bulk of the expected value is from prizes that occur with less than one in a million probability. A wealth level of $1 million is needed in Case A to justify $1 ticket. The corresponding wealth in Case B is over $150,000.

We can calculate the chance that the investor will double, quadruple or increase tenfold this fortune before it is halved using Kelly and fractional Kelly strategies for Cases A and B respectively. These chances are in the 40–60% and 55–80% ranges for Cases A and B, respectively. With fractional Kelly strategies in the range of 0.00000004 and 0.00000025 or less of the investor's initial wealth, the chance of increasing one's initial fortune tenfold before halving it is 95% or more with Cases A and B respectively. However,

[8] An estimate of the number of tickets sold versus the carryover in millions is proportional to the carryover to the power 0.811. Hence, the growth is close to 1:1 linear. See Ziemba *et al.* (1986)

it takes an average of 294 billion and 55 billion years respectively to achieve this goal assuming there are 100 draws per year as there are in the Canadian 6/49 and UK 6-49.

An investor can have a 95% plus probability of achieving the $10 million goal from a reasonable initial wealth level with the quarter Kelly strategy for Cases A and B. Unfortunately the mean time to reach this goal this is 914 million years for Case A and 482 million years for Case B. For Case A with full Kelly it takes 22 million years on average and 384 million years with half Kelly for Case A. For Case B it takes 2.5 and 19.3 million years for full and half Kelly, respectively. It takes a lot less time, but still millions of years on average to merely double one's fortune: namely 2.6, 4.6 and 82.3 million years for full, half and quarter Kelly, respectively for Case A and 0.792, 2.6 and 12.7 for Case B. We may then conclude that millionaires can enhance their dynasties' long-run wealth provided their wagers are sufficiently small and made only when carryovers are sufficiently large (in lotto games around the world). There are quite a few that could be played.

What about a non-millionaire wishing to become one? The aspiring investor must pool funds until $150,000 is available for Case B and $1 million for Case A to optimally justify buying only one $1 ticket per draw. Such a tactic is legal in Canada and in fact is highly encouraged by the lottery corporation which supplies legal forms for such an arrangement. Also in the UK, Camelot will supply model agreement forms for syndicates to use, specifying who must pay what, how much, and when, and how any prizes will be split. This is potentially very important for the treatment of inheritance tax with large prizes. Our aspiring millionaire puts up $100,000 along with nine others for the $1 million bankroll and when they reach $10 million each share is worth $1 million. The syndicate must play full Kelly and has a chance of success of nearly 50% assuming that the members agree to disband if they lose half their stake. Participants do not need to put up the whole $100,000 at the start. The cash outflow is easy to fund, namely 10 cents per draw per participant. To have a 50% chance of reaching the $1 million goal, each participant (and their heirs) must have $50,000 at risk. It will take 22 million years, on average, to achieve the goal.

The situation is improved for Case B players. First, the bankroll needed is about $154,000 since 65 tickets are purchased per draw for a $10 million wealth level. Suppose our aspiring nouveau riche is satisfied with $500,000 and is willing to put all but $25,000/2 or $12,500 of the $154,000 at risk. With one partner he can play half Kelly strategy and buy one ticket per Case B type draw. The probability of success is about 0.95. With initial wealth of $308,000 and full Kelly it would take million years on average to achieve this goal. With half Kelly it would take, on average, 2.7 million years and with quarter Kelly it would take 300 million years.

The conclusion is that except for millionaires and pooled syndicates, it is not possible to use the unpopular numbers in a scientific way to beat the lotto and have high confidence of becoming rich; these aspiring millionaires will also most likely be residing in a cemetery when their distant heirs finally reach the goal.

What did we learn from this exercise?

1. Lotto games are in principle beatable but the Kelly and fractional Kelly wagers are so small that it takes virtually forever to have high confidence of winning. Of course, you could win earlier or even on the first draw and you do have a positive mean on all bets. The largest jackpots contain about 47% of the nineteen most unpopular numbers in 1986 versus 17% unpopular numbers in the smallest jackpots. Hence, if you play, emphasizing unpopular numbers is a valuable strategy to employ. But frequently numbers other than the unpopular ones are drawn. So the strategy of focussing on three or four unpopular numbers and then randomly selecting the next two numbers might work. Gadgets to choose such numbers are easy to devise. But you need deep pockets here and even then you might ruin. The best six numbers in our lotto 6/49 book (Ziemba *et al.*, 1986), once won a $10 million unshared jackpot in Florida. Could you bet more? Sorry: log is the most one should ever bet.
2. The Kelly and fractional Kelly wagering schemes are very useful in practice but the size of the wagers will vary from very tiny to enormous bets. My best advice: never over bet; it will eventually lead to trouble unless it is controlled somehow and that is hard to do!

2.3. Good and Bad Properties of the Kelly Criterion

What are the good and bad properties of the Kelly expected log capital growth criterion?[9] If your horizon is long enough then the Kelly criterion is the road, however bumpy, to the most wealth at the end and the fastest path to a given rather large fortune.

The great investor Warren Buffett's Berkshire Hathaway actually has had a growth path quite similar to full Kelly betting over a 50+ year

[9]See MacLean *et al.* (2010, 2011, 2012).

horizon. Buffett also had a great record from 1977 to 1985 turning 100 into 1429.87, and 65,852.40 in April 2000 and 296,400.31 on December 23, 2017,

The main disadvantages result because the Kelly strategy is very very aggressive with huge bets that become larger and larger as the situations are most attractive. The optimal Kelly bet is the mean edge divided by the odds of winning. As I repeatedly argue, the mean counts by far the most. Good mean estimates are essential in any portfolio decision problem. There is about a 20-2:1 ratio of expected utility loss from similar sized errors of means, variances and covariances, respectively.[10]

Returning to Buffett who gets the mean right, better than almost all, notice that the other funds he outperformed are not shabby ones at all. Indeed they are George Soros' Quantum, John Neff's Windsor, Julian Robertson's Tiger and the Ford Foundation, all of whom had great records as measured by the Sharpe ratio. Buffett made 32.07% per year net from July 1977 to March 2000 versus 16.71% for the S&P500. Those of us who like wealth prefer Warren's path but his higher standard deviation path (mostly winnings) leads to a lower Sharpe (normal distribution based) measure. Ziemba (2005), reprinted in Ziemba (2016) with an analysis of Renaissance Medallion and the entire UMASS hedge fund database, proposes a modification of the Sharpe ratio to not penalize gains. This improves Buffet's evaluation. Since Buffett and Keynes are full or close to full Kelly bettors their means must be even more accurate. With their very low risk tolerances, the errors in the mean are 100+ times as important as the co-variance errors.

Kelly betting has very low risk aversion, hence it yields very large, risky bets.[11] Hence it never pays to bet more than the Kelly strategy because then risk increases (lower security) and growth decreases so is stochastically dominated. As you bet more and more above the Kelly bet, its properties become worse and worse. When you bet exactly twice the Kelly bet, the growth rate is zero plus the risk free rate. If you bet more than double the Kelly criterion, then you will have a negative growth rate. With derivative positions one's bet changes continuously so a set of positions amounting to a small bet can turn into a large bet very quickly with market moves. Long Term Capital is a prime example of this overbetting leading to disaster but the phenomenon occurs all the time all over the world. Overbetting plus a

---

[10]See Chopra and Ziemba (1993).

[11]Kelly betting has essentially zero risk aversion since its Arrow-Pratt absolute risk aversion index is $-u''(w)/u'(w) = 1/w$, which is essentially zero.

bad scenario leads invariably to disaster. Thus you must either bet Kelly or less. We call betting less than Kelly fractional Kelly, which is simply a blend of Kelly and cash. So half Kelly is half the full Kelly wager and half cash.[12]

The good properties

- Maximization of the expected log of final wealth maximizes the maximizes the asymptotic rate of asset growth and never risks ruin. Ruin means zero wealth.
- The expected time to reach a preassigned goal is asymptotically as wealth increases least with a strategy maximizing the expected log of final wealth.
- The absolute amount bet is monotone in wealth and maximizes the median.
- The Kelly bettor is never behind any other bettor on average in 1, 2, ... trials.
- The Kelly bettor has an optimal myopic policy. He does not have to consider prior nor subsequent investment opportunities to obtain the optimal decision. This is a crucially important result for practical use. The myopic policy obtains for dependent investments with the log utility function. For independent investments and power utility a myopic policy is optimal.
- The chance that a Kelly wagerer will be ahead of any other wagerer after the first play is at least 50%.
- Simulation studies show that the Kelly bettor's fortune pulls way ahead of other strategies wealth for reasonable-sized samples. The key again is risk.
- If you wish to have higher security by trading it off for lower growth, then use a negative power utility function or fractional Kelly strategy. We can compute the correct coefficient to stay above the growth path with given probability.

---

[12]Consider the negative power utility function $\delta\omega^\delta$ for $\delta < 0$. This utility function is concave and when $\delta \to 0$ it converges to log utility. As δ gets more and more negative, the investor is less aggressive since his Arrow-Pratt risk aversion is also higher. For a given δ and $\alpha = 1/(1-\delta)$ between 0 and 1, will provide the same portfolio when α is invested in the Kelly portfolio and $1-\alpha$ is invested in cash. For example, half Kelly is $\delta = -1$ and quarter Kelly is $\delta = -3$. So if you want a less aggressive path than Kelly pick an appropriate δ. This result is correct for lognormal investments and approximately correct for other distributed assets. See MacLean *et al.* (2005).

The bad properties

- False Property: If maximizing the expected log of final wealth almost certainly leads to a better outcome then the expected utility of its outcome exceeds that of any other rule provided the number of periods is sufficiently large.[13]
- If the Kelly bettor wins then loses or loses then wins with coin tosses, he is behind. The order of the wins and losses is immaterial.[14]
- The bets are extremely large when the wager is favorable and the risk is very low. For single investment worlds, the optimal wager is proportional to the edge divided by the odds. Hence for low risk situations and corresponding low odds, the wager can be extremely large. There, in the inaugural 1984 Breeders' Cup Classic $3 million race, the optimal fractional wager on the 3–5 shot Slew of Gold was 64%. There was also a 74% future bet on the January turn of the year effect, see Ziemba (2012), *Calendar Anomalies and Arbitrage*. Thorp and I actually made this place and show bet and won with a low fractional Kelly wager. Slew finished third but the second place horse Gate Dancer was disqualified and placed third. Luck (a good scenario) is also nice to have in betting markets. Wild Again won this race; the first great victory by the masterful jockey Pat Day.
- One overinvests when the problem data is uncertain. Investing more than the optimal capital growth wager is dominated in a growth-security sense. Hence, if the problem data provides probabilities, edges and odds that may be in error, then the suggested wager will be too large.
- The total amount wagered swamps the winnings — that is, there is much churning.
- The unweighted average rate of return converges to half the arithmetic rate of return. As with the above bad property, this indicates that you do not seem to win as much as you expect.
- Betting double the optimal Kelly bet reduces the growth rate of wealth to zero plus the risk free rate.[15]

---

[13] *Counter Example:* $u(x) = x, 1/2 < p < 1$, Bernoulli trials $f = 1$ maximizes $EU(x)$ but $f = 2p - 1 < 1$ maximizes $ElogX_N$.

[14] The order of the wins and losses is immaterial for one, two, ..., sets of trials since $(1+\gamma)(1-\gamma)X_0 = (1-\gamma^2)X_0 < X_0$. This is not true for favorable games.

[15] See Stutzer (1998) and Janecek (1999). Proof that betting exactly double the Kelly criterion amount leads to a growth rate equal to the risk free rate. This result is due to Thorp (1997), Stutzer (1998) and Janacek (1998) and possibly others. The following simple proof is due to Harry Markowitz as reprinted in Ziemba (2003).

- Despite its superior long-run growth properties, it is possible to have very poor return outcome. For example, making 700 wagers all of which have a 14% advantage, the least of which had a 19% chance of winning can turn \$1,000 into \$18. But with full Kelly 16.6% of the time \$1,000 turns into at least \$100,000. Half Kelly does not help much as \$1,000 can become \$145 and the growth is much lower with only \$100,000 plus final wealth 0.1% of the time.
- It can take a long time for a Kelly bettor to dominate an essentially different strategy. In fact this time may be without limit.[16]

In continuous time

$$g_p = E_p - \frac{1}{2} V_p$$

E_p, V_p, g_p are the portfolio expected return, variance and expected log, respectively. In the CAPM

$$E_p = r_o + (E_M - r_0)X$$

$$V_p = \sigma_M^2 X^2$$

where X is the portfolio weight and r_0 is the risk free rate. Collecting terms and setting the derivative of g_p to zero yields

$$X = (E_M - r_0)/\sigma_M^2$$

which is the optimal Kelly bet with optimal growth rate

$$\begin{aligned} g^* &= r_0 + (E_M - r_0)^2 - \frac{1}{2}[(E_M r_0)/\sigma_M^2]^2 \sigma_M^2 \\ &= r_0 + (E_M - r_0)^2/\sigma_M^2 - \frac{1}{2}(E_M - r_0)^2/\sigma_M^2 \\ &= r_0 + \frac{1}{2}[(E - M - r))/\sigma_M]^2. \end{aligned}$$

Substituting double Kelly, namely $Y = 2X$ for X above into

$$g_p = r_0 + (E_M - r_0)Y - \frac{1}{2}\sigma_M^2 Y^2$$

and simplifying yields

$$g_0 - r_0 = 2(E_M - r_0)^2/\sigma_M^2 - \frac{4}{2}(E_M - r_0)^2/\sigma_M^2 = 0.$$

Hence, $g_0 = r_0$ when $Y = 2S$.

The CAPM assumption is not needed. For a more general proof and illustration, see Thorp (2006).

[16]Suppose $\mu_\alpha = 20\%$, $\mu_\beta = 10\%$, $\sigma_\alpha = \sigma_\beta = 10\%$. Then in five years A is ahead of B with 95% confidence. But if $\sigma_\alpha = 20, \sigma_\beta = 10\%$ with the same means, it takes 157 years for A to beat B with 95% confidence. In a coin tossing suppose game A has an edge of 1.0% and game B 1.1%. It takes two million trials to have an 84% chance that game A dominates game B, see Thorp (2006).

Chapter 3

Rating Batters in Baseball

Leonard C. MacLean and William T. Ziemba

In this chapter we evaluate the greatest batters in baseball. We do this several ways using stochastic dominance, by allowing the batters to bat in all nine positions, and finally how many standard deviations their batting average is above that of the average baseball player. This latter idea is used for other sports such as basketball (Chapter 6), hockey (Chapter 8) and NFL football (Chapter 16).[1]

3.1. Introduction: Who is the Best?

People are naturally competitive and opinionated. A good deal of space is devoted to discussion over the "best" at a particular sporting activity. This may be supported by evidence garnered from the mountains of statistics collected in data bases covering the decades of competition. Since the records (including video) on sporting events are almost complete, it is reasonable to expect that the information on superior performance is available for analysis. The game with the longest record of statistical comparisons is baseball (James, 1994). Let's consider batting in baseball. The standard batting performance statistic is batting average:

$$BA = \frac{Nh}{Nb},$$

where Nh is the number of hits, and Nb is the number of at bats. Bases on balls and sacrifices are not included as an at bat. The celebrated batters are players with high BA' s. All baseball aficionado' s know that Ty Cobb had the highest ever batting average at 0.367. Is Ty the top performing hitter?

[1]Thanks to Steven Moffitt for helpful comments.

Over the years, the overall batting average is about 0.260. Meanwhile, the pitching has gotten tougher and tougher. Rarely does a pitcher go the full 9 innings (complete game). The current pitching pattern is for five strong innings for the "starter", followed by a parade of flame throwers to secure a lead. So the batters face top pitching every inning and need to prepare to keep up.

A good way to evaluate the best players is to compare them to a suitable benchmark computed from statistics on hitters playing at the same time. For example, batting average could be standardized using the league average and standard deviation. A player is rated by how many standard deviations they are better than the league average. In the early part of the 20th century, a number of players were able to hit over .400 including Ty Cobb, Rogers Hornsby (.424 in 1924 and .403 in 1925), Hugh Duffy (highest: .438 in 1894), and others. However, the league average in 1894 was .303. League averages were high in the Ruth era. The National League average was .303 in 1930.

Later, Ted Williams hit .406 in 1941, when the American League average was .266. Williams, sure of himself, went into the last day of the season with an average of .3995. His manager said you can sit out today and finish with a rounded .400. Williams wanted to really earn the .400, so played a double header and had six hits in eight bats. No one has reached 400 since, although George Brett's .390 in 1980 was close. Williams won three MVP awards but did not win in 1941. In that year Joe DiMaggio set the record of 56 consecutive games with a hit, another record not ever reached again. Pete Rose was close at 44 in 1978.

There are a number of players in baseball who were three standard deviation hitters in a season, including Ted Williams, Ty Cobb, Rogers Hornsby, George Brett and Barry Bonds. But there are no 4 BA Hitters. Ruth was also a very good hitter. He hit .392 in 1923, .376 in 1920, .378 in 1921, .372 in 1926, .378 in 1924, and ended with a career average of .342. Williams had a career average of .344. Ruth's batting average record is phenomenal but it is not four standard deviations. However, for home runs Babe Ruth was more than 4 standard deviations above the league average. We all know that he hit 60 in 1927, but he hit 59 in 1921 and 54 in 1920 and 1928. What's impressive is that when Ruth was hitting 50+ home runs per year, the other best players were far below (next highest of 19 in 1920, 24 in 1921, 47 in 1927, 27 in 1928).

Another four standard deviation player was Wayne Gretzky in hockey in 1981–82 to 1986–87. In that span of seasons, Gretzky's points were more

Table 3.1. Legends of baseball — career.

Name	AV	OBP	SLG	OERA
Ted Williams	0.344	0.480	0.634	13.200
Babe Ruth	0.342	0.471	0.690	13.190
Lou Gehrig	0.340	0.445	0.632	11.190
Jimmie Foxx	0.325	0.427	0.609	10.140
Hank Greenberg	0.313	0.410	0.605	9.440
Mickey Mantle	0.298	0.422	0.557	9.310
Stan Musial	0.331	0.416	0.559	9.152
Ty Cobb	0.367	0.429	0.512	9.148
Billy Hamilton	0.344	0.449	0.432	9.010
Tris Speaker	0.344	0.422	0.500	8.810

Table 3.2. Season statistics — TopTen.

Name	Year	AV	OBP	SLG	OERA
Ted Williams	1941	0.406	0.549	0.735	19.62
Babe Ruth	1923	0.393	0.542	0.764	19.13
Babe Ruth	1920	0.376	0.528	0.847	18.71
Ted Williams	1957	0.388	0.523	0.731	17.34
Babe Ruth	1921	0.378	0.509	0.846	17.22
Babe Ruth	1926	0.372	0.513	0.737	16.51
Babe Ruth	1924	0.378	0.510	0.739	16.32
Rogers Hornsby	1924	0.424	0.506	0.696	15.80
Hugh Duffy	1894	0.438	0.501	0.690	15.58
Rogers Hornsby	1925	0.403	0.487	0.756	15.15

than 50% higher than the next best scorer, see Chapter 8. Other candidates for four sigma status are: Aaron Rodgers QB rating in NFL football, Roger Federer and Serena Williams in tennis, Pele in soccer, and Michael Phelps in swimming (23 olympic medals).

One challenge in comparing performance is the rating on multiple criteria. In baseball hitting is traditionally rated by average, home runs and runs batted in. It is rare that a player leads in all three (triple crown), although N. Lajoie, T. Cobb, R. Hornsby, L. Gehrig. J. Fox, T. Williams, M. Mantle and M. Cabrera have accomplished the feat. A single performance statistic was proposed by Cover and Keilers (1977). Clearly runs win games. The offensive earned run average (OERA) in baseball is the expected number of earned runs per game a player would score if he batted in all nine positions. To calculate this, it is assumed the sacrifices do not count, errors are counted as outs, runners do not advance on outs, singles advance a runner two bases, a double scores a runner from first base, and there are no double plays. Of course this is hypothetical.

Well, who is the best by OERA? Table 3.1 presents the top 10 results. The OBP is the on base percentage, which includes walks. The SLG is the slugging percentage, which is the total bases achieved divided by at bats.

Great hitters excel over many years, but some years stand out. In Table 3.2 are the best seasons by the OERA statistic. Williams has the best season in 1941, but Ruth had 5 of the 10 best seasons.

3.2. Stochastic Dominance

The OERA analysis is hypothetical. There is a wealth of actual performance data on baseball games, teams and players. Sports games are games of chance. In baseball an at bat is a contest between the batter and pitcher. The outcomes vary: {out, sacrifice, base on balls, single, double, triple, home run}. Each of those outcomes has a chance of occurrence: $\{p_0, p_1, p_2, p_3, p_4, p_5, p_6, p_7\}$, with the chances depending on the hitter. Of course other factors may affect the chances in an at bat (pitcher, park, time of day, score), but we will assume over the long run those systematic factors affect batters equally. A random variable is a mapping of outcomes to the real numbers, with corresponding probabilities. Table 3.3 gives a mapping, which reflects judgement of the hitting impact.

Stochastic dominance is an ordering of random variables based on characteristics of the distribution as defined by the values and probabilities. (Levy, 1973; MacLean and Ziemba, 2015).

1. **First order dominance** is a comparison of the inverse cumulative distributions for two random variables. If one inverse cumulative is above another then the higher random variable dominates. This is a partial order since distributions may intersect. A total order is found by

Table 3.3. Batting impact score.

Value	Description	Probability
0	Out	p_0
1	Sacrifice or Base on balls or Single	p_1
2	Double	p_2
3	Triple	p_3
4	Home run	p_4

calculating the area below the inverse cumulative as shown in Figure 3.1. The area is reported as the measure γ_1.

2. **Second order dominance** is a comparison of Lorenz curves (Lorenz, 1905). The Lorenz curve is the integrated inverse cumulative distribution to each probability value. Again, a complete order is determined from the area under the Lorenz curve as shown in Figure 3.1. The area is reported as the measure γ_2.

The stochastic dominance measures were calculated for the 10 hitting legends in Table 3.2, and the results are in Table 3.4.

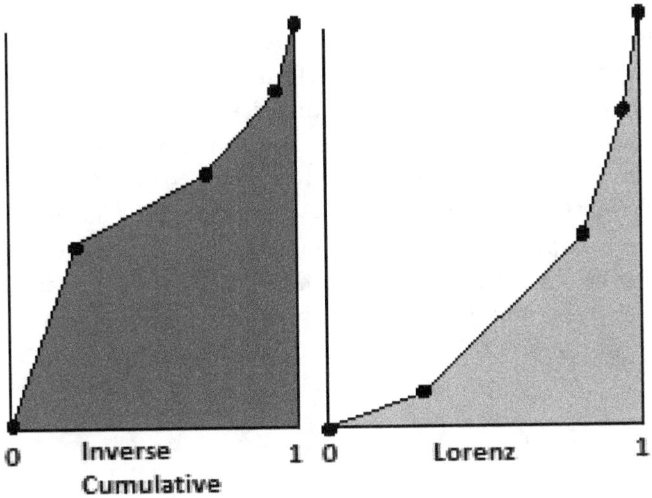

Figure 3.1. Stochastic dominance.

Table 3.4. Legends.

Name	OERA	γ_1	γ_2
Ted Williams	13.200	0.709109	0.521113
Babe Ruth	13.190	0.750025	0.530537
Lou Gehrig	11.190	0.691018	0.496958
Jimmie Foxx	10.140	0.667696	0.477017
Hank Greenberg	9.440	0.660297	0.468738
Mickey Mantle	9.310	0.635186	0.460323
Stan Musial	9.152	0.615210	0.454712
Ty Cobb	9.148	0.560437	0.450395
Billy Hamilton	9.010	0.522825	0.455458
Tris Speaker	8.810	0.562180	0.447876

There is a lot of agreement between the rankings on the measures OERA, γ_1 and γ_2. However, Babe Ruth jumps ahead of Ted Williams (largely based on his home run numbers). On γ_2, Billy Hamilton passes Ty Cobb, and this is based on walks — on base percentage. The strength of the measures γ_1 and γ_2 is the foundation on stochastic dominance.

3.3. Benchmarking

We cannot finish without commenting on the line-up presented by the analysis. All the listed hitters are white and from decades well past. Comparisons across eras are fraught with problems. Early African American players such as Josh Gibson and Sachel Page are omitted. Advances in training, technology, and rewards raises the performance level, and for all competitors. We simply need to look at the statistics on sports where competition is against the clock or tape measure. Track athletes run faster and jump higher than ever. This advance equally applies to players on teams. The accomplishments of recent standouts such as Roger Clemens and Barry Bonds need the proper context for analysis. The challenge is to use the appropriate benchmark against which an athlete should be compared. The gap between Babe Ruth and his benchmark may still be larger than the gap for Barry Bonds. Let's see what the data tells us.

Chapter 4

The Expected Utility of Performance: Dominant Batting Seasons in Baseball

Leonard C. MacLean, William T. Ziemba and Austin Krogan

The random output or production from alternative systems is usually compared using principles of expected utility or stochastic dominance. The output from batting in a baseball season is a random variable, which for comparability is transformed to a benchmark season to adjust for seasonal factors. In this chapter, the performance of three great baseball hitters: Babe Ruth, Ted Williams and Barry Bonds, is standardized for season and then compared using measures of stochastic dominance.

4.1. Introduction

Hitting a round ball with a round bat is a challenge. In major league baseball the ball is thrown at great speed and rotation and there are eight players in the field covering much of the ground. It is small wonder the success rate overall is approximately a quarter of at bats. In spite of the difficulty in hitting there are exceptional batters in every season. A popular statistic for summarizing batting performance is OPS - on-base percentage plus slugging percentage. In Table 4.1 are listed the top 10 hitting seasons by players as determined by OPS.

The hitters listed in Table 4.1 were wonders in their time and were feared by opposition pitchers. Bonds, Ruth and Williams were also leaders in bases on balls. They were often walked intentionally rather than suffer the consequences of challenging them with hitable pitches. Former ballplayer Ray Henningsen says "the really good hitters whom I have seen have had the ability to wait on pitches. This means they have had to be very strong, very quick with their hands ("quick bat") and it means that throwing them an off speed pitch or breaking ball is doing them a favor. Bonds, I think, was

Table 4.1. Top OPS seasons.

Rank	Name	OPS	Year
1	Barry Bonds	1.4217	2004
2	Barry Bonds	1.3807	2002
3	Babe Ruth	1.3791	1920
4	Barry Bonds	1.3785	2001
5	Babe Ruth	1.3586	1921
6	Babe Ruth	1.3089	1923
7	Ted Williams	1.2875	1941
8	Barry Bonds	1.2778	2003
9	Babe Ruth	1.2582	1927
10	Ted Williams	1.2566	1957

unbelievable at waiting, like no other hitter I have ever seen. He hardly ever swung at bad pitches and he hit left and right handed pitchers equally well. I had seen Williams mostly after he had retired. I saw him at spring training one year put a glove standing up in right center field and then asked a bunch of us standing around the batting cage if we believed he could knock that glove over in five swings. Amazingly he did it in four swings, hitting it on one bounce on the fourth swing. That cost me a hundred bucks."

In this chapter, we evaluate the performance of these great hitters. An aggregate performance measure is defined which incorporates the components of the triple crown: average, power, runs batted in. A comparison of players from differing eras is problematic. We will adjust for the performance in an era by standardizing in the fashion of rates in epidemiology. Of course this adjustment is a numbers game and is not intended to diminish the outstanding accomplishments.

4.2. Aggregate Performance

For a batting system at times $\{0, 1, \ldots, T\}$ there are successes at random times, with $A(T) = \{t_1 < \cdots < t_n \leq T\}$ = the set of success times. We use the term *success* to refer to an *at bat*. Each success has a random impact defined as $X_{t_i}, t_i \in A(T)$. It will be assumed that impacts are real valued, $X_{t_i} \in \Re$, defined by the production of the success. The batting event is repeated in scheduled games over the course of a season and a career. The accumulation of success impacts to time T is the total impact. Consider, then, the accumulated impact to time T:

$$Y(T) = \sum_{t_i \in A(T)} X_{t_i}. \tag{4.1}$$

Table 4.2. Batting score sheet.

						t						
		1	2	3	4	5	6	7	8	9	10	Y^*
	0		√	√		√		√		√	√	0
	1	√					√					2
	2								√			4
X	3											4
	4				√							8
	5											8
	6											8
	7											8
	Y	1	1	1	5	5	6	6	8	8	8	

The stochastic process $\{Y(t), t = 0, 1, \ldots, T\}$ is the accumulated impact process. It is also referred to as the *batting process*. $Y(T)$ is random in two respects: it has a random number of successes; each of the impacts is a random variable.

Consider an observed trajectory from the batting process to time T, denoted by $y(T) \in Y(T)$. The trajectory is determined by the set $\{(t_i, x_{t_i}), i = 1, \ldots, n(T)\}$, where $n(T)$ is the number of successes, t_i is a success time, and x_{t_i} is the impact of the success at time $t_i, i = 1, \ldots n(T)$. The value of the process at time T for the trajectory is

$$y(T) = \sum_{i=1}^{n(T)} x_{t_i}.$$

If $n(T, x)$ is the number of successes with impact x, then an alternative or *complementary* representation of the observed batting process value is

$$y^*(T) = \sum_{x \geq 0} n(T, x) \cdot x,$$

where $n(T, x)$ is the number of successes with impact x. It is clear that $y(T) = y^*(T)$. An illustration of the alternative representations of the batting process is presented in Table 4.2, where a tick indicates the impact class. The time axis is discretized to indicate trials (at bats), and impact of an event (plate appearance) is restricted to a 7 point scale. The zero impact is the batting failure. This is a traditional scoring card for the batting process. The margins show the accumulated impact either to a point in time (column) or to a impact level (row). With zero the impact of an out, then $\frac{1}{T} y^*(T) = \frac{1}{T} \sum_{x \geq 0} n(T, x) \cdot x = \frac{1}{T} \sum_{i=1}^{7} n(T, i) \cdot i =$

$\left[\frac{n(T)}{T}\right] \times \left[\sum_{i=1}^{7} \frac{n(T,i)}{n(T)} \cdot i\right]$. In this format the batting process is the product of the success rate (on base percentage) and the expected impact of a successful at bat.

4.2.1. *Batting Impact*

The effects of batting success vary depending on the role it plays in the outcome of the game. Impact is a score corresponding to the beneficial effect and incorporates the various contributions to game success. Let

$$X_t = \text{impact of a batting success at plate appearance } t. \tag{4.2}$$

The impact of a batting success is a non-negative number which may depend on the state of the system (opponent, inning, score, runners) at the time of batting. The hitting component is recorded by X_{1t} =number of bases achieved. The runs scored component is given by X_{2t} =runners plated in addition to the hitter. An impact score based on the bases achieved and the runs scored is $X_t = X_{1t} + X_{2t}$. A variation on this impact measure is discussed in Hardegree (2015). An illustration is given in Table 4.3. The notation is: O — out; S — sacrifice to gain a run or base; kB — k bases achieved; HR — home run; jR — j additional runs scored. Note that a "walk" and "hit by pitch" are recorded as $X = 1$, since first base is achieved.

The impact defined in Table 4.3 incorporates the standard batting performance measures $\{OBP$: on base percentage, SLG: slugging percentage, RBI: runs batted in$\}$, in a single measure. The "runs batted in" are assigned to the batter, so that $X = X_1 + X_2$. It is possible to assign partial credit to the batter with $X = X_1 + \alpha X_2$. The usual practice is to attribute RBI's to the batter and the "Triple Crown" of batting is the set {Avg, HR, RBI}.

Table 4.3. Impact score.

Score	**Description**
0	{O}
1	{O+S} or {1B}
2	{2B} or {1B + 1R}
3	{3B} or {2B + 1R} or {1B + 2R}
4	{HR} or {3B + 1R} or {2B + 2R}
5	{HR + 1R} or {3B + 2R} or {2B + 3R}
6	{HR + 2R} or {3B + 3R}
7	{HR + 3R}

Underlying the impact score is the probability of each specific value at a plate appearance. The probability could depend on the batting scenario or state. Let the conditional distribution for impact X_t at plate appearance t, given the state Φ_t, be $H_t(x|\Phi_t) = Pr[X_t \leq x|state = \Phi_t]$, and let the corresponding density be $h_t(x|\Phi_t)$. Given T total appearances, the conditional density for the sequence of impacts is $g(x_1, \ldots, x_T|A^T) = [h_1(x_1|\Phi_1) \times \ldots \times h_T(x_T|\Phi_T)]$. Now the conditional density can be used to define the density $g(T, x)$ for each severity value x in T appearances. Consider $I^T =$ the class of all sets A^T, and $R^{T/j} = x_1, \ldots, x, \ldots, x_T$ the set of T-tuples with x in the jth position. Let $X(T)$ be the random variable of impacts in T appearances. Then the density for impact value x in T appearances is

$$g(T, x) = \sum_{j=1}^{T} \int_{I_t^n \times R^{T/j}} g(x_1, \ldots, x, \ldots x_T|A^T) dx_1 \ldots dx_T dP[A^T].$$

With this density for impact values, the overall number of successes can be decomposed into successes by impact level. If the number of appearances is T, and the density for the impact distribution is $g(T, x)$, then the impact specific number of successes in T appearances is $N(T, x) = T \cdot g(T, x)$. This conditional number of successes for a given impact level is a key component of the batting process. The data record will provide T and $n(T, x)$ and the estimated impact distribution up to appearance T is $\hat{g}(T, x) = (n(T, x))/T)$.

4.2.2. *Dominance and Utility*

Consider the distribution functions F_1 and F_2, with the inverse cumulative distributions $F_1^{-1}$and F_2^{-1}, respectively. Let $T(\alpha) = \int_0^\alpha [F_1^{-1}(p) - F_2^{-1}(p)]dp$, the area between the distributions in the $\alpha-$tail. A utility function u for which: $\{T(\alpha) \geq 0, 0 \leq \alpha \leq 1\} \Rightarrow Eu(X_1) \geq Eu(X_2)$, is *concave.* (Rothschild and Stiglitz, 1970.) The area/integration condition implies that the utility has decreasing first derivatives (negative second derivatives). So the risk averter has a concave utility.

Stochastic dominance is an ordering of random variables based on characteristics of the distribution as defined by the values and probabilities. (Levy, 1973; MacLean and Ziemba, 2015).

1. **First order dominance** is a comparison for two random variables of the inverse cumulative distributions, F_1^{-1} and F_2^{-1}. If one inverse cumulative is above another then the higher random variable dominates, that

is $[F_1^{-1}(p) - F_2^{-1}(p)] \geq 0, 0 \leq p \leq 1$. This is a partial order since distributions may intersect. A total order is found by calculating the area below the inverse cumulative as shown in Figure 4.1. The area is reported as the measure γ_1. The area under the inverse cumulative is the mean: $\int_0^1 F^{-1}(p)dp = \mu$.

2. **Second order dominance** is a comparison of Lorenz curves (Lorenz, 1905). The Lorenz curve is the integrated inverse cumulative distribution to each probability value. The Lorenz tracts the incomplete means up to the full mean: $L(\alpha) = \int_0^\alpha F^{-1}(p)dp, 0 \leq \alpha \leq 1$. If one Lorenz curve is above another then it is dominant, that is $\int_0^\alpha [F_1^{-1}(p) - F_2^{-1}(p)]dp \geq 0, 0 \leq \alpha \leq 1$. The Lorenz is a convex curve below the diagonal line from the origin to the complete mean. Again, a complete order is determined from the area under the Lorenz curve as shown in Figure 4.1. The area under the diagonal is half the mean, so it is usual to double the area under the Lorenz. The double area is reported as the measure γ_2.

The orders of stochastic dominance above are defined from the inverse cumulative distribution. It is well known that equivalent definitions follow from nested classes of utility functions: monotone increasing, monotone increasing concave, etc. (Levy, 1973). So random variable X_1 first order dominates X_2 if $E(u(X_1)) \geq E(u(X_2))$ for all monotone increasing utilities: $\{u' > 0\}$, with at least one strict inequality. Also X_1 second order dominates X_2 if $E(u(X_1)) \geq E(u(X_2))$ for all monotone increasing concave utilities: $\{u' > 0, u'' < 0\}$, with at least one strict inequality. A utility function for which $\{\int_0^\alpha [F_1^{-1}(p) - F_2^{-1}(p)]dp \geq 0, 0 \leq \alpha \leq 1\} \Rightarrow Eu(X_1) \geq Eu(X_2)$ is concave. (Rothschild and Stiglitz, 1970.) An interesting aspect of the

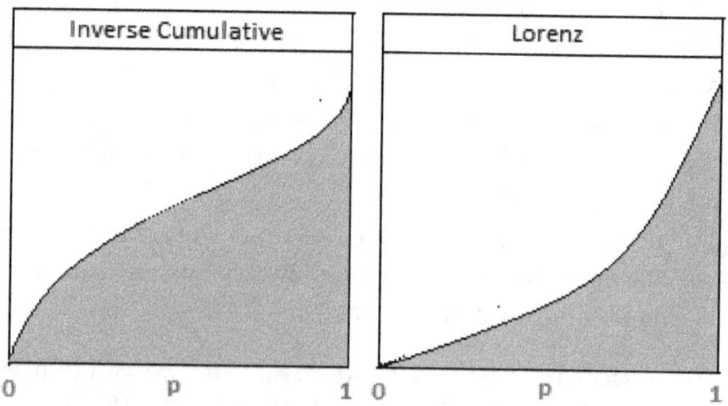

Figure 4.1. Stochastic dominance.

concave utility is the decrease in incremental value for higher impact scores. That makes sense for batting scores since "grand slams", for example, are dramatic but are likely associated with blow outs rather than game deciding hits.

4.2.3. *Standardization*

Although a players production within a baseball season is quite stable, there are factors which affect performance that vary across seasons (Petersen *et al.*, 2011). Adjustment procedures are any of a variety of procedures performed during data analysis to attempt to remove the effect of extraneous sources of variation (Meinert, 1980). By calculating the relative production at different factor levels for each player, those relative rates can be applied for all players to the same theoretical or benchmark season. This standardization is common practice in epidemiology for comparing illness distributions in disparate regions. (Rothman, 2002).

Let X_{ik} be the production of player i in season k. The density for X_{ik} is $g_{ik}(x)$ and for notational convenience let $g_{ik}(x) = p_{xik}$. With n_{ik} plate appearances we have $n_{xik} = p_{xik} \times n_{ik}$. For the performance relative to all m players in season k, we compute the weighted average $X_{\cdot k}$ for season k over all players, where

$$p_{x \cdot k} = \sum_{i=1}^{m} w_{ik} p_{xik}.$$

The weights are $w_{ik} = \frac{n_{ik}}{\sum_{i=1}^{m} n_{ik}}$.

The performance distributions are shown in Table 4.4.

The benchmark is also shown. The benchmark distribution is arbitrary, but a reasonable choice is the long term average.

Table 4.4. Standardized performance.

X	**Player** i	**All Players**	**Benchmark**	**Standardized** i
0	p_{0ik}	$p_{0 \cdot k}$	p_0	$\tilde{p}_0$
1	p_{1ik}	$p_{1 \cdot k}$	p_1	$\tilde{p}_1$
2	p_{2ik}	$p_{2 \cdot k}$	p_2	$\tilde{p}_2$
3	p_{3ik}	$p_{3 \cdot k}$	p_3	$\tilde{p}_3$
4	p_{4ik}	$p_{4 \cdot k}$	p_4	$\tilde{p}_4$
5	p_{5ik}	$p_{5 \cdot k}$	p_5	$\tilde{p}_5$
6	p_{6ik}	$p_{6 \cdot k}$	p_6	$\tilde{p}_6$
7	p_{7ik}	$p_{7 \cdot k}$	p_7	$\tilde{p}_7$

The player i seasonal relative for impact x in season k is $r_{xik} = \frac{p_{xik}}{p_{x \cdot k}}$. Applying the relative to the benchmark and correcting to get total probability 1, the standardized production for player i is $\tilde{X}_{ik}$, where

$$\tilde{p}_{xik} = \frac{r_{xik} \times p_x}{\sum_x r_{xik} \times p_x}. \tag{4.3}$$

So $\tilde{X}_{ik}$ has probabilities $\tilde{p}_{xik} = Pr\left[\tilde{X}_{ik} = x\right]$. This is the impact in the benchmark season if the performance of player i relative to other players in season k holds.

4.3. Comparison of Batters

Consider the impact $X = X_1 + X_2$, which includes both bases achieved and additional runs scored for the great hitters in Table 4.1. Babe Ruth's self acknowledged best season is 1923. His performance numbers, the numbers for Ted Williams great season in 1941 when he hit .406, and Barry Bonds 2001 season when he hit 73 HRs are given in Table 4.5. The raw data for the impact calculations are taken from Retrosheet.

The performance statistics for the great hitters follow in Table 4.6. In addition to the standard production statistics are the dominance measures γ_1 and γ_2. The various statistics in Table 4.6 show the excellence of the great hitters, with support for Bonds'01 being better. The measure γ_2 has the hitters almost equivalent. The better on base percentages are dominated by the slugging percentages in γ_1, but the path of incomplete means to the total mean is sensitive to the lower successes in OBP. So γ_2 presents a more balanced picture.

There is a difference in the calculation for the performance statistics. Suppose the impact is calculated from the number of bases achieved plus

Table 4.5. Hitting impact.

Impact	Ruth' 23	Williams' 41	Bonds' 01
0	0.455	0.447	0.485
1	0.386	0.401	0.347
2	0.061	0.056	0.038
3	0.020	0.028	0.015
4	0.019	0.010	0.008
5	0.022	0.015	0.059
6	0.023	0.028	0.032
7	0.014	0.015	0.017

Table 4.6. Performance: Ruth'23, Williams'41, Bonds'01.

Statistic	Ruth'23	Williams'41	Bonds'01
AV	0.393	0.406	0.328
OBP	0.545	0.553	0.515
SLG	0.764	0.735	0.863
OPS	1.309	1.288	1.379
RBI	130	120	137
γ_1	1.490	1.485	1.608
γ_2	0.844	0.848	0.841

Table 4.7. League hitting impact.

Impact	All' 23	All' 41	All' 01
0	0.6362	0.6577	0.667
1	0.2507	0.2361	0.223
2	0.0684	0.0584	0.059
3	0.0230	0.0216	0.017
4	0.0138	0.0161	0.021
5	0.0057	0.0070	0.008
6	0.0019	0.0025	0.003
7	0.0003	0.0006	0.001

the number of runs scored in an appearance, $X = X_1 + X_2$. Then $E(X) = \frac{totalbases}{appearances} + \frac{totaladditionalruns}{appearances}$ and with $OBP = \frac{successes}{appearances} = \frac{N(T)}{T}$, $\gamma_1 = E(X) = \frac{1}{T}Y^*(t) = OBP \times PSL + OBP \times SRS$. The statistics *per success slugging (PSL)* and the *per success additional runs scored (SRS)* are a variation on per at bat statistics such as $SLG = \frac{totalbases}{atbats}$. Then $\gamma_1 = \frac{atbats}{appearances}[OBP \times SLG + OBP \times ARS]$, where ARS is the additional runs per at bat, not counting a run by the batter (counted in SLG). Obviously γ_1 and $OPS = OBP + SLG$ have common components, but the calculation is different and the additional component of runs scored is included. Statistics which include runs scored have a much higher correlation with team win percentage than statistics based only on slugging. (Hardegree, 2014).

Not all baseball seasons are the same, and that is the rationale for standardizing performance by considering the league performance in the relevant seasons. The performance of the league in the corresponding years is shown in Table 4.7. The data for the league performance comes from Retrosheet. These numbers are estimates, since not all players are included

Table 4.8. Standardized batting impact.

Impact	SRuth' 23	SWilliams' 41	SBonds' 01
0	0.463	0.454	0.485
1	0.333	0.379	0.347
2	0.051	0.057	0.038
3	0.014	0.022	0.015
4	0.028	0.013	0.008
5	0.030	0.017	0.059
6	0.035	0.034	0.032
7	0.045	0.025	0.017

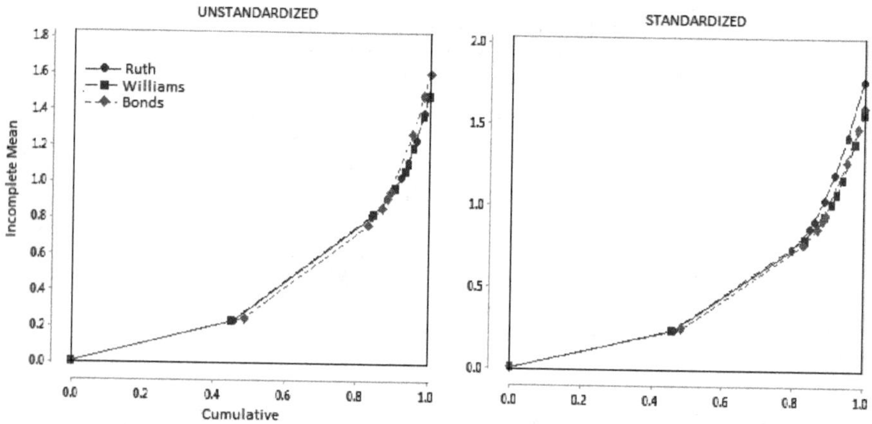

Figure 4.2. Lorenz curves.

in the Retrosheet tabulations. However, the majority are included and the estimates are valid.

The standardization considers a player relative to the league in the same season, and converts that performance to the same benchmark season for each player. In this case the benchmark was taken as the 2001 season, the one where Bonds broke the home run record with 73. The standardized performance statistics for the great hitters follows in Table 4.8. Obviously Bonds statistics remain the same, but there is a significant shift in the distribution over impact for Ruth and Williams. Probability is shifted to higher impact values.

Since the measure γ_2 has special interest, the Lorenz curves of incomplete means are plotted in Figure 4.2. When the distributions are standardized it can be seen that Ruth'23 is second order stochastically dominant.

Table 4.9. Standardized performance: Ruth'23, Williams'41, Bonds'02.

Statistic	SRuth'23	SWilliams'41	SBonds'01
AV	0.364	0.397	0.328
OBP	0.535	0.551	0.515
SLG	0.837	0.803	0.863
OPS	1.372	1.354	1.379
RBI	134	124	137
γ_1	1.769	1.573	1.608
γ_2	0.893	0.857	0.841

The curves are close for the batters, but the standardized evidence supports Ruth.

The various batting statistics were computed for standardized seasons in Table 4.9. The case for Ruth'23 being the best season is pretty clear.

4.4. Conclusion

In this chapter we discussed the batting performance of three legendary hitters in their best baseball season. The distinguishing features of our approach are: (1) including "runs batted in" as a component of production; (2) accounting for the variation in league batting performance/conditions across time by standardizing yearly performance to a common benchmark season; (3) basing the comparison of standardized distributions on principles of stochastic dominance. The methods provide some additional insight into the performance of batters, and contribute to a comparison of all time greats.

Chapter 5

Jai Alai arbitrage strategies*

DANIEL LANE[1] and WILLIAM T. ZIEMBA[2]

[1] *School of Management, University of Ottawa, Ottawa, ON K1N 6N5, Canada*
[2] *Sauder School of Business, University of British Columbia, Vancouver, BC V6T 1Z2, Canada and MIT Sloan School of Management, 50 Memorial Drive, Cambridge, MA 02142, USA*
E-mail: ziemba@interchange.ubc.ca

This paper presents arbitrage and risk arbitrage betting strategies for Team Jai Alai. This game is the setting for the analysis and most results generalize to other sports betting situations and some financial market applications. The arbitrage conditions are utility free while the risk arbitrage wagers are constructed according to the Kelly criterion/capital growth theory that maximizes asymptotically long-run wealth almost surely.

Keywords: arbitrage, risk arbitrage, hedging, sequential investing

1. INTRODUCTION

This paper develops arbitrage and risk arbitrage strategies for betting in the game of team Jai Alai.[1] The game originated in the Basque region of Spain and is played in Mexico City and other locales. It is played in a large enclosed rectangular court called a fronton between two opposing teams, each having two players. Players serve each point in turn and single points are scored by one team winning a rally off the serve as in tennis, squash or racquetball. Games are usually played to thirty points. At the fronton, bets may be placed on either team to win the game before every point is played at fixed locked-in odds, until the outcome of the game. Payoffs on bets made during the game are settled at the end of the game based on the quoted house odds at each betting point. We are concerned with the construction of arbitrage and risk arbitrage bets that have zero or little risk while at the same time yielding a positive return. Sklansky (1983) discusses the concept of *hedging bets* in sporting events, which we call arbitrage.

Perfect arbitrage occurs in strategies where the net gain of all bets is always non-negative and sometimes positive and involves no risk of losing. Conditions that lead to arbitrage in various circumstances are studied in Kallio and Ziemba (2003). Risk arbitrages may yield losses, but occur more frequently and have higher mean returns. We develop these arbitrages for team Jai Alai. Section 2

[1] Goodfriend and Friedman (1975, 1977) have analysed the game of individual Jai Alai.

*This article originally appeared in *The European Journal of Finance*, **10**, pp. 353–369.

provides conditions for arbitrage. Risk arbitrage is discussed in Section 3. Their application to other areas is discussed in Section 4.

Assume that

1. the Jai Alai fronton bet payout rate is the constant $Q \in (1, 0)$; and
2. the two teams' relative ability is known and defined by the probability of winning a single point – team A wins with probability p, and B with $q = 1 - p$.

These probabilities are assumed to be score invariant.

With p known, the probability of A reaching K points before B, given that A currently has $0 \leqslant m < K$ points and B has $0 \leqslant n < K$ points, is (according to Montmort, see Epstein [1977, p. 109]):

$$\begin{aligned} P_a &= P_a(m, n) \\ &= p^{K-m}\left[1 + q(k-m) + q^2\frac{(k-m)(K-m+1)}{2} \right. \\ &\quad \left. + \cdots + q^{K-n-1}\frac{(2K-m-n-2)!}{(K-m-1)(K-n-1)!}\right] \\ &= p^{K-m}\left[\sum_{i=0}^{K-n-1} q^i \binom{K-m+i-1}{i}\right] \end{aligned}$$

For $K = 30$, P_a is the probability that team A will win the game given that the current score is m to n. A schedule of P_a and P_b, with $P_a + P_b = 1$, for all values of m and n over the 30 point game in abbreviated form appears as Table 1 for the case of $p = 0.5$.

For given fixed Q, a schedule, as shown in Table 2, can be computed of the consistent house odds over the game since

$$P_a = Q/(O_a + 1), \quad P_b = Q/(O_b + 1) \text{ or } O_a = \frac{Q}{P_a} - 1 = \frac{Q - P_a}{P_a} \text{ and}$$

$$O_b\frac{Q}{P_b} - 1 = \frac{Q - P_a}{P_a} \tag{1}$$

In (1) O_a and O_b are the consistent house odds for teams A and B respectively, when the score is (m, n). Odds of 1.5 to 1 means 1.5 profit plus the original bet or 2.5, is returned for each 1 bet, etc. Consistent odds are those that return $1 - Q$ for the house's profit regardless of which team A or B wins. Then the expected return per dollar bet on each team is Q. Since $P_a + P_b = 1$ independent of Q, the odds then reflect the actual value of Q through (1). Hence

$$O_aO_b = (Q - P_a)(Q - P_b)/P_aP_b = 1 - [Q(1 - Q)/P_aP_b] \tag{2}$$

For given Q and odds on A of O_a to 1, consistent odds on B may fail to exist that guarantee the house advantage $1 - Q$. In that case, if there is a minimum payout of 1, that is you just get your money back, then there is a *minus pool* and the house's actual take is less than $1 - Q$. A minus pool is defined to be this situation where the house take is $1 - Q^* < 1 - Q$, where $Q^* > Q$. So the effective Q, namely Q^*, is higher and the odds on B always exist since at their lowest the odds on O_b

Table 1. Probability that Team A wins when the score is A = m and B = n and the single point probability is $p = 0.5$

n/n	0	1	2	3	4	5	6	7	8	9	10	11	12	13	14	15	16	17	18	19	20	21	22	23	24	25	26	27	28	29
0	.50	.55	.60	.66	.70	.75	.79	.83	.87	.90	.92	.94	.96	.97	.98	.99	.99													
1	.45	.50	.55	.61	.66	.71	.76	.80	.84	.87	.90	.93	.95	.96	.98	.98	.99	.99												
2	.40	.45	.50	.55	.61	.66	.71	.76	.80	.84	.88	.91	.93	.95	.97	.98	.99	.99												
3	.34	.39	.45	.50	.56	.61	.66	.72	.76	.81	.85	.88	.91	.94	.96	.97	.98	.99	.99											
4	.30	.34	.39	.44	.50	.56	.61	.67	.72	.77	.81	.85	.89	.92	.94	.96	.97	.98	.99	.99										
5	.25	.29	.34	.39	.44	.50	.56	.61	.67	.72	.77	.82	.86	.89	.92	.95	.96	.98	.99	.99										
6	.21	.24	.29	.34	.39	.44	.50	.56	.62	.67	.73	.78	.83	.87	.90	.93	.95	.97	.98	.99	.99									
7	.17	.20	.24	.28	.33	.39	.44	.50	.56	.62	.68	.73	.79	.83	.87	.91	.93	.96	.97	.98	.99	.99								
8	.13	.16	.20	.24	.28	.33	.38	.44	.50	.56	.62	.68	.74	.79	.84	.88	.91	.94	.96	.97	.99	.99								
9	.10	.13	.16	.19	.23	.28	.33	.38	.44	.50	.56	.63	.69	.74	.80	.84	.89	.92	.94	.96	.98	.99	.99							
10	.08	.10	.12	.15	.19	.23	.27	.32	.38	.44	.50	.56	.63	.69	.75	.80	.85	.89	.93	.95	.97	.98	.99							
11	.06	.07	.09	.12	.15	.18	.22	.27	.32	.37	.44	.50	.57	.63	.70	.76	.81	.86	.90	.93	.96	.97	.99	.99						
12	.04	.05	.07	.09	.11	.14	.17	.21	.26	.31	.37	.43	.50	.57	.64	.70	.76	.82	.87	.91	.94	.96	.98	.99	.99					
13	.03	.04	.05	.06	.08	.11	.13	.17	.21	.25	.31	.37	.43	.50	.57	.64	.71	.77	.83	.88	.92	.95	.97	.98	.99					
14	.02	.02	.03	.04	.06	.08	.10	.13	.16	.20	.25	.30	.36	.43	.50	.57	.64	.71	.78	.84	.89	.92	.95	.97	.99	.99				
15	.01	.02	.02	.03	.04	.05	.07	.09	.12	.15	.20	.24	.30	.36	.43	.50	.57	.65	.72	.79	.95	.89	.93	.96	.98	.99				
16	.01	.01	.01	.02	.03	.04	.05	.07	.09	.11	.15	.19	.24	.29	.36	.43	.50	.58	.65	.73	.80	.86	.91	.94	.97	.98	.99			
17		.01	.01	.01	.02	.02	.03	.04	.06	.08	.11	.14	.18	.23	.29	.35	.42	.50	.58	.66	.74	.81	.87	.92	.95	.98	.99			
18				.01	.01	.01	.02	.03	.04	.06	.07	.10	.13	.17	.22	.28	.35	.42	.50	.58	.67	.75	.82	.88	.93	.96	.98	.99		
19					.01	.01	.01	.02	.03	.04	.05	.07	.09	.12	.16	.21	.27	.34	.42	.50	.59	.68	.76	.83	.89	.94	.97	.99		
20							.01	.01	.01	.02	.03	.04	.06	.08	.11	.15	.20	.26	.33	.41	.50	.59	.69	.77	.85	.91	.95	.98	.99	
21								.01	.01	.01	.02	.03	.04	.05	.08	.11	.14	.19	.25	.32	.41	.50	.60	.70	.79	.87	.93	.97	.99	
22										.01	.01	.01	.02	.03	.05	.07	.09	.13	.18	.24	.31	.40	.50	.60	.71	.81	.89	.95	.98	
23												.01	.01	.02	.03	.04	.06	.08	.12	.17	.23	.30	.40	.50	.61	.73	.83	.91	.96	.99
24													.01	.01	.01	.02	.03	.05	.07	.11	.15	.21	.29	.39	.50	.62	.75	.86	.94	.98
25															.01	.01	.02	.02	.04	.06	.09	.13	.19	.27	.38	.50	.64	.77	.89	.97
26																	.01	.01	.02	.03	.05	.07	.11	.17	.25	.36	.50	.66	.81	.94
27																			.01	.01	.02	.03	.05	.09	.14	.23	.34	.50	.69	.88
28																					.01	.01	.02	.04	.06	.11	.19	.31	.50	.75
29																								.01	.02	.03	.06	.13	.25	.50

*This table is symmetric in the sense that Prob(A wins) with score m, n equals Prob(B wins) with score n, m. This occurs if and only if $p = 0.5$.

Table 2. Consistent odds for Team B (O_b to 1) given odds for Team A (O_a to 1) and payback rate Q

House odds	Payback rate, Q						
O_a to 1	1.000	0.950	0.900	0.850	0.800	0.750	0.700
0.100	10.0000	5.9667	3.9500	2.7400	1.9333	1.3571	0.9250
0.111	9.0090	5.5556	3.7389	2.6182	1.8579	1.3082	0.8922
0.125	8.0000	5.1071	3.5000	2.4773	1.7692	1.2500	0.8529
0.143	6.9930	4.6262	3.2333	2.3159	1.6659	1.1813	0.8061
0.167	5.9880	4.1090	2.9337	2.1292	1.5439	1.0989	0.7493
0.200	5.0000	3.5600	2.6000	1.9143	1.4000	1.0000	0.6800
0.250	4.0000	2.9583	2.2143	1.6563	1.2222	0.8750	0.5909
0.333	3.0030	2.3064	1.7707	1.3459	1.0008	0.7148	0.4741
0.500	2.0000	1.5909	1.2500	0.9615	0.7143	0.5000	0.3125
1.000	1.0000	0.8095	0.6364	0.4783	0.3333	0.2000	0.0769
1.500	0.6667	0.5323	0.4063	0.2879	0.1765	0.0714	na
2.000	0.5000	0.3902	0.2857	0.1860	0.0909	na	na
2.500	0.4000	0.3039	0.2115	0.1226	0.0370	na	na
3.000	0.3333	0.2459	0.1613	0.0794	na	na	na
3.500	0.2857	0.2042	0.1250	0.0479	na	na	na
4.000	0.2500	0.1728	0.0976	0.0241	na	na	na
4.500	0.2222	0.1484	0.0761	0.0054	na	na	na
5.000	0.2000	0.1287	0.0588	na	na	na	na
5.500	0.1818	0.1126	0.0446	na	na	na	na
6.000	0.1667	0.0992	0.0328	na	na	na	na
6.500	0.1538	0.0878	0.0227	na	na	na	na
7.000	0.1429	0.0780	0.0141	na	na	na	na
7.500	0.1333	0.0695	0.0066	na	na	na	na
8.000	0.1250	0.0621	na	na	na	na	na
8.500	0.1176	0.0556	na	na	na	na	na
9.000	0.1111	0.0497	na	na	na	na	na
9.500	0.1053	0.0445	na	na	na	na	na
10.000	0.1000	0.0398	na	na	na	na	na

na = consistent house odds for this Q and O_a, that guarantee the house take of $1 - Q$, do not exist and there is a minus pool. If there is a minimum odds payoff of \$1 for each dollar wagered, then consistent odds always exist for this $Q^* = 1$. With a minimum payoff above odds of zero, then consistent odds on O_b for all O_a and for all $Q^* < 1$ may not exist.

are the reciprocal of the odds on A. That is the case where the payback is all the money wagered and the house makes no profit since $Q^* = 1$. In general, these odds are possibly as low as the minimum guarantee, that is $O_b = 1/O_a$. In a typical minus pool, the odds on B are higher than $1/O_a$. For example, if the minimum payout is 1.05 as is typical then consistent odds on O_b may fail to exist. In this case, the odds on A are too large given the $1 - Q^*$ demanded by the minimum guarantee so that the odds on B do not exist. Let O_b be $Q = 1$ consistent odds and O_{bh} be any odds offered for some other Q. Then O_b and O_{bh} are related by $O_{bh} = Q^* O_b - (1 - Q^*)$. Actual house odds, O_{ah} may differ from the consistent odds O_a and O_b for a number of reasons, including the desire of the oddsmakers to balance their books, competition among individual bookies for larger shares of the total pool, or additional information about teams' performances. This then adjusts the actual $1 - Q^*$ that the house receives.

For team A, or respectively B, we refer to the house odds as: $O_{ah} = O_a$ (consistent), $O_{ah} > O_a$ (favourable), and $O_{ah} < O_a$ (unfavourable).

2. THE PERFECT ARBITRAGE

The *perfect arbitrage* is the proverbial sure bet. For each betting point of a K point game with a utility function U and betting wealth W, optimal arbitrage bets can be found by solving

$$\max_{B_a \geqslant 0, B_b \geqslant 0} E[U(B_a, B_b)] \tag{3}$$

$$\text{s.t.} \quad B_a + B_b \leqslant W$$
$$B_a O_{ah} + B_a \geqslant B_a + B_b$$
$$B_b O_{bh} + B_b \geqslant B_a + B_b$$

where B_a and B_b are the amounts bet on A and B, respectively, W is initial wealth and E is the expectation operator. Besides the budget constraint, the arbitrage constraints indicate that the return if either A or B wins is never less than the total bet on A and B. This reduces to the perfect arbitrage betting condition at every point of the game. These constraints yield,

$$1/O_{ah} \leqslant B_a/B_b \leqslant O_{bh}, \; B_b \neq 0 \tag{4}$$

which demonstrates:

Theorem 1. The perfect arbtirage exists iff

$$O_{ah} O_{bh} \geqslant 1. \tag{5}$$

The arbitrage condition (5) is utility free and holds for all U. Both B_a and B_b must be positive or both zero.

The constraints in (3) imply that

$$B_a/B_b \leqslant W/B_b - 1.$$

By (4),

$$1/O_{ah} \leqslant W/B_b - 1.$$

Hence

$$B_b \leqslant O_{ah} W/(1 + O_{ah}).$$

Similarly,

$$B_a \geqslant W/(1 + O_{ah}).$$

We consider betting strategies using the strategy variable $f \geqslant 1$, using

$$B_a = fW/(1 + O_{ah}) \text{ and } B_b = W(1 - f + O_{ah})/(1 + O_{ah}).$$

When $f = 1$, then $O_{ah} O_{bh} = 1, B_a = W/(1 + O_{ah}),\; B_b = O_{ah} W/(1 + O_{ah})$.

To guarantee the arbitrage, the profit must be non-negative regardless of which team wins:

$$\begin{aligned} \text{profit if A wins} &= W(O_{ah} f - (1 - f) - O_{ah})/(1 + O_{ah}) \geqslant 0 \\ &= W(f - 1) \geqslant 0 \end{aligned} \tag{6}$$

$$\begin{aligned} \text{profit if B wins} &= W(O_{bh}(1 - f) + O_{bh} O_{ah} - f)/(1 + O_{ah}) > 0 \\ &= W(O_{bh}(1 + O_{ah}) - f(1 + O_{bh}))/(1 + O_{ah}) > 0. \end{aligned} \tag{7}$$

To satisfy conditions (5)–(7)

$$f_{\min} \equiv 1 \leqslant f \leqslant (1 + O_{ah})/(1 + O_{bh}) \equiv f_{\max}. \tag{8}$$

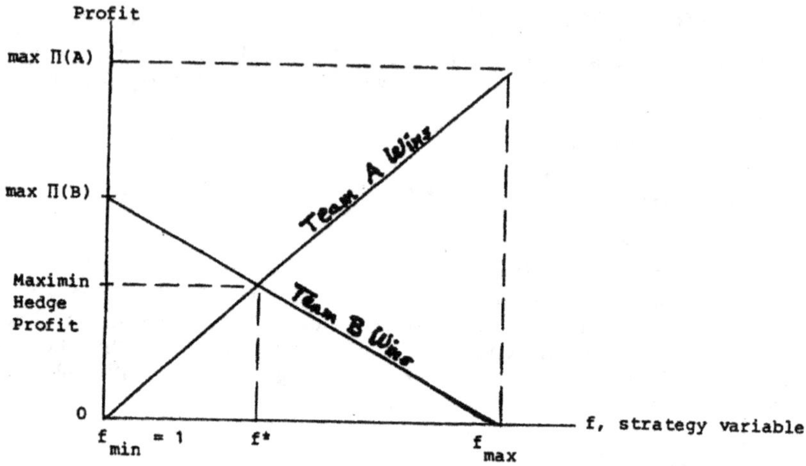

Fig. 1. Profits for Teams A and B for initial betting wealth of 1 unit versus strategy variable f, when $O_{ah} > O_{bh}$ and $O_{ah}O_{bh} > 1$.

Figure 1 illustrates how the net payoffs vary with f. At

$$f^* = (O_{ah} + 1)(O_{bh} + 1)/(1 + O_{ah} + O_{bh} + 2) \tag{9}$$

one maximizes the minimum arbitrage profit, namely

$$W(O_{ah}O_{bh} - 1/O_{ah} + O_{bh} + 2)$$

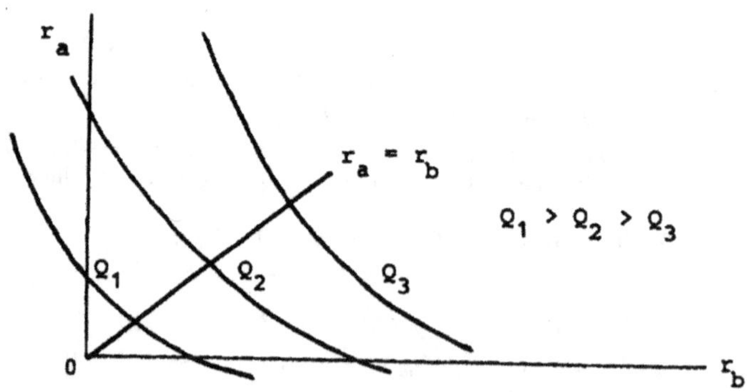

Fig. 2. House odds favourability regions.

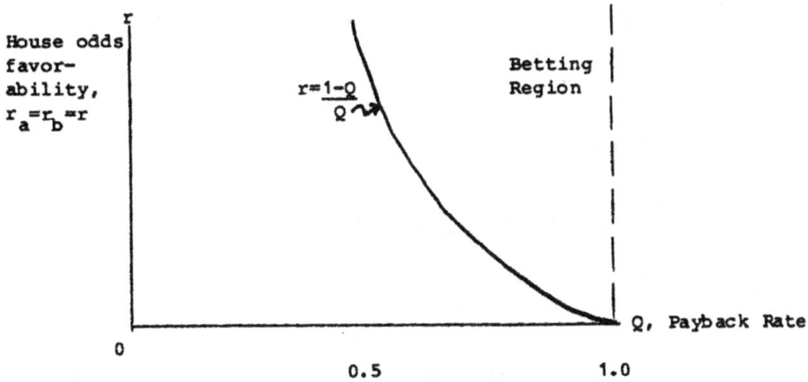

Fig. 3. Betting region of Q versus r.

More insight about the perfect arbitrage betting condition (5) may be obtained by comparing it to consistent odds at each betting point. They require that

$$O_a O_b = (Q - P_a)(Q - P_b)/P_a P_b = 1 - [Q(1 - Q)/P_a P_b]. \tag{10}$$

The house odds favourability factors $r_a > 0$ and $r_b > 0$ for favourable odds are defined by

$$O_{ah} \equiv O_a(1 + r_a) \text{ and } O_{bh} \equiv O_b(1 + r_b). \tag{11}$$

Then condition (5) implies that

$$O_a(1 + r_a)O_b(1 + r_b) > 1. \tag{12}$$

Note that $r_a > 0$ and $r_b > 0$, although typical, is not required for (12); see also Fig. 2.

If $r_a = r_b = r$, the schedule of Q versus r and the region of betting under the perfect hedge is as shown in Fig. 3.

For typical values for Q of about 0.85 the required favorability for house odds quoted on both teams is nearly 20%. Such discrepancies occur occasionally in actual betting. More frequently, however, one needs to take added risk to get good bets so we now turn to the construction of risk arbitrages.

3. RISK ARBITRAGES

Two approaches are considered for constructing risk arbitrage positions. They exploit the observed house odds favourability conditions to find *good* arbitrage strategies.

A model encompassing these approaches is

$$\max_{B_a(i)\geqslant 0, B_b(i)\geqslant 0} E_g[\log W(g)] \tag{13}$$

$$\text{s.t.} \quad \sum_{i\in g} B_a(i) + B_b(i) \leqslant W_0, \forall g \in G$$

$$\sum_{i\in g} B_a(i)O_{ah}(i) \geqslant \alpha \sum_{i\in g} B_b(i), \alpha > 0$$

$$\sum_{i\in g} B_b(i)O_{bh}(i) \geqslant \alpha \sum_{i\in g} B_a(i), \alpha > 0$$

where E_g represents mathematical expectation with respect to the game path g, G is the set of game paths from (0,0) to the final outcome, and the constant α is the relative degree of risk of the bettor in the arbitrage. For example, if $\alpha = 1/2$, the bettor requires that total returns must cover at least 50% of total bets in any game. With $\alpha = 1$, the goal is to find an arbitrage to cover all bets and a premium is required for betting in any game if $\alpha > 1$. The log utility function corresponds to the Kelly (1956) system of betting which maximizes the long-run rate of growth of the bettor's fortune. See Thorp (1975), MacLean, Ziemba and Blazenko (1992) and MacLean and Ziemba (1999) for a summary of results concerning such betting strategies.

The first approach to the risk arbitrage problem is a model which analyses the objective function over all feasible paths of the game and computes the bets B_a, B_b which maximize (13). This presupposes that information is known in advance about the odds O_{ah} and O_{bh}, actually set by the house throughout the game. This information may be a probability distribution or a function for O_{ah}, and O_{bh} over the scores of the game. The drawback is that the cardinality of G is very large

	Game			
		Betting Points		
Points in the Game	Total Betting Points	Min	Max	Number of Game Paths
1	1	1	1	2
2	4	2	3	6
3	9	3	5	20
4	16	4	7	70
5	25	5	9	252
..	.	.	.	
..	.	.	.	
..	.	.	.	
30	900	30	59	5.91×10^{16}

Calculations for two and three point games using $\alpha = 1$, $Q = 0.85$, and $p = 0.5$ appear in Table 3. These calculations utilize the following probability distributions

Table 3. Sample results for two and three point games

House odds type	W	σ	Games bet/ games played	Ave % bet of W/ Game Bet	Ave value fund/ game played
		Two point games			
1	1	0	0/1	0	0
	1	.1	1/10	100	0.0005
	1	.2	5/10	84	0.0073
2	1	0	0/1	0	0
	1	.1	0/10	0	0
	1	.2	2/10	100	0.0119
		Three point games			
1	1	0	0/1	0	0
	1	.1	0/10	0	0
	1	.2	7/10	80	0.0193
2	1	0	0/1	0	0
	1	.1	3/10	75	0.0098
	1	.2	5/10	60	0.0059

for the house odds favourability factors $r_a = r_b = r$:

1. $r \sim N(0, \sigma^2)$ is iid for all scores of the game; and
2. $r \sim N(r(i), \sigma^2)$, depends upon the size of the lead and the number of points the leader is away from winning the game, where

$$r(i) = \begin{cases} \exp(-M/D) - 1 & \text{if team i is leading by M points} \\ \exp(pM/D) - 1 & \text{if team i is trailing by M points.} \end{cases}$$

D is the number of points the leader is away from winning the game, namely K-S(leader).

The results yield insights which may be useful in the construction of good heuristic strategies for 30 point games. For the normally distributed favorability factors there is an intrinsic threshold value for the odds favorability below which no initial bet is placed. This threshold is about a 20% odds favourability. Secondly, betting almost always takes place in natural-arbitrage pairs, where a bet on one team at one point of a particular game path is paired with a compensating bet on the other team later in the game along the same game path. Where perfect arbitrages could be constructed, these dominated all other possible bet points. As variance increases, the number of lucrative bets also increases both in number and size of bet.

Many betting points occurred in pairs of tied scores and trailing team bets, where the higher odds for the trailing team boost the combined bet pair over the arbitrage condition requirements. In these situtations gains could be realized on a team which came from behind to win and strategies can concentrate on this possible event occurring while hedging *a priori* that the leading team wins.

In the exponential function distribution the high relative favourability of the trailing team contributes to still greater emphasis on betting on the trailer to come from behind to win while hedging (usually early in the game, or at a tied point) on the leader to win. As in the normal case, the initial bet favourability threshold value of 20% continues to manifest itself in the results.

Our additional calculations showed modest expected total gains in the range of 1–2% using this method for sets of 25 games. The gains in the three point game are larger than the two point game for the same level of variance, which suggests that higher gains could be anticipated as the game size increases and more betting opportunities arise.

We now utilize these insights in a second approach to risk arbitrage by constructing single arbitrage bets for the 30 point game. A single arbitrage is a bet on one team and subsequently a bet on the opposing team later on in the game such that the constraints of (13) hold. Unlike the perfect arbitrage, which required betting both teams at the same time, this risk arbitrage does not require concurrent bets. Rather, the idea is to exploit the favourability of quoted odds on one team at some point in the game and take the risk that the house odds will become attractive enough on the opposing team later on so that an arbitrage may be constructed. However, the second half of this bet will not always materialize. Volatility and prediction models are useful here. This hedge may be formulated by examining the constraints on the bets B_a and B_b and

$$\begin{aligned} B_a(S_a)O_{ah}(S_a) &\geqslant \alpha B_b(S_a),\ \alpha > 0 \\ B_b(S_b)O_{bh}(S_b) &\geqslant \alpha B_a(S_b) \end{aligned} \tag{14}$$

where S_a and S_b are the scores of the game at the time a bet is made on team A and B, respectively.

The approach taken in the construction of the single hedge is to simulate the passage of the 30 point game using the same assumptions about odds favourability as with the 2 and 3 point game model.

The simulation model of the 30 point game generates at each point an odds favorability for each team, and the winner of the point using a uniform distribution on p. Bets were generated by first initializing a threshold favourability value which is used as the basis for placing the initial bet. Once the initial bet is placed whose amount is determined by criteria discussed below, the game continues until a new betting point for the opposing team is found such that the arbitrage condition (5) is satisfied. At the end of the game the bets are settled and the results recorded. Each simulation run is a set of 30 point games.

To find better strategies, and study the sensitivity of the model, different sets of games were simulated and compared in order to find the threshold favourability values which gave consistent positive expected net gains over the entire set of games. The results are highly sensitive to the value of this parameter. Low threshold values typically mean early betting points and more likely completion of the single hedge. However, early bets typically mean low odds and thus a small hedge margin (the amount by which $O_{ah}O_{bh}$, actually exceeds 1) and consequently smaller net gains. Higher values mean delayed betting points with a greater chance of not completing the second half of the hedge. However, potential loss due to unhedged or single bet games is compensated for by higher hedge margins (due to later game scores, larger point spreads and higher odds) and hence more potential net gains when the risk arbitrage is successfully completed. Sample results for these single arbitrage betting pairs appear in Table 4. In two games the risk arbitrage was completed. One leads to a positive gain, the other to a breakeven situation. In the other game the risk arbitrage was not completed and leads to a

Table 4. Sample results for single risk arbitrage betting pairs

Game number	Bet	Team	Amount Bet	Score A	Score B	Actual odds	House odds	Favourability
10	1.	B	0.8581	18	23	0.1288	0.1654	0.2838
	2.	A	0.1419	19	24	6.2963	7.6719	0.2185
		Final score	Bets	Payoff				
	Team A	31	0.1419	1.0886				
	Team B	29	0.8581	−0.8531				
			Net betting payoff = 0.2304					
11*	1.	A	0.0306	14	23	25.7480	31.6751	0.2302
		Final score	Bets	Payoff				
	Team A	15	0.0306	−0.0306				
	Team B	31	0.0	0.0				
			Net betting payoff = −0.0306					
21	1.	B	0.6493	0	3	0.4466	0.5401	0.2094
	2.	A	0.3507	1	5	2.0653	1.9782	−0.0422
		Final score	Bets	Payoff				
	Team A	17	0.3507	−0.3507				
	Team B	30	0.6493	0.3507				
			Net betting payoff = 0.0000					

*Arbitrage condition not realized, only one bet placed.

loss. If a risk arbitrage is not completed, it invariably leads to a loss because the team that you would like to bet on to complete the risk-arbitrage remains ahead throughout the game.

Figure 4 gives a profile of three different sets of games under various initial bet threshold favourability values for the normally distributed case.

In the cases illustrated and described above, the implicit assumption in the construction of the hedge and the determination of the amounts bet, was that the arbitrage condition (5) is satisfied as an equality, i.e. $O_{ah}O_{bh} = 1$. Thus the arbitrage margin was assumed to be zero in the construction of the arbitrage bet pair. However, if a margin, $m > 0$ exists, such that

$$O_{ah}O_{bh} = 1 + m$$

then the effect is to permit bets to place more emphasis on one team or the other or neither within the limits of satisfying the constraint set of (13) (see Fig. 1 for the arbitrage case). The perceived existence of a risk arbitrage margin allows the bettor to express the bet as a function of the score at the time of the bet placement, or as merely a prediction about the eventual outcome of the game. The actual margin cannot be known until the arbitrage condition is satisfied at

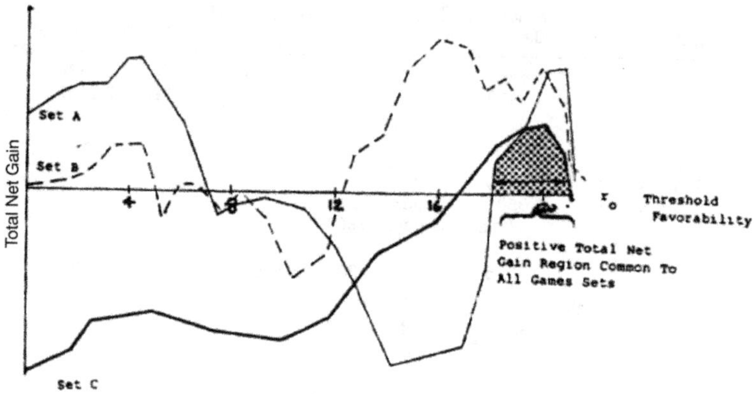

Fig. 4. Thirty point game, single risk arbitrage simulation r_0 search.

the second betting point. However, because the value of the margin affects the initial bet, it must be anticipated by some estimate.

If a margin exists, then the arbitrage, if it has been successfully constructed, satisfies all the conditions required for a member of the infinite set of betting pairs defined by the single betting strategy variable, f of Fig. 1. However, if the margin should not materialize, then the risk is that the risk arbitrage will not be completed and the game may end with an unpaired bet that may be lost. If on the other hand the anticipated margin understates the actual margin, then there is an opportunity loss due to the wrongly specified betting split. Hence even though the bet is not lost, we could have done better had we known the exact margin value.

This model was used in this second way to search for best values for the anticipated margin factor, m and the threshold favorability factor, r_0 values for the different sets of games described above. In the first instance, a constant betting strategy was employed independent of the score at the time of the initial bet. The strategy variable used here corresponds to the upper, and lower limits of f, as well as f^*.

Typical results for various m values are in Table 5.

When the anticipated margin is zero, the results of the three strategies are identical since the zero margin assumption uniquely defines the bets for each team (given by $f = 1$).

For some (m, r_0) pairs the $f_{\min}$ strategy yields better results while for other pairs $f_{\max}$ is superior. The f^* results always take intermediate positions between $f_{\min}$ and $f_{\max}$ for all (m, r_0). The results for all three strategies however are not significantly different for any (m, r_0). This performance is not unexpected and for larger game

Table 5. Total gain values for a 100 game set exponential function favourability, $\sigma = 0.2$ constant strategy

	f_{min}				f^*				f_{max}			
$m \backslash r_0$	0	0.05	0.10	0.20	0	0.05	0.10	0.20	0	0.05	0.10	0.20
0	1.41	0.47	−0.22	2.22	1.41	0.47	−0.22	2.22	1.41	0.47	−0.22	2.22
0.05	2.22	1.09	−0.02	3.35	2.01	0.93	−0.05	3.50	1.92	0.86	−0.10	3.89
0.10	2.67	2.43	−0.02	3.18	2.32	2.25	−0.08	3.62	2.07	1.92	−0.15	4.27
0.20	1.19	0.08	−1.47	3.09	0.78	−0.03	−1.50	4.09	0.17	−0.68	−1.57	5.17

sets it is expected that there would be less difference between the results of these three strategies.

As m increases for constant r_0, the total gain rises and then falls off as the second half of the bet pair is more difficult to complete. Low r_0 returns are in general positive with low variance since bets are placed early and the pairs are completed early generally with low odds. High r_0 yield better mean returns with larger variances. Intermediate r_0 reduce the returns. The results of this strategy for the same set of games used in Table 5 appear in Table 6.

Comparing the automatic versus constant strategy variable strategies shows that the automatic strategy dampens the extreme results of the f_{min} and f_{max} strategies of Table 5 while improving on the more conservative results of f^*. While these results may not be considered as being significantly different, the trend of the automatic strategy is toward a more stable and profitable outcome. More importantly, the variance of the expected gains is reduced by about a third from 6 to 4 over the comparable results in Table 5. Finally, the automatic strategy being score dependent is more intuitive and appealing and is the preferred policy for the single hedge construction problem in the 30 point game.

While the single risk arbitrage Jai Alai results are encouraging, the gains which occur for the simulated game sets are modest. There is greater potential for larger gains in longer games as there is more opportunity for inefficiency to manifest itself through volatility.

Combining the results of the two risk arbitrages, our final analysis examines the policy of betting over the 30 point game through the construction of a series of arbitrage bet pairs.

Table 6. Single hedge construction; total gain over 100 games sets using an automatic strategy variable

	Threshold favorability, r_0			
m	0	0.05	0.10	0.20
0	1.41	0.47	−0.22	2.22
0.05	2.11	1.03	−0.02	3.55
0.10	2.49	2.33	0.02	3.61
0.20	0.94	0.02	−1.24	3.12

The simulation model discussed above was modified to accommodate a series of single arbitrage bets. The same amount was assumed available for each arbitrage bet pair with a maximum total bet availability requirement of 60 betting units.

The algorithm proceeds by requiring that the preset threshold favorability factor value is satisfied before the initial bet of any pair is made. Priority over initializing the first half of a new risk arbitrage is given to matching unmatched hedges. The automatic strategy policy is used for the construction of all pairs.

Table 7 describes the bets in a typical game where 24% of a betting unit is the total profit. A summary of the results of this simulation appears in Table 8. The results are encouraging. Depending on the anticipated margin and the threshold

Table 7. Betting summary: multiple quasi-hedge bets

Bet	Team	Amount Bet	Score A	Score B	Actual odds	House odds	Favourability
1	A	0.5459	1	0	0.6894	0.8733	0.2668
1	B	0.4541	1	0	1.0480	1.2047	0.1495
2	A	0.5230	1	1	0.8500	0.9356	0.1007
2	B	0.4770	4	2	1.3188	1.4157	0.0735
3	A	0.5350	2	1	0.6869	0.9127	0.3288
3	B	0.4650	2	1	1.0519	1.1600	0.1028
4	A	0.6342	4	2	0.5479	0.6057	0.1055
4	B	0.3658	9	6	1.7590	1.7204	−0.0219
5	B	0.3139	10	7	1.7899	2.1853	0.2209
5	A	0.6861	10	9	0.6606	0.7306	0.1059
6	B	0.3855	11	9	1.4189	1.5938	0.1233
6	A	0.6145	12	11	0.6517	0.6392	−0.0192
7	B	0.3167	12	10	1.4385	2.1578	0.5000
7	A	0.6833	12	10	0.5022	0.5551	0.1052
8	A	0.4782	12	12	0.8500	1.1168	0.3139
8	B	0.5218	25	24	1.4049	1.0277	−0.2685
9	A	0.2919	19	21	1.7751	2.4262	0.3668
9	B	0.7081	19	21	0.4070	0.4617	0.1344
10	A	0.2301	19	22	2.6866	3.3467	0.2457
10	B	0.7699	21	23	0.3706	0.3380	−0.0880
11	A	0.4152	22	23	1.3005	1.4085	0.0831
11	B	0.5848	23	23	0.8500	0.7379	−0.1319
12	A	0.4123	23	24	1.3452	1.4254	0.0596
12	B	0.5877	25	25	0.8500	0.8935	0.0512
13	B	0.4613	24	24	0.8500	1.1942	0.4049
13	A	0.5387	24	24	0.8500	0.9764	0.1487
14	A	0.4969	25	25	0.8500	1.0372	0.2203
14	B	0.5031	26	25	1.4898	1.5992	0.0734
15	B	0.5303	26	26	0.8500	0.9089	0.0693
15	A	0.4697	28	29	2.5500	3.3276	0.3049
16	B	0.5080	29	29	0.8500	0.9926	0.1678

	Final score	Bets	Payoff
TEAM A	29	7.5549	−7.5549
TEAM B	30	7.9532	8.7968
	Net Betting Payoff = 1.2419		

Table 8. Exponential function favourability, $\sigma = 0.3$; 100 game set hedge series construction

Threshold favourability, r_0				
m	0	0.05	0.1	0.2
0	−1.96	2.12	11.29	17.21
0.05	−0.76	4.51	13.27	19.12
0.1	−0.79	3.77	10.34	17.26
0.2	2.83	4.74	8.19	14.17

value chosen, the number of hedges completed in the simulated games can range from 1 to 20 with never more than 3 uncompleted bet pairs among this series. Losses may be incurred on any particular game under this imperfect hedge strategy due to the possibility of uncompleted bet pairs. Such losses never exceeded 1 betting unit for any of 14 the simulated games. Whereas the single game gain has ranged as high as 3 units. Game sets are divided approximately 60–40 in terms of winning to losing games for the sets examined. The total gain over the entire set of games is increased relative to the single hedge strategy and the instance of loss is reduced. As the odds favourability variance increases the potential for more profitable bets occurs and the expected gains and variance rise accordingly, positive net gains occur regularly for similar values of the standard deviation of the odds favourability distribution. The variance of the expected gains are larger than for the single hedge case (40 versus 6) as expected.

4. FINAL REMARKS

It appears possible to construct a profitable arbitrage strategies for the 30 point Jai Alai game. Modest returns may be realized under strategies of arbitrage and risk arbitrage single bet pair constructions. Mathematical programming results imply that series of bet pairs may be optimal for games of this kind. Simulation results suggest that improved gains may be obtained under such strategies where bet placements are dependent on the favourability of quoted odds and the score. Further analysis of this situation might concentrate on more detailed investigation into the actual distribution of quoted house odds during the game. This will involve more intensive data collection at Jai Alai frontons. Our preliminary data collection in Mexico City indicates that there are substantial inefficiencies. The formulation here has assumed score invariant single point win probabilities. A more refined but possibly unmanageable analysis might consider score variant probabilities possibly using Markov chains. More study should also be undertaken with respect to the reaction of the oddsmakers to shifts in score and an examination of their individual objective functions. Parayre (1986) has some results along these lines for win and perfecta bets based on player strength and post positions. These results follow ideas in Ziemba and Hausch (1986).

The methodology and insights found for team Jai Alai also have potential applications in other situations where one has non-marketable financial instruments.

These include certain horseracing (especially on betting exchanges), currency exposure and production situations. Risk arbitrage in traded options and warrants markets is an additional example. See Shaw, Thorp and Ziemba (1995) for one such application related to the Japanese Nikkei put warrant in 1989–90.

In England and other European and Commonwealth countries legalized bookies set odds that various horses will win a given race both on-course and off-course. These odds may differ across bookies at a particular moment of time. The odds change during the twenty or so minutes before a race is run as opinions are altered in light of new information such as the horses' appearances and because the bookies would like to simultaneously balance their books to guarantee a profit no matter what horse wins, and maximize the number of tickets sold. This situation from the bettor's perspective mirrors the Jai Alai situation, once extended to multiple outcomes, assuming that he has an independent estimate of the probability that each horse will win obtained by a handicapping or statistical procedure.

A key feature of the team Jai Alai and racing situations is that the tickets once purchased are not marketable except perhaps at a substantial discount. Other situations share these features and we will describe two of them briefly here.

Consider a company with substantial foreign accounts receivable at a future date. The standard way to hedge against possible devaluations is through a futures contract in the country's currency. However, in many cases this is not possible because the currency does not have an active futures market or the time horizon is too long. The currencies of Italy, Thailand and Turkey are examples of the former. Even for established heavily traded currencies such as the euro and the Mexican Peso such contracts will not cover a multiple year exposure. Negotiations with a bank might produce a special forward contract for part of the exposure. Such a contract would be difficult to sell except at a substantial discount. As time goes on the company may add additional contracts to cover more of the exposure with the original or other banks. In terms of the Jai Alai formulation one may think of the original exposure and any subsequent accounts receivable as bets on A and the covering as bets on B.

Farmers often have fixed contracts for delivery of the crops from their acreage at a specified time. Both the price he will receive and quantity he will have available are likely uncertain. In a publicly traded commodity such as corn or wheat he could hedge against these uncertainties. However, active futures markets are not available for most commodities. Lettuce and raspberries are two such examples. The farmer can consider his crop as bets on A and contracts he makes with other farmers of specific quantitites at fixed prices as bets on B.

Some analyses of problems similar to these two examples using hedging arguments for static problems appear in Anderson and Danthine (1981), Feiger and Jacquillat (1979), McKinnon (1967) and Rolfo (1980) and for a two period problem in which additional information becomes available in Baesel and Grant (1982).

ACKNOWLEDGMENT

This research was partially supported by the Natural Sciences and Engineering Research and the Social Science and Humanities Research Councils of Canada.

Thanks are due to Ian Howard and friends for taking WTZ to the Mexico City fronton where the idea for this paper was born, and to Donald Hausch and Jerry Kallberg for helpful discussions.

REFERENCES

Anderson, R.A. and Danthine, J.P. (1981) Cross hedging, *Journal of Political Economy*, **89**, 1182–96.

Baesel, J. and Grant, D. (1982) Optimal sequential futures trading, *Journal of Financial and Quantitative Analysis*, **17**, 683–95.

Epstein, R.A. (1977) *The Theory of Gambling and Statistical Logic*, 2nd edn. Academic Press.

Feiger, G. and Jacquillat, B. (1979) Currency option bonds, puts and calls on spot exchange and the hedging of contingent foreign earnings, *Journal of Finance*, **34**, 1124–40.

Goodfriend, M.J. and Friedman, J.H. (1975) A Monte-Carlo analysis of Jai Alai. Paper presented at the ORSA/TIMS Joint National Meeting, Nov. 17–19.

Goodfriend, M.J. and Friedman, J.H. (1977) Some further analyses of Jai Alai. Paper presented at the ORSA/TIMS Joint National Meeting, Atlanta, Georgia, Nov. 7–9.

Hausch, D.B. and Ziemba, W.T. (1986) *Betting at the Racetrack*. San Luis Obispo, CA: Dr Z Investments, Inc.

Kallio, M. and Ziemba, W.T. (2003) Arbitrage pricing simplified. Working Paper, Helsinki School of Economics.

Kelly, J. (1956) A new interpretation of information rate, *The Bell System Technical Journal*, **35**, 917–26.

MacLean, L.C. and Ziemba, W.T. (1999) Growth versus security tradeoffs in dynamic investment analysis, *Annals of Operations Research*, **85**, 193–226.

MacLean, L.C., Ziemba, W.T. and Blazenko, G. (1992) Growth versus security in dynamic investment analysis, *Management Science*, **38**, 1562–85.

McKinnon, R.I. (1967) Futures markets, buffer stocks and income stability for primary producers, *Journal of Political Economy*, **75**, 844–61.

Parayre, R. (1986) A study of Jai-Alai betting. Term paper in UBC Commerce 612, Faculty of Commerce, University of British Columbia.

Rolfo, J. (1980) Optimal hedging under price and quantity uncertainty: the case of a cocoa producer, *Journal of Political Economy*, **88**, 100–16.

Shaw, J., Thorp, E.O. and Ziemba, W.T. (1995) Convergence to efficiency of the Nikkei put warrant market of 1989–1990, *Applied Mathematical Finance*, **2**, 243–71.

Sklansky, D. (1983) Hedging and middling, *Gambling Times*, January.

Thorp, E.O. (1975) Portfolio choice and the Kelly criterion, in W.T. Ziemba and R.G. Vickson (eds), *Stochastic Optimization Models in Finance*. Academic Press, pp. 599–619.

Ziemba, W.T. (2003) *The Stochastic Programing Approach to Asset Liability and Wealth Management*. AIMR and Appendix.

Chapter 6

The Game Box Score in Basketball: Linking Statistics to Game Outcomes

Leonard C. MacLean and William T. Ziemba

In this chapter we use game box scores to evaluate the actual contribution to team success of specific players. Those who contribute the most are not necessarily the best offensive players. Defensive players like the famous Bill Russell who won 11 championships in 13 years with the Boston Celtics, can have greater impact than offensive giants like Wilt Chamberlin who won only two. Using data from the 1989–1990 NBA season, Dennis Rodman, Bill Lambier, A. C. Green and Vlade Divac standout above the legendary great player Magic Johnson.

6.1. Introduction

Assessing the performance of athletes on teams has a long tradition in sport. The top performers in recognized game statistics such as points scored receive awards and are compensated with fame and fortune. The complexity of elite performance in team sports is high, since team members frequently have different roles and different performance expectations, but also have an associated goal of winning. There are many scenarios during a game and person's role within the team would be scenario dependent. It is likely that the abilities that produce superior performance for an elite offensive player may differ from those of an elite defensive player.

When reports show individual differences in the measured performance for different types of essential situation related activities, it is typical to separately measure and analyze performance in these activities. The typical report of individual performance in separate activity dimensions is called the box score for a game. If investigators were to measure a composite index of performance by averaging all the many types of activities, then expert performance in essential domains would not be evident. The ability to explain both the skills that mediate performance and how these skills are acquired would be reduced or even eliminated.

The rapid reactions of athletes, such as hockey goalies, tennis players, and baseball batters, have been found to reflect acquired skills that involve anticipation of future events. Expert athletes do not simply acquire superior anticipation skills, but they also acquire superior control over their motor actions. Expert performance is facilitated by acquired mental representations that allow the athlete to anticipate, plan, and reason alternative courses of action. These mental pictures provide athletes with increased control of the abilities that are relevant to generating superior performance.

In many types of sports, athletes rapidly select actions in game situations. Expert performers gain an advantage from being able to foresee consequences of their actions and their opponents' actions (see Tenenbaum, Chapter 8; Williams & Ward, Chapter 9). For performers to actually improve their ability to anticipate and plan, it is necessary for them to set up practice tasks where their planning and selected actions can be evaluated against the actions of better performers in the same situations. Instead, the expert performance approach proposes that these improvements actually correspond to changes both in the cognitive mechanisms that mediate how the brain and nervous system control performance and in the degree of adaptation of the body's physiological systems. This approach also argues that these changes are induced by practice activities that are specifically designed to modify the current mechanisms so that performance can be incrementally improved.

Once we conceive of expert performance as mediated by complex integrated systems of representations for the execution, monitoring, planning, and analyzes of performance, it becomes clear that the acquisition of expert performance requires an orderly and deliberate approach. Deliberate practice is therefore designed to improve specific aspects of performance in a manner that assures participants that attained changes can be successfully integrated into representative performance. Compelling evidence now exists that many abilities of the elite performers are not signs of innate talent, but rather, they are the results of extended practice, sometimes amplified by early starts of practice during childhood. Similarly, it is quite possible that when coaches perceive a relation between high levels of motivation and attained performance, their ratings of motivation may really reflect the athletes' willingness to engage in deliberate practice with higher quantity and quality. Other personality characteristics, such as selfconfidence and anxiety, might at least in part be viewed not as causes of performance but rather as consequences of success or failure during past competitions and practice sessions that were designed to improve aspects of performance.

The evidence indicates that preparation through deliberate practice is a major factor in athlete performance. In a team competition there are numerous scenarios and players execute skills to gain advantage in situations. The score card for the competition will record those events which directly effect the outcome of the competition. For example, in basketball one team has possession of the ball. The possession ends if the team scores or losses possession of the ball. Loss of possession occurs with an expiration of possession time or a failed score attempt or a ball turnover. So the basketball score card records attempts, success/failure, reason for loss of possession. Player performance on a possession as documented on the scorecard is multidimensional.

6.2. Performance Measurement: The Box Score

The particular performance of interest in this paper is focused on competitive games in sports. An athlete or team of athletes compete in a structured game, following rules of play. Typically a game is composed of a sequence of head to head events, with the game outcome being the aggregate of the event outcomes. For example, in basketball the event is a ball possession for a team and that possession continues until the opposing team takes possession, either from a score or turnover. The outcome of an event is defined by classes which delineate the various possible occurrences in the event. Of course the event occurs over a period of time and the variety of things that happen in "play by play" are complex.

A box score is a structured summary of the results from a sport competition. The box score lists the game score as well as individual and team achievements in the game.The box score data is derived from a statistics sheet, and is then summarized into a contingency table, also known as a cross tabulation or cross tab or as a basic set of averages. This is used to help determine the relationship between elements, and in sports, certain percentages often help define the success of a team. This information is then correlated to a player, or a team where it is read to obtain a general idea of how the game was played or how the player performed during the game, a season, or their career. The box score statistics are used to determine the best performers in a game or over a season. That is, the leaders in offensive and defensive statistics are determined from game box scores.

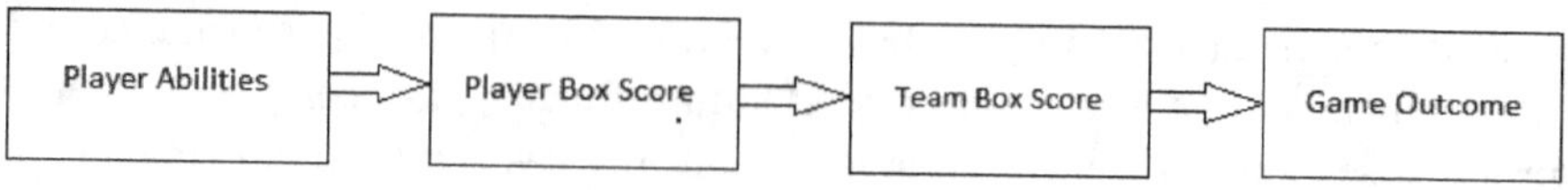

Figure 6.1. Outcome relationships.

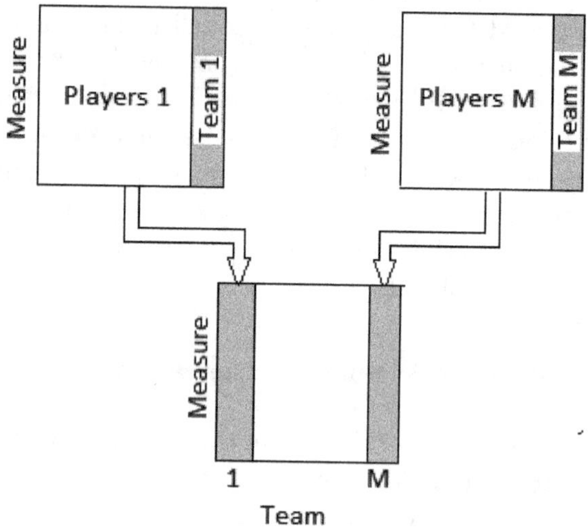

Figure 6.2. Hierarchial relationship.

The approach here is simplified, so that the information in the "box score" for a game is defined by the outcome classes. It is considered that the box score for competing teams is a sufficient description of in-game activities and are determinants of game outcome (win/loss). A depiction of the approach is given in Figure 6.1.

Underlying the statistics in the box score are the physical and mental characteristics of expert performance. The many hours of deliberate practice will condition a players actions in game situations and that is reflected in the player box score. It is estimated that 10,000 hours of practice are usual for elite performers (Ericsson, 1996). The exceptional performers in sports create favorable opportunities on offense and defense. In a team sport like basketball the players on the floor coordinate their activities on offense and defense to get a favorable team result. The player box scores aggregate to a team box score, and players are nested within a team for the game. Individual player activities on each possession generate the game box score for players and the team as shown in Figure 6.2. The game outcome is a team result, so it is natural to relate game outcome to team box score. It is clear that very different player box scores could aggregate to the same team box score. So attributing team success to individual players presents a challenge. An example of that effect in basketball is the performance of Wilt Chamberlain of the Philadelphia Warriors. Chamberlain's box score dominated the Warrior's box score and indeed all other player box scores. However, the Warrior's box did not dominate the Boston Celtic's box and Boston routinely won the NBA championship during Chamberlain's career. Team composition in football is shown to be significant, and in particular defensive players are critical to winning (MacLean and Ziemba, 2020). It is likely the same is true in basketball.

The analysis of the relationship of box scores to game outcomes will be in two stages: (1) the effect of the team box score on game outcome; (2) the contribution of individual players to team box scores.

6.2.1. *Event outcomes*

A competitive game is composed of a sequence of events. In basketball the event is a possession of the ball. The possession ends when the ball is turned over to the competing team. So possessions alternate. The play on an offensive possession is intricate, with the five players having important roles. For example, the classic pick and roll is an offensive play in which a player sets a screen for a teammate handling the ball and then moves toward the basket to receive a pass. The legendary pair of John Stockton (guard) and Karl Malone (forward) used the play to devasting effect. On defense the effect of blocking out offensive players around the basket produces successful rebounds and a change of possession. Although the on-floor choreography is complicated, the end result is clear — a change of possession with a score or change of possession without a score. The score card for the possession will record those activities which directly effect the outcome. A focus on the score card and box score assumes that the strategic movements and physical abilities of players lead to favorable offensive and defensive opportunities, and that in turn produces a winning box score. The hours of deliberate practice and sophisticated game plans are accounted for indirectly.

Consider the multidimensional outcome for player j on team h, from a possession in a game as displayed in Table 6.1. The possessions are alternating, and roles switch from offense to defense.

If $X_j' = (X_{j1}, \ldots, X_{jK})$, where X_{jk} = the number of instances of class k during a possession and the observed result from possession i is $X_{ij}' = (X_{ij1}, \ldots, X_{ijK})$, then the game box score for player j for the total of n possessions in the game is $Y_j' = \sum_{i=1}^{n} X_{ij}'$.

Table 6.1. Player j score card.

	Action		
Possession	C_1	$\cdots$	C_K
1	✓		
2			✓
⋮			
n			
Game Box Score	Y_{j1}	$\cdots$	Y_{jK}

PLAYER	TEA	MATCH UP	W/L	MIN	PTS	FGM	FGA	3PM	3PA	FTM	FTA	ORE	DRE	AST	STL	BLK	TOV	PF
B King	WAS	WAS @ CHH	W	34	19	7	14	0	0	5	9	5	1	5	1	0	2	4
C Jones	WAS	WAS @ CHH	W	13	2	1	2	0	0	0	0	1	2	1	0	2	0	4
D Walker	WAS	WAS @ CHH	W	38	12	4	9	0	0	4	7	2	9	8	6	0	1	3
E Horton	WAS	WAS @ CHH	W	5	2	0	1	0	0	2	2	0	0	0	0	0	1	0
H Grant	WAS	WAS @ CHH	W	16	5	2	5	0	0	1	2	0	1	0	1	0	2	5
J Malone	WAS	WAS @ CHH	W	33	28	11	21	0	0	6	6	0	6	3	0	0	0	1
J Williams	WAS	WAS @ CHH	W	35	24	8	18	0	1	8	8	1	10	2	2	0	5	0
L Eackles	WAS	WAS @ CHH	W	15	8	3	6	0	0	2	2	1	1	1	1	0	3	1
M Alarie	WAS	WAS @ CHH	W	21	10	5	9	0	0	0	0	5	2	2	0	0	3	4
S Colter	WAS	WAS @ CHH	W	10	0	0	0	0	0	0	0	1	2	0	0	0	2	0
T Hammond	WAS	WAS @ CHH	W	20	6	2	8	0	0	2	3	5	5	0	0	1	0	5

Figure 6.3. NBA game box: Players on team

A game involves two teams each with a roster of players. There is a game box score for each of the players on the competing, defined as $Y'_{hj} = (Y_{hj1}, \ldots, Y_{hjK})$, for player j on team h. The players are nested on teams, and assuming a team roster in a game has M players , the team has a game box score $Y'_h = \sum_{j=1}^{M} Y'_{hj}$.

An illustration of the box score array for players on a team for a game is displayed in Figure 6.3. The data is taken from the site NBA.com. Obviously the player boxes total to the team box and the game boxes total to the season box. Usually the season box is averaged over the number of games. It is assumed that the team box score in a game is directly related to team success in the game. Achieving the successful team box score is complex. A successful team could be composed of specialists, with individual players excelling in specific dimensions of the event outcome X. Alternatively, a team could have versatile players who cover most roles and are flexible and interchangeable. So the player profile on successful teams is significant.

The box score is the routine data collected on players and teams in a competition. There is a lot more information about play by play than the statistics in the box score. The availability of box score data for a long history of sport competitions makes that game summary a convenient basis for comparing players and teams.

6.2.2. *Composite measures*

Although the box score for a game is a summary it has a substantial array of numbers. The individual components can be compared for players and teams, and that is very traditional. The season leaders in points scored per game, assists per game and rebounds per game are distinguished. However, it is the multidimensional profile for players and teams which is of interest, and in particular the link of that profile to game success that will be explored. The usual approach to multivariate analysis is to study linear combinations of the many variables for structural and causal relationships. Following that approach we will consider linear combinations of the box score components as composite measures of performance. In the analysis it is important to recognize that players are nested on teams, and the team success results from the coordinated activities of team players. We will work on two levels: (1) the link between the team box score and team success (winning a game); (2) The structure of the player box scores which aggregate to the team box score, and the structure for winning teams.

6.2.3. *Team value*

Using the multidimensional profile in the box score, a composite measure can be constructed (Winston, 2009). The approach is to generate a linear combination of the box score components with weights $\beta = (\beta_0, \ldots, \beta_L)$. The weights capture the relative importance of a component to team success. Teams differ in their composition, with varying player abilities and strategies for game success. So relative importance of the box score components should differ by team. If we have H teams, then define the team indicators: $T_j, j = 1, \ldots, H-1$, where $T_j = 1$ for team j and $T_j = 0$ otherwise, except $T_j = -1$ for team H. Consider team h with K_h players and a player box score set

$[Y_{hjl}, l = 1, \ldots, L, j = 1, \ldots, K_h]$. Then the composite score for player $j, j = 1, \ldots, K_h$ on team h is

$$U_{hj} = \left[\beta_0 + \sum_{l=1}^{L} \beta_l Y_{hjl}\right] + \left[\sum_{j=1}^{H-1} T_j \left(\beta_{L+j} + + \sum_{l=1}^{L} \beta_{L+M-1+j+l} Y_{hjl}\right)\right].$$

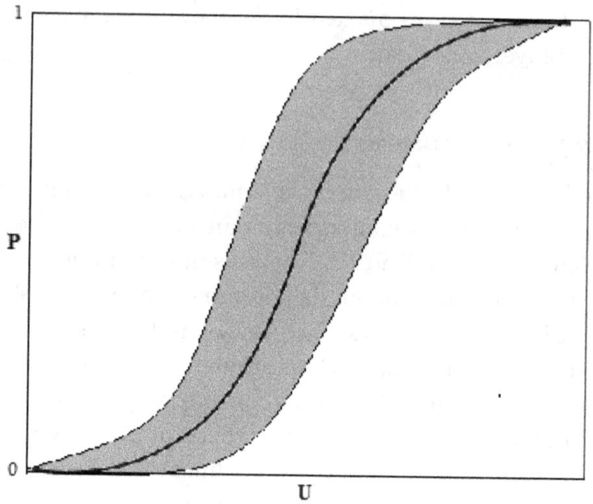

Figure 6.4. Win probability vs. team value.

The box score value U_{hj} represents the contribution of the multidimensional team profile to "success" in the competitive game. The aggregate of player scores gives the team score, $Y_{hl} = \sum_j Y_{hjl}$. So team h has a box score value for a game,

$$U_h = \beta_0^h + \beta_1^h Y_{h1} + \ldots + \beta_L^h Y_{hL}.$$

In the linear function, $\beta_0^h = \beta_0 + \beta_{L+h}$, $\beta_l^h = \beta_l + \beta_{L+M+h}$. The games are taken as repetitions, so the box score for each game provides player scores $\{U_{ihj}, i = 1, \ldots, n\}$ and team scores $\{U_{ih}, i = 1, \ldots, n\}$.

The objective in a competition is to "win" the game, so the objective is to find weights β that define a value U which is closely related to winning. Of course the box score is an incomplete profile of game play and there is an element of chance in winning, so value is $V = U + \varepsilon$, where ε is random with expectation $E(\varepsilon) = 0$. With a specific box score there is a chance of winning, with the assumption that the chance increases as the value increases. Let P =the probability of winning, and consider the relationship between P and U represented in Figure 6.4. The sigmoid shape is a theoretical function for the improvement in performance with learning/training. The improvement through practice is a player phenomenon, and the team improves with individual player development.

Winning in a team competition is a team success and the initial hypothesis is that as the team box score value increases, the success rate increases - implied by the sigmoid function. With game i team h statistics $Y_{ih} = (Y_{ih1}, \ldots, Y_{ihL}) = \left(\sum_{j=1}^{K_h} Y_{ihj1}, \ldots, \sum_{j=1}^{K_h} Y_{ihjL}\right)$, the total of player box scores for a team, then $V_{ih} = \beta_0^h + \beta_1^h Y_{ih1} + \cdots + \beta_L^h Y_{ihL} + \varepsilon_i$. If the team value is V_{ih}, consider the team win probability in game i defined by the logistic/sigmoid function for probability (Bradley-Terry, 1952):

$$P_{ih} = \frac{1}{1 + e^{-V_{ih}}} = \frac{1}{1 + e^{-\left(\beta_0^h + \beta_1^h Y_{ih1} + \cdots + \beta_L^h Y_{ihL} + \varepsilon_i\right)}}.$$

With $L = ln\left(\frac{P}{1-P}\right)$, L is the logarithm of the odds ratio and is called the logit. The logit linearizes the probability model as

$$L_{ih} = \beta_0^h + \beta_1^h Y_{ih1} + \cdots + \beta_L^h Y_{ihL} + \varepsilon_i.$$

So $L = V = U + \varepsilon$, the composite box score value plus random variation. The logit transformation sets the model in the framework of logistic regression. With team box scores for n games $\{Y_{ih}, i = 1, \ldots, n, h = 1, \ldots, H\}$. the weights are estimated as $\left(\hat{\beta}_0^h, \ldots, \hat{\beta}_L^h, h = 1, \ldots, H\right)$, The estimation is from the full model, with fitted values

$$\hat{U}_{ih} = \hat{\beta}_0 + \sum_{l=1}^{L} \hat{\beta}_l Y_{ihl} + \sum_{h=1}^{H-1} T_h \hat{\beta}_{L+j} + \cdots + \sum_{l=1}^{L} \hat{\beta}_{L+M-1+j+l} \left(T_h \times Y_{ihl}\right).$$

The fitted team values for games $\hat{U}_{ih}$ are directly related to wins and losses. By inverting the logit we have $\hat{p}_{ih} = \frac{1}{1+e^{-\hat{U}_{ih}}}$, the estimated win probability for team h in game i. The estimated probability can be converted to predicted wins $\hat{W}$ and losses $\hat{L}$ and a comparison of predicted and actual W/L for the set of n games is a validation of the team values $\hat{U}_{ih}$ and the estimated linear weights.

6.2.4. *The estimated player contribution*

The contribution of individual players to the team win may not be reflected in the team box score. In a game each player has as box score as shown in Figure 6.3. *We will assume the team linear weights for components reflect the importance of each component in the box score.* Those weights can be used with player box scores to calculate the player contribution to the team box score. The player aggregate score for game i is $\hat{U}_{ihj} = \beta_0^h + \beta_1^h Y_{ihj1} + \cdots + \beta_L^h Y_{ihjL}$. Then we have $\sum_{j=1}^{K_h} \hat{U}_{ihjk} = \beta_0^h + \beta_1^h \sum Y_{ihj1} + \cdots + \beta_L^j \sum Y_{ihjL} = \hat{U}_{ih}$, so the total of player scores on a team in a game is equal to the team score for the game. The pattern in player scores $\{\hat{U}_{ihj}, j = 1,\ldots,K_h\}$ may be important to the game outcome. Summary statistics for the pattern over a season will provide additional evidence for game success.

6.3. The 1989–1990 NBA Season

The NBA team and player analysis will be applied to the game box score data for the 1989–1990 regular season. The data is found on the site NBA.com/boxscores. The layout is as shown in Figure 6.3, with data for every game - game result, player statistics, team statistics. The estimated logistic regression results for the team box scores for each game are provided in Table 6.2. Only the statistically significant components in the box score are shown. The nonsignificant weights are taken as $\beta_l = 0$. Many of the weights are the same for teams. The cases where team weights differ are in larger print.

6.3.1. *Team value*

The team linear weights were applied to the team box scores for each game in the 1989–1990 season, to give fitted logit values $\hat{U}_{ih},\ i = 1,\ldots 82$. The logits were classified by winning team and losing teams. The plot of winning and losing logits is shown in Figure 6.5. Clearly there is a difference between winning and losing logits and by implication a difference between winning and losing box scores. The linear weights produce an aggregate score which discriminates between winning and losing.

The logit is converted to a probability of winning/losing with $\hat{p}_{ih} = \frac{1}{1+e^{-\hat{U}_{ih}}}$. Obviously $\hat{U}_{ih} = 0 \Rightarrow \hat{p}_{ih} = 0.5$, and $\hat{U}_{ih} < 0 \Rightarrow \hat{L}, \hat{U}_{ih} > 0 \Rightarrow \hat{W}$. In Table 6.3 the classification of actual wins/losses and predicted wins/losses is given. The association is very high (88%). The evidence is strong that creating an aggregate score from team box scores using linear weights is warranted.

The logits are legitimate team descriptors, and the comparison of teams using the logit is valid. The box plot of the distribution of fitted logits for each team is presented in Figure 6.6. The positioning of the boxes is a display of team strength. The Detroit Pistons are highlighted with a green box. The other outstanding team is the Los Angeles Lakers. Although the upside of the Pistons is greater than the Lakers, a higher fraction of the distribution for the Lakers is above zero, and in fact the Lakers had

Table 6.2. Fitted weights by NBA team: 1989–1990.

	PTS	FGA	3PA	FTA	ORB	DRB	STL	BLK	TOV	PF
ATL	0.2319	−.3381	−.1859	−0.0987	.1365	0.3332	0.0663	0.0855	−0.2273	0.0579
BOS	0.2319	−.3381	−.1859	−0.0987	0.3006	0.3332	0.3343	0.0855	−0.2273	−0.1511
CHH	0.2319	−.3381	−.1859	−0.0987	0.3006	0.3332	0.3343	0.0855	−0.2273	−0.1178
CHI	0.2319	−.3381	−.1859	−0.0987	0.3006	0.3583	0.3343	0.0855	−0.2273	−0.1178
CLE	0.2319	−.3381	−.1859	−0.0987	0.3485	0.3332	0.3343	0.0855	−0.2273	−0.1178
DAL	0.2319	−.3381	−.1859	−0.0987	0.3006	0.3332	0.3343	0.0855	−0.2273	−0.1178
DEN	0.2319	−.3381	−.1859	−0.0987	0.5615	0.3332	0.3343	0.0855	−0.4398	−0.1178
DET	0.2319	−0.1659	−0.5339	−0.0987	0.3006	0.3332	0.3343	0.0855	−0.2273	−0.5038
GOS	0.2319	−.3381	−.1859	−0.0987	0.3006	0.3332	0.3343	0.0855	−0.2273	−0.1178
HOU	0.2319	−.3381	0.1251	−0.0987	0.3006	0.485	0.3343	0.0855	−0.2273	−0.4608
IND	0.2319	−.3381	−.1859	−0.0987	0.3006	0.3332	0.3343	0.0855	−0.2273	−0.1178
LAC	0.2319	−.3381	−.1859	−0.1585	0.3006	0.3332	0.3343	0.0855	−0.2273	−0.1178
LAL	0.2319	−0.2834	−.1859	−0.0987	0.3006	0.3332	−0.0497	0.0855	−0.2273	−0.1178
MIA	0.2319	−.3381	−0.4359	−0.0987	0.3006	0.3332	0.3343	0.0855	−0.2273	−0.1178
MIL	0.2319	−.3381	−.1859	−0.0987	0.3006	0.3332	0.3343	0.4142	−0.2273	−0.1178
MIN	0.2319	−.3381	−.1859	−0.0987	0.2359	0.3332	0.3343	0.0855	−0.2273	−0.1178
NJN	0.2000	−.3381	−.1859	−0.0987	0.4129	0.3332	0.3343	0.0855	−0.2273	−0.1178
NYK	0.2319	−.3381	−.1859	−0.0987	0.3006	0.3332	0.3343	0.0855	−0.2273	−0.1178
ORL	0.2319	−.3381	0.4191	−0.0987	0.3006	0.3332	0.3343	0.0855	−0.2273	−0.1178
PHL	0.2319	−.3381	−.1859	−0.0987	0.3006	0.3332	0.3343	0.0855	−0.2273	−0.1178
PHX	0.2319	−.3381	−.1859	−0.0987	0.4817	0.3332	0.3343	0.0855	−0.2273	−0.2541
POR	0.2319	−.3381	0.2771	−0.0987	0.3006	0.5547	0.3343	−0.3045	−0.2273	−0.1178
SAC	0.2319	−.3381	0.0261	−0.0987	0.3006	0.3332	0.3343	−0.2535	−0.2273	−0.1178
SAN	0.2319	−.3381	−.1859	−0.0987	0.3006	0.3332	0.3343	0.0855	−0.2273	−0.1178
SEA	0.2319	−.3381	−0.0681	−0.0987	0.3006	0.3332	0.3343	0.0855	−0.2273	−0.1178
UYH	0.2319	−.3381	−.1859	−0.0987	0.3006	0.3332	0.3343	0.0855	−0.2273	−0.1178
WAS	0.2319	−.3381	−.1859	−0.0987	0.3006	0.3332	0.3343	0.0855	−0.2273	−0.1178

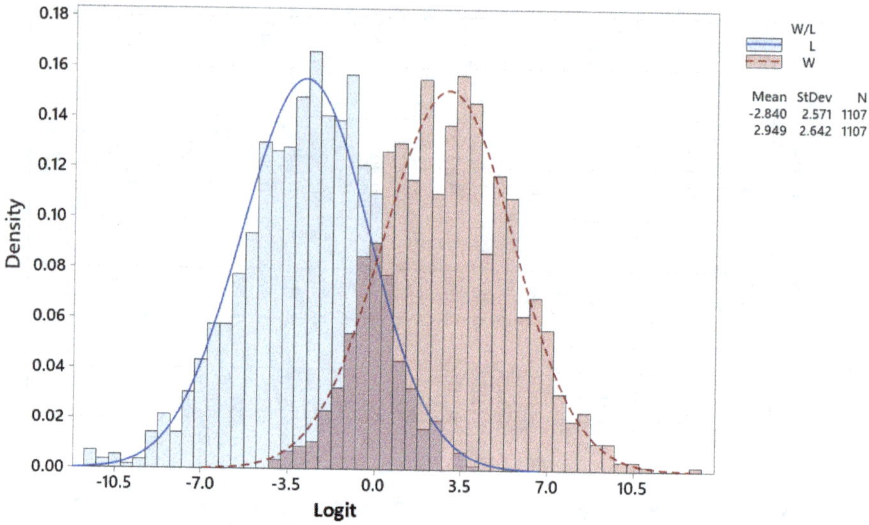

Figure 6.5. Game logits by win/loss result.

Table 6.3. Model prediction.

	$\widehat{L}$	$\widehat{W}$	
L	**970**	137	1107
W	149	**958**	1107
	1119	1095	2214

the best winning percentage in the regular 1989–1990 season. However, the Pistons beat the Lakers in the playoff final to win the NBA Championship. Again, this display shows the success of the linear weights in describing team strength and performance.

6.3.2. *Player contribution*

The contribution of individual players to the team win may not be reflected in the team box score. In a game each player has a box score as shown in Figure 6.3. Player scores were computed for each game in the 1989–1990 season using the team weights in Table 6.2. The player profiles $\{\hat{U}_{ihj},\ j = 1, \ldots K_h,\ h = 1, \ldots, 27\}$ were summarized with the mean and standard deviation. The means were adjusted by substracting the team score, so the values shown reflect deviation from the mean. The player

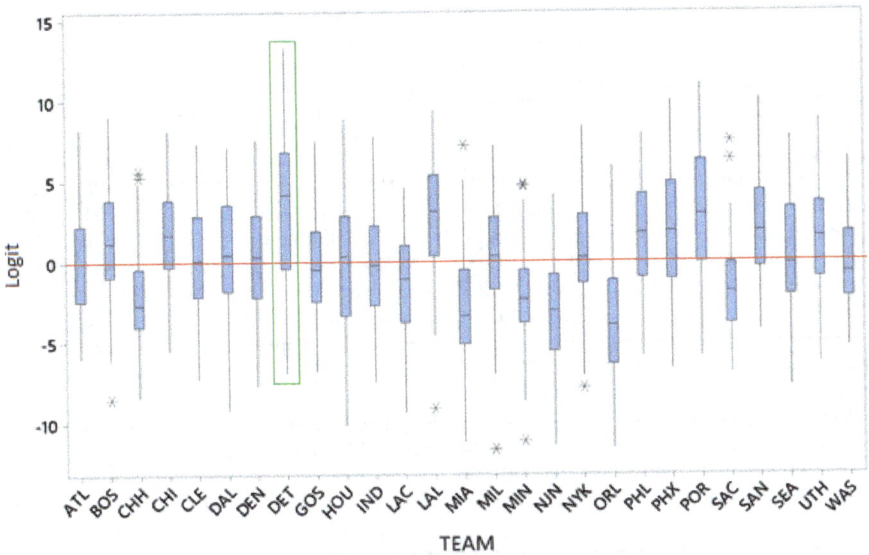

Figure 6.6. Game logits for NBA teams: 1989–1990.

scores for the distinguished teams (Pistons, Lakers) are shown in Table 6.4. The statistics are averages for all the games played and don't necessarily reflect the player contributions to success in individual games. The objective here is to highlight players with a positive effect on average: Dennis Rodman, Bill Lambier (Pistons) and A. C. Green, Vlade Divac (Lakers) are notable. The logit certainly picks up defensive performance.

The play of successful teams involves player coordination and interaction. So the full set of box scores for a team are a factor. In Table 6.4 the player box score is summarized with a logit. It is hypothesized that the within game variability of the player logits $\{\hat{U}_{ihj},\ j = 1, \ldots, K_h, h = 1, \ldots, 27\}$ would be an additional factor in team success in a game.

6.4. Discussion

The box score from an NBA game has a long tradition as the summary of in-game activities. The numbers in the box score have been used to distinguish player excellence since the very beginning of basketball competitions. Partly that comes from the observation of remarkable skill. When Michael Jordan attacked the rim, evading larger defenders and hammering home a "thunderous dunk", everyone understood they witnessed elite skill. When

Table 6.4. Players: Pistons and lakers.

Lakers				Pistons			
Name	**Games**	**Mean**	**SD**	**Name**	**Games**	**Mean**	**SD**
Bill Laimbeer	81	0.740	1.750	A.C. Green	82	1.378	1.563
David Greenwood	37	−0.097	0.655	Byron Scott	77	−0.843	1.168
Dennis Rodman	82	1.160	1.427	James Worthy	80	0.781	1.169
Gerald Henderson	46	−0.5322	0.6479	Jawann Oldham	3	−0.912	0.351
Isiah Thomas	81	−0.878	1.488	Jay Vincent	24	−0.851	0.578
James Edwards	82	−0.073	1.285	Larry Drew	80	−1.1310	0.8293
Joe Dumars	75	0.376	1.360	Magic Johnson	79	0.412	1.378
John Salley	82	0.024	1.314	Mark McNamara	33	−0.578	0.598
Mark Aguirre	78	−0.316	1.399	Mel McCants	13	−1.028	0.500
Ralph Lewis	4	−0.346	0.347	Michael Cooper	80	−1.013	0.910
Scott Hastings	40	−0.4164	0.5933	Mike Higgins	6	−0.9146	0.1568
Stan Kimbrough	10	−0.147	0.564	Mychal Thompson	70	0.876	1.120
Vinnie Johnson	82	−0.241	1.329	Orlando Woolridge	62	−0.048	0.983
William Bedford	42	−0.244	0.791	Steve Bucknall	18	−1.1807	0.3679
				Vlade Divac	82	0.638	1.330

Stephen Curry "drops jimmers" from way beyond the arc, eyes widen and joy erupts. The statistics in the box score reflect the elite performance of Jordan and Curry. Of course, Jordan's Bulls and Curry's Warriors were winning teams and it is natural to attribute the team success to the individual. However, there are many examples where individual performance did not translate into team success. The little things, the subtly of team play, the mental skill to assess high percentage plays, are a big part of success. It was no coincidence that Bill Russell and Tim Duncan, players with elite intellectual and defensive skill, led perennial winning teams. It is possible that the box score misses the subtleties of the game. It is also possible that the strategy and dynamics of in-game play place the elite players in optimal situations and their box scores stand out. This paper explores the link between the box score and team success in a season of games in the NBA.

Basketball is a game with complex spatio-temporal dynamics and strategies. The analyzes of NBA data is classified into two categories: those utilizing simple, box-score type statistics and those built around more extensive data measurements such as per-possession data, lineup-based data, or even extensive data containing player positions, shot types, etc. NBA analytics utilizing game statistics without an inherent court geometry context tend toward displays in which communication is valued over interactive/exploratory analysis. With the availability of new sources of data, increasing computational capability, and methodological innovation, our ability to characterize these dynamics with statistical and machine learning models is improving. Structured hierarchical models which incorporate more prior knowledge about basketball and leverage correlations across time and space will continue to be an essential part of disentangling player, team, and chance variation.

Regardless of the calculation methodology, we demonstrate some of the common uses of win probability and show how win probability can be used to evaluate the overall impact of NBA players by wins added to their respective teams. What is presented here constitutes just a few of the possibilities win probability values introduce. The paramount statistic in all sporting competition is wins, so accurate estimation of win probability and analyzes designed to increase win probability and consequently number of wins are invaluable to sports analytics.

We explore building on the fact that the box score somehow inherently incorporates both help and competition in its statistics. Whereas our initial direction was to view the league as a function of two teams to a win or loss, we realized plus-minus at the team level leads to a slightly different, and more easily managed paradigm. That is, a game is a function from two teams to a measure of team plus-minus ("winness"). This gives us a much better target for correlative analysis. Just as importantly, instead of analyzing and attempting to quantify exactly how plus-minus handles all the subtleties of competition, we simply leverage whatever it is with all other stats as well. Starting with box-score data, we calculate on a per game basis, the team plus-minus for all stats; all calculations and visualizations are based on different comparisons of these plus-minus statistics. For all results in this paper, NBA box-score data from the 1989–1990 season is used.

We have found many advanced statistics to be variations of linear weighting of singular statistics that are averages or accumulations. Often, this leads to the notion of value being akin to "more is better." It is possible for this to be the optimal or even correct approach. If linear weighting of box score components is sufficient for analyzing game outcome, then the historical records of game competition can be the basis for a comparison of legendary teams and players across eras.

Chapter 7

Risk Arbitrage in the 2021 NBA Championship

William T. Ziemba

The NBA playoffs and finals are ideal games to watch as they are very competitive and they have many lead changes so mean reversion risk arbitrage is an ideal way to bet and watch these games. I start discussing the general risk arbitrage principles and its application to various sports betting, political and stock market mean reverting situations, then apply it to the NBA playoffs and finals.

7.1. What is Risk Arbitrage?

Leonard MacLean and I both like NBA and NFL games. MacLean likes hockey. I don't like the violence that the fans seem to want. It's beautiful to watch but the low scores can lead to betting problems as a silly and controversial penalty can give the victory to the weaker team and you lose your bet. I did set the line for the BC Lotto Corporation in 1982 in the regular season and the playoffs and did watch some games. In 1982 when I was a visiting professor at UCLA, my wife and I went to an Oilers Kings game. That was in Wayne Gretsky's peak period with a great team filled with many outstanding players. Not surprising the score became 5–0 for Edmonton. Then people left so you could actually talk. Kings owner Jerry Buss left. But there was massive mean reversion and the Kings rallied 5–1 then 5–2 etc and the game ended 6–5 with Los Angeles winning.

The master of risk arbitrage is Ed Thorp. In his Princeton Newport hedge fund run from 1968–1988 he used risk arbitrage plus other strategies with risk control to gain about 20% gross and 16% net for his investors. The fee was a standard 20% incentive fee plus a small management fee. There were only three monthly losses in those twenty years so Ed got a rating of 13.8 on my DSSR symmetric Sharpe ratio, see Ziemba (2005) and Gergaud and Ziemba (2012) and reprinted in *Great Investment Ideas*, Ziemba (2017). This book also contains full and fractional Kelly simulations with Thorp and a response to Professor Paul Samuelson's critique of full Kelly strategies.

Thorp invested early in Berkshire Hathaway stock and clued me in to its advantage and I also have done well owning the stock long and augmenting with put and call option positions. I knew about Berkshire Hathaway the original company Buffett bought because there was one of their factories in my home town Adams, Massachusetts and my mother worked there and we bought some of the fabric products made there.

I knew Thorp was a Kelly optimization fan as he used it in his 1960 Beat the Dealer Blackjack book that changed that industry. For every card counter who made gains playing Thorp's or other systems there are many who lose so despite the casinos hating card counters they made much more profit because of the few successful card counters. Thorp used risk arbitrage in his 1966 book *Beat the Market* focusing on warrant risk arbitrage namely sell high and buy low similar or identical securities. Mathematically if OA are the US odds on A and B is the similar or same security with odds OB then, see Lane and Ziemba (2004, 2008), there is an arbitrage if (OA-1) (OB-1) is positive for US odds. Its called risk arbitrage since the arbitrage might not exist.

Thorp deserved the Nobel prize in Economics along with Robert Merton and Myron Scholes because he had the approximate but not analytic solution to fairly price options and was using his model to successfully trade warrant options. Thorp discussed this in the 1966 book seven years before the Black Scholes 1973 paper that Gene Fama and Merton Miller got it accepted in the University of Chicago's *Journal of Political Economy* after it was rejected by four other journals. It is typical that breakthrough papers are not well received by top journals.

But by saying that Samuelson, who also was searching for an option pricing formula, and he could find a solution in this book Samuelson who wanted to discover everything himself was severely displeased.

Samuelson was a complex person. He was a fellow for three years at the Harvard Economics Department for his PhD in the late 1930s. He then had about twenty five papers all in the top journals so assumed he would be hired at Harvard on the Economics faculty but because he was Jewish he was not hired. He then joined MIT where he helped build a department comparable to Harvard. Since Samuelson was so important that killed any chance for Thorp to get the Economics Nobel prize.

Samuelson was very friendly to me and over the years wrote me on various topics including three letters on his Kelly critique which I responded to with my response to Samuelson paper in the *Journal of Portfolio Management* reprinted in my *Great Investment Ideas.* Samuelson had some papers in my 1975 Ziemba Vickson *Stochastic Optimization Models in Finance* book.

Thorp also had his 1971 Kelly paper reprinted in that book so I got to know him from that. We did have other Kelly type papers in that book. Later Thorp wrote the forward to the Ziemba and Hausch (1984) *Beat the Racetrack*, saying that this book contains one of the few gambling systems that actually works. In the fall of 1984 Thorp, Bruce Fauman, a UBC colleague, and I went together to the first Breeders' Cup which was held at Hollywood Park in Los Angeles. The story of our day including the successful bets we made with the place and show system and the color of the Hollywood stars attending is in my 2018 memoir book *Adventures of a Modern Renaissance Academic in Investing and Gambling*, available from World Scientific or Amazon. That book discusses consulting, research and travel for academic professional or personal which were often combined so has about 100 color pictures for places around the world.

I learned about risk arbitrage somewhat independent of Thorp. In 1982 I was designing sports lottery games for the government sponsored Canadian Sports Pool. These were games based on hockey, basketball, basketball and other sports made into lotteries with an edge for the government. Ian Howard, the head of the project in Vancouver, and I went to Mexico City. There we visited the Jai Alai fronton where we saw the scores and prices moving up and down continuously. So with the help of UBC PhD student Dan Lane, we developed theory and Dan did simulations, discussed in Lane and Ziemba (2008). That taught me risk arbitrage. Later Thorp and I along with Julian Shaw of Toronto's Gordon Capital did a Nikkei Put warrant arbitrage. I had just returned from a year in Japan where I studied Japanese anomalies and stock market crashes. I discovered that the Nikkei put warrants were trading for 3–4 times their value. So we sold them and bought fair priced warrant options to hedge that were in the stock exchange. I executed the trades and wrote the Shaw, Thorp, and Ziemba (1995) paper with a more chatty version in *Wilmott* in 2018 which explained what we did. Thorp won the over $1 million *Barrons'* institutional investor contest and Shaw and I did well in our trading as well.

On Betfair the usual commission is 5% taken only on the bet winnings. That's a flaw in the business model as its better to get a cut of the total bet and this has caused Betfair to lose business such as shutting down business in some countries such as Canada. The bookies have taken over some of this business.

I explain the arbitrage formula as follow: Suppose A is 3–1, so in UK odds by betting 1 we collect 3. US odds are British odds plus one. To be fair if A is 3–1 then the odds on B who is favored must be less than even money namely 1/3rd so three times 1/3rd = 1 our 1 pound bet. We, of course, are looking for an arbitrage where OaOb > 1 with British odds or (Oa-1)(Ob-1) > 1 for US odds. So we search for an Ob like 2/3rd to give the edge and the arbitrage where you cannot lose. This usually happens when A gets enough ahead of B, that B is now 2/3rd. Since the arbitrage might not exist its called risk arbitrage.

Another way to do risk arbitrage is to bet on A at long odds and then cover later, that is sell at a lower price. These are situations where you think events might lower the odds. A good example was the 2021 Super Bowl. Clearly quarterbacks Tom Brady (Tampa Bay) or Patrick Mahomes (Kansas City) were the most likely to be MVP. Mahomes was last year when Kansas City won and Brady was MVP four times when New England won. But the good bet was on Rob Gronkowski. Gronkowski holds the NFL Super Bowl records for Super Bowl TD's by a tight end and all of these were from Brady passes. Gronkowski retired from New England but Brady convinced him to return to Tampa Bay. Brady did a terrific job building the team around him, getting other star players as well such as star receiver Antonio Brown, running back Leonard Fournette and defensive star Jason Pierre-Paul.

Gronkowski was not used much during the season except for blocking which he is also good at. Brady focused on other receives such as Brown and Mike Evans. But this was the Super Bowl and it made perfect sense for Brady to get Gronk more involved. Since Gronkowski was not used much his MVP odds were 188–1. Well these odds fell considerably when the first touchdown for Tampa Bay was a Brady to Gronkowski pass. Then there was a second Brady to Gronkowski TD pass and the odds for to be MVP were now 6–1. Since it was still obvious that Brady would be MVP if Tampa Bay won the game. And that was the result Tampa Bay won and Brady was MVP for the fifth time. Cashing out at 6–1 gave a gain of a whopping 182 points so the gain on a 100 pound bet was 1820£ less 5%. Again the key is find a situation with long odds that can come down in odds if something quite reasonable happens.

This strategy combines analysis of the situation and good betting. A political one is the US 2024 presidential election. The Democrat Joe Biden, the current president, is doing a very good job dealing with COVID-19. He wants to help all Americans even those who did not vote for him. This includes non whites and legal immigrants. He wants to cooperate with the Republican opposition. But the Republicans do not want to cooperate and they want a white dominated society without immigrants. They will not accept defeat even though the vote was 81–74 million for Biden who also won the Electoral College. Now November 2024 is a long way off and Biden is currently 78 years old. Vice President Harris is a strong candidate but there are frictions with her staff and the White House.

Trump still claims the votes were faulty yet there is no such evidence. Trump's many followers are sticking with the *big lie* as it's called in the press. Meanwhile Trump's company and, possibly, his family are in legal and financial trouble. But he could as he has for the last 30 years escape the trouble.

The Betfair odds on July 21, 2021 were along with bets I made so far follow in Figure 7.1.

To win I need the odds to get longer as I am short. Remember only one person can be president so with N shorts, $N-1$ must win and all N can win if none of the shorts are elected president.

67 selections	88.2%		Back all	Lay all		75.5%
Kamala Harris £1,500.99	6 £298	6.2 £15	6.4 £108	6.6 £70	6.8 £56	7 £111
Joe Biden £1,500.99	5.1 £51	5.2 £36	5.3 £8	5.5 £86	5.6 £100	5.7 £140
Donald Trump -£3,154.12	8.8 £105	9 £812	9.2 £764	9.6 £1267	9.8 £846	10 £64
Ron DeSantis -£2,989.31	11.5 £40	12 £261	12.5 £95	13.5 £53	14 £695	14.5 £20
Nikki Haley -£2,905.40	20 £124	21 £88	22 £3	24 £4	26 £11	27 £4
Dwayne Johnson -£1,349.01	44 £6	80 £3	85 £7	90 £55	95 £26	100 £11
Mike Pence -£2,990.93	27 £38	28 £5	29 £13	30 £8	32 £231	34 £13
Mike Pompeo -£2,859.76	65 £7	75 £32	80 £10	90 £3	95 £34	100 £16
Tucker Carlson -£3,242.61	80 £5	85 £11	90 £5	100 £7	110 £5	120 £9
Pete Buttigieg -£2,237.51	50 £31	55 £28	60 £9	75 £45	80 £43	85 £26
Elizabeth Warren -£2,499.01	55 £18	60 £53	75 £8	90 £2	95 £7	100 £4
Candace Owens -£499.01	70 £9	80 £3	85 £5	100 £2	110 £21	150 £5
Kristi Noem -£1,859.01	55 £74	60 £41	65 £33	75 £19	80 £506	100 £15
Ted Cruz -£3,298.06	60 £32	65 £32	70 £27	90 £4	95 £12	100 £6
Ivanka Trump -£2,147.11	100 £29	110 £9	120 £6	150 £13	160 £206	180 £270
Josh Hawley -£3,349.01	75 £30	80 £19	85 £2	95 £7	100 £36	110 £25
Alexandria Ocasio-Cortez £1,500.99	85 £9	90 £7	100 £4	140 £20	150 £15	160 £8

Figure 7.1. Betfair odds on the winner of the US presidency, 2024, on July 21, 2021.

The highest probability scenario currently favors the Democrats as Biden might get re-elected or Harris might win. Trump might avoid serious legal trouble and get back into favor with the majority of US voters but most likely not, So I am short Trump and many other Republicans and Democrats who I think won't win, but not Biden or Harris.

7.2. The NBA Playoffs

The regular season ended with the following standings as shown in Figure 7.2. The Philadelphia 76ers led the Eastern conference followed by the Brooklyn Nets then the Milwaukee Bucks and the New York Knicks. The Utah Jazz led the Western conference followed by the Phoenix Suns and then the Denver Nuggets and the Los Angeles Clippers.

The playoff tree is shown in Figure 7.3. Like other sports the high rated teams from the regular season play the lower ranked teams and have more home games.

7.3. The NBA Finals

The layout of this column is to discuss first the NBA finals and after that discuss the earlier rounds that led the Milwaukee Bucks and the Phoenix Suns to the finals. Neither teams had won in a long time. The Suns were in the NBA finals in 1993 led by Charles Barclay. They lost to the Michael Jordan led Chicago Bulls. Comparing these two greats:

	Points	Rebounds	Assists	Wins
Jordan	41.0	8.5	6.3	4
Barclay	27.3	13.0	5.5	2

Barclay was the regular season MPV in 1993. The Suns have never been NBA champions.

7.3.1. *Game 1: Milwaukee Bucks vs. the Phoenix Suns in Phoenix*

The Suns were 2nd n the West vs. the Bucks 3rd in the East and were five point favorites at home. The Suns won game 1 of the Western Conference finals 118–105. Chris Paul had 32 points and 9 assists. He along with Devin Booker's 27 points and 6 assists and Deandre Ayton with 19 rebounds and 22 points led the Suns to the victory.

Team	W	L	Pct	GB	Conf	Home	Away	L10	Strk
1 76ers	49	23	.681	-	31-11	29-7	20-16	8-2	W2
2 Nets	48	24	.667	1.0	26-16	28-8	20-16	6-4	W5
3 Bucks	46	26	.639	3.0	30-12	26-10	20-16	8-2	L1
4 Knicks	41	31	.569	8.0	25-17	25-11	16-20	7-3	W3
5 Hawks	41	31	.569	8.0	24-18	25-11	16-20	7-3	W4
6 Heat	40	32	.556	9.0	24-18	21-15	19-17	8-2	W1
7 Celtics	36	36	.500	13.0	20-22	21-15	15-21	4-6	L1
8 Wizards	34	38	.472	15.0	16-26	19-17	15-21	6-4	W2

(a) Eastern

Team	W	L	Pct	GB	Conf	Home	Away	L10	Strk
1 Jazz	52	20	.722	-	28-14	31-5	21-15	7-3	W2
2 Suns	51	21	.708	1.0	30-12	27-9	24-12	7-3	W3
3 Nuggets	47	25	.653	5.0	26-16	25-11	22-14	6-4	L1
4 Clippers	47	25	.653	5.0	27-15	26-10	21-15	4-6	L2
5 Mavericks	42	30	.583	10.0	21-21	21-15	21-15	7-3	L1
6 Trail Blazers	42	30	.583	10.0	23-19	20-16	22-14	8-2	W1
7 Lakers	42	30	.583	10.0	25-17	21-15	21-15	6-4	W5
8 Grizzlies	38	34	.528	14.0	19-23	18-18	20-16	6-4	L1

(b) Western

Figure 7.2. The NBA standings of the 16 teams in the playoffs.

For the Bucks, Giannis had 17 rebounds and 4 assists, Brook Lopez with 17 points and 6 rebounds and Khris Middleton had 29 points, 7 rebounds and 4 assists but that was not enough to win the game. Jrue Holiday was largely ineffective with only 10 points but got 9 assists. The bench did not provide much but added 22 points the same as the Suns bench led by Cameron Johnson and Cameron Payne who both had 10 points. The key was Holliday not able to guard Paul and Booker.

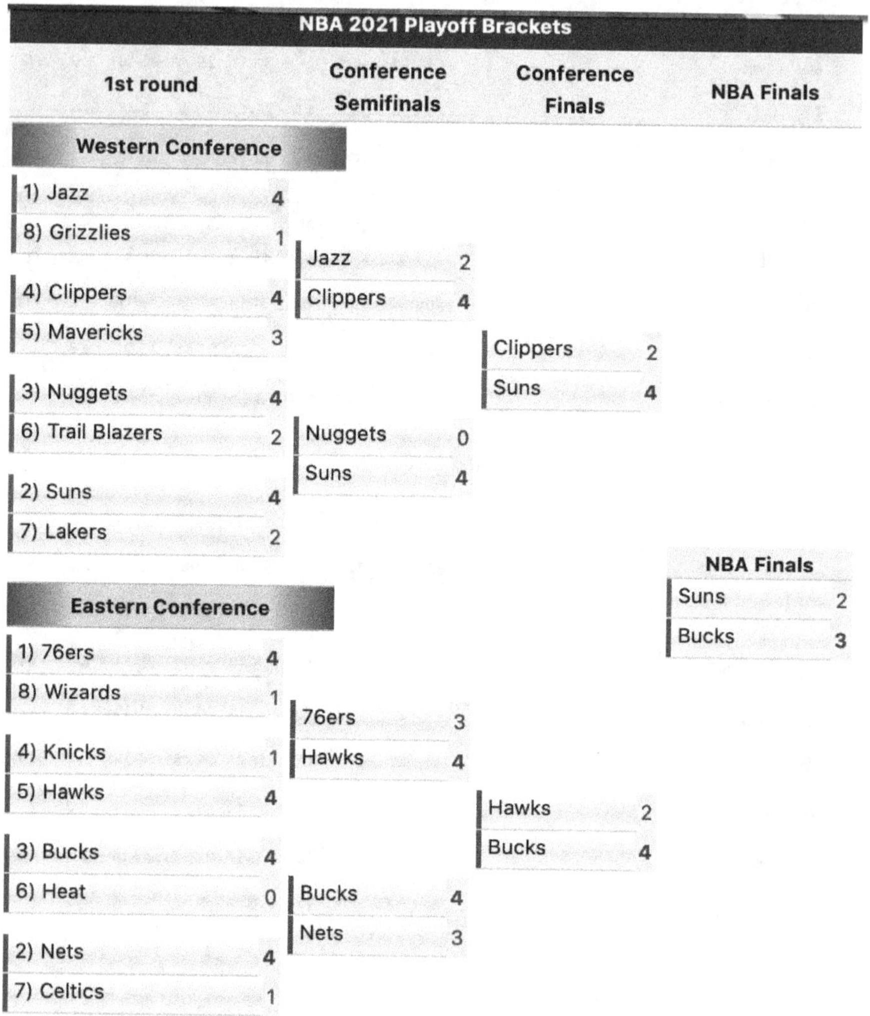

Figure 7.3. The NBA playoff tree going into game 6 of the finals.

7.3.2. *Game 2: Milwaukee Bucks vs. the Phoenix Suns in Phoenix*

Phoenix won again 118–108 to go up 2–0 in the series winning both home games. Phoenix was a $4\frac{1}{2}$ point favorite. Giannis had 42 points and 12 rebounds in a losing effort. He simply did not get enough help from the other Bucks. Khris Middleton had 11 points, 6 rebounds and 8 assists, Jrue

Holiday had 17 points and 7 assists and Brook Lopez had only 8 points and 9 rebounds. Pat Connaughton had 14 points and 7 rebounds off the bench. But the rest of the bench had only 11 points from Teague, Forbes and Portis. Meanwhile Devin Booker's 31 points along with Chris Paul's 23 and Mikhail Bridges 27 along with 11 from Jae Crowder and 10 from Deandre Ayton who also had 10 and 11 rebounds, respectively.

7.3.3. *Game 3: Milwaukee Bucks vs. the Phoenix Suns in Milwaukee*

The Bucks were a $4\frac{1}{2}$ point favorite and did win easily 120–100 to move the series to 2–1 in favor of Phoenix. Giannis had 41 points and both Middleton with 18 and Holiday's 21 plus Lopez's and Portis with 11 each and Connaghtan's 8 were enough for the victory. The key though was Holiday holding star Devin Booker to 10 points on a miserable 4/18 shooting and led to his benching in Q4. Paul had 19 and 9 assists. Crowder and Ayton each had 18 and the Cameron's Johnson 14 and Payne 7 and that was not good enough to win.

7.3.4. *Game 4: Phoenix Suns vs. the Milwaukee Bucks*

The series was 2–1 in favor of the Suns. They won their two home games and then the Bucks won game 3 in Milwaukee. I made two bets on Betfair 50£ long on the Bucks to win the series @ 3.1-1 and 100 long on the game @1.57-1 as Milwaukee was favored. Oscar Robertson and Kareen Abdul-Jabbar (formerly known as Lew Alcinder) who were the stars on the 1971 Milwaukee team that won the championship 50 years ago were at the game.

The game was tight the whole way. Devin Booker who was held to 10 points and benched based on poor 3/14 shooting returned to his greatness scoring 42 points. He had 20 at the half and ended up 17/28 shooting. He has had three 40+ point games in this postseason. Booker now has the most postseason points of a first time player namely 542 beating Rick Barry's 1967 record of 521. Jae Crowder added 15 but Chris Paul had only 10 and had 5 turnovers. The Suns had 17 turnovers vs. only 5 for the Bucks. Deandre Ayton had 17 rebounds but only 6 points and 3 blocks. Cameron Johnson off the bench added 10 and Cameron Payne 9 more. But it was the Booker which got the Suns a 9 point lead which was not enough to win the game.

Milwaukee pulled ahead in the last minutes and won 109–103. Giannis had a decent game with 14 rebounds, 8 assists, 3 steals, 2 blocks and 26 points. He made a spectacular block on Ayton that helped the Bucks win the game. Phoenix led with $2\frac{1}{2}$ minutes to go but Middleton scored twice to give the Bucks a 101–99 lead. Near the end Booker fouled Giannis but the referees missed that even though it was obvious and it turned out better for the Bucks as Giannis scored then. Otherwise he would have had to shoot free throws and he only makes about half of those. Booker really should have fouled out.

The star of the game was Khris Middleton who scored 40 and rallied them to the win.and had 10 straight points to turn the tide towards the Bucks. He was 15/33 shooting. Brook Lopez added 14 but only one rebound. Jrue Holiday was strong on defense and guarded Chris Paul well. Stopping Booker was impossible. Jrue is always good on defense. But like Middleton is streaky on offense. In this game he got 13 points but had 7 assists and 7 rebounds. But the 4/20 shooting was very poor. Pat Connaghton added 11 points and 9 rebounds. Fan favorite Bobby Portis did play 20 minutes but was a non factor scoring only 3 points but did get 5 rebounds. P J Tucker had 5 rebounds and played defense but got no points. Milwaukee is the better bigger rebounding team and Phoenix are the smaller, better shooters. Milwaukee's physicality is a big advantage.

7.3.5. *Game 5: Phoenix Suns vs. Milwaukee Bucks in Phoenix*

All four games were won by the home team: Phoenix won the first two games and Milwaukee won the next two. So game 5 was a pivotal must win game for both teams. Phoenix was favored at home by 4 points. I bet 170£ on Milwaukee +4 points at British odds of 1.89-1. That meant I would win 152 if the bucks won or lost by three points or less. I also bet 100 on Milwaukee at 2.5-1 odds. That would collect 150 if the bucks won. For the series I was −1186.43 loss if the Suns were champions and +1664.54 if Milwaukee were victories.

The series odds were Suns 1.72–1.77; Bucks 2.28–2.36, and for game 5 in Phoenix, Bucks 2.52–2.58, Suns 1.64–1.66.

The Suns were on fire in quarter 1 with Deven Booker and Jae Crowder hitting basically all their shots. Quarter 1 ended Suns ahead 37–21. The Suns shot 14/19 vs. the Bucks 9/21. Quarter 2 saw a big turnaround. The Bucks whittled down the 16 point advantage and took the lead a few times, the first at 50–49. For the Bucks to win they needed all three superstars to play outstanding. Yannis is always good a big threat on offense and defense and Holiday is always a great defender. But Holliday and Middleton are streaky on offense. Fortunately for Milwaukee all three stars were outstanding and the Bucks are a bigger more rugged team vs. the smaller superior shooting Suns quarterbacked by Chris Paul. The Bucks scored 43 vs. 24 for the Suns in Q2 to end the half at 64–61 for the Bucks on 17/24 shooting. Holiday was strong on defense limiting Paul to not much and was 8/11 shooting for 19 points at the half. In the 3rd quarter Milwaukee pulled ahead and when they were 10 points ahead at 85–75.

I started hedging my Milwaukee long bets. First I hedged out the 100 pound long bet at 2.5 to move it to +88 if Milwaukee won that game and +50 if the Suns prevailed.

The 3rd quarter ended 96–83. So I could now begin to exit my long Milwaukee bet by shorting 400 Milwaukee at 1.5–1 so the bet for the series was now −386.43 Suns and +1224.54 Bucks. Then shorting 386.43 short at 1.4–1 moved the bet to Suns 0 and Bucks +1069.97. The Bucks stayed ahead. Throughout the 4th quarter but the Suns fought back and at 1.47 to go the Suns were only behind at 120–117. Yannis missed both free throws at 1.09 to go. At the 53 second mark it was 120–119 and the Suns had a big chance to win the game. Booker who was outstanding all game was charging but then was tied up and Holiday made a brilliant steal of the ball and threw it to Yannis who dunked it in for a 123–119 lead. That was Holiday's 13th assist. There was only 9.8 seconds left and then the game ended Bucks winning 123–119.

For the series the Betfair odds widened to 1.39–4.6 for the Suns and 1.2–1.44. I won my bet on the Bucks plus 4 and surprisingly Betfair settled the Atlanta Bucks risk arbitrage bets gaining about 1200£.

Giannis had 32 points 9 rebounds and 6 assists. Khris Middleton scored 7 of his 29 points in the final 3.25 to that suppressed Phoenix's comeback effort. Jrue Holiday had 27 points. Booker scored 40 points for the second straight game but it was not enough to win either game. Again Chris Paul was off but he still scored 10 of his 21 points in the failed Q4.

7.3.6. *Game 6: Milwaukee Bucks vs. the Phoenix Suns at Milwaukee*

The key to the game, with the Bucks a 5 point favorite, was which big three will prevail. In game 4 the Bucks big three Giannis, Middleton and Holiday had 88 points, 24 assists and twenty rebounds. With their assists they were involved in 115 of the Bucks 123 points. Yannis is averaging 32.2 points, 13 rebounds and 5.6 assists shooting 61.2% from the field. Very good guarding of Paul by Holiday helped the Bucks win the last three games. Still Paul is averaging 21.0 points shooting 54.3% overall and 52.4% from three point land. But Paul has turned the ball over 18 times in the Milwaukee series vs. 22 times in the previous three series to get to the finals. Paul's best game closed out the Los Angeles Clippers, scoring 41 points with 8 assists and no turnovers. Paul had 5 turnovers in the game 3 and 4 losses but in game 5 also lost he had 11 assists and just two turnovers. So the key to the game is which big three will prevail.

Paul, Booker and Deandre Ayton have played well too.

I went into this game with a series bet where I lose zero if Phoenix wins games 6 and 7 and +1069.97£ less the 5% commission on winning bets if Milwaukee wins, as I suspect they will.

On the game 6 itself the odds on Milwaukee were 1.55–1 and I bet 500 long on Milwaukee hoping to gain 270.05 again less the 5%. For the MVP I went with Giannis but he is a big favorite so I could only get 11 bet long at 1.28–1 risking 43.22 should Paul or Booker be named MVP.

Booker was 17/28 for 42 points and 17/33 for 40 points in the game 4 and 5 losses, respectively. So the key for the Suns is whether Ayton, Booker and Paul can outduel the Bucks big three. We know that Yannis is always the big star and is outstanding on defense as well as offense. The deer district fans were packed in like covid sardines and there were about 65,000 of them cheering on plus the 17,000 in the stadium.

The Bucks are 9–1 at home during the playoffs and the Suns are a good road team.

The game see sawed throughout with lots of mean reversion. The quarterly scores were

Suns	16	31	30	21	98
Bucks	28	13	35	28	105

with the Bucks closing out the series 4–2 with a strong Q4. The keys to the game were a super MVP performance by Yannis who scored 50 points (64% shooting). He tied an NBA finals record closeout game along with Bob Pettitt, plus 14 rebounds and 5 blocks plus superior defense. Yannis averaged 35.2 points, 13.2 rebounds and 5 assists in the series. He was 16/25 shooting and a remarkable 17/19 free throws, well above expectation and the Sun's strategy to foul him. He was easily the MVP and I won my bet +25.65.

Yannis joined Michael Jordon, LeBron James, Jerry West, and Elgin Baylor who also got 50 points in a finals playoff game. Yannis at 26 was the 2nd youngest finals MVP only exceeded by Kawai Leonard at 22 in 2012.

The Bucks got 16 points from fan favorite Bobby Portis on 6/10 shooting and Brock Lopez added 10 on 5/10 shooting and 8 rebounds. Middleton had a decent game with 17 points, 5 rebounds, 5 assists and a very useful 4 steals. Holliday had a miserable game shooting 4/19 21.1% for 12 points but he was strong on defense and, had 9 rebounds, 11 assists and 4 valuable steals. Pat Connaughton had no points but 8 rebounds. P J Tucker also had no points but 6 rebounds plus good defense. A big key to the game plus Yannis's super performance was the Bucks 53 rebounds to the Suns 37 a 16 advantage which contributed greatly to the win. Both teams shot about 45% with the Bucks 37/82 and the Suns 38/86. Chris Paul had a good game with 26 points, 2 rebounds and 5 assists. Booker had 19 points, 3 rebounds and 5 assists, Crowder had 15 points and 13 rebounds, Ayton had 12 points and only 6 rebounds, Payne and Bridges had 10 and 7 points, respectively. The Suns were close but the bigger better rebounding Bucks with the clear superstar prevailed.

This was a great victory for Yannis who joined the Bucks in 2013 as an 18 year old from Greece with Nigerian parents. Then he did not know where his next meal would come from. Now he has a super max contract for $228 million.

I also won +867.68 on the series with my long Bucks bet and +256.55 on my long Bucks bet on game 6. Table 7.4 below has all the bets. In total I won 1758.78.

Basketball: £1,758.78 Total P&L: £1,758.78

Basketball — Showing **1** - **20** of 27 markets

Market	Start time	Settled date	Profit/Loss (£)
Basketball / NBA Finals MVP : Winner	08-Jul-21 01:05	21-Jul-21 04:54	25.65
Basketball / NBA : NBA Championship 2020/2021	25-Mar-21 15:43	21-Jul-21 04:44	867.68
Basketball / Phoenix Suns @ Milwaukee Bucks : Moneyline	21-Jul-21 02:11	21-Jul-21 04:42	256.55
Basketball / Milwaukee Bucks @ Phoenix Suns : Handicap	18-Jul-21 02:10	18-Jul-21 04:34	145.02
Basketball / Milwaukee Bucks @ Phoenix Suns : Moneyline	18-Jul-21 02:10	18-Jul-21 04:34	83.62
Basketball / Phoenix Suns @ Milwaukee Bucks : Moneyline	15-Jul-21 02:11	15-Jul-21 04:41	53.20
Basketball / Milwaukee Bucks @ Phoenix Suns : Handicap	09-Jul-21 02:11	09-Jul-21 04:32	-40.00
Basketball / Milwaukee Bucks @ Phoenix Suns : Moneyline	09-Jul-21 02:11	09-Jul-21 04:32	-100.00
Basketball / Milwaukee Bucks @ Phoenix Suns : Handicap	07-Jul-21 02:11	07-Jul-21 04:28	-150.00
Basketball / Milwaukee Bucks @ Atlanta Hawks : Handicap	04-Jul-21 01:34	04-Jul-21 03:57	15.20
Basketball / Milwaukee Bucks @ Atlanta Hawks : Moneyline	04-Jul-21 01:34	04-Jul-21 03:57	229.85
Basketball / Atlanta Hawks @ Milwaukee Bucks : Moneyline	02-Jul-21 01:33	02-Jul-21 03:58	49.32
Basketball / NBA : Western Conference Winner	25-Mar-21 15:43	01-Jul-21 04:50	111.59
Basketball / Phoenix Suns @ Los Angeles Clippers : Handicap	01-Jul-21 02:16	01-Jul-21 04:47	-100.00
Basketball / Milwaukee Bucks @ Atlanta Hawks : Handicap	30-Jun-21 01:34	30-Jun-21 03:53	14.14
Basketball / Milwaukee Bucks @ Atlanta Hawks : Moneyline	30-Jun-21 01:34	30-Jun-21 03:53	-127.50
Basketball / Los Angeles Clippers @ Phoenix Suns : Handicap	29-Jun-21 02:16	29-Jun-21 04:38	-14.39
Basketball / Los Angeles Clippers @ Phoenix Suns : Moneyline	29-Jun-21 02:16	29-Jun-21 04:38	284.98
Basketball / Milwaukee Bucks @ Atlanta Hawks : Moneyline	28-Jun-21 01:33	28-Jun-21 03:57	135.61
Basketball / Phoenix Suns @ Los Angeles Clippers : Moneyline	27-Jun-21 02:16	27-Jun-21 04:59	-150.00

Figure 7.4. Settlement of Betfair bets.

7.4. The Road the Finals

7.4.1. *Round 1 East*

Philadelphia 76ers vs. Washington Wizards: The top rated 76ers team beat the 8th rated Wizards 4–1 to win the series. Philadelphia looked strong in spite of Ben Simmons' shooting problems.

New York Knicks vs. Atlanta Hawks: The 4th rated Knicks were defeated 4–1 by the 5th rated Hawks. The Hawks Trae Young was too much for the Knicks to handle.

Milwaukee Bucks vs. the Miami Heat: Milwaukee won all four games with six different players averaging at least ten points per game. Giannis Antetokounmpo averaged 23.5 points, 15.0 rebounds and 7.8 assists. This avenged last years defeat by the Heat. Giannis guarded Heat star Jimmy Butler holding him to 14.5 points per game on less than 30% shooting. In 2019 Milwaukee got to the eastern Conference finals, only to be eliminated by eventual the champion the Toronto Rapters. During that series the Rapter's guard Fred Van Fleet had the greatest three game shooting stretch in NBA playoff history hitting 14/17 three pointers in games 4–6 all won by Toronto.

Brooklyn Nets vs. the Boston Celtics: Brooklyn had way too much firepower for the Celtics. The Nets won games 1 and 2 but the Celtics won game 3 125–119. But the Nets won games 4 and 5 easily namely 141–126 and 123–109, respectively. So the Nets won the series 4–1 and then faced the Milwaukee Bucks. Kevin Durant, James Harden and Kyrie Irving were all on their best games and were the favorites to win the NBA championships. Durant had a 42 point game, hitting 14–20 from the field.

7.4.2. *Round 1 West*

Utah Jazz vs. Memphis Grizzlies: Utah first in the West, easily beat the eighth rated Grizzlies 4–1. Utah looked like title contenders.

Los Angeles Clippers vs. Dallas Maverick: The games were close but the Clippers, rated fourth in the West, beat the Mavericks (rated 5th), 4–3. Luca Doncic was outstanding for Dallas, but hs did not have enough support.

Denver Nuggets vs. Portland Trailblazers: Denver, rated 3rd, beat Portland, rated 6th, 4–2. Even without Jamal Murray, the Nuggets were too good for Portland.

Phoenix Suns vs. Los Angeles Lakers: The 7th rated Lakers had too many injuries including stars LeBron James and Anthony Davis, so the 2nd rated Suns, beat the Lakers 4–2. Without Davis and a hobbled James, the Lakers size advantage disappeared.

7.4.3. *Conference Semi-Finals: East*

Philadelphia 76ers vs. the Atlanta Hawks

Philadelphia was rated first in the regular season and the Hawks fifth, but the Hawks won the series 4–3. All the series games were close. The Hawks won game 5 109–106. The 76ers won game 6 104–99. In the final game, the Hawks won 103–96. They were led by Huerter with 27 points, Trae Young 21 points and 10 assists, Gallinaro 17 points, and Cappella 13 points. Joel Embiid led the 76ers with 31 points aided by Harris with 24 and Curry with 16.

Brooklyn Nets vs. Milwaukee Bucks

The Golden State were champions in 1975 and then recently during 2015–2018. They were led by the splash brothers Stephan Curry and Klay Thompson who were dynamite three point shooters and Kevin Durant an all around offensive superstar. Plus they had defensive and rebounding star Draymond Green. But then they had a sequence of bad scenarios. It started with a season ending injury to Klay Thompson. This was followed by a season ending injury to Kevin Durant. The market value of the very top players is so great that when Durant asked to be traded to the Brooklyn Nets they gave him a maximum salary, even though he had to skip one season due to the injury. Brooklyn was assembling a super team by signing former MVP and perennial scoring champion who specializes in long distance three point shots the bearded James Hardin who wanted to leave the Houston Rockets. They also signed Boston Celtics guard Kyrie Irving. They added to these three superstars Blake Griffin from the Detroit for defense, rebounding and some more offense. On paper they looked invincible but I know from big favorites that lost that they run races at the track not on the computer. The same is true in NBA basketball where they play on the court.

Then bad scenarios started to appear. Kyrie Irving got injured so was out of the playoffs. Then James Harden was also injured and only played the last part of the Milwaukee series. Blake Griffin stepped up as did other players especially Kevin Durant (arguably the best NBA player according to Milwaukee's Greek Freak, Giannis), the current major rival as top NBA player.

The Los Angeles Lakers typically at the top had minor injuries to both of their superstars Anthony Davis and LeBron James. LeBron has been at the top ever since he joined the NBA in 2003, winning championships in Miami (2012, 2013), Cleveland (2016) and Los Angeles (2020). But the top players in 2021 were Durant, Yannis and the Denver Nuggets Nikola Jokic who was awarded the 2021 regular season MVP.

The series went to the full seven games with Milwaukee winning the deciding game 7 at 118–111. Milwaukee had won game 6 at 104–89 to tie the series at 3–3. The Nets had won game 5 at 114–108 to go 3–2. Durant was spectacular in carrying the team scoring a record 48 points in game 5. Khris Middleton is very streaky, either hot or cold. He can score 35 points then 15 averaging about 20 points a game. Yannis is steady getting 30–40 points per game. He scores close to 90% near the basket. But he misses a lot from further out and especially when he tries to shoot threes. The coach, Mike Budenholzer, has been criticized as not being able to make within game adjustments, something made famous by New England Patriots coach Bill Belichick. Since the Milwaukee Bucks lost early in the playoffs the past two years they added defensive and playmaking ace Jrue Holliday. Holiday did help the Bucks defeat the Nets.

7.4.4. *Conference Semi-Finals: West*

Utah Jazz vs. Los Angeles Clippers

The Clippers won game 6 131–119 to close out the series 4–2. Kawai Leonard was injured but Mann had 39 points, Jackson 27 and George 28 to seal the win. Mitchell led the Jazz in a losing effort, scoring 39 with 9 rebounds and 9 assists. Clarkson had 21, Gopert 12, Bogdanovic 14, and O'Neale 21 in 10 rebounds.

Denver Nuggets vs. Phoenix Suns

The 3rd rated Nuggets sere simply outplayed by the sharp shooting Suns. The fourth game that ended the series in a 4–0 sweep was 125–118. Denver was led by MVP Jokic with 22, Porter 20, Morris 19, and Barton 25 in a losing effort. The Suns were led by star guard Chris Paul in his 16th year in the NBA who had 37 points and 7 assists, and rising super star Devin Booker who had 34 points and 11 assists.

7.4.5. *Conference Finals*

Eastern Conference Finals: Atlanta Hawks vs. Milwaukee Bucks

There was a lot of mean reversion risk arbitrage in the seesaw finals. Atlanta won game 1 in Milwaukee 116–113, behind a career high 48 point super performance with 11 assists and 7 rebounds by Trae Young, aided by double doubles from John Collins and Clint Capela. Giannis had 34 points, 12 rebounds and 9 assists. Jrue Holiday added 33 points, 10 assists and 5 rebounds in the losing effort. Khris Middleton had a poor game, shooting 6/23 for only 15 points and was 0/9 from 3 point land. Milwaukee bounced back in game 2, winning 125–91, leading by 40 at one time scoring 20 straight points late in Q2 to break open the game. Giannis had 25 points, and Holliday 20 to lead the Bucks to victory. Young only scored 15 on 6/16 shooting with only 1 of 8 from three point land. Thus the series was tied 1–1 but the odds moved considerably with Atlanta at low odds following game 1 and then the Bucks at low odds after game 2. In game 3 Young bounced back and scored 32 points but was injured. With 30 seconds left in Q3 he stepped on referee Sean Wrights foot twisting his ankle.

Khris Middleton took over in Q4 scoring 20 of his 38 points to lead the Bucks to a 113–102 win in game 3 and a 2–1 series lead and long odds on Atlanta to win the overall series so I went long Atlanta putting in shorts much lower that would be filled for the risk arbitrage should Atlanta make a comeback with they did. In game 3 Khris scored 11 in a two minute stretch and had 11 rebounds and 7 assists. Giannis had 33 points, and 11 rebounds, and Portis added 15 off the bench. Holiday had another dismal shooting game 2/11 but had 12 assists. The Hawks never trailed in game 4 winning 110–88. Trae Young was out with his ankle injury and Giannis hurt his knee late in the game trying to block a Clint Capela dunk. Middleton was only 6/16 shooting for 16 points, missing all 7 three point attempts. Lopez had 16 and Middleton had 15 along with 8 assists and 7 rebounds. Lou Williams replaced Young and scored 21. Bogdanovic added 20 and Reddish 12.

In game 5 with Yannis out with his knee injury others stepped up, especially Brook Lopez who got 33 points, and three other starters got over 20 points to win 123–112 and go up 3–2 in the series.

In game 6 Khris Middleton was the star again, scoring 32 points including 16 straight in the decisive 3rd quarter that led to a 118–107 Bucks win and a 4–2 series victory. Observe that the risk arbitrage — long Atlanta short later is for the overall series not game 6 so it does not get settled by Betfair until later.

Giannis was still out in game 6 with his knee injury. The Bucks won with a balanced attack. Middleton had 23 in Q3 and got the Bucks to a commanding 91–72 lead. Holiday scored 27 and had 9 assists and 9 rebounds. Lopez added 13, Portis 12, Connaughnot 13 and Teague 11. Trae Young, who missed the last two games, never got it going in game 6, scoring only 14 points with 9 assists. The others carried the load but it was not enough to win. Bogdanovic had 20, Capela 14, Collins 13, Reddish 21 and Gallinaro 13.

Conference Finals West: Los Angeles Clippers (4th) vs. Phoenix Suns (2nd)

The Suns won game 1, 120–114 and they won the second game 104–103. The Clippers rallied back to win game 3 106–92. Then Phoenix won game 4 84–80 to lead the series 3–1. The Clippers won game 5 116–102. Paul George was 15/20 with 6 three-pointers for 41 points and had 13 rebounds and 6 assists. Marcus Morris added 20, Reggie Jackson 21 and Nick Batum 18. For the Suns, Devon Booker led with 31, Chris Paul had 22, Cameron Johnson 14 and Deandre Ayton 10 in a losing cause. This win sent the 3-2 series to a series to game 6.

Phoenix won game 6 130–103 to win the series 4–2 and now move on to their first finals since 1993 to face the Milwaukee Bucks. Chris Paul had a spectacular game, scoring 41 points with 8 assists. Booker added 22, Ayton 16 and Crowder 19 in the winning effort. For the Clippers, Paul George had 21 points, Marcus Morris 26, Reggie Jackson 13, Patrick Beverly 11, De Marcus Cousins 12 and Nicolas Baluas 10 in a losing effort.

Acknowledgements

Many thanks to my colleague Leonard MacLean for helpful discussions and comments on an earlier draft of this chapter.

Chapter 8

Winning Hockey: Team and Player Impact in the NHL

Leonard C. MacLean and William T. Ziemba

Ice hockey is a fast physically demanding game, with the outcome of a contest between teams being determined by a few key events. A spectator can usually detect the key plays which affect game outcome. As well statistics on player activity in each game is recorded in a box score. This paper considers the game box score and the problem of identifying box score statistics for teams and players which materially affect outcome. The box score variables are separated into two levels: team level variables which directly affect outcome; player level variables which impact the important team level variables . The team level analysis uses logistic regression to link outcome to team variables and the player level analysis uses multiple regression to identify player variables which impact team variables. The methods are applied to games in the National Hockey League during the 2021 regular season. The teams in the Canadian Division are featured.

8.1. Introduction

Player performance in hockey is difficult to quantify due to the continuity of play, frequent line changes, and the infrequency of goals. Historically, the primary measure of individual skater performance has been the plus-minus value: the number of goals scored by a player's team minus the number of goals scored by the opposing team while that player is on the ice. More complex measures of player performance have been proposed to take into account game data beyond goal scoring, such as hits or face-offs. Examples include the adjusted minus/plus probability approach of Schuckers (2010) and indices such as Corsi and DeltaSOT, as reviewed by Vollman (2010).

Unfortunately, analysts do not generally agree on the relative importance of the added information. While it is possible to statistically infer additional variable effects in a probability model for team performance (Thomas *et al.*, 2012), in the low-scoring world of hockey, such high-dimensional estimation relies heavily upon model assumptions that are difficult to validate. As a result, complex scores provide an interesting new source of commentary but have yet to be adopted as consensus performance metrics or as a basis for decision making. Due to its simplicity, the plus-minus remains the most popular measure of player performance. It has been logged for the past fifty years and is easy to calculate from the current resolution of available game data, which consists of the identities of each player on the ice at any time point of the game as well as the times when goals were scored. However, a key weakness is that the plus-minus for each player does not just depend on their individual ability but also on other factors, most obviously the abilities of teammates and opponents. In statistical terms, plus-minus is a marginal effect: it is an aggregate measure that averages over the contributions of opponents and teammates. Since the quality of the pool of teammates and opponents that each player is matched with on-ice can vary dramatically, the marginal plus-minus for individual players are inherently polluted. Another disadvantage is that plus-minus does not control for sample size, such that players with limited ice-time will have high variance scores that soar or sink depending on a few chance plays. A better measure of performance would be the partial effect of each player, having controlled for the contributions of teammates, opponents and possibly other variables. To this end, we propose a logistic regression model to estimate the credit or blame that should be apportioned to each player when a goal is scored. In keeping with the spirit of plus-minus (and using the same publicly available data), we focus on the list of players on the ice for each goal as our basic unit of analysis.

Our approach to evaluating teams and players is based on the box score summary of game activities. We consider that the variables in the box score can be partitioned into primary and secondary sets. The primary set are team level variables which are directly related to game outcome. The secondary set are player level variables which are determinants of the primary variables. The secondary variables are shots, shooting percentage, missed shots, and blocked shots, turnovers and giveaways while on ice. These statistics were chosen because each of them has been shown to be a good indicator of performance at the team level (Likens, 2011; Ferrari, 2009). If a team has more shots, missed shots, and blocked shots than their opponents, it is most likely an indication of a territorial advantage and an advantage in terms of puck possession. In order to take a shot, a player must possess the puck, and typically that player is also in the offensive zone.

8.2. Winning Profiles

In a sporting competition the ultimate goal is to win. In a team sport such as ice hockey the win is a team achievement. That is not to say that individual excellence is secondary in a team game, but dominant individual play in a losing team effort needs context. Advantage is gained by skilled play and disadvantage acquired by poor play. Consistently winning requires exploiting advantage situations and eliminating disadvantage situations. Some perspective on winning in the National Hockey League is provided in Table 8.1. The information covers the seasons since 2000, with a focus on Stanley Cup wins — the measure of team success in a season. The winning team has the names of team players engraved on the famous silver cup. So a player could have their name engraved multiple times. The legendary Montreal Canadiens have most of the names on the cup (Henri Richard: 11; Jean Béliveau: 10, Yvon Cornyuoer: 9; Maurice Richard: 8, and so on). It has become much harder to string together winning seasons in professional sport, but there are still elite teams and players. The list of names on the cup since the year 2000 has 385 players, and 103 players appear multiple times. We have filtered out those with 3 or more cup wins. The star players, that is players with many individual awards, are highlighted in blue. Obviously the best offensive player, Sydney Crosby, and defensive player, Nick Lidstrom, are listed. More than half the list is composed of solid (non-star) players.

Are the top individual performers on the cup winning team each season? Let's look at the awards in Table 8.2. The awards are based on regular season play and are voted prior to the playoffs. The Stanley Cup playoffs are a two month tournament, with a team playing up to 28 games over 4 different rounds.

Of the 114 awards in the seasons between 2001 and 2020, 15 were awarded to players on cup winning teams. In 6 of the 19 seasons the winning team had no player awards! It is possible that a team with all players better than average (Lake Wobegon?) and a hot goaltender takes the Stanley Cup. Confronted with this paradox, we will focus on the regular season play in the NHL.

Table 8.1. Stanley cup wins by player: 2000–2020.

Name	Team	Wins	Awards
Draper, Kris	Detroit Red Wings	4	0
Kunitz, Chris	Anaheim Ducks; Pittsburgh Penguins	4	0
Lidstrom, Nicklas	**Detroit Red Wings**	**4**	**8**
Maltby, Kirk	Detroit Red Wings	4	0
Roy, Patrick	**Montreal Canadiens; Colorado Avalanche**	**4**	**11**
Brodeur, Martin	**New Jersey Devils**	**3**	**10**
Brylin, Sergei	New Jersey Devils	3	0
Chelios, Chris	**Montreal Canadiens; Detroit Red Wings**	**3**	**3**
Crosby, Sidney	**Pittsburgh Penguins**	**3**	**11**
Cullen, Matt	Carolina Hurricanes; Pittsburgh Penguins	3	0
Daneyko, Ken	New Jersey Devils	3	0
Fedorov, Sergei	**Detroit Red Wings**	**3**	**4**
Fleury, Marc-Andre	Pittsburgh Penguins	3	0
Hossa, Marian	Chicago Blackhawks	3	0
Kane, Patrick	**Chicago Blackhawks**	**3**	**5**
Keith, Duncan	**Chicago Blackhawks**	**3**	**3**
Letang, Kris	Pittsburgh Penguins	3	0
Madden, John	New Jersey Devils 2; Chicago Blackhawks	3	1
Malkin, Evgeni	**Pittsburgh Penguins**	**3**	**6**
Rafalski, Brian	New Jersey Devils; Detroit Red Wings 2	3	0
Recchi, Mark	Pittsburgh Penguins; Carolina Hurricanes; Boston Bruins	3	0
Seabrook, Brent	Chicago Blackhawks	3	0
Sharp, Patrick	Chicago Blackhawks	3	0
Toews, Jonathan	**Chicago Blackhawks**	**3**	**2**
Williams, Justin	Carolina Hurricanes; Los Angeles Kings	3	1
Yzerman, Steve	**Detroit Red Wings**	**3**	**4**

Note: Multiple award winners are in bold.

8.3. Team and Player Value

The particular performance of interest in this chapter is focused on competitive games in sports. An athlete or team of athletes compete in a structured game, following rules of play. Typically a game is composed of a sequence of head to head events, with the game outcome being the aggregate of the event outcomes. For example, in basketball the event is a ball possession

Table 8.2. Top players by season.

Season	Ross	Richard	Hart	Selke	Norris	Vezina	Cup
01	Jagr	Bure	**Sakic**	Madden	Lidstrom	Hasek	**Col**
02	Iginla	Iginla	Theodore	Peca	**Lidstrom**	JTheodore	**Det**
03	Forsberg	Hejduk	Forsberg	Lehtinen	Lidstrom	**Brodeur**	**N J**
04	**St. Louis**	Nash, Kovalchuk, Iginla	**St. Louis**	K Draper	Niedermayer	Brodeur	**T B**
05	NA	NA	NA	NA	NA	NA	**NA**
06	Thornton	Cheechoo	Thornton	**Brind'Amour**	Lidstrom	Kiprusoff	**Car**
07	Crosby	Lecavalier	Crosby	Brind'Amour	Lidstrom	Brodeur	**Ana**
08	Ovechkin	Ovechkin	Ovechkin	**Datsyuk**	**Lidstrom**	Brodeur	**Det**
09	**Malkin**	Ovechkin	Ovechkin	Datsyuk	Chara	Thomas	**Pitt**
10	Sedin	Crosby, Stamkos	Sedin	Datsyuk	**Keith**	Miller	**Chi**
11	Sedin	Perry	Perry	Kesler	Lidstrom	**Thomas**	**Bos**
12	Malkin	Stamkos	Malkin	Bergeron	Karlsson	Lundqvist	**L A**
13	St. Louis	Ovechkin	Ovechkin	**Toews**	Subban	Bobrovsky	**Chi**
14	Crosby	Ovechkin	Crosby	Bergeron	Keith	Rask	**L A**
15	Benn	Ovechkin	Price	Bergeron	Karlsson	Price	**Chi**
16	Kane	Ovechkin	Kane	Kopitar	Doughty	Holtby	**Pitt**
17	McDavid	**Crosby**	McDavid	Bergeron	Burns	Bobrovsky	**Pitt**
18	McDavid	**Ovechkin**	Hall	Kopitar	Hedman	Rinne	**Was**
19	Kucherov	Ovechkin	Kucherov	**O'Reilly**	Giordano	Vasilevskiy	**S L**
20	Draisaitl	Pastrnak, Ovechkin	Draisaitl	Couturier	Josi	Hellebuyck	**T B**

Note: Players on Cup winner are in bold.

for a team and that possession continues until the opposing team takes possession, either from a score or turnover. The outcome of an event is defined by classes which delineate the various possible occurrences in the event. Of course the event occurs over a period of time and the variety of things that happen in "play by play" are complex.

A box score is a structured summary of the results from a sport competition. The box score lists the game score as well as individual and team achievements in the game.The box score data is derived from a statistics sheet, and is then summarized into a contingency table, also known as a cross tabulation or cross tab or as a basic set of averages. This is used to help determine the relationship between elements, and in sports, certain percentages often help define the success of a team. This information is then correlated to a player, or a team where it is read to obtain a general idea of how the game was played or how the player performed during the game, a season, or their career. The box score statistics are used to determine the best performers in a game or over a season. That is, the leaders in offensive and defensive statistics are determined from game box scores.

The approach here is simplified, so that the information in the "box score" for a game is defined by the activity classes. It is considered that the box score for competing teams is a sufficient description of in-game activities and are determinants of game outcome (win/loss). A depiction of the approach is given in Figure 8.1.

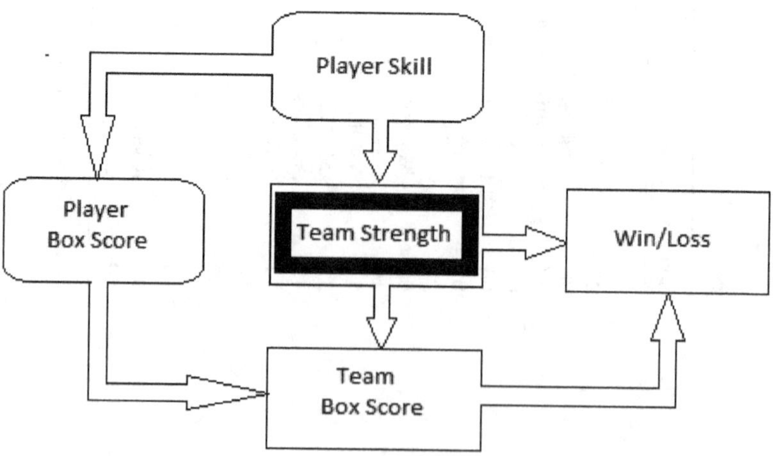

Figure 8.1. Outcome relationships.

Underlying the statistics in the box score are the physical and mental characteristics of expert performance. The many hours of deliberate practice will condition a player's actions in game situations and that is reflected in the player box score. It is estimated that 10,000 hours of practice are usual for elite performers. (Ericsson, 1996). The exceptional performers in sports create favorable opportunities on offense and defense. In a team sport like ice hockey the players on the ice coordinate their activities on offense and defense to get a favorable team result. The player box scores aggregate to a team box score, and players are nested within a team for the game. Individual player activities on each possession generate the game box score for players and the team as shown in Figure 8.2. The game outcome is a team result, so it is natural to relate game outcome to team box score. It is clear that very different player box scores could aggregate to the same team box score. So attributing team success to individual players presents a challenge. An example of that effect in basketball is the performance of Wilt Chamberlain of the Philadelphia Warriors. Chamberlain's box score dominated the Warrior's box score and indeed all other player box scores. However, the Warrior's box did not dominate the Boston Celtic's box and Boston routinely won the NBA championship during Chamberlain's career. Team composition if football is shown to be significant, and in particular defensive players are critical to winning (MacLean and Ziemba, 2020). It is likely the same is true in hockey.

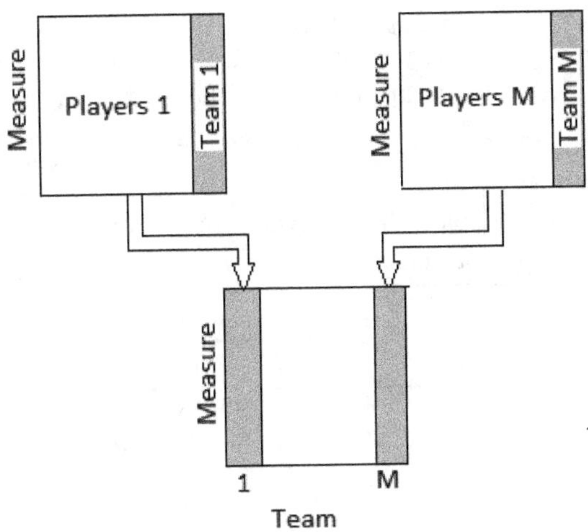

Figure 8.2. Hierarchical relationship.

The analysis of the relationship of box scores to game outcomes will be in two stages: (1) the effect of the team box score on game outcome; (2) the contribution of individual players to team box scores.

8.3.1. *Event outcomes*

A competitive game is composed of a sequence of events. In ice hockey the three forwards on a line and the two defensemen usually play as a unit, The game is physically demanding and the unit plays a shift of approximately one minute. Depending on conditions the shift change is made to get fresh legs on the ice. During the shift there are actions by the players in a unit which are recorded. The score card for the shift will record those activities which directly effect the outcome. A focus on the score card and box score assumes that the strategic movements and physical abilities of players lead to favorable offensive and defensive opportunities, and that in turn produces a winning box score. The hours of deliberate practice and sophisticated game plans are accounted for indirectly.

Consider the multidimensional actions for player j on team i, from a shift in a game as displayed in Table 8.3. The puck changes possession during a shift and there are actions with the puck (offense) and without the puck (defense).

If $X'_{ij} = (X_{ij1}, \ldots, X_{ijK})$, where X_{ijk} = the number of instances of action class k during a shift and the observed result from shift s is $X'_{sij} = (X_{sj1}, \ldots, X_{sjK})$, then the game box score for player j for the total of n_j shifts in the game is $Y'_{ij} = \sum_{s=1}^{n_j} X'_{sij}$.

A game involves two teams each with a roster of players. There is a game box score for each of the players on the competing teams, defined as $Y'_{ij} = (Y_{ij1}, \ldots, Y_{ijK})$, for player j on team i. The players are nested on

Table 8.3. Player j on team i score card.

	Action		
Shift	C_1	$\cdots$	C_K
1	✓		
2			✓
$\vdots$			
n_j			
Game Box Score	Y_{ij1}	$\cdots$	Y_{ijK}

Table 8.4. NHL game box.

Player	SHF	ge	Pos	Date	Tm▲		Opp		G	A	PTS	+/-	PIM	EV	PP	SH	GW	S
Sam Steel	22	22-346	C	2021-01-14	ANA	@	VEG	L	0	1	1	0	0	0	0	0	0	1
Adam Henrique	23	30-343	C	2021-01-14	ANA	@	VEG	L	0	0	0	-2	0	0	0	0	0	1
Troy Terry	23	23-126	C	2021-01-14	ANA	@	VEG	L	0	0	0	0	0	0	0	0	0	2
Max Comtois	24	22-006	LW	2021-01-14	ANA	@	VEG	L	2	0	2	1	0	2	0	0	0	2
Jakob Silfverberg	24	30-093	LW	2021-01-14	ANA	@	VEG	L	0	0	0	-2	0	0	0	0	0	1
Rickard Rakell	25	27-254	RW	2021-01-14	ANA	@	VEG	L	0	0	0	-2	0	0	0	0	0	2
Josh Manson	28	29-099	D	2021-01-14	ANA	@	VEG	L	0	0	0	-1	0	0	0	0	0	0
Cam Fowler	30	29-040	D	2021-01-14	ANA	@	VEG	L	0	0	0	-1	0	0	0	0	0	1
Hampus Lindholm	30	26-360	D	2021-01-14	ANA	@	VEG	L	0	0	0	-1	0	0	0	0	0	0
Kevin Shattenkirk	32	31-351	D	2021-01-14	ANA	@	VEG	L	0	0	0	-1	0	0	0	0	0	3

teams, and assuming a team roster in a game has Q players , the team has a game box score $Y_i' = \sum_{j=1}^{Q} Y_{ij}'$. An illustration of a game partial box score for players on Anahiem Ducks in a loss to the Vegas Knights is shown in Table 8.4.

8.3.2. *Performance measure I: Elo*

A strength rating based on wins/losses is the Elo rating system pioneered by Arpad Elo (2008). Suppose a game between team i and team h is scheduled to commence at time $t; t = 1, \ldots, T$. We assume the teams have up to date ratings of $\theta_i(t)$ and $\theta_h(t)$, respectively. Also suppose heading into the competition team i has a prior chance of winning against team h of $p_{ih}(t)$: So $p_{ih}(t) + p_{hi}(t) = 1$. If there is no basis for favoring one team then $p_{hi}(t) = p_{ih}(t) = 0.50$. However, with strength ratings we have the chance of winning the game at time t calculated as $p_{ih}(t) = \frac{1}{1+e^{-(\theta_i(t)-\theta_h(t))}}$.

The outcome of the game is $x_{ih}(t)$, where $x_{ih}(t) = 1$ for a win for team i and $x_{ih}(t) = 0$ for a loss for team i. The formula for updating team ratings based on the game result is

$$\theta_i(t+1) = \theta_i(t) + \alpha(x_{ih}(t) - p_{ih}(t)).$$

The change in rating is $\alpha(x_{ih}(t) - p_{ih}(t))$, which weights the difference in actual and expected outcome by the smoothing parameter α. The parameter determines how much the most recent game result contributes to the revision of the rating. With the revised (posterior) values of the strength parameters the probabilities for the next game against team g are

$$p_{ig}(t+1) = \frac{1}{1 + e^{-(\theta_i(t+1) - \theta_g(t+1))}}.$$

The initial value of the parameter θ and the α are to be determined. We will start with $\theta_i = 0$. A single win shouldn't move the probability very much, and we found a reasonable choice to be $\alpha = 20$.

8.3.3. *Performance measure II: The LOGIT*

The approach to connecting the box score to game outcome has the same link function as the ELO. The objective in a game is to win, so that is the final performance measure and the basis of the ELO. However, the players generate the W/L with their activities in the game and it is expected that game outcome is dependent on the box score. The standard model for the relationship between a binary classification variable and independent variables is the logistic function.

That is, if $p_{ih}(t) = Prob\left[x_{ih}(t) = 1\right]$, the probability team i wins the game with team h at time t, and there are independent box score variables $(Y_{i1}(t), \ldots, Y_{iM}(t))$ for team i in the game against team h at the time t, then

$$p_{ih}(t) = \frac{1}{1 + e^{-(\beta_0 + \beta_{i1} Y_{i1}(t) + \cdots + \beta_{iM} Y_{iM}(t) + \varepsilon)}}.$$

If $U_i(t) = \beta_{i0} + \beta_{i1} Y_{i1}(t) + \cdots + \beta_{iK} Y_{iM}(t)$, then $p_{ih}(t) = \frac{1}{1+e^{-(U_i(t)+\varepsilon)}}$ and $\ln\left[\frac{p_{ih}(t)}{1-p_{ih}(t)}\right] = \beta_0 + \beta_{i1} Y_{i1}(t) + \cdots + \beta_{iM} Y_{iM}(t) + \varepsilon$. The value $\ln\left[\frac{p_{ih}(t)}{1-p_{ih}(t)}\right]$ is the logit and it's direct link to the game outcome W/L shows how to relate the variables $(Y_{i1}(t), \ldots, Y_{iM}(t))$ to outcome. If there are n games for team i at times $\{t_{i1}, \ldots, t_{in}\}$,the coefficients can be chosen to optimize the relationship across the games. Logistic regression calculates weights $\left(\hat{\beta}_{i0}, \ldots, \hat{\beta}_{iM}\right)$ which maximize the correlation between $\{U_i(t), t = t_{i1}, \ldots, t_{in}\}$ and $\left\{\hat{U}_i(t), t = t_{i1}, \ldots, t_{in}\right\}$, with $U_i(t_{il}) + \epsilon = \ln\left[\frac{p_{ih}(t_{il})}{1-p_{ih}(t_{il})}\right]$ for game against team h at time il, and $\hat{U}_i(t_{il}) = \hat{\beta}_0 + \hat{\beta}_{i1} Y_{i1}(t_{il}) + \cdots + \hat{\beta}_{iK} Y_{iM}(t_{il})$. We will define $\hat{U}_i(t_{il})$ as a team i rating of performance in the game against team h at time t_{il}.

Logistic regression models are fitted using the method of maximum likelihood – i.e. the parameter estimates are those values which maximize the likelihood of the data which have been observed. McFadden's R squared measure is defined as $R^2_{\text{McFadden}} = 1 - \frac{\log(L_c)}{\log(L_{\text{null}})}$, where L_c denotes the (maximized) likelihood value from the current fitted model, and L_{null} denotes the corresponding value but for the null model — the model with only an intercept and no covariates. If the model has no predictive ability, the ratio of the two log-likelihoods will be close to 1, and R^2_{McFadden} will be close to zero. If the model explains virtually all of the variation in the outcome, $\hat{p}_{ih}(t_{il}) \to x_{ih}(t_{il})$, the likelihood value for each observation is close to 1.

So the log-likelihood value $log(L_c)$ will be close to 0. Then R^2_{McFadden} will be close to 1.

8.3.4. *Connecting rating measures*

As depicted in Figure 8.1, the team strength and box score should both capture the determinants of game outcome. That is, the ELO and logit should be strongly related. The ELO is an aggregate measure, so it is the change in ELO from the game at time t which is connected to the logit at time t.

Let $\theta_i(t+1) = \theta_i(t) + \Delta\theta_i(t)$ be the rating after the game against team h at time t, with the change

$$\Delta\theta_i(t) = \theta_i(t+1) - \theta_i(t).$$

So

$$\Delta\theta_i(t) = \alpha(x_{ih}(t) - p_{ih}(t)).$$

If the logistic model is strong, the fitted values $\hat{p}_{ih}(t) = \frac{1}{1+e^{-\hat{U}_i(t)}}$ are close to the observed valuers $x_{ih}(t)$ and there is a strong relationship between $\Delta\theta_i(t)$ and $\hat{p}_{ih}(t)$.

8.3.5. *Rating teams and players*

Wins and losses are team outcomes and the ELO is a team measure of strength. Box scores are recorded for each team player and the aggregate yields the team box score. If the logistic model from team box scores is strong, i.e. the deviance R^2 is high, then working with box scores is sufficient to characterize the performance of a team in a game. So the logit $\hat{U}_i(t_{il}) = \hat{\beta}_0 + \hat{\beta}_{i1}Y_{i1}(t_{il}) + \cdots + \hat{\beta}_{iM}Y_{iM}(t_{il})$ is the team performance value, which is predictive of game outcome: $\hat{p}_{ih}(t_{il}) \to x_{ih}(t_{il})$.

The link between the player box score and the team value and/or game outcome is complex. Our approach is to relate the individual players activities while on the ice to the significant team box score components. In this approach it is assumed that the box score components will partition into primary and secondary levels. The primary components are important at the team level, and the secondary components define player level activities which affect the primary components. That is, primary components win games, but secondary activities produce the primary components.

For example, goals are the determinants of game outcome and thus are primary. However, player activities (shots, blocks turnovers, etc...) produce the goals.

So we will determine the primary components at the team level analysis based on the team box score for the games. Let $Y_a' = (Y_{1^*}, \ldots, Y_{M^*})$ be the primary components at the team level. Then $Y_b' = (Y_{1_*}, \ldots, Y_{M_*})$ are the secondary components, with $M^* + M_* = K$. We will find the relationships $Y_{k^*} = \beta_{0k^*} + \beta_{1k^*}Y_{1_*} + \cdots + \beta_{M_*k^*}Y_{M_*} + \varepsilon, k^* = 1^*, \ldots, M^*$. The predicted values $\hat{Y}_{ik^*} = \hat{\beta}_{0k^*} + \hat{\beta}_{1k^*}Y_{i1_*} + \cdots + \hat{\beta}_{M_*k^*}Y_{iM_*}, k^* = 1, \ldots, M^*$, will give an estimate of an individual player primary components scores based on their scores on the secondary components. Inputing the estimated primary component scores into the level I equation

$$\hat{U}_i(t) = \hat{\beta}_0 + \hat{\beta}_{i1^*}\hat{Y}_{i1^*}(t) + \cdots + \hat{\beta}_{iM^*}\hat{Y}_{iM^*}(t)$$

gives an individual player value, calculated from the team value equation.

8.4. NHL 2021

The alternative measures ELO and logit will be considered for regular season games in the National Hockey League (NHL) during the most recent 2021 season. That season is unusual because of the public health complications caused by the COVID-19 pandemic. This required that teams play in arenas without fans and the season was reduced to 56 games. The US–Canada border was closed to travel, so Canadian teams only played in Canadian cities, and US teams played in US cities.

8.4.1. *NHL teams*

The regular season began on January 13, 2021. The alignment of teams by division are shown in Table 8.5. Teams played games within their division only. The teams in the three U.S. divisions played each of their seven division opponents eight times. Due to limitations on travel into and out of Canada, the seven Canadian teams were aligned into a single North division. The seven teams in the North Division played each other nine or ten times. To further reduce travel, a "baseball-style" schedule was used where teams played each other twice or thrice consecutively in the same location.

For the latest season the divisions were like leagues, analogous to the traditional American League and National League in Major League Baseball. Although the teams only played within division in the regular season,

Table 8.5. 2021: NHL teams by division.

North	East	Central	West
Calgary Flames	Boston Bruins	Carolina Hurricanes	Anaheim Ducks
Edmonton Oilers	Buffalo Sabres	Chicago Blackhawks	Arizona Coyotes
Montreal Canadiens	New Jersey Devils	Columbus Blue Jackets	Colorado Avalanche
Ottawa Senators	New York Islanders	Dallas Stars	Los Angeles Kings
Toronto Maple Leafs	New York Rangers	Detroit Red Wings	Minnesota Wild
Vancouver Canucks	Philadelphia Flyers	Florida Panthers	San Jose Sharks
Winnipeg Jets	Pittsburgh Penguins	Nashville Predators	St. Louis Blues
	Washington Capitals	Tampa Bay Lightning	Vegas Golden Knights

in the post season (playoffs) division winners compete in semi-final and final series.

NHL North Division: Comparing Measures: Since the divisions are essentially leagues, we focus on the North Division and the statistics for the games involving the seven teams in that "league". We have two measures of performance: (1) ELO and (2) Logit. The ELO is a team strength measure based on the accumulated wins and losses to date and the logit is a single game measure based on the statistics (box scores) from that game.

(1) ELO: The formula $\theta_i(t+1) = \theta_i(t)+\alpha(x_{ih}(t)-p_{ih}(t))$ was calculated for the teams in the North Division, using parameter values: $\theta_i(0) = 0, \alpha = 20$. The January 2021 ELO's are shown in Table 8.6 and Figure 8.3 shows the progression of those values.

The ELO's are determined by game outcomes: $x_{ih}(t) = 1$ for a win for team i and $x_{ij}(t) = 0$ for a loss for team i. The W/L records for two teams stand out — Toronto for wins, Ottawa for losses.

(2) Linear Weights: LOGIT: An illustration of the box score data recorded for each NHL game is provided in Figure 8.4. Actually that table is part of a more extended table on the game between Anaheim and Vegas on January 14, 2021. All active players are included and saves, shot blocks, hits and turnovers are recorded. The site Stathead (2021) has complete data on games and that is the source for our information. The analysis will proceed

Table 8.6. January ELO's.

Date	ELOCa	ELOEd	ELOMo	ELOOt	ELOTo	ELOVa	ELOWi
J13	0	-0.01	-0.01	0	0.01	0.01	0
J14	-0.01	-1E-04	-0.01	0	0.01	0	-0.01
J15	-0.01	-0.0001	-0.01	0.01005	-0.00005	0	-0.01
J16	0.00005	-0.01005	4.95E-05	0	0.01	-0.01005	-0.01
J17	0.00005	-0.01005	4.95E-05	0	0.01	-0.01005	-0.01
J18	0.01	-0.01995	0.01	0	0.02	-0.02	-0.02
J19	0.01	-0.01995	0.01	-0.0101	0.02	-0.02	-0.0099
J20	0.01	-0.00975	-0.00015	-0.0101	0.0098	-0.00985	-0.0099
J21	0.01	-0.00975	0.009802	-0.0202	0.0098	-0.0098	9.9E-05
J22	0.01	-0.01965	0.009802	-0.0202	0.019702	-0.0098	9.9E-05
J23	0.01	-0.01965	0.019703	-0.0301	0.019702	-0.0197	0.0098
J24	4.85E-05	-0.0095	0.019703	-0.0301	0.029654	-0.0197	-0.00035
J25	4.85E-05	-0.0095	0.019703	-0.04035	0.029654	-0.00975	-0.00035
J26	-0.01995	-0.01946	0.019703	-0.04035	0.039506	-0.00975	0.009607
J27	-0.01995	-0.01946	0.019703	-0.05019	0.039506	9.21E-05	0.009607
J28	-0.02975	-0.02916	0.029505	-0.05994	0.049212	0.009841	0.009607
J29	-0.02975	-0.02916	0.029505	-0.05994	0.049212	0.009841	0.009607
J30	-0.02005	-0.01955	0.019801	-0.05994	0.039603	0.01984	-0.00039
J31	-0.02005	-0.00975	0.019801	-0.06974	0.039603	0.01984	-0.00039

in stages, with team level statistics considered initially, and then players within teams will be considered. The variables in the team box score are provided in Table 8.7. The variables represent a comprehensive description of the on-ice activities of players during a game.

The statistics on January 2021 games by Calgary Flames in the North Division are shown in Table 8.8. This partial list of variables were sufficient to analyze the factors affecting wins and losses in a game.

The team level analysis considered the Outcome (W/L) against (G, PP, S, PIM, PPGA, SHGA, PPO, PPOA, SA). The impact of goaltending is a major factor in game outcome, so save percentage was calculated as $SP = 100(1 - \frac{G}{S}), SPA = 100(1 - \frac{GA}{SA})$. The logistic regression models which were the best fits to the observed box scores only needed G =goals and SP = save percent. With the logit for game with team i against team h, $U_i(t) = log_e\left[\frac{p_{ih}(t)}{1-p_{ih}(t)}\right]$, the fitted models were $\hat{U}_i = \hat{\beta}_{i0} + \hat{\beta}_{i1} \times G + \hat{\beta}_{i2} \times SP$. Table 8.9 contains the coefficient estimates for the North Division teams, as well as an overall model.

Although the coefficients appear to vary by team, there is simply a scale effect. The deviance R^2 for the overall model is 91.51% and for a number

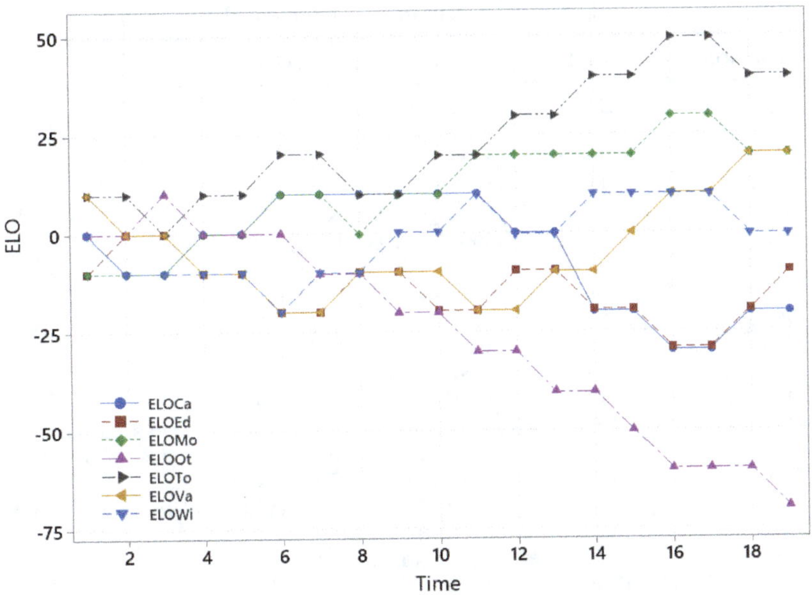

Figure 8.3. ELO trend.

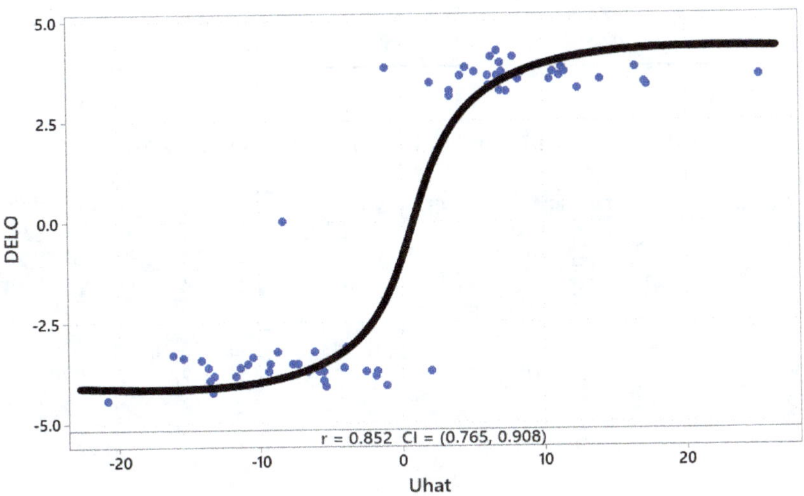

Figure 8.4. ELO and value.

Table 8.7. Team box score: NHL.

Variable	Label	Definition
Y_1	GF	Goals For
Y_2	GA	Goals Against
Y_3	S	Shots For
Y_4	PIM	Penalty Minutes For
Y_5	PPGF	Power Play Goals For
Y_6	PPOF	Power Play Goals Against
Y_7	SHGF	Shorthanded Goals For
Y_8	SA	Shots Against
Y_9	PIMA	Penalty Minutes Against
Y_{10}	PPGA	Power Play Goals Against
Y_{11}	PPOA	Power Plays Against
Y_{12}	SHGA	Shorthanded Goals Against
Y_{13}	CF	(Shots+Misses+Blocks) For at even strength
Y_{14}	CA	(Shots+Misses+Blocks) Against at even strength
Y_{15}	FF	(Shots+Misses) For at even strength
Y_{16}	FA	(Shots+Misses) Against at even strength
Y_{17}	FOW	Face Offs Won
Y_{18}	FOL	Face Offs Lost
Y_{19}	BLK	Blocks
Y_{20}	HIT	Hits
Y_{21}	TK	Takeaways
Y_{22}	GV	Giveaways
Y_{23}	oZS%	oZS% faceoffs in Offensive Zone
Y_{24}	dZS%	oZS% faceoffs in Defensive Zone

Table 8.8. Calgary flames team box: January 2021.

Outcome	G	PP	SH	S	PIM	GA	PP GA	SH GA	PPO	PPOA	SA	Opp PIM
W	2	1	0	33	14	0	0	0	6	5	37	16
L	2	1	0	25	13	4	2	1	4	3	21	15
L	3	1	0	26	4	4	1	0	4	2	21	10
L	2	1	0	33	8	3	1	0	4	4	32	8
W	5	2	0	32	8	2	0	1	7	4	27	14
W	3	3	0	35	8	0	0	0	6	4	32	12
L	3	1	0	26	10	4	1	0	3	4	34	8

of the team models it exceeded 95%. The predictability/discrimination of the model is very high, and the maximum likelihood solution to the logistic regression is almost on the boundary. There is some instability in the coefficient estimates and scale changes would provide the same discrimination between W and L. We use the ALL estimates, with teams combined.

Table 8.9. 2021: NHL North: team weights.

Team	**Constant**	**G**	**SP**
Calgary Flames	−364	14.77	354
Edmonton Oilers	−438	15.87	430
Montreal Canadiens	−112.3	4.27	109.7
Ottawa Senators	−565	18.52	551
Toronto Maple Leafs	−118.8	3.569	119.8
Vancouver Canucks	−402	13.77	393
Winnipeg Jets	−475	18.59	463
ALL	**−119.2**	**4.430**	**117.6**

The important point is that goals and save percentage characterize wins and losses across all teams. Of course the other activities in the box score contribute to goals (offense) and save percent (defense), and we will consider that relationship at the player level.

(3) Comparison: The Logit model

$$\hat{U}_i(t) = -119.2 + 4.430 \times G_i(t) + 117.6 \times SP_i(t)$$

was used to calculate fitted values — logits. The change in the ELO's by game outcome (DELO) were compared with the fitted logits for that game and the results are shown in Figure 8.4 for the January Logits and DELOs. The logistic relationship between $\hat{U}$ and $\Delta\theta$ is strong ($r = 0.852$), and transforming the logits to probabilities by $\hat{p}_{ij}(t) = \frac{1}{1+e^{-\hat{U}}}$ provides an almost perfect linear relationship ($r = 0.938$, Figure 8.5) The fact that the measures are almost equivalent is reassuring, and validates the use of box scores for analyzing team and player performance.

8.5. NHL North: Teams Values

The fitted values for the 2021 regular season were determined from $\hat{U}_i(t) = -119.2 + 4.430 \times G_i(t) + 117.6 \times SP_i(t)$. The separation between win games and loss games is clear, and the centroids for the win and loss clusters is given in Table 8.10. As noted the contrast is the same across teams.

In Figure 8.7, the contrasting distributions of $\hat{U}$ values for wins and losses is displayed for all teams. The figure provides additional evidence of the ability of box score variables (Goals, Save%) to distinguish wins from losses.

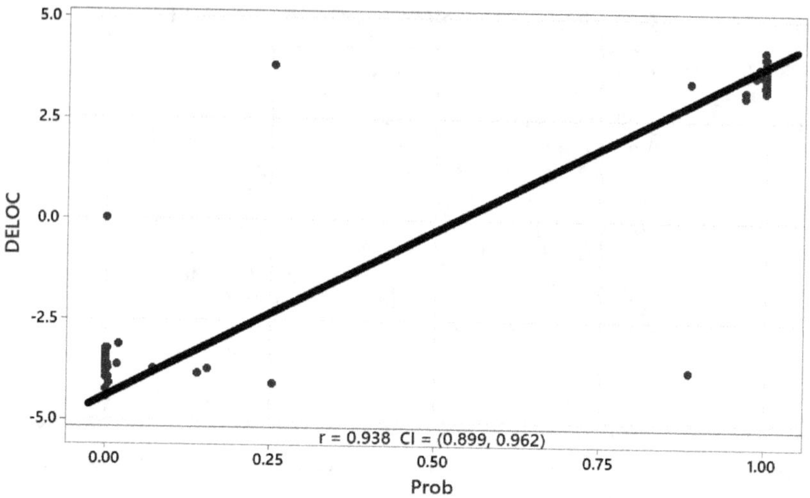

Figure 8.5. ELO and probability.

Table 8.10. Key box statistics by outcome.

Team	Outcome	Avg. Goals	Avg. Save %
Cal	W	4.017	0.93526
	L	1.730	0.86468
Edm	W	4.214	0.93704
	L	1.926	0.85991
Mon	W	4.018	0.93192
	L	2.057	0.86683
Ott	W	4.085	0.93643
	L	1.936	0.86923
Tor	W	4.137	0.93352
	L	2.286	0.85964
Van	W	4.409	0.94030
	L	1.696	0.86908
Win	W	4.152	0.94143
	L	1.742	0.87000
ALL	**W**	**4.0718**	**0.93664**
	L	**1.8315**	**0.86293**

In Table 8.11, we present a summary of the game logits by team for the 2021 season, using the Logit model $\hat{U}_i(t) = -119.2 + 4.430 \times G_i(t) + 117.6 \times SP_i(t)$. The average logit for each team is a measure of season performance. Edmonton Oilers and Toronto Maple Leafs standout as the strong teams in the North Division. Figure 8.6 shows the team value for win/loss levels.

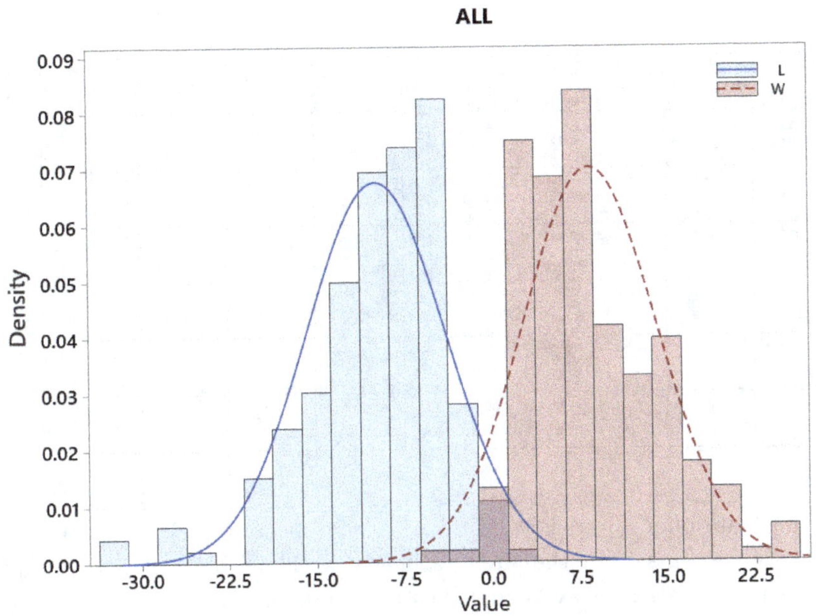

Figure 8.6. Team value for W/L.

Table 8.11. Value statistics by Team: 2021.

Team	Mean	Standard Deviation
Edmonton	1.82	11.21
Toronto	1.55	9.58
Winnipeg	0.22	11.12
Vancouver	−1.91	11.29
Montreal	−2.00	10.71
Ottawa	−2.44	10.05
Calgary	−2.87	11.38

8.6. NHL North: Player Effects

The empirical evidence indicates that the predicted outcome of a game between competing teams in ice hockey is defined by a simple model based on goals scored and save percentage. This is a logical result of the defining feature of team offense and defense. Of course the scoring of a goal or denial of a goal against involves actions of the players on the ice when that event occurs. So we will turn to player box scores to relate player activities

Table 8.12. Toronto player box score: 2021.

Player	G/G	BLK/G	TK/G	GV/G	FF/G	FA/G	SH%	SV%	oZS%	dZS%	TOI/Gm
Alexander Kerfoot	0.125	0.535714	0.25	0.446429	7.232143	7.767857	8.6	91.8	51.3	48.7	12.3
John Tavares	0.232143	0.482143	0.535714	0.892857	10.96429	9.589286	11.1	91.9	55.2	44.8	15.6
T.J. Brodie	0.017857	1.392857	0.339286	0.803571	12.42857	11.73214	11.6	93.2	52.3	47.7	19.1
Morgan Rielly	0.071429	1.053571	0.321429	1.142857	13.71429	12.25	11	90.7	56.6	43.4	20.3
Justin Holl	0.035714	1.196429	0.25	0.625	11.76786	11.58929	11.9	90.2	49.5	50.5	18.4
Mitch Marner	0.357143	0.660714	0.785714	1	11.73214	10.39286	13.4	90.1	55.8	44.2	17.4
Ilya Mikheyev	0.125	0.428571	0.232143	0.446429	7.857143	7.946429	7.5	93.9	34.2	65.8	12.5
Jason Spezza	0.160714	0.160714	0.267857	0.464286	5.75	5.392857	11.4	90.4	59.3	40.7	8.9
Jake Muzzin	0.035714	1.321429	0.339286	0.946429	11.82143	10.76786	11.7	91	47.3	52.7	18.5
Auston Matthews	0.553571	0.803571	0.75	0.803571	12.16071	9.946429	13.6	89.2	56.9	43.1	18.2
Travis Dermott	0.035714	0.607143	0.071429	0.464286	7.321429	7.321429	7.2	92.2	55.8	44.2	12.8
William Nylander	0.232143	0.267857	0.517857	0.589286	9.25	7.607143	10.4	92	59.1	40.9	14.2
Zach Bogosian	0	0.482143	0.125	0.267857	7.107143	6.714286	8.8	92.6	50.5	49.5	13
Joe Thornton	0.089286	0.178571	0.196429	0.482143	6.5	5.071429	10.3	89.7	66.4	33.6	11.8
Zach Hyman	0.214286	0.357143	0.285714	0.25	8.928571	7.625	12.5	93.1	46.6	53.4	15.9
Pierre Engvall	0.125	0.214286	0.107143	0.339286	5.892857	5.589286	7.8	92.2	38.3	61.7	11.3
Wayne Simmonds	0.071429	0.267857	0.214286	0.303571	4.714286	4.178571	4.7	94.1	49.7	50.3	10.2
Jimmy Vesey	0.089286	0.142857	0.071429	0.071429	3.214286	3.607143	9.5	89.2	47.3	52.7	10
Alex Galchenyuk	0.071429	0.160714	0.089286	0.160714	4.196429	4.017857	10.6	87	52.6	47.4	12.9
Travis Boyd	0.035714	0.160714	0.035714	0.071429	1.839286	2.232143	15.2	89.9	54.8	45.2	8.8

to the team offense (goals) and defense (save percentage). The player box scores also come from the site Stathead (2021). Table 8.12 shows player activities statistics — average values per game for players on the Toronto Maple Leafs, at even strength when the player is on the ice. In the notation: FF/G is the (shots + misses for) while player is on-ice; FA/G is the (shots + misses against) while player is on-ice; SV%/ is the save percentage while the player is on-ice; SH% is shooting percentage; OZ% is percent of on-ice time in offensive zone; OZ% is percent of on-ice time in defensive zone; TOI is time on ice per game. From the team level analysis G and SV% are the determining factors in W/L. That is, the logit model used those components as independent variables. At the player level, we want to consider the game activities which effect those team statistics.

Multiple linears regression models were estimated from Toronto box score data for 2021, with goals scored when the player is on-ice and save percentage when the player is on-ice as dependent variables. This will provide an estimate of the individual player contribution to G (goals) and SV% (save percentage).

(1) Goals: The fitted regression equation for goals when the player is on the ice is

$$\hat{G} = -0.0702 + 0.02176 \times FF + 0.00775 \times SH\% - 0.1038 \times BLK$$
$$+ 0.1865 \times TK - 0.1205 \times GV.$$

The other variables in the box score were not significant. The fit is very good with $R^2 = 66.71\%$. As expected, the play on ice determines goals.

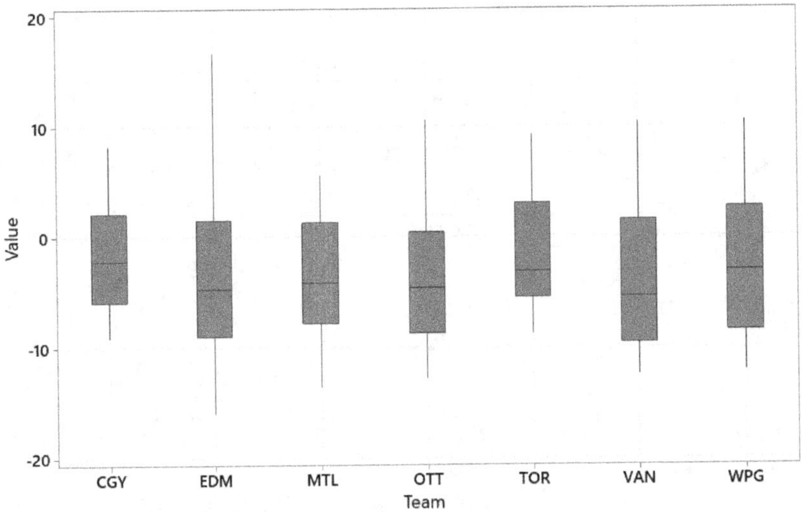

Figure 8.7. NHL North players value by team.

(2) Save Percentage: The fitted regression equation for save percentage when the player is on the ice is

$$\hat{SP} = 91.29 + 0.0555dZS - 0.323TOI + 1.465BLK + 0.955GV.$$

In the case of save percentage the fit was significant but the contribution from on ice play was much less, with $R^2 = 18.14\%$. The goaltender is the major factor in SV%, but the skaters contribute.

(3) Player Value: With the prediction equations for goals and save percentage we calculated each players contribution to goals and save percentage using the players box score statistics. With the player predictions $\left(\hat{G}_i, S\hat{V}_i\%\right)$ for each game, the predictions were input to the value (logit) equation

$$\hat{U}_i = -119.2 + 4.430 \times \hat{G}_i + 117.6 \times S\hat{P}_i.$$

The distribution of player values for each team in the North Division are presented with box plots in Figure 8.7.

Toronto has a slightly better array of player values. In Table 8.13 are presented the individual player values per game for the Toronto Maple Leafs.

The goals and save percentage numbers are for the time the player is on the ice. The value of the star players Auston Matthews, and Mitch Marner

Table 8.13. Toronto player values.

Name	Pos	Team	Pred G	Pred S%	Pred Val
T.J. Brodie	D	TOR	2.238609	0.905635	-2.78031
Morgan Rielly	D	TOR	2.525463	0.897638	-2.45
Justin Holl	D	TOR	2.502721	0.90487	-1.70027
Mitch Marner	RW	TOR	4.926567	0.900343	8.505043
Ilya Mikheyev	F	TOR	2.077009	0.919492	-1.86657
Jason Spezza	C	TOR	2.411015	0.913455	-1.09693
Jake Muzzin	D	TOR	1.79403	0.910669	-4.15778
Auston Matthews	C	TOR	5.187506	0.897361	9.3103
Travis Dermott	D	TOR	0.784172	0.909321	-8.78999
William Nylander	C	TOR	4.187752	0.899185	5.095862
Zach Bogosian	D	TOR	1.871582	0.907908	-4.13896
Joe Thornton	C	TOR	2.220342	0.900566	-3.45737
Zach Hyman	C	TOR	4.13968	0.898689	4.824641
Pierre Engvall	LW	TOR	1.505664	0.916936	-4.69823
Wayne Simmonds	RW	TOR	0.88672	0.914611	-7.71354
Jimmy Vesey	LW	TOR	1.264137	0.912541	-6.28501
Alex Galchenyuk	C	TOR	1.676409	0.901334	-5.77668
Travis Boyd	C	TOR	1.379107	0.912522	-5.77791

stands out. Keep in mind the values are on a logit scale, where positive values imply an increase in win probability and negative values imply a decrease in win probability. Defensive players are at a disadvantage in this calculus since their lower goals contribution is not compensated by the contribution to save percentage. The variation in save percentage is small compared to the variation in goals. The goaltender is the major factor in save percentage and the same goaltender applies to all skaters.

8.7. Discussion

The methods presented in this chapter describe models for evaluating the value of teams and players in ice hockey. The basis for evaluation is the box score, the statistical summary of key activities in game play. The fact that team value in a game is characterized by goals scored and save percentage is not at all surprising. The on-ice activities of players are related to goals scored and save percentage, and that relationship is the method for assigning player values. The analysis applies to skaters, but not goaltenders.

The absence of the goaltender effect is certainly a shortcoming in player evaluation. The team featured in the analysis of the NHL North Division, the Toronto Maple Leafs, is very strong on offense. However, the goaltending was shaky at times. Compensating for weak goaltending with a flood of goals was somewhat successful in the regular season. The other offensive juggernaut with spotty goaltending, the Edmonton Oilers, also had a strong regular season. Players on both teams will do well in the end of season awards. However, both Toronto and Edmonton were eliminated in the first round of the post season playoffs. Their opponents were stronger in goal and also stymied the offensive stars with defensive play (tight checking, borderline illegal obstruction-hooking,holding). Referees tend to "swallow their whistles" is the playoffs. The all time great, Mario Lemieux, famously referred to the NHL as a garbage league, where skill is neutralized with obstruction. Of course "Super Mario" still light up the scoreboard, so exceptional skill overcomes obstacles. It is not that today's stars (Austin Matthews, Conner McDavid) are overrated based on regular season games. They need a supporting cast, and in particular a solid goalkeeper are an important part of playoff success against top teams.

Chapter 9

NFL Analytics I

Leonard C. MacLean and William T. Ziemba

In this chapter and Chapter 10 we discuss a number of interesting ideas including some from the class notes of our Stanford colleague Tom Cover who died in 2016 at 73. Tom was a brilliant professor of statistics and electrical engineering who supervised an astounding 64 PhD dissertations. He was arguably the top information theory expert in the US. In addition, he was interested in various gambling games and sports statistics. He taught a course in Sports Statistics and interested numerous students in the topic. We had discussed doing a sport statistics book together, but now can only dedicate our book to him and record for a larger audience some of his results and add our thoughts along the way. Analytics is popular in today's sports analysis, and Tom was ahead of his time in bringing mathematics and statistics to decision making in sports. The examples of sports analytics are taken from American baseball and football.

9.1. Expected Value of Field Position in Football

In American football the playing field is 100 yards long. When the offense takes possession of the ball at the x yard line, there is $100 - x$ yards to cross the goal line for a touchdown. For strategy purposes it is important to understand the chance $p(x)$ of a touchdown on that possession starting at the x yard line. Assuming the convert is automatic, the outcomes on that possession drive are: 7 points with probability $p(x)$ or 0 points with probability $(1 - p(x))$. The expected number of points $= 7 \times p(x)$. In Figure 9.1 is displayed the average number of points for starting positions during NCAA football games in the Big Ten Conference over the 2013–2014 seasons. Similar plots exist for NFL games.

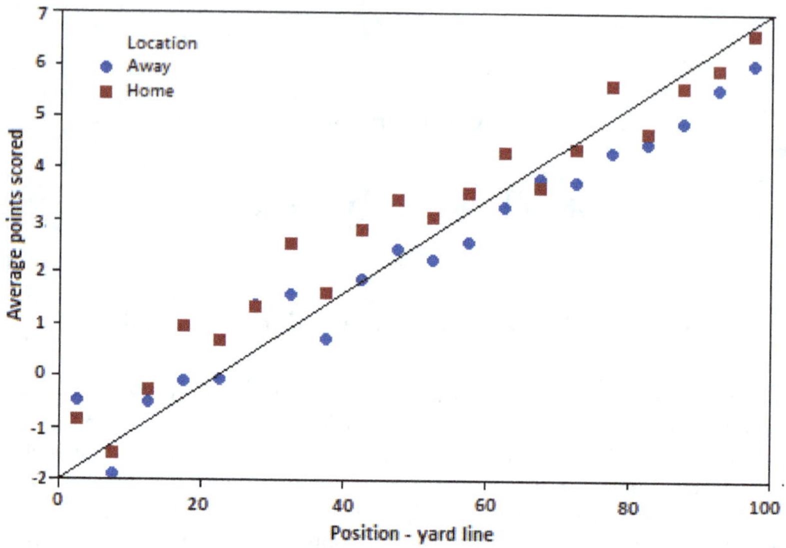

Figure 9.1. Field position and points scored.

The remarkable feature of the plot is the simple pattern. If a line is drawn as shown from the "0" yard line (a touchback costing -2 points) to the "100" yard line (a touchdown paying $+7$ points) the straight line almost passes through the middle of the points. With this observation the expected value of field position x, defined as $V(x)$, is approximately

$$V(x) = -2 + 0.09x.$$

This formula can be used to support decision making by the offensive team depending on field position. (See Carter and Macholl (1978); Carroll *et al.* (1988); Quinn (2012)). We illustrate this with some examples.

1. *Kicking*: It is 4th down and 5 yards to a first down on the opponents 30 yard line. The options are to kick a field goal for 3 points or attempt to advance the ball at least to the 25 yard line for a first down. It is estimated that the chance of a successful field goal from the 30 (actually a 47 yard kick) is 0.5. The chance of a first down x yards past the 25 yard line is 0.4 and the chance of falling y yards short of the 25 is 0.6. Assume if the field goal is missed the opponent takes over at their 30 yard line, and if the field goal is successful the ball is placed at the 20 (a touchback). The expected value of kicking the field goal is

$$EV = 0.5 \times (3 - V(20) + 0.5 \times (-V(30)) = 1.25.$$

Table 9.1. Logit model.

	A	$\bar{A}$
B	p_{AB}	$p_{\bar{A}B}$
$\bar{B}$	$p_{A\bar{B}}$	$p_{\bar{A}\bar{B}}$

The expected value of going for the first down is

$$EV(x, y) = 0.4 \times V(75 + x) + 0.6 \times V(100 - (70 + y)) \geq 1.48.$$

So the best option is to go for the first down.

2. *Passing*: A team has first down at the x yard line and they are interested in the distance an intercepted pass needs to be thrown (assuming it is downed immediately) so that the expected value field position of the offense at x yards equals the expected value of the opposition from intercepting the pass at y yards. The distance the ball was thrown is $y - x$. The change in value from the interception is

$$\Delta = V(x) - (-V(100 - y)) = 5 - 0.09(y - x).$$

If $\Delta = 0$, then $y - x \approx 55$. Of course that is quite a throw and equal to the distance of a good punt. Most passes are much shorter and the value of an interception is negative. The chance of a completion, incompletion or interception for passes of each distance would would be used to calculate the expected value of a pass attempt of $y - x$ yards.

9.2. Combining Odds Ratios

A popular model for the probability of an event is the Bradley–Terry model (Bradley and Terry, 1952). Let $p = Pr[A]$ for event A. Then p is defined by the formula

$$p = \frac{e^\beta}{1 + e^\beta}.$$

As β ranges from $-\infty$ to $+\infty$ we have p moving from 0 to 1. For the parameter β we have $\beta = ln\left(\frac{p}{1-p}\right)$, where $\frac{p}{1-p}$ is the odds ratio and $ln\left(\frac{p}{1-p}\right)$ is called the logit. The logit transformation has the effect of linearizing probability and a linear model for logits is justified. Consider a simple 2-factor linear model for logits as shown in Table 9.1.

Then in expectation $\beta_{AB} = \beta_{A\cdot} + \beta_{\cdot B} - \beta_{\cdot\cdot}$. In terms of logits

$$ln\left(\frac{p_{AB}}{1-p_{AB}}\right) = ln\left(\frac{p_{A\cdot}}{1-p_{A\cdot}}\right) + ln\left(\frac{p_{\cdot B}}{1-p_{\cdot B}}\right) - ln\left(\frac{p_{\cdot\cdot}}{1-p_{\cdot\cdot}}\right)$$

and for odds ratios

$$\frac{p_{AB}}{1-p_{AB}} = \frac{p_{A\cdot}}{1-p_{A\cdot}} \times \frac{p_{\cdot B}}{1-p_{\cdot B}} \times \frac{1-p_{\cdot\cdot}}{p_{\cdot\cdot}}.$$

In these expressions, p_{AB} is the joint probability for A and B, $p_{A\cdot}$ is the marginal probability for A, $p_{\cdot B}$ is the marginal probability for B, and $p_{\cdot\cdot}$ is the overall probability. The odds ratios for the margins generate the odds ratio for the specific AB event. Obviously there are many ways to combine odds ratios based on the Bradley-Taylor model and linear factor models. This is a general and powerful method for developing the chance for an particular outcome from a competition.

As an example of the use of a 2-factor model, let p_{AB} = batting average of player A against pitcher B. Then $p_{A\cdot}$ = the batting average of A against all pitchers, $p_{\cdot B}$ = the batting average of all batters against pitcher B, and $p_{\cdot\cdot}$ = the league batting average. If batter A is facing pitcher B, then the batting average (chance of a hit) can be determined from the knowledge of his batting average, the league average and the pitchers batting against average, statistics which are known.

For illustration consider a good hitter with $p_{A\cdot} = .320$ facing a poor pitcher with $p_{\cdot B} = .270$, and a league average $p_{\cdot\cdot} = .250$. Then

$$\frac{p_{AB}}{1-p_{AB}} = \frac{.320}{.680} \times \frac{.270}{.730} \times \frac{.750}{.250} = .522,$$

and $p_{AB} = .343$.

This use of marginal probabilities to generate probabilities for specific scenarios can be used to make strategic decisions in batting and pitching. Of course, it can also be used to calculate the chance for an outcome from any head to head competition, where the characteristics of the competitors is known.

9.3. Game Point Spread: Predicting Success

Leading up to a sporting competition there is a lot of "expert" opinion expressed about the eventual outcome of the competition. One type of opinion or judgement is manifest in betting on the outcome, a very popular activity worldwide. In a sporting event almost every game has a favorite and an underdog. Let $F =$ the number of points scored by the favorite, and $U =$ the number of points scored by the underdog. Then the point spread is

$$P = F - U.$$

The general purpose of spread betting is to create an active market for both sides of a binary wager. The point spread is essentially a handicap towards the underdog and the wager becomes "Will the favorite win by more than the point spread?" The point spread is set at a level to create an equal number of participants on each side of the wager. This allows a bookmaker to act as a market maker by accepting wagers on both sides of the spread. Spread betting is a judgement on the likely outcome of a game.

Of course the points by the favorite and underdog are uncertain and the margin of victory over/under the point spread is a variable. Let M be the margin over the point spread

$$M = F - U - P.$$

In Figure 9.2 is displayed an empirical distribution of M for NFL games covering 1981–1984 (Stern, 1991).

The shape of the distribution is very close to a normal, and normality is supported by statistical tests. The mean of the distribution is $\overline{M} = 0.07$, and the standard deviation is $s_M = 13.86$. For simplicity we assume

$$M \propto N(0, 14).$$

With a given point spread $P = p$, the chance of the favorite winning can be calculated as

$$Pr\left[F > U \mid P = p\right] = Pr\left[M > -P \mid P = p\right] = 1 - \Phi\left(\frac{-p}{14}\right),$$

where Φ is the normal cumulative distribution.

For example in a game between San Francisco 49ers and Oakland Raisers, the 49ers are favored by 4 points. Then the chance of the 49ers winning the contest is $1 - \Phi(-0.2857) = 0.6124$. So the spread is converted into a chance of winning.

The standard deviation, which determines the distribution of M, would depend on the sport (e.g., football, baseball, basketball, hockey), but the information on margin of victory compared to point spread is available and the standard deviation can be estimated. The expert judgement as revealed in the point spread can be used to estimate the chance of a team winning a game or even a series of games.

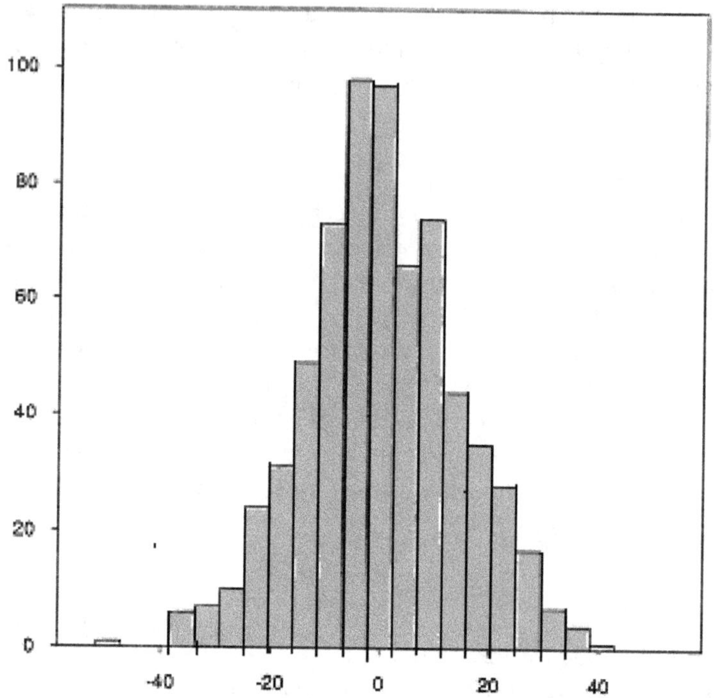

Figure 9.2. Margin over point spread.

Table 9.2. Aggregation.

	Season 1	**Season 2**
Avg: A	p_{A1}	p_{A2}
AtBats: A	n_{A1}	n_{A2}
Avg: B	p_{B1}	p_{B2}
AtBats: B	n_{B1}	n_{B2}

9.4. Aggregation of Performance Measures

The overall evaluation of a player in a sport such as baseball or basketball is an aggregation of performance statistics across seasons. When highlighting Hall of fame performers it is usual to emphasize aggregate career statistics. The aggregation is more complicated than a simple average of season statistics. Consider data on batting averages in baseball for two seasons in Table 9.2.

Table 9.3. Simpsons paradox.

	Season 1	Season 2
Avg: A	.667	.100
AtBats: A	30	100
Avg: B	.333	0
AtBats: B	30	10

The aggregate average for A is

$$p_A = \frac{n_{A1}}{n_{A1} + n_{A2}} \times p_{A1} + \frac{n_{A2}}{n_{A1} + n_{A2}} \times p_{A2},$$

and the aggregate for B is

$$p_B = \frac{n_{B1}}{n_{B1} + n_{B2}} \times p_{B1} + \frac{n_{B2}}{n_{B1} + n_{b2}} \times p_{B2}.$$

It is possible that $p_{A1} > p_{B1}$ and $p_{A2} > p_{B2}$ but $p_A < p_B$. That is, player A has a better average in both seasons but a lesser average in the combined seasons. This effect is an example of Simpsons paradox (Simpson, 1951) and is generated by the disparity in at bats (attempts) between players.

To observe the paradox consider the data in Table 9.3.

Then combining seasons we have

$$p_A = \frac{30}{130} \times .667 + \frac{100}{130} \times .100 = .231$$

and

$$p_B = \frac{30}{40} \times .333 + \frac{10}{40} \times .000 = .250.$$

So $(p_{A1}, p_{A2}) > (p_{B1}, p_{B2})$ and $p_A < p_B$. Although this example is based on small numbers, it is possible to find the same effect for large numbers if the attempts (at bats) are disproportionate.

9.5. Performance Measures: QB Rating

A sports contest (game) is composed of many events or individual contests, with the result of each contest being a failure or a success. The failure/success can have a variety of consequences. Consider, for example, an attempt (down) in football. The offensive team had possession of the ball and seeks to advance the ball at each attempt. The critical offensive player is the quarterback, since he takes possession of the ball and manages the forward thrust. About half of the attempts involve moving the ball through passing to an eligible receiver. The passing game has come to dominate football. The quarterback performance is measured by successes and failures of passing attempts. The simplest classification has a success as: completed pass of x yards or completed pass for a touchdown (score). A failure is classified as: an incomplete pass or an interception by the defense.

In the National Football League the aggregate passing performance over games is measured by four variables: x_1 = completion per attempt, x_2 = yards per attempt, x_3 = touchdowns per attempt, and x_4 = interceptions per attempt. The multidimensional score $X = (x_1, x_2, x_3, -x_4)$ is the basis of performance measurement. (Note that x_4 is a failure statistic and is negative in ranking X.)

In addition to reporting performance on each of the four dimensions, a combined passer rating score is completed. First, each of the x_i variables is scaled to a value between 0 and 2.375, with 1.0 being statistically average (based on league data between 1960–1970). The four separate calculations can be expressed in the following equations:

$$z_1 = max\left\{min\left\{(x_1 - .3) \times 5, 2.375\right\}, 0\right\}$$

$$z_2 = max\left\{min\left\{(x_2 - 3) \times .25, 2.375\right\}, 0\right\}$$

$$z_3 = max\left\{min\left\{x_3 \times 20, 2.375\right\}, 0\right\}$$

$$z_4 = max\left\{min\left\{2.375 - (x_4 \times 25), 2.375\right\}, 0\right\}.$$

Second, the separate scores are aggregated with the formula:

$$Y = \frac{100}{6}\left(z_1 + z_2 + z_3 + z_4\right).$$

A perfect passer rating (158.3) requires at least: 77.5% completion percentage, 12.5 yards per attempt, 11.875% touchdown percentage, and no interceptions.

The rating score Y reduces the four dimensional representation to a single dimension. The rating is from the pro football Hall of Fame official site. The formula does not include rushing statistics or fumbles, nor does it put added weight on performance in situations like third downs or fourth-quarter scoring tries. The rating does not account for the quality of receivers or protection from the offensive line. The rating does not measure a quarterback's contributions to team wins. The highest career passing rating is 104.0 by Aaron Rodgers, 2005–2016. He also holds the one-season highest rating of 122.5 in 2011. Peyton Manning holds the record for the most games (4) with a perfect passer rating. Phil Simms holds the record for the highest passer rating in a Super Bowl of 150.92 in Super Bowl 21. Ben Roethlisberger holds the record for the lowest passer rating to win a Super Bowl at 22.6 in Super Bowl 40.

There are desired properties of any aggregate rating score and we will mention three.

1. **Consistency:** Any ranking by Y should be consistent with the partial ranking by $X = (x_1, x_2, x_3, -x_4)$. That is if $X_1 \leq X_2$ then $Y_1 \leq Y_2$.
2. **Order Preserving:** If $Y_1 \leq Y_2$ and $Y_2 \leq Y_3$, then $Y_1 \leq Y_3$.
3. **Distance Preserving:** If d is a distance function, then $d(X_1, X_2) \leq d(X_2, X_3) \Rightarrow d(Y_1, Y_2) \leq d(Y_2, Y_3)$.

The passer rating score Y actually fails the consistency property. Consider game data on two quarterbacks as shown in Table 9.4.

So quarterback B threw an extra pass which was intercepted. The scoring for dimensions and the combined rating are in Table 9.5.

The anomaly in rating where $X_A > X_B$ whereas $Y_A \leq Y_B$ is created by the benchmark figure 2.375.

There has been much criticism of the QB rating formula. (Byrne, 2011). Consider a quarterback who is 3/10 for 30 yards, with 0 touchdowns and 1 interception. At that point, with $x_1 = 0.3$, $x_2 = 3.0$, $x_3 = 0$, $x_4 = 0.1$, the rating is $Y = 0$. Suppose the quarterback then throws an incomplete pass. The statistics are $x_1 = 0.272$, $x_2 = 2.272$, $x_3 = 0$, $x_4 = 0.09$, and

Table 9.4. Quarterback performance.

	$\mathbf{x_1}$	$\mathbf{x_2}$	$\mathbf{x_3}$	$\mathbf{x_4}$
A	9/10	300/10	3/10	1/10
B	9/11	300/11	3/11	2/11

Table 9.5. Quarterback rating.

	$\mathbf{z_1}$	$\mathbf{z_2}$	$\mathbf{z_3}$	$\mathbf{z_4}$	**Y**
A	2.375	2.375	2.375	0	118.75
B	2.375	2.375	2.375	1.7	120.45

$Y = 1.705$. The rate has improved by throwing an incompletion, because the interception rate improved.

A recent illustration of the quarterback rating shortcomings come from the 2017 Superbowl (Ziemba, 2017c). Some Super Bowl statistics: Tom Brady was 43 of 62 for 466 yards with two TDs, one interception, and a 95.2 rating. Matt Ryan was 17 of 23 for 284 yards with two TDs, no interceptions, five sacks, and one fumble for a 144.1 rating. The reason Ryan's rating was so much more than Brady's can be seen from the rating formula and the statistics counted in the formula. Of course, statistics can lie. Performance in crucial game situations by Brady is missed with the total game statistics. Brady is pleased and Ryan is not with the outcome of the game.

Wikipedia lists a number of attempts at alternative rating formulas for quarterbacks, but none of them seem to capture the full essence of the quarterback concept, which is very complex. We will add our contribution to a more complete QB rating formula in our forthcoming Sports Statistics book.

Chapter 10

NFL Analytics II

Leonard C. MacLean and William T. Ziemba

This chapter discusses several topics. First is an interesting sports decision situation, namely, an analysis of a crucial play late in a playoff game against Peyton Manning's Indianapolis Colts on 4th down to pass, run or punt that was the correct decision but lost the top NFL game of the year by New England coach Bill Belichick. We then discuss the jet lag effect and how to calculate the home field advantage. Then we discuss the decision of what to do on 4th down on the 1 yard line. Finally we discuss when to go for 1 or 2 point conversions after a touchdown.

10.1. Introduction

As I write on Sunday November 22, 2010, I am watching the TV analysts discuss this controversial decision on Sunday, November 15. They are all ex-NFL star players together with an announcer. Their analysis is seat of the pants. But is that the right way to analyze complex decision situations? So it is a good example for us to look at.

The setting was the showdown of the year, pitting the two "best" quarterbacks, Peyton Manning of the 9–0 Indianapolis Colts at home versus Tom Brady of the 6–2 New England Patriots and winner of three Super Bowls. Between them they have won most of the recent MVP honors. Manning has won the MVP of the season four times. Both teams have very good receivers and plenty of them for these superb quarterbacks to run down the field with.

Dr Z's bets were long New England at match odds — Indianapolis was favored and New England $+2\frac{1}{2}$ and $+3\frac{1}{2}$ points on Betfair in London. The Colts got a fast touchdown then New England got three touchdowns plus a field goal so moved out to a 24-7 lead. I then hedged my match odds bets, the larger ones to lock in a sure profit no matter who wins.

See Lane and Ziemba (2008) for an analysis of these types of bets where you can lock in odds on A then on B to guarantee a profit on a sports betting and some financial market situations. See Hausch and Ziemba (2008) and Hausch *et al.* (2008) for many studies of sports betting analyses.

I kept the $+2\frac{1}{2}$ and $+3\frac{1}{2}$ bets as 17 points seemed a huge lead. But I knew from past Patriots-Colts games that mean reversion comebacks are frequent. Indeed, the Colts rallied. With 2.08 left to play, the Patriots were ahead by 6 points (34-28) on their 28 yard line with 4th down. Normally it is conservative football wisdom with a 6-point lead to kick and move the ball down the field to say the Indianapolis 25 yard line. But the Patriots pass defense was not effective against Manning's fast accurate passes so they could easily move down the field and win the game. The Patriots traded two great defensive players Richard Seymour and Mike Vrabel plus some other key defense players including Teddy Bruski and Junior Sean had retired. So the Patriots were weaker on defense than usual. They had just seen Manning run through the defense for two long touchdowns.

Should the Patriots go for it and get the first down they likely could run out the clock or get a field goal to go ahead by an insurmountable 9 points. What to do?

The play was similar to a 2-point conversion after a touchdown but with a longer field. Coach Belichick was familiar with and accepted the conclusions of a paper by Berkeley Economics Professor David Romer (2006) which argues that going for it on 4th down is optimal much more frequently than coaches actually go for it.[1] And indeed Belichick has gone for it much more then the league average. So Belichick ordered Brady to try to pass for a 3 yard gain to get the first down 2 yards away.

Brady delivered a good pass to Kevin Faulk but Faulk bobbled the ball and was then pushed back so he did not gain the needed 2 yards when he hit the ground. Manning, of course, drove the Colts in 4 plays from the

[1] Romer looks at extensive data and does a good analysis recognizing that these decisions are really the first step of a dynamic situation so Bellman dynamic programming is involved. But it is complex with the number of things that can happen in the future and future decisions. With great players such as Brady and Manning involved it is even more complex to get the data right. We are reminded why Wayne Gretzy was essentially the only player four standard deviation sports better than average. He knew where the opposing player was going even before the player did. Here you are facing the greatest fast passing quarterback in history, Manning. So no matter where you leave him timewise and on the field, his chances of scoring are high. And as we see below, he managed the clock perfectly to not give Brady a chance to win the game with a field goal or touchdown.

New England 29 with 1.57 to go. With all 3 timeouts available, this is an eternity for the 3 time MVP to a score using up all the time left except a few (13) seconds. So Brady had no time to rally back for a game winning field goal. To use the clock Manning ran on three plays then hit favorite target Reggie Wayne for the winning touchdown. Belichick had used up 2 of his 3 time outs prior to the 4th down failed play.

So the Colt's won 35–34. Manning said "we were preparing to go 60, 70 yards. It was a great play by the defense, shortened our field." I won all my bets. But the big issue is the criticism leveled against Belichick for a so-called stupid decision. One coach, Brian Belick, fired last year as Baltimore coach, said "it's 50–50" you either make it or not. Other coaches pooh-poohed the Romer analysis saying they flunked calculus in college.

Of course, the analysis is very simple. It is just expected value arithmetic in this application.

For example, Brian Burke of Advanced NFL Statistics calculated that there was a 70% probability that the Patriots would win if they punted. But it was 79% if they went for it assuming that the chance that the Patriots get the first down was 60%. Burke writes:

> A team picks up 4th and 2 about 60 percent of the time – and we all know that a fourth down conversion in this case means certain victory. On the flip side: A team would score a game-winning touchdown from the 30 about 53 percent of the time. This leads to this formula – the first part is the 60 percent multiplied by 1 (1 signifying the certain victory if the play is converted). The second part is 40 percent multiplied by the chance of winning the game if the 4th down play fails:
>
> $$(.60\,^*1) + (.40^*(1 - .53)) = 78.8\% \text{ chance of winning.}$$
>
> ... Burke then estimates the chance of winning if Belichick punts – that is the chance of a team going 66 yards for a touchdown in the final two minutes. He says, historically, teams get that about 30 percent of the time. So a punt gives the Patriots a 70 percent chance of winning.
>
> ... Now, you probably are saying the numbers do not sound all that authentic. The Peyton Manning Colts would have a much better than 53 percent chance of scoring from the 30 (and, as it played out, the Colts scored so easily and left so little time on the clock it seemed just about automatic). But, you have to figure the Colts also had a much better than 30 percent chance of scoring had the Patriots punted – no doubt this was weighing on Belichick's mind. And for that matter, you have to

> figure that Brady has a better chance than 60 percent chance of converting on fourth down and two.
>
> Really, no matter how you play with the numbers, it will come out about the same. Try it. There is almost no way – without suppressing the numbers – to make the percentages even out. The Patriots' best percentage chance was to go for it on fourth down. Of course, football is not really a percentage game for most of us, is it? No, it's a game about emotion and passion and momentum.
>
> When the game ended and Belichick's gamble failed, people lined up to bash him – and normally I'd be all for this. Former Patriots player Rodney Harrison called it the worst coaching move Belichick ever made. Former Patriots player Teddy Bruschi wrote that Belichick dissed his defense by not believing they could stop the Colts over 70 yards. Tony Dungy said, "You have to punt there. You just have to punt there."

More or less, this analysis is ok but it is possible for the Pats to get the first down and still lose and the 53% versus 30% chances under these circumstances are likely much closer. And the situation is dynamic. Still it looks like Belichick made the right decision.

A Vancouver friend of mine who is a professional sports bettor related the following to me:

> There was a big bet in NYC late overnight on the "correctness" of the call. a jury of five top poker players/sports bettors gave their probability estimates for four questions:
>
> - probability of NE fourth-down conversion
> - Colts win probability after successful conversion
> - Colts win probability after failed conversion
> - Colts win probability after punt
>
> A friend of mine laid −1000, to win 100k, that the jury would return a verdict, based on their inputs above, of "correct to go for it". The estimates were varied, especially for item two, but all five supported the call. They are doing a second round of west-coast jurors today. I already voted (62%, 6%, 58%, 33%, respectively).

His 56% = 62%−6% is more than 50% so with essentially any reasonable utility function, the decision to go for it is optimal. Observe that since we are so close to the end of the game, so this two-stage modeling approach approximates the dynamic situation. One could add the probability that the Colts score with the Pats having enough time left to win with a field goal or touchdown.

My friend adds:

> Yes, what all the talking heads don't understand is that all of Indy's wins come off the second leg of a parlay, if NE goes for it, and that they're a solid underdog on the first leg. (Parlay = NE fail to convert, Indy score TD, NE fail to kick FG). Yes and Indy gets PAT. They just look at the gap between prob(score from NE28) and prob(score from Indy25), without realising it's conditioned on NE not converting, in which case NE wins outright. Yes and Prob(score from Indy25) might be close to Prob(score from NE28). It's a trivial problem, but it's funny to see how much sound and fury is expended by folks thinking the (trivially) correct choice is a punt. Yes former Indy coach Tony Dungy said that so did Rodney Harrison former Patriot player on the commentary after the game. There might be as much as a 8–9% swing in overall win probability by going for it, which is huge.

The goal is to win the Super Bowl and making the playoffs with a first week bye, and having home field advantage throughout the playoffs is paramount. At 6–3, New England is leading their division so are on track to have a chance to get the bye and one home field advantage but 9–0 Indianapolis looks poised to have an easy trip to the Super Bowl with a bye and home field advantage till the Super Bowl. Should both teams so progress, they would meet for the American Conference final in Indianapolis and not in the snow of Foxboro. Both teams won the following Sunday so the Patriots were 7–3 and the Colts 10–0.

The debate continues with most of the commentary and former football player stars who are experts on TV still blaming Belichick for a bad decision. Indeed they did lose the game. However, essentially all the sports bettors and sophisticated fans favored Belichick's decision. Again, getting the mean right is crucial and the key is the probability of getting the first down.

The league average for two-point conversions is about 45%. But on the 28th yard line, with Brady passing, it is at least 55–60% with 65% likely the upper bound.

It is too bad with the billions at stake that professional sports teams do not use statistical and economic analysis more. Billy Ball as it is called, is a notable exception where the Oakland A's usually have a top team with a low budget. But they have not won a World Series. See Lewis (2003) and the Brad Pitt movie, *Moneyball*, which discusses Billy Bean's strategy. The strategy is basically to assemble players that produce runs assuming that the more runs you have, the more games you will win. This means instead of batting average go for players who were on base very often. The Yankees, who have won by far the most World Series, have a simple formula for success: buy the best players. But this approach can lead to suboptimal behavior because the best players may not be the ones producing the most runs. In the Oakland A's application they put together less expensive players who together produce a lot of runs. Ziemba found similar behavior in lotteries where he consulted for 30+years. Most games are designed by non-analysts but when there are bugs they call on us.

10.1.1. *The jet lag effect*

There are many edges that can be used to successfully wager on NFL games. A powerful edge is mean reversion and risk arbitrage. This we show in multiple seasons of the NFL throughout the season, playoffs and Super Bowl. Here we discuss the jet lag effect.

We all face jet lag when we travel. We know also that the home team very often has an advantage. For example, the Seattle Seahawks are often undefeated at home. During the 2016 season, they were 8–0 but yet they lost many games on the road. It is often said that the stadiums are built to help the home team and in the case of Seattle the loud crowd, one of the very loudest in the NFL along with Kansas City and Denver, is known as the 13th player. Why then do they lose more often on the road? DiFilippo, Krieger, David and Fodor (2014) shows for the 2005–2010 regular seasons that there is a significant jet lag effect. What they find is that the effect is strongest when teams go from west to east over several time zones and then play and wind up losing those games. A Seattle example was in the 2017 playoffs when they went to Atlanta and lost.

The effect is strongest during afternoon games and when teams are in different divisions. However the effect does not seem to be there if it is a night game and it is less when the teams go east to west and when they are in the same division.

10.1.2. *How to calculate the home field advantage*

I have mostly worked with simple models. Complicated models do not necessarily improve prediction accuracy. I used a simple model focusing on home advantage to win 74% in the NHL against Roxys 50–50 line and used it to set the line for the BC lotto corp. But keeping track of some other things can be useful.

We use the following formulas to get our probabilities that a given team wins adjusting for the home field advantage. This probability can be compared to the probability of winning based on the odds makers spread, which is discussed as follows.

If Team A has true strength R_A and Team B has true strength R_B, the exact formula (using the logistic curve) for the chance of winning for Team A is

$$p_A = \frac{1}{1 + 10^{(R_B - R_A)/200}}.$$

Similarly the expected score for Team B is

$$p_B = \frac{1}{1 + 10^{(R_A - R_B)/200}}.$$

yielding

$$p_A = \frac{Q_A}{Q_A + Q_B}$$

and

$$p_B = \frac{Q_B}{Q_A + Q_B}$$

where $Q_A = 10^{R_A/200}$ and $Q_B = 10^{R_B/200}$ and $p_A + p_B = 1$. In the latter case, the same denominator applies to both expressions. This means that by studying only the numerators, we find out that the expected chance of winning for Team A is Q_A/Q_B times greater than the expected chance of winning for Team B. It then follows that for each 200 rating points of advantage over the opponent, the chance of winning is magnified ten times in comparison to the opponent's chance of winning.

Since the true strength of each team is unknown, the forecasted probabilities are calculated using the team's current ratings.

10.1.3. *The decision on what to do on fourth down on the one yard line*

In 2017, La Garette Blount of the New England Patriots scored 18 TDs and many of these were one or two yard plunges to the end zone to score these TDs. During the off season, the 250 pound Blount went from New England to the Philadelphia Eagles, the highest rated team. Previously he had gone to New England after being cut by Pittsburgh. In the 2017–2018 year, Blount had a very good running game, sharing duties on the Eagles with Jai Alai and he has had more of these one yard TDs.

In many cases, the decision on what to do on fourth on one is crucial to winning or losing a close game. Tom Brady, of New England, has a high effect rate nearing 90% and he has used the play some of the time. The classic case in the 2015 Super Bowl with Seattle on the one yard line on the first down with the possibility to run three times the powerful running back Marshan Lynch, who excels at this. The coaches elected not to do this and Russell Wilson's pass was intercepted and lost the game. Why did they do this when it seems non-optimal.

Another example was 2018 in the Pittsburgh home playoff game against Jacksonville. Twice the Steelers had the ball on the one yard line on the fourth down. Their QB, Big Ben Roethlisberger, at 250 pounds, is a good candidate to QB sneak the ball. He is 18 of 19 in fourth and one rush attempts in his career. This is the highest success rate (94.7%) for any player with over ten attempts in his career including the playoffs. But Big Ben is not allowed to change the plays designed by the offensive coordinator and coach Mike Tomlin. In this game, in the two times they were on the one yard line on fourth down, the decision was to run LéVeon Bell, who failed and to have Ben pass, which also failed. This cost them the game and a chance to meet New England in the AFC championship. One wonders why the Pittsburgh coaches do this.

There were also other dubious coaching decisions that did not seem optimal that cast doubt on the Pittsburgh management. For example, the final 47 seconds against the Jaguars in 2018 were basically wasted although they almost pulled out a victory. There have been other instances of wasted time in Pittsburgh games.

There are rumblings from some minor Steelers owners about this alleged poor coaching, but the major owner, Art Rooney II, likely will not make any coaching changes since historically Pittsburgh coaches have long, 10+ year contracts. One source argued that Pittsburgh would be undefeated if Belichick were the coach given the talent on the bench.

10.1.4. *The two versus one extra point fallacy*

Walker *et al.* (2018) describe a behavioral finance fallacy where coaches focus too much on the possibility of an immediate loss. They avoid risking instant defeat even when taking that risk offers the best chance to win the game. This is highly related to the previous section on going for it on fourth and one. The authors used ten years of NFL data focusing on a last minute TD with the scoring team being one point behind with little time left in the game. The choice is to kick a field goal to send the game into overtime or attempt a two point conversion by running or passing.

What is optimal? And what do coaches actually do? In 47 such incidences over the 10 years, the team kicked 42 times, which is 89% of the time. Teams who kicked won 40% of the games, which is below the average success rate for two point conversions which would have won the game rather than go into overtime. Of course, Some players like Brady and Big Ben are 90% which is much higher than the about 50% for two point conversions in the league.

The authors show that the ad hoc bias is also in NBA basketball. It is similar to the Belichick fourth down situation discussed above. They argue that the bias is involved with the tendency to treat problems in isolation rather than as part of a larger whole, that is, they are myopic. In lab experiments they found that decisions were uncorrelated with how teams would perform in overtime. The idea is to minimize the chance of losing now.

Chapter 11

Stop Shy of the First Down

Peter Cotton

On the first down, an NFL player should stop shy of the first down marker unless they can make several extra yards on the play. The decision can be clarified by introducing the notion of implied yards per possession. Strategies for 2nd and 3rd down with 1 yard are discussed. The often used strategy of pass on 2nd and run on 3rd is not optimal. The value of various field positions for success is also studied.

11.1. The First Down

The year 2020 marked the 100th anniversary of the National Football League. The game has undergone many changes, but statistical analysis of strategy has been something of a late starter although some teams have analysts. For example, half that history expired before a serious discussion of punting strategy occurred and to this day, some armchair statisticians are driven to distraction by questionable fourth-down decision making.

Here I go after a different sacred cow — the first down. I argue that players are making a mid-play strategy error on the first down that is materially impacting their team's chance of winning the game. The error isn't a lack of aggression, as with punting too much, but the opposite. They are fighting their way to the first down marker too often.

While *not* getting first downs may seem like an odd ambition for a football team, and hard to accept for player's conscious of their individual statistics, it's often optimal. I suggest that on a first-down play, no team should want a first down completion *unless a few extra yards are thrown into the bargain.*

11.2. The Choice

Even a casual observer of the NFL will notice that commentators, fans, and coaches alike uniformly encourage their players to lunge, stretch, hurdle, or bulldoze their way across that last yard to move the chains and get a first down. Getting the first down is a motherhood issue. It's applauded. For example, how often do we see a wide receiver break the imaginary yellow plane in an acrobatic fashion, often one arm outstretched, as they careen out of bounds?

But using data from the 2009–2013 NFL seasons, I question this "decision" (or perhaps we should call it a non-decision). It is a decision made every time a player decides to put their body on the line to reach the first down marker.

Let me be clear about this scenario. First, we are only talking about the first of four downs.[1] Second, I assume a player with the ball is certain he can't progress terribly far beyond the first down marker. We're talking about that last effort to break the plane. Obviously, a player in full flight who is likely to achieve the first down and also many extra yards would be silly to stop 1 yard short.

Under my stated conditions, in choosing to complete the first down, or not, I shall assume that the ball carrier is determining which of these two outcomes will ensue:

1. Second down and 1 yard.
2. First down and 10 yards (but with the line of scrimmage 1 yard further down the field).

The second possibility seems to be the strongly preferred option, given two seeming advantages:

- The field position is advanced 1 yard.
- The team will have one extra down.

However, there is one big disadvantage. The number of yards required for the next down reset will be ten, rather than one. I ask the reader to focus

[1]The "first down" refers to the first of four attempts to advance 10 yards, and also refers to the act of achieving the 10-yard advance, thereby resetting the down count back to the first down. Due to penalties, the first attempt may sometimes require 5 or 15 yard gain in order for a completion of a first down to occur, but usually completion of a first down is synonymous with a 10 yard gain or more.

on this downside when considering the completion of the first down. Conversely, there is a positive spin to a perceived "failure" to get the first down: *you are probably going to get it anyway, just further down the field.*

Due to this likely symmetry, it's clear that the tradeoff comes down to how much we value yards gained as compared to the small chance of losing possession. To formalize this and provide what I hope is a simple perspective, this article is broken down as follows.

1. A brief comment on ways to estimate the empirical value of possession, measured in yards.
2. An estimate of *implied yards per possession* when a player chooses to complete the first down, based on second and third down completion statistics.

I suggest that by completing the first down, players, and by implication coaching staff, are valuing possession far too highly relative to yards. I consider it my duty to convince the NFL offensive coordinators to order their players to do what seems most unnatural.[2] Instead of reaching for the first down, players should slide, run out of bounds, or otherwise stop the advance at the 9-yard line. This makes for quite the break in tradition.

Conversely, defensive coordinators should not be cursing players who allow a 10 yard gain when a 9 yard stop seemed possible. Those players have done their team a favor in conceding the first down. As controversial as this may sound, the logic is simple granted an upper bound on the value of possession relative to yards.

Rather than present a definitive calculus for possession value, I'll mention several ways to come at this that are all more than adequate. The decision to stop shy of the first down is in not predicated on a precise estimate of points per yard, and a rough number will do.

11.3. The Value of Possession, in Yards

The value of possession versus yards is old topic. I'm not going to get into endgame analysis or special situations, nor the value of the clock when one team is ahead — though I think it should be clear how the rationale extends to these situations.

[2]Actually, some certainly appreciate this already, based on their initial reaction to this idea.

THE EXPECTED POINT VALUES OF POSSESSION OF THE FOOTBALL WITH FIRST DOWN AND TEN YARDS TO GO FOR VARIOUS TEN-YARD STRIPS

Center of the ten-yard strip (yards from the target goal line): X	Expected point value: $E(X)$
95	−1.245
85	−0.637
75	+0.236
65	0.923
55	1.538
45	2.392
35	3.167
25	3.681
15	4.572
5	6.041

Figure 11.1. Table of field position values from Carter and Machol (1970).

I shall be content with somewhat typical field and game position, which, if you prefer, can be assumed to occur in the first three-quarters of a relatively even game. I assume that the game is not so lopsided that one team has significantly diverged from a strategy that maximizes mean points scored.

The value of field position in points was considered by Virgil Carter and Robert E. Machol back in 1970. Their table of field position values is presented in Figure 11.1 and, while some improvements are possible, we can read off the difference between 15 and 85 yards. This provides a very loose estimate of how expected points varies — namely one point per 12 yards. Combined with some reasoning about punts, even this early analysis may suffice.

Coming at things another way, the value of a yard is arguably easier to estimate on fourth downs rather than first — at least if the team is in field goal range and will with certainty kick. Then, the value of a yard can be inferred from field goal kicking probability (the blue line's slope in Figure 11.2) since the only value of a yard is a reduction in the probability of missing.

Since the slope clearly varies, so does the value of a yard. The value of a yard on first down might be viewed as an averaging of these results, somewhat smoothing out the differences in slope, but we will still have different values of points per yard.

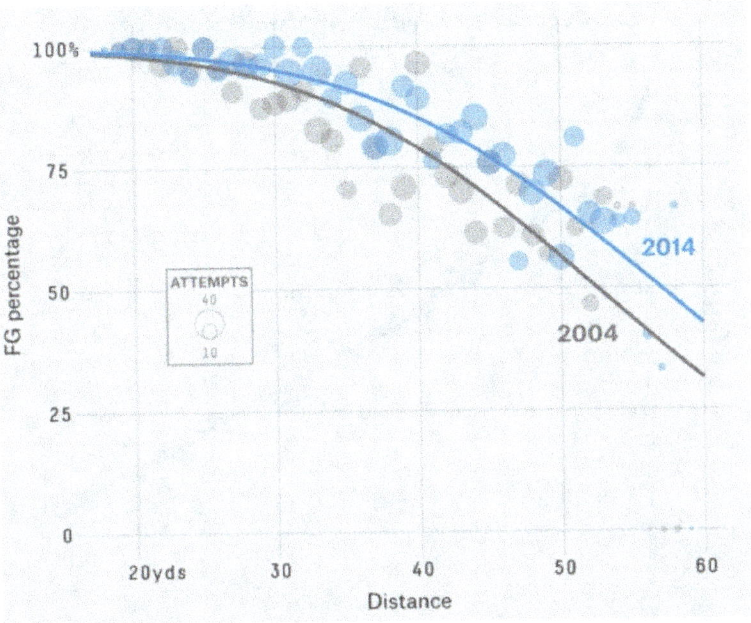

Figure 11.2. Field goal percentage as a function of distance. The value of a yard on the fourth down, measured in points, can be estimated from the slope of the curve. Plot by Benjamin Morris (2015) from the website 538.

Incidentally you can also see that the value of "a" yard (or at least some yards on the field, within reasonable field goal range) changed between 2004 and 2014. As kickers got better, the value of a yard on fourth down decreased.

To proceed to a slightly more careful estimate of first down field position, a value function approach could be taken, as is common in control theory. For example, Figure 11.3 shows the expected points as a function of field position in a Markov model for football authored by Brian Burke (Burke, 2008). We can read the value of possession from this plot or the accompanying data, as follows.

Notice that 66 yards (i.e., our own 34-yard line) corresponding to +1 points, assuming we have possession. Now imagine we punt it to our opposition. They start their next play on their own 34-yard line after an entirely plausible, if unspectacular, net punt of 32 yards. So now they are +1 points. Net, we have lost two points.[3]

[3]Or perhaps the punt is better. They start at their own 20 instead, corresponding to an expected 0.5 points per possession. Net, we have lost 1.5 points. These illustrations are

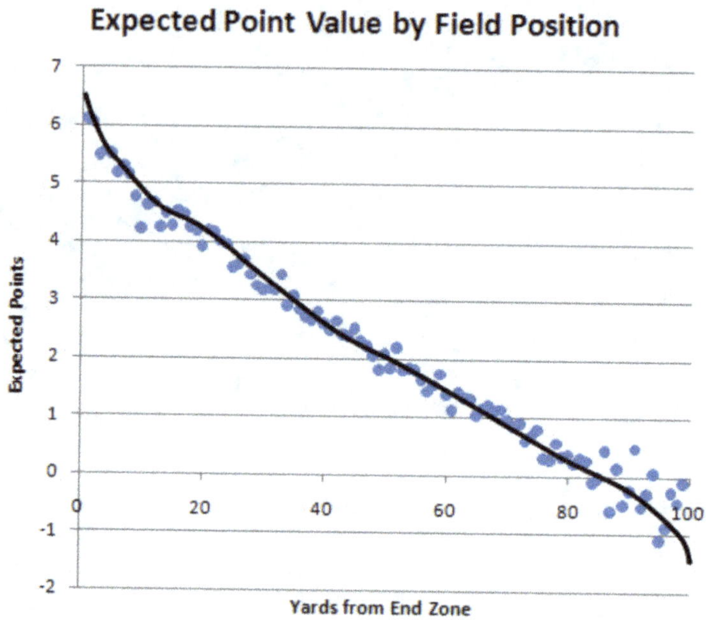

Figure 11.3. Expected value by field position, from an article by Brian Burke (2008). This is indicative of the value of a yard in points on the first down.

To emphasize the role of the punt, notice that the intercept with the x-axis occurs near the 85 yard line. Let's place a Herculean punter there who can always pin an opposition to their own 15-yard line (for an amazing net 70-yard punt). What a handy asset that punter would be. A team transferring possession in this manner has lost absolutely nothing!

We also note that the value of possession on first down varies a little less than it does for fourth down, as we expect given the kernel smoothing effect of the three proceeding plays. Granted, there is still some variation here that has not been eliminated completely. Look closely and you will see the field goal effect is still there — intermingled with touchdown possibilities.

We can read the value of a yard too. You can see that between the red zones (i.e. not within 20 yards of the end zone) it takes about 60 yards to go from four points to zero. This translates to 15 yards per point. The takeaway: from the value of possession in points and the value of a yard

intended only to make the point that in the upper envelope of estimates, a possession is still only worth a little more than two points on average.

in points we reason that a possession is *unlikely to be worth substantially more than 30 yards.*[4]

11.4. Third and One

Armed with that basic observation, we return to our key strategy question and reconsider "opting out" of a completion of the first down on the first attempt. This choice, which I have asserted is the superior one, might lead to a first down completion on the next play. Of course, we might also find ourselves in a third and one — a situation we must analyze too.

Strictly speaking these aren't the only possibilities — and the reader will note there is a small chance of a loss on the second down play, or a catastrophic turnover. However one can, for the sake of argument, assume a running play, where the possibility of a loss is greatly diminished. Whether running or passing is chosen, the under-appreciated upside is the number of yards gained on a successful second and one play, or if needed, a successful third and one play.

For avoidance of any doubt, I refer to the conditional averages, not the average including unsuccessful plays that don't advance the line of scrimmage. The data reveals that when rushing, this conditional average gain for a third down play is about 5 yards. When passing, it is a shockingly large 12.75 yards.

Another aside: this is a large discrepancy between passing and running and it suggests that teams might consider passing on third and one more often than they do. Passing plays are only successful 61% of the time, versus 72% when rushing. However, an 11% chance of lost possession corresponds to only a few yards, according to our analysis above. And this gets swamped by the massive 7.75 yard differential when passing. Side conclusion: teams should use passing plays on third and one more often!

Third and one strategy is certainly interesting, but the only thing we need to take from this analysis is that a successful third and one results in an advance of field position of almost 5 yards, even if you choose to run the

---

[4] A small flaw in the use of "expected points" is the value of possession conceded after a score is made — though as can be inferred on the plot, this is small near the region where the defence are likely to restart play. Thus, the notion of expected next score is quite similar to a value function approach, as is common in control theory. The discrepancy does not warrant an extended discussion here since we require only a rough estimate of possession value.

ball. Perhaps that's worth rephrasing for those who fear the third down. *Third and one is probably first and six, on average.*

11.5. Second and One

With that in mind, let's roll back one play. How should we feel about finding ourselves in second and one? When we look at second and one plays, rather than third and one, we find that the rushing play percentage goes even higher — up to 80% — though the average number of yards drops slightly (down to 4.73). That isn't surprising, since the defensive team has less incentive to prevent the first down completion.

Another aside: the differential between passing and rushing yards gained decreases, as compared with the same differential for third and one, with passing leading to only 6.5 yards of gain on average compared with 7.75 for passing on third down. The natural urge to pass on second and run on third might be working against the better interest of teams.

That's interesting — but not crucial to the case I make for stopping shy of the first down. What's important, and now evident by multiplication (assuming conditional independence of third down play outcomes) is that if you tell your team to run on second and one, and then again from third and one (should that be necessary) then you will have a 94.5% chance of getting the first down. In the process you will advance an average of 4.75 valuable yards.

Perhaps it is apparent why you don't want those chains moved on the first down.

11.6. Implied Value of Possession

Our star receiver takes a catch a yard short of the first down. Flat-footed, he turns to see a defensive player bearing down at great speed. Risking a season-ending injury he can, most certainly, dive forward with outstretched hands and make the hero play — securing the first down. Alternatively, he can casually step out of bounds, leaving his team at second and one.

Or perhaps a tight end has broken one tackle and staggers toward the first down marker dragging a defender who has grasped his leg. Should he break the plane or voluntarily stop his progress, if he knows he won't get any extra yards beyond the first down?

For a potentially controversial topic, the calculus is alarmingly easy and I frame it in terms of implied yards per possession. Using the values above,

Table 11.1. The value of a possession, measured in yards, implied by a player's "decision" to achieve the first down on the first down.

Extra yards on first down	Implied value of a possession	Assessment
0	64 yards	Incorrect
1	48 yards	Incorrect
2	30 yards	Break-even
3	13 yards	Correct

the wide receiver's lunge suggests that a 5.5% chance of losing possession in this series of downs is more important than 3.75 yards of field position. He is wrong! Since 5.5% is roughly 1 in 18, this means that possession must be 17 times more important than 3.75 yards. The receiver implies a value of possession of $17*3.75 = 63.75$ yards! But there is no way on God's green football field that a possession is worth over 60 yards. It is closer to half that number, as we have seen.

The results in Table 11.1 imply that a player might instead stop 1 yard shy of the first down marker, leaving his team at second and one. It also assumes a "typical" game and (middle) field position, and that a punt will be taken on fourth down. The implied yards per possession is conservative for several reasons. It assumes running plays will be chosen on second and third downs — though our discussion suggests this is sub-optimal. It doesn't take into account gains of less than a yard on second down. It also ignores the possible option value of running or passing on the fourth down, and it applies a conservative estimate of a gain of 4.75 yards conditional on success (on either down). This represents a conditional mean gain of 3.75 yards — averaged over 17 of 18 occasions when possession is maintained.

It becomes difficult to justify achieving the first down even if some gain is made. Some values are tabulated in Table 11.1. If possession is valued at 30 yards, it is clear that players should "decline" the first down (voluntarily stop progress of the ball) quite often. There may be additional reasons to do so, such as reduced risk of injury. Going for the first down isn't even worth it if you get to the 11-yard line. The calculus would then read $2.75*17 = 46.75$, which is still way too high a value (in yards) to put on possession.

Thus, contrary to commonly accepted wisdom, a celebration is only warranted if a player can advance 3 yards past the first down marker. A marginal first down completion could be setting the team up for failure.

Conversely, defensive players need not suffer one extra concussion to bring about an abrupt deceleration of the ball carrier. Let them get the

10 yards, or eleven if necessary. And the implication extends beyond individual player decisions. Offensive and defensive teams should design plays to make the +13 and +9 yard gains more likely, and the middle ground less so. Are they?

11.7. Evidence of Poor Strategy

Now that we know what is optimal, let's take a look at what happens on the field. Figure 11.4 show a histogram of first down yards gained rushing, where for simplicity we are restricting attention to cases where it is first and ten. One would think that with a rushing play, the offensive ball carrier would have good ability to aim for 9 yards or 12, but not accidentally end up in between.

The data, which shows *some* mass moved from 10-yard gains back to 9 yard gains, seems to indicate one of two things:

1. Some offensive players are aware that second and one is better than first and ten, and they are deliberately acting so as to achieve more 9 yard gains than they otherwise would (though not to the extent they should).

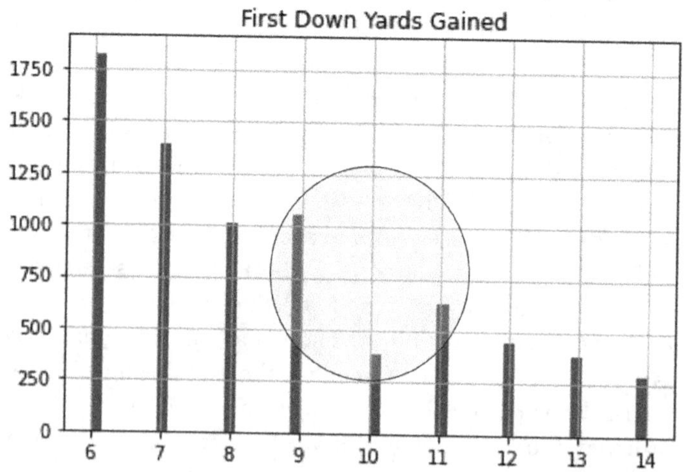

Figure 11.4. The empirical distribution of yards gained on the first down.
Note: Figure 11.4 preponderance of 9 yard gains relative to 10 yard gains suggests that both offensive and defensive teams are making a strategy error. Defenses should be allowing 10 and 11 yard gains. Offenses should be aiming for 9 yard gains, unless they can get to 13.

2. Defensive players are trying too hard to prevent the first down, mistakenly believing that a stop at 9 yards is better than conceding 10.

I'm not sure how we can disentangle these two effects but the latter is more culturally plausible. However, one thing is clear, and that is that there is plenty of room for improvement in strategy by both offense and defense. Defensive teams could very easily allow players to make a 10 yard advance, and they are clearly not doing that. Conversely, offensive teams really should have very little probability on the 10-yard advances.

From the perspective of the offensive team, the fact that 12-yard advances are less common than 11-yard advances is also a clear sign of poor strategy. That mass on the 11-yard gain should be moved back to 9 yards. Injury risking heroics used to get to 10 yards should, in fact, be reserved for going from 11 to 12, or 12 to 13, when the opportunity arises.

One could also consider passing plays. The yards gained increases — especially for third downs as noted — and the success probability falls. But after accounting for these offsetting effects the data is so similar that I'll save one plot.[5]

The point is that whether we are talking passing or rushing, both offensive and defensive teams clearly need to improve their strategy. Defensive teams can no doubt benefit from coverage patterns that deliberately allow the first down if a player is likely to make 9 yards. These changes, both to plays and execution, are likely to bring other benefits, such as reducing the chance of being caught flat footed by a long pass, or completely missing a tackle when trying to stop a ball carrier at nine yards rather than 10.

A more scathing indictment of strategy, both offensive and defensive, is delivered by Figure 11.5 which shows first down yards gained on the rarer occasions when, due to a defensive penalty, we are at first and 5 yards to go. There ought to be more ability to control yardage gained, and design a play to achieve 4 yards with high probability. Instead, teams are mistakenly attempting to get to 5 yards.

What are they thinking?! My data suggest that teams' chances of making 4 yards when they want it is significantly higher than their chance of making 5 yards (when they think they want it) — about 10% higher. For this, we have to use second down data due to a dearth of first and four

[5]If it were not similar, we would have unearthed a completely different type of suboptimal decision making.

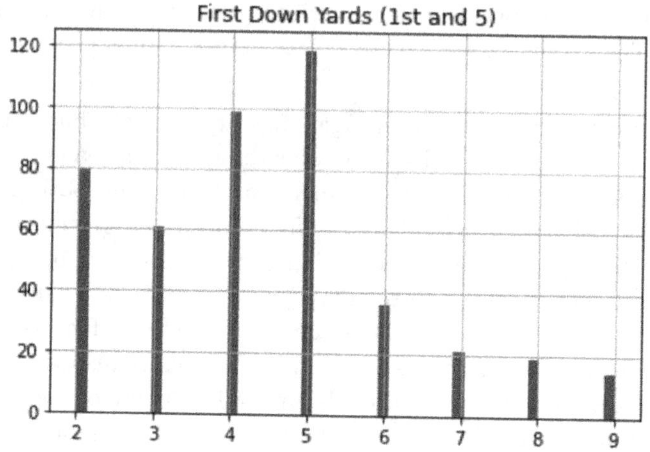

Figure 11.5. Yards gained on first down when there is 5 yards required.
Note: The scenario in Figure 11.5 results from a penalty applied to the defense. As with first and 10, the implementation of optimal strategy by either offensive or defensive coordinators should preclude what we see — namely the abnormally large number of 5 yard gains. Compared to Figure 11.4, this provides even more dramatic evidence that teams do not appreciate the relative value of yards and possession.

situations. But it is clear that teams are running riskier plays to achieve a worse outcome.

11.8. Conclusion

The lunge for the first down is part of football culture, and it seems almost distasteful to point out that this act fails to assist a team's chances of winning — at least on the first down. It is unfortunate that under optimal strategy, the great game of football is not as clean as fans might like. Team advantage is not monotonic in yards gained on the first down.

I have explained the calculation as a trade-off between yards and possession, with the likely valuable yardage gain outweighing a the small risk of losing possession. I've couched this by noting that a player who stretches out his arm to break the plane of the first down marker is only justified in doing so if a possession is believed to be worth 50 or 60 yards. This strains credulity, given that the value of possession appears to be roughly half that number, however computed.

But there are other ways to convince skeptical players. Indeed, stopping at 9 yards can be seen as a way of maintaining possession — whereas completion of the first down sets up the stiffer challenge: the necessity to make 10 yards on three plays. So, the calculation I present should not be viewed as an opinion on possession. Even coaches and players who believe in "possession at all cost" should come around to this way of thinking.

Stopping shy is not defeatist as it will almost certainly lead to a first down completion further down the field. Offensive coordinators should ask their running backs if they would prefer five downs to make eleven yards (with 95% probability), or 3 to make 10.

I hope that this provokes a more rigorous treatment of offensive and defensive strategy. Playbooks need to be rewritten, with a view to maximizing the nine yard gain. Though I have not tried to cover all situations, this should not present an excuse. Each case deserved careful consideration. For example when touchdowns have a high probability, remaining downs are more valuable — but so is the marginal value of a yard.

There are other directions for research. Though the data set used here did not facilitate it, a future analysis might consider more granular yardages, and even the possibility of stopping shy of the first down marker on the second down, not just the first.

Chapter 12

Efficiency in NFL Betting Markets

Leonard C. MacLean and William T. Ziemba

In this chapter we investigate whether or not the NFL odds are weak form efficient. Using data from the 2017 season, we show that it is. So to win you need to have superior handicapping and/or superior betting. We focus on the latter and show that with scores changing a lot, thus changing prices, the strategy of mean reversion risk arbitrage usually leads to winning outcomes. This is useful in various sports and financial markets and we use it for three NFL seasons in Chapters 13–15. Ten more seasons are in our *NFL Guidebook*, Ziemba and MacLean (2018). We also discuss odds of winning, point spreads and the ELO system for ranking teams.

12.1. Introduction

Market efficiency refers to the degree to which market prices reflect all available, relevant information. If markets are efficient, then all information is already incorporated into prices, and so there is no way to "beat" the market because there are no under- or overvalued opportunities available. Market efficiency was developed in 1960's by economist Eugene Fama (Fama, 1965a, 1965b), whose theory of an efficient market hypothesis (EMH) stated it is not possible for an investor to outperform the market, and that market anomalies should not exist because they will immediately be arbitraged away. The investment process incurs costs and the return is adjusted for transactions costs.

There are theories other than EMH which have gained support by investors. Ziemba and Ziemba (2013) have clustered theories into five camps. The EMH camp is populated by academics. Closely related are the risk focused group, which is a spin off from EMH. The systematic return is not simply from the total market, but rather dependent as well on various risk factors. Members of this camp are disciples of Fama-French (1992). The appeal of this approach is clear, since knowledge of market characteristics will help to reduce uncertainty in investment outcomes. Successful practitioners aren't believers in the EMH theory. They are confident in their knowledge and judgement, and identify favorable opportunities and focus their investment on that set of instruments. E. O. Thorp (1962) is famous as a gambler and investor because of his success in selecting favorable opportunities. Another camp is composed of believers in anomalies in markets. There is strong evidence of behavioral bias in decision making and these generate deviations from the efficient market. These deviations are temporary, but provide "risk arbitrage" opportunities at various times in market dynamics. W. T. Ziemba has lived in this anomalies camp.

The focus of this column is the efficiency of betting markets. *If the NFL betting market is efficient, then win probabilities will reflect all relevant information about competing teams.* A gambling site will determine win probabilities (odds), and based on the odds will specify a spread, which is the expected difference in the score of the favorite and the underdog. VegasInsider.com is an online gambling company which operates out of Las Vegas. To bet on NFL football, the bettor specifies the team they wish to bet, with the point spread and the amount of the wager. In Las Vegas type betting the house bears risk and they need to balance longs and shorts with their posted odds. The payout, unless stated otherwise, is figured at odds of 10/11. This means that a wager of \$11 would win \$10 and return \$21. This is called a straight bet. A straight bet is the most common type of football bet and this column considers such bets. When betting on football, the team you bet on must "cover the spread". This means the team must win or not lose by a predetermined margin of points.

Example:

Bet Line has Jets at Dolphins with a spread of -6. If you bet the Dolphins, the Dolphins must win by seven points for you to win your bet. If you bet the Jets, any of the following will declare you a winner. (a) The Jets win the game. (b) The game ends in a tie. (c) The Jets lose the game by not more than six points. If the Dolphins win by exactly six points, the wager is declared a push and all money is refunded.

Point spreads change constantly. The listed point spread at the time you make your bet may be different from the point spread when the game starts. The point spread that is listed on your ticket is your official spread. We will use point spreads and win probabilities which are applicable to the start of a game.

This column is about odds and available information and whether the odds reflect all relevant information. The information we access is from the site 538, which reports NFL team strength ratings prior to a game. We will check to find if the odds and spreads based on that information are fair.

12.2. Components of the Betting Decision

12.2.1. *Odds and win probabilities in games*

A NFL season is a tournament of games between teams, with each game having a win/loss outcome. If X_{ij} is the outcome of a game between team i and team j, then consider $X_{ij} = 1$ if team i wins and $X_{ij} = 0$ if team j wins. The score $W_i = \sum_{j \neq i} X_{ij}$ defines the performance of team i against other teams. The outcome of a game is uncertain, so consider $p_{ij} = Prob\left[X_{ij} = 1\right]$. Considering that the team standings in a season depend only on $\{W_i, i = 1, \ldots, N\}$ for N teams, then the outcome probabilities can be defined by

$$p_{ij} = \frac{1}{1 + e^{-(\theta_i - \theta_j)}},$$

for parameters θ_i and θ_j for teams i and j (Buhlmann and Huber, 1963). Of course the values for the parameters θ_i and θ_j in a head to head competition are unknown. If the parameters reflect the relative strengths of the teams, then elements of team composition, strategy and management would factor into competitiveness. In this article the Elo method of estimating team strength from W will be described and applied to games in the 2017 NFL season.

Related to the win probabilities are the odds. In statistics, odds are an expression of relative probabilities, generally quoted as the odds ratio or odds in favor. The odds (in favor) of an event is the ratio of the probability that the event will happen to the probability that the event will not happen. Given probabilities p = Prob of Win and q = Prob of Loss, the odds in favor o_f is:

$$o_f = \frac{p}{q}.$$

In gambling, odds represent the ratio between the amounts staked by parties to a wager or bet. Thus, odds of 6 to 1 mean the first party (normally a betting agency or bookmaker) stakes six times the amount staked by the second party. In simplest terms, 6 to 1 odds means if you bet a dollar (the "1" in the expression), and you win you get paid six dollars (the "6" in the expression), or 6×1 plus the 1. If you lose you would lose the dollar. The odds are determined by the total amount that has been bet on all of the possible events. They reflect the balance of wagers on either side of the event, and include the deduction of an agency's brokerage fee. The odds on display do not represent the true chances that the event will or will not occur, but are the amount that the betting agency will pay out on a winning bet, together with the required stake. In formulating the odds, the bookmaker will have included a profit margin which effectively means that the payout to a successful bettor is less than that represented by the true chance of the event occurring.

In a football game, for example, the true probabilities of each of the teams winning based on their relative abilities may be 60%, and 40% . The true odds against winning for each of the two teams are 2:3 and 3:2, respectively. In order to generate a profit on the wagers accepted, the agency/bookmaker may decide to increase the values to 70%, 50% for the two teams. This represents the posted odds against each, which are 3:7, and 1:1, in order. These values now total 120%, meaning that the book has an overround of 20. This value of 20 represents the amount of profit for the betting agency if they receive bets in correct proportions on each of the teams. To see this suppose the wagers are 60% bet on team 1 and 40% bet on team 2, and each bet is for \$1. Then the expected value of the agency profit is $0.6[1 + (1 - 7/3)] + 0.4[1 + (1 - 1)] = 0.20$. The art of bookmaking is in setting the odds low enough so as to have a positive expected value of profit while keeping the odds high enough to attract customers, and at the same time attracting enough bets for each outcome to reduce his risk exposure.

There are important points to consider in working with the odds posted by a bookmaker. If the odds for competing teams are given and the profit margin is known, then the probabilities of winning for the teams can be estimated. Suppose the posted odds for are o_f and the markup is δ. Then $o_f = \frac{\hat{p}+\delta}{\hat{q}+\delta} = \frac{\hat{p}+\delta}{(1-\hat{p})+\delta}$, and solving for $\hat{p}$ gives

$$\hat{p} = \frac{o_f}{(1 + o_f)} - \delta.$$

In the example above, $o_f = 7/3, \delta = 0.1$, and the calculation gives $p = 0.6$.

In the calculation, *it is assumed that the betting market is efficient*, that is wagers on teams and the odds adjusted for fees produces the true chances of winning, or $E(\hat{p}) = p$.

12.2.2. *Point spread*

Many NFL games are matches between strong and weak teams and the uncertainty in the outcome is not attractive for wagers. The point spread is a forecast of the number of points by which a stronger team is expected to defeat a weaker one, used for betting purposes. The general purpose of spread betting is to create an active market for both sides of a binary wager, even if the outcome of an event may appear prima facie to be biased towards one side or the other. The point spread is essentially a handicap towards the underdog.

Professional NFL bettors spend time building power ranking systems to evaluate teams' relative strengths and calculate who will have the advantage in any given game. This is then measured against the spreads and odds offered by bookmakers – looking for discrepancies that represent value. Let F = points scores by the favorite, and U = points scores by the underdog. If the spread is s, then the margin over the spread is $M = [F - U] - s$. The margin over the spread for NFL games covering 1981–84 (Stern, 1991) is shown in Figure 12.1.

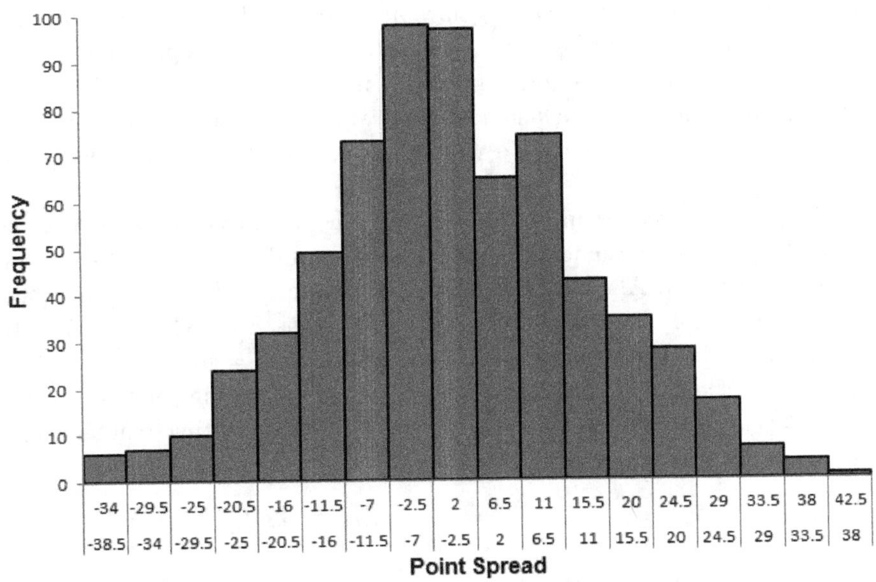

Figure 12.1. Margin over spread.

Based on Figure 12.1, a very good fit to the distribution is the normal: $M \propto N(0,14)$. With the point spread $S = s$, the probability of the favorite winning is $P(s) = Pr\,[M > -s] = 1 - \Phi(\frac{-s}{14})$, where Φ is the normal cumulative. This relationship is closely approximated by $P(s) = 0.5 + \frac{1}{32}s$. That is, there is an almost perfect relationship between chance of winning and the spread in points between the winning team and losing team. The function can be inverted to give $S(p) = -16 + 32p$.

The win probabilities reflect all available information about competing teams in an efficient market. Considering the functional relationship between probabilities and spreads, an efficient market will have spreads which reflect all available information. *That is $E(M) = 0$, and half the time the difference between scores for the favorite and underdog will exceed the spread in an efficient market.*

12.3. Team Strength Ratings: The Elo System

Without accounting for the talents of individual players and coaches, the pattern of wins and losses to date indicate the relative strengths of teams heading into a match. A strength rating based on wins/losses is the Elo rating system pioneered by Arpad Elo (1986), a Hungarian-born American physicist. The rating evolves as games are completed. Following a match, the rating for each competitor is adjusted up or down depending on the outcome. Victories over strong opponents increases one's rating the most. Other factors such as home field advantage are also considered. The amount a team's rating improves with a victory depends on the way the system is tuned.

If a game between team i and team j is scheduled to commence at time $t, t = 1, \ldots, T$, we assume the teams have up to date ratings of $\theta_i(t)$and $\theta_j(t)$, respectively. Also suppose heading into the competition team i has a prior chance of winning against team j of $p_{ij}(t)$. So $p_{ij}(t) + p_{ji}(t) = 1$. If there is no basis for favoring one team then $p_{ij}(t) = p_{ji}(t) = 0.50$. The outcome of the game is $x_{ij}(t)$, where $x_{ij}(t) = 1$ for a win for team i and $x_{ij}(t) = 0$ for a loss for team i. The formula for updating team ratings based on the game result is

$$\theta_i(t+1) = \theta_i(t) + \alpha(x_{ij}(t) - p_{ij}(t)).$$

The change in rating is $\alpha(x_{ij}(t) - p_{ij}(t))$, which weights the difference in actual and expected outcome by the smoothing parameter α. The parameter

Table 12.1. Sensitivity to α.

α	.01	.02	.03	.04	.05	.06	.07	.08	.09	.10
$p_{ij}(t+1)$	.5025	.5050	.5075	.5100	.5125	.5150	.5175	.5200	.5225	.5250

α determines how much the most recent game result contributes to the revision of the rating. It will depend on whether the game is at home or away.

With the revised (posterior) values of the strength parameters the probabilities for the games in the next week, $t+1$, are calculated as

$$p_{ij}(t+1) = \frac{1}{1+e^{-(\theta_i(t+1)-\theta_j(t+1))}}.$$

The initial value of the parameter θ and the α are to be determined. If the teams are evenly matched, with $\theta_i(t)-\theta_j(t) = 0$ and $p_{ij}(t) = 0.5$, and team i wins: $x_{ij}(t) = 1$, then $\theta_i(t+1) - \theta_j(t+1) = \alpha$ and $p_{ij}(t+1) = \frac{1}{1+e^{-\alpha}}$. Each additional unit of 0.01 added to α adds 0.0025 to $p_{ij}(t+1)$ as shown in Table 12.1. A single win shouldn't move the probability very much, and a reasonable choice is $\alpha = 0.02$. Some adjustment in α is necessary to account for home field advantage, player injuries and travel.

12.4. Efficiency in the 2017 NFL Season

We will consider the ability to predict game results using the pregame Elo rating for team matchups each week in the 2017 NFL season. There are two aspects of the game outcome we consider: (1) the win/loss; (2) the difference between winning and losing scores. The pregame Elo rating will be used to calculate probabilities of winning for the competing teams, as well as the expected point spread between the favorite and underdog. The actual game score, i.e. the difference in points scored between the favorite and underdog, will determine the margin over the spread. *If the Elo accounts for all the relevant information about competing teams, then the efficient market hypothesis implies that the spread is covered half the time.*

12.4.1. *538 Elo NFL Ratings for 2017*

The website FiveThirtyEight (sometimes referred to as 538), whose name derives from the number of electors in the US electoral college, focuses on opinion poll analysis, politics, economics, and sports blogging (Silver, 2015). The 538 website NFL coverage uses Elo ratings. As indicated, teams gain and lose ground based on the final score of each game and how unexpected the result was in the eyes of the pregame ratings. Under Elo, teams pick up where they left off in the previous season.

The scale of the 538 Elo ratings is magnified by a factor of 400, so we will use notation R_i for team strength. The benchmark rating is 1500. The initial team ratings for 2017 are by definition the same as last season's end-of-year ratings, but are more compressed because of reversion toward the mean — each team's rating is shrunk to the mean by one-third, with the league average team clocking in slightly above 1500. If $R_i(0)$ is the team i Elo at the start of the season and $\bar{R}(0)$ is the league average, then Elo for team i at game $t = 1$ is $R_i(1) = 0.7 \times R_i(0) + 0.3 \times \bar{R}(0)$. The updating equation during the season is

$$R_i(t+1) = R_i(t) + K(X_{ij}(t) - p_{ij}(t)),$$

where the sensitivity parameter K is scaled appropriately.

In calculating win probabilities for the game between team i and team j, 538 uses a base 10, and the formula is

$$p_{ij}(t+1) = \frac{1}{1 + 10^{-\frac{1}{400}(R_i(t+1) - R_j(t+1))}}.$$

Since $10^{-a} = e^{-(log_{10}e)\times a}$ the sensitivity factor is $K \approx 20 = \frac{400\times.02}{(log_{10}e)}$ in the above formula. The K factor is adjusted for home field advantage and player injuries.

To visualize the dynamics of the Elo rating by 538 for each team in 2017, we have the plot in Figure 12.1.

An inspection of Figure 12.2 shows teams with a consistently increasing rating:

{Carolina, Jacksonville, L.A.Chargers, L.A.Rams, Minnesota, NewEngland, NewOrleans, Philadelphia, Pittsburgh},

and teams with a consistently decreasing rating:

{Arizona, Cincinnati, Cleveland, Denver, GreenBay, Houston, Indianapolis, N.Y.Giants, Oakland, TampaBay}.

It appears that the ingredients of truly strong/weak teams (players, coaches) are present throughout the football season. For 60% of the NFL teams the performance in the weeks leading up to a game is a very good indication of the chance of winning that weeks game. There are also up

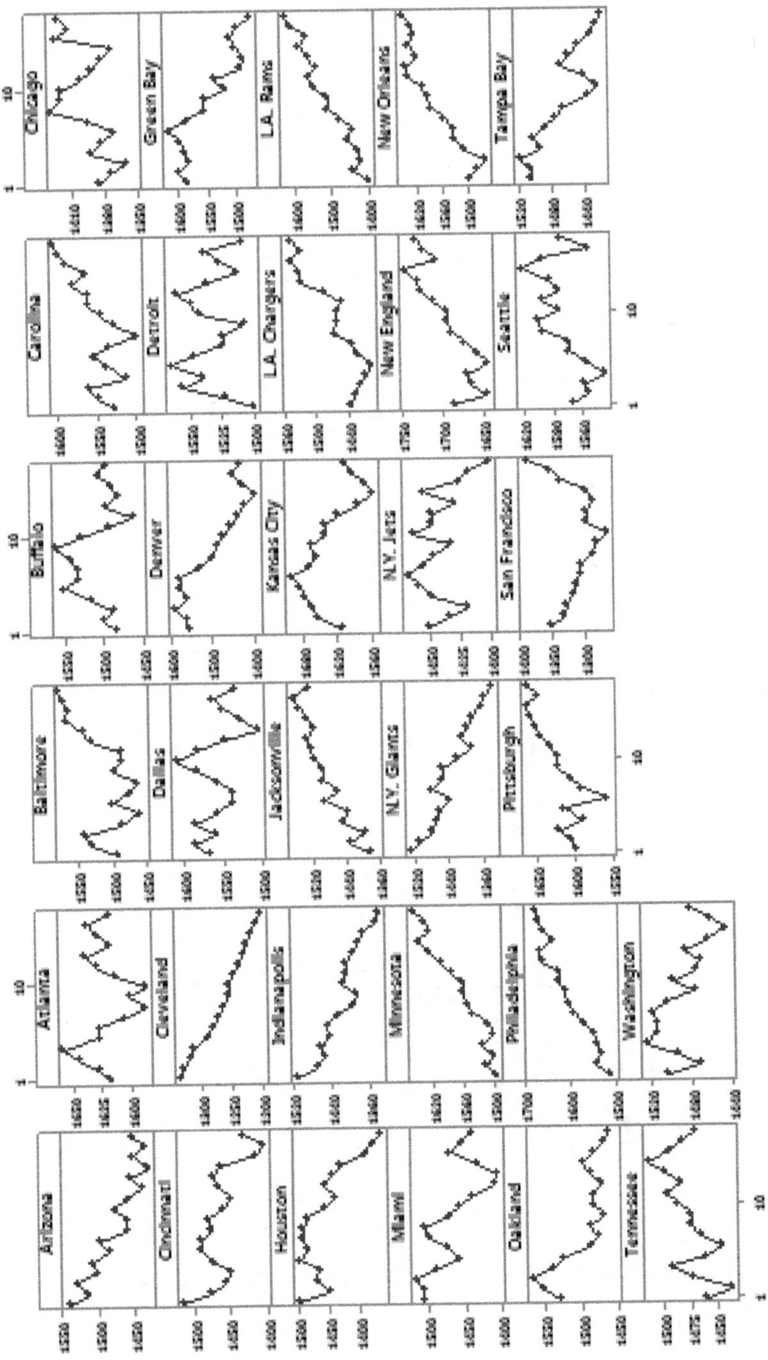

Figure 12.2. Elo ratings by week.

Table 12.2. Weekly game results.

Wk	St	1	2	3	4	5	6	7	8	9	10	11	12	13	14	15	16
	P	0.55	0.79	0.54	0.82	0.55	0.60	0.51	0.67	0.66	0.52	0.73	0.56	0.5	0.66	0.60	
1	S	1.45	9.4	1.1	10.2	1.7	3.2	0.3	5.3	5.1	0.7	7.4	1.8	0	5.3	3.4	
	D	9	6	−20	3	−12	10	13	−22	−39	8	20	16	10	3	−15	
	P	0.54	0.56	0.65	0.72	0.62	0.68	0.57	0.50	0.76	0.66	0.61	0.54	0.55	0.78	0.53	0.52
2	S	1.1	2.0	4.9	7.2	4.0	5.8	2.2	0.1	8.3	5.2	3.58	1.2	1.5	9.0	1.1	0.6
	D	−4	3	7	16	17	22	6	21	14	24	2	−25	7	3	11	14
	P	0.62	0.69	0.65	0.82	0.63	0.68	0.53	0.75	0.64	0.58	0.64	0.62	0.68	0.80	0.60	0.54
3	S	4.0	6.2	4.7	10.2	4.0	5.9	0.9	8.1	4.4	2.4	4.5	3.8	5.7	9.7	3.3	1.4
	D	2	−37	−10	−6	4	3	−17	3	−14	3	−21	−6	3	14	−17	11
	P	0.76	0.53	0.70	0.68	0.71	0.52	0.71	0.5	0.64	0.54	0.74	0.68	0.53	0.53	0.61	0.70
4	S	8.3	0.9	6.3	5.9	6.9	0.7	6.8	0	4.7	1.2	7.7	5.9	1.1	1.1	3.4	6.5
	D	21	20	−6	25	−5	7	−3	−3	15	−43	3	2	1	6	28	9
	P	0.69	0.61	0.73	0.54	0.68	0.50	0.59	0.56	0.73	0.59	0.64	0.56	0.74	0.67		
5	S	6.2	3.6	7.3	1.3	5.7	0.05	3.0	2.0	7.4	3	4.4	2.0	7.8	5.3		
	D	5	−4	3	−3	3	−6	−3	27	−21	−12	6	4	8	3		
	P	0.53	0.70	0.65	0.51	0.75	0.77	0.68	0.77	0.51	0.57	0.69	0.59	0.69	0.50		
6	S	0.8	6.5	4.7	0.5	8.0	8,6	5.6	8.5	0.3	2.4	6.2	2.9	6.2	0.1		
	D	5	−3	−13	−14	7	2	−3	16	−5	−10	−6	−1	−13	−14		
	P	0.75	0.58	0.69	0.75	0.54	0.55	0.53	0.56	0.60	0.79	0.63	0.64	0.64	0.60	0.60	
7	S	8.0	2.6	6.1	8.1	1.4	1.6	1.0	1.9	3.1	9.4	4.2	4.5	4.4	3.2	3.3	
	D	−1	3	−14	3	−9	27	−33	3	8	30	17	15	−21	16	10	
	P	0.57	0.84	0.58	0.62	0.78	0.72	0.69	0.86	0.55	0.65	0.57	0.61	0.71			
8	S	2.2	11.0	2.4	3.8	9.0	6.9	6.0	11.6	1.5	4.7	2.3	3.7	6.9			
	D	−40	17	20	1	8	8	5	23	14	3	14	5	10			

(Continued)

Table 12.2. *(Continued)*

Wk	St	1	2	3	4	5	6	7	8	9	10	11	12	13	14	15	16
	P	**0.67**	**0.53**	**0.72**	**0.58**	**0.67**	**0.60**	**0.53**	**0.64**	**0.74**	**0.68**	**0.62**	**0.51**	**0.57**			
9	S	**5.5**	**1.0**	**7.0**	**2.7**	**5.4**	**3.2**	**0.8**	**4.6**	**7.5**	**5.8**	**3.7**	**0.3**	**2.3**			
	D	−13	−3	20	34	28	−3	16	−6	10	−3	−11	−3	−13			
	P	0.65	0.61	0.64	0.84	0.54	0.77	0.56	0.59	0.58	0.63	0.53	0.71	0.78	0.62		
10	S	**4.9**	**3.7**	**4.6**	**10.9**	**1.3**	**8.5**	**1.9**	**2.9**	**2.6**	**4.1**	**1.1**	**6.6**	**9.1**	**3.9**		
	D	**6**	**37**	**7**	**14**	**4**	**3**	**−5**	**8**	**3**	**26**	**−20**	**−10**	**25**	**24**		
	P	0.68	0.72	0.53	0.70	0.53	0.58	0.81	0.83	0.50	0.56	0.79	0.51	0.56	0.51		
11	S	**5.8**	**7.1**	**0.9**	**6.5**	**0.8**	**2.5**	**10.0**	**10.6**	**0.1**	**1.8**	**9.2**	**0.4**	**2.0**	**0.5**		
	D	**23**	**3**	**−10**	**3**	**17**	**−23**	**−3**	**12**	**10**	**−30**	**25**	**−3**	**28**	**3**		
	P	0.57	0.59	0.59	0.79	0.61	0.71	0.83	0.71	0.65	0.86	0.84	0.64	0.64	0.55	0.70	0.60
12	S	**1.9**	**2.7**	**2.7**	**8.9**	**3.2**	**6.5**	**10.2**	**6.6**	**4.7**	**11.3**	**10.6**	**4.4**	**4.2**	**1.3**	**6.3**	**2.9**
	D	**7**	**−22**	**10**	**14**	**4**	**−6**	**28**	**14**	**8**	**18**	**11**	**−6**	**−3**	**7**	**3**	**7**
	P	0.52	0.79	0.71	0.51	0.63	0.53	0.51	0.54	0.68	0.57	0.85	0.57	0.63	0.66	0.61	0.74
13	S	**0.7**	**9.4**	**6.6**	**0.2**	**4.3**	**0.9**	**0.5**	**1.3**	**5.6**	**2.4**	**11.1**	**2.1**	**4.1**	**5.1**	**3.4**	**7.5**
	D	**24**	**20**	**−7**	**24**	**−1**	**−26**	**−5**	**6**	**20**	**11**	**9**	**10**	**7**	**16**	**−14**	**3**
	P	0.54	0.68	0.64	0.58	0.60	0.83	0.63	0.62	0.70	0.59	0.60	0.62	0.57	0.62	0.63	0.86
14	S	**1.2**	**5.9**	**4.5**	**2.7**	**3.1**	**10.6**	**4.1**	**4.0**	**6.3**	**2.8**	**3.2**	**3.9**	**2.3**	**3.9**	**4.2**	**11.5**
	D	**−3**	**−10**	**6**	**11**	**3**	**6**	**−26**	**−7**	**20**	**−23**	**17**	**−5**	**8**	**−6**	**1**	**−7**
	P	0.58	0.65	0.53	0.50	0.72	0.53	0.76	0.88	0.78	0.85	0.61	0.55	0.71	0.56	0.60	0.77
15	S	**2.6**	**4.6**	**1.0**	**0.1**	**7.1**	**0.9**	**8.4**	**12.1**	**8.9**	**11.3**	**3.4**	**1.5**	**6.9**	**2.1**	**3.1**	**8.2**
	D	**12**	**10**	**17**	**−5**	**38**	**8**	**11**	**17**	**27**	**5**	**7**	**−35**	**−2**	**3**	**3**	**3**
	P	0.79	0.69	0.76	0.50	0.73	0.68	0.51	0.65	0.78	0.69	0.69	0.78	0.51	0.61	0.83	0.76
16	S	**9.2**	**6.1**	**8.3**	**0.1**	**7.4**	**5.9**	**0.3**	**4.9**	**8.9**	**6.1**	**6.0**	**8.9**	**0.5**	**3.6**	**10.4**	**8.4**
	D	**7**	**16**	**17**	**10**	**3**	**4**	**16**	**7**	**21**	**16**	**−9**	**=11**	**−9**	**23**	**28**	**9**
	P	0.80	0.54	0.87	0.55	0.70	0.93	0.70	0.73	0.62	0.58	0.60	0.70	0.52	0.80	0.69	0.80
17	S	**9.6**	**1.2**	**11.6**	**1.5**	**6.3**	**13.9**	**6.4**	**7.4**	**3.9**	**2.5**	**2.9**	**6.4**	**0.6**	**9.5**	**5.7**	**9.5**
	D	**13**	**−9**	**20**	**24**	**−6**	**4**	**−8**	**3**	**20**	**6**	**-5**	**-4**	**12**	**−21**	**−3**	**−7**

Table 12.3. Times spread exceeded each week.

Week	Games	Correct Predictions	Beat the Spread
1	15	9	7
2	16	14	12
3	16	9	3
4	16	11	8
5	14	8	4
6	15	4	2
7	15	10	9
8	13	12	8
9	13	5	5
10	14	11	10
11	14	9	7
12	16	12	11
13	16	11	9
14	16	8	5
15	16	13	11
16	16	13	10
17	16	8	6
ALL	257	167	127

and down teams, where in season dynamics alter performance and the Elo rating reverses direction. It is a reasonable assumption that the Elo rating provides the relevant information to assess the chances for teams competing each week, and the expected point spreads based on each team's probability of winning creates a fair betting situation.

12.4.2. *Probabilities and spreads from the Elo*

The formulas for win probability and point spread were used with the Elo ratings from 2017. Table 12.2 shows for the games each week the following:

P = win probability for the favorite; S = the point spread for the favorite; D = difference in scores for the favorite minus the underdog.

The calculation $\Delta = D - S$ in the weekly game results will show if the actual score of a game "beat the spread". The spread is the expected score differential and to win a bet you need $\Delta > 0$. Table 12.3 shows how often $\Delta > 0$.

We see that 65% of the outcomes of games are correctly predicted. In terms of beating the spread the percent is 49.5%, which is basically a flip of the coin. The conclusion is that the Las Vegas betting market in NFL games in 2017 was efficient.

12.5. Conclusion

The analysis of the 2017 season in the NFL supports the conclusion that the strait betting market is basically efficient. The odds based on 538 Elo's take into account factors which traditionally affect outcomes, such as player injuries, home field effects, travel, etc. Beating the spread with the posted odds presumably would require some additional information not openly available.

Opportunities exist for wagering on NFL games where the chance of winning is much better that 50/50. There are many examples in our book (Ziemba and MacLean, 2018) where you actually win money through betting. The key is the within game dynamics. Obviously the scores frequently go up and down, with many games having three or four or more lead changes. Some betting exchanges (Betfair, Pinnacle, Betdaq) change the odds throughout most games based on the current score. (Note that Betfair *et al.* bear no risk, but take a cut of net winnings.) However, there is an expectation of mean reversion of scores as the game progresses. At points in the game there are "risk arbitrage" opportunity bets using the mean reversion of the odds. It is called risk arbitrage since it may not work, but the method described in our book will provide profits most of the time even if the team you bet on to start loses the game in the end.

Chapter 13

National Football League: 2018–2019 Season

Leonard C. MacLean and William T. Ziemba

In this chapter we review the 2018–2019 NFL season analyzing strategies, prediction models, odds and discussing bets Ziemba made. We predict the number of games various teams will win and compare the predictions with the results. We discuss the top players and the awards and the playoffs and Superbowl.

13.1. Introduction

In the sporting world in North America the NFL is the most popular by far and is also popular in Mexico and the UK where some NFL games are played. TV networks, newspapers, magazines and the internet are filled with stories about teams and players, analyzes and predictions. September is the time to get out the paraphernalia of our favorite team and look forward to NFL Sunday, or Monday and Thursday night football. January is the time to regret the performance of lifelong favorites and cheer for other teams as the playoffs get under way leading to Superbowl.

13.1.1. *2018 Regular season: Teams*

Every team starts with a 0–0 record and looks ahead to a positive season, with a possible run to the Superbowl or at least an improvement on the previous campaign. In Table 13.1, we provide the preseason predictions for all NFL teams in 2018. In each division there are favorites, largely based on performance in the 2017–2018 season. The most notable teams are

Table 13.1. NFL teams: 2018 predictions and results.

Division	Team	2017 Record	2018 Prediction	2018 Record
AFC East	Patriots	13–3	12–4	11–5
	Jets	5–11	9–7	4–12
	Dolphins	6–10	7–9	7–9
	Bills	9–7	4–12	6–10
AFC North	Steelers	13–3	11–5	9–1–6
	Ravens	9–7	7–9	10–6
	Browns	0–16	4–12	7–8
	Bengals	7–9	4–12	6–10
AFC South	Jaguars	10–6	10–6	5–11
	Texans	4–12	9–7	11–5
	Titans	9–7	8–8	9–7
	Colts	4–12	5–11	10–6
AFC West	Chargers	9–7	10–6	12–4
	Broncos	5–11	8–8	6–10
	Chiefs	10–6	7–9	12–4
	Raiders	6–10	5–11	4–12
NFC East	Eagles	13–3	11–5	9–7
	Giants	3–13	8–8	5–11
	Cowboys	9–7	8–8	10–6
	Redskins	7–9	5–11	7–9
NFC North	Packers	7–9	11–5	6–1–9
	Vikings	13–3	11–5	8–1–7
	Lions	9–7	10–6	6–10
	Bears	5–11	7–9	12–4
NFC South	Falcons	10–6	12–4	7–9
	Saints	11–5	11–5	13–3
	Panthers	11–5	7–9	7–9
	Buccaneers	5–11	5–11	5–11
NFC West	Rams	11–5	10–6	13–3
	49ers	6–10	9–7	4–12
	Seahawks	9–7	7–9	10–6
	Cardinals	8–8	4–12	3–13

Blue: The Chiefs, Bears, Seahawks and Texans certainly had better than predicted seasons. In the case of the Chiefs the offense, led by Patrick Mahomes, was outstanding and made them the most exciting team to watch each week. The Bears and Texans both featured dominant defenses and emerging quarterbacks. The Browns and Colts also exceeded expectations with exciting teams. The comeback season of Andrew Luck and the rookie season of Baker Mayfield were very positive. The Seahawks had a lot of player turnover from their great team of 2013–2014 (see Ziemba and MacLean, 2018), but good draft choices, a solid running game and Russell Wilson produced a winning team.
Green: The Patriots just keep chugging. At 41 years old, Tom Brady is remarkably the same outstanding quarterback as always. The Saints and Rams also delivered the top seasons that were predicted. For the Saints Drew Brees doesn't have the Brady number of championship trophies, but he is consistently excellent.
Red: Aaron Rodgers return to health created high expectations for the Packers, but the season and Rodgers performance were a disappointment. The Falcons and Jaguars also faltered unexpectedly. The Steelers were good but in the end fell short, with the holdout of top running back Le'Veon Bell hard to overcome. Other teams such as the Giants, Jets and 49'ers preformed in line with the previous season rather than expectations for improvement.

highlighted: blue for exceeding expectations; green for meeting high expectations; red for falling short of expectations.

13.1.2. *Players*

Football is a team game and, like most sports, one player cannot deliver a championship. However, each season players standout for their performance compared to other players at their position. We list three players on offense and defense who were outstanding during the 2018 season and worthy candidates for league MVP.

Offense

1. Patrick Mahomes, quarterback, Kansas City Chiefs — He was the most impressive player all season long, expanding the possibilities of a given play due to his escapability, creativity and arm strength. It can no longer be claimed without challenge that Aaron Rodgers is the most talented quarterback in football. No player put up better raw numbers. No player was more exciting to watch. No player was more valuable to his offense in 2018. Mahomes is a worthy favorite for MVP honors. Mahomes placed at, or near, the top of most passing categories: finished first in touchdown passes, second in passing yards, passer rating, yards per game and yards per attempt.
2. Drew Brees, quarterback, New Orleans Saints — The soon-to-be 40-year-old quarterback completed a league- and career-best 74.4 percent of his passes. Not even Mahomes could top his 115.7 passer rating — sixth-highest in league history. Brees led the league with seven game-winning drives, and although he was eight yards short of 4,000 through the air, Brees tied for sixth in passing touchdowns with 32 and with only five interceptions. In 2018, he set the NFL career passing records for yardage (74,437) and completions (6586). With 501 career touchdown passes he is only 19 behind the all time leader Peyton Manning.
3. Tom Brady, quarterback, New England Patriots — Brady finished the season completing 375 of 570 passes (a 65.8% completion rate), 4,355 yards, 29 touchdowns and 11 interceptions. In week 15, Brady reached 70,000 passing yards, becoming only the fourth quarterback in NFL history to accomplish the feat. In this season he threw a touchdown to an NFL-record 71st different player. The pieces change around Brady, but the Patriots are consistently at the top of the class in the NFL.

Defense

1. Aaron Donald, defensive lineman, Los Angeles Rams — Donald is the single most unblockable defender in football. On January 4, 2019, he was named to the AP All-Pro First Team, being the only unanimous selection. He led the NFL with 20.5 sacks — all from the interior — and lapped the field with 106 total pressures, per PFF, 11 more than the next closest defender and the most any player has recorded since J.J. Watt notched 119 in 2014. His sacks for the season total broke the record for most sacks in a season by a defensive tackle. Disrupting quarterback play is arguably the most important ingredient in game outcome, so Donald was a big factor in the Rams successfull season.
2. Kahlil Mack, defensive lineman, Chicago Bears — It is a remarkable thing when one NFL player being traded can change the fate of two different NFL teams. Not only has Mack been an absolute force since joining the Bears his departure left a huge hole on the Raiders defense this year as well. The trade set both of these teams on two very different paths this season: Bears went from 5–11 to 12–4, Raiders from 6–10 to 4–12. The Bears won with defense and Mack was the leader. The Bears are the first team since the 2006 Ravens with at least 45 sacks and 25 interceptions in a season.
3. J. J. Watt, defensive end, Houston Texans — Watt was the Comeback Player of the Year candidate after having missed 11 games in 2017 due to a broken leg. All he did in 2018 was finish second in the league in sacks (16.0) and was tied for first with a career-high seven forced fumbles. His sack total was the third-highest of Watt's career. Defense was a strength of the Texans, with the team finishing third in the NFL in rush defense.

13.2. Playoffs Teams in 2019

From each conference six teams qualify for the playoffs. The regular season record is a factor since homefield advantage is very important. Also the two conference teams with the best record get a bye in the first round (Wildcard weekend). The quarterback is the architect of the offense and it is natural that media and fan attention is focused on that position. Table 13.2 provides statistics for the quarterbacks of the playoff teams. Carson Wentz is marked in red since he is injured and will be replaced by Nick Foles. Any rating above 100 is very good, so the qb position is strong for all teams. Tom Brady is in the 9th position, but the rating doesn't account for winning and Brady is the ultimate closer.

Table 13.2. Quarterbacks: 2019 playoffs.

Name	Team	TD	INT	YDS	Rating
Brees	NO	32	5	3992	115.7
Mahomes	KC	50	12	5092	113.8
Wilson	SEA	35	7	3448	110.9
Rivers	LAC	32	12	4308	105.5
Watson	HOU	26	9	4165	103.1
Wentz	PHI	21	7	3074	102.2
Goff	LAR	32	12	4688	101.1
Luck	IND	39	15	4593	98.7
Brady	NE	29	11	4355	97.7
Prescott	DAL	22	8	3885	96.9
Foles	PHI	7	4	1413	96.0
Trubisky	CHI	24	12	3223	95.4
Jackson	BAL	6	3	1261	84.5

Table 13.3. NFL playoff teams, 2019: Superbowl odds.

Conference	Team	Odds	Offensive Rank	Defensive rank
	NE	6/1	4	6
	KC	9/2	1	23
AFC	LAC	16/1	6	11
	IND	25/1	5	8
	BAL	14/1	13	2
	HOU	25/1	11	5
	NO	5/2	3	12
	LAR	5/1	2	20
NFC	DAL	25/1	23	7
	PHI	25/1	18	9
	SEA	25/1	8	14
	CHI	8/1	9	1

The odds for the playoff teams are given in Table 13.3. The regular season rank in scoring for (offense) and against (defense) is also shown. The Chiefs and Patriots are favorites in the AFC and the Saints and Rams are favorites in the NFC. Chicago looks like a team to watch. It is natural if all eyes are on the Chiefs with their explosive offense led by Patrick Mahomes. The old maxim that defense wins in the playoffs could be their achiles heel.

13.3. Wild Card Games

The matchups for the first round of playoff games are in Table 13.4.

The wildcard games were very competitive, with the exception of the Colts–Texans match. Andrew Luck was excellent with three touchdown

Table 13.4. Wild card results, January 2019.

Conference	Home	Away	Score	Comment
AFC	Texans	Colts	7–21	Colts have Luck
	Ravens	Chargers	17–23	Costly Ravens turnovers
NFC	Bears	Eagles	15–16	Foles strickes again!
	Cowboys	Seahawks	24–22	Elliott impressive

Table 13.5. Division results, January 2019.

Conference	Home	Away	Score	Comment
AFC	Chiefs	Colts	31–13	Mahomes is ready
	Patriots	Chargers	41–28	Patriots impressive
NFC	Saints	Eagles	20–14	Nick Foles magic ends
	Rams	Cowboys	30–22	Strong running game by Rams

passes against a strong Houston defense. DeShaun Watson was ineffective at qb for Houston. The other games could have gone either way. The Ravens moved the ball very well in the second half against the Chargers, but turnovers by Jackson at qb were too much to overcome. The Bears actually had the game in hand against the Eagles, but a missed short field goal as time expired broke Chicago hearts. The magic of Nick Foles continues. The Cowboys and Seahawks are similar teams and the game was close, but touchdowns by Elliott and Prescott in the 4th quarter were enough for the win.

13.4. Division Champions

In Table 13.5 are the results of the second round of playoff games.

The maligned Chiefs defense successfully shut down Andrew Luck and the potent Indianapolis Colts. Mahomes and the high-powered offense took care of the rest, rolling to a 31–13 victory in the divisional round to end 25 years of playoff frustration for the Chiefs. The Patriots blew out the Chargers. A couple of garbage time TD's by the Chargers made the score respectable. The Eagles started well, but Brees and the superior Saints team dominated after the first quarter. However, Nick Foles brought some late excitement by moving deep into Saints territory only to have an on-target pass to Jeffery slip through his hands and be intercepted. The Rams

Table 13.6. Conference results, January 2019.

Conference	Home	Away	Score	Comment
AFC	Chiefs	Patriots	31–37	Game of the year — last possession wins!
NFC	Saints	Rams	23–26	Poor refereeing cost Saints the game

running game, with Gurley and Anderson each over 100 yards, was too much for Dallas. The Cowboys scored late in the 4th quarter to get within a score, but didn't get another chance. All the favored teams won.

13.5. Conference Champions

The early playoff rounds actually turned out as expected. The remaining teams for the conference titles were the favorites and the top teams during the regular season. The results of the games are in Table 13.6.

Two overtime games decided the conference championships and the competing teams for the Superbowl. The Saints were robbed when a clear pass interference was not called inside the Rams 5 yd line with less than two minutes remaining. The Saints settled for a field goal to lead by three with more than a minute remaining for the Rams. They moved the ball into field goal position to send the game to overtime. An unexpected interception on Brees in his own end led to the winning field goal for the Rams. In addition to fouls on that deciding play, there were other missed calls by referees earlier in the game. Saints fans appealed to the league to undo the wrong, but there are numerous other cases in sports where flagrant missed calls decided a championship game. Sports fans recall the "hand of God" goal by Maradona against England in the World Cup, and the goal crease winner by Brett Hull in the Stanley Cup of hockey.

The Patriots–Chiefs game was a barn burner. The Chiefs were stymied in the first half, but Mahomes came alive in the second half. A record setting 38 points in total were scored in the fourth quarter and the game went to overtime. The Patriots won the coin toss to get the ball and marched the field for the winning touchdown. Brady was terrific on 3rd downs in the winning drive. How great are the Patriots? In Table 13.7 are conference championship game results for the last 10 years. The Patriots have played in the AFC Championship every year from 2011 – 2018, winning five times. They also won the AFC Championship 4 times between 2001 and 2007. That dominance is unprecedented in professional football.

Table 13.7. Conference champions, 2008–2017.

Year	AFC	NFC
2017	*Patriots* 24 Titans 20	Eagles 38 Vikings 7
2016	*Patriots* 36 Steelers 17	Falcons 44 Packers 21
2015	Broncos 20 *Patriots* 18	Panthers 49 Cardinals 15
2014	*Patriots* 45 Colts 7	Seahawks 28 Packers 22 (OT)
2013	Broncos 26 *Patriots* 16	Seahawks 23 49'ers 17
2012	Ravens 28 *Patriots* 13	49'ers 28 Falcons 24
2011	*Patriots* 23 Ravens 20	Giants 20 49'ers 17 (OT)
2010	Steelers 24 Jets 19	Packers 21 Bears 14
2009	Colts 30 Jets 17	Saints 31 Vikings 28 (OT)
2008	Steelers 23 Ravens 14	Cardinals 32 Eagles 25

13.6. Superbowl LIII

The culmination of the NFL season is the Superbowl, a game contested by the winners of the conference championships. Traditionally the SB is the premier sporting event in North America, with more than 100 million viewers on television in the US. The cheapest ticket near game time was $2300. The spectacle includes a half-time show featuring the gliterati of entertainment, such as Lady Gaga, Beyonce and Justin Timberlake (the infamous "indecent exposure"). Television ads during the game cost $5.2 million for each 30 seconds.

Superbowl LIII in Atlanta featuring The New England Patriots and the Los Angeles Rams had the Patriots as a 2.5 point favorite. The expectation was for a tight game matching a top Rams offence and a balanced Patriots team. The actual game was a snoozefest. The game had the fewest total points and the most consecutive punts in superbowl history. With seven minutes left in the 4th quarter the score was tied at three points per team, the result of two field goals, one for each team. Of course, if coach Belichick was told before the game that after 53 minutes the game would be tied he couldn't hide his delight — maybe even smile! The New England dynasty's five previous Super Bowl victories came by 3, 3, 3, 4 and 6 points. Two were decided on the last play. The other three came down to the final minutes. The Patriots are masters of the end of game marches engineered by quarterback Tom Brady. To little surprise they did it again. The game statistics are given in Table 13.8. Although the score was close New England was much better. They controlled the ball and had a tired Los Angeles defense at the end when it counted.

Table 13.8. SB LIII: Game statistics.

Statistic	**Patriots**	**Rams**
Points	13	3
TD	1	0
FG	2	1
First Downs	22	14
Total yds	407	260
Rushing yds	154	62
Passing yds	253	198
Completions	21/35	19/38
Interceptions	1	1
Unrecovered Fumbles	1	1
Punts	5	9
Penalties	3	9
Time of Possession	33:10	26:50

The Superbowl LIII MVP was Julian Edelman. He had 10 catches for 141 yards, many of them to extend ball possession and downs. But the big story of the Patriots Superbowl victory was the Patriots' underrated defence. Jared Goff, the Rams quarterback, was under constant pressure and the vaunted Los Angeles Rams offense managed only three points. Defense is coach Belichick's specialty, and he and linebackers coach Brian Flores planned a masterful game. A three-time coach of the year, Belichick has not won the award since 2010. He has been Superbowl winner coach six times and Superbowl winner defensive coordinator another two times. The Rams' young coach Sean McVey admitted he was outcoached by Belichick, and he has plenty of company among NFL coaches over the last two decades.

13.7. Awards

On the same weekend as the Superbowl, the NFL 2018 season awards are announced. The 2018 winners are shown in Table 13.9. We also have the 2017 winners to check for repeats — only Aaron Donald, Defensive Player of the Year repeated.

Football is a team game and it is noteworthy that New England Patriots did not receive any awards. But all Patriot team members received a Superbowl LIII ring. Also announced on Superbowl weekend were the latest additions to the NFL Hall of Fame.

Table 13.9. NFL awards: 2017 & 2018 seasons.

Award	2017 Recipient	2018 Recipient
MVP	T. Brady, NE	P. Mahomes, KC
Defensive Rookie of the Year	M. Lattimore, NO	D. Leonard, IND
Defensive Player of the Year	A. Donald, LAR	A. Donald, LAR
Comeback Player of the Year	K. Allen, LAC	A. Luck, IND
NFL Coach of the Year	S. McVey, LAR	M. Nagy, CHI
NFL Offensive Rookie of the Year	A. Kamara, NO	S. Barkley, NYG
Offensive Player of the Year	A. Kamara, NO	P. Mahomes, KC
Sportmanship	L. Kuechly, CAR	D. Brees, NO
Walter Payton Man of the Year	J.J. Watt, HOU	C. Long, PHI
Assistant Coach of the Year	P. Shurmur, MIN	V. Fangio, CHI
Offensive Air Player of the Year	C. Wentz, PHI	P. Mahomes, KC
Offensive Ground Player of the Year	T. Gurley, LAR	S. Barkley, NYG

NFL Hall of Fame Inductees: Champ Bailey, CB; Pat Bowlen, contributor; Gil Brandt, contributor; Tony Gonzalez, TE; Ty Law, CB; Kevin Mawae, C; Ed Reed, S; Johnny Robinson, S.

It is fitting that many of the 2019 inductees are defensive players.

13.8. Conclusion

The 2018–2019 NFL season wrapped up with a somewhat disappointing game and show on Superbowl Sunday. The New England Patriots are once again champions. However, it is fair to say that many teams believe they can dethrone the Patriots and the closeness of games support that belief. The NFL is not like the other cultural phenomena, the National Basketball Association. where most NBA teams do not believe they can compete with the Golden State Warriors in 2019.[1] The NFL has a cohort of young stars who could lead their team to the title in 2019. There is another exciting season to anticipate a championship performance from many teams. It is also expected that new rules around video replay will be introduced to avoid errors in referee calls. In the meantime football fans will cheer for teams in basketball, ice hockey or soccer. A committed sports fan can even enjoy watching a game of darts.

[1]But in 2021, with injuries and trades, they are no longer the best.

Chapter 14

Review of the NFL 2019/20 Season, Playoffs and Superbowl

Leonard C. MacLean and William T. Ziemba

This chapter reviews the 2019–2020 NFL season focusing on the regular season, the playoffs and the Superbowl. We start with pre-season predictions and compare with the regular season results. We then study the playoffs including the great games and betting on them. In the Superbowl, Kansas City won and Patrick Mahomes was the MVP. We conclude with a discussion about the new breed of scrambling quarterbacks and the new NFL contract.

14.1. Introduction

In many dimensions the year 2019 was confusing and stressful. Events in politics, entertainment, health, the economy and the environment were a cause for worry. For many people there is solace in the stories of favorite sports teams and players. Sporting events world-wide are major cultural experiences. Identifying with national sports teams raises emotions in a shared commitment to conquest.

Soccer is the world's most popular spectator sport. It is also the main focus of a huge sports betting industry, and it's estimated that soccer makes up 70% of the $1 trillion bet on sports each year. If we focus on North America, the National Football League is king. Bets on the NFL make up almost half of all sports bets placed, with the Super Bowl being the single most popular television and betting event during the sporting year. More than 100 million viewers tune in to the Super Bowl, with many watching at Super Bowl parties. The half time show is a major entertainment event and ads during the game cost several millions per 30 seconds. In 2020, the average ticket cost \$4320 on Stubhub. This was more than other sports. The most expensive tickets close to the field with pregame hospitality cost \$30–50,000.

The Super Bowl is the culmination of a football tournament (season), with 32 teams playing a 16 game regular season to determine the qualifiers for single game elimination playoffs — a loss and you are done for the season. The NFL is organized into two conferences (American, National), with four divisions (North, South, East, West) in each conference. For the regular season the NFL's s formula schedules games so that a team: (i) plays two games against the other three teams in their division; (ii) play one game against each team in a matched division in their conference; (iii) play one game against each team in a matched division in the opposing conference; (ii) play one game against the team from the nonmatched divisions from your conference that finished in the same place in their respective divisions as you did in your division in the previous season.

Although each team starts the season tied at zero wins, there are expectations and predictions based on the previous season, the team roster, and schedule strength. In Table 14.1, we provide a rating of teams prior to the start of the season games. The basis of the rating is the ELO system (Chapter 12). The initial rating is set to 1500. The rating evolves as games are completed. Following a match, the rating for each competitor is adjusted up or down depending on the outcome. Because of home field advantage (which has an adjustment), victories over strong opponents in the opponent's stadium increase one's rating the most. The amount one's rating improves with a victory depends on the way the system is tuned. If $R_i(t)$ is the rating for team i, the updating equation is

$$R_i(t+1) = R_i(t) + K(X_{ij}(t) - p_{ij}(t)).$$

In week t, $X_{ij}(t) = 1$ for a win in game i, j and 0 for a loss, and $p_{ij}(t)$ is the probability of a win. The sensitivity parameter K accounts for varying game conditions.

The win probability in week t uses the ELO and the Bradley-Terry (1952) probability model. In calculating win probabilities for the game between team i and team j, the logistic formula is

$$p_{ij}(t) = \frac{1}{1 + 10^{-\frac{1}{400}(R_i(t) - R_j(t))}}$$

The predictions are provided in Table 14.1. In addition to the ELO score, the table predicts the won-loss record and the chance of winning the Super

Table 14.1. Preseason predictions.

Division	**Team**	**W/L 2018**	**ELO**	**Predicted W/L 2019**	**Pob Win Super Bowl**
AFC East	New England	11-5	1620	11-5	14%
	Buffalo	6-10	1475	8-8	1%
	New York J	4-12	1452	7-9	1%
	Miami	7-9	1389	6-10	<1%
AFC North	Pittsburgh	9-6-1	1569	9-7	5%
	Baltimore	10-6	1527	8-8	3%
	Cleveland	7-8-1	1516	8-8	3%
	Cincinnati	6-10	1414	6-10	<1%
AFC South	Houston	11-5	1533	8-8	3%
	Tennessee	9-7	1502	8-8	2%
	Jacksonville	5-11	1498	8-8	2%
	Indianapolis	10-6	1479	7-9	1%
AFC West	Kansas City	12-4	1615	10-6	9%
	L. A. Chargers	12-4	1580	10-6	6%
	Denver	6-10	1462	7-9	1%
	Oakland	4-12	1413	6-10	<1%
NFC East	Philadelphia	9-7	1586	10-6	7%
	Dallas	10-6	1547	9-7	4%
	N. Y. Giants	5-11	1424	6-10	1%
	Washington	7-9	1427	6-10	<1%
NFC North	Chicago	12-4	1566	9-7	5%
	Minnesota	8-7-1	1540	8-8	3%
	Green Bay	6-9-1	1522	8-8	3%
	Detroit	6-10	1458	7-9	1%
NFC South	New Orieans	13-3	1604	10-6	8%
	Atlanta	7-9	1533	8-8	3%
	Carolina	7-9	1515	8-8	3%
	Tampa Bay	5-11	1446	7-9	1%
NFC West	L.A. Rams	13-3	1588	10-6	7%
	Seattle	10-6	1545	9-7	4%
	San Francisco	4-12	1480	7-9	1%
	Arizona	3-13	1389	5-11	<1%

Bowl. The ELO is a blend of the overall score and the specific team score, akin to James–Stein estimation, which blends the individual mean with the overall mean. The win predictions for the 2019–2020 season are close to the final records for teams in the 2018 season. The favorites were New England, Kansas City and the L.A. Chargers in the AFC, and Philadelphia, New Orleans, Seattle and the L.A. Rams in the NFC.

A factor in the ELO score and the game by game success is the quarterback of a team. Football is unique in team sports in that one player

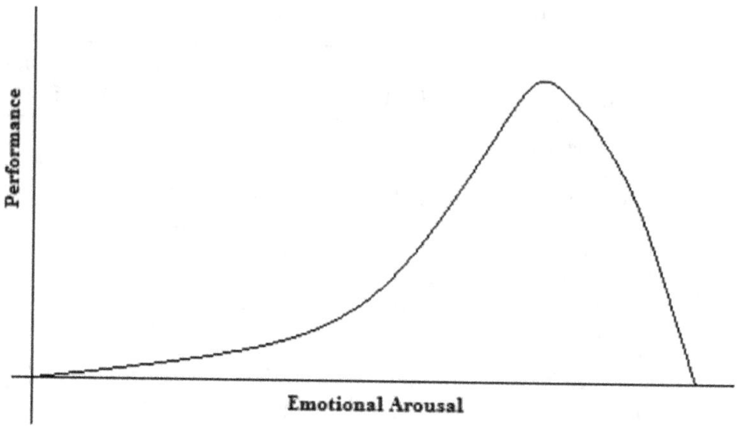

Figure 14.1. Performance pattern.

is the architect of most offensive plays. The mental skill and toughness of the quarterback is critical, particularly in big games. Mental skills and toughness are the ingredients in clutch performance. As the season progresses the importance of games and moments within games increases. Players and especially the quarterback experience an emotional arousal, which affects performance. Increased arousal creates a situational awareness and an improvement in performance. However, at some arousal level performance peaks and more stress leads to a rapid decline in performance. (Swan *et al.*, 2016). Figure 14.1 shows a generic curve of the arousal-performance relationship.

The arousal-performance relationship is different for individuals. The reaction to stress at crucial points in a football game is most observable in the quarterback. The clearest example of mental toughness and clutch performance under pressure is the New England quarterback Tom Brady. He made the difficult plays look routine most of the time. Brady led NE to six Super Bowls wins in nine appearances (both NFL records), mostly leading an end of game winning score.

It is proposed that mental toughness has four dimensions: (1) Composure; (2) Concentration; (3) Confidence; and (4) Commitment. (Vernacchia, 2003.) Clearly, Tom Brady encapsulates those characteristics. However, there is we think a new sheriff in town. The Kansas City quarterback, Patrick Mahomes, has very early shown he possesses the 4 C's. You can tell a lot about a player's emotional arousal level by how they react to mistakes and difficult situations.

Great athletes aren't great because they are perfect, rather they have the best reaction to their mistakes and difficult situations such as large deficits in a game. We will review the 2019–2020 NFL season with a focus on the performance of Mahomes and will look for his reaction to challenges.

14.2. NFL Regular Season: The Round Robin

Each NFL team plays 16 games over 17 weeks from September to December. Football is a very physical and strategic game and a week between contests is usually needed to rest and prepare. The results of the regular season for 2019–2020 are shown in Table 14.2. The actual results are somewhat in line with expectations/predictions in Table 14.1. The comparison in Figure 14.2 shows the agreement between predictions and actual wins (the correlation is 0.557), considering the natural variation in a season.

New England, Kansas City, and New Orleans had very good seasons, and coasted to the playoff round. Baltimore was expected to be good, but was outstanding, with the best record in the league at 14–2, and the Superbowl favorite. The offense led by Lamar Jackson was the best in the NFL (winner of the regular season MVP) and, as usual, their defense was solid. Green Bay 13–3 won a lot of close games, and they depended on the stellar play of their quarterback, Aaron Rodgers. The real surprise was San Francisco at 13–3. There were questions about the San Francisco offense, but they led the National Conference with a strong running game, dominant defence and reliable play from quarterback Jimmy Garoppolo.

The LA Chargers were a disappointment, with only five wins. Many of their eleven losses were in close games and the usually reliable quarterback Philip Rivers made too many errors, with almost as many interceptions as touchdowns. He then retired from the Chargers and moved his family to Florida. He subsequently joined the Indianapolis Colts for 2020. Detroit and Cincinnati were worse than expected.

What about Mahomes? He had a strong season with an 11–3 record in the games he started. Mahomes injured his knee in week 7 and missed two games. He lost his first game upon return, but then reeled off six straight wins to finish the regular season. There were not many critical games since KC was well ahead in its division. However, seeding in the playoff round is important and the winning streak and particularly a win in New England in week 14 augured well for the playoffs. With receivers Travis Kelsey, Tyreek Hill and Sammy Watkins, Mahomes had talented passing targets and with his ability to escape the pass rush, there was reason for confidence.

Table 14.2. NFL regular season results (2019).

Division	Team	W/L 2019	Points For	Points Against
AFC East	**New England**	**12-4**	**420**	**225**
	Buffalo	**10-6**	**314**	**259**
	New York J	7-9	276	359
	Miami	5-11	308	494
AFC North	Pittsburgh	8-8	289	303
	Baltimore	**14-2**	**531**	**282**
	Cleveland	6-10	335	393
	Cincinnati	2-14	279	420
AFC South	**Houston**	**10-6**	**378**	**385**
	Tennessee	**9-7**	**402**	**331**
	Jacksonville	6-10	300	397
	Indianapolis	7-9	361	373
AFC West	**Kansas City**	**12-4**	**451**	**308**
	L. A. Chargers	5-11	337	345
	Denver	7-9	282	316
	Oakland	7-9	313	419
NFC East	**Philadelphia**	**9-7**	**385**	**354**
	Dallas	8-8	434	321
	N. Y. Giants	4-12	341	451
	Washington	3-13	266	435
NFC North	Chicago	8-8	280	298
	Minnesota	**10-6**	**407**	**303**
	Green Bay	**13-3**	**376**	**313**
	Detroit	3-12	341	423
NFC South	**New Orleans**	**13-3**	**458**	**341**
	Atlanta	7-9	381	399
	Carolina	5-11	340	470
	Tampa Bay	7-9	458	449
NFC West	L. A. Rams	9-7	394	364
	Seattle	**11-15**	**405**	**398**
	San Francisco	**13-3**	**479**	**310**
	Arizona	5-10	361	442

14.3. The 2019–2020 NFL Playoffs

As we review the playoffs, we will include the pre-game wagers of sports bettors. The betting market is efficient (MacLean and Ziemba, 2019), so the odds determined from wagers are a good indication of win probabilities. Of course, personal bias and emotion also play into wagers. A bettor named *Mattress Mack* consistently bets against Kansas City. He lost $550,000 on the Superbowl and $1,000,000 on them in the division game, when they beat Houston in a game where Houston got ahead by 20–0 and lost when

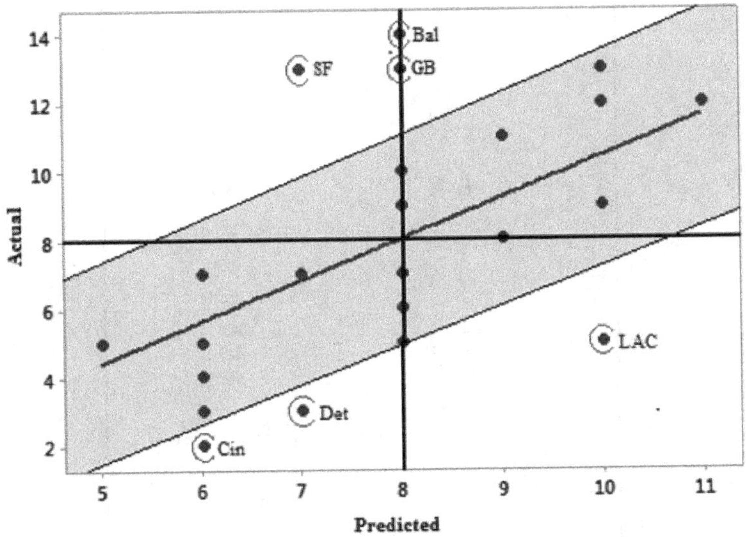

Figure 14.2. Actual vs. predicted.

Kansas City and Mahomes got 7 straight TDs to win 51–31. He lost another \$1,000,000 when KC beat Tennessee 35–24 in the AFC championships.

The qualifying teams for the NFL playoffs in 2019–2020 are in bold in Table 14.2. The seeding of the playoff teams in each conference is given in Table 14.3.

Mattress Mack is Jim McIngvale from Houston who owns the Gallery Furniture Empire. He also owns the stallion Run Happy at Claiborne Farm who is advertised everywhere and has a \$10,000 stud fee. Mattress Mack also bets on other sports. Previously he lost \$12,000,000 on the 2018 Baseball World Series betting on the Houston Astros to win after they had won in 2017. In the 2021 Kentucky Derby he bet about \$2.3 million on the favorite Essential Quality who had won all five of his races and was sired by leading stallion Tapit whose stud fee is \$185,000 in 2021 and was as high as \$300,000 when Essential Quality was conceived. Mattress Mack often uses sports insurance where he sells products and gives a refund if a certain event occurs in his furniture business.

The playoff round is a single game knock out, so it is win or be eliminated. The pressure is greatly increased, and the expectation is each team can go to the Super Bowl. The first round is four games, with the wild cards vs. the lower ranked division leaders. The Betfair bid and ask British odds going into the wildcard round were:

Table 14.3. NFL Playoffs 2019–2020.

Conference	Team	Seed	Wildcard		Division		Conference		SB
	Tennessee	6	**Tennessee**	**20**					
	New England	3	New England	13	**Tennessee**	28			
	Baltimore	1			Baltimore	12			
American									
							Tennessee	**24**	
							Kansas City	35	Kansas City
	Kansas City	2			**Kansas City**	**51**			
	Houston	4	**Houston**	**22**	Houston	31			
	Buffalo	5	Buffalo	19					
	Minnesota	6	**Minnesota**	**26**					
	New Orleans	3	New Orleans	20	**Minnesota**	10			
	San Francisco	1			**San Francisco**	**27**			
National									
							San Francisco	**37**	San Francisco
							Green Bay	20	
	Green Bay	2			**Green Bay**	**28**			
	Seattle	4	**Seattle**	**17**	Seattle	23			
	Philadelphia	5	Philadelphia	9					

To win the Superbowl — Baltimore 4.3–4.4, New England 4.9–5.1, New Orleans 7.4–7.6, San Francisco 8.6–8.8, Seattle 14–14.5, Kansas City 15–16, Minnesota 25–27, the rest much longer odds.

> These are British odds, so 4.3 means bet 1 to receive 4.3 if you win, otherwise lose 1. The odds are determined by the total amount that has been wagered on the possible event outcomes by bettors. They reflect the balance of wagers on either side of the event, and include the deduction of an agency's brokerage fee, which for Betfair only applies on net winning bets and not on losing bets. The odds on display do not represent the true chances that the event will or will not occur, but are the amount that the betting agency will pay out on a winning bet, together with the required stake. However, the odds from betting are fairly accurate in determining the probabilities of outcomes.

The 3rd seeding proved to be unlucky. The preseason favorites for the Super Bowl were New England and New Orleans, and they both unexpectedly lost to wildcard teams.

In New England's case, the ground game of the Tennessee Titans made a difference. Derrick Henry ran roughshod, with more than 200 yards on the ground. Both teams had elite defenses and that was the deciding factor. Tom Brady couldn't engineer a late game drive. To be fair, New England didn't have the receiving weapons to complement Brady. The offense sorely missed pro-bowler Rob Gronkowski (retirement), and departures of Antonio Brown and Josh Gordon, both of whom had off-the-field problems.

A big clue to their demise was a week 17 loss to Miami so they did not get a playoff bye. In all six of their Superbowl winning seasons, they had a bye from Wildcard weekend. Ryan Fitzpatrick threw a 5 yard TD to Mike Gesiki with 24 seconds left to win the game. New England was 12–3 and ahead of 11–4 Kansas City, but the 27–24 loss to Miami gave Kansas City the bye when they beat the LA chargers. So New England had to play in the Wildcard round. They ended the season 12–4 after an 8–0 start largely based on superior defense. Miami was a 16 point underdog but still won. Brady had 2 TDs and one pick-six interception and was 15–1 against Miami at home. The Patriots had beaten Miami 43–0 on September 15, 2019 in Miami.

Drew Brees had another great season with New Orleans. Unfortunately, they had a rematch of last year's wild card game against Minnesota. Brees was so-so, but still led NO to 10 fourth quarter points to tie the game. However, the Minnesota Vikings won the coin toss and scored in overtime to complete the upset.

The other wildcard games went as expected, although Houston needed to rally from a 16 point deficit in the second half to beat Buffalo. The game was tied in regulation time and Houston scored on a field goal on its first possession in overtime. Seattle controlled the game against Philadelphia. That became easier when Philly QB Carson Wentz was knocked out of the game on a sack in quarter 1.

There were 8 teams remaining in the playoffs, and going into the division round the Betfair odds for the Superbowl were: Baltimore 3–3.15; Kansas City 4.7–4.8; San Francisco 4.6–4.7; Green Bay 11–11.5; Seattle 7.5–18; Minnesota 19–19.5; Tennessee 32–34; Houston 42–44.

14.3.1. *Division round*

The Betfair odds on the Division games were as follows:

- Tennessee at 4.7–4.9 vs. Baltimore at 1.27–1.28, so Baltimore was a heavy favorite. The Point Spread is a forecast of the number of points by which a stronger team is expected to defeat a weaker one. The general purpose of spread betting is to create an active market for both sides of a binary wager. The point spread is essentially a handicap towards the underdog. The spread was +8.5 points, so adjusting for spread the odds of winning a bet were Tennessee 2.03–2.06. So the bet is close to a toss-up. It was very tempting to take Tennessee, with a great runner and QB who is hot (rating 117 in wildcard).
- Minnesota at 3.75–3.85 vs. San Francisco at 1.35–1.36. The spread was +7 points for Minnesota. Adjusting for the spread, the odds for Minnesota were 1.99–2.00, which makes the bet fair.
- Houston at 4.7–4.8 vs. Kansas City at 1.26–1.27. The spread for Houston was +9.5 points, and the adjusted odds for a bet were 1.95–1.97. Again this is a fair betting game.
- Seattle at 2.88–2.9 vs. Green Bay at 1.53–1.54. So this is viewed as the most competitive game, and the spread was +4 to Seattle. The betting odds for Seattle were 2.02–2.06, and the spread bet is fair.

The division round had more excitement in store. Tennessee was matched against the top team in the NFL and Super Bowl favorites, the Baltimore Ravens, led by their dynamic quarterback Lamar Jackson. Again, Derrick Henry was a force for Tennessee, accounting for more than 200 yards. However, the real story was mistakes by the Baltimore offense. Jackson's numbers were off the charts, with 365 yards passing on 59 attempts with two interceptions and 143 yards rushing. Those record setting statistics only produced 12 points! Baltimore turned the ball over seven times, including 4 times on downs. Successful plays at critical moments just weren't there. A great season by Jackson ended in disappointment.

The Kansas City — Houston game was a contrast. KC was slow out of the gate and fell behind 24–0 in the first quarter. In a remarkable show of mental toughness/clutch play, Mahomes led Kansas City to seven consecutive touchdowns and a field goal. The Texans became the first team in 100 years to have a 24 point lead in the first half and be behind at half time. Mahomes threw 5 TD passes and ran for one and KC scored seven straight TDs to win 51–31. He is the first player in NFL history with 300+ passing yards, 50+ rushing yards, and five touchdown passes. The KC Coach Andy Reed had many playoff disappointments in a long career, so he must have wondered if Mahomes could pull this rabbit out of the hat. But there was no panic, only calm and confidence. Deshaun Watson is the only QB in the Superbowl era to lose a playoff game despite having 300+ pass yards, 3+ total TDs and 0 giveaways.

Rodgers was clutch at the end and managed to run out the clock. Seattle's running game was absent as their key players Chris Carson and CJ Prosise were injured. So they brought in the twice retired Marshawn Lynch who did score 1 yard TDs but did not do much else. They brought him in after a 27–13 loss to lowly Arizona.

In the other division game San Francisco dominated Minnesota, with advantages of 21 to 7 in first downs and 308 to 147 in yards gained. They won with a so-so quarterback performance by Garropolo, 11 for 19, 1 TD and 1 interception with a 74.9 rating. It was defense and running that won the game. The 49ers under general manager John Lynch and coach Kyle Shanahan have built a powerful team mostly through outstanding draft picks.

If you wagered on the "underdog" in spread betting, Tennessee paid off, but Minnesota, Houston and Seattle lost by more than the spread.

14.3.2. *Conference round*

The conference finals featured teams whose fans had not experienced an NFL championship in a long time. In the AFC Tennessee has no titles and the last Kansas City Super Bowl championship was in 1970. Of course, Tennessee was the surprise team, having knocked off the AFC favorites New England and Baltimore. Still Kansas City was a 7.5 point favorite. In the championship game Kansas City followed form by falling behind early 10-0. Again, Mahomes brought KC back and held a 21–17 lead at half time. In the second half Kansas City took over and the final score was 35–24. Mahomes passed for 295 yards and three touchdowns and KC outgained Tennessee 404–295 total yards. Derrick Henry was held in check by a strong KC defense, and only gained about 60 yards. Previously in a week 10 game they had 188 yards on the ground against the Chiefs. But the inspired Kansas City defense basically shut Henry down. Mahomes demonstrated the composure and confidence which allowed him to make the big plays when needed.

In the NFC the game was even less competitive. San Francisco RB Raheem Mostert went through the Green Bay line like a hot knife through butter. He rushed for 220 yards and four touchdowns. Jimmy Garoppolo only threw the ball 8 times. Green Bay scored a couple of touchdowns late to make the game seem respectable, but it was a rout. Previously in November in San Francisco, they beat the Packers 37–8.

The AFC and NFC teams were set for the Super Bowl and both teams looked forward to the contest with confidence.

14.4. Super Bowl

The NFL championship, Super Bowl LIV, was played on February 2, 2020 at Hard Rock Stadium, Miami, Florida. It was the first meeting between the Kansas City Chiefs and San Francisco 49ers in the Super Bowl. The SB is the biggest sporting event, but it is also a major entertainment spectacle. A stunning "Take it to the House" commercial at the start of the game broadcast featured a kid running across the US onto the football field, past football legends who were in attendance as living members of the NFL's 100th Anniversary All-Time Team. It was a treat to see Jim Brown, Joe Montana, Jerry Rice and other stars. The game also had to compete with a spectacular half-time show featuring singers Jennifer Lopez and Shakira.

Table 14.4. Box score of the 2020 superbowl.

	1	**2**	**3**	**4**	**Total**
San Francisco	3	7	10	0	20
Kansas City	7	3	0	**21**	31

Table 14.5. Game statistics.

Statistic	**San Francisco**	**Kansas City**
First Downs	21	26
Total Plays	**53**	**71**
Plays: Rushing/Passing	22/31	29/42
Yards Rushing	141	129
Yards Passing	210	286
Passing completions	20/31	26/42
Interceptions	2	2
Sacks	1	4
Time of Possession	**26:47**	**33:13**

Table 14.6. Fourth quarter scoring.

Team	**Time**	**Plays**	**Yards**	**Result**
SF	3:04	5	20	Punt
KC	**2.40**	**10**	**68**	**TD**
SF	1.03	3	5	Punt
KC	**2.26**	**7**	**65**	**TD**
SF	1.19	7	32	TO (Downs)
KC	**0.13**	**2**	**42**	**TD**
SF	0.15	2	0	Int
KC	0.57	4	−15	End

The Super Bowl game itself was worthy of the hoopla. It was competitive and intense, with game deciding plays to the end. The box score for the game is shown in Table 14.4.

Kansas City was the champ with a huge 4th quarter. The statistics for the game are in Table 14.5.

Kansas City had a significant advantage in number of plays and time of possession. A look at the dominant 4th quarter is provided in Table 14.6.

Kansas City scored on three successive possessions to take control. Every one of those possessions was critical to the outcome. Patrick Mahomes was

Table 14.7. Mahomes clutch performance.

Composure	Concentration	Confidence	Commitment
X	X	X	X

at his best when the game was on the line. If we go back to the 4 C's of clutch performance, he gets a tick in each box (Table 14.7).

There were times in the quarter when SF could have kept the ball, eaten up clock time and denied KC the opportunity to score the winning points. It just didn't happen.

14.4.1. *Awards*

The 2019–2020 NFL season gave the football fan many enjoyable moments. Popular coach Andy Reed finally got a Super Bowl ring. There were outstanding performances by individual players at each position. The Associated Press All Pro team is listed in Table 14.8.

Kansas City had one player on the first team (defense) and two players on the second team (offense). The Baltimore Ravens had the most players on the All Pro Team with six.

The Associated Press selects players in various categories for AP Awards. The recipients in major categories are listed in Table 14.9.

Lamar Jackson, the dynamic quarterback of Baltimore, was the Most Valuable Player and Air Player of the Year. He was also a serious candidate for Ground Player of the year, with more than 1200 running yards, the most ever for a quarterback.

14.5. Conclusion: Looking Ahead

The NFL was fortunate to complete its season. The other major professional sports leagues, NBA, NHL, MLB, are on hiatus as a result of the global pandemic caused by the COVID 19 virus. March Madness in NCAA basketball was cancelled and the 2020 Olympics in Tokyo were postponed. For the time being we will have to be satisfied with memories of Super Bowl LIV.

Looking ahead to the next season, there are some significant changes.

(1) The New NFL Contract

The new arrangement for the next 11 years to 2030 was accepted but just barely — 1019 yes to 955 no. The main changes are:

Table 14.8. AP all pro teams.

Position	**First Team**	**Second Team**
Offense		
Quarterback	Lamar Jackson, Baltimore	Russell Wilson, Seattle
Running back	Christian McCaffrey, Carolina	Derrick Henry, Tennessee
Flex	Christian McCaffrey, Carolina	Derrick Henry, Tennessee
Tight End	George Kittle, San Francisco	**Travis Kelce, Kansas City**
Wide Receiver	Michael Thomas, New Orleans DeAndre Hopkins, Houston	Julio Jones, Atlanta Chris Godwin, Tampa Bay
Left Tackle	Ronnie Stanley, Baltimore	David Bakhtiari, Green Bay
Right Tackle	Ryan Ramczyk, New Orleans	**Mitchell Schwartz, Kansas City**
Left Guard	Quenton Nelson, Indianapolis	Joel Bitonio, Cleveland Joe Thuney, New England
Right Guard	Zack Martin, Dallas	Marshal Yanda, Baltimore
Center	Jason Kelce, Philadelphia	Rodney Hudson, Oakland
Defense		
Edge Rusher	Chandler Jones, Arizona T. J, Watt, Pittsburgh	Shaq Barrett, Tampa Bay Cameron Jordon, New Orleans
Interior Lineman	Aaron Donald, L.A. Rams Cam Heyward, Pittsburgh	Grady Jarrett, San Francisco Deforest Buckner, San Francisco
Linebacker	Bobby Wagner, Seattle Demarco Davis, New Orleans Eric Kendricks, Minnesota	Luke Kuechly, Carolina Darius Leonard, Indianapolis T. J. Watt, Pittsburgh
Cornerback	Stephon Gilmore, New England Tre'Davious White, Buffalo	Richard Sherman, San Francisco Marcus Peters, Baltimore
Safety	Jamal Adams, New York J Minkah Fitzpatrick, Pittsburgh	Justin Simmons, Denver Tyrann Mathieu, Kansas City
Defensive Back	Marcus Peters, Baltimore **Tyrann Mathieu, Kansas City** Marlon Humphrey, Baltimore	
Special Teams		
Placekicker	Jason Tucker, Baltimore	Josh Lambo, Jacksonville
Punter	Brett Kern, Tennessee	Tress Way, Washington
Kick Returner	Cordarrelle Patterson, Chicago	Mecole Hardman, Kansas City
Punt Returner	Deonte Harris New Orleans	Diontae Johnson, Pittsburgh
Special Teamer	Matthew Slater, New England	Cordarrelle, Patterson, Pittsburgh J. T. Gray, New Orleans

Table 14.9. Associated press awards (2019–2020).

Award	Recipient
MVP	Lamer Jackson, QB, Baltimore
Walter Payton Man of the Year	Calais Campbell, DL, Jacksonville
Offensive Player of the Year	Michael Thomas, WR, New Orleans
Defensive Player of the Year	Stephon Gilmore, CB, New England
Rookie of the Year	Nick Bosa, DE, San Francisco
Air Player of the Year	Lamar Jackson, QB, Baltimore
Ground Player of the Year	Derrick Henry, RB, Tennessee
Offensive Rookie of the Year	Kyler Murray, QB, Arizona
Defensive Rookie of the Year	Nick Bosa, DE, San Francisco
Comeback Player of the Year	Ryan Tannehill, QB, Tennessee
Coach of the Year	John Harbaugh, Baltimore
Assistant of the Year	Greg Roman, Baltimore
NFL Hall Of Frame — Class of 2020	Steve Atwater, Safety
	Isaac Bruce, Wide Receiver
	Steve Hutchinson, Offensive Guard
	Edgerrin James, Running Back
	Troy Polamalu, Safety

- a 17 game regular season with three rather than four pre-season games,
- the playoffs have 14 teams rather than the current 12,
- only one team in each conference will get a bye with the other six playoff teams in each conference playing three games on Wildcard weekend,
- expanded rosters to 55 from 53, and game day rosters of 48 from 46,
- players' percentage of revenues will be 48.5 vs. 47,
- rookie minimum is \$610,000 vs. \$510,000 now in 2020 rising to \$1.1 million in 2030, also players with 1–7 years experience have higher minimums of \$675,000 – \$1.05 million in 2020 to \$1.19 million – \$1.48 million in 2030,
- benefits to active and retired players were increased,
- marijuana is no longer a reason for suspension, and
- the Commissioner's powers in players disputes is lessened.

(2) Possible quarterback changes in the 2020–2021 season

Though it was thought that the NFL 2020–2021 season might not be affected by the pandemic, it was as we see in chapter 15. When it begins, there is likely to be a changing of the guard at the quarterback position. Stars of the past decade are aging. In Table 14.10, the top 10 of the all-time passing yards by quarterbacks are listed. Out of 10 the 2019–2020 players occupy six positions, and at the top are Drew Brees and Tom Brady.

Table 14.10. Lifetime passing yardage leaders.

Rk	Player	Yds
1	DREW BREES	77,416
2	TOM BRADY	74,571
3	Peyton Manning	71,940
4	Brett Favre	71,838
5	Dan Marino	61,361
6	PHILIP RIVERS	59,271
7	ELI MANNING	57,023
8	BEN ROETHLISBERGER	56,545
9	John Elway	51,475
10	MATT RYAN	51,186

The passing leaders have been the face of their teams, but 2020–2021, will bring changes.

- Tom Brady: The 42-year-old signed a two-year contract with the Tampa Bay Buccaneers. In 2020–2021, Brady will have two of the best receiving options he's ever had in his career in Pro Bowl wideouts Mike Evans and Chris Godwin. Why did he leave New England after 20 years and great success when he frequently took a salary cut to help the team sign other top players? There was conflict between Brady and coach Belichick, following an October 2017 Belichick attempt to trade Brady to San Francisco and keep Jimmy Garoppolo as the quarterback. San Francisco sought Garoppolo but Belichick offered Brady, who had been MVP of the previous Superbowl for winning a game in spectacular fashion when they were behind 28–3. This was quite an insult to Brady who was under contract for two more years. The trade did not materialize, and it was Garoppolo, who is not Brady, who was traded to San Francisco. But the damage to the relationship was done. Brady, always the polished gentleman, did not announce the rift, but as soon as his contract ended he was a free agent and decided to leave. The Patriots owner has blamed Belichick for losing Brady (Kruk, 2020a). Belichick is widely regarded as the smartest coach in the NFL but his ruthless behavior towards players to save money by bringing in cheaper players has led to problems. Malcolm Butler provides one such example. The hero of Superbowl 48 against Seattle was not used in the 2018 Superbowl, which New England lost to Philadelphia, because of a minor disagreement and soon Butler was traded.

The Brady & Belichick tandem has been like Lennon & McCartney, with varying opinions on who is the success driver. It is likely that the combination was more than the sum of their individual talents, and the separation will diminish the legacy of these legends — greatest of all time. The 2020–2021 NFL season should be revealing. It sure was, see chapter 15 for the story.

- Drew Brees: The long time Saint has re-signed with the team on a two-year deal. The partnership between Brees and coach Sean Payton is strong, and at 41-years-old, Brees appears intent on finishing his career in New Orleans. Brees' regular season success has not transferred to the playoffs. Of course *winning it all* is tough and one critical play in a very close playoff can determine the outcome. The amazing thing is that Brady has made those critical plays.
- Philip Rivers: After 16 seasons with the Los Angeles Chargers, Rivers has signed a one year deal with the Indianapolis Colts. Jacoby Brissett, who started for the Colts in two of the past three seasons, will presumably move to the bench. Although Rivers is only one year from a pro-bowl season, he will be on a short leash with the Colts. No quarterback has lost more one score games than Rivers, and a slow start will bring on Brissett who can extend plays with his legs.
- Eli Manning retired from New York Giants after two Super Bowl MVP awards. Manning was always better in the playoffs and in big games. In 16 years, he was 117–117 as a starter, completing 60.3% of his passes for 57,023 yards, 366 TDs and a so-so 84.1 rating. He was very popular and received the Walter Payton Man of the Year Award.
- Ben Roethlisberger is to be returning from injury in Pittsburgh. Big Ben led the Steelers to two Super Bowl wins. If Pittsburgh can add another weapon to make up for the absence of wide receiver Antonio Brown and running back LeVeon Bell, Roethlisberger is still capable of putting together a productive season. They did pretty well as discussed in chapter 15.
- Matt Ryan is secure in Atlanta. His sustained success over the past few years indicates that he should be able to bounce back once he gets better protection. Ryan was pressured on 269 dropbacks, 26 more than any other quarterback in 2019–2020.

Here is a rundown of other quarterbacks who have agreed to deals and some that are available.

- Joe Flacco was released by Denver: He quarterbacked Baltimore to two Super Bowl wins, but was replaced by Jackson.
- Cam Newton is available to be traded: Newton, a former NFL MVP, is arguably the best quarterback option remaining although he has had various injuries. He should be able to find another starting qb job. He did in New England with only mediocre success with more interceptions than TDs. Again another who is not Brady.
- Teddy Bridgewater: Bridgewater is joining the Carolina Panthers on a three year deal.
- Ryan Tannehill: Tannehill has a four year contract with Tennessee Titans and is doing well.
- Marcus Mariota: Mariota is joining the now-Las Vegas Raiders, as long-time starter Derek Carr's backup.
- Jameis Winston: Winston will almost certainly not be returning to Tampa Bay now that the Bucs have landed Brady. He went to backup Drew Brees in New Orleans.
- Andy Dalton is leaving Cincinnati, and was signed by the Dallas Cowboys as the starter and later backup to Dak Prescott who is returning from an injury.
- Brian Hoyer has signed with New England. Besides Hoyer, the Patriots also have on their roster former Auburn quarterback Jarrett Stidham, who is entering his second year, and journeyman Cody Kesler. (See Kruk, 2020c).
- Jacksonville traded Nick Foles to Chicago. Foles will be a back-up, and should provide support and mentoring to the talented Mitch Trubisky.
- The US colleges have some promising quarterbacks available in the draft. Joe Burrow, QB, LSU, should be the top pick, and went to Cincinnati which has the first pick. Tua Tagovailoa, QB, Alabama, went to Miami, and Justin Herbert, QB, Oregon, went to the Los Angeles Chargers and became offensive rookie of the year.

14.5.1. *Scrambling*

The 2019–2020 season was dominated by scrambling quarterbacks, who used their athletic ability to escape defensive pressure and succeed in moving the ball downfield. The designed passing play is based on a pocket created by the offensive line to protect the quarterback and provide time to survey the field and get the ball to a designated receiver. This is planned

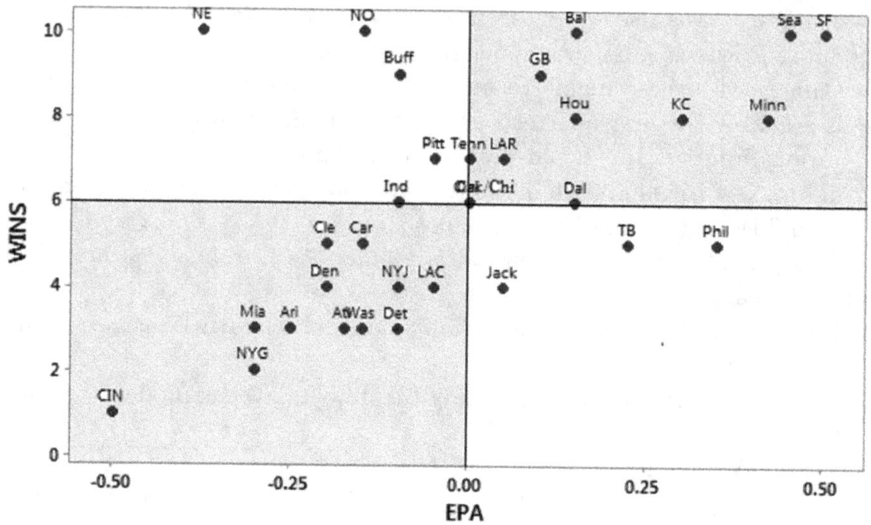

Figure 14.3. EPA vs. WINS at 3/4 mark of 2019–2020 season.

as a standard drop back with a stationary pocket, or a rollout with the quarterback and pocket moving to the right/left. Scrambling by the quarterback occurs when the defense breaks the pocket or more time is needed for a receiver to get open for a pass.

The most underappreciated aspect of a football game is the play at the line of scrimmage. Players on the line are big and strong, but keeping back the on-rushing defense, particularly the defensive ends, can only last at best 7 seconds. (It is noteworthy that some of the highest paid players are defensive ends.) The New England Patriots, the most successful team in the last two decades, has mastered the skill of maintaining the pocket and protecting the star quarterback Tom Brady — kudos to coach Belichick.

As containing the defense becomes more difficult, there is a need for the quarterback to evade the rush by going out of the pocket. In Figure 14.3, the average points added per play outside the pocket (EPA) is plotted against WINS for each of the NFL teams. The data covers the games up to the 13th week of 2019–2020 season.[1]

The picture is incomplete, with the teams like Baltimore and Kansas running the table over the final quarter of the season. It is clear that *play outside the pocket* was important for team success. The out of pocket play for quarterbacks on leading teams is given in Table 14.11.

[1]*Source*: ESPN.

Table 14.11. Quarterback rating: Total QBR 2019–2020.

Quarterback	Out of Pocket	In Pocket	Total
Jackson, Balt	72.1	76.9	81.6
Mahomes, KC	75.2	74.6	76.6
Prescot, Dal	81.1	70.8	72.9
Wilson, Sea	92.8	63.4	72.1
Wilson, Hou	84.7	68.0	71.9
Stafford, Det	15.1	82.7	68.5
Wentz, Phil	94.4	57.9	64.3
Brees, NO	8.6	72.8	61.0
Cosins, Minn	66.5	66.7	60.5
Murray, Ariz	23.7	64.0	59.6
Garappolo, SF	87.5	63.8	58.4
Rogers, GB	66.1	55.5	55.9
Ryan, Atl	28.3	58.0	54.5
Tannehill, Tenn	18.3	49.8	52.9
Brady, NE	12.1	54.4	52.5

Table 14.12. Seattle record in Russell Wilson seasons.

Year	W	L	T	Playoffs
2012	11	5	0	Lost Divisional playoffs
2013	13	3	0	Won Super Bowl XLVIII
2014	12	4	0	Lost Super Bowl XLIX
2015	10	6	0	Lost Divisional playoffs
2016	10	5	1	Lost Divisional playoffs
2017	9	7	0	Missed playoffs
2018	10	6	0	Lost Wild Card playoffs
2019	11	5	0	Lost Divisional playoffs

The Total QBR rates the quarterback on a 0–100 scale, adjusted for strength of opposing teams. (ESPN Stats and Information). The top five ratings are filled by quarterbacks who are scramblers. The number of outside the pocket plays is not shown, but those five do scramble a lot. (In contrast Wentz and Garoppolo are not scramblers.)

The statistics highlight the value of Russell Wilson to Seattle. Wilson is frequently a passing quarterback, but he often passes outside the pocket. He led Seattle to a win in Super Bowl XLVIII, and should have won in the following year. In our guidebook, Ziemba and MacLean (2018), we discuss the demise of Seattle after losing Superbowl XLIX. Tables 18.3–18.8 in

Table 14.13. NFL quarterback and team status 2021. (Top 7 in each conference in bold).

Division	Team	QB Status	QB Rank	SB 2021 Odds Ratio	SB Win%
AFC East	**New England**	**Building**	**12**	**20/1**	**14.8**
	Buffalo	**Good**	**6**	**26/1**	**13.8**
	New York J	Good	28	80/1	11.2
	Miami	Building	27	100/1	11.0
AFC North	**Pittsburgh**	**Uncertain**	**16**	**25/1**	**13.8**
	Baltimore	**Excellent**	**2**	**6.75/1**	**22.1**
	Cleveland	Good	17	40/1	12.4
	Cincinnati	Building	31	135/1	10.7
AFC South	Houston	Very Good	15	50/1	12.0
	Tennessee	**Good**	**7**	**30/1**	**13.2**
	Jacksonville	**Good**	30	150/1	10.6
	Indianapolis	**Good**	**19**	**31/1**	**13.2**
AFC West	**Kansas City**	**Excellent**	**1**	**5.25/1**	**25.6**
	L. A. Chargers	Building	22	40/1	12.4
	Denver	Good	21	66/1	11.5
	Oakland	Good	25	45/1	12.2
NFC East	**Philadelphia**	**Good**	**9**	**14.5/1**	**16.5**
	Dallas	**Good**	**5**	**16/1**	**15.9**
	N. Y. Giants	Hoping	26	85/1	11.2
	Washington	Building	32	150/1	10.6
NFC North	Chicago	Hoping	20	35/1	12.8
	Minnesota	Good	10	33/1	13.0
	Green Bay	**Very Good**	**8**	**17/1**	**15.6**
	Detroit	Good	24	80/1	11.2
NFC South	**New Orleans**	**Very Good**	**3**	**10.5/1**	**18.7**
	Atlanta	Good	18	55/1	11.8
	Carolina	Good	29	70/1	11.4
	Tampa Bay	**Very good**	**13**	**11.5/1**	**18.0**
NFC West	L. A. Rams	Hoping	14	33/1	13.0
	Seattle	**Very Good**	**11**	**18/1**	**15.3**
	San Francisco	**Good**	**4**	**9/1**	**20.0**
	Arizona	Good	23	60/1	11.6

the book details this year by year. Table 14.12 shows Seattle's record with Wilson at quarterback, and the success continued despite the departure of key players.

In 2019 Seattle rebuilt their outstanding defense with the key signing of Jadeveon Clowney, but he may be leaving after one year (Condotta, 2020) and he did leave the Tennessee Titans. Regardless Seattle will be strong so long as Wilson is behind center.

Table 14.14. Betfair odds for superbowl 2021 (March 29, 2020).

Team	Back All	Lay All	Team	Back All	Lay All
Kansas City	7.6	7.8	Tennessee	32	34
Baltimore	8.4	8.6	Green Bay	32	36
San Francisco	12	12.5	Cleveland	44	46
New Orleans	14.5	16	LA Ram	48	50
New Orleans	14.5	16	Minnesota	38	46
Tampa Bay	19	19	Chicago	46	50
Philadelphia	21	23	Atlanta	44	55
New England	25	27	LA Chargers	50	80
Dallas	29	32	Houston	55	75
Pittsburgh	27	28	Denver	50	80
Buffalo	29	30	Las Vegas	55	70
Seattle	30	34	Arizona	60	70
Indianapolis	29	34	NY Jets	95	100

14.5.2. *Prospects for 2020–2021*

The many changes at the quarterback position reflect the importance of the qb to team success. In Table 14.13, we give the current qb status of the NFL teams in their planning for the 2020–2021 season. The addition of Tom Brady has elevated Tampa Bay prospects, and they are among the list of betting favorites as shown in Table 14.14. Although Houston has a very good quarterback (D. Watson), they traded arguably the best receiver in the league (D. Hopkins) when he demanded to renegotiate his contract with 3 years to go.

It is a long way to the 2020–2021 NFL season, but the teams with the most favorable quarterback status are the early favorites for Super Bowl LIVI. The team rankings and betting SB odds against are from the Las Vegas betting site The Lines. As one would expect the betting odds are long, with the early favorites in bold. The NFL is adding one additional playoff team in each conference, so seven teams are bolded. In the coming season there will only be one bye in each conference in the wildcard round.

A range of odds for Super Bowl 2021 from Betfair are provided in Table 14.14. (The very long shots are not shown). The team order of preferences is almost the same, but the odds are a bit higher.

There were other notable rooster changes after the completion of the 2019–2020 NFL season which affect team strength. Todd Gurley, star running back of the LA Rams but less effective recently, being cut and going to

Atlanta. He was in college at Georgia. LA also did not renew defensive coordinator Wade Philips. Star receiver Emanuel Sanders, who San Francisco got from Denver, is off to New Orleans.

Both LA Rams and New England got rid of 16 of 28 defensive players over the past two seasons, so are rebuilding. New England's defensive coordinator, Brian Flores, left in 2019 to become Miami's coach. All this was the aftermath of Superbowl 53 between New England and LA Rams, with a final score 13-3 and New England winning on superior Belichick coaching. The Rams got rid of 8 of 11 defensive starters and 8 of 17 reserves and New England exited 4 of 11 starters and 12 of 17 backups. (Kruk, 2020b).

Chapter 15

The COVID-19 NFL Playoffs and Super Bowl, 2020–2021

Leonard C. MacLean and William T. Ziemba

The 2020–2021 NFL season took place in the COVID-19 era, so the lack of fans in the stands was the norm. Here we discuss the effects of COVID-19 on the NFL teams. Still, the season went well. Tom Brady left the New England Patriots to join Tampa Bay Buccaneers and recruited several key players. It paid off as they had a good season and they won the Superbowl. In the chapter we discuss several topics including the popularity of the NFL with fans and the NFL business, the Hall of Fame inductees, the player awards, a forecast of the playoffs, the results of the playoffs and Superbowl. We also discuss the path the of Betfair odds through the season and the bets Ziemba made along with the Betfair odds during the playoffs and Superbowl and a forecast for the 2021–2022 season We close with with a discussion of future happenings for the next season.

Brady and Gronkowski at the Super Bowl.

15.1. The NFL 2020–2021 Setting

There are so many issues vying for attention in our modern world, but interest in football at all levels is near the top. Eight of the top 10 highest-rated US TV shows of 2020 were football games, and the NFL is the richest league in US sports. As Figure 15.1 shows, TV revenue alone has grown exponentially over the decades.

In 2020, the league revenue was about $16.5 billion. League revenue is generated by broadcasting rights and national merchandising and licensing deals. And unlike local revenue, every team gets an equal share. That added up to almost $3 billion for each of the NFL's 32 teams. Team revenue is also generated by ticket sales, merchandise, concessions, local sponsorships and other game-related revenue streams. Forbes reported that teams collectively generated $5.5 billion in local revenue in 2018.

So the National Football League is a big business, and shocks to its operations touch players, fans and an American way of life. Of course, such a shock occurred in 2020–2021 with the coronavirus pandemic. The COVID-19 pandemic, and the actions associated with attempting to arrest its spread, has greatly impacted sport. Professional leagues were forced to cancel regular season games. The National Basketball Association and National Hockey League concluded their seasons with playoffs in a "bubble" — at a single site without live spectators. Teams suffered an immediate

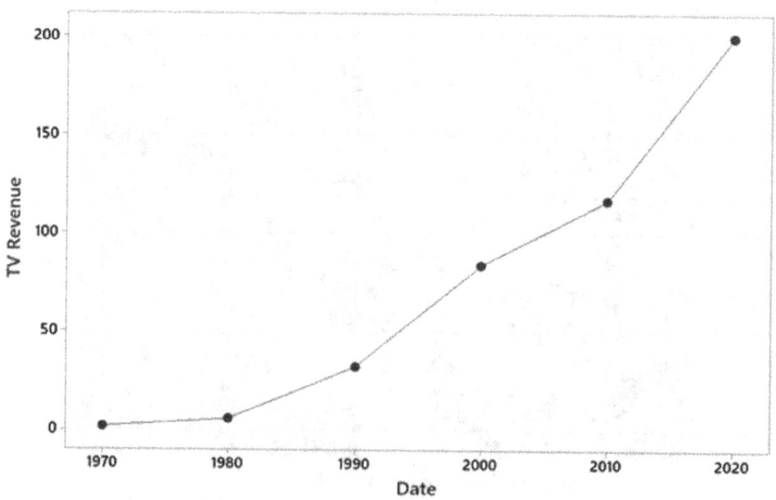

Figure 15.1. Annual TV Revenue in $millions per Team: NFL.

financial impact with losses without fans in the stands. As well, the effect of raucous crowd touches the players (particularly home teams) and viewers on TV across the world, who believe they can directly influence the outcome of a game with loyalty and enthusiasm.

The NFL was less affected initially since its season really begins in the fall. However, the pandemic was still raging in the fall, so the league had to plan operations for a very challenging time. Given the physical demands of the game and the need to rest and recover between games, a compressed schedule is not possible in football. So a regular weekly schedule of games was planned. It was possible that the NFL would play its 2020 season without spectators in its stadiums. Ultimately some teams allowed up to 20,000 fans into games, but the Denver Broncos, Philadelphia Eagles, Green Bay Packers, Las Vegas Raiders and Seattle Seahawks all banned fan attendance for the season. The season was a bumpy ride. On 3 February 2021, the NFL's chief medical officer reported that COVID-19 had infected 262 players and 463 other personnel. By season's end 31 of the NFL's 32 teams (96%) had COVID-19 cases. Numerous games were either been postponed or rescheduled due to outbreaks.

The impact of the pandemic on the NFL in 2020 was felt financially and in the character of games. A simple comparison of successive seasons is provided in Table 15.1. The monetary effect is clear. In terms of game play, the statistics for teams in 2019 and 2020 were similar. The mid-season report on injuries showed a 16% increase, mostly soft tissue injuries. That has been attributed to the cancellation of preseason games and the possibility players were not as physically prepared early in the season. One noteworthy effect was the percentage of wins by road teams — 50%. With few or no fans, the home field advantage was diminished. This actually was the experience by the NBA and NHL with games in a "bubble". In a sense

Table 15.1. The COVID effect.

Measure	**2019**	**2020**
Attendance	17 million	1 million
TV viewers	16.5 m	15.4 m
Revenue	15.26 billion	12.56 billion
Injuries	477	555
Road Win (%)	47.8	50.0
Team Rushing AYPG	112.9	118.9
Team Passing AYPG	235.0	240.2
Team Points APG	22.8	24.8

games are more fair and the champions were the best teams. Certainly, the Los Angeles Lakers (NBA) and Tampa Bay Lightening (NHL) were preseason favorites and won.

In the Appendix we list by team the major effects of COVID-19 which were not as much as one might expect. Also, likely of greater importance, are injuries as shown in Figure 15.14.

15.2. NFL Super Bowl Betting 2021

In Nevada the 184 sports books handled \$136 million in 2020, some 12% below the \$154.7 million wagered in 2019. They gained \$12.6 million (9.2%) vs. \$18.8 million in 2019 (12.1%). This was lower because of COVID-19 restrictions since attendance in sports books was much lower. The Super Bowl in 2018 generated a record \$158.6 million in wagers. The record profit from the Super Bowl was in 2014 when they made \$19.7 million. In terms of big bets, the investor that bet \$2.3 million on Tampa Bay to win \$2 million with a 3.5 spread as Kansas City was favored by about 3.5 points, won his bet. The 2 vs. 2.3 accounts for the Las Vegas take plus the difference in odds from 3.5 depending on the betting handle. I made similar but smaller bets on Betfair. There were other large bets that were at odds of £1.88 to one, namely bet one to collect 1.88 or 0.88 gain and you win if Tampa Bay wins or loses by three points or less.

I missed one super Super Bowl bet. I saw that before the game Gronkowski had 188–1 Betfair odds to win the MVP. I thought that in such a big game Brady would rely on his top receiver who had been lightly used all season and mostly as a superior blocker, but he holds many NFL Super Bowl and playoff receiving and TD records. Since there was not much on offer at 188 but there was much a bit lower, I mistakenly passed on this. I was pretty sure Brady would be the MVP if Tampa Bay won. But if Gronkowski did well the 188 would drop a lot. Well he caught the first two Brady TDs and the 188-1 became 6–1. So a £10 bet would have gained about £1600.

BetMGM reported on some large bets on the Chiefs that all lost. These included \$188,000 to win \$100,000 and \$115,000 and \$110,000 on the Chiefs at −3.5 points that lost. BetMGM was happy to get the \$2.3 million bet on Tampa Bay since most of the bets were on Kansas City. These bets helped balance their book. In the Green Bay — Tampa Bay game a majority of the bet (75%) was on Green Bay. When Tampa Bay won, that was the best outcome of a single event in the year for BetMGM.

Brady has not been a Super Bowl underdog in the last 19 years even though this was his 10th Super Bowl appearance. The only previous time Brady was an underdog the Patriots won as a 14 point underdog to the St. Louis Rams. Tampa Bay started out 60–1 to win the Super Bowl and when Brady was signed it fell to 16–1. While Tampa Bay was a long shot to win the Super Bowl, there was a lot bet on them to win at these odds. And only Kansas City had more bet on them to win the Super Bowl. In Brady's nine previous Super Bowl's he was 6–3 to win the game and 4–5 against the spread showing again that the oddsmakers are pretty accurate.

In the 2021, NFL Hall of Fame class, the highlight was that they showed each recipient being told in person that they were selected by Hall of Fame president David Baker. The Pro Football Hall of Fame did a good job of keeping its newest class of inductees secret until Saturday night's announcement on TV during the NFL honors show. The star was Peyton Manning who will headline the enshrinement ceremony for the class of 2021 on August 8 in Canton, Ohio. Manning played 18 seasons, went to four Super Bowl's and won two of them, one with Indianapolis and one with Denver. He won five MVP awards, one Super Bowl MVP award, two offensive of player of the year awards, one comeback player of the year award and a Walter Payton man of the year award. Manning held multiple NFL records at the time of his retirement including career passing yards (71,009), career passing touchdowns (539) and consecutive seasons with at least 25 passing touchdowns (13). He made the NFL's 100th anniversary team in 2019 and is one of the 10 greatest quarterbacks in NFL history.

Other stars were nominated including Charles Woodson and Calvin Johnson. Also nominated were John Lynch, Alan Faneca, Drew Pearson, Tom Flores and Bill Nunn. Woodson was a nine time Pro bowl selection in 18 season with two teams, the Oakland Raiders and the Green Bay Packers. He was also a four time all-pro and defensive rookie of the year in 1998 and defensive player of the year in 2009. He finished his career with 65 interceptions, fifth all time with 13 defensive TDS.

Johnson, who is referred to as Megatron, finished his career ranked 31st all time in receiving yards with 11,006 in 9 seasons, all with the Detroit Lions. He was a six-time Pro bowl selection and three-time All-Pro. Johnson will be the third player inducted at 35 years or younger, joining a small club with Gale Sayers and Jim Brown.

Woodson was a nine time Pro Bowler and six-time All-Pro in 13 seasons with the Pittsburgh Steelers, New York Jets and Arizona Cardinals. Drew Pearson played 11 seasons with the Dallas Cowboys and was a three-time pro-bowl selection and three-time All-Pro. John Lynch was a nine time pro-bowl selection in 15 seasons with Tampa and Denver. Flores is one of only two people to win the Super Bowl rings as a head coach player and assistant coach joining Mike Ditka for his 2 Super Bowls as coach of the Oakland raider. Nunn was the scouting dynamo for the 1970s Steelers who died in 2014 after 45 seasons with the Pittsburgh organization. The August inductions will also include the class of 2020 and the Centennial class both of which were canceled last year due to the COVID-19 pandemic.

The 10th annual NFL honors TV show was different because it was done in the COVID-19 era so was held remotely. Offensive rookie of the year was Los Angeles Charger quarterback Justin Herbert who was drafted six overall behind fellow quarterbacks Joe Borrow and Tua Tagovailoa, the left handed Alabama star. Herbert was not the initial starter for the Chargers but he ended up the season as the best offensive rookie of the year with 31 touchdowns and 4336 passing yards.

He beat out Minnesota Viking's receiver Justin Jefferson, who set a record for receiving yards for a rookie. Defensive rookie of the year was Washington's football defensive end Chase Young. He had an immediate impact on the team that won the NFC East with 7.5 sacks and was a major force during the year. The defensive player of the year was Los Angeles Rams defensive tackle Aaron Donald who was slightly favored over Pittsburgh Steeler's edge rusher T.J. Watt. Donald has now won three defensive player of the year awards tying Lawrence Taylor and J.J. Watt for the record. This year he had 13.5 sacks, his fourth straight double-digit sack season for the Rams that made the playoffs. Donald who has six All-Pro selections and seven Pro Bowls in seven seasons and also won defensive player of the year in 2017 and 2018.

Offensive player of the year was, not surprisingly, Tennessee Titans running back Derrick Henry who won his second straight rushing title by rushing to 250 yards in the Titan's final game and 2027 yards for the season, the fifth most in NFL history and the seventh runner to have 2000 or more yards in a regular season.

The coach of the year was Kevin Stefanski who led the Cleveland Browns to the playoffs with an 11–5 record for the first time since 1999. The salute to service award went to Steve Cannon CFO of the Atlanta Falcons. The man of the year award, named for Walter Payton who won in 1977, was given to Seattle Seahawks quarterback Russell Wilson who, besides being a great team leader, is a great contributor to the Seattle community. The play of the year was the famous Hail Murray when Tyler Murray, in the last seconds of a game against Buffalo, threw a pass to the end zone and Arizona Cardinals wide receiver DeAndre Hopkins leapt up and caught the pass with three Buffalo Bills defenders around him to win the game.

The Art Rooney sportsmanship award went to quarterback Teddy Bridgewater of the Carolina Panthers. The Deacon Jones award went to T.J. Watt who had 15 sacks in 15 games for the Pittsburgh Steelers. The comeback player of the year was the remarkable Alex Smith who had 17 operations over 728 days to repair a broken leg that was in terrible shape from a November 2018 accident. Smith regained the quarterback position for the Washington football team.

The Bud Light Celly of the year was Pittsburgh. A special award went to Dr Laurent Tardif of the Kansas City Chiefs is also a medical doctor. He took the year off to work in Montreal hospitals on COVID-19. The draft King's fantasy player of the year was Josh Allen of the Buffalo Bills. Assistant coach of the year was Brian Daboll of the Bills. The NFL fan of the year presented by Subway was Brenda Galloway of the Tennessee Titans.

The MVP had three quarterbacks in the competition: Josh Allen, Patrick Mahomes, and the winner was Green Bay Packer quarterback Aaron Rodgers. Rodgers, who is now a three time MVP, had 46 TDs with only five interceptions. Beginning in week 9, he completed 75.1% of his passes with 28 TDs and three interceptions with a 129.2 quarterback rating and led Green Bay to a 8–1 record in that period enabling them to win the NFC North and the NFC bye in the playoffs.

In the NFL there were expectations for each team before the 2020–2021 season began. Table 15.2 presents the expected regular season wins by teams, based on the ELO score calculated by the site 538. These scores are largely determined by the previous season performance. There is a shrinkage to the mean component and the expected wins are a bit low for strong teams and a bit high for weak teams. This is a version of the favorite-longshot bias found in horseracing and other sports betting, see Ziemba (2021). The expected leaders in each division are in bold. Table 15.2 also contains the actual wins/losses for the 2020 season and the resulting seedings for the playoff ranking beginning in January 2021.

The teams which qualified for the playoff (elimination) round are shown in Table 15.2, and their seeding in their conference is shown in green. While the season win/loss record is a good indication of team strength, it could be misleading for strength in the playoffs. Pittsburgh started with 11 wins but only won 1 game in their final 5 games. As a test on the season win/loss

Table 15.2. Preseason predictions and 2020 record.

Division	Team	ELO Preseason	Predicted W/L (2020)	Actual W/L (2020)	
AFC East	**New England**	**1552**	**9 - 7**	7 - 9	
	Buffalo	1533	8 - 8	**13 - 3**	2
	New York J	1456	7 - 9	2 - 14	
	Miami	1435	6 - 10	10- 6	
AFC North	Pittsburgh	1573	10 - 6	**12 - 4**	3
	Baltimore	**1647**	**11 - 5**	**11 - 5**	5
	Cleveland	1496	8 - 8	**11 - 5**	6
	Cincinnati	1390	5 - 11	4 – 11 - 1	
AFC South	Houston	1501	8 - 8	4 - 12	
	Tennessee	**1549**	**9 - 7**	**11 - 5**	4
	Jacksonville	1383	5 - 11	1 - 15	
	Indianapolis	1525	9 -7	**11 - 5**	
AFC West	**Kansas City**	**1658**	**11 - 5**	**14 – 2**	1
	L. A. Chargers	1462	7 - 9	7 - 9	
	Denver	1485	7 - 9	5 - 11	
	Las Vegas	1466	7- 9	8 - 8	
NFC East	Philadelphia	1548	9 - 7	4 – 11 - 1	
	Dallas	**1561**	**9- 7**	6 - 10	
	N. Y. Giants	1419	6 - 10	6 - 10	
	Washington	1372	5 - 11	**7 - 9**	4
NFC North	Chicago	1526	8 - 8	**8 - 8**	7
	Minnesota	1544	9 - 7	7 - 9	
	Green Bay	**1556**	**9 - 7**	**13 - 3**	1
	Detroit	1453	7 - 9	5 - 11	
NFC South	**New Orleans**	**1614**	**10 - 6**	**12 - 4**	2
	Atlanta	1465	7 - 9	4 - 12	
	Carolina	1428	6 - 10	5 - 11	
	Tampa Bay	1540	9 - 7	**11 - 5**	5
NFC West	L.A. Rams	1541	9 - 7	**10 - 6**	6
	Seattle	1548	9 - 7	**12 - 4**	3
	San Francisco	**1601**	**10 - 6**	6 - 10	
	Arizona	1465	7 - 9	8 - 8	

record of teams we have calculated the expected wins based on the points for and points against in the 2020 season. The calculation uses a formula known as the Pythagorean projection (Miller, 2007). This projected number is given by the equation

$$E(Wins) - \frac{P_0^{2.37}}{(P_0^{2.37} + P_a^{2.37})} * 16.$$

Table 15.3. Pythagorean wins.

Team	W	PF	PA	Py(W)	Team	W	PF	PA	Py(W)
Ari	8	410	367	9	LAC	7	384	426	7
Atl	4	396	414	8	LAR	10	372	296	10
BAL	11	468	303	12	LV	8	434	478	7
Buf	13	501	375	11	Mia	10	404	338	9
Car	5	350	402	7	Min	7	430	475	7
Chi	8	372	370	8	NE	7	326	353	7
ClN	4	311	424	5	NO	12	482	337	11
Cle	11	408	419	8	NY	2	243	457	3
Dal	6	395	473	6	NYG	6	280	357	6
Den	5	323	446	5	Phil	4	334	418	6
Det	5	377	519	5	Pitt	12	416	312	11
GB	13	509	369	11	Sea	12	459	371	10
Hou	4	384	464	6	SF	6	376	390	8
Ind	11	451	362	10	TB	11	492	355	11
Jack	1	306	492	4	Ten	11	491	439	9
KC	14	473	362	10	Was	7	335	329	8

The expected Pythagorean wins are given in Table 15.3. Based on the expected wins, Green Bay and Kansas City seem to have over performed during the regular season, the result of winning close games. That could be a red flag heading into the playoffs and neither won the Super Bowl. Pittsburgh and New Orleans were also compromised and did not do well in the playoffs.

The seeding round of games to determine qualifiers for the playoff round began in September. It ran for 17 weeks and in-season factors affect the outcome of games. Factors of special interest in 2020 are (i) COVID-19 infections and (ii) injuries. In the Appendix is a list COVID-19 affected teams. The virus brought about many changes in daily life — face masks, social distancing, forced shutdown of many businesses, working from home. Football nevertheless proceeded with scheduled games. The list in the Appendix shows some effects of COVID-19 by team, but the games went on without too much of a downside. Baltimore had a mini-slump when star quarterback Lamar Jackson was sidelined. Pittsburgh had three games rescheduled which may have contributed to a late season decline.

15.3. The Evolution of the Betfair Odds Before and During the Playoffs and Super Bowl

Figure 15.2 has the Betfair odds on December 27, 2020. Of these 16 teams, 14 would make the playoffs with the exception of Arizona and Miami.

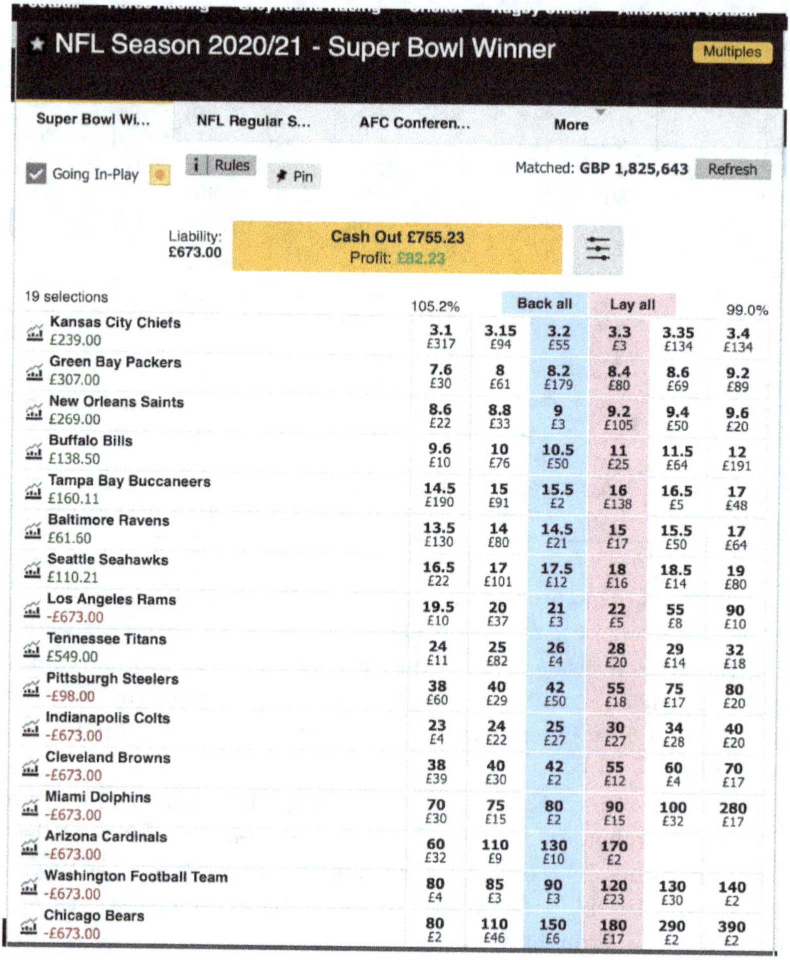

★ NFL Season 2020/21 - Super Bowl Winner Multiples

Super Bowl Wi... | NFL Regular S... | AFC Conferen... | More

Going In-Play | Rules | Pin | Matched: **GBP 1,825,643** | Refresh

Liability: **£673.00** | **Cash Out £755.23** Profit: £82.23

19 selections	105.2%		Back all	Lay all		99.0%
Kansas City Chiefs £239.00	3.1 £317	3.15 £94	3.2 £55	3.3 £3	3.35 £134	3.4 £134
Green Bay Packers £307.00	7.6 £30	8 £61	8.2 £179	8.4 £80	8.6 £69	9.2 £89
New Orleans Saints £269.00	8.6 £22	8.8 £33	9 £3	9.2 £105	9.4 £50	9.6 £20
Buffalo Bills £138.50	9.6 £10	10 £76	10.5 £50	11 £25	11.5 £64	12 £191
Tampa Bay Buccaneers £160.11	14.5 £190	15 £91	15.5 £2	16 £138	16.5 £5	17 £48
Baltimore Ravens £61.60	13.5 £130	14 £80	14.5 £21	15 £17	15.5 £50	17 £64
Seattle Seahawks £110.21	16.5 £22	17 £101	17.5 £12	18 £16	18.5 £14	19 £80
Los Angeles Rams -£673.00	19.5 £10	20 £37	21 £3	22 £5	55 £8	90 £10
Tennessee Titans £549.00	24 £11	25 £82	26 £4	28 £20	29 £14	32 £18
Pittsburgh Steelers -£98.00	38 £60	40 £29	42 £50	55 £18	75 £17	80 £20
Indianapolis Colts -£673.00	23 £4	24 £22	25 £27	30 £27	34 £28	40 £20
Cleveland Browns -£673.00	38 £39	40 £30	42 £2	55 £12	60 £4	70 £17
Miami Dolphins -£673.00	70 £30	75 £15	80 £2	90 £15	100 £32	280 £17
Arizona Cardinals -£673.00	60 £32	110 £9	130 £10	170 £2		
Washington Football Team -£673.00	80 £4	85 £3	90 £3	120 £23	130 £30	140 £2
Chicago Bears -£673.00	80 £2	110 £46	150 £6	180 £17	290 £2	390 £2

Figure 15.2. The Betfair odds on December 27, 2020.

Kansas City was favored at 3.2–1, so if you bet 1 and they win the Super Bowl, you collect 3.2 and gain 2.2. My bets then are listed mostly long with some short on the weaker teams and ones I thought would not win the Super Bowl.

15.3.1. *Super Wildcard weekend January 9–10, 2021*

There were seven teams in each conference who were in the playoffs. Kansas City and Green Bay got the byes and the other six teams in each conference

Liability: £1,732.17 — Cash Out £1,823.36 — Profit: £91.19

selections	101.4%		Back all	Lay all		96.6%
Kansas City Chiefs £174.33	3.65 £184	3.7 £292	3.75 £163	3.8 £51	3.85 £345	3.9 £31
Green Bay Packers £662.63	5.8 £289	5.9 £124	6 £60	6.2 £381	6.4 £636	6.6 £143
Buffalo Bills £202.33	7.6 £10	8 £69	8.2 £20	8.6 £176	8.8 £233	9 £308
New Orleans Saints £204.83	9 £14	9.2 £53	9.4 £28	9.8 £851	10 £70	10.5 £98
Baltimore Ravens £187.43	11 £74	11.5 £279	12 £495	12.5 £466	13 £49	13.5 £287
Tampa Bay Buccaneers £69.46	12 £201	12.5 £81	13 £3	13.5 £149	14 £78	15 £100
Seattle Seahawks £273.56	15.5 £23	16 £161	16.5 £309	20 £104	21 £100	28 £89
Pittsburgh Steelers -£487.17	27 £77	28 £11	29 £101	30 £70	32 £134	34 £58
Los Angeles Rams -£1,153.71	40 £635	42 £10	44 £64	50 £16	55 £103	110 £50
Tennessee Titans £239.83	36 £50	38 £167	40 £170	42 £34	44 £20	55 £100
Indianapolis Colts -£1,462.17	50 £302	55 £37	60 £64	65 £98	70 £50	85 £44
Cleveland Browns -£1,732.17	55 £182	60 £24	65 £101	75 £89	80 £50	110 £61
Washington Football Team -£982.17	90 £68	100 £14	110 £9	170 £4	180 £11	200 £20
Chicago Bears £288.33	110 £38	120 £68	130 £26	140 £14	180 £17	190 £3

Figure 15.3. The Betfair odds for the Super Bowl going into Super Wildcard Weekend.

met on Wildcard weekend. The higher rated teams faced the lower rated team. These rankings of the teams were are in Figure 15.3.

Figure 15.4 has the Betfair odds going into the playoffs. Kansas City remained the favorite to repeat as Super Bowl champion. The Las Vegas point spreads reflect these odds but the betting can shift the line as the bookmakers must control their risk. As of February 5, the Tampa Bay Buccaneers and the Pittsburgh Steelers were attracting nearly 90% of the money bet as favorites. The betting public was favoring the favorite in 4 of the 6 games in their bets.

15.3.2. *AFC Games*

Indianapolis at Buffalo: The Bills were favored by 6.5 points and they were perhaps the NFL's hottest team winning seven of their last eight games with the only loss to Arizona when Kyler Murray passed to the end zone

Sat 9 Jan — Multiples

Coming up			Matched	1		2	
Today 18:05	Indianapolis Colts / Buffalo Bills	1	£22,062	3.6 £13	3.65 £882	1.38 £871	1.39 £1499
Today 21:40	Los Angeles Rams / Seattle Seahawks	1	£12,688	2.52 £58	2.56 £335	1.64 £1458	1.66 £185

Sun 10 Jan — Multiples

Coming up			Matched	1		2	
Sun 01:15	Tampa Bay Buccaneers / Washington Football Team	3	£24,800	1.28 £686	1.29 £2088	4.5 £40	4.6 £480
Sun 18:05	Baltimore Ravens / Tennessee Titans		£7,241	1.6 £1670	1.62 £845	2.62 £280	2.66 £523
Sun 21:40	Chicago Bears / New Orleans Saints	1	£6,636	5.7 £14	5.8 £385	1.21 £1011	1.22 £1846

Mon 11 Jan — Multiples

Coming up			Matched	1		2	
Jan 11 01:16	Cleveland Browns / Pittsburgh Steelers		£6,101	3.45 £232	3.5 £35	1.4 £88	1.41 £848

Figure 15.4. The Betfair odds going into the Super Wildcard games, January 9, 10.

in the last second and DeAndre Hopkins made a spectacular catch while being surrounded by three Bill's players to win the game.

The spread odds vary with the betting, see our guidebook Ziemba and McLean (2018) for formulas to convert spreads to probabilities of winning. The Buffalo Bill's quarterback Josh Allen had a spectacular throwing and running year and was in the MVP running. The Bill's were 13–3. In week they 17 beat the Dolphins 56 to 26 to knock Miami out of the playoffs with may starters resting. The Colts, led by quarterback Philip Rivers, have been solid on offense and defense but likely not good enough to beat the powerful Bills.

Indeed Buffalo won the game 27–24 and I won my bet. This was Buffalo's first playoff win in 25 years. Rivers, who played well and is a sure Hall of Fame quarterback, retired after the game to close out his 17 year career. But like many players who retire, he might come back to play for another team in the future.

Cleveland at Pittsburgh: The Cleveland Browns were a six point underdog to the Pittsburgh Steelers. The Steelers had two seasons, namely an 11–0 start and then the shaky last five games, losing four of them to finish at 12–4. It was the Browns' first playoff appearance since 2002. The Steelers played well in their first game, losing 24 to 22 after missing a two point conversion in the final two minutes that would have tied the game that was also against Cleveland.

The playoff game started out with huge miscue when the center Maurice Pouncey threw the ball over quarterback Ben Roethlisberger's head and the Browns scored a touchdown in the end zone to create a 7–0 lead. More miscues and a good Browns' play and Pittsburgh's turnovers led to a 28–0 lead in quarter one. Pittsburgh came back to some extent but lost 48–37 and I lost my bet. Pittsburgh was a difficult team to bet on all season because you did not know if they were good or not. Pouncey and his twin brother, another center, both retired.

MF Stewart had an interception one of four by Ben Roethlisberger. Ben had a tough day and looked to have trouble in the future as Pittsburgh's quarterback but that got resolved by the team and Ben with a restructured contract. Kareem Hunt scored two TDs and MJ Stewart caught a Baker Mayfield pass for a touchdown. The Browns had the early 28–0 lead in quarter one and were 35–10 at half time and coasted to victory.

Baltimore at Tennessee: The Baltimore Colts were a three point favor over the home team Tennessee Titans. After a slow start, Baltimore finished strong and were 11–5 as was Tennessee for the season. Baltimore's last year's MVP quarterback Lamar Jackson was a major running threat with over 1000 yards for the second time and was the first player to ever do this and he was a passing threat but his playoff record has been poor.

Tennessee had a balanced attack with top runner Derrick Henry who gained over 2000 yards for this season plus a good passing game led by quarterback Ryan Tannehill who was the top rated quarterback last year and was a better passer than Jackson and had the same number of running TDs as Jackson. Tennessee was strong on offense but weak on defense and actually of the 184 teams to make the playoffs since 2006, they were rated 183rd on defense. However, the Titans led the NFL in the turnover differential. Baltimore won the game 22–13. The key was limiting Henry to 40 yards rushing on 20 carries. It was Lamar Jackson's first playoff win and I won the bet on Baltimore.

15.3.3. *NFC Games*

Chicago at New Orleans: The Chicago Bears were a 10 point underdog after an 8–8 season to the New Orleans Saints who had a powerful offensive team led by quarterback Drew Brees, all around runner Alvin Kamara (who scored a record six TDs on Christmas Day and could have had seven), and top receivers like last year's offensive player of the year wide receiver Michael Thomas. In the game, Bears quarterback Mitch Trubisky was 19 of 29 for 199 yards and one meaningless TD to Jimmy Graham late in the game. The Bears only converted one of 10 third downs and had nine penalties. They held the flying Saints offense to seven first half points but the Saints pulled away in the second half. Brees was 28 of 39 passing for two TDs and Kamara had 99 yards rushing and 23 carries and another TD. I won my bet on New Orleans.

Los Angeles Rams at Seattle: The Los Angeles Rams were a three point underdog to hometown Seattle Seahawks. Before the game, the focus was on quarterback Jared Goff, who was injured with a bruised thumb versus John Woolford as the starting Los Angeles quarterback offered but got a neck injury in the first quarter so Goff returned. Running back Cam Acres ran for 176 yards in the TD and was the offensive player of the week for Los Angeles. Russell Wilson, the Seattle quarterback, was all right but not special like he was early in the season when he was perhaps the leading MVP candidate. The Rams defense was strong and Darius Williams, who was the defensive player of the week, got a pick six on a Wilson interception. The Rams won 32–20 and I lost my bet on Seattle.

Later the Rams gave up on Goff and traded him to Detroit and got Matthew Stafford in exchange as their new quarterback.

Tampa Bay at Washington: Tampa Bay was improving game by game after a 7–5 season. They were 7–2 and then had three losses which had a lot to do with no practice because of COVID-19 precautions and a new system with many new players brought in with the hiring of Tom Brady. Tampa were favored by eight points over the Washington footfall team. Brady brought with him receivers Rob Gronkowski out of retirement, Antonio Brown on his off field troubles, Leonard Fournette out of retirement and star defensive lineman Jason Pierre-Paul, plus a spirit of cooperative winning. Washington was led by star linebacker Chase Young and quarterback Taylor Hannity, the backup to the remarkable Alex Smith who had a good year recovering from his terrible leg injury that required 17 operations. He threw for one TD and one interception and 306 yards passing in 20 of 46 passes but it was not enough as Tom Brady threw three TDs and 381 yards and Fournette ran for 93 yards and another TD. Tampa Bay won 31–25 and I won by bet. Washington was 7–9 and the only team to win their division with a losing record. They had a credible defense but the offense was not strong enough to compete with Tampa Bay.

15.4. Divisional Round, January 16, 17

Figure 15.5 shows the Betfair Super Bowl odds and my bets in the middle of the New Orleans - Tampa Bay game where New Orleans was eliminated. I was long all five teams.

Figure 15.6 shows the NFC championship odds before the New Orleans — Tampa Bay game.

Baltimore at Buffalo: The weak play of 2019 regular-season MVP Lamar Jackson continued. He was 14 of 24 passing but had one interception. Lamar ran for 34 yards on nine carries but his 3.8 yards per carry did not help much. Tyler Huntley, the backup quarterback added 60 yards on 6 of 13

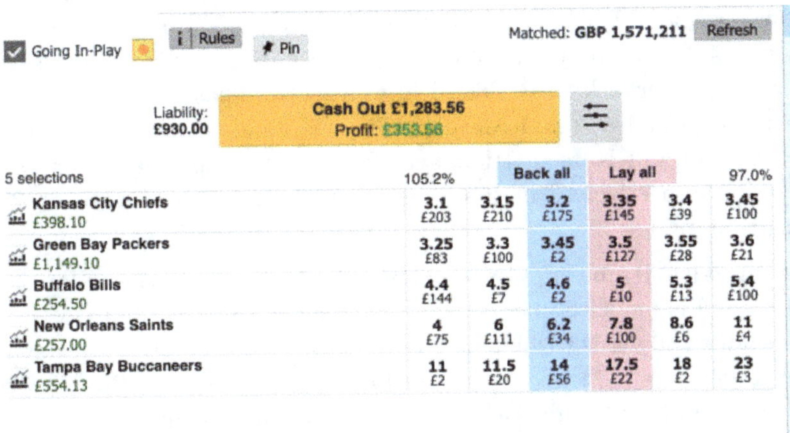

Going In-Play · Rules · Pin · Matched: GBP 1,571,211 · Refresh

Liability: £930.00 · Cash Out £1,283.56 · Profit: £353.56

5 selections	105.2%		Back all	Lay all		97.0%
Kansas City Chiefs £398.10	3.1 £203	3.15 £210	3.2 £175	3.35 £145	3.4 £39	3.45 £100
Green Bay Packers £1,149.10	3.25 £83	3.3 £100	3.45 £2	3.5 £127	3.55 £28	3.6 £21
Buffalo Bills £254.50	4.4 £144	4.5 £7	4.6 £2	5 £10	5.3 £13	5.4 £100
New Orleans Saints £257.00	4 £75	6 £111	6.2 £34	7.8 £100	8.6 £6	11 £4
Tampa Bay Buccaneers £554.13	11 £2	11.5 £20	14 £56	17.5 £22	18 £2	23 £3

Figure 15.5. The Betfair Super Bowls odds, January 17.

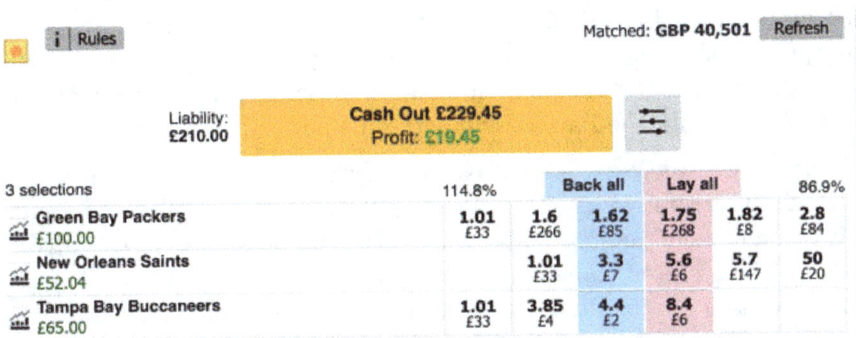

Rules · Matched: GBP 40,501 · Refresh

Liability: £210.00 · Cash Out £229.45 · Profit: £19.45

3 selections	114.8%		Back all	Lay all		86.9%
Green Bay Packers £100.00	1.01 £33	1.6 £266	1.62 £85	1.75 £268	1.82 £8	2.8 £84
New Orleans Saints £52.04		1.01 £33	3.3 £7	5.6 £6	5.7 £147	50 £20
Tampa Bay Buccaneers £65.00	1.01 £33	3.85 £4	4.4 £2	8.4 £6		

Figure 15.6. The Betfair odds for the NFC championship, January 17.

passing and 32 yards rushing on three carries for 10.7 average. Baltimore's rushing by Gus Edwards and JK Dobbins helped a little as both gained 42 yards on 10 carries. Josh Allen was 23 of 37 passing for one TD and star receiver Stephan Diggs gained 106 yards on eight catches for 13.2 average and a TD. John Brown added 62 yards and 8 carries. Buffalo won 17 to 3 and I won my bet.

Cleveland at Kansas City: The Chiefs, who were a 10-point favorite, started strong and led after the first quarter 6–3 and 19–3 at halftime. They maintained the lead throughout the game. Patrick Mahomes, as usual, was sharp with one TD passing and no interceptions going 21 of 30 passing and one running TD. The running game was strong with Darrell Williams gaining 78 yards on 13 carries Mercole Hardman added 58 yards on four receptions. Both Tyreek Hill and Travis Kelsey went over 100 yards receiving with 110 and 109 yards on only eight receptions for each, respectively. Brown's quarterback Baker Mayfield was 23 of 37 passing for one TD and one interception by Tyrann Mathieu. The dual tandem of top running backs Nick Chubb and Kareem Hunt averaged 5.3 yards per carry for 69 and 32 yards, respectively. But that was not enough as the Chiefs won 22–17 and I won my bet.

Los Angeles Rams at Green Bay: The Rams quarterback Jared Goff had a good game with one TD passing going 21 of 27 for 174 yards. Cam Akers added 90 yards rushing on 18 carries and another TD. Josh Reynolds gained 65 yards and three receptions for a 21.7 average and Robert Woods added 48 yards and eight carries. But this was not enough to compensate for the high-powered Packers offense led by Aaron Rodgers who was 23 of 36 passing with two TDs and 296 yards and one rushing TD. Aaron Jones ran for 99 yards on 14 carries and Jamaal Williams had 65 in 12 rushing attempts. Allen Lazard, Devante Adams and Robert Tonyan, Jr caught four, nine and four of Rodgers passes for 96, 66 and 60 yards, respectively. Green Bay led at the half 19 to 10 and led the entire game. The final score was 32 to 18 with the Packers winning so I won my bet.

Tampa Bay at New Orleans: New Orleans at home was a 3-point favorite. Tom Brady was sharp throwing 2 TDs to Leonard Fournette and Mike Evans and running for another TD. The passing was well diversified as eight players caught passes. Cameron Brate and Chris Goodwin had four each for 50 and 34 yards, respectively and Fournette had five for 44 yards. The defense remained strong and caught 3 Drew Brees interceptions by Devon White, Sean Bunting and Mike Edwards. Fournette and Ronald Jones had 63 and 62 yards, respectively, on 17 and 13 carries which helped, but Brady was the star once again. The usually accurate Drew Brees was only 19 of 34 for 134 yards and those three interceptions. He did throw for one TD and Jamis Winston, the backup quarterback, threw for another TD in a spectacular play. All around back Alvin Kamara rushed for 85 yards on 18 carries and caught three passes for 20 more yards but that was not enough. The Buccaneers led 6–0 after the first quarter but pulled away in the rest of the game. The Saints came back and tied it after three quarters but Tampa Bay scored 10 points in the final quarter as Brady threw for one touchdown and they got a field goal so Tampa Bay one 32–20 and I won my bet on the Buccaneers and I was able to win all four bets in the divisional round.

15.4.1. *The Conference Championship Games*

Figure 15.7 has the Betfair odds and my bets on the AFC Championship game. I bet mostly on Kansas City and they won 38–24.

AFC: Kansas City Chiefs 38, Buffalo Bills 24

Kansas City overcame an early 9–0 deficit scoring 38 points and 439 total yards as they advanced to their second consecutive Super Bowl (see Table 15.4)

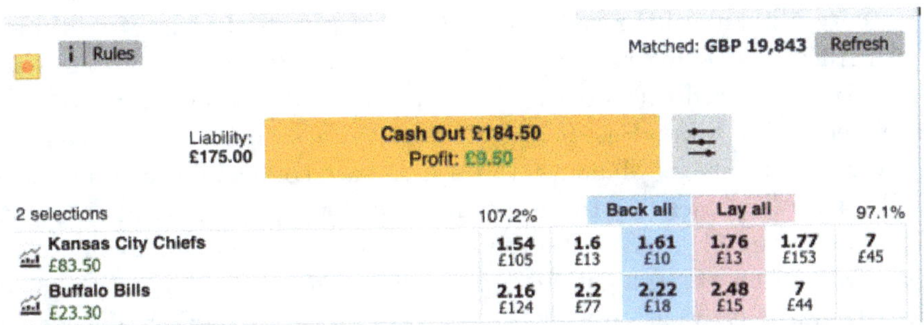

Figure 15.7. The Betfair odds and my bets on the AFC Championship game, January 17.

Table 15.4. Buffalo Bills vs. Kansas City Chiefs: Game Summary.

	1	2	3	4	Total
Bills	9	3	3	9	24
Chiefs	0	21	10	7	38

Buffalo opened up the scoring with Tyler Bass' 51-yard field goal, at the end of a 10-play, 42-yard drive, and the Bills forced the Chiefs to go three-and-out. The Bills also had to punt on their next drive, but returner Mecole Hardman muffed the kick and Taiwan Jones recovered it for Buffalo on the Chiefs' 3-yard line. On the next play, Josh Allen threw a touchdown pass to tight end Dawson Knox, making the score 9–0 after Bass missed the extra point. Kansas City advanced 80 yards on their next drive in which Patrick Mahomes completed 10 passes, one of them a 9-yard completion to running back Darrel Williams on 4th and 1. With 14:20 left in the half, Mahomes' 3-yard touchdown completion to Hardman made the score 9-7. The next time Kansas City got the ball, Hardman's 50-yard gain on an end-around run pre-empted a 6-yard touchdown run by Williams, giving the Chiefs a 14–9 lead. Following another Bills punt, Mahomes completed passes to tight end Travis Kelce for gains of 11 and 17 yards, along with a 33-yard completion to Tyreek Hill. Clyde Edwards-Helaire finished the drive with a 1-yard touchdown run, increasing the team's lead to 21–9. Buffalo took the ball back and drove 73 yards to the Chiefs' 2-yard line, featuring a 20-yard reception by running back T. J. Yeldon. On 4th and goal with 14 seconds left, the Bills decided to settle for Bass' 20-yard field goal and a 21–12 halftime score.

Mahomes started the third quarter completing 7 of 8 passes for 50 yards on the way to a 45-yard Harrison Butker field goal, bringing the Chiefs' lead up to 24–12. The Bills responded with a drive to the Chiefs' 8-yard line, with Allen completing passes of 23 yards to Cole Beasley and 17 yards to John Brown. Faced with 4th and 3 on the Chiefs' 8-yard line, Buffalo once again elected to take a Bass field goal, making the score 24–15. On the next play from scrimmage, Mahomes threw a 71-yard completion to Hill on the Bills' 4-yard line, leading to his 1-yard touchdown pass to Kelce that put Kansas City up 31–15. Chiefs cornerback Rashad Fenton then intercepted a pass from Allen, returning it 30 yards to the Chiefs' 42-yard line with 13:20 left. Kansas City went on to drive 58 yards and score another touchdown with Mahomes' 5-yard pass to Kelce, increasing their lead to 38–15 with 7:36 remaining. On their next drive, Buffalo drove 63 yards in 10 plays, including a 27-yard completion from Allen to Stefon Diggs on 3rd and 13, to score on Allen's 6-yard touchdown pass to Isaiah McKenzie; a 2-point conversion was unsuccessful, keeping the score at 38–21. Buffalo recovered the ensuing onside kick, and Allen's 34-yard completion to Diggs set up Bass' fourth field goal of the day on a 51-yard kick. Buffalo's second attempt at an onside kick was unsuccessful and the Chiefs ran out the rest of the clock.

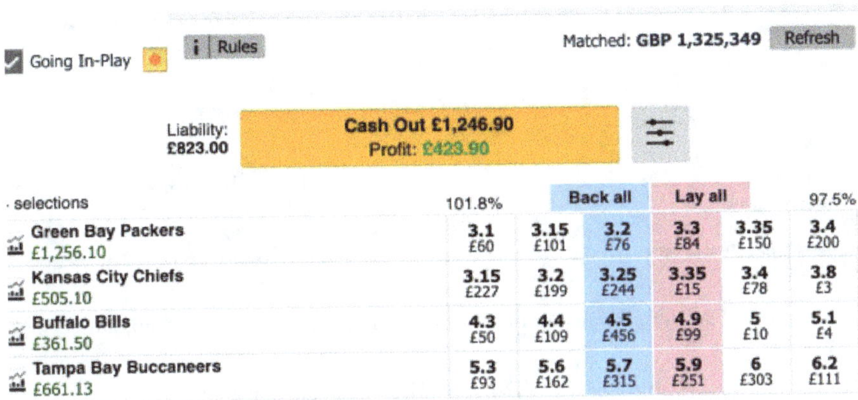

selections	101.8%		Back all	Lay all		97.5%
Green Bay Packers £1,256.10	3.1 £60	3.15 £101	3.2 £76	3.3 £84	3.35 £150	3.4 £200
Kansas City Chiefs £505.10	3.15 £227	3.2 £199	3.25 £244	3.35 £15	3.4 £78	3.8 £3
Buffalo Bills £361.50	4.3 £50	4.4 £109	4.5 £456	4.9 £99	5 £10	5.1 £4
Tampa Bay Buccaneers £661.13	5.3 £93	5.6 £162	5.7 £315	5.9 £251	6 £303	6.2 £111

Figure 15.8. The Betfair odds to win the Super Bowl and my bets going into the Championship games, January 17.

I won my bets on the Chiefs.

Mahomes completed 29 of 38 passes for 325 yards and three touchdowns, Hill had nine receptions for a franchise record 172 yards, and Kelce caught 13 passes for 118 yards and two touchdowns — the most receptions by a player in a Conference Championship game. Defensive tackle Frank Clark had two of Kansas City's four sacks in the game. Allen finished the day 28-for-48 for 287 yards with two touchdowns and an interception, and was the game's leading rusher with seven carries for 88 yards.

This was the fourth postseason meeting between the Chiefs and Bills. The Bills had won two of the prior three meetings, including the 1993 AFC championship game.

Figure 15.8 has the Betfair odds to win the Super Bowl and my bets going into the Conference Championship games. My strategy was to win the bet regardless of who wins the Super Bowl.

Tampa Bay Buccaneers vs. Green Bay Packers: Figure 15.9 has the Betfair odds and my bets to win the NFC championship as of January 17. I bet mostly on Tampa Bay who were not favored but they won 31–26 and I won my Tampa bets.

Despite giving up more yards and having more turnovers than Green Bay, Tampa Bay's 18 point lead early in the second half helped them weather a comeback by Green Bay, as Tampa Bay's defense held Green Bay to just six points off three Brady interceptions. (See Table 15.5)

Tampa Bay took the opening kickoff and drove 66 yards on a drive that featured three third down conversions. First, Tom Brady converted a 3rd and 4 with a 27-yard pass to Mike Evans. Then on 3rd and 9, he

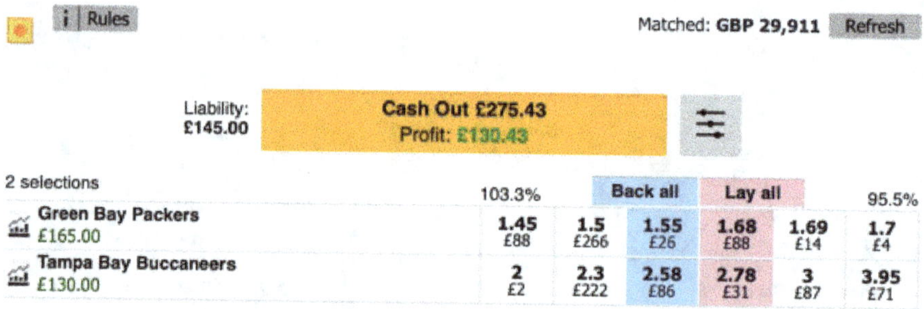

Figure 15.9. The Betfair odds and my bets to win the NFC championship, January 17.

Table 15.5. Tampa Bay Buccaneers vs. Green Bay Packers: Game Summary.

	1	2	3	4	Total
Buccaneers	7	14	7	3	31
Packers	0	10	13	3	26

threw a 14-yard completion to Chris Godwin. Finally, Brady finished the possession with a 15-yard touchdown pass to Evans on 3rd and 7, giving the Buccaneers a 7–0 lead. Following a punt from each team, Green Bay tied the score at 7–7 on a 90-yard drive in which Aaron Rodgers converted a 3rd and 15 with a 23-yard pass to Allen Lazard before throwing a 50-yard touchdown completion to Marquez Valdes-Scantling. Tampa Bay took the ball back, and made another big 3rd down conversion with Brady's 52-yard pass to Godwin on 3rd and 9. On the next play, Leonard Fournette's 20-yard touchdown run made the score 14–7 with 12:24 left in the half. Green Bay responded by driving 69 yards in 15 plays to cut the score to 14–10 with Mason Crosby's 24-yard field goal. Their defense then forced a punt, but on the Packers' next drive, Sean Murphy-Bunting intercepted a pass from Rodgers on the Buccaneers' 49-yard line with 28 seconds left in the half. Tampa Bay then drove to a 4th and 4 on the Packers' 45-yard line, managing to convert it with a 6-yard catch by Fournette. With eight seconds remaining, Tampa Bay decided against kicking a long field goal, and Brady threw a 39-yard touchdown pass to Scotty Miller, ending the half with the Buccaneers ahead 21–10. In the first half, Brady completed 13 of 22 passes for 202 yards and two touchdowns.

Two plays into the third quarter, safety Jordan Whitehead forced a fumble from Packers running back Aaron Jones. Devin White recovered it for Tampa Bay and returned it 21 yards to the Green Bay 8-yard line. On the next play, Tampa Bay fooled the Packers defense with a play-action pass, with Brady faking a backfield handoff before throwing the ball to tight end Cameron Brate for a touchdown and a 28–10 lead. On Green Bay's next drive, Rodgers completed 5 of 6 passes for 68 yards and finishing the drive with an 8-yard touchdown throw to tight end Robert Tonyan, making the score 28–17. Then safety Adrian Amos intercepted a pass from Brady on the Packers' 32-yard line, sparking a 13-play, 68-yard drive that ended with Rodgers' 2-yard touchdown completion to Davante Adams with 24 seconds left in the quarter; receiver Equanimeous St. Brown dropped Rodgers' pass on a 2-point conversion attempt, and the score remained 28–23. Tampa Bay then drove to the Packers' 28-yard line, only to lose the ball again when Brady threw an interception to cornerback Jaire Alexander. Green Bay could not get a first down and had to punt after Shaquil Barrett sacked Rodgers for a 10-yard loss on 3rd and 5. Then Brady was picked off for the third time, throwing another interception to Alexander. Green Bay's next possession resulted in Rodgers again being sacked by Barrett and the team again going three-and-out. Tampa Bay took the ball back on their own 28-yard line, and went on to drive 44 yards in 8 plays, the longest a 29-yard gain on a screen pass from Brady to Rob Gronkowski. On the last play, Ryan Succop's 46-yard field goal gave the Buccaneers a 31–23 lead with 4:42 left.

Green Bay then drove to a first and goal from the Buccaneers' 8-yard line. After two incompletions, Rodgers appeared to have room to run toward the end zone, but he chose to throw the ball to a well covered Adams, which resulted in another incompletion. Packers head coach Matt LaFleur elected not to attempt a tying touchdown and 2-point conversion on 4th and goal from the 8-yard line with 2:09 left; Crosby kicked a field goal that cut the Packers' deficit to five points, 31–26. But this was thought by Rodgers and many others including us to be a major error since Green Bay had the MVP quarterback. LaFleur thought that his defense would get the ball back. But that was poor thinking. You don't give Brady the ball this late in the 4th quarter when he is ahead.

Tampa Bay went on to run out the rest of the clock with three first downs; they started the drive with a 9-yard pass from Brady to Evans as the clock ran down to the 2-minute warning. Green Bay deliberately committed an encroachment penalty, on 2nd and 1, giving the Buccaneers a first down. Two plays later on 3rd and 4, Brady's threw an incomplete pass, but the officials threw a late flag against defensive back Kevin King for pass interference while trying to cover Tyler Johnson, giving the Buccaneers another first down to clinch the game. Tampa Bay finished the game with a run by Godwin on third and 5.

The final score was 31–26 and I won my bets on Tampa Bay.

Brady completed 20 of 36 passes for 280 yards with three touchdowns and three interceptions in his 14th conference championship game (and first in the NFC) as he advanced to his 10th Super Bowl in 21 seasons. Godwin was his top target with five receptions for 110 yards. White had nine tackles, six assists, and a fumble recovery. Barrett had three sacks, while linebacker Jason Pierre-Paul had two sacks. Rodgers completed 33 of 48 passes for 346 yards and three touchdowns, with one interception, as he lost his second consecutive conference championship game and fell to 1–4 overall in Conference title games over his 16 seasons [80]. Valdes-Scantling caught four passes for 115 yards and a score. Nose tackle Kenny Clark had six tackles (1 for loss), two assists, and a sack. With the win, the Buccaneers reached their second Super Bowl in franchise history and became the first team to play a Super Bowl in their home stadium.

15.5. The Super Bowl LV, February 7, 2021

First half: Kansas City won the coin toss and deferred possession to the second half. The opening kickoff from Chiefs kicker Harrison Butker was returned to the Tampa Bay 24-yard line. The Buccaneers' opening drive stalled to a three-and-out, and the resulting Bradley Pinion punt was downed at the Kansas City 33-yard line. The Chiefs' first drive ended similarly, with the offense able to gain only one first down and Tommy Townsend's punt resulting in a touchback. Tampa Bay's second drive started with a promising 13-yard rush by Ronald Jones II, but stalled from there and resulted in another punt by Pinion, this one downed at the Chiefs' 38-yard line. Kansas City's ensuing drive took them 31 yards in eight plays, culminating in the first points of the game: a 49-yard field goal by Butker. On the next drive, Buccaneers running back Leonard Fournette rushed four times for 26 yards on an eight-play, 70-yard drive that ended on Tom Brady's 8-yard touchdown pass to Rob Gronkowski, giving Tampa Bay a 4-point lead. This was the 13th postseason touchdown pass from Brady to Gronkowski, setting a new record, which they had previously shared with Joe Montana and Jerry Rice. It was also the first time in Brady's 10 Super Bowls that he threw a touchdown pass in the first quarter. The Chiefs' next drive, which started on their own 37-yard line, ended in a three-and-out, and the Buccaneers took over on their own 30-yard line following the punt.

On their first drive of the second quarter, Brady's 31-yard completion to Mike Evans gave Tampa Bay a first and goal at the Chiefs 6-yard line. However the Bucs were only able to reach the Chiefs' 1-yard line with their next three plays, and Ronald Jones II was stopped short of the goal line on a fourth down rushing attempt (a ruling that was challenged by Tampa Bay and upheld), giving the ball over on downs to Kansas City. The Chiefs were unable to capitalize off of the stop. The Chiefs' Tommy Townsend punted deep into Tampa Bay territory, but Kansas City was flagged for a holding call and had to punt again. Townsend's follow-up punt went out-of-bounds at the Chiefs' 38-yard line, for a net of only 29 yards. On the next drive, Brady threw a 17-yard touchdown pass to Gronkowski, increasing the Buccaneers' lead to 14–3. The Buccaneers' drive was aided by two significant penalties - first, an interception by the Chiefs' Tyrann Mathieu was negated by defensive holding call. Later, after Kansas City stopped the Buccaneers on third down, the Chiefs' Mecole Hardman was called for offsides during the ensuing field goal attempt, giving the Buccaneers a first down as a result of the 5-yard penalty. Kansas City responded by moving the ball 61 yards in 10 plays, with Patrick Mahomes completing three passes to Travis Kelce for 36 yards and rushing for 11. Butker finished the possession with another field goal, this from 34 yards, making the score 14–6. Tampa Bay's final first half drive began on their own 29-yard line with just over a minute on the clock, and increased their lead to 21–6 with a five-play, 71-yard drive, the longest a 15-yard catch by Fournette. Brady finished it with a 1-yard touchdown pass to Antonio Brown with six seconds to play. Again, Tampa Bay was aided by penalties - in particular a 34-yard pass interference call against Bashaud Breeland who was covering Evans, and an 8-yard pass interference call against Mathieu in the end zone. All told, in the first half the Chiefs were penalized eight times for 95 yards — the most penalties called on any team in one half in any game of the 2020–2021 NFL season, while the Buccaneers were flagged for one 5-yard penalty [123]. At halftime, the Buccaneers led the Chiefs 21–6.

Second half: The second half began with a kickoff by Pinion, which was returned to the Chiefs' own 19-yard line. On the next play, Clyde Edwards-Helaire rushed for a 26-yard gain. Edwards-Helaire also had a 10-yard run on the drive, which went for 47 yards in seven plays and concluded with a 52-yard field goal, Butker's third of the game, making the score 21-9.

Tampa Bay stormed right back with a six-play, 74-yard drive, featuring a 25-yard completion from Brady to Gronkowski. On the next play, Fournette's 27-yard touchdown burst increased the Bucs lead to 28–9. Following a touchback, Kansas City began their drive on their own 25-yard line, but an interception by Antoine Winfield Jr. at the Chiefs' 45-yard line gave Tampa Bay the ball back. Despite the fact that the Buccaneers were only able to gain eleven yards on their next eight plays, they were able to capitalize on the turnover, as Succop ended the drive with a 52-yard field goal, increasing their lead to 31–9. On the next drive, Tampa Bay forced a turnover on downs at their own 11-yard line with 13:43 left in the game, stuffing a running play for a 1-yard gain and then forcing Mahomes to throw three straight incompletions.

The Chiefs defense forced Tampa Bay to punt for just the third time, allowing their offense to take the ball at their own 8-yard line. They got the ball across midfield, but turned the ball over to Tampa Bay on downs at the Bucs' 27-yard line. The Buccaneers then went three-and-out, and punted the ball to the Kansas City 42-yard line. Kansas City drove the ball to the Buccaneers 10-yard line, but Mahomes threw an interception to Devin White with 1:33 left in the game, which was downed in the end zone for a touchback. Brady then kneeled the ball three times for Tampa Bay, running out the clock, ending the game at 31–9. Brady, who completed 21 of 29 passes for 201 yards and three touchdowns, won the Super Bowl Most Valuable Player Award for a record fifth time in his career, extending his previous record of four. It was a reminder that NFL football is a team game and the ultimate clutch team player, Tom Brady, prevailed. (See Table 15.6.)

I won on two sets of bets, namely the long run Super Bowl winner bets where I had about \$1100 on Tampa Bay and a bit less, about \$1000 on Kansas City. So I won that amount with a little more moved from Kansas City to Tampa as it was pretty clear Tampa Bay was winning early. More of this switching would have increased the gain on Tampa. I did win the two bets for \$200 on tampa $+3\frac{1}{2}$ at 1.88 odds to win the Super Bowl game.

Table 15.6. Game summary.

	1	**2**	**3**	**4**	**Total**
Chiefs (AFC)	3	3	3	0	9
Buccaneers (NFC)	7	14	10	0	31

Fournette was the game's leading rusher with 16 carries for 89 yards and a touchdown, while also catching four passes for 46 yards. Gronkowski, who caught only two passes in Tampa Bay's previous three postseason games, was the team's leading receiver with six receptions for 67 yards and two touchdowns. White had eight tackles (two for a loss), four assists, and an interception. Mahomes finished the day 26-of-49 for 270 yards and two interceptions, while also rushing for 33 yards. Kelce caught 10 passes for 133 yards, setting a new Super Bowl record for receiving yards by a tight end. Out of 110 Super Bowl teams, Kansas City became just the third to finish the game without scoring a touchdown, joining the Miami Dolphins in Super Bowl VI and the Los Angeles Rams in Super Bowl LIII. Buccaneers coach Bruce Arians became the oldest coach to win a Super Bowl, at 68 years and 127 days, while the team became the first to score at least 30 points in four games during the same postseason. (See Table 15.7.)

15.5.1. *Commentary*

Momentum: Tampa Bay on a roll but Kansas City scrambling: Kansas City was a 3-point favorite based on their best in their regular season record of 14–2. However, in the last seven they escaped with narrow 4-point wins, depending always on some Mahomes magic. In contrast Tampa Bay was getting better game by game and Kansas City was squeaking by opponents mostly winning by a few points often late in the game.

Table 15.7. Final statistics.

Statistic	Kansas City Chiefs	Tampa Bay Buccaneers
First downs	22	26
Total net yards	350	340
Net yards rushing	107	145
Rushing attempts	17	33
Yards per rush	6.3	4.4
Yards passing	243	195
Passing-completions/attempts	26/49	21/29
Times sacked-total yards	3-27	1-6
Interceptions thrown	2	0
Interceptions-total return yards	0-0	2-0
Penalties-yards	11-120	4-39
Time of possession	28:37	31:23
Turnovers	2	0

Table 15.8. Momentum.

	KC		TB	
Week	Opponent	Score	Opponent	Score
14	@Mia	W33–27	Minn	W26–14
15	@NO	W32–29	@Atl	W31–27
16	Atl	W17–14	@Det	W47–7
17	LAR	L38–21	Atl	W44–27
WC	Bye		@Was	W31–23
DIV	Cle	W22–17	@NO	W30–20
CONF	Buff	W38–24	@GB	W31–26
Av D		+2.17		+11.29

Table 15.8 shows the progress. Kansas City won by just 2.17 points per game and Tampa Bay by 11.29.

Mahomes: Patrick Mahomes left Super Bowl LV battered, bruised and brought low by a ferocious and unassailable Tampa Bay Buccaneers defense during the Kansas City Chiefs' humbling 31–9 loss. At the same time, the Chiefs quarterback was easily the team's best player and did everything in his power to keep his squad competitive despite obvious disadvantages.

Mahomes twirled and pranced and attempted nearly impossible passes from improbable angles only to have everyone around the quarterback let him down. "Until the last snap, he was trying to win the football game," head coach Andy Reid told reporters about his quarterback after the team's disappointing performance.

Coaching: The defining moment of Super Bowl LV on Sunday wasn't so much one play as it was one drive, namely the Tampa Bay Buccaneers' 55-second touchdown march that closed the first half. The drive increased Tampa Bay's lead to 21-6 and punctured any momentum the Chiefs hoped to build entering halftime. Kansas City would score only three points the rest of the way. The drive will be remembered for two reasons, one being Chiefs Coach Andy Reid twice calling timeout in an attempt to get the ball back. (The clock stoppages merely gave Tom Brady and Co. more time to work.) But two pass-interference penalties called by referee Carl Cheffers's crew proved to be just as important.

What went wrong for the Chiefs and Patrick Mahomes in a brutal Super Bowl defeat: Facing first and 10 from his team's 42-yard line with the clock ticking, Brady fired a deep ball toward wide receiver Mike Evans, who was defended by cornerback Bashaud Breeland. The two appeared to get their feet tangled and both went down, but Breeland was flagged for pass interference, a 34-yard penalty that gave Tampa Bay a first down at the Chiefs' 24-yard line. Gene Steratore, a former NFL referee and CBS's officiating analyst, said during the broadcast that the call had to be made.

Two plays later, Chiefs safety Tyrann Mathieu was called for pass interference on Evans in the end zone even though the pass from Brady did not appear to be catchable. With the ball spotted at the 1-yard line, Brady found Antonio Brown in the end zone on the next play, giving the Bucs a lead they would hold comfortably for the rest of the night. In the second quarter alone, the Chiefs were flagged for 90 penalty yards, the most in one quarter in Super Bowl history and the most in a quarter of any NFL game since Week 1 of the 2018 season.

Cheffers led the officiating crew in three Chiefs games this season. (He was not working with his usual crew Sunday; Super Bowl officiating teams feature the highest-rated officials from the regular season.) His crew called 11 penalties against Kansas City on Sept. 20 vs. the Los Angeles Chargers, 10 on Nov. 22 vs. the Las Vegas Raiders and 11 on Sunday in the Super Bowl. Kansas City averaged 6.6 penalties per game during the regular season; only three teams averaged more.

"Now, the referee that's working our game, Carl Cheffers, he's done a couple of our games this year, so he knows us, we know him. And Bryan, the umpire, we know him - the back judge, all these guys have worked our games and/or have been at our training camps in years past," he said. "I think [Bucs Coach Bruce Arians] would tell you the same thing: By the time you get to this one, they know you, they kind of know your players, and they've watched tape and so on, so they've got a pretty good feel on things. But no, I think they let you play within reason. They're still going to call holdings and do those things, but within reason they'll let you play."

Cheffers's history with the Chiefs goes a little deeper than that. He was the head official during an AFC second-round playoff game between the Chiefs and Pittsburgh Steelers in January 2017. Pittsburgh won, 18-16, after Kansas City had a successful 2-point conversion attempt negated by a holding penalty on tackle Eric Fisher. Kansas City tight end Travis Kelce did not hide his disgust with Cheffers after that game, saying he "shouldn't be able to wear a zebra jersey ever again. He shouldn't even be able to work at [expletive] Foot Locker." Nevertheless, the NFL appointed Cheffers as the referee of Super Bowl LI a few weeks later.

15.5.2. *Final comments on betting*

My bets on the Super Bowl were designed to make profits regardless who of the group of six or some top teams wins. So as shown in figures in this column the strategy was implemented successful. So for the Super Bowl game itself the gain was about +1100 pounds if Tampa Bay won and about +950 pounds if if Kansas City won. Some minor switching from Kansas City bets to Tampa Bay bets was done as the game went greatly in Tampa Bay's favor and the defense shut down Mahomes *et al.* These moves are a judgment call. So the result was about 1000+ plus the 200 bet on Tampa Bay plus 3 1/2 point at 1.88 −1. As explained in our book Ziemba and McLean (2018) the Las Vegas odds are basically correct so the market is weak form efficient. So to win and beat the take, one needs superior handicapping which is not easy or what we suggest in the book and this paper, namely, mean reversion risk arbitrage to adjust the bets as the game progresses. The goal was to bet on A with odds O_a to 1 and later get a bet on B at odds of O_b to 1 so O_a times 0_b is greater than one. Then you have an arbitrage and you repeat this as much as possible. In many games there are three or four switches near the end of the game in the scores so that you can do a lot of this successfully. See examples of 10 years of such successful betting in our book.

Figure 15.10 has the results of the playoffs and the Super Bowl.

15.5.3. *Epilogue*

Some of the future and events and happenings were:

Tom Brady continues to amaze and confound. A religious person might believe he is the second coming. He is in the right place at the right time. Players with sublime physical talent such as Aaron Rodgers (or Jim Brown in an earlier era) don't often get to the top. Brady leads a team rather than carries them, and that is a difference maker.

Brady's departure from the Patriots in 2020 into free agency seemed to reflect both Belichick and Brady wanting Brady to be traded to San Francisco. Belichick apparently was happy to exit Brady (even though he had just won the SuperBowl and was the MVP) for the younger Jimmy Garoppolo (former backup for Brady on the Patriots), who had never won a SuperBowl. Rumor has it that Belichick wanted to trade Brady as early as right after the 2017 SuperBowl where Brady engineered a dramatic comeback from a 28 to 3 deficit in the 3rd quarter against Atlanta and won the MVP that year. We think that Brady wanted to go to the San Francisco

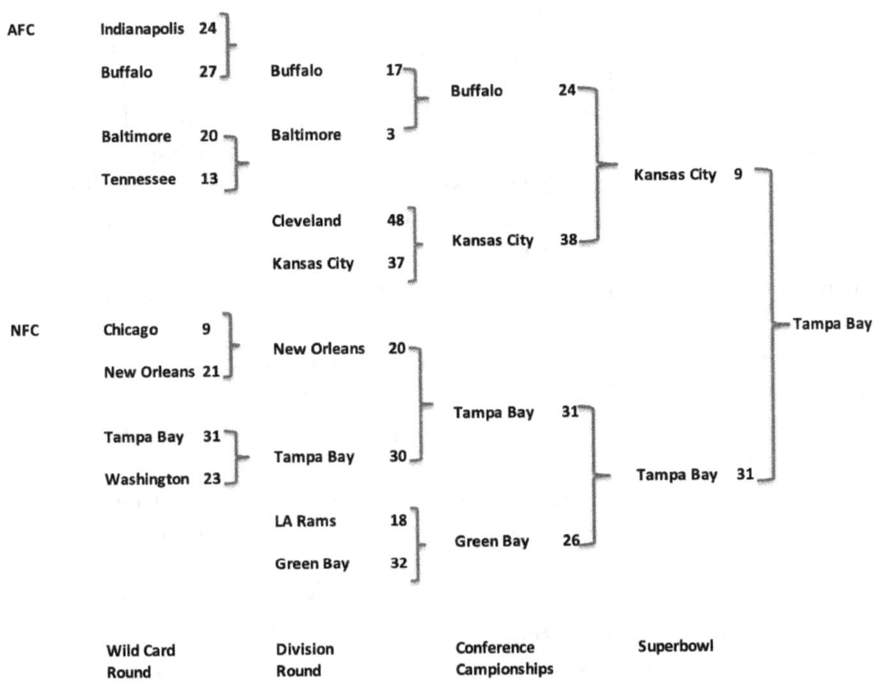

Figure 15.10. Playoff tree, 2021.

Forty-niners as it was close to where he grew up as a child idolizing San Francisco great Joe Montana. However, SF rejected that trade, preferring to stick with the younger Jimmy Garoppolo whose record is so-so over Brady, a seven time SuperBowl winner and four times MVP. Brady was upset and is quoted as saying "You're sticking with that motherf-fer?" quoted in Florio (2021), having been rejected by both Belichick and the Forty-niners. The gainer here is Tampa Bay and the losers are the San Francisco 49ers and the New England Patriots.

Injuries are a big factor in game outcomes. Drew Brees did not play up to his standard in the Division championship, but he was compromised by rib injuries and apparently a separated shoulder. Three of the four starters on Kansas City's offensive line were injured. It is small wonder Mahomes had so many Tampa Bay defensive linemen in his backfield.

Defense wins championships. That axiom is true in all competitive games. It has been commented that the real MVP of Super Bowl LV, along with Brady, was the defensive so-coordinator for Tampa Bay.

Referee's can influence the flow of a game. In the Super Bowl there were critical penalties called on Kansas City. Pass interference calls led to 2 TB touchdowns and another eliminated a Brady interception. In the second quarter alone, the Chiefs were flagged for 90 penalty yards, the most in one quarter in Super Bowl history and the most in a quarter of any NFL game since Week 1 of the 2018 season. The calls were marginal, and gave Tampa Bay a cushion which allowed the defense to take over. In all the Chiefs had 11 penalties for 120 yards. The same referee called 10 penalties on KC in a game against LV during the regular season, a game the Chiefs lost.

Coaching decisions can be confusing. Andy Reid, the KC coach, called several time-outs in the closing minute of the first half, when Tampa Bay had the ball. The saved time helped Tampa Bay score a decisive touchdown just before half-time.

Both Russell Wilson and Aaron Rodgers are unhappy with their coaches. Wilson does not like getting so many sacks and wants better protection. Green Bay with two minutes left in the game did not go for a game-tying TD and two point extra point rather the coach went for a field goal assuming incorrectly that his defense would give them one more chance. This seemed like a very poor decision given that Green Bay has the MVP quarterback. The ball was at the 8 yard line on fourth down and to tie the game all they needed a TD and the two point conversion. All year Rodgers has played under the circumstance of Green Bay using a first-round pick to pick a quarterback to possibly replace Rodgers in the future. But a top receiver or good lineman might've been the better choice.

We doubt Wilson or Rodgers will be traded but changes likely will be made. Also most likely Ben Roethlisberger will remain quarterback of the Pittsburgh Steelers with a restructured contract.

The Houston Oilers are falling apart after another losing season. Quarterback DeSean Watson wants to be traded. Three-time defensive player of the year J.J. Watt has asked for his release and he has joined the Arizona Cardinals for $31 million over two years, a high salary for a lineman, but he's a star. The coach and general manager were fired largely because of the turmoil and poor performance. The David Johnson trade to move DeAndre Hopkins to Arizona favored Arizona much more.

32 selections	102.9%		Back all	Lay all		96.9%
Kansas City Chiefs	6.4 £301	6.6 £121	6.8 £63	7 £290	7.2 £113	7.4 £44
Tampa Bay Buccaneers	10.5 £139	11 £14	11.5 £15	12 £392	12.5 £12	14 £5
Green Bay Packers	14 £29	14.5 £9	15 £5	15.5 £9	16 £70	17.5 £18
Buffalo Bills	12 £25	15.5 £82	16 £23	16.5 £8	17 £2	17.5 £15
Los Angeles Rams	14.5 £7	15.5 £13	16 £25	16.5 £5	17 £27	17.5 £19
San Francisco 49ers	17 £110	17.5 £6	18 £12	18.5 £42	19 £2	19.5 £2
Baltimore Ravens	15.5 £2	18 £5	18.5 £22	19 £182	19.5 £2	20 £3
New Orleans Saints	26 £2	27 £13	28 £20	29 £10	30 £21	32 £2
Cleveland Browns	23 £12	24 £97	25 £28	26 £42	27 £105	28 £2
Indianapolis Colts	22 £15	23 £22	24 £27	25 £122	26 £40	27 £13
Miami Dolphins	26 £9	28 £20	29 £18	30 £2	32 £13	34 £25
Seattle Seahawks	27 £113	28 £11	29 £14	30 £374	40 £20	55 £2
Dallas Cowboys	30 £124	34 £17	38 £16	40 £20	42 £4	46 £20
Tennessee Titans	38 £6	40 £90	42 £13	44 £96	46 £34	60 £15
Los Angeles Chargers	34 £41	40 £9	42 £13	44 £13	48 £9	65 £31
New England Patriots	40 £2	44 £7	46 £9	50 £2	55 £5	60 £3
Pittsburgh Steelers	4 £4	40 £77	44 £9	48 £6	50 £3	55 £59
Arizona Cardinals	4 £4	40 £49	46 £25	48 £20	50 £2	55 £11
Washington Football Team	4 £4	50 £31	55 £11	75 £6	85 £3	150 £2
Minnesota Vikings	55 £2	60 £6	65 £17	70 £6	100 £5	160 £2
Chicago Bears	65 £5	70 £10	75 £9	85 £50	95 £5	100 £30

Figure 15.11. The Betfair odds for the 2022 Super Bowl as of February 22, 2021.

Carson Wentz, who had a poor season with 16 TDs and 15 interceptions was traded as he wanted to be. That was to Indianapolis to replace the retired Philip Rivers for minor compensation, namely a 2021 third round pick plus a 2022 second round pick that could be upgraded to a first-round pick if Wentz played a lot. Wentz is now reunited with Frank Reich, the former Eagles offensive coordinator. Maybe he can get Wentz back to his 2017 form where he had 33 TDs and seven interceptions and was in the MVP running.

Jared Goff with his massive salary was traded by the LA Rams along with some draft picks in exchange for the Detroit Lions quarterback Matthew Stafford. Goff is 26, Stafford is 33. Both are solid but can either win a Super Bowl? To us that seems unlikely.

16 selections	126.6%		Back all	Lay all	
Kansas City Chiefs	1.01 £100	3.55 £49	3.6 £25	4 £99	4.5 £50
Buffalo Bills	1.01 £100	5.9 £25	6 £12		
Baltimore Ravens	1.01 £100	7.2 £20	8 £8		
Cleveland Browns	1.01 £100	10 £6	12.5 £11		
Tennessee Titans	1.01 £100	13.5 £10	16 £5	26 £2	
Miami Dolphins	1.01 £100	12 £7	13.5 £10		
Pittsburgh Steelers	1.01 £100	14.5 £10	15 £6		
Indianapolis Colts		1.01 £100	13.5 £51	18 £30	
Los Angeles Chargers		1.01 £100	16.5 £10	38 £10	40 £2
New England Patriots	1.01 £100	16 £6	19.5 £10		
Las Vegas Raiders	1.01 £100	24 £4	32 £10		
Houston Texans	1.01 £100	38 £10	40 £2	95 £2	
Denver Broncos		1.01 £100	10 £2	36 £8	
New York Jets	1.01 £100	44 £10	50 £2	100 £2	
Jacksonville Jaguars		1.01 £100	32 £3	65 £8	70 £2
Cincinnati Bengals	1.01 £100	44 £10	50 £2	80 £2	100 £2

Figure 15.12. The Betfair odds for the 2022 AFC Championship as of February 22, 2021.

The Patriots had quarterback troubles this year and had a losing year, their first in a long time, as Cam Newton had many more interceptions than TDs. He did run well though.

Some big contracts need to be settled such as Dak Prescott with the Dallas Cowboys. That's complicated since Dak, after a good season, got a season ending injury.

The Betfair odds for the 2022 Super Bowl and AFC and NFC Championships are in Figures 15.11–15.13. Not surprisingly the Super Bowl contestants of 2021 are the favored teams for 2022, namely the Kansas City and Tampa Bay. Kansas City is favored but historically the Super Bowl loser does not do well after that loss. Green Bay and Buffalo follow next, then the LA Rams responding to the new quarterback. This seems over bet. San Francisco, Baltimore, New Orleans and Cleveland follow as the top teams. So more or less the odds follow the previous year's and similarly in the AFC and NFC odds.

16 selections	134.8%		Back all	Lay all	
Tampa Bay Buccaneers	**1.01** £100	**5** £20	**5.4** £28	**7** £20	**10** £2
Green Bay Packers		**1.01** £100	**5.5** £20	**5.9** £3	
Los Angeles Rams	**1.01** £100	**6.8** £21	**7** £12		
San Francisco 49ers	**1.01** £100	**7.2** £20	**8** £11	**10** £32	
New Orleans Saints	**1.01** £100	**8.8** £16	**9** £9		
Seattle Seahawks	**1.01** £100	**9.2** £15	**10** £9		
Dallas Cowboys	**1.01** £100	**14.5** £10	**16** £5	**25** £10	
Minnesota Vikings	**1.01** £100	**19.5** £10	**20** £4		
Arizona Cardinals	**1.01** £100	**16** £5	**20** £10		
Carolina Panthers	**1.01** £100	**22** £10	**24** £4		
Philadelphia Eagles		**1.01** £100	**12** £2		
Atlanta Falcons	**1.01** £100	**20** £5	**22** £10		
Chicago Bears	**1.01** £100	**22** £4	**25** £10		
New York Giants	**1.01** £100	**30** £3	**34** £10		
Washington Football Team		**1.01** £100	**12** £2	**48** £20	**50** £2
Detroit Lions	**1.01** £100	**50** £2	**60** £10		

Figure 15.13. The Betfair odds for the 2022 NFC Championship as of February 22, 2021.

15.5.4. *Appendix: The COVID-19 and injury effects*

The list of infections by team:

Arizona: The Cardinals largely avoided major disruptions. Veteran receiver Larry Fitzgerald missed a loss to New England while on the COVID-19 list.

Atlanta: Little impact. The team cancelled practice and held virtual meetings three times because of virus protocols. Atlanta won all three contests following its shutdowns. A handful of players spent time on the COVID-19 list, most notably first-round pick cornerback A.J. Terrell and D.E. Dante Fowler Jr. Baltimore An outbreak among the Ravens and staff followed an overtime loss to Tennessee and decimated Baltimore's roster heading into a pivotal Thanksgiving rematch with the Steelers.

Buffalo: The Bills had three games rescheduled. Tight end Tommy Sweeney tested positive and missed the remainder of the season.

Carolina: Some half-dozen players were on the COVID-19 list, notably CB Rasul Douglas for two games. The Panthers twice have been in intense protocol.

Chicago: Nose tackle Eddie Goldman opted out of the season, damaging the inside defence.

Cincinatti: Assistant coaches Nick Eason (defensive line), Steven Jackson (cornerbacks), Al Golden (linebackers), Bob Bicknell (receivers) and Mark Duffner (defensive assistant) missed games. Regular cornerbacks Trae Waynes and Mackensie Alexander, and defensive end Margus Hunt have been on the list. Cincinnati shut down its practice facility midweek in early November after two players tested positive.

Cleveland: The Browns spent the better part of the past month dealing with facility shutdowns, virtual meetings and practices being moved or cancelled on a nearly daily basis. They've placed several players, including star D.E. Myles Garrett, on the COVID-19 list; he missed two games. The Browns also were without starting linebacker Sione Takitaki and fullback Andy Janovich because of positive cases.

Dallas: QB Andy Dalton's positive test forced him to missed two straight games, after he had been sidelined for one with a concussion.

Denver: Eight players have gone on the reserve/COVID-19 list, three assistant coaches have been infected defensive co-ordinator Ed Donatell missed all of November and was hospitalized at one point with respiratory complications. Denver essentially lost its bye week because of New England's issues, and the Broncos lost to the Saints without any quarterbacks.

Detroit: The Lions practiced without Matthew Stafford when they played at Minnesota in early November because the quarterback was deemed a close COVID-19 contact.

Green Bay: Leading to a November 5 game at San Francisco, rookie RB A.J. Dillon tested positive and fellow running back Jamaal Williams also was placed on the COVID-19 list as a close contact.

Houston: A handful of players have missed time because of the virus. The Texans played at Jacksonville without linebackers Whitney Mercilus, Jacob Martin and Dylan Cole after Martin tested positive. Offensive tackle Max Scharping tested positive for the virus during the team's bye week, forcing the closure of the facility, and he missed one game.

Indianapolis: D.E. Denico Autry, who leads Indy with six sacks, went on the COVID-19 list two weeks ago. Last week, 2019 Pro Bowl D.T. DeForest Buckner and Rookie R.B. Jonathan Taylor joined Autry on the list.

Jacksonville: With the most players (12) on the COVID-19 list to open training camp, the Jaguars have done better than others since. R.B. Ryquell Armstead was placed on the list twice, was hospitalized twice and dealt with respiratory issues. Armstead is expected to make a full recovery.

Kansas City: The Chiefs have been remarkably clear of COVID-19 positives. They lost W.R. Mecole Hardman for a game in Week 10. L.T. Eric Fisher and R.T. Mitchell Schwartz tested positive along with backup O.L. Martinas Rankin, but Fisher was cleared to return.

LA Chargers: One of the teams not to have a player opt out for the season, and no player went on the COVID-19 list until late October.

LA Rams: Only one outbreak, with three practice squad players affected during the season.

Las Vegas: Players, coaches and the organization have been fined more than $1.2 million and docked a sixth-round pick for COVID-19 violations. The team practiced the entire week before the Tampa Bay game without the starting offensive line after tackle Trent Brown tested positive. The other four linemen returned the morning of the game and the Raiders lost 45–20. Defensive lineman Clelin Ferrell tested positive leading up to the Kansas City game.

Miami: Several key assistants missed consecutive games: outside linebackers coach Austin Clark, quarterbacks coach Robby Brown, defensive line coach Marion Hobby and offensive quality control coach Kolby Smith. Defensive backs coach Gerald Alexander missed one match. Only one starter has missed playing time due to the virus: D.T. Christian Wilkins sat out two games.

Minnesota: Receiver Adam Thielen was the first player of significance to miss a game. The biggest impact of the virus might have come in July when new nose tackle Michael Pierce opted out of the season due to asthma-related health concerns.

New England: The Patriots' Week 4 matchup against the Chiefs was postponed a day after QB Cam Newton tested positive. New England's game the following week against Denver was twice postponed following positive tests by several players, including star cornerback Stephon Gilmore. They had several key players who opted out.

New Orleans: The organization was fined $500,000 and stripped of a seventh-round draft pick for repeated protocol violations. Individual players missed games intermittently, most notably receiver Emmanuel Sanders and left tackle Terron Armstead. Coach Sean Payton contracted the virus in the off-season.

NY Giants: LG Will Hernandez tested positive and he missed two games. All O-linemen but RG Kevin Zeitler had to isolate because of close contact. The regulars came back without missing any games. Kicker Graham Gano tested positive and was sidelined for a game.

NY Jets: Top LB C.J. Mosley opted out. Only tight end Ross Travis, on the practice squad at the time, has been on the list during the regular season. They had four players on it during training camp, rookie CB Bryce Hall, now a starter, the only one still with the team.

Philadelphia: The Eagles haven't had any starters miss games because of COVID-19, but coach Doug Pederson had it in training camp.

Pittsburgh: The Steelers recently sent to the COVID-19 list a group that includes tight end Vance McDonald and running back James Conner. A number of their games were rescheduled.

Seattle: Seattle was the only NFL team with no players on the COVID-19 list until Saturday, when injured defensive lineman Bryan Mone went on it.

San Francisco: Receivers Kendrick Bourne and Brandon Aiyuk and left tackle Trent Williams were idle for a loss to Green Bay; several players then were placed on the COVID-19 list after defensive lineman Arik Armstead tested positive.

Tampa Bay: Only one starter has spent time on the COVID-19 list, DL William Gholston, and he didn't miss a game. Special teams player Jaydon Mickens missed a game.

Tennessee: The Titans had the NFL's first outbreak that forced the first postponement and then rescheduling of a game this season. Their outbreak affected 24 players and personnel and postponed a second game against Buffalo.

Washington: Only one player, already on IR, has tested positive for COVID-19. The scheduling change from other disruptions saw Washington's game at Pittsburgh shifted from Sunday to Monday.

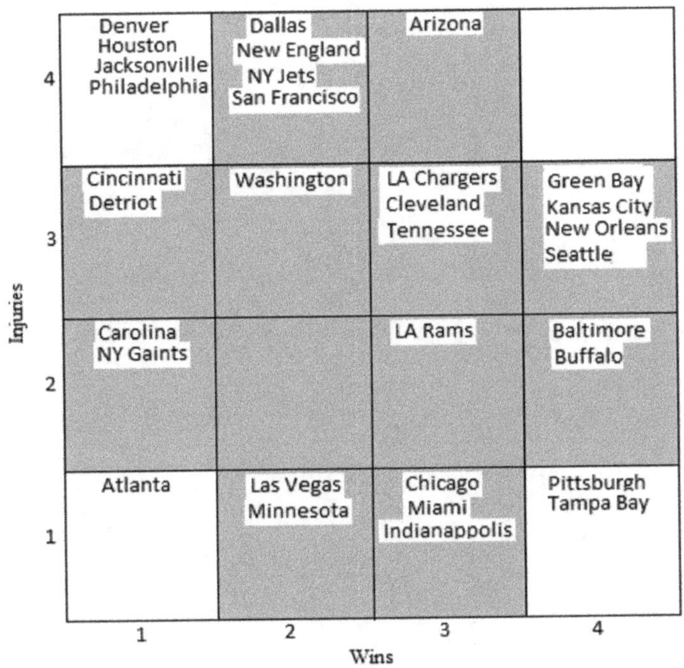

Figure 15.14. Wins vs. injuries: NFL 2020.

Injuries: The most overlooked factor and key to winning is staying healthy. If a team has a rash of injuries, it is likely that team is in trouble. Certainly injury to key/irreplaceable players like a quarterback is devastating. However, losing players on the offensive or defensive line will affect team success. MacLean and Ziemba (2019) considered team composition and found quality defensive ends were a significant factor in the chance of winning. Without considering positions, the number of injuries in 2020 is related to the number of wins in Figure 15.14. The axes are divided into quartiles.

It could be argued that some teams (Baltimore, Cleveland, New England, Las Vegas) were adversely affected by the virus. The picture on injuries shows some high preforming teams with injury issues (GB, KC, NO). Tampa Bay and Pittsburgh looked to be in good shape heading to the playoffs. Another COVID-19 factor was the loss of players who took the offer of lower salary and sat out the year This affected the New England Patriots.

Chapter 16

Team Composition: Are the Best Players on the Best Teams?

Leonard C. MacLean and William T. Ziemba

We investigate whether or not the best players are on the best teams. We isolate those players who contribute the most to success and find that they are not necessarily the best players. Also having several good players is usually preferable to having one superstar. We use player ranking data from *Sports Illustrated* and from NFL players' rankings. Defensive players are often more important than widely believed.

16.1. Introduction

In team sports the individual players occupy defined positions in the field of play. If a team has superior players at every position or even most positions then success is likely. There are team dynasties which attest to this fact – the Montreal Canadiens in ice hockey, the New York Yankees in baseball, the Boston Celtics and Los Angeles Lakers in basketball, and the Green Bay Packers, the San Francisco 49ers, Dallas Cowboys and New England Patriots in different eras in football were all dominant over a period of time. We are focusing on football and note that the Pittsburgh Steelers, San Francisco 49ers, Dallas Cowboys and New England Patriots have all achieved periods of dominance. It also true that the players "Hall of Fame" for each of the major North American sports is crowded with players from these legendary teams. At the same time there are teams with modest success which have great players at their designated position. The running back Jim Brown is, in many minds, the greatest football player ever, but had only a single championship. The great Ted Williams never played on a championship team. Wilt Chamberlain won two championships but that didn't reflect his dominance in basketball. Even Bobby Orr only won 2 Stanley cups. Confounding the team versus individual accomplishment is the impact of coaching and game strategy on team results.

We consider the great player-great team connection in NFL football. For individual players we take the rating determined by NFL players and/or expert rankers. Team rating is defined by the win percentage in games. We analyze the 2017 NFL season, with the player ratings before the season began and the win percentage at the end of the season. Many events during the course of the season are critical to success. The loss of a key player (Aaron Rodgers), the unanticipated emergence of a star (Carson Wentz) do not factor into preseason ratings, but have a major impact on team success.

16.2. Top Ranked Players

16.2.1. *Number of top 400 players by team in 2017 by Sports Illustrated*

Sports Illustrated publishes a ranking of the top 400 NFL players at the start of each season, compiled by Andy Benoit (2017). The ranking is based on player comparisons using game films of games from the previous season. The stated criterion is "Does player A do his job better than player B?" There are algorithms for generating a ranking of players from pairwise comparisons (Negahban and Shah, 2012). The SI rankings are subjective rather than algorithm based. We consider the distribution of the "Top 400" players by team. There are 53 active players on a team roster, so we split the ranks into groups of 50. Under complete parity each team would expect to have a player in each rank group. The top players are well distributed across teams, but some teams are "stacked". Seattle had 6 top 50 players and Atlanta, Dallas and Pittsburgh have 4. The distribution of top players at the beginning of the 2017 season is in Table 16.1.

The notation for rank group is as follows: G1:1–50; G2:51–100; G3:101–150; G4:151–200; G5:201–250; G6:251–300; G7:301–350; G8:351–400.

A preliminary look at the team composition and team success is in Table 16.2. There is support for an association between team success and the number of top 400 players. The teams with the most top players (green) generally have high win percentages, and teams with fewer top players (red) have low win percentages. However, the correlation is only 0.392, so top players only explain 15% of the variation in win percentage.

Table 16.1. Top 400 by team.

Team	G1	G2	G3	G4	G5	G6	G7	G8
Arizona Cardinals	3	0	2	1	2	0	2	1
Atlanta Falcons	4	2	3	2	2	2	0	1
Baltimore Ravens	1	2	4	0	0	2	2	1
Buffalo Bills	0	1	0	3	1	2	4	0
Carolina Panthers	2	3	0	1	1	4	3	2
Chicago Bears	0	1	1	0	4	1	0	1
Cincinnati Bengals	1	1	1	2	1	2	1	2
Cleveland Browns	1	0	2	1	2	1	1	1
Dallas Cowboys	4	4	0	0	3	0	1	2
Denver Broncos	2	2	2	2	0	2	2	3
Detroit Lions	0	1	2	3	1	4	3	2
Green Bay Packers	1	3	2	3	2	1	0	0
Houston Texans	2	1	0	2	0	1	3	2
Indianapolis Colts	1	1	1	0	1	1	1	4
Jacksonville Jaguars	1	2	0	3	1	1	0	0
Kansas City Chiefs	3	2	0	4	2	3	2	3
Los Angeles Chargers	1	3	1	2	1	0	2	1
Los Angeles Rams	1	2	3	0	1	0	1	1
Miami Dolphins	0	2	2	3	1	1	3	0
Minnesota Vikings	1	2	1	3	2	1	0	1
New England Patriots	3	1	5	1	1	3	5	1
New Orleans Saints	1	0	1	2	3	2	1	2
New York Giants	1	3	3	3	1	0	1	1
New York Jets	0	2	1	0	0	0	1	1
Oakland Raiders	1	1	4	1	3	2	0	1
Philadelphia Eagles	1	3	2	0	2	1	1	4
Pittsburgh Steelers	4	2	2	2	2	0	2	0
San Francisco 49ers	0	0	0	0	2	4	1	4
Seattle Seahawks	6	1	2	2	0	0	0	1
Tampa Bay Buccaneers	1	1	1	2	5	3	3	0
Tennessee Titans	1	0	0	1	2	3	3	4
Washington Redskins	2	1	2	1	1	2	0	0

16.2.2. *NFL top 100*

There are other rankings of NFL players. The NFL top 100 lists the top one hundred players as chosen by fellow NFL players. The rankings are based on an off-season poll organized by the NFL, where players vote on their peers based on their projected performance for the next NFL season. Only players that will be active in the next season are eligible for consideration. A strong case can be made that the best rating of players comes from other players. The tradition of experts and sports reporters ranking teams and players

Table 16.2. SI and win % (2017).

Team	Win PCT	Number
Arizona	0.5000	11
Atlanta	0.6250	16
Baltimore	0.5620	12
Buffalo	0.5620	11
Carolina	0.6880	16
Chicago	0.3120	8
Cincinnati	0.4380	11
Cleveland	0.0322	9
Dallas	0.5620	14
Denver	0.3120	15
Detroit	0.5620	16
Green Bay	0.4380	12
Houston	0.2500	11
Indianapolis	0.2500	10
Jacksonville	0.6250	8
Kansas City	0.6250	19
LA Chargers	0.5620	11
LA Rams	0.6880	9
Miami	0.3750	12
Minnesota	0.8120	11
New England	0.8120	20
New Orleans	0.6880	12
NY Giants	0.1880	13
NY Jets	0.3120	5
Oakland	0.3750	13
Philadelphia	0.8120	14
Pittsburgh	0.8120	14
San Francisco	0.3750	11
Seattle	0.5620	12
Tampa Bay	0.3120	16
Tennessee	0.5620	14
Washington	0.4380	9

still rules the day. For comparison the top 100 from Sports Illustrated and the NFL are shown in Table 16.3.

The top 100 from the NFL ranking is split into deciles and the number of players in each decile by team is in Table 16.4. Teams with higher numbers are highlighted.

The connection of top 100 players to team winning percentage is in Table 16.5. The correlation is 0.292, reduced from the top 400 result as would be expected with fewer players per team. Again, the teams with more top 100 players (green) have high win percentages and the teams with less top 100 players (red) have low win percentages.

Table 16.3. Top 100 NFL players in 2017 by Sports Illustrated and NFL players.

SI				NFL			
1	Tom Brady	51	Ndamukong Suh	1	Tom Brady	51	Andrew Luck
2	J.J. Watt	52	LeSean McCoy	2	Von Miller	52	Gerald McCoy
3	Von Miller	53	Marcus Peters	3	Julio Jones	53	Amari Cooper
4	Luke Kuechly	54	Telvin Smith	4	Antonio Brown	54	Janoris Jenkins
5	Le'Veon Bell	55	Geno Atkins	5	Khalil Mack	55	Ndamukong Suh
6	Aaron Rodgers	56	Ezekiel Elliott	6	Aaron Rodgers	56	Cliff Avril
7	Rob Gronkowski	57	Olivier Vernon	7	Ezekiel Elliott	57	Jameis Winston
8	Khalil Mack	58	Mike Daniels	8	Odell Beckham Jr.	58	Zack Martin
9	Julio Jones	59	Kyle Long	9	Le'Veon Bell	59	Josh Norman
10	Antonio Brown	60	A.J. Bouye	10	Matt Ryan	60	Dez Bryant
11	Tyron Smith	61	Ryan Shazier	11	Derek Carr	61	T.Y. Hilton
12	Earl Thomas	62	Maurkice Pouncey	12	David Johnson	62	Cameron Wake
13	Aaron Donald	63	David Bakhtiari	13	Eric Berry	63	Chris Harris Jr.
14	Patrick Peterson	64	Whitney Mercilus	14	Dak Prescott	64	Casey Hayward
15	David Johnson	65	Thomas Davis	15	Aaron Donald	65	Jordan Reed
16	Ben Roethlisberger	66	Kelechi Osemele	16	Drew Brees	66	Xavier Rhodes
17	Michael Bennett	67	Jason Verrett	17	AJ Green	67	Greg Olsen
18	Travis Frederick	68	Robert Quinn	18	Tyron Smith	68	Geno Atkins
19	Bobby Wagner	69	Marshal Yanda	19	Patrick Peterson	69	Jay Ajayi
20	Joey Bosa	70	Mike Evans	20	Luke Kuechly	70	Kirk Cousins
21	Travis Kelce	71	Ryan Kalil	21	Richard Sherman	71	Julian Edelman
22	Chris Harris	72	Jimmy Graham	22	Ben Roethlisberger	72	Taylor Lewan
23	Odell Beckham Jr.	73	Byron Jones	23	Rob Gronkowski	73	Philip Rivers
24	Zack Martin	74	Leonard Williams	24	Russell Wilson	74	Harrison Smith
25	Trent Williams	75	Dez Bryant	25	Joe Thomas	75	Delanie Walker
26	Fletcher Cox	76	Aqib Talib	26	Travis Kelce	76	Justin Houston
27	Eric Berry	77	Kawann Short	27	LeSean McCoy	77	Ha Ha Clinton-Dix
28	Matt Ryan	78	T.J. Ward	28	Landon Collins	78	Brian Orakpo
29	Sean Lee	79	Jason Witten	29	Mike Evans	79	Sean Lee
30	Andrew Luck	80	Mike Pouncey	30	Earl Thomas	80	LeGarrette Blount
31	K.J. Wright	81	Josh Norman	31	Matthew Stafford	81	Alex Smith
32	Alex Mack	82	Andrew Whitworth	32	Marcus Peters	82	Clay Matthews
33	A.J. Green	83	Mitchell Schwartz	33	DeMarco Murray	83	Calais Campbell
34	Jordan Reed	84	Lane Johnson	34	Kam Chancellor	84	Mike Daniels
35	Calais Campbell	85	Terrell Suggs	35	JJ Watt	85	Chandler Jones
36	Devin McCourty	86	Dont'a Hightower	36	Tyreek Hill	86	Jurrell Casey
37	Drew Brees	87	Xavier Rhodes	37	Aqib Talib	87	Travis Frederick
38	Joe Thomas	88	Philip Rivers	38	Fletcher Cox	88	Doug Baldwin
39	Justin Houston	89	Alshon Jeffery	39	Bobby Wagner	89	Thomas Davis
40	Harrison Smith	90	Janoris Jenkins	40	Vic Beasley	90	Malcolm Jenkins
41	Jurrell Casey	91	Tevin Coleman	41	Devonta Freeman	91	Lorenzo Alexander
42	Greg Olsen	92	Devonta Freeman	42	Jarvis Landry	92	Everson Griffen
43	Kam Chancellor	93	Muhammad Wilkerson	43	Marshal Yanda	93	Brandon Graham
44	Desmond Trufant	94	Damon Harrison	44	Cam Newton	94	Dont'a Hightower
45	Tyrann Mathieu	95	Melvin Ingram	45	Larry Fitzgerald	95	Kelechi Osemele
46	Cliff Avril	96	Linval Joseph	46	Michael Bennett	96	Damon Harrison
47	Brandon Williams	97	Jordy Nelson	47	Trent Williams	97	David DeCastro
48	Jadeveon Clowney	98	Brandon Graham	48	Jordy Nelson	98	Adrian Peterson
49	Gerald McCoy	99	Ziggy Ansah	49	Jadeveon Clowney	99	Malcolm Butler
50	David DeCastro	100	Vontae Davis	50	Marcus Mariota	100	Joey Bosa

16.2.3. *Comparison of SI and NFL rankings*

How does the top 100 from Sports Illustrated compare to that provided by the NFL players? The players on both lists are shown in Table 16.6. About two-thirds of the top 100 are on both lists. However, the rankings are quite mixed. The correlation between ranks is only 0.456, so there is much disagreement. Some notable examples of different rankings are Russell Wilson in Seattle and J. J. Watts in Houston.

Table 16.4. NFL top 100 by decile and team.

Team	**D1**	**D2**	**D3**	**D4**	**D5**	**D6**	**GD7**	**D8**	**D9**	**D10**	**All**
Arizona Cardinals	0	2	0	0	1	0	0	0	1	0	4
Atlanta Falcons	2	0	0	1	1	0	0	0	0	0	4
Baltimore Ravens	0	0	0	0	1	0	0	0	0	0	1
Buffalo Bills	0	0	1	0	0	0	0	0	0	1	2
Carolina Panthers	0	1	0	0	1	0	1	0	1	0	4
Chicago Bears	0	0	0	0	0	0	0	0	0	0	0
Cincinnati Bengals	0	1	0	0	0	0	1	0	0	0	2
Cleveland Browns	0	0	1	0	0	0	0	0	0	0	1
Dallas Cowboys	**1**	**2**	**0**	**0**	**0**	**2**	**0**	**1**	**1**	**0**	**7**
Denver Broncos	1	0	0	1	0	0	1	0	0	0	3
Detroit Lions	0	0	0	1	0	0	0	0	0	0	1
Green Bay Packers	1	0	0	0	1	0	0	1	2	0	5
Houston Texans	0	0	0	1	1	0	0	0	0	0	2
Indianapolis Colts	0	0	0	0	0	1	1	0	0	0	2
Jacksonville Jaguars	0	0	0	0	0	0	0	0	1	0	1
Kansas City Chiefs	**0**	**1**	**1**	**2**	**0**	**0**	**0**	**1**	**1**	**0**	**6**
Los Angeles Chargers	0	0	0	0	0	0	1	1	0	1	3
Los Angeles Rams	0	1	0	0	0	0	0	0	0	0	1
Miami Dolphins	0	0	0	0	1	1	2	0	0	0	4
Minnesota Vikings	0	0	0	0	0	0	1	1	0	1	3
New England Patriots	**1**	**0**	**1**	**0**	**0**	**0**	**0**	**2**	**0**	**2**	**6**
New Orleans Saints	0	1	0	0	0	0	0	0	0	1	2
New York Giants	1	0	1	0	0	1	0	0	0	1	4
New York Jets	0	0	0	0	0	0	0	0	0	0	0
Oakland Raiders	1	1	0	0	0	1	0	0	0	1	4
Philadelphia Eagles	0	0	0	1	0	0	0	0	1	1	3
Pittsburgh Steelers	2	0	1	0	0	0	0	0	0	1	4
San Francisco 49ers	0	0	0	0	0	0	0	0	0	0	0
Seattle Seahawks	**0**	**0**	**3**	**2**	**1**	**1**	**0**	**0**	**1**	**0**	**8**
Tampa Bay Buccaneers	0	0	1	0	0	2	0	0	0	0	3
Tennessee Titans	**0**	**0**	**0**	**1**	**1**	**0**	**0**	**3**	**1**	**0**	**6**
Washington Redskins	0	0	0	0	1	1	2	0	0	0	4

16.3. Modeling the Dependence of Team Win Percentage on Top Players

We would expect that having elite players would translate into better team performance. However, the correlations between team win percentage and number of top players is rather low. Of course the player rankings are from performance in prior seasons, not 2017. So this is an attempt to anticipate performance based on team composition at the start of the 2017 season.

Table 16.5. Number of top 100 NFL players and win %.

Team	Win PCT	Number
Arizona	0.5000	4
Atlanta	0.6250	4
Baltimore	0.5620	1
Buffalo	0.5620	2
Carolina	0.6880	4
Chicago	0.3120	0
Cincinnati	0.4380	2
Cleveland	0.0322	1
Dallas	0.5620	7
Denver	0.3120	3
Detroit	0.5620	1
Green Bay	0.4380	5
Houston	0.2500	2
Indianapolis	0.2500	2
Jacksonville	0.6250	1
Kansas City	0.6250	6
LA Chargers	0.5620	3
LA Rams	0.6880	1
Miami	0.3750	4
Minnesota	0.8120	3
New England	0.8120	6
New Orleans	0.6880	2
NY Giants	0.1880	4
NY Jets	0.3120	4
Oakland	0.3750	0
Philadelphia	0.8120	3
Pittsburgh	0.8120	4
San Francisco	0.3750	0
Seattle	0.5620	8
Tampa Bay	0.3120	3
Tennessee	0.5620	6
Washington	0.4380	4

Team composition is much more complex than a simple count of top players, but we explore the relationship in more detail.

16.3.1. *Number of top players from Sports Illustrated*

If we consider the number of top players, without taking into account player position, the relationship between team win percentage and team top players can be analyzed. Consider the breakdown of SI's top 400. Let

Table 16.6. Comparison of rankings.

SI		NFL		SI		NFL	
13	Aaron Donald	15	Aaron Donald	9	Julio Jones	3	Julio Jones
6	Aaron Rodgers	6	Aaron Rodgers	41	Jurrell Casey	86	Jurrell Casey
30	Andrew Luck	51	Andrew Luck	39	Justin Houston	76	Justin Houston
10	Antonio Brown	4	Antonio Brown	43	Kam Chancellor	34	Kam Chancellor
76	Aqib Talib	37	Aqib Talib	66	Kelechi Osemele	95	Kelechi Osemele
16	Ben Roethlisberger	22	Ben Roethlisberger	8	Khalil Mack	5	Khalil Mack
19	Bobby Wagner	39	Bobby Wagner	5	Le'Veon Bell	70	Kirk Cousins
98	Brandon Graham	93	Brandon Graham	74	Leonard Williams	9	Le'Veon Bell
35	Calais Campbell	83	Calais Campbell	52	LeSean McCoy	27	LeSean McCoy
22	Chris Harris	63	Chris Harris Jr.	4	Luke Kuechly	20	Luke Kuechly
46	Cliff Avril	56	Cliff Avril	53	Marcus Peters	32	Marcus Peters
94	Damon Harrison	96	Damon Harrison	69	Marshal Yanda	43	Marshal Yanda
15	David Johnson	12	David Johnson	28	Matt Ryan	10	Matt Ryan
92	Devonta Freeman	41	Devonta Freeman	17	Michael Bennett	46	Michael Bennett
75	Dez Bryant	60	Dez Bryant	58	Mike Daniels	84	Mike Daniels
86	Dont'a Hightower	94	Dont'a Hightower	70	Mike Evans	29	Mike Evans
37	Drew Brees	16	Drew Brees	51	Ndamukong Suh	55	Ndamukong Suh
12	Earl Thomas	30	Earl Thomas	23	Odell Beckham Jr.	8	Odell Beckham Jr.
27	Eric Berry	13	Eric Berry	14	Patrick Peterson	19	Patrick Peterson
56	Ezekiel Elliott	7	Ezekiel Elliott	88	Philip Rivers	73	Philip Rivers
26	Fletcher Cox	38	Fletcher Cox	7	Rob Gronkowski	23	Rob Gronkowski
55	Geno Atkins	68	Geno Atkins	68	Robert Quinn	24	Russell Wilson
49	Gerald McCoy	52	Gerald McCoy	29	Sean Lee	79	Sean Lee
42	Greg Olsen	67	Greg Olsen	65	Thomas Davis	89	Thomas Davis
40	Harrison Smith	74	Harrison Smith	1	Tom Brady	1	Tom Brady
48	Jadeveon Clowney	49	Jadeveon Clowney	18	Travis Frederick	87	Travis Frederick
90	Janoris Jenkins	54	Janoris Jenkins	21	Travis Kelce	26	Travis Kelce
38	Joe Thomas	25	Joe Thomas	25	Trent Williams	47	Trent Williams
20	Joey Bosa	100	Joey Bosa	11	Tyron Smith	18	Tyron Smith
34	Jordan Reed	65	Jordan Reed	3	Von Miller	2	Von Miller
97	Jordy Nelson	48	Jordy Nelson	87	Xavier Rhodes	66	Xavier Rhodes
81	Josh Norman	59	Josh Norman	24	Zack Martin	58	Zack Martin

T_1 = number of top 50 players at the start of 2017
T_2 = number of top 100 players at the start of 2017
T_3 = number of top 150 players at the start of 2017
T_4 = number of top 200 players at the start of 2017
T_5 = number of top 250 players at the start of 2017
T_6 = number of top 300 players at the start of 2017
T_7 = number of top 350 players at the start of 2017
T_8 = number of top 400 players at the start of 2017.

So $T_j, j = 1, \ldots, 8$ captures the accumulation of top players in descending rank.

With P = team win fraction in 2017, let

$$Y = ln\left(\frac{P}{1-P}\right).$$

Y is the logarithm of the odds ratio and is called the logit. The logit linearizes the usual Bradley-Terry (1952) model for probability.

Table 16.7. Fitted logistic model for win %.

Variable	R^2	β_1	t	P
T_1	10.41	0.045	1.87	0.072
T_2	15.03	0.041	2.30	0.028
T_3	11.72	0.028	2.00	0.055
T_4	12.20	0.026	2.04	0.050
T_5	11.94	0.025	2.02	0.053
T_6	14.94	0.028	2.30	0.028
T_7	15.66	0.025	2.36	0.025
T_8	15.38	0.025	2.33	0.026

The model $Y = \beta_0 + \beta_1 T_j + \varepsilon$ is equivalent to

$$P = \frac{e^{\beta_0+\beta_1 T_j+\varepsilon}}{1+e^{\beta_0+\beta_1 T_j+\varepsilon}}.$$

Then the relationships between win percentage and number of top players are given in Table 16.7.

The effect of top ranked players on performance is significant, but rather small. We previously noted that the top 400 accounted for around 15% of the variation in win % P. T_8 confirms that effect. The number of top 100 players (T_2) seems to have the most impact. Beyond the top 100 there is not an increase in R^2 percent explained. We will concentrate on the top 100 in subsequent analysis. It is not surprising that in a team game it is better to have a roster of good players than a small subset of stars. This is similar to stud prices for thoroughbred stallions (Cameron, 2010; Ziemba, 2017). The price is determined by having many good offspring, not by having a few great ones.

16.3.2. *Weighting by position*

Football is a team game, but the importance of each position to success is not equal. Obviously the quarterback position is crucial, since the QB is "the player with the ball" most of the time, makes decisions on each down, and is the key factor in successful offense. Figure 16.1 summarizes the salary for top players at each position. We assume that salary is a proxy for the importance of the position to team success.

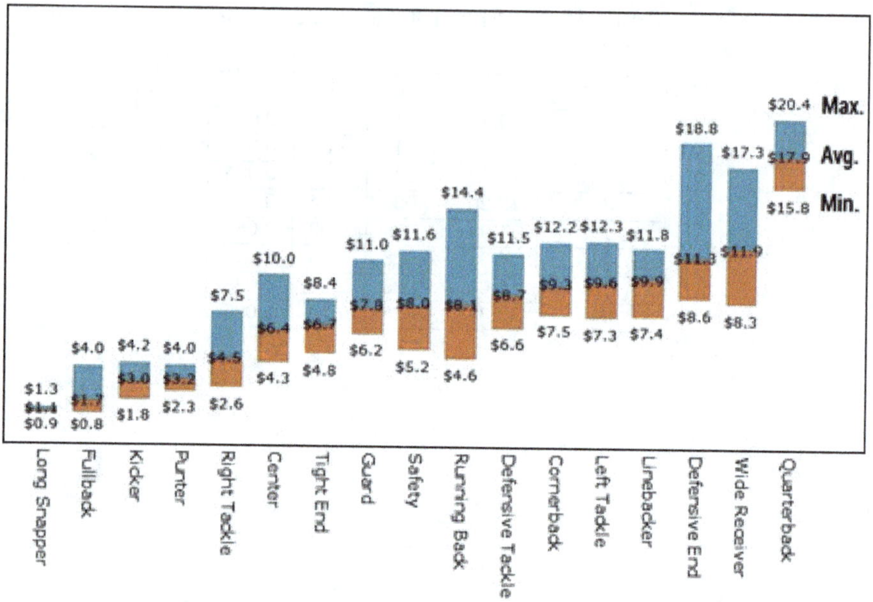

Figure 16.1. Salary of top 10 players by position-Source.

Source: Spotrac.com

If the average salary of the top 10 at each position is taken as a player weight, then the weighted value for the top 100 players as determined by the NFL can be calculated. Let

X_1 = players ranked from 1 to 10 weighted by average position salary

X_2 = players ranked from 10 to 20 weighted by average position salary

X_3 = players ranked from 21 to 30 weighted by average position salary

X_4 = players ranked from 31 to 40 weighted by average position salary

X_5 = players ranked from 41 to 50 weighted by average position salary

X_6 = players ranked from 51 to 60 weighted by average position salary

X_7 = players ranked from 61 to 70 weighted by average position salary

X_8 = players ranked from 71 to 10 weighted by average position salary

X_9 = players ranked from 81 to 90 weighted by average position salary

X_{10} = players ranked from 91 to 100 weighted by average position salary.

Table 16.8 shows the weighted score by ranking decile for each team. Some teams with high scores are flagged. It is important to keep in mind that these rankings and scores are before the actual 2017 season started. However, the marked teams were favorites in each division at the start of the season.

16.3.3. *Team performance: Predicted and actual*

Can the team performance in 2017 be predicted based on the weighted player rankings from Table 16.8? We analyze team performance with the logistic model where

Table 16.8. Weighted score for top players by team.

Team	X_1	X_2	X_3	X_4	X_5	X_6	X_7	X_8	X_9	X_{10}
Arizona Cardinals	0.0	17.4	0.0	0.0	11.9	0.0	0.0	0.0	9.9	0.0
Atlanta Falcons	29.8	0.0	0.0	9.9	8.1	0.0	0.0	0.0	0.0	0.0
Baltimore Ravens	0.0	0.0	0.0	0.0	7.8	0.0	0.0	0.0	0.0	0.0
Buffalo Bills	0.0	0.0	8.1	0.0	0.0	0.0	0.0	0.0	0.0	9.9
Carolina Panthers	0.0	9.9	0.0	0.0	17.9	0.0	6.7	0.0	9.9	0.0
Chicago Bears	0.0	0.0	0.0	0.0	0.0	0.0	0.0	0.0	0.0	0.0
Cincinnati Bengals	0.0	11.9	0.0	0.0	0.0	0.0	8.7	0.0	0.0	0.0
Cleveland Browns	0.0	0.0	8.7	0.0	0.0	0.0	0.0	0.0	0.0	0.0
Dallas Cowboys	8.1	26.6	0.0	0.0	0.0	19.7	0.0	9.9	6.4	0.0
Denver Broncos	9.9	0.0	0.0	9.3	0.0	0.0	9.3	0.0	0.0	0.0
Detroit Lions	0.0	0.0	0.0	17.9	0.0	0.0	0.0	0.0	0.0	0.0
Green Bay Packers	17.9	0.0	0.0	0.0	11.9	0.0	0.0	8.0	18.6	0.0
Houston Texans	0.0	0.0	0.0	11.3	11.3	0.0	0.0	0.0	0.0	0.0
Indianapolis Colts	0.0	0.0	0.0	0.0	0.0	17.9	11.9	0.0	0.0	0.0
Jacksonville Jaguars	0.0	0.0	0.0	0.0	0.0	0.0	0.0	0.0	11.3	0.0
Kansas City Chiefs	0.0	8.0	6.7	21.2	0.0	0.0	0.0	9.9	17.9	0.0
Los Angeles Chargers	0.0	0.0	0.0	0.0	0.0	0.0	9.3	17.9	0.0	11.3
Los Angeles Rams	0.0	8.7	0.0	0.0	0.0	0.0	0.0	0.0	0.0	0.0
Miami Dolphins	0.0	0.0	0.0	0.0	11.9	8.7	19.4	0.0	0.0	0.0
Minnesota Vikings	0.0	0.0	0.0	0.0	0.0	0.0	9.3	8.0	0.0	11.3
New England Patriots	17.9	0.0	6.7	0.0	0.0	0.0	0.0	20.0	0.0	19.2
New Orleans Saints	0.0	17.9	0.0	0.0	0.0	0.0	0.0	0.0	0.0	8.1
New York Giants	11.9	0.0	8.0	0.0	0.0	9.3	0.0	0.0	0.0	8.7
New York Jets	0.0	0.0	0.0	0.0	0.0	0.0	0.0	0.0	0.0	0.0
Oakland Raiders	11.3	17.9	0.0	0.0	0.0	11.9	0.0	0.0	0.0	7.8
Philadelphia Eagles	0.0	0.0	0.0	8.7	0.0	0.0	0.0	0.0	8.0	11.3
Pittsburgh Steelers	20.0	0.0	17.9	0.0	0.0	0.0	0.0	0.0	0.0	7.8
San Francisco 49ers	0.0	0.0	0.0	0.0	0.0	0.0	0.0	0.0	0.0	0.0
Seattle Seahawks	0.0	0.0	35.2	17.9	11.3	11.3	0.0	0.0	11.9	0.0
Tampa Bay Buccaneers	0.0	0.0	11.9	0.0	0.0	26.6	0.0	0.0	0.0	0.0
Tennessee Titans	0.0	0.0	0.0	8.1	17.9	0.0	0.0	25.3	8.7	0.0
Washington Redskins	0.0	0.0	0.0	0.0	8.7	9.3	24.6	0.0	0.0	0.0

Table 16.9. Logistic model: ANOVA.

Source	*DF*	*Seq SS*	*Contribution %*	*Adj SS*	*F*	*P*
Regression	10	12.4513	**39.87**	12.4513	1.39	0.250
X_1	1	0.9129	2.92	0.1245	0.14	0.713
X_2	1	0.6561	2.10	1.0848	1.21	0.283
X_3	1	0.0202	0.06	0.0134	0.01	0.904
X_4	1	0.6596	2.11	0.7128	0.80	0.382
X_5	1	0.0248	0.08	0.1979	0.22	0.643
X_6	1	2.5340	8.11	0.6410	0.72	0.407
X_7	1	0.3532	1.13	0.3025	0.34	0.567
X_8	1	2.0209	6.47	0.0061	0.01	0.935
X_9	1	0.3526	1.13	1.0288	1.15	0.296
X_{10}	**1**	**4.9170**	**15.74**	**4.9170**	**5.50**	**0.029**
Error	21	18.7791	60.13	18.7791		
Total	31	31.2303	100.00			

$Y = ln\left(\frac{P}{1-P}\right)$ and $X = X_1, \ldots, X_{10}$. So

$$Y = B^{'}X + \varepsilon,$$

for $P =$ team win fraction. The a multiple linear regression of Y on X gives

$$Y = -0.746 + 0.0087X_1 + 0.0301X_2 - 0.0037X_3 + 0.0292X_4 + 0.0173X_5$$
$$-0.0254X_6 + 0.0192X_7 - 0.0026X_8 + 0.0426X_9 + 0.1088X_{10}.$$

The analysis of variation in Y shows that almost 40% is accounted for by the relationship to X. So accounting for player position increases the explanatory power of top players. The data has the unusual result that the tenth decile values are the strongest predictors as shown in Table 16.9.

To pursue that effect we looked at all combinations of predictors. The best subsets of independent variables are in Table 16.10.

For the NFL player ranking data the 9th and 10th deciles are sufficient to account for most of the variation in team performance. The model equation with X_9, X_{10} is

$$Y = -0.535 + 0.0627X_9 + 0.1015X_{10}.$$

The analysis of variance for the reduced model is in Table 16.11.

The fact that the 9th and 10th deciles are so important for team success is curious, so Table 16.12 lists the players involved. The players have above

Table 16.10. Best Subsets: Y vs. X.

p	R^2	$adjR^2$	S	X_1	X_2	X_3	X_4	X_5	X_6	X_7	X_8	X_9	X_{10}
1	19.2	16.5	0.91693										√
2	**30.9**	**26.1**	**0.86265**									√	√
3	33.1	26.0	0.86355						√			√	√
4	35.4	25.9	0.86420		√				√			√	√
5	37.1	25.0	0.86946		√		√		√			√	√
6	38.7	23.9	0.87540		√		√		√	√		√	√
7	39.4	21.7	0.88789		√		√	√	√	√		√	√
8	39.8	18.9	0.90397	√	√		√	√	√	√		√	√
9	39.8	15.2	0.92405	√	√	√	√	√	√	√		√	√
10	39.9	11.2	0.94564	√	√	√	√	√	√	√	√		√

Table 16.11. Reduced model.

Source	*DF*	*Seq SS*	*Contribution %*	*Adj SS*	*F*	*P*
Regression	2	9.650	30.90	9.650	6.48	0.005
X_9	1	1.608	5.15	3.642	4.89	0.035
X_{10}	**1**	**8.042**	**25.75**	**8.042**	**10.81**	**0.003**
Error	29	21.581	69.10	21.581		
Total	31	31.2303	100.00			

Table 16.12. 9th and 10th decile players: NFL ranking.

Rank	**Player**	**Position**	**Team**	**Weight**
80	LeGarrette Blount	RB	Patriots	8.1
81	Alex Smith	QB	Chiefs	17.9
82	Clay Matthews	**LB**	Packers	9.9
83	Calais Campbell	**DE**	Jaguars	11.3
84	Mike Daniels	**DT**	Packers	8.7
85	Chandler Jones	**LB**	Cardinals	9.9
85	Jurrell Casey	**DT**	Titans	8.7
87	Travis Frederick	C	Cowboys	6.4
88	Doug Baldwin	WR	Seahawks	11.9
89	Thomas Davis	**LB**	Panthers	9.9
90	Malcom Jenkins	**S**	Eagles	8.0
91	Lorenzo Alexander	**LB**	Bills	9.9
92	Everson Giffen	**DE**	Vikings	11.3
93	Brandon Graham	**DE**	Eagles	11.3
94	Dont'a Hightower	**LB**	Patriots	9.9
95	Kelechi Osamele	G	Raiders	7.8
96	Damon Harrison	**DT**	Giants	8.7
97	David DeCastro	G	Steelers	7.8
98	Adrian Peterson	RB	Saints	8.1
99	Malcom Butler	**CB**	Patriots	9.3
100	Joey Bosa	**DE**	Chargers	11.3

average position weight. The striking observation is that the defensive positions (in bold) are prominent. Half the players are defensive ends or linebackers. It is well known that these positions are the key to disrupting quarterback play. The 2018 Superbowl was decided by a quarterback strip of Tom Brady by the defensive end Brandon Graham.

16.3.4. *Model predictions*

There is a lot of unexplained variation, but the reduced model is significant. The observed and predicted win percentages (from the reduced model) are in Table 16.13.

Table 16.13. Model predictions.

Team	Observed Win Rate	Predicted Win Rate
Arizona	0.5000	0.5215
Atlanta	0.6250	0.3694
Baltimore	0.5620	0.3694
Buffalo	0.5620	0.6154
Carolina	0.6880	0.5215
Chicago	0.3120	0.3694
Cincinnati	0.4380	0.3694
Cleveland	0.0322	0.3694
Dallas	0.5620	0.4666
Denver	0.3120	0.3694
Detroit	0.5620	0.3694
Green Bay	0.4380	0.6527
Houston	0.2500	0.3694
Indianapolis	0.2500	0.3694
Jacksonville	0.6250	0.5431
Kansas City	0.6250	0.6427
LA Chargers	0.5620	0.6484
LA Rams	0.6880	0.3694
Miami	0.3750	0.3694
Minnesota	0.8120	0.6484
New England	0.8120	0.8042
New Orleans	0.6880	0.5713
NY Giants	0.1880	0.5861
NY Jets	0.3120	0.3694
Oakland	0.3750	0.5639
Philadelphia	0.8120	0.7527
Pittsburgh	0.8120	0.5639
San Francisco	0.3750	0.3694
Seattle	0.5620	0.5526
Tampa Bay	0.3120	0.3694
Tennessee	0.5620	0.5025
Washington	0.4380	0.3694

Table 16.14. Fitted logistic model: SI rankings.

Source	*DF*	*Seq SS*	*Contribution %*	*Adj SS*	*F*	*P*
Regression	10	10.5145	33.67	10.5145	1.07	0.428
Z_1	1	2.4480	7.84	2.1031	2.13	0.159
Z_2	1	1.1373	3.64	0.5941	0.60	0.446
Z_3	1	0.0316	0.10%	0.3124	0.32	0.580
Z_4	1	0.9206	2.95%	1.0219	1.04	0.320
Z_5	1	0.0099	0.03%	0.2122	0.22	0.648
Z_6	1	0.0055	0.02%	0.1944	0.20	0.662
Z_7	1	0.3164	1.01%	0.0080	0.01	0.929
Z_8	1	0.1387	0.44%	0.2546	0.26	0.617
Z_9	**1**	**5.3247**	**17.05%**	**4.8768**	**4.94**	**0.037**
Z_{10}	1	0.1817	0.58%	0.1817	0.18	0.672
Error	21	20.7158	66.33%	20.7158		
Total	31	31.2303	100.00			

The highlighted teams have reasonable predictions from the reduced model. If we go back to the data on deciles, the predicted poor performance is from teams with no players in the bottom deciles of the top 100, and the strong performers had multiple players in the bottom deciles.

16.3.5. *The Sports Illustrated list: Top 100*

We used the NFL list of top 100 players for the analysis of team performance. The top 100 from the SI list had an overlap of about 2/3rds of players with the NFL list, but the ranking of individual players in the lists differed (see Table 16.6). Although we lean towards the NFL list, it is informative to analyze the deciles from the Sports Illustrated list for their effect on Y.

Let

Z_1 = players ranked from 1 to 10 by SI, weighted by average position salary

Z_2 = players ranked from 10 to 20 by SI, weighted by average position salary

Z_3 = players ranked from 21 to 30 by SI, weighted by average position salary

Z_4 = players ranked from 31 to 40 by SI, weighted by average position salary

Table 16.15. 9th decile of SI Top 100 players.

Rank	Player	Position	Team	Weight
81	Josh Norman	CB	Redskins	9.3
82	Andrew Whitworth	LT	Rams	8.7
83	Mitchell Schwartz	RT	Chiefs	8.7
84	Lane Johnson	RT	Eagles	8.7
85	Terrell Sugs	LB	Ravens	9.9
86	Dont'a Hightower	LB	Patriots	9.9
87	Xavier Rhodes	CB	Vikings	9.3
88	Philip Rivers	QB	Chargers	17.9
89	Alshon Jeffery	WR	Eagles	11.9
90	Janoris Jenkins	CB	Giants	9.3

Table 16.16. Best subsets: Y vs. Z.

p	R^2	$adjR^2$	S	Z_1	Z_2	Z_3	Z_4	Z_5	Z_6	Z_7	Z_8	Z_9	Z_{10}
1	14.1	11.2	0.94586									√	
2	22.8	17.5	0.91163	√								√	
3	27.9	20.2	0.89667	√	√							√	
4	**31.5**	**21.4**	**0.88991**	√	√		√					√	
5	31.9	18.8	0.90424	√	√	√	√					√	
6	32.4	16.1	0.91922	√	√	√	√				√	√	
7	32.7	13.1	0.93554	√	√	√	√	√			√	√	
8	33.1	9.8	0.95339	√	√	√	√	√	√		√	√	
9	33.6	6.5	0.97056	√	√	√	√	√	√		√	√	√
10	33.7	2.1	0.99321	√	√	√	√	√	√	√	√	√	√

Z_5 = players ranked from 41 to 50 by SI, weighted by average position salary

Z_6 = players ranked from 51 to 60 by SI, weighted by average position salary

Z_7 = players ranked from 61 to 70 by SI, weighted by average position salary

Z_8 = players ranked from 71 to 10 by SI, weighted by average position salary

Z_9 = players ranked from 81 to 90 by SI, weighted by average position salary

Z_{10} = players ranked from 91 to 100 by SI, weighted by average position salary.

The logistic regression equation is

$$Y = -0.805 + 0.0486Z_1 + 0.0236Z_2 - 0.0201Z_3 + 0.0426Z_4 + 0.0211Z_5 + 0.0194Z_6 + 0.0046Z_7 + 0.0171Z_8 + 0.0804Z_9 + 0.0182Z_{10}.$$

The model has less predictive power. Of course since most of the same players are on both lists the results have comparable R^2 with the 10 deciles included (Table 16.14). However, the contrasting rankings produce a different important decile. In the SI list it is the players ranked from 81 to 90 who have the big impact. Those players are listed in Table 16.15. There is a split between offensive and defensive players. The defense positions (LB, CB) have high weights.

It is again the case that a reduced model accounts for most of the variation. The model with Z_1, Z_2, Z_4, Z_9 is identified in Table 16.16.

16.4. Conclusion

The data on pre-season player rankings and team success in 2017 yielded the following conclusions:

- An association exists between team success and the number of top 400 players. However, the correlation is 0.392, so top players only explain 15% of the variation in win percentage.
- The teams with the most top players generally have high win percentages, and teams with fewer top players have low win percentages.
- The connection of top 100 players to team winning percentage is most important. The correlation is 0.292, reduced from the top 400 result as would be expected with fewer players per team.
- The correlation between ranks of top 100 players on the Sports Illustrated list and the NFL players list is 0.456, so there is quite bit of disagreement.
- Weighting players by position value increases the explanatory power of top players.
- For the NFL player ranking data the lower deciles are sufficient to account for most of the variation in team performance.
- The lower deciles emphasize the defensive positions, and they are key factors in team success.

Chapter 17

Primer on Dosage and the 2012 Triple Crown

William T. Ziemba

This chapter describes a very useful breeding concept. Certain horses called *chef-de-race* tend to determine the breed speed-stamina characteristics consistently in their offspring. Then a *dosage index* can be used to better evaluate individual horses in particular races, especially the Kentucky Derby and the Belmont Stakes where the horses have never run that distance before. I also discuss the 2012 Triple Crown races.

17.1. Introduction to Dosage

Investing in traditional financial markets has many parallels with racetrack and lottery betting and much of the analysis is similar. Behavioral anomalies such as the favorite-longshot bias are pervasive and also exist and are exploitable in the S&P500 and FTSE100 futures and equity puts and calls options markets, see Tompkins, Ziemba and Hodges (2008) and Ziegler and Ziemba (2015). I use this in personal and private managed accounts and in a futures fund. Biases there favor buying high probability favorites and selling low probability longshots just like the high probability low payoff racing wagers. But in complex low probability high payoff exotic wagers such as the Pick 6, the bias reverses to overbet the favorite so one must include other value wagers in the betting program. Fundamental information such as breeding is important as well and is especially useful for the Kentucky Derby and Belmont Stakes where horses have never run that far before.

Dosage as championed by Steve Roman has been a valuable tool in analyzing various races, especially the Kentucky Derby and the Belmont Stakes partially because the horses have never run this far a forecast of how they might do from their breeding is helpful. The idea is that there are specific stallions that impart consistent speed and stamina in their offspring. The idea is that more stamina is needed to win these races from the sires in the horses lineage. Bain, Hausch and Ziemba (2006) studied this by merging the odds (prices) with expert opinion (breeding measured by dosage). See also Gramm and Ziemba (2008) and Roman (2016), the definitive source.

During the period 1929 to the early 2000s, the predictions were spectacular. Indeed, I once was invited by *Fortune* magazine to do a story about the place and show system. In 1997, I was invited to give asset-liability talks at Cornell and Stanford universities. I volunteered as well to give a Kentucky Derby talk which largely focused on dosage. The script said that the best horse was Silver Charm (his pedigree is in Chapter 18; the second best horse was Captain Bodgit and the third horse was Free House. Later, I went to the Kentucky Derby with the *Fortune* reporter. She was paid $2000 to follow me around and take photos. Previously she had done a story about Bo Derek and next story was about the Silk Road so I was flattered. I did play the place and show system which was successful and by a combination of skill and luck, the finish of the race was exactly according to the script 1–2–3. I was able to win $5000 to beat the reporter's daily fee. I then went to Hong Kong consulting for the Paul Makin betting syndicate and wrote a 25 page fax to the reporter explaining how the dosage theory related to financial markets. In particular, stock market anomalies. Unfortunately she was called off to another story and my story never appeared. When I wrote to get the photos she had taken, there was no response.

Another great example was in 1985 when the two horses ranked 1–2, namely, Spend a Buck first over Stephan's Odyssey second. They actually came in 1–2 in this exact order and provided a huge exacta, $82 for a $2 bet. The favorite in that race, who was favored in all three Triple Crown races and won none of them, but finished in the money in each race, was two-year-old champion Chief's Crown whose dosage was 5, above the historically determined 4 limit. It was like that year by year in the 1980s and 1990s until the breed started changing in the early 2000s. In some years, the finish was 1–2–3 with these being the only dual qualifiers. These predictions are similar to the turn-of-the-year effect which I traded successfully in 21 of 22 years, see Ziemba (2012). This effect is strongest with a Democratic president though it still works successfully for a Republican president. The 2020–2021 Biden year was an especially strong turn of the year.

In the period 1929 to the early 2000s, no horse with a dosage index above 4.0 won the Kentucky Derby. There were no exceptions. But, recently,

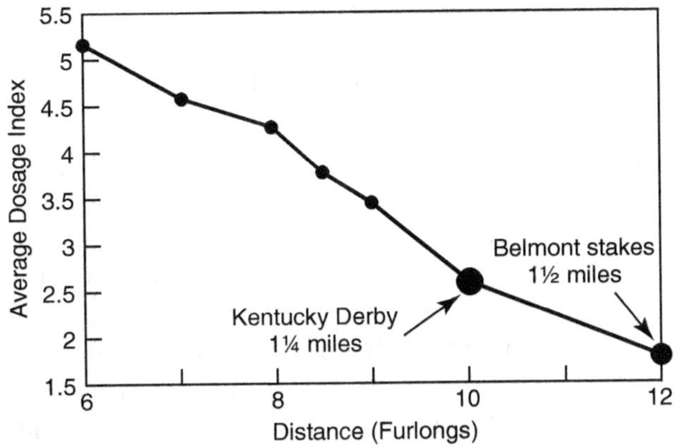

(a) $25,000+purses from historical data

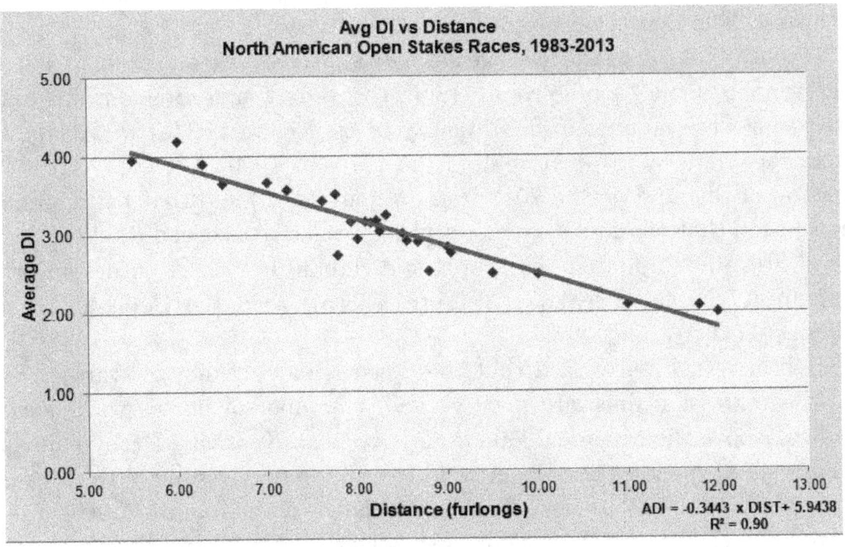

(b) Open stakes winners, 1983–2013

Figure 17.1. Average dosage of winners by distance.

Source: Steve Roman, chef-de-race.com.

past the early 2000s, the US breed of thoroughbreds has changed more towards speed. That means that horses with dosage above 4 have been able to win the Kentucky Derby, see Figures 17.2 and Roman's (2016) marvelous book. The speed-stamina tradeoff for a particular horse is measured by the dosage index discussed below. This is calculated from the chefs-de-race in that particular horse's pedigree. Two-year old form is also important. For example, the last two horses who won the Kentucky Derby who had not run as two-year-olds were Justify (2018) and Apollo (1882). There were no other horses who won the Kentucky Derby without having run a two-year-old race in those 130 years. We measure two-year-old form from the experimental free handicap evaluated by the Jockey Club. If a horse is within of 10 pounds of the top rated horse it is said to be a dual qualifier, so it has good dosage (<4) and good two-year-old form. One very interesting thing about dual qualifiers is that they have traditionally been very important is the Belmont Stakes. One interesting example is dual qualifiers who had a terrible three-year-old year leading up to the Kentucky Derby and did very poorly, skipped the Preakness and were the lone dual qualifier in the Belmont Stakes which they won. There are three such example: Lemon Drop Kid (1999), Birdstone (2004) and Union Rags (2012, as discussed in this chapter). The first two were at long odds of about 30–1.

Figure 17.2 shows the average dosage or speed over stamina for the average winner of the $1\frac{1}{4}$ mile Kentucky Derby and $1\frac{1}{2}$ mile Belmont stakes as well as a large number of high quality races. Figure 17.1(a) was compiled from race data by Steve Roman in the 1970s to 1990s. Figure 17.1(b) is a version of this updated to 2013 from Roman (2016) and that has a similar conclusion that winners have more stamina relative to speed the longer the race. Steve has updated the graphs individually for the Kentucky Derby (Figure 17.2), the Preakness (Figure 17.3(a)), and the Belmont Stakes (Figure 17.3(b)).

Observe in Figures 17.2 that the breed is moving more towards speed as the regression lines are positive and a number of horses with dosage indices above the historical 4.0 cutoff have been Kentucky Derby winners. Figure 17.2(a) shows that from 1940 to 1990 ***every*** Kentucky Derby winner had a DI of 4.00 or less. Then from 1990 to 2009, Figure 17.2(b), there were some Kentucky Derby winners with DI over 4.0. Figure 17.2(c) has the Derby winners from 1940–2014 showing rising rising dosage among the winners over time. Figure 17.2(d) shows that the median dosage of Kentucky Derby entrants has been rising and is now close to 3.0.

But, observe that in the long $1\frac{1}{2}$ mile Belmont all the recent winners since 2003 have had low dosage of 3.00 or less. It is not clear how useful Steve's regression line is here as there is a lot of noise in the system.[1] The

[1]Union Rags with DI = 2.14 won the 2012 Belmont, Palace Malice won in 2013 with a DI = 1.88 and Tonalist won in 2014 with a DI = 2.78, but these three are not on the graph in Figure 17.3(b).

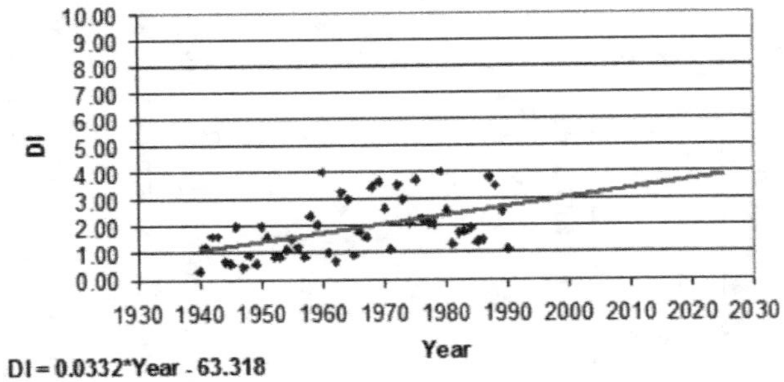

(a) Derby winners DI, 1940–1990

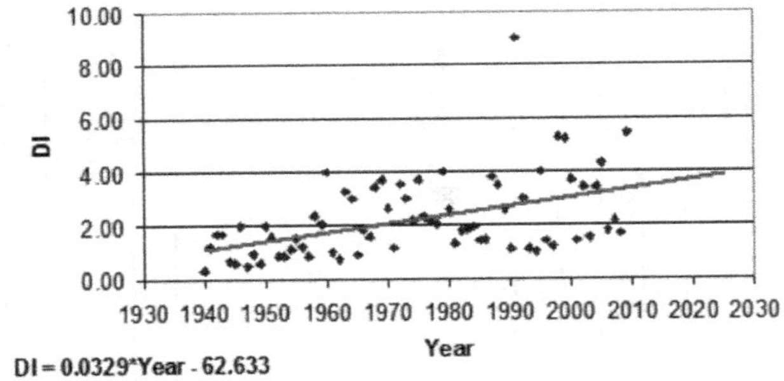

(b) Derby winners, 1940–2009

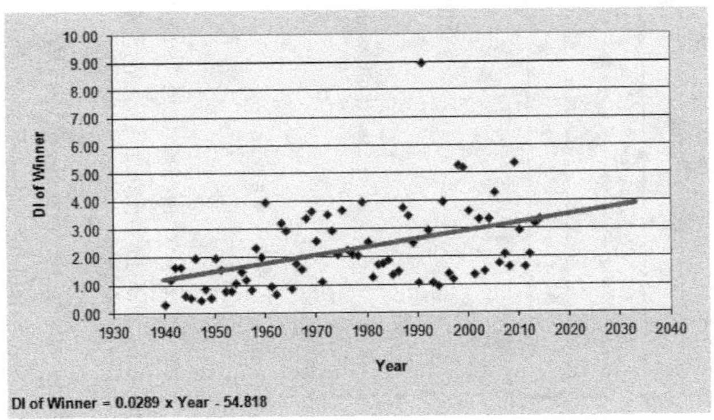

(c)Derby winners, 1940–2014

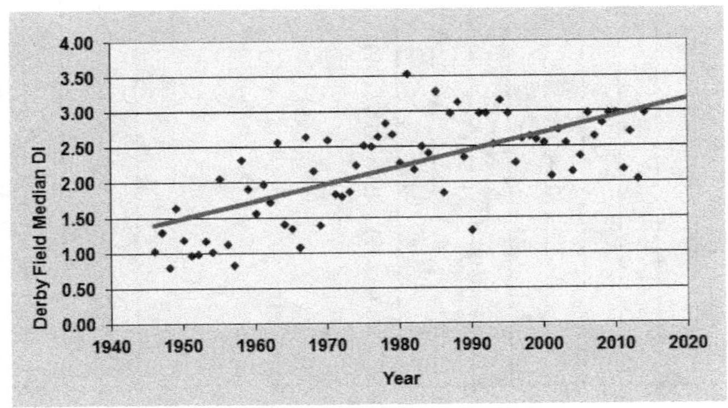

(d) Kentucky Derby Median DI of entrants by Year, 1946–2014

Figure 17.2. Dosage indices.

Source: Steve Roman, chef-de-race.com.

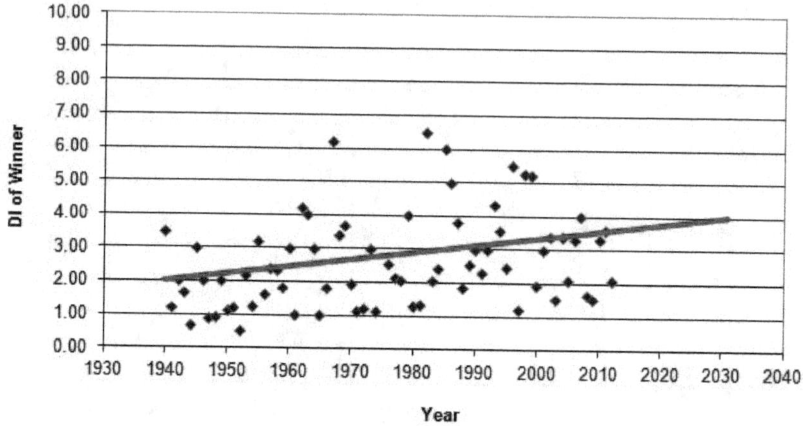

DI = 0.022 x Year - 39.99

(a) Preakness winners, 1940–2012

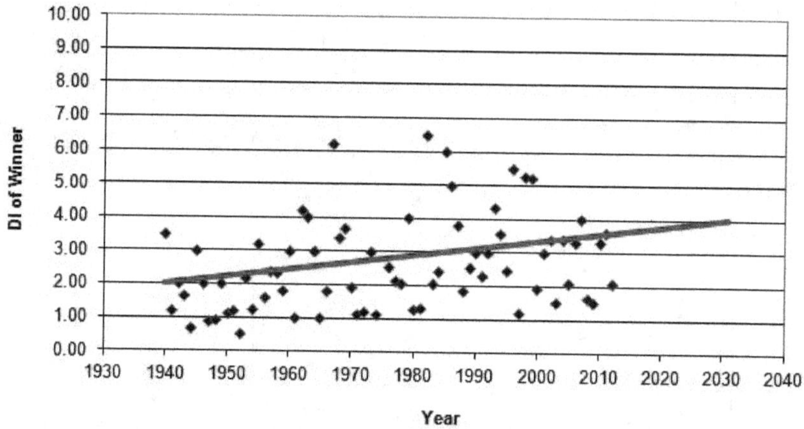

DI = 0.022 x Year - 39.99

(b) Belmont winners, 1940–2012

Figure 17.3. Dosage indices.

Source: Steve Roman, chef-de-race.com.

breed has changed toward speed and that shows up more in the Kentucky Derby and less in the Belmont. Gramm and Ziemba (2008) study this as well.

Great races used to be seen on Roman's website, chef-de-race.com. Unfortunately, this website has been shut down, I have downloaded them for personal use. Outstanding ones are Personal Ensign (1988 Breeders' Cup

Distaff), Zenyatta (2009 and 2010 Breeders' Cup Classics), Affirmed-Alydar Triple Crown battles (1978) and Secretariat (1973) possibly the greatest performance since Man O'War in the 1920s. Secretariat's 31 length victory win in a dirt race when he ran every quarter mile faster than the previous quarter, is very impressive. Of course, Man O'War once won a race by 100 lengths at odds of 1 to 100. If you go to the Kentucky Horse Park near Lexington, you will find the strides of the great gelding John Henry (24.5 ft) which was very long, then longer is that of Secretariat (26 ft)and much longer is Man O'War (28 ft). The place bet on Secretariat in the Belmont of 2.40 per $2 bet when he paid 2.20 to win is one of the greatest bets in history.

However, in the long $1\frac{1}{2}$ mile Belmont all the recent winners have had low dosage. 2012 was no exception as the lone dual qualifier, Union Rags, with a dosage index of 2.14 won the race and the favorite, Dullahan, with a 4.20 dosage, finished seventh. In 2013, Palace Malice won with a DI of 2.64. In 2014, Tonalist won with a 2.78 dosage. There have been horses with DI above 3.5 who won the Belmont such as Commendable (5.00 in 2000) and Sarava (4.50 in 2002). The last twelve winners from 2014 back to 2003 had dosage indices of 2.64, 2.14, 2.56, 1.75, 2.56, 2.43, 3.00, 3.00, 2.11, 1.77, 1.88, 2.64 and 2.78.

The winners of the Belmont Stakes from 2015 to 2021 were as follows:

2015 American Pharoah with dosage 4.33, slightly above four but this Triple Crown winner was so good he easily beat all the horses he faced, except one defeat in Saratoga.

2016 Creator, 3.00.

2017 Tapwrit, 3.00.

2018 Justify, the last Triple Crown winner, 3.00.

2019 Sir Winston, 2.71.

2020 Tis the Law, 4.33, again so good, a bit high dosage but he still won. Also because of COVID-19 health concern, the Belmont was shortened to $1\frac{1}{8}$ mile and held before the other two Classics. So dosage is not very relevant.

2021 Essential Quality, 3.00.

Four of the last 8 Belmont winners were sired by Tappit who was born in 2001. HIs dosage index is 2.75, with dosage profile 13–19–24–2–2. You can see from this profile how he could easily be a super star stallion. When he ran, he had 6 races, 3 wins and 3 out of the money earning $557,300. The Gainesway Stallion's pedigree is Pulpit, AP Indy and Seattle Slew on the male side and with dam sires Unbridled, Fappiano, and Mister Prospector. You see why Tappit is so good and deserving of his about $200,000 stud fee.

Even the great Sunday Silence with a 3.8 dosage got crushed in the Belmont by Easy Goer. It is not clear how useful Steve's regression line is here as there is a lot of noise in the system. It is believed that the breed has changed toward speed and that shows up more in the Kentucky Derby and less in the Belmont. Gramm and Ziemba (2008) study this as well.

A horse named *Stay Thirsty* in race 12 on Travers Day in 2012 has a dosage profile of 4–6–16–0–0. That is four brilliant points (pure speed); six intermediate points, 16 classic points, zero solid and zero professional points. These are categories on the speed-stamina space. You can think of this as a discrete probability distribution. Now each chef-de-race stallion (that is a stallion which breeds consistent characteristics in their offspring) in the horse's pedigree counts: 16 for first generation sires, eight each for the second generation, four each for the four third generation and finally two for the eight fourth generation sires. So each generation is equally important. If a chef is in two categories, the points are split. Some generations may have no chefs. The dosage index is then

$$\text{DI} = \frac{\text{Brilliant} + \text{Intermediate} + 1/2\ \text{Classic}}{\text{Solid} + \text{Professional} + 1/2\ \text{Classic}}$$

Despite its simplicity and crude weighting, the index does seem to work. An example of the pedigree and dosage of the 2005 Belmont Stakes winner, Afleet Alex, is in Tables 17.1 and 17.2.

Table 17.1. Pedigree for the 2005 Belmont Stakes Winner Afleet Alex.

Northern Afleet	Afleet	Mr. Prospector (B/C)	Raise a Native (B)
			Gold Digger
		Polite Lady	Venetian Jester
			Friendly Ways
	Nuryette	Nureyev (C)	Northern Dancer (B/C)
			Special
		Stellarette	Tentam
			Square Angel
Maggy Hawk	Hawkster	Silver Hawk	Roberto (C)
			Gris Vitesse
		Strait Lane	Chieftain
			Level Sands
	Qualique	Hawaii	Utrillo II
			Ethane
		Dorothy Gaylord	Sensitivo
			Gaylord's Touch

Table 17.2. Dosage Index Calculation for 2005 Belmont Stakes Winner Afleet Alex.

Generation	Sire	Brilliant	Intermediate	Classic	Solid	Professional
1	Northern Afleet					
2	Afleet					
	Hawkster					
3	Mr. Prospector	2		2		
	Nureyev			4		
	Silver Hawk					
	Hawaii					
4	Raise a Native	2				
	Venetian Jester					
	Northern Dancer	1		1		
	Tentam					
	Roberto			2		
	Chieftain					
	Utrillo II					
	Sensitivo					
	Total	**5**	**0**	**9**	**0**	**0**

Note: Dosage Index $= (5 + 0 + 9/2)/(0 + 0 + 9/2) = 2.11$.

A dual qualifier is a horse whose dosage index is 4.00 or lower, which is the limit suggested for maximum speed for Kentucky Derby winner, and within 10 pounds of the top two year old horse on the experimental free handicapping ratings. Gramm and Ziemba (2008), Bain, Hausch and Ziemba (2006) and on the website chef-de-race.com show that such horses have superior performance in the Kentucky Derby and Belmont Stakes. An asterisk qualifier has dosage less than 4.00 and won a major grade I race as a three year old.

Tables 17.3–17.5 has some dual qualifier and asterisk qualifier results plus win odds of the winner for the Kentucky Derby, Preakness and Belmont Stakes from 1946 to 2014.[2]

[2]Experimental free handicap listings were taken from the *American Racing Manual, The Blood Horse* magazine (print and online at www.bloodhorse.com), the Thoroughbred Times (www.thoroughbredtimes.com) and Roman's website (chef-de_race.com) The Results of the Kentucky Derby were taken from the *Daily Racing Form* both print and online (www.drf.com), press materials from Churchill Downs, and from Chew (1974). Recent results charts were obtained from the following websites: About.com Inc (horseracing.abuut.com), Sportsline.com Inc (www.sportsline.com), CNN/Sports Illustrated (sportsillustrated.cnn.com), Equibase Company, LLC (www.equibase.com), Daily Racing Form, LLC (www.drf.com). The results for the major races prior to the

Afleet Alex going into the 2005 Belmont Stakes which he won as a dual qualifier.

As a student and trader of anomalies in the financial markets, I know that advantages may persist for a long time but might trend or change slightly over time. For example, in the January turn of the year effect, the advantage was there from mid December to mid January for futures traders. Then it moved gradually forward partly due to futures anticipation. Currently the effect is totally in December. However most finance books and papers have just said that the effect no longer exists. But my gains in the last five years have been, if anything, higher than in the 14 previous years I won on the effect. The 19/19 had a gap because of a contract change and liquidity. See Ziemba (2013). It is similar with dosage as Steve Roman's research has shown. In the 1980s and 1990s, the advantage to those betting with DI was strong in the Kentucky Derby. Now it is much less, but the advantage for the longer Belmont Stakes remains strong. Dual qualifiers, that is those with DI of 4.00 or less and two year old form within ten pounds of the top rated horse on the Experimental Free Handicap have had a very good record, especially in the Belmont.

Derby for the asterisk qualifiers were taken from the *American Racing Manual* and lists from the following websites: Blue Grass Stakes (www.keeneland.com/liveracing/history.asp), Flamingo Stakes (hialeahpark.com/99/HalloFame/flamingo.htm), Florida Derby (www.thoroughbredchampions.com/library/fladerby.htm), Santa Anita Derby (www.revistahipodromo.com/santaanita.html), Wood Memorial Stakes (www.nyra.com/aqueduct/index2.html) and the out of date site www.iglou.com/tbread/tc97/preps, which was run by the *Thoroughbred Times*.

Table 17.3. Kentucky Derby Winners and Dual Qualifiers (1946–2014).

Year	Horse	Odds	DQ	Year	Horse	Odds	DQ	Year	Horse	Odds	DQ
1946	Assault*	8.2	5	1970	Dust Commander*	15.3	4	1993	**Sea Hero**	12.9	3
1947	**Jet Pilot**	5.4	4	1971	Canonero II	8.7	1	1994	**Go For Gin**	9.1	5
1948	**Citation**	0.4	4	1972	**Riva Ridge**	1.5	3	1995	**Thunder Gulch**	24.5	6
1949	Ponder	16	5	1973	**Secretariat**	1.5	2	1996	Grindstone	5.9	6
1951	Count Turf	14.6	2	1974	**Cannonade**	1.5	1	1997	**Silver Charm**	4	2
1952	**Hill Gail**	1.1	2	1975	**Foolish Pleasure**	1.9	1	1998	Real Quiet	8.4	0
1953	Dark Star	24.9	3	1976	**Bold Forbes**	3	4	1999	Charismatic	31.3	6
1954	**Determine**	4.3	5	1977	**Seattle Slew**	0.5	4	2000	Fusaichi Pegasus*	2.3	5
1955	Swaps*	2.8	2	1978	**Affirmed**	1.8	3	2001	Monarchos*	10.5	3
1956	**Needles**	1.6	4	1979	**Spectacular Bid**	0.6	3	2002	War Emblem	20.5	3
1957	**Iron Leige**	8.4	5	1980	**Genuine Risk**	13.3	5	2003	Funny Cide	12.8	0
1958	Tim Tam*	2.1	1	1981	**Pleasant Colony**	3.5	4	2004	Smarty Jones	4.1	5
1959	**Tomy Lee**	3.7	8	1982	**Gato del Sol**	21.2	3	2005	Giacomo	50.3	2
1960	**Venetian Way**	6.3	5	1983	**SunnyÕs Halo**	2.5	3	2006	Barbaro*	6.1	2
1961	**Carry Back**	2.5	3	1984	**Swale**	3.4	3	2007	**Street Sense**	4.9	8
1962	Decidedly	8.7	2	1985	**Spend A Buck**	4.1	2	2008	Big Brown*	2.4	3
1963	Chateaugay*	9.4	3	1986	**Ferdinand**	17.7	2	2009	Mine that Bird	50.6	3
1964	**Northern Dancer**	3.4	6	1987	**Alysheba**	8.4	5	2010	**Super Saver**	8	10
1965	Lucky Debonair*	4.3	5	1988	Winning Colors *	3.4	3	2011	Animal Kingdom*	20.9	2
1966	Kauai King	2.4	2	1989	Sunday Silence*	3.1	3	2012	I'll Have Another*	15.3	8
1967	Proud Clarion	30.1	4	1990	**Unbridled**	10.8	4	2013	Orb*	5.40	4
1968	Forward Pass*	2.2	4	1991	Strike The Gold*	4.8	4	2014	California Chrome*	9.20	2
1969	Majestic Prince*	1.4	3	1992	Lil E. Tee	16.8	3				

Note: **Bold** indicates dual qualifier, *indicates asterisk qualifier.

Table 17.4. Preakness Stakes Winners and Dual Qualifiers (1946–2014).

Year	Horse	Odds	DQ	Year	Horse	Odds	DQ	Year	Horse	Odds	DQ
1946	Assault*	1.4	2	1970	Personality*	4.5	3	1993	Prairie Bayou	2.2	1
1947	**Faultless**	4.2	4	1971	Canonero II	3.4	3	1994	**Tabasco Cat**	3.6	3
1948	**Citation**	0.1	3	1972	Bee Bee Bee	18.7	2	1995	Timber Country	1.9	2
1949	**Capot**	2.5	2	1973	**Secretariat**	0.3	1	1996	Louis Quatorze	8.5	2
1950	**Hill Prince**	0.7	2	1974	Little Current	13.1	1	1997	**Silver Charm**	3.1	1
1951	Bold	4.1	1	1975	Master Derby	23.4	2	1998	Real Quiet	2.5	0
1952	Blue Man*	1.6	3	1976	**Elocutionist**	10.1	4	1999	Charismatic	8.4	2
1953	**Native Dancer**	0.2	1	1977	**Seattle Slew**	0.4	1	2000	Red Bullet	6.2	2
1954	**Hasty Road**	5	2	1978	**Affirmed**	0.5	3	2001	Point Given	2.3	3
1955	**Nashua**	0.3	2	1979	**Spectacular Bid**	0.1	3	2002	War Emblem	2.8	0
1956	Fabius	2.5	1	1980	Codex*	2.7	2	2003	Funny Cide	1.9	0
1957	**Bold Ruler**	1.4	3	1981	**Pleasant Colony**	1.5	1	2004	Smarty Jones	0.7	1
1958	Tim Tam*	1.1	2	1982	AlomaÕs Ruler	6.9	1	2005	**Afleet Alex**	3.3	3
1959	**Royal Orbit**	6.6	4	1983	Deputed Testamony	14.5	0	2006	Bernardini	12.9	1
1960	**Bally Ache**	1.7	3	1984	Gate Dancer	4.8	1	2007	Curlin	3.4	
1961	**Carry Back**	1	2	1985	TankÕs Prospect	4.7	0	2008	Big Brown	0.2	
1962	Greek Money	10.9	2	1986	Snow Chief	2.6	2	2009	Rachel Alexandra	1.8	
1963	**Candy Spots**	1.5	2	1987	**Alysheba**	2	2	2010	Looking at Lucky	2.4	
1964	**Northern Dancer**	2.1	4	1988	Risen Star	6.8	2	2011	Shackelford	12.1	
1965	**Tom Rolfe**	3.6	2	1989	Sunday Silence*	2.1	2	2012	I'll Have Another	3	
1966	Kauai King	1	3	1990	**Summer Squall**	2.4	2	2013	Oxbow	1.5	
1967	Damascus	1.8	3	1991	**Hansel**	9.1	2	2014	California Chrome	0.5	
1968	Forward Pass*	1.1	0	1992	**Pine Blu?**	3.5	1				
1969	Majestic Prince*	0.6	1								

Note: **Bold** indicates dual qualifier, *indicates asterisk qualifier.

Table 17.5. Belmont Stakes Winners and Dual Qualifiers (1946–2014).

Year	Horse	Odds	DQ	Year	Horse	Odds	DQ	Year	Horse	Odds	DQ
1946	Assault*	1.4	1	1970	**High Echelon**	4.5	2	1993	Colonial Affiair	13.9	2
1947	**Phalanx**	2.3	2	1971	**Pass Catcher**	34.5	3	1994	**Tabasco Cat**	3.4	2
1948	**Citation**	0.2	4	1972	**Riva Ridge**	1.6	3	1995	**Thunder Gulch**	1.5	1
1949	**Capot**	5.6	2	1973	**Secretariat**	0.1	1	1996	**EditorÕs Note**	5.8	3
1950	**Middleground**	2.7	3	1974	Little Current	1.5	1	1997	Touch Gold	2.65	1
1951	Counterpoint	5.15	3	1975	Avatar*	13.2	2	1998	Victory Gallop	4.5	1
1952	One Count	12.8	2	1976	**Bold Forbes**	0.9	1	1999	**Lemon Drop Kid**	29.75	3
1953	**Native Dancer**	0.45	1	1977	**Seattle Slew**	0.4	1	2000	Commendable	18.8	0
1954	High Gun	3.45	2	1978	**Affirmed**	0.6	3	2001	**Point Given**	1.35	3
1955	**Nashua**	0.15	1	1979	Coastal	4.4	3	2002	Sarava	70.25	0
1956	**Needles**	0.65	2	1980	Temperence Hill	53.4	4	2003	Empire Maker*	2	0
1957	Gallant Man	0.95	1	1981	Summing	7.9	1	2004	**Birdstone**	36	1
1958	Cavan	4.5	0	1982	Conquistador Cielo	4.1	1	2005	**Afleet Alex**	1.15	2
1959	**Sword Dancer**	1.65	3	1983	**Caveat**	2.6	1	2006	Jazil	6.2	0
1960	Celtic Ash	8.4	2	1984	**Swale**	1.5	1	2007	Rags to Riches	4.3	
1961	Sherluck*	65.05	4	1985	Creme Fraiche	2.5	1	2008	Da'Tara	38.5	
1962	**Jaipur**	2.85	1	1986	**Danzig Connection**	8	2	2009	Summer Bird	11.9	
1963	Chateaugay*	4.5	1	1987	**Bet Twice**	8	2	2010	Drosselmeyer	13	
1964	**Quadrangle**	6.55	3	1988	Risen Star	2.1	1	2011	Ruler on Ice	24.75	
1965	Hail to All	2.65	1	1989	**Easy Goer**	1.6	3	2012	Union Rags	2.75	
1966	Amberoid	5.5	2	1990	Go And Go	7.5	2	2013	Palace Malice	13.8	
1967	Damascus	0.8	1	1991	**Hansel**	4.1	3	2014	Tonalist	9.2	
1968	Stage Door Johnny	4.4	1	1992	**A.P. Indy**	1.1	2				
1969	Arts and Letters	1.7	1								

Note: **Bold** indicates dual qualifier, * indicates asterisk qualifier.

A more powerful test would be to score with money. It is clear that the DIs, especially in the Belmont, have high value added with a number such as Thunder Gulch, Birdstone and Lemon Drop Kid at very high odds. The latter two at odds of about 30–1. Steve Roman on his chef-de-race site summarizes the results on IV or relative advantage:

> The data reveal that between 1973 and 1999, each decade and each Triple Crown race has an IV greater than 1.00, from IV 1.45 for the Preakness in the 1980's to IV 4.57 for the Kentucky Derby in the 1970's. The pattern continues into the new millennium except for the Derby. The IV for the Derby has declined in each decade between the 1973 and 2009, but the IV's for the Preakness and Belmont have held up well. The overall IV of 2.55 for all the Triple Crown races in which a Dual Qualifier started since 1973 supports the notion that Dual Qualifier characteristics are indeed an advantage in classic performance.

So if 20% of the horses are DQs and 30% win, then the IV is 1.50.

17.2. The 2012 Triple Crown

The lone dual qualifier wins the Belmont again!

For the 2012 Belmont Stakes, I was in Istanbul, where I have taught an applied stock market course at Sabanci University each June. There was a lot of hype going into the Belmont as I'll Have Another had won the Kentucky Derby and Preakness piloted by an unknown 25 year old Mexican jockey Mario Gutierrez. Thoughts of a triple crown winner abounded. But in the 34 years since Affirmed won all three races in 1978, there have been seven horses that went into the Belmont with a chance to win all three classic races. They are: Spectacular Bid, Silver Charm, Sunday Silence, Smarty Jones, Charismatic, Real Quiet, and Big Brown. An 8th who lost was California Chrome in 2014. In addition, there were some great horses who won the last two legs but had lost the Derby such as Risen Star, Afleet Alex and Point Given. The record of the dual qualifies in all three triple crown races from 1973–2013 is in Table 17.6.

I'll Have Another had a relatively weak two-year-old campaign but did have one win and one second in three races with Beyers of 83, 84 and a dismal 40 in the Grade I Hopeful at Saratoga.

I presume that Mario got the mount on at Santa Anita because the horse did not look that good and the top jockeys had other mounts. Mario had been in Vancouver at the old Hastings Park where Donald Hausch and I did a lot of our early research on racetrack betting in the late 1970s and 1980s.

Table 17.6. The record of dual qualifiers in the triple crown races (1973–2013).

YEARS		DERBY	%	PREAKNESS	%	BELMONT	%	ALL	%
2010-2013	Races	4		4		4		12	
	Winners	1	25.0%	1	25.0%	1	33.3%	3	25.0%
	DQs	23	29.5%	9	19.6%	7	20.0%	42	24.3%
	DQ Winners	4.3%		11.1%		10.0%		7.1%	
	Starters	78		46		49		173	
	IV	0.85		1.28		1.23		1.03	
YEARS		DERBY	%	PREAKNESS	%	BELMONT	%	ALL	%
2000-2009	Races	9		7		5		21	
	Winners	1	11.1%	3	42.9%	3	60.0%	7	33.3%
	DQs	34	18.2%	17	23.0%	9	18.8%	60	19.4%
	DQ Winners	2.9%		17.6%		33.3%		11.7%	
	Starters	187		74		48		309	
	IV	0.61		1.87		3.20		1.72	
YEARS		DERBY	%	PREAKNESS	%	BELMONT	%	ALL	%
1990-1999	Races	9		9		10		28	
	Winners	5	55.6%	6	66.7%	6	60.0%	17	60.7%
	DQs	38	25.0%	19	19.2%	21	20.0%	78	21.9%
	DQ Winners	13.2%		31.6%		28.6%		21.8%	
	Starters	152		99		105		356	
	IV	2.22		3.47		3.00		2.77	
YEARS		DERBY	%	PREAKNESS	%	BELMONT	%	ALL	%
1980-1989	Races	10		10		10		30	
	Winners	8	80.0%	2	20.0%	5	50.0%	15	50.0%
	DQs	33	19.3%	13	13.8%	14	13.5%	60	16.3%
	DQ Winners	24.2%		15.4%		35.7%		25.0%	
	Starters	171		94		104		369	
	IV	4.15		1.45		3.71		3.08	
YEARS		DERBY	%	PREAKNESS	%	BELMONT	%	ALL	%
1973-1979	Races	7		7		7		21	
	Winners	7	100.0%	5	71.4%	4	57.1%	16	76.2%
	DQs	21	21.9%	15	26.8%	11	20.4%	47	22.8%
	DQ Winners	33.3%		33.3%		36.4%		34.0%	
	Starters	96		56		54		206	
	IV	4.57		2.67		2.81		3.34	
YEARS		DERBY	%	PREAKNESS	%	BELMONT	%	ALL	%
1973-2013	Races	39		37		36		112	
	Winners	22	56.4%	17	47.2%	19	52.8%	58	51.8%
	DQs	149	21.8%	73	20.0%	65	18.1%	287	20.3%
	DQ Winners	14.8%		23.3%		29.2%		20.2%	
	Starters	684		369		360		1413	
	IV	2.59		2.32		2.92		2.55	

Source: Chef-de-race.com.

He then moved to the big time at Santa Anita. I'll Have Another won the R. B. Lewis Grade II at $1\frac{1}{16}$ on February 4 by $2\frac{3}{4}$ lengths with a 96 Beyer at 43–1. He then won the Grade I Santa Anita Derby by a nose with a Beyer of 95 at 4–1. I'll Have Another was lightly raced and famed jockey Gary Stevens pointed out that he might improve. In the Derby he was overlooked by most handicappers as his Beyer speed and other figures were not that strong compared to the competition. It was a big item in the Vancouver Sun and my wife thought the whole story of this underdog meant that he would do well in the Derby. She suggested I bet on him but I did not. She was right and he ran down the favorite Bodemeister who had run a Beyer 108 in the Arkansas Derby at $1\frac{1}{8}$ miles uncontested to win by $9\frac{1}{2}$ lengths. But in the Kentucky Derby he was in a speed dual with Trinniberg for the first mile with Bodemeister leading, Trinniberg then faded to 11th and then 17th at 44.9 to 1. After a perfect trip, I'll Have Another beat Bodemeister by $1\frac{1}{2}$ lengths with a Beyer of 101. Again, he was at long odds, 15.3–1 and was an asterisk qualifier winner of the Kentucky Derby. Bodemeister had a 99 Beyer. Dullahan with his 4.2 dosage finished third at 12.1 to 1, with Went the Day Well fourth at 30.6 to 1 and Union Rags was seventh at 5.1 to 1. The payoffs were large with the \$2 exacta \$306.60. The \$2 trifecta for \$3065.60 and the \$2 super for \$96,092.80. The \$2 Pick 6 paid \$675,148.00. In the Preakness, Mike Smith had a perfect trip with Bodemeister leading all the way and running back to the Arkansas Derby level at 109 Beyer. But I'll Have Another improved to a slightly better 109 and won again. Creative Cause finished third and Zetterholm fourth. So the finish was 9–7–6–8. The charts for both of these races follow.

Legendary trainer Bob Baffert did not run Bodemeister in the Belmont. I suppose there were several reasons for this. First, Bodemeister was unable to win even with the perfect Preakness trip. Second, he likely needed a rest and third, Baffert had a fresh horse, Paynter, who had run a 106 Beyer, ready to take his place again with Mike Smith aboard.

The hype was intense then dropped like a thud when it was announced that I'll Have Another had a minor tendon injury that did not affect him much but was a danger when fully extended. So he was scratched. He was also retired. I assume that was because he was worth more now for breeding than he might be in a year or so after the injury healed. There is the risk that he would not regain his Derby and Preakness form. Also there are many costs such as insurance and the time value of money with earnings not that much and stud fees more. Again, an example of fast rushing to stud. Regarding the betting, I had a loss in the Derby, collecting on the place and show bets on Bodemeister but losing the win bets and the exotics.

Table 17.7. Kentucky Derby Bets.

Amount	Runners	Bet	Payout
50.00	6 win	50.00	0.00
50.00	6 place	50.00	155.00
100.00	6 show	100.00	280.00
25.00	3 show	25.00	0.00
10.00	15/6	10.00	0.00
10.00	15/6/4	10.00	0.00
5.00	15/6/4/8,13	10.00	0.00
40.00	6/10	40.00	0.00
25.00	6/15	25.00	0.00
10.00	6/4,8,15	30.00	0.00
10.00	6/15/8/13	10.00	0.00
10.00	4/6,15	20.00	0.00
3.00	3/4-6,8,10,14,15	21.00	0.00
2.00	3/4-6,8,10,14,15/4-6,8,10,14,15	84.00	0.00
1.00	3/4-6,8,10,14,15/4-6,8,10,14,15/4-6,8,10,14,15	210.00	0.00
3.00	6/3-5,8,10,14,15	21.00	0.00
2.00	6/3-5,8,10,14,15/3-5,8,10,14,15	84.00	0.00
1.00	6/3-5,8,10,14,15/3-5,8,10,14,15/3-5,8,10,14,15	210.00	0.00
3.00	4/3,5,6,8,10,14,15	21.00	0.00
2.00	4/3,5,6,8,10,14,15/3,5,6,8,10,14,15	84.00	0.00
1.00	4/3,5,6,8,10,14,15/3,5,6,8,10,14,15/ 3,5,6,8,10,14,15	210.00	0.00
3.00	15/3-6,8,10,14	21.00	0.00
2.00	15/3-6,8,10,14/3-6,8,10,14	84.00	0.00
1.00	15/3-6,8,10,14/3-6,8,10,14/3-6,8,10,14	210.00	0.00
100.00	6 win	100.00	0.00
50.00	6 place, show	100.00	295.00
	Total	1840.00	730.00

In the Preakness, I recalled that the Derby 1–2 finishers are often 1–2 or 2–1 in the Preakness. See Table 17.7 for the bets and the chart of the race.

So I was heavily on both of them but with more on Bodemeister than I'll Have Another, partially because of that 108 Beyer in the Arkansas Derby but also by the six handicapping services I use which favored Bodemeister and his hall of fame trainer Bob Baffert and hall of fame jockey Mike Smith.

The 2–1 finish was good enough to make a profit in the bets which are listed in Table 17.9 before the rebate even though I lost the superfecta. My bets (including my wife's) in the Peakness totaled $2422.00 and returned $3131.60 plus rebate. They are listed in Table 17.8 followed by the chart of the race. I had place and show in both of the 1–2 finishers and some on the trifecta. I focused on Went the Day Well along with Creative Cause behind the two tophorses with a

CHURCHILL DOWNS - May 5, 2012 - Race 11
STAKES Kentucky Derby Presented by Yum! Brands Grade 1 - For Thoroughbred Three Year Old
One And One Fourth Miles On The Dirt **Track Record:** (Secretariat - 1:59.40 - May 5, 1973)
Purse: $2,000,000 Guaranteed
Available Money: $2,219,600
Value of Race: $2,219,800 1st $1,459,600, 2nd $400,000, 3rd $200,000, 4th $100,000, 5th $60,000
Weather: Cloudy **Track:** Fast
Off at: 6:31 **Start:** Good for all except 16

EQUIBASE COMPANY

Video Race Replay

Last Raced	Pgm	Horse Name (Jockey)	Wgt	M/E	PP	1/4	1/2	3/4	1m	Str	Fin	Odds	Comments
7Apr12 ^{6}SA^{1}	19	I'll Have Another (Gutierrez, Mario)	126	LA	19	6^{Head}	$7^{2\ 1/2}$	6^{1}	$4^{1/2}$	2^{2}	$1^{1\ 1/2}$	15.30	4 wide 1/4 pl
14Apr12 ^{11}OP^{1}	6	Bodemeister (Smith, Mike)	126	LA	6	1^{Head}	1^{1}	1^{1}	1^{3}	1^{3}	2^{Neck}	4.20*	fast pace, gamely
14Apr12 ^{11}KEE^{1}	5	Dullahan (Desormeaux, Kent)	126	LA	5	$11^{1/2}$	11^{Head}	$13^{1\ 1/2}$	$7^{1/2}$	5^{1}	$3^{3/4}$	12.10	broke in, bmpd, 7w 1/4
24Mar12 ^{10}TP^{1}	13	Went the Day Well (Velazquez, John)	126	LA b	13	$17^{1/2}$	17^{1}	$15^{1/2}$	$14^{1\ 1/2}$	9^{Head}	$4^{1/2}$	30.60	bumped, 7w 1/4 pl
7Apr12 ^{6}SA^{2}	8	Creative Cause (Rosario, Joel)	126	L	8	10^{Head}	$10^{1/2}$	$11^{1/2}$	$5^{2\ 1/2}$	$3^{1/2}$	5^{4}	11.90	in close 7/8, 8w 1/4
7Apr12 ^{6}SA^{6}	20	Liaison (Garcia, Martin)	126	LA b	20	$9^{1/2}$	8^{Head}	7^{1}	6^{Head}	6^{Head}	$6^{1/2}$	56.20	4 wide, tired
31Mar12 ^{11}GP^{3}	4	Union Rags (Leparoux, Julien)	126	LA	4	$18^{1\ 1/2}$	$18^{1/2}$	17^{1}	$16^{1\ 1/2}$	$13^{2\ 1/2}$	$7^{3/4}$	5.10	squeezed, took up
1Apr12 ^{10}FG^{3}	7	Rousing Sermon (Lezcano, Jose)	126	LA b	7	14^{Head}	14^{Head}	9^{Head}	9^{1}	$8^{1\ 1/2}$	8^{2}	40.70	waited, blocked
14Apr12 ^{11}KEE^{2}	14	Hansen (Dominguez, Ramon)	126	LA	14	3^{Head}	3^{1}	$3^{1\ 1/2}$	3^{Head}	$4^{1\ 1/2}$	$9^{1\ 1/4}$	13.10	carried in early,tired
25Mar12 ^{12}SUN^{1}	10	Daddy Nose Best (Gomez, Garrett)	126	LA	10	$8^{1\ 1/2}$	$9^{1\ 1/2}$	10^{1}	8^{2}	7^{1}	$10^{1/2}$	14.00	forced in, steadied
14Apr12 ^{11}OP^{6}	2	Optimizer (Court, Jon)	126	LA	2	12^{2}	12^{2}	$12^{1/2}$	$13^{1/2}$	$10^{1/2}$	$11^{7\ 1/4}$	42.40	steadied 1/4 pl
7Apr12 ^{9}AQU^{2}	11	Alpha (Maragh, Rajiv)	126	LA f	11	13^{1}	$13^{1/2}$	14^{Head}	$15^{1/2}$	$15^{1\ 1/2}$	$12^{3/4}$	19.60	awkward st, no menace
31Mar12 ^{11}GP^{4}	16	El Padrino (Bejarano, Rafael)	126	LA	16	20	20	20	18^{4}	17^{2}	$13^{3\ 1/2}$	29.40	steadied, roughed
7Apr12 ^{8}HAW^{1}	17	Done Talking (Russell, Sheldon)	126	LA	17	19^{2}	19^{2}	18^{Head}	17^{Head}	$16^{1/2}$	$14^{1\ 1/4}$	39.40	in tight, jostled
14Apr12 ^{11}OP^{3}	18	Sabercat (Nakatani, Corey)	126	LA	18	16^{Head}	15^{3}	$16^{1/2}$	11^{1}	$12^{1/2}$	$15^{5\ 1/4}$	37.80	5 wide early
7Apr12 ^{9}AQU^{1}	15	Gemologist (Castellano, Javier)	126	LA	15	$5^{2\ 1/2}$	$5^{1\ 1/2}$	$5^{1/2}$	10^{Head}	14^{2}	$16^{1\ 1/2}$	8.60	drifted out, came in
7Apr12 ^{9}AQU^{1}	9	Trinniberg (Martinez, Willie)	126	LA f	9	$2^{1\ 1/2}$	$2^{1\ 1/2}$	2^{3}	2^{Head}	11^{2}	17^{3}	44.90	chased fast pace
14Apr12 ^{11}KEE^{6}	12	Prospective (Contreras, Luis)	126	L b	12	$15^{1/2}$	16^{Head}	19^{Head}	19^{10}	19^{14}	$18^{15\ 1/2}$	57.90	clipped heels early
31Mar12 ^{11}GP^{1}	3	Take Charge Indy (Borel, Calvin)	126	L b	3	7^{1}	6^{1}	$4^{1/2}$	12^{Head}	18^{3}	19	11.90	inside, gave way
31Mar12 MEY^{1}	1	Daddy Long Legs (O'Donoghue, Colm)	126	LA	1	4^{Head}	4^{2}	$8^{1/2}$	20	20	---	26.00	eased

Fractional Times: 22.32 45.39 1:09.80 1:35.19 **Final Time:** 2:01.83
Split Times: (23:07) (24:41) (25:39) (26:64)
Run-Up: 34 feet

Winner: I'll Have Another, Chestnut Colt, by Flower Alley out of Arch's Gal Edith, by Arch. Foaled Apr 01, 2009 in Kentucky.
Breeder: Harvey Clarke. **Winning Owner:** Reddam Racing LLC

Scratched Horse(s): My Adonis (Also-Eligible)

Total WPS Pool: $56,626,629

Pgm	Horse	Win	Place	Show
19	I'll Have Another	32.60	13.80	9.00
6	Bodemeister		8.20	5.60
5	Dullahan			7.20

Wager Type	Winning Numbers	Payoff	Pool	Carryover
$2.00 Exacta	19-6	306.60	23,827,020	
$2.00 Trifecta	19-6-5	3,065.60	28,767,230	
$2.00 Superfecta	19-6-5-13	96,092.80	10,864,365	
$2.00 Daily Double	1-19	817.60	1,138,854	
$2.00 Daily Double	OAKS/DERBY 9-19	731.20	2,351,108	
$2.00 Pick 3	6-1-19 (3 correct)	3,297.40	1,442,960	
$0.50 Pick 3	OAKS/WDFRD/DERBY 9-1-19 (3 correct)	3,492.45	642,736	
$2.00 Pick 4	10-6-1-19 (4 correct)	31,124.40	2,757,964	
$0.50 Pick 5	4-10-6-1-19 (5 correct)	23,923.80	1,074,309	
$2.00 Pick 6	2-4-10-6-1-19 (5 correct)	3,161.80	0	
$2.00 Pick 6	2-4-10-6-1-19 (6 correct)	675,148.00	1,789,046	
$1.00 Super High Five	19-6-5-13-8		341,917	276,914
$2.00 Future Wager	FUTURE EXACTA POOL 1 13-24	257.80	137,041	
$2.00 Future Wager	FUTURE EXACTA POOL 2 12-3	1,661.00	111,794	
$2.00 Future Wager	FUTURE EXACTA POOL 3 10-2	1,351.40	124,304	
$2.00 Future Wager	FUTURE POOL 1 - 13	60.20	494,263	
$2.00 Future Wager	FUTURE POOL 2 - 12	48.20	299,574	
$2.00 Future Wager	FUTURE POOL 3 - 10	45.60	303,043	

Trainers: 19 - O'Neill, Doug; 6 - Baffert, Bob; 5 - Romans, Dale; 13 - Motion, H.; 8 - Harrington, Mike; 20 - Baffert, Bob; 4 - Matz, Michael; 7 - Hollendorfer, Jerry; 14 - Maker, Michael; 10 - Asmussen, Steven; 2 - Lukas, D.; 11 - McLaughlin, Kiaran; 16 - Pletcher, Todd; 17 - Smith, Hamilton; 18 - Asmussen, Steven; 15 - Pletcher, Todd; 9 - Parboo, Bisnath; 12 - Casse, Mark; 3 - Byrne, Patrick; 1 - O'Brien, Aidan

Owners: 19 - Reddam Racing LLC; 6 - Zayat Stables, LLC, Moreno, Mike and Moreno, Tiffany; 5 - Donegal Racing; 13 - Team Valor International and Ford, Mark; 8 -Heinz Steinmann; 20 - Arnold Zetcher LLC; 4 - Chadds Ford Stable; 7 - Williams, Mr. and Mrs. Larry D.; 14 - Hansen, Kendall, M.D. and Skychai Racing, LLC; 10 - Zollars, Cathy and Bob; 2 - Bluegrass Hall LLC; 11 - Godolphin Racing LLC; 16 - Let's Go Stable; 17 - Skeedattle Associates; 18 - Winchell Thoroughbreds LLC; 15 - WinStar Farm LLC; 9 - Shivananda Racing; 12 -John C. Oxley; 3 - Chuck and Meribeth Sandford LLC; 1 - Magnier, Mrs. John, Tabor, Michael and Smith, Derrick;

Footnotes
I'LL HAVE ANOTHER angled in early and gained a forward position, eagerly pulled his rider up between rivals late on the backstretch, continued to make progress on the second turn, came four wide into the stretch, reeled in the leader near the sixteenth marker and drew clear late. BODEMEISTER vied for the early lead near the rail, took over before a half, led the field through a fast pace into the second turn, increased his lead under urging approaching the stretch, stayed on gamely to the final sixteenth but could not cope with the winner late. DULLAHAN broke in and bumped UNION RAGS, was in tight entering the first turn when reserved, continued under a rating hold for six furlongs, commenced his rally three wide once in the second turn, came seven wide into the stretch and closed well late. WENT THE DAY WELL bumped at the start, was outrun for a half four wide, angled in into the second turn, moved back out seven wide entering the stretch and closed well between rivals. CREATIVE CAUSE in hand early mid pack, was in close quarters three wide entering the first turn, angled to the outside on the backstretch, made an eight wide run out of the second turn and finished willingly. LIAISON within striking distance four wide, held on well to midstretch, bumped with DADDY KNOWS BEST soon after and tired. UNION RAGS bumped and squeezed back at the start, was outrun along the rail, took up once in the second turn behind DADDY LONG LEGS, angled outside that one, swung to the outside for the drive and made a late gain. ROUSING SERMON unhurried early, saved ground after five furlongs, waited off the inside with three furlongs to go, was blocked when attempting to split rivals in upper stretch, angled back in and showed some late interest. HANSEN carried in early, was a bit eager when forwardly placed between rivals, made a mild run into the stretch but tired. DADDY NOSE BEST steadied when forced in early, gained good position soon after, made a good run between rivals to the quarter mile marker, was bumped in midstretch and tired. OPTIMIZER reserved early along the inside, steadied approaching the stretch after angling out a bit, moved back to the inside for the drive but could not threaten. ALPHA awkward at the start, was outrun early, raced six wide into the stretch and could not menace. EL PADRINO rank when breaking slowly, trailed for five furlongs, was roughed between rivals near the half mile marker then passed tiring rivals. DONE TALKING in tight at the start, was outrun while wide, came in to soundly bump EL PADRINO near the half mile marker then failed to menace. SABERCAT outrun early five wide, made a mild run to the quarter mile marker but tired in the drive. GEMOLOGIST drifted out at the start, came in carrying several rivals in soon after, raced close up three wide and faded. TRINNIBERG chased a fast pace, held well to the stretch and gave way. PROSPECTIVE bumped at the start, clipped heels and stumbled in traffic in the initial furlong, was outrun early, bumped EL PADRINO near the half mile marker and faded. TAKE CHARGE INDY within striking distance along the inside, gave way. DADDY LONG LEGS close up along the inside, failed to respond when hard ridden late on the backstretch, stopped and was eased.

Table 17.8. Preakness bets.

Amount	Runners	Bet	Payout
200.00	7 win	200.00	0.00
400.00	7 place	400.00	640.00
200.00	7 show	200.00	280.00
200.00	9 place	200.00	380.00
200.00	9 show	200.00	280.00
100.00	5 show	100.00	0.00
25.00	7/9	25.00	0.00
25.00	7/9	25.00	0.00
25.00	7/9	25.00	0.00
25.00	7/9	25.00	0.00
30.00	9/7	30.00	279.00
20.00	9/5,7	40.00	186.00
12.00	5/7,9	24.00	0.00
8.00	9/5,7	16.00	74.40
10.00	7/9/5	10.00	0.00
10.00	7/9/5	10.00	0.00
10.00	7/9/5	10.00	0.00
10.00	7/9/5	10.00	0.00
10.00	7/9/5	10.00	0.00
8.00	9/5-7/5-7	48.00	283.20
20.00	7/5,6,9/ 5,6,9	120.00	0.00
10.00	9/7/5,6	20.00	354.00
7.00	5/7,9/6,7,9	28.00	0.00
4.00	7,9/7-9/ 7-9	16.00	0.00
20.00	7/9/5,6	40.00	0.00
5.00	7/8/5,6,9	15.00	0.00
25.00	7/ 9/ 5/ 6	25.00	0.00
8.00	7/9/8/5	8.00	0.00
8.00	7/9/8/6	8.00	0.00
6.00	7,9/5,6/5,6/8	24.00	0.00
6.00	9/5-7/5-8/5-8	108.00	0.00
8.00	7/5,6,9/5,6,8,9/5,6,8,9	144.00	0.00
3.00	5/7,9/6-9/ 6-9	36.00	0.00
2.00	7,9/ 5-7,9/5-7,9/5-7,9	24.00	0.00
1.00	7,9/5-9/5-9/5-9	48.00	0.00
15.00	9 win	45.00	112.50
35.00	9 win, place, show	105.00	262.50
	Total	2422.00	3131.60

TWELFTH RACE
Pimlico
MAY 19, 2012

$1\frac{3}{16}$ MILES. (1.52^{2}) 137TH RUNNING OF THE PREAKNESS. Grade I. Purse $1,000,000 FOR THREE-YEAR-OLDS, $10,000 TO PASS THE ENTRY BOX, STARTERS TO PAY $10,000 ADDITIONAL. 60% of the purse to the winner, 20% to second, 11% to third, 6% to fourth and 3% to fifth. Weight 126 pounds for Colts and Geldings. A replica of the Woodlawn Vase will be presented to the winning owner to remain his or her personal property.

Value of Race: $1,000,000 Winner $600,000; second $200,000; third $110,000; fourth $60,000; fifth $30,000. Mutuel Pool $20,136,607.00 Exacta Pool $10,679,092.00 Superfecta Pool $6,648,721.00 Super High Five Pool $359,708.00 Trifecta Pool $12,557,107.00

Last Raced	Horse	M/Eqt.	A.	Wt	PP	St	¼	½	¾	Str	Fin	Jockey	Odds $1
5May12 ^{11}CD^{1}	I'll Have Another	L	3	126	9	6	$4^{\frac{1}{2}}$	4^{hd}	$3^{\frac{1}{2}}$	$2^{3\frac{1}{2}}$	1^{nk}	Gutierrez Mario	3.20
5May12 ^{11}CD^{2}	Bodemeister	L	3	126	7	3	1^{1}	1^{1}	$1^{1\frac{1}{2}}$	1^{3}	$2^{3\frac{3}{4}}$	Smith M E	1.70
5May12 ^{11}CD^{5}	Creative Cause	L	3	126	6	4	$3^{1\frac{1}{2}}$	2^{1}	$2^{2\frac{1}{2}}$	$3^{5\frac{1}{2}}$	3^{3}	Rosario J	6.30
6Apr12 ^{8}Aqu^{1}	Zetterholm	L	3	126	4	8	$9^{2\frac{1}{2}}$	$9^{3\frac{1}{2}}$	$7^{1\frac{1}{2}}$	$4^{1\frac{1}{2}}$	$4^{3\frac{1}{4}}$	Alvarado J	20.50
7Apr12 ^{9}Aqu^{3}	Teeth of the Dog	L	3	126	2	1	7^{1}	$6^{\frac{1}{2}}$	6^{1}	$5^{1\frac{1}{2}}$	5^{nk}	Bravo J	15.50
5May12 ^{11}CD^{11}	Optimizer	L	3	126	10	10	10^{1}	$10^{1\frac{1}{2}}$	10^{3}	6^{hd}	$6^{2\frac{1}{4}}$	Nakatani C S	23.30
14Apr12 ^{11}OP^{4}	Cozzetti	L	3	126	11	7	$8^{\frac{1}{2}}$	$8^{\frac{1}{2}}$	$9^{2\frac{1}{2}}$	7^{6}	$7^{7\frac{1}{2}}$	Lezcano J	27.30
7Apr12 ^{9}Aqu^{4}	Tiger Walk	L bf	3	126	1	2	5^{1}	$5^{2\frac{1}{2}}$	5^{1}	$8^{\frac{1}{2}}$	$8^{2\frac{1}{4}}$	Dominguez R A	23.40
5May12 ^{11}CD^{10}	Daddy Nose Best	L	3	126	8	11	11	11	11	9^{3}	$9^{3\frac{1}{4}}$	Leparoux J R	11.10
5May12 ^{11}CD^{4}	Went the Day Well	L b	3	126	5	9	6^{1}	7^{2}	8^{hd}	10^{hd}	$10^{3\frac{3}{4}}$	Velazquez J R	5.70
5May12 ^{10}Pim^{1}	Pretension	L bf	3	126	3	5	2^{hd}	$3^{1\frac{1}{2}}$	4^{hd}	11	11	Santiago Javier	33.70

OFF AT 6:20 Start Good. Won driving. Track fast.

TIME :23^{3}, :47^{3}, 1:11^{3}, 1:36^{3}, 1:55^{4} (:23.79, :47.68, 1:11.72, 1:36.69, 1:55.94)

$2 Mutuel Prices:				
	9–I'LL HAVE ANOTHER	8.40	3.80	2.80
	7–BODEMEISTER		3.20	2.80
	6–CREATIVE CAUSE			3.60

$2 EXACTA 9–7 PAID $18.60 $1 SUPERFECTA 9–7–6–4 PAID $424.30 $2 SUPER HIGH FIVE 9–7–6–4–2 PAID $3,667.60 $2 TRIFECTA 9–7–6 PAID $70.80

Ch. c, (Apr), by Flower Alley – Arch's Gal Edith, by Arch. Trainer O'Neill Doug. Bred by Harvey Clarke (Ky).

I'LL HAVE ANOTHER relaxed in the clear while removed from the inside, edged closer leaving the far turn while still within himself, responded when given his cue leaving the five sixteenths marker, closed relentlessly under stout right handed pressure and forged ahead of BODEMEISTER in the final strides. BODEMEISTER advanced wide to a clear lead through the opening quarter, dropped in about a path from the rail and set comfortable fractions under rating, opened up when set down entering the stretch, remained clear approaching the sixteenth pole, kept on gamely but could not withstand the winner's charge. CREATIVE CAUSE was steadied off BODEMEISTER'S heels nearing the first turn, angled out a bit and stalked three wide, came under strong left handed pressure leaving the five sixteenths marker, failed to kick on and faded in the final furlong. ZETTERHOLM, fractious in the gate, was rated back from between rivals soon after the start, saved ground leaving the five eighths pole, angled out to advance four wide between foes into the stretch, shifted back in then had no significant late response. TEETH OF THE DOG, three wide racing inside WENT THE DAY WELL nearing the half mile pole, continued off the inside into the stretch and had no rally. OPTIMIZER lacked speed, angled four wide leaving the far turn and passed tiring rivals. COZZETTI settled back early, angled out and made mild progress five wide approaching the quarter pole then flattened out. TIGER WALK, taken back a bit under firm handling nearing the clubhouse turn, angled out leaving the three quarter pole, gained ground racing between horses into the far turn then tired. DADDY NOSE BEST, away slowly after bobbling, lagged well back, saved ground into the lane and failed to threaten. WENT THE DAY WELL, in close soon after the break, moved up into a forward position four wide, failed to respond when called upon into the far turn then retreated. PRETENSION angled inside early to force the early pace, continued willingly into the far turn then dropped back.

Owners– 1, Reddam Racing LLC; 2, Zayat Stables LLC Moreno Mike and Moreno Tiffany; 3, Steinmann Heinz; 4, Winter Park Partners; 5, JW Singer LLC; 6, Bluegrass Hall LLC; 7, Albaugh Family Stables LLC; 8, Sagamore Farm; 9, Zollars Cathy and Bob; 10, Team Valor International and Ford Mark; 11, Kidwells Petite Stable

Trainers– 1, O'Neill Doug; 2, Baffert Bob; 3, Harrington Mike; 4, Dutrow Richard E Jr; 5, Matz Michael R; 6, Lukas D Wayne; 7, Romans Dale; 8, Correas Ignacio IV; 9, Asmussen Steven M; 10, Motion H Graham; 11, Grove Christopher W

Table 17.9. Belmont bets.

Amount	Runners	Bet	Payout
50.00	9 win, place, show	150.00	225.00
7.00	9/3	7.00	0.00
15.00	9/5	15.00	0.00
15.00	9/5/3	15.00	0.00
7.00	9/3/5	7.00	0.00
4.00	9/ 5/ 3/ 1,2,12	12.00	0.00
2.00	9/ 3/ 5/ 1,2,12	6.00	0.00
400.00	9 win	400.00	0.00
500.00	9 place	500.00	1275.00
600.00	9 show	600.00	1170.00
100.00	9/5	100.00	0.00
40.00	9/3	40.00	0.00
20.00	3,5/ 3,5,9	80.00	314.00
10.00	9/5/3	10.00	0.00
10.00	9/5/3	10.00	0.00
10.00	9/5/3	10.00	0.00
10.00	9/5/3	10.00	0.00
10.00	9/5/3	10.00	0.00
20.00	9/3/5	20.00	0.00
5.00	3,5/ 3,5,9/ 3,5,9	20.00	0.00
10.00	9/ 5/ 3/ 1,2,12	30.00	0.00
10.00	9/ 5/ 3/ 1,2,12	30.00	0.00
10.00	9/ 5/ 3/ 1,2,12	30.00	0.00
10.00	9/ 5/ 3/ 1,2,12	30.00	0.00
1.00	3,5/ 3,5,9/ 3,5,9/ 1,2,12	12.00	0.00
1.00	3,5/ 3,5,9/ 3,5,9/ 1,2,12	12.00	0.00
1.00	3,5/ 3,5,9/ 3,5,9/ 1,2,12	12.00	0.00
10.00	9/ 3/ 5/ 1,2,12	30.00	0.00
10.00	9/ 3/ 5/ 1,2,12	30.00	0.00
	Total	2238.00	2984.00

small amount on number 8, Daddy Nose Best at 11.1–1 who also was never in contention. Went the Day Well at 5.70 to 1 with J. R. Velasquez aboard was never in the race. Quinn was the only handicapper picking Zetterholm but I did not use him. The $1 superfecta paid $424.30 with Zetterholm at 20.5 to 1. The $2 super high five getting the first five finishers in correct order paid $3,667.60 with Teeth of the Dog at 15.5 to 1 finishing fifth. Again my wife got it perfect betting win, place and show on the winner.

ELEVENTH RACE
Belmont
JUNE 9, 2012

1½ MILES. (2.24) 144TH RUNNING OF THE BELMONT. Grade I. Purse $1,000,000 FOR THREE YEAR OLDS. By subscription of $600 each, to accompany the nomination, if made on or before January 21, 2012, or $6,000, if made on or before March 24, 2012. $10,000 to pass the entry box and $10,000 additional to start. All entrants will be required to pay entry and starting fees; but no fees, supplemental or otherwise shall be added to the purse. The purse to be divided 60% to the winner, 20% to second, 11% to third, 6% to fourth and 3% to fifth. Colts and Geldings, 126 lbs.; Fillies, 121 lbs. The winning owner will be presented with the August Belmont Memorial Cup to be retained for one year as well as a trophy for permanent possession and trophies to the winning trainer and jockey.

Value of Race: $1,000,000 Winner $600,000; second $200,000; third $110,000; fourth $60,000; fifth $30,000. Mutuel Pool $20,544,942.00 Exacta Pool $10,199,514.00 Trifecta Pool $11,942,148.00 Superfecta Pool $6,573,393.00

Last Raced	Horse	M/Eqt.	A.	Wt	PP	¼	½	1	1¼	Str	Fin	Jockey	Odds $1
5May12 ^{11}CD^{7}	Union Rags	L	3	126	3	$5^{1\frac{1}{2}}$	5^{1}	$3^{\frac{1}{2}}$	2^{hd}	2^{hd}	1^{nk}	Velazquez J R	2.75
19May12 ^{4}Pim^{1}	Paynter	L	3	126	9	1^{1}	$1^{1\frac{1}{2}}$	1^{1}	1^{1}	1^{1}	$2^{1\frac{3}{4}}$	Smith M E	4.30
5May12 ^{1}CD^{1}	Atigun	L	3	126	4	7^{hd}	$8^{\frac{1}{2}}$	6^{2}	$3^{\frac{1}{2}}$	$3^{3\frac{1}{2}}$	$3^{5\frac{1}{4}}$	Leparoux J R	20.50
12May12 ^{9}Bel^{3}	Street Life	L b	3	126	1	11	11	10^{15}	10	$5^{\frac{1}{2}}$	$4^{2\frac{1}{2}}$	Lezcano J	9.80
18Apr12 ^{3}Aqu^{4}	Five Sixteen	L b	3	126	7	8^{1}	$6^{\frac{1}{2}}$	$8^{\frac{1}{2}}$	7^{1}	$6^{\frac{1}{2}}$	5^{1}	Napravnik R	19.30
27Apr12 ^{3}Bel^{1}	Unstoppable U	L f	3	126	2	2^{1}	3^{1}	$2^{2\frac{1}{2}}$	4^{3}	4^{4}	6^{hd}	Alvarado J	11.90
5May12 ^{11}CD^{3}	Dullahan	L	3	126	5	$9^{\frac{1}{2}}$	9^{hd}	9^{1}	$6^{\frac{1}{2}}$	$7^{1\frac{1}{2}}$	$7^{7\frac{1}{4}}$	Castellano J J	2.50
5May12 ^{10}Pim^{3}	My Adonis	L b	3	126	11	4^{hd}	4^{1}	4^{1}	5^{2}	8^{4}	$8^{3\frac{3}{4}}$	Dominguez R A	19.70
10Mar12 ^{11}Tam^{5}	Ravelo's Boy	b	3	126	6	$6^{\frac{1}{2}}$	7^{hd}	$7^{\frac{1}{2}}$	8^{2}	9^{1}	$9^{8\frac{3}{4}}$	Solis A	27.00
19May12 ^{12}Pim^{6}	Optimizer	L	3	126	10	3^{2}	$2^{\frac{1}{2}}$	5^{1}	9^{1}	10	10	Nakatani C S	14.40
27Apr12 ^{3}Bel^{2}	Guyana Star Dweej	L bf	3	126	8	10^{1}	$10^{2\frac{1}{2}}$	11	—	—	—	Desormeaux K J	23.20

OFF AT 6:41 Start Good. Won driving. Track fast.

TIME :23^{3}, :49^{1}, 1:14^{3}, 1:38^{4}, 2:04^{1}, 2:30^{2} (:23.72, :49.23, 1:14.72, 1:38.85, 2:04.39, 2:30.42)

$2 Mutuel Prices:				
	3 – UNION RAGS	7.50	4.20	3.40
	9 – PAYNTER		5.10	3.90
	4 – ATIGUN			10.60

$2 EXACTA 3–9 PAID $31.40 $2 TRIFECTA 3–9–4 PAID $496.00
$2 SUPERFECTA 3–9–4–1 PAID $1,906.00

B. c, (Mar), by Dixie Union – Tempo, by Gone West. Trainer Matz Michael R. Bred by Phyllis M Wyeth (Ky).

UNION RAGS tucked quickly along the rail, contently tracked the front runners under a good hold from the rider for the opening mile, was let out a notch at the five-sixteenths pole and closed the gap, cut the corner into the lane, idled behind PAYNTER lacking optimal clearance along the rail, gained sufficient passage when the previously mentioned rival drifted outward, in response to some left handed stick work, slipped by in the vicinity of the sixteenth pole to draw abreast, wore down PAYNTER in the final seventy yards under strong handling. PAYNTER came away in good order and grabbed control early under his own power, was sent over to the inside, rated kindly while carving the pace, continued along on the same scenario until the quarter pole, came under intensified pressure at that juncture and was let out in response, dug in well to hold the advantage during the ensuing furlong, began to drift outward approaching the sixteenth marker, just after some left handed shots, was switched to a strong hand ride as the top one drew alongside, relinquished but continued on willingly to save the place. ATIGUN sat reserved from off the inside in midpack, was lightly coaxed along departing the backstretch, paused in hand off rivals near the seven-sixteenths pole before commencing to advance, was put to urging angling four wide from the five-sixteenths marker, reached the eighth pole just off the leader, got out finished in the late stages. STREET LIFE swung three wide into the backstretch, was kept well off the inside thereafter, picked up the pace nearing the end of the far turn, fanned seven wide into upper stretch, got straightened away and improved position belatedly. FIVE SIXTEEN raced three wide around both turns, commenced the stretch drive five wide, lacked the needed response. UNSTOPPABLE U broke out a step at the break, settled into a forward position, forced his way into the two path taking over that position from OPTIMIZER proceeding down the backstretch, was rated while attending the pacesetter until the quarter pole, tired steadily after turning for home. DULLAHAN between rivals for much of the initial stages, ducked over to the rail coming to the end of the backstretch, felt the whip midpoint on the far turn, attempting to pick up the pace, was taken outward approaching the top of the lane, settling into the five path, flattened out soon after finishing the move. MY ADONIS underwent a three wide journey and tired. RAVELO'S BOY three wide around the first turn, continued from off the rail, left the three-eighths pole from the five path under encouragement, failed to make headway on the front runners. OPTIMIZER accompanied the pacesetter from the outside for nearly a half, yielded the two path to UNSTOPPABLE U midway down the backstretch, remained prominently placed to the half mile pole before backing away. GUYANA STAR DWEEJ strung out four wide on the opening bend, remained well off the inside, advanced into midpack early down the backstretch, failed to sustain the bid, lost contact with the field and was eased.

Owners– 1, Chadds Ford Stable; 2, Zayat Stables LLC; 3, Shortleaf Stable Inc; 4, Magnolia Racing Stable LLC and Hidden Brook Farm; 5, MeB Racing Stables LLC; 6, Magdalena Racing (Susan McPeek) and Mojallali Stables Inc; 7, Donegal Racing; 8, Hall George and Lori; 9, Korina Stable; 10, Bluegrass Hall LLC; 11, Shivmangal Racing Stable LLC

Trainers– 1, Matz Michael R; 2, Baffert Bob; 3, McPeek Kenneth G; 4, Brown Chad C; 5, Schettino Dominick A; 6, McPeek Kenneth G; 7, Romans Dale; 8, Breen Kelly J; 9, Azpurua Manuel J; 10, Lukas D Wayne; 11, Shivmangal Doodnauth

Scratched– I'll Have Another (19May12 ^{12}Pim^{1})

Table 17.10. Table of handicapper rankings.

Quinn	PSR	HTR	Beyer	Equiform
Paynter	Paynter 113	Paynter	I'll Have Another 109	Paynter $77\frac{1}{2}$
Dullahan	I'll Have Another 108	I'll Have Another	Paynter 106	Dullahan $76\frac{3}{4}$
Union Rags	Dullahan 102	Dullahan	Dullahan 98	Union Rags $76\frac{1}{2}$
Street Life	Union Rags 101	Union Rags	Union Rags 95	My Adonis 74
	My Adonis 99	Street Life		Street Life $73\frac{1}{4}$*
				Atigun 72
				Others 72

Note: *New pace top

Table 17.11. Betting results with rebate for the Triple Crown races (2012).

	Kentucky Derby	Preakness	Belmont	Triple Crown	Second Rebate Shop for Belmont
Wagered	$2,860.00	$2,712.00	$2,953.00	$8,525.00	$1648.00
Return	$1,339.20	$3,208.00	$3,247.00	$7,794.20	$2184.00
Win/Loss	($1,520.80)	$496.00	$294.00	($730.80)	$564.00
Rebate	$140.82	$154.88	$168.04	$463.74	$146.00
Net W/L	($1,379.99)	$650.88	$462.04	($267.07)	$710.00

The Belmont shaped up to favor Paynter and indeed all six handicappers favored him as Table 17.10 shows. Table 17.11 has betting results with rebate for all three triple crown races. Table 17.12 has the odds, dosage profiles, dosage indices and experimental free handicap of the horses. Observe that very few horses were rated as two years old.

Dullahan and Union Rags looked the next best. I did not downgrade Dullahan enough with his dosage of 4.2. This seems way to high to win the Belmont. There have been horses with dosage above 3.5 who won the Belmont Stakes such as Commendable (5.00 in 2000) and Sarava (4.50 in 2002). However, the last ten winners from 20124 back to 2003 had dosage indices of 2.14, 2.56, 1.75, 2.56, 2.43, 3.00, 3.00, 2.11, 1.77, 1.88, 2.64 and 2.78. Even the great Sunday Silence with a 3.8 dosage got crushed in the Belmont.

So Paynter was the pick and he was 7–1 in the morning line and a hefty 4–1 at the racetrack. His Equiform numbers were trending nicely: $70\frac{1}{4}$, 73, 75, and $77\frac{1}{2}$ with Beyers of 79, 89, 100 and 106. His sire, Awesome Again,

Table 17.12. Dosage profiles, indices, experimental free handicap ratings and odds: 2012 Belmont Stakes.

Post Position	Name	Odds to 1	Dosage Profile	Dosage Index	EFH
1	Street Life	9.80	5–3–8–0–0	3.00	nr
2	Unstoppable U	11.90	5–4–9–0–0–	3.0	nr
3	Union Rags	2.75	9–1–10–2–0	2.14	126 (DQ)
4	Atigun	20.50	5–3–12–0–0	2.33	nr
5	Dullahan	2.50	8–8–10–0–0	4.20	119
6	Ravelo's Boy	27.00	2–2–4–0–0	3.00	nr
7	Five Sixteen	19.30	2-0–4–0–0	2.00	nr
8	Guyana Star Dweej	23.00	9–12–9–2–2	3.00nr	
9	Paynter	4.30	6–0–8–0–0	2.50	nr
10	Optimizer	14.40	10–9–17–0–0	3.24	115
11	My Adonis	19.70	2–9–10–0–1	2.67	109
	Dropouts				
	Bodemeister		9–9–12–0–2	3.00	nr
	I'll Have Another		2–4–7–1–0	2.11	111

Note: nr=not rated.

won the Breeders' Cup Classic in 1996 and sired the fastest horse in the last 20+ years, Ghostzapper, who ran four Equiform 84's, the highest I have seen, and won the 2004 Breeders' Cup Classic in record time, under two minutes. I could not check Betfair odds as it is blocked in Turkey. Dullahan and Union Rags looked next best. But Union Rags had another angle. He was the lone dual qualifier in the race. And he had the same pattern as Lemon Drop Kid (at 29.75–1) had in 1999 and Birdstone in 2004 (at 36–1). That is, a terrific two year old year with high earnings and a high experimental free handicap rating, then a very poor three year old year, a very poor Derby followed by skipping the Preakness and a 30–1+ win in the Belmont over Charismatic and Smarty Jones, the two horses that had won the Kentucky Derby and the Preakness, respectively. So I had to have some Union Rags first — but he was 5–2, the second choice behind Dullahan also at 5–2. Given the disappointing 2012 season experienced by Union Rags, these were very short odds.

In the race, as the chart indicates, Mike Smith ran Paynter just as he did Bodemeister in the previous two legs of the triple crown. And the same thing happened. Union Rags came on the inside, which Smith could have blocked but did not. Smith took the blame for the loss because of this.

The finish was

3 Union Rags	9 Paynter	4 Atigun	1 Street Life
5–2	4–1	20–1	9–1

Not surprising, Dullahan's 4.20 dosage proved a correct indicator again as he finished seventh.

There was $2,109,525 to win on Paynter out of $13,327,049 wagered; for place $610,379 out of $3,919,209 and for show $494,600 out of $3,298,667.

My bets were $350 place and $450 show on Paynter and a $20 exacta Union Rags/Paynter which collected $2184 plus $146 rebate.

My losing bets were

#9 $250 win, $ 350 place, and $ 450 show

$115 exacta 9/5 $47 exacta 9/3 $20 exacta 3,5/ 3,5,9

$65 tri 9/5/3 $27 tri 9/3/5 $5 tri 3,5/3,5,9

$44 super 9/5/3/ 1,2,12

$22 super 9/3/5/ 1,2, 12

$3 super 3,5/3,5,9/3,5,9/1, 2, 12

So the total bet was $1648 and $2330 was collected on the Belmont stakes at one rebate shop. At another rebate shop, $2953 was bet and $3247 collected plus a rebate of $168.04, so the total gain with rebate was $710.

For a record of the bets, payouts and rebate of the three races at one rebate shop plus a second rebate shop for the Belmont, see Table 17.11.

Chapter 18

An Application of Expert Information to Win Betting on the Kentucky Derby, 1981–2005*

RODERICK S. BAIN*, DONALD B. HAUSCH** & WILLIAM T. ZIEMBA†

*Ottawa, ON, Canada, **School of Business, University of Wisconsin, Wisconsin, USA, †Sauder School of Business, University of British Columbia, Vancouver, Canada and Sloan School of Management, Massachusetts Institute of Technology, Massachusetts, USA

ABSTRACT *The Kentucky Derby features top three-year-old thoroughbred horses. Run at $1\frac{1}{4}$ miles, it is typically at least 1/8 mile longer than any of the horses has raced before. This extra distance, combined with a large field, makes the race a difficult test of stamina for horses this young. Bettors, because there is no direct evidence of whether a horse has the stamina to compete effectively at $1\frac{1}{4}$ miles, are also challenged. The informational content of one publicly available, pedigree-based measure of stamina, the Dosage Index, is used with simple performance measures to identify a semi-strong-form inefficiency, and to create a betting scheme based on the optimal capital growth model that merges these criteria with the public's opinion. Statistically significant profits, net of transaction costs, could have been achieved during the period 1981 to 2005.*

KEY WORDS: Semi-strong market efficiency, capital growth theory, speculative investments, sports betting

1. Introduction

The Kentucky Derby annually gathers many of the top three-year-old thoroughbred horses at Churchill Downs in Louisville Kentucky on the first Saturday in May. For the horses entered, the race is a new challenge since its distance of $1\frac{1}{4}$ miles is typically at least 1/8 mile longer than any of them have ever raced. The extra distance of the Kentucky Derby, usually combined with a large field that includes many top-flight contenders, presents a significant test of stamina for these young horses. For the Kentucky Derby, the uncertainty about each horse's stamina increases the difficulty for the public of establishing accurate win odds. This potential source of semi-strong-form inefficiency in the Kentucky Derby win-betting market is the focus of this paper.

Roberts (1967) defined a market as being 'weak-form', 'semi-strong-form' or 'strong-form' efficient if it is not possible to devise a profitable investment scheme net of transactions costs based on prices (or, for the racetrack, publicly available odds), based on all publicly available information, or based on all information, respectively. For traditional financial markets, there is considerable evidence that points to weak-form and semi-strong-form efficiency, but little evidence for strong-form efficiency (see Fama, 1970, 1991 and Keim and Ziemba, 2000 for surveys).

Correspondence Address: William T. Ziemba, Sauder School of Business, University of British Columbia, Vancouver, BC V6T 1Z2, Canada. Email: ziemba@interchange.ubc.ca

1351-847X Print/1466-4364 Online/06/000001-19 © 2006 Taylor & Francis
DOI: 10.1080/13518470500531051

---

*This article originally appeared in *The European Journal of Finance*, **12**, pp. 283–301.

Weak-form efficiency of the racetrack's win market means that betting systems based solely on the public's win odds, established through pari-mutuel betting, are not profitable. Evidence from many tracks over many years has pointed to weak-form efficiency (Ali, 1977; Asch *et al.*, 1982).[1] Weak-form efficiency of the win-betting market is a consequence of four of its features. First, transaction costs are high, about 13–20%, depending on track location, so a bettor needs to be considerably more successful than the average bettor just to break even.[2] Second, while the challenge is substantial, the concept of the win bet is relatively simple. Thus, bettors have no confusion about their task. Third, many racetrack bettors approach their wagering very seriously and some are very sophisticated. Fourth, for this serious audience, there is usually an abundance of relevant information, including records of past performances and workouts for all the horses, breeding, earnings, jockey records, etc.

For the Kentucky Derby, the first two of these criteria are satisfied for the win market. While the third criterion is met, the Kentucky Derby also receives much more interest in North America from casual fans than any other race. Because, typically, none of the Derby entrants has raced at $1\frac{1}{4}$ miles, it can be argued that the fourth criterion is not fully met.

The main objective of this paper is to determine whether the informational content of one particular pedigree-based measure of stamina that is publicly available, namely the Dosage Index, in conjunction with simple performance measures, is captured in the pari-mutuel win odds and, if not, whether it can be used to develop a profitable betting scheme.

The operation of the racetrack market is discussed in the following section. Section 3 describes the Dosage Index and performance measures, and their application to the Kentucky Derby. The data used in the analysis are discussed in Section 4. Section 5 develops a scheme for estimating each betting interest's win probability based on the public's odds, the Dosage Index and the performance measures. The betting model is described and analysed in Section 6, and conclusions given in Section 7.

2. The Racetrack as a Sequence of Markets

Prior to a race, bettors engage in markets that establish prices for the various betting opportunities for that race. Betting closes immediately before the race begins, and payouts are calculated immediately following the race. We focus on the market for win betting. Suppose there are N betting interests in a race. Let W_i be the total amount bet to win on betting interest $i = 1, \ldots, N$.[3] The total win pool for the race is

$$W = \sum_{i=1}^{N} W_i. \tag{1}$$

The 'track payback' Q (generally 0.80 to 0.87) is the fraction of each dollar bet that is returned to the bettors. The commission or 'track take' is $1 - Q$. If betting interest k wins the race, then win bets on betting interests $i \neq k$ return zero, while each dollar bet on betting interest k returns approximately QW/W_k. The actual profit per dollar is rounded down to the nearest nickel or dime (this is called 'breakage'). Together the track take and breakage constitute the transaction costs.[4]

Typically, each horse in a race runs as a separate betting interest. However, two or more horses in a race that have common ownership typically run as a single betting interest known as an 'entry'. In addition, in a race where there would be more betting interests than a preset maximum, the horses with the least-impressive credentials are grouped as a single betting interest known as the 'Field'. A bet to win on an entry or the Field pays off if any member of that betting interest wins the race.

Both have been common in the Kentucky Derby. However, the long-time restrictions in Kentucky changed in 2001, so there were no entries and no Field in the Kentucky Derby from 2001 on.

3. The Dosage Index and Performance Measures

The fact that usually no Derby entrant has raced at $1\frac{1}{4}$ miles prior to the race has led to the search for relevant information from alternative sources, including the horse's pedigree. One method of evaluating a thoroughbred's pedigree, commonly known as Dosage Theory, has its roots in the work of French cavalry officer Lt.-Col. Jean-Joseph Vuillier, who studied the pedigrees of exceptional thoroughbreds of the late 19th and early 20th centuries (Vuillier, 1902, 1906, 1928). The concept of thoroughbred dosage evolved through Varola, who developed a patented classification of prominent stallions according to the type of offspring that they produced in a series of articles in The British Racehorse (Varola, 1974, 1980).

Roman's (1981) modifications of Varola's work are known as Dosage Theory. His work was outlined in Leon Rasmussen's Bloodlines column in the *Daily Racing Form* beginning before the 1981 Kentucky Derby. One product of Roman's pedigree analysis is the Dosage Index (*DI*), which is based on the categorization of prominent stallions in terms of whether they consistently sire offspring with distance proficiencies that are incongruous with the dosage profiles of those offspring when that stallion is excluded. Classified stallions are called *chefs-de-race* (or simply *chefs*)[5]; see Ziemba and Hausch (1987), Roman's Web site, http://www.chef-de-race.com for the rationale behind the selection of recent chefs, and Roman (2002).

There are five categories for *chef* classification in Roman's system: Brilliant, Intermediate, Classic, Solid and Professional. The categorization is based on 'where they (sires) must lie on the speed-stamina spectrum to bring the figures of their descendants back in line with those of horses in the general population exhibiting similar performance traits' (Roman, 2001). A *chef* can be placed in one or two categories. Each time a *chef* appears in a four-generation pedigree, points are awarded in the appropriate category. Points are assigned on a scale of 16 for the first-generation sire, 8 for each second-generation sire, 4 for each third-generation sire, and 2 for each fourth-generation sire. Sires that are classified in two categories have their points split. After the fifteen sires have been assigned points, the total for each category is entered into the Dosage Index formula

$$\mathrm{DI} = \frac{\text{Brilliant} + \text{Intermediate} + 1/2 \text{ Classic}}{\text{Solid} + \text{Professional} + 1/2 \text{ Classic}} \qquad (2)$$

It is evident that horses with a high *DI* have a pedigree that is weighted towards Brilliant and Intermediate *chefs*, that is, sires who tend to produce offspring with greater sprinting ability than their pedigrees would suggest if that sire was eliminated from the pedigree. Horses with a low *DI* are predicted to have stamina. Very seldom will a stakes-quality horse have no dosage points, though some have so few that the *DI* is unreliable. The dosage profile for 1997 Kentucky Derby winner Silver Charm is shown in Table 1.

After the initial classification of *chefs* in 1981, Roman found that no Kentucky Derby winner from 1940 to 1980 had a *DI* exceeding 4.0, despite about 1 in 7 entrants having a *DI* that high (over the interval 1946–1980 considered here).

The Dosage Index is not a direct measure of the quality of a horse. One quality measure is the 'Experimental Free Handicap' (EFH), an annual ranking of two-year-old thoroughbreds that raced in select races in the USA (see http://www.jockyclub.com/experimental.asp). Conducted since 1933 by the Jockey Club, the EFH assigns the top runners a figurative weight on a scale that usually has the two-year-old champion weighted at 126 pounds.[6] Exceptional horses have

Table 1. Dosage Index calculation for 1997 Kentucky Derby winner Silver Charm

Generation	Sire	Brilliant	Intermediate	Classic	Solid	Professional
1	Silver Buck					
2	Buckpasser			8		
	Poker					
	Tom Fool		2	2		
3	Hail to Reason			4		
	Round Table				4	
	Wise Margin					
	Menow					
	War Admiral			2		
	Turn-to	1	1			
4	Mahmoud		1	1		
	Princequillo		1		1	
	Nasrullah	2				
	Market Wise					
	Faultless					
	Total	3	5	17	5	0

Dosage Index $= (3 + 5 + 17/2)/(5 + 0 + 17/2) = 1.22$.

been weighted up to 130 pounds. Other top horses are assigned lower weights based on perceived ability until a cutoff is reached at about 100 pounds beyond which no more are classified. Usually there are 15 to 30 horses classified within 10 pounds of the top-weighted horse. Roman (1981) observed that starting in 1972 most Kentucky Derby winners were rated within 10 pounds of the top-weighted horse. This observation led to the designation 'dual qualifier' for any horse that was weighted within 10 pounds of the top-weighted horse on the EFH (indicating the quality of the horse) and had a *DI* less than or equal to 4.0.[7]

Professional handicapper James Quinn offered a second measure of quality to add late-developers to the list. He defined what we call an 'asterisk qualifier' to be any horse that: (1) won at least one of a selection of premier races prior to the Kentucky Derby; (2) had a *DI* less than or equal to 4.0; and (3) was not rated within 10 pounds on the EFH. A horse is a 'dual-or-asterisk' qualifier if it qualifies for one of these two categories.

Our objective was neither to judge these measures nor to refine them. Instead, our objective was to study whether any predictive power there may be in these widely publicized measures was incorporated into the public's pari-mutuel win odds. If not fully incorporated, then a further objective was to investigate whether these measures could be used to determine win probability estimates that are sufficiently superior to the public's so that a profitable wagering scheme based on win betting could be developed, despite the significant transaction costs.

4. Data Acquisition

This section discusses the nature of the data, while the sources of the data are described in the Appendix.

The public's win betting pool and results were collected for the period 1946 to 2005. For 52 of these years, dollar amounts that the public wagered were found, so we had precise values for q_i. For the other eight years, only the final win odds for each betting interest were available. In these cases it was possible to back out win probabilities that were consistent with these odds.

The Experimental Free Handicap listing and pedigree information for each Derby participant was collected for each year from 1946 to 2005. The original list of *chefs* was published in 1981. For years prior to 1981, this list was used, which means that the classification of *chefs* for 1946 to 1980 is not completely out of sample. However, the hypothetical betting begins in 1981, so all betting is based on lists of *chefs* that were out of sample. For the period 1981–1986, the 1981 list was used (see Appendix for explanation). After 1986, an updated list of *chefs* was used each year.

The major races for asterisk-qualifier status, with their 2005 graded stakes classification and the years that they have been run over the interval 1946–2005, were the Blue Grass Stakes (G1) (1946–2005), Flamingo Stakes (currently not run) (1946–1989,1992–2001), Florida Derby (G1) (1952–2005), Santa Anita Derby (G1) (1946–2005) and the Wood Memorial Stakes (G1) (1946–2005). The Flamingo Stakes declined in importance before being cancelled, but was included because historically it was an important prep race.

5. Application of Breeding Information and Performance Measures to Refine Estimated Win Probabilities

Two models were developed for estimating win probabilities that depended on whether a betting interest was a dual qualifier or a dual-or-asterisk qualifier.

The 1995 Kentucky Derby is used in Table 2 to illustrate the required information. Most of the possibilities in terms of qualifying are presented in Table 2. Also evident is a complication with regard to accounting for pedigree with entries (and the Field): the horses in an entry may not have the same qualifier status. This difficulty was handled using the following scheme:

1. If all members of an entry had the same qualifier status, then the entry was considered as one horse with that qualification.
2. If one member of the entry was a dual qualifier plus had won any of the designated major races prior to the Kentucky Derby, the entry was considered to be a dual qualifier regardless of the qualifications of the other member(s) (based on the presumption that in most cases most of the public's attention on the entry was due to that horse).
3. If the members of an entry did not all have the same qualifier status, but each was either a dual qualifier or an asterisk qualifier, then the entry was viewed as a dual-or-asterisk qualifier.
4. In all other cases the entry was considered to be neutral, i.e. neither a qualifier nor not a qualifier.

The qualifier status of the Field was determined in the same manner. For the dual-qualifier model there are 67, 0, 10 and 22 betting interests in the respective categories, and for the dual-or-asterisk-qualifier model there are 57, 2, 10 and 30 betting interests in the respective categories.

With respect to the dual-qualifier model, of the winners there are 29 that are qualifiers, 26 that are not qualifiers, and 3 that are part of a neutral entry. With respect to the dual-or-asterisk-qualifier model, of the winners there are 41 qualifiers, 16 that are not qualifiers, and 3 that are part of a neutral entry. In 1998 and 2003 there were no dual qualifiers so those years were ignored in the dual-qualifier modeling.

We began our modelling with a base-case model that related a betting interest's win probability to the public's wagering to see if looking solely at the pools without the 'expert information' could lead to a profitable betting scheme.

Let W_i^j be the public's win bet on betting interest i, W^j be the win pool in race j, and N^j be the number of betting interests in race j. For race j, define p_i^j to be the probability that betting

Table 2. Sample input data: 1995 Kentucky Derby field

Horse	W_i/W	Entry	EFH	Won specified race	*DI*	Qualifier status	
						Dual	Asterisk
Jambalaya Jazz	0.044	1	115		1.15		
Pyramid Peak			–	Flamingo	3.00		•
Serena's Song	0.189	2	122		2.11	•	
Timber Country			126		3.29	•	
Mecke			107		4.50		
Knockadoon			–		3.57		
Citadeed	0.066	Field	–		1.60		
In Character			–		1.77		
Ski Captain			–		3.67		
Lake George			–		4.50		
Thunder Gulch	0.033		116	Florida Derby	4.00	•	
Tejano Run	0.087		121		2.38	•	
Jumron	0.126		115		3.80		
Eltish	0.070		123		3.00	•	
Afternoon Deelites	0.086		124		5.00		
Suave Prospect	0.059		113		4.60		
Talkin Man	0.167		114	Wood Memorial	3.00		•
Dazzling Falls	0.029		111		6.20		
Wild Syn	0.042		–	Blue Grass	4.33		

W_i/W	Post-time fraction of win pool.
Entry	Entry number or Field.
EFH	Experimental Free Handicap weight. Blank implies not weighted. (High weight for two-year-olds from 1994 was 126 pounds.)
Won specified race	Winner of a major race prior to Kentucky Derby.
DI	Dosage Index: see Equation (2).
Qualifier status	• implies meets qualifier requirements.

interest i wins and define $q_i^j \equiv W_i^j / W^j$ to be the fraction of the win pool bet on betting interest i. For this base case, the following model was used for each race

$$p_i^j = \frac{(q_i^j)^\delta}{\sum_{m=1}^{N^j} (q_m^j)^\delta}. \tag{3}$$

If δ is 1 then p_i^j equals q_i^j.

We used a standard maximum-likelihood approach to estimate optimal values of δ. Consider R independent races and define $K \equiv (k_1, \ldots, k_R)$ to be an R-tuple representing the winners of the R races, i.e., k_j is the number of the betting interest that won race j. Let $p_{k_j}^j$ represent the estimated probability based on Equation 3, evaluated before race j, that betting interest k_j wins race j. The probability that the vector $\boldsymbol{K}$ corresponds to the winners of the R races is

$$\mathrm{P}(\boldsymbol{K}|\delta) = \prod_{j=1}^{R} p_{k_j}^j. \tag{4}$$

Treating Equation 4 as a likelihood function that depends on δ gives

$$\ell(\delta|\boldsymbol{K}) \propto \prod_{j=1}^{R} p_{k_j}^{j}. \tag{5}$$

A maximum-likelihood point estimate for δ, namely δ_{ML}, can be found by maximizing the likelihood as a function of δ. Our first value for δ_{ML} was calculated using the first 10 years of data, namely 1946–1955 inclusive. Thereafter, the value of δ_{ML} was updated for each year using data from 1946 to that year. The win pool fraction for the winner and values for δ_{ML} calculated after each year's race are shown in Fig. 1.

The values for δ_{ML} are less than 1.0 for the years prior to 1974. This is a consequence of the public's more favored betting interests winning less often during this period than would have been expected based on the public's odds. The winners from 1972 to 1979 were dominated by favourites, culminating with Spectacular Bid in 1979, so δ_{ML} increases over this interval, reaching a maximum value of 1.12. During the period 1980–2005, the public's favourite seldom won, so δ_{ML} tends to decrease to it final value 0.92.[8]

With values of δ_{ML} close to 1.0, Equation 3 generates revised win probabilities that differ only slightly from the fraction of the win pool. The greatest ratio p_i^j/q_i^j over the interval 1981–2005 is 1.12. This 12% edge is insufficient to offer a positive expected return on a win bet after accounting for the transaction costs; hence this simple model points to weak-form efficiency of the win-betting market over this period.

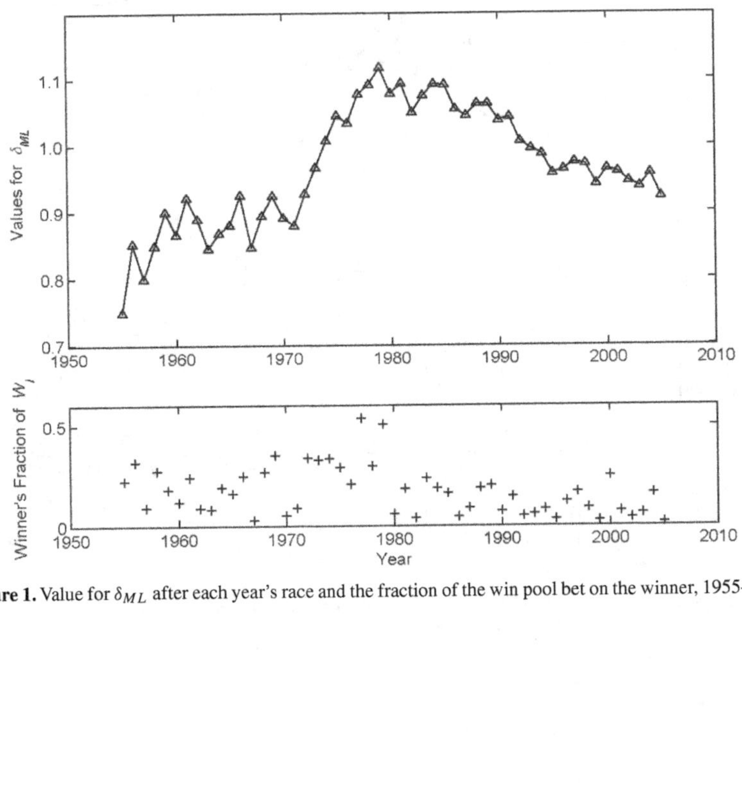

Figure 1. Value for δ_{ML} after each year's race and the fraction of the win pool bet on the winner, 1955–2005

Our main objective was to use this same procedure to create models that modified the win probability for each betting interest based on whether or not it was considered a dual qualifier or considered a dual-or-asterisk qualifier.

For this case, the probability of betting interest i winning is

$$p_i^j = \frac{(q_i^j)^{\gamma_i}}{\sum_{m=1}^{N^j} (q_m^j)^{\gamma_m}}, \quad \gamma_i, \gamma_m = \alpha, \beta \text{ or } 1. \tag{6}$$

The variable γ_i equals α if betting interest i was a dual qualifier (or dual-or-asterisk qualifier depending on the test), β if it was classified as not a dual qualifier (or not a dual-or-asterisk qualifier if applicable), and 1 if the betting interest was an entry or Field classified as being neutral.

Based on Equation 6, maximum-likelihood values for α and β, denoted as α_{ML} and β_{ML}, were calculated each year. The initial estimate was to predict for 1956, using the first ten years of data (1946–1955). Figure 2 illustrates the progression of α_{ML} and β_{ML} values for the dual-qualifier model, and figure 3 shows α_{ML} and β_{ML} values for the dual-or-asterisk-qualifier model.

In these two figures, the critical pattern is the relative magnitude of α_{ML} and β_{ML}. In Fig. 2, for nearly 20 years, α_{ML} exceeds β_{ML}. Consequently, for this period, the revised win probability for each dual qualifier is less than the fraction of the money bet on it in the win pool. This implies

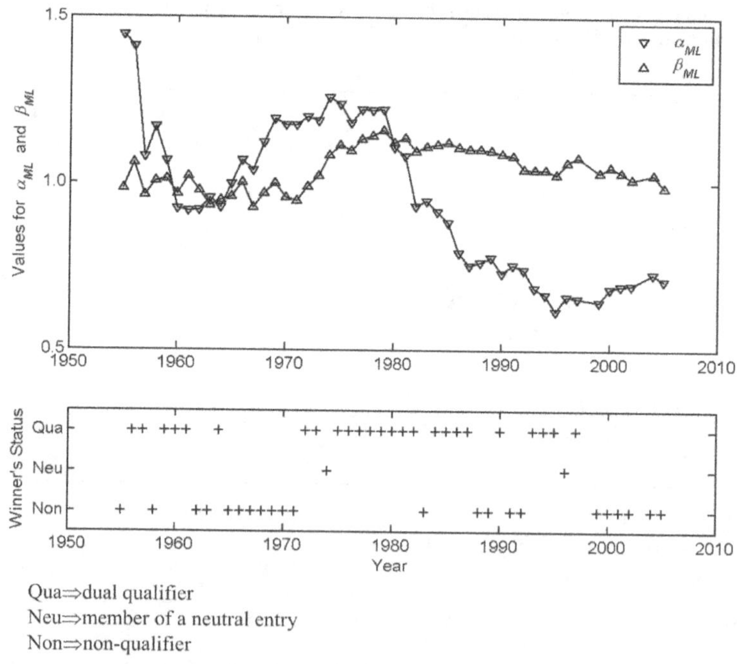

Figure 2. Values for α_{ML} and β_{ML} for dual-qualifier model after each year's race, 1955–2005

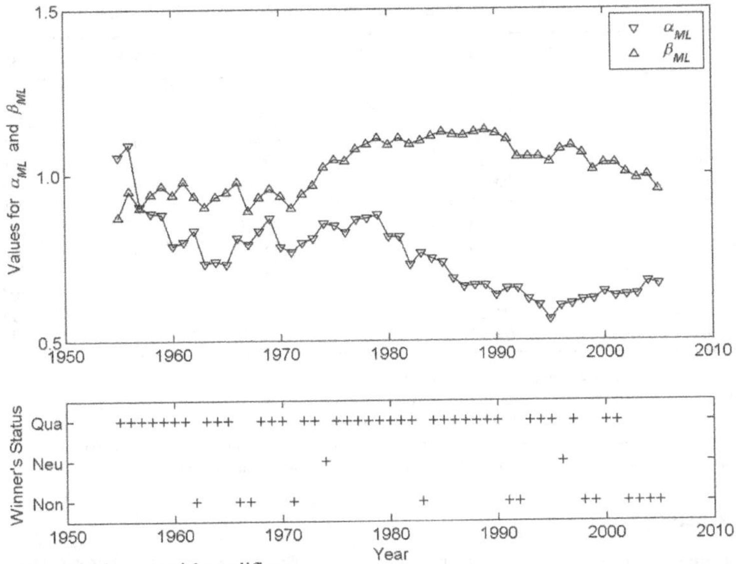

Qua⇒dual-or-asterisk qualifier
Neu⇒member of a neutral entry
Non⇒non-qualifier

Figure 3. Value for α_{ML} and β_{ML} for dual-or-asterisk qualifier model after each year's race, 1955–2005

that betting on dual qualifiers, if they had been known, would not have been advantageous during that period. In the mid-1970s, dual qualifiers began to win consistently, eventually leading to β_{ML} exceeding α_{ML} for the remainder of the study period. For this later period, the revised win probabilities for dual qualifiers exceed their fraction of the win pool. Figure 3 for dual-or-asterisk qualifiers shows a similar pattern, although β_{ML} begins to exceed α_{ML} after only three years. Thus, after the third year, the model predicts win probabilities for dual-or-asterisk qualifiers that exceed their fraction of the win pool. For example, the original and revised estimates of win probabilities for 1995 are in Table 3.

In Table 3 a betting interest's estimated win probability rises if it meets the qualifier criterion. (This is not necessarily the case if there are many qualifiers because the sum of the probabilities is unity.) The effect of considering asterisk qualifiers is demonstrated by Talkin Man, an asterisk qualifier but not a dual qualifier. His estimated win probability varies from 0.114 to 0.204 depending on the criterion used.

The revised win probability estimates are occasionally sufficiently greater than the fraction of the win pool to allow a positive expected return even considering transaction costs.

The percentage increase in the win probability over the fraction of the win pool for Thunder Gulch is much greater than for Entry 2. There is a general tendency for p_i/q_i to increase for qualifiers as q_i decreases, which is a consequence of the power function model in Equation 6 together with values of $\alpha < \beta$ and $\alpha < 1$.

Table 3. Original and revised estimated win probabilities for the 1995 Kentucky Derby

Betting Interest	W_i/W	DQ	p_{DQ}	DAQ	p_{DAQ}
Entry 1	0.044	−1	0.029	0	0.027
Entry 2	0.189	1	0.242	1	0.220
Field	0.066	−1	0.044	−1	0.035
Thunder Gulch	0.033	1	0.075	1	0.076
Tejano Run	0.087	1	0.144	1	0.137
Jumron	0.126	−1	0.085	−1	0.068
Eltish	0.070	1	0.125	1	0.121
Afternoon Deelites	0.086	−1	0.057	−1	0.046
Suave Prospect	0.059	−1	0.039	−1	0.031
Talkin Man	0.167	−1	0.114	1	0.204
Dazzling Falls	0.029	−1	0.019	−1	0.015
Wild Syn	0.042	−1	0.027	−1	0.022

W_i/W fraction of win pool bet on the betting interest.
DQ indicator is 1 for dual qualifiers, 0 for unclassified entries and −1 for non-qualifiers.
p_{DQ} revised estimated win probability based on dual-qualifier model.
DAQ indicator is 1 for dual-or-asterisk qualifiers, 0 for unclassified entries and −1 for non-qualifiers.
p_{DAQ} revised estimated win probability based on dual-or-asterisk qualifier model.

6. The Betting Model

Betting amounts were determined using the optimal capital growth model (OCGM) which maximizes the expected logarithm of wealth on a race-by-race basis. This approach was developed by Kelly (1956) (and is commonly called the 'Kelly criterion'), and was extended and rigorously proved by Breiman (1961). Among its properties are: (1) it maximizes the asymptotic growth rate of wealth; (2) it asymptotically minimizes the expected time to reach any specific sufficiently large wealth level; and (3) in the long run it outperforms any other essentially different betting strategy almost surely and provides infinitely more final wealth than any other essentially different strategy. (See MacLean *et al.*, 1992, 2006; Rotando and Thorp, 1992; and Thorp, 2006 for further properties, and Ziemba and Hausch, 1986 for simulation results for shorter time horizons.)

The revised probability of betting interest i winning based on dual-qualifier or dual-or-asterisk qualifier status is p_i. Let r_i be the gross return per dollar bet based on the win odds established by the public. (As in Section 2, we are suppressing the superscript indicating the race number.) The OCGM requires solving the following optimization problem for each race

$$\underset{f\in\Re^N}{\text{maximize}} \sum_{i=1}^{N} p_i \log\left(1-\sum_{m=1}^{N} f_m + f_i r_i\right) \quad \text{s.t. } f_i \geq 0\,\forall i=1,\ldots,N \quad \text{and} \quad \sum_{i=1}^{N} f_i \leq 1. \quad (7)$$

The decision variable f_i is the fraction of the current wealth to bet on betting interest i. Suppose that the bettor's initial wealth is w and betting interest i wins. Then wf_ir_i is returned to the bettor after having invested $w\sum_{m=1}^{N} f_m$, for a final wealth of $w(1-\sum_{m=1}^{N} f_m + f_ir_i)$. The objective function determines the logarithm of final wealth for each betting interest winning, weighted by the probability of that betting interest winning. The actual initial wealth, w, can be disregarded in the formulation by having the decision variables be the fraction of wealth that is bet on each betting interest. The constraints comprise a budget constraint and non-negativity.[9]

This formulation assumes that the bets are sufficiently small so that they do not influence the payout on any betting interest, i.e. the bets on betting interest i do not reduce r_i. For the Kentucky

Derby, the win betting pool is so large that a typical bet is very unlikely to influence payouts.[10] The large pools also permit this assumption because the percentage bet on each betting interest is assumed to vary little in the final few minutes.

Revised probabilities for the base-case model based on Equations 3 to 5 are sufficiently close to the public's win probabilities that expected returns are negative on all betting interests over the period 1981–2005. Solving Equation 7 with these revised probabilities leads to no bets.

For the models based on Equation 6 and on status as a dual or dual-or-asterisk qualifier, the betting started with an initial wealth of $2,500 in 1981. It was updated after each year based on the bets made and the actual outcome of the race. The wealth history for betting over 1981 to 2005 is shown in Fig. 4 for dual qualifiers and for dual-or-asterisk qualifiers. Overall results are summarized in Table 4. For the years up to the mid-1980s any advantage identified by the model is small and results in small bets. Comparing the values in Fig. 4 with those in Figs 2 and 3 shows that α_{ML} and β_{ML} are relatively close over that interval. As the model predicts a greater advantage, the amount per bet, and consequently the volatility, grows.

For comparison, betting $2500 on the favourite to win from 1981 to 2005 would yield a loss of $41,500; betting $200 to win on each dual qualifier would yield a profit of $12,920 on $13,200 bet; and a $200 bet to win on each dual-or-asterisk qualifier would yield a profit of $7,780 on $23,000 bet (neutral entries excluded as qualifiers). The improved return on investment compared to the OCGM in the short run is mostly due to a few huge profits on qualifiers Gato del Sol (1982), Ferdinand (1986), and Thunder Gulch (1995).

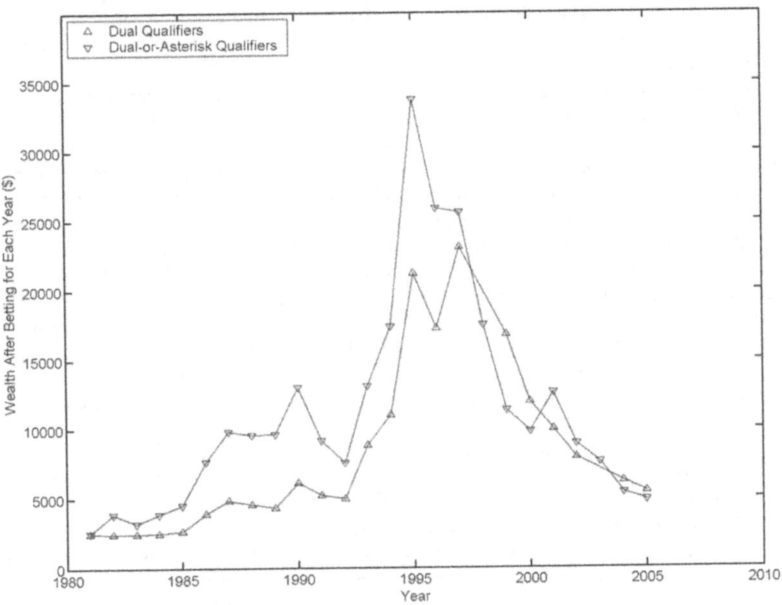

Figure 4. Wealth level history for Kelly win bets, 1981–2005

Table 4. Profits from both models based on Kelly bets and revised win probabilities

	Model based on qualifier type	
	Dual	Dual-or-asterisk
Number of bets	61	107
Total amount bet	$32,828	$66,467
Number of bet that won	9	14
Initial wealth	$2,500	$2,500
Final wealth	$5,514	$4,889
Total profit	$3,014	$2,389
Percentage return on investment	9.2	3.6

For both models the betting scheme produced profits over the 1980s and up to the mid-1990s, but the performance has been poor since. Several possibilities can be considered for this:

1. The sample space is too small. This could mean that the sequence of successes for qualifiers for both models from 1972 to 1997 was a short-term run, so that in the long run there is nothing to be gained from using either model developed here.
   The limited sample space also implies that the final wealth is sensitive to individual race results. To give an idea of the scope, two extreme examples are (i) if a non-dual-qualifier had won in 1995, instead of Thunder Gulch, the final wealth for the dual-qualifier model would be $2221, i.e. a slight loss overall, and (ii) if 2005 winner Giacomo had a favourable change of a single dosage point in any category, he would have been a dual qualifier and the final wealth would have been $13,877.
2. It is extremely difficult to make a proper assessment of all of the two-year-olds, so the EFH can omit suitable horses. A pointed example occurred in 2003 where eventual 2004 Derby winner Smarty Jones was not rated on the EFH. Yet, he had overwhelmed a field of state-bred two-year-olds at Philadelphia Park, but that race is not counted when determining the EFH. Roman (2005a) lists other Derby winners such as Winning Colors and Sunday Silence who were superior two-year-olds but were not rated on the EFH.
3. Classification of *chefs* is an ongoing exercise. For example, Alydar was classified as a *chef* subsequent to Strike The Gold winning the Derby in 1991, so Strike The Gold, who won the Blue Grass Stakes, is not considered as an asterisk qualifier here ($DI = 9.00$), yet when Alydar was classified, Strike The Gold's DI was reduced to 2.60. Ziemba (1991) wrote a column about this prior to the 1991 Derby arguing that Alydar should be a classic *chef* as he had numerous classic distance winners. The reclassification of Alydar, and at what point, would possibly change other pedigrees. However, here we go with Roman's classification so Strike the Gold is not a dual or asterisk qualifier.
4. Roman (2005b) has pointed out the gradual rise in the DI of Derby winners over time, so the failure of the system in the last few years of the study may reflect a shift of the overall breed in North America towards speed at shorter distances. Real Quiet (1998), Charismatic (1999) and Giacomo (2005) all had DI values greater than 4.00.
5. The Flamingo Stakes decreased in significance in the final years that it was run. Including the Flamingo winner as an asterisk qualifier in recent years was unwarranted in retrospect. Two possible solutions are to drop the Flamingo at some point in the analysis, or switch to the Arkansas Derby as the fifth significant prep race.

Random betting generates expected losses in excess of 16%, due to the 16% track take plus breakage. Our results showed both qualifier designations approximately doubling wealth over the betting period. However, in light of the variation in wealth displayed in Fig. 4, it is important to address the statistical significance of these profits. We do so with two approaches. The first treats a betting interest's win or loss as a binomial random variable and then uses a Normal approximation. The second approach simulates the set of races assuming random wagering.

Before considering the first approach, observe that the data in Fig. 4 are not ideal for addressing the statistical significance. Wealth generally grows until the mid-to-late 1990s, and then dramatically falls. This pattern of wins and losses leads to wealth that is highly variable. Focusing on just the dual-qualifier case, Fig. 5 superimposes on Fig. 4 the wealth level history assuming that the races were run in reverse order, i.e. we started in 2005 with $2,500, then updated wealth based on our results in 2005 and went to the 2004 race, and so on. Thus, the string of large losses occurs early with lower wealth, after which wins are more common. The final wealth is identical, since the optimal capital growth system simply determines the optimal fraction of wealth to bet each year. (For example, losing 10% one year and gaining 20% the other year leads to an overall return of 8%, whatever the order of the win and the loss.) Despite the final wealth being the same, the wealth histories are very different, as is the appearance of any statistical significance to the profits.

Our goal is to assess the profitability of this system. To eliminate the effect of varying wealth, which can dampen or intensify the variance in profits, our test of statistical significance uses bets and returns in each race assuming an identical initial wealth each race. We do not update wealth year by year (as in Fig. 4); instead the initial wealth each year is assumed to be $2,500.

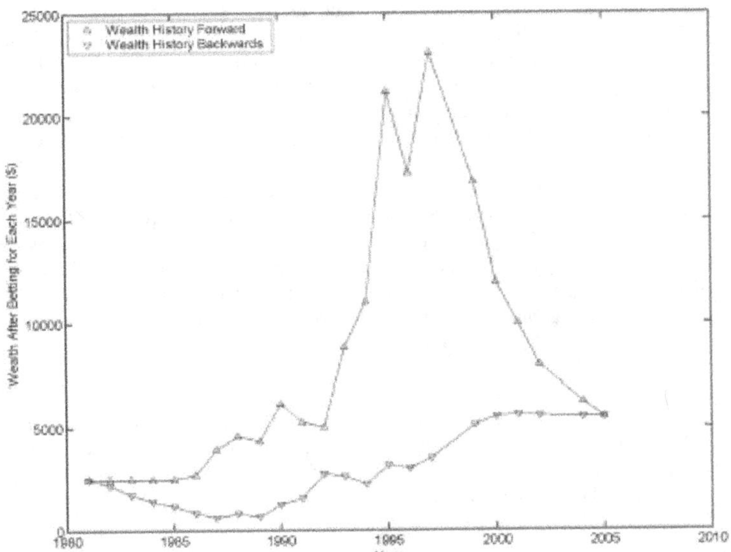

Figure 5. Betting wealth for Kelly win bets on dual qualifiers with races run forward (1981–2005) and run backwards (2005–1981)

Let q be the probability of winning a bet in each trial, n be the number of trials, c be the amount wagered each trial, and r be the gross return upon winning,[11] and let X be the random variable representing the number of wins. The probability of profits exceeding a constant π is

$$\mathrm{P}\left[rX - nc > \pi\right]. \tag{8}$$

Assume that the trials are independent. For bets in different races, this assumption is reasonable. For multiple bets on the same race – which are common – wins are negatively correlated since if one betting interest wins then the others must lose. Negative correlation leads to a tighter distribution of wins, so in this way our analysis based on independent trials will underestimate the statistical significance of our results. Since X is binomially distributed, the Normal distribution approximates equation (8) as

$$1 - \Phi\left[\frac{((\pi + nc)/r) - nq}{\sqrt{nq(1-q)}}\right], \tag{9}$$

where Φ is the cumulative distribution function of a standard N(0,1) variable.

For dual qualifiers and assuming an initial wealth of \$2,500 each year, there were 61 bets totaling \$7,079, and of these bets, 9 won for a gross return of \$11,357 and a profit of \$4, 278. Thus, $c = 7079/61 = 116.0$ and $r = 11,357/9 = 1262$. If the system were no better than random betting, then q satisfies $rq - c = -0.16c$, recognizing the 16% track take, giving $q = 0.07725$. Then, by Equation 9, the probability of profits of at least the observed level of \$4,278 given random betting is 2.0%. Suppose instead that the system is better than random betting but only good enough to offer zero expected profits. Then q solves $rq - c = 0$, or $q = 0.09192$, and, by Equation 9, the probability that such a system would produce at least the observed profits is 6.7%.

For dual-and-asterisk qualifiers, with initial wealth of \$2,500 each year, there were 107 bets totaling \$13,268; 14 of these bets won for a gross return of \$18,253 and a profit of \$4,985. Thus, $c = 124$ and $r = 1304$. If the system were no better than random betting, then $q = 0.07988$ and the probability of profits of at least the observed level is only 2.6%. Assuming instead that the system is better than random betting but only good enough to offer zero expected profits, then $q = 0.09509$ and the probability that such a system would produce at least the observed profits is 10.4%.

Our second approach to addressing the statistical significance of the results involved two simulations for each qualifier designation. The first simulation dealt with the question of how likely it would be that profits at the observed level would have been generated if our approach is vacuous and, therefore, is essentially nothing beyond random wagering. The second simulation asked how likely it would be that the observed profits would have been generated if the system is able to improve upon random wagering, but only enough to achieve zero expected return on each wager (excluding breakage). The algorithm for the first simulation was

1. Start with a betting wealth of \$2,500 in 1981.
2. Determine the fraction of wealth to wager on each betting interest i for the current year based on the Kelly criterion and the (wrong) assumption that our probability estimate, p_i, is correct.
3. Randomly select the winner, with the probability of winning for betting interest i being q_i.
4. Based on the simulated winner, its payout and our wagers, update wealth.
5. Repeat steps 2 to 4 for each year in order up to 2005.

The second simulation differed only in step 3, where the simulation used q_i/Q as the correct win probability for any betting interest i that received a wager in step 2. The expected return on

Table 5. Results from 10,000 betting simulations with $2,500 initial wealth

	Dual qualifier		Dual-or-asterisk qualifier	
	Simulation 1	Simulation 2	Simulation 1	Simulation 2
Final wealth ≤ $1,000 (%)	54.3	37.0	73.8	49.3
Final wealth ≤ $2,500 (%)	84.2	72.6	91.5	76.1
Final wealth ≥ System's Final wealth (Table 4) (%)	3.9	9.2	3.1	11.4
Mean final wealth	$1,555	$2,449	$1,030	$2,473
Median final wealth	$892	$1,371	$450	$1,022
Maximum final wealth	$67,601	$161,777	$97,336	$409,294

every wager was zero, before accounting for breakage. The collective win probability of the other betting interests was such that probabilities summed to one. For example, in a three-horse race with $[q_1, q_2, q_3] = [0.42, 0.21, 0.37]$ and Kelly bets having been placed on the first two horses based on $[p_1, p_2, p_3]$, the probability that the simulation would select each betting interest as the winner was [0.42, 0.21, 0.37] for Simulation 1, and was [0.5, 0.25, 0.25] for Simulation 2 after dividing the first two fractions by 0.84. The simulations were run 10,000 times each. The results are in Table 5.

For all simulations, losses occurred more than 70% of the time. For Simulation 2 and for both types of qualifiers, the mean final wealth was close to $2,500, which is expected given the modification in step 3 of this simulation. For dual qualifiers, only 3.9% of the time did Simulation 1 realize profits as high as our observed profit. For Simulation 2, the corresponding value is 9.2%. For dual-or-asterisk qualifiers, these values for Simulations 1 and 2 are, respectively, 3.1% and 11.4%.

As a final test the analyses were conducted using limited data. For example, if the year being considered was 1997 and the interval was 25 years, only information from 1972 to 1996 would have been applied. For the dual-qualifer model, using the entire data set produced the greatest final wealth; while for the dual-or-asterisk model, using an interval of 56 years produced a final wealth of $5305.

7. Conclusions

The racetrack is a useful financial market for testing market efficiency and considerable evidence exists, including results in this paper, in support of the track's win market being weak-form efficient, i.e. no profitable system can be developed based on the odds established by the public. This paper tests whether the win market is also semi-strong efficient, i.e. no profitable system can be developed based on the public's odds and other publicized information.

We focus on a particular aspect of the Kentucky Derby, which is that the Derby's distance of $1\frac{1}{4}$ miles is typically farther than any entrant has ever raced. This lack of direct evidence of an entrant's stamina for this race has motivated the search for indirect evidence. Dosage Theory, which analyses a horse's pedigree, has been offered as such evidence but it has also been controversial, both in general and in its relation to the Kentucky Derby. Other evidence that has been offered includes well-publicized rankings of horses and results from recent high-calibre races.

Our goal has not been to evaluate the criticisms or the justifications offered for the dosage concept and for the ranking of two-year-olds, nor do we attempt to refine their application to the Kentucky Derby. Instead, we developed a model that takes this information, which is readily available to the public and receives much attention, and merges it with the public's win odds to establish win probabilities. We then tested these win probabilities within a betting system based on the optimal capital growth model and showed statistically significant profits.

A specific application of the procedure would be for the $1\frac{1}{2}$ mile Belmont Stakes which is run weeks after the Kentucky Derby. This analysis is the planned focus of future work. It is known though from our preliminary analysis that during the period in the 1980s to mid-1990s when the dual qualifiers were having very good success in the Derby their results in the Belmont were not as good. However, in recent years the situation has reversed with much better results in the Belmont than the Derby. In a more general context, the betting systems detailed here are two of many 'angles' used by bettors. The procedure outlined shows that given the pools from a set of races for which the angle is applicable, the simple model given in Equation 6 can be used to test the validity of the angle.

Acknowledgements

The authors would like to thank Richard P. Waterman of the University of Pennsylvania for discussions regarding the development of the model, Hilda P. Marshall for her assistance in constructing pedigrees and the referees and editor for helpful comments on a previous version of the paper.

Notes

1 An exception may be extreme favourites at odds of 3–10 or less, which, while quite rare, have been shown to produce a small average profit (Ziemba and Hausch, 1986). Inefficiencies in other more complex markets are more common; see Hausch *et al.* (1994) for such evidence.

2 Large bettors can reduce this take by betting at rebate sites that return a portion of the bet to make the actual take about 10%. We do not deal with such bettors here nor with those outside the USA who wager on Betfair or other betting exchanges against other bettors directly rather than in a pari-mutuel pool as discussed here.

3 Our notation deals with one race only. In Section 5, to deal with several races simultaneously, we will add a superscript to our notation to identify the race number.

4 For each track there is a minimum payout, usually 5%, that the track must return even if there are insufficient funds available in QW.

5 Mares are not included because they are considered to have too few offspring to identify distance proficiencies, while it is not unusual for a stallion to sire over 100 offspring in a year.

6 Ranking horses by weight is a familiar concept at the racetrack. In handicap races, the top horses carry greater weight (jockey + saddle + additional weights if necessary) than the less-qualified horses. Handicapping of this sort occurs only in select races and is intended to make the race more competitive.

7 Some people expand the dual qualifier category to include any horse that is declared a champion in a country other than the USA and has a *DI* less than or equal to 4.0. In this paper, only the first definition was used.

8 Griffith (1949), McGlothlin (1956), Ali (1977) Asch *et al.* (1982) and Ziemba and Hausch (1986), among others, have demonstrated that the public's wagering has a strong and stable bias of underbetting the favourites and overbetting the longshots. This results in $\delta > 1.0$. Ziemba and Hausch (1987) provided evidence that this 'favourite-longshot bias' is exhibited at the Kentucky Derby but it is weaker, that is more flat, than in these earlier studies. The recent advent of rebate and betting exchange wagering has led to a flattening of the favourite-longshot bias in recent data since about 1998 (Ziemba, 2004).

9 The solution for Equation 7 was obtained using the Fortran package DONLP2 written by Professor Peter Spellucci which is available from NetLib (<http://www.netlib.org>).

10 See Hausch *et al.* (1981) for a formulation that does account for the bettor's effect on payouts.

11 In practice, q, c, and r vary across races and even within races if there are multiple wagers. We approximate the sequence of wagers by using the average values of these parameters.

References

Ali, M. M. (1977) Probability and utility estimates for racetrack bettors, *Journal of Political Economy*, 85, pp. 803–815.

American Produce Records (Lexington, KY: Bloodstock Research Information Services Inc.).

American Racing Manual (New York: Daily Racing Form, Daily Racing Form, LLC).

Asch, P., Malkiel, B. G. and Quandt, R. E. (1982) Racetrack betting and informed behavior, *Journal of Financial Economics*, 10, pp. 187–194.

Bloodstock Research Information Services, Lexington, Kentucky.

Breiman, L. (1961) Optimal gambling system for favorable games, in: *Proceedings 4th Berkeley Symposium on Mathematical Statistics and Probability*, Vol. 1, pp. 63–68.

Camerer, C. F. (1998) Can asset markets be manipulated? A field experiment with racetrack betting, *Journal of Political Economy*, 106, pp. 457–482.

Chew, P. (1974) *The Kentucky Derby: The First 100 Years* (Boston, MA: Houghton Mifflin Company).

Daily Racing Form, Daily Racing Form, LLC, New York.

Fama, E. (1970) Efficient capital markets: a review of theory and empirical work, *Journal of Finance*, 25, pp. 383–417.

Fama, E. (1991) Efficient capital markets: II, *Journal of Finance*, 46, pp. 1575–1617.

Griffith, R. M. (1949) Odds adjustments by American horse-racing bettors, *American Journal of Psychology*, 62, pp. 290–294.

Hausch, D. B., Ziemba, W. T. and Rubinstein, M. (1981) Efficiency of the market for racetrack betting, *Management Science*, 27, pp. 1435–1452.

Hausch, D. B., Lo, V. and Ziemba, W. T. (Eds) (1994) *Efficiency of Racetrack Betting Markets* (New York: Academic Press).

Keim, D. B. and Ziemba, W. T. (Eds) (2000) *Security Market Imperfections in Worldwide Equity Markets* (Cambridge: Cambridge University Press).

Kelly, J. L. (1956) A new interpretation of information rate, *Bell System Technical Journal*, 35, pp. 917–926.

MacLean, L. C., Ziemba, W. T. and Blazenko, G. (1992) Growth versus security in dynamic investment analysis, *Management Science*, 38, pp. 1562–1585.

MacLean, L. C. and Ziemba, W. T. (2006) Capital growth theory and practice, in: S.A. Zenios and W. T. Ziemba (Eds) *Handbook of Asset and Liability Management, Volume A* (North Holland, in press).

McGlothlin, W. H. (1956) Stability of choices among uncertain alternative, *American Journal of Psychology*, 69, pp. 604–619.

Roberts, H. (1967) Statistical versus clinical prediction of the stock market. Mimeo, University of Chicago.

Roman, S. A. (1981) Dosage: a practical approach, *Daily Racing Form*, May.

Roman, S. A. (2001) Personal communication to R. S. Bain. 17 May 2001.

Roman, S. A. (2002) *Dosage: Pedigree and Performance* (Neenah, Wisconsin: The Russell Meerdink Company Ltd).

Roman, S. A. (2005a) Dosage and two-year-old form: a predictor of classic performance, http://www.chef-de-race.com/dosage/classics/di_and_2yo_form.htm

Roman, S. A. (2005b), Dosage figures for kentucky derby winners since 1940, http://www.chef-de-race.com/dosage/classics/derby_dosage.htm

Rotando, L. M. and Thorp E. O. (1992) The Kelly Criterion and the stock market, *American Mathematical Monthly*, pp. 922–931.

The Blood-Horse, The Blood-Horse Inc., Lexington, Kentucky.

The British Racehorse, Turf Newspapers, London (no longer published).

The Courier-Journal, Louisville, Kentucky.

The Pedigree Program, Heath & Field Inc., Dallas, Texas (no longer published).

Thoroughbred Times, Thoroughbred Times Co. Inc., Lexington, Kentucky.

Thorp, E. O. (2006) The Kelly criterion in blackjack, sports betting and the stock market, in: S. A. Zenios and W. T. Ziemba (Eds) *Handbook of Asset and Liability Management, Volume A* (North Holland, in press).

Varola, F. (1974) *Typology of the Race Horse* (London: J. A. Allen).

Varola, F. (1980) *Functional Development of the Thoroughbred* (London: J. A. Allen).

Vuillier, J.-J. (1902) *Les Croisements Rationnels dans la Race Pur* (Paris: Legoupy).

Vuillier, J.-J. (1906) *Les Croisements Rationnels dans la Race Pur* (Paris: Legoupy).

Vuillier, J.-J. (1928) *Les Croisements Rationnels dans la Race Pur* (Paris: Maulde).

Ziemba, W. T. (2004) Behavioral finance, racetrack, betting and options and futures trading. Presentation to the Mathematical Finance Seminar, Stanford University, January.

Ziemba, W. T. and Hausch, D. B. (1986) *Betting at the Racetrack* (Los Angeles: Dr. Z Investments Inc.).

Ziemba, W. T. and Hausch, D. B. (1987) *Dr. Z's Beat the Racetrack* (New York: William Morrow).
Ziemba, W. T. (1991) Triple crown dosage analysis review, *Win Magazine* (August, written 28 April 1991, one week before the 1991 Kentucky Derby).

Appendix: Data Sources

(1) *Public's Wagering*

For races from 1946 to 1991, betting data were taken from tables published in *The Courier-Journal*, a Louisville Kentucky newspaper, usually on the Sunday after the Kentucky Derby. The pools for 1970 could not be found. There were several discrepancies in the data for which the published pools did not sum to the totals, or did not correspond with published win odds. Adjustments were made for errors for which an apparent revision could be made. For 1999–2002, complete pools were obtained from the Bloodstock Research Information Services Web site <http://www.bris.com>. In 2001, the pools also appeared on the Web site for the home of the Kentucky Derby, Churchill Downs, <http://www.churchilldowns.com>. The 2003 pools were sent directly by Churchill Downs, and the 2004 and 2005 pools were obtained courtesy of John Swetye who obtained them from Philadelphia Park's Phonebet service. From 1992 to 1998, the pools recorded in *The Courier-Journal* did not have all of the bets included. While these totals are not available, win odds based on total wagering are available. Therefore, for 1970 and 1992–1998 we estimated the total win pool and backed out a set of win pool fractions that are consistent with the published win odds. There were no dual qualifiers in 1998 and 2003 so those years were excluded from the dual-qualifier modeling.

(2) *Pedigrees*

Pedigree information was taken from *The Blood-Horse* magazine, the *American Produce Records*, a software database called *The Pedigree Program*, the pedigree query Web site <http://owl.netscout.com/pedigree> (no longer active), the Del Mar Turf Club Web site <http://www.dmtc.com/dmtc98/Pedigree/>, thoroughbred registries, and Roman's Web site <http://www.chef-de-race.com>. The 2004 data were sent by personal communication from Roman to John Swetye who forwarded them to us.

(3) *Chef-de-Race Listings*

Classifications of *chefs* were taken from the original 1981 list (Roman, 2000), the *American Racing Manual* for each year from 1986 (the first year that the list was included) to 1993, and from Roman's Web site. For the period 1981–1986, the 1981 list was used. For years prior to 1981, the original list was used. For 2001 to 2003, and 2005, Dosage Indices and EFH rankings tabulated by Roman were taken from his Web site, <http://www.chef-de-race.com>, and for 2004 they were sent via e-mail from Roman (see (2)).

(4) *Experimental Free Handicap Listings*

The EFH listings were taken from the *American Racing Manual*, *The Blood-Horse* magazine (print and on line <http://www.bloodhorse.com>), the *Thoroughbred Times* Web site <http://www.thoroughbredtimes.com>, and Roman's Web site <http://www.chef-de-race.com>.

(5) *Results of the Kentucky Derby and Major Races Prior to the Kentucky Derby*

The results of the Kentucky Derby were taken from the *Daily Racing Form*, both print and on line (<http://www.drf.com>), press materials from Churchill Downs, and from Chew (1974). Recent results charts were obtained from the following Web sites:

About.com Inc.	<http://horseracing.about.com>
Sportsline.com Inc.	<http://www.sportsline.com>
CNN/Sports Illustrated	<http://www.sportsillustrated.cnn.com>
Equibase Company, LLC	<http://www.equibase.com>
Daily Racing Form, LLC	<http://www.drf.com>

The results for the major races prior to the Derby were taken from the *American Racing Manual* and lists from the following Web sites:

Blue Grass Stakes:	<http://www.keeneland.com/liveracing/history.asp>
Flamingo Stakes:	<http://hialeahpark.com/99/HallofFame/flamingo.htm>
Florida Derby:	<http://www.thoroughbredchampions.com/library/fladerby.htm>
Santa Anita Derby	<http://www.revistahipodromo.com/santaanita.html>
Wood Memorial Stakes	<http://www.nyra.com/aqueduct/index2.html>

and the out-of-date site http://www.iglou.com/tbred/tc97/preps which was run by the *Thoroughbred Times.*

Chapter 19

Stochastic Programming and Optimization in Horserace Betting

William T. Ziemba

This chapter discusses the stochastic optimization approach to racetrack betting pioneered by the author with the help of Donald Hausch and Mark Rubinstein and used by the professional syndicate teams in Hong Kong, the US and elsewhere. The ideas are from financial theory and portfolio theory applications. One prices the bets and then wagers intelligently on the good ones. I discuss key topics such as the importance of good mean estimates, the favorite-longshot bias, various wagers such as place and show, and the Pick 2, 3, 4, 5 and 6.

Racetrack betting is simply an application of portfolio theory. The racetrack offers many bets that involve the results of one to about ten horses. Each race is a special financial market with betting then a race that takes one or a few minutes. Unlike the financial markets, one cannot stop the race when one is ahead or having the market going almost 24/7. There is a well-defined end point. Like standard portfolio theory, the key issues are to get the means right in this case, it is the probabilities of say ijkl finishes for a superfecta or ijk for place and show bets, and to bet well. For the latter, the Kelly capital growth criterion is widely used and that maximizes the expected logarithm of final wealth. Transaction and price pressure odds changes fit well into the stochastic programming models.

Professional syndicates or teams have been successful as hedge funds with gains approaching one billion over several years for the most successful. In the modern era, there are two features used extensively. First, there are rebates for large bettors of the track take similar to discounts at Costco. So instead of facing a 13–30% transaction cost, it's more like 10%. So to win, the bettors must make back this 10% disadvantage before profits ensue.

And this is not easy as the markets are quite efficient. Also over half the betting is not recorded in the pools until the race is being run. This is because monies are bet near the start of the race and come from many off track sites which are combined with the on-track bets into the track pool. All this takes time. So estimates of future prices are crucial. Secondly, betting exchanges such as Betfair in London allow short as well as standard long bets. This allows for more arbitrage and the ability to take advantage of known biases. I have been involved in this research since the late 1970s with six books and a number of articles.

In this chapter I relate the theory, computations and examples of real races and experiences for various bets such as win, place and show, exactas, triactors, superfectas, super hi five, place Pick all, double, pick 3, 4, 5 and 6. In the Halifax presentation I showed two of the greatest races ever by two undefeated female horses, one that was still then running (Zenyatta) and one retired (Personal Ensign) in 1988. The previous undefeated horse running at major tracks in the e US with at least ten races was Colin in 1907!

19.1. Introduction

Racetrack betting is simply an example of portfolio analysis. The investment horizon is short with betting for a period and then a race for about 1–2 minutes. Some of the bets involve multiple horses in a given race while others involve multiple races. The wagers are basically of two types: high probability of winning low payoff bets and low probability high payoff bets. The latter can return a million dollars or more. Table 19.1 describes a number of the bets.

Table 19.1. Common US and Canadian racetrack wagers.

High probability low payoff	Win
Low probability high payoff	Pick 3–6
One horse is involved	Win
Two horses are involved	Place, exacta
Three horses are involved	Show, triactor
Four horses are involved	Superfecta
Two races are involved	Double
Three races are involved	Pick 3
Four races are involved	Pick 4
Five races are involved	Pick 5
Six races are involved	Pick 6
N races are involved place	Pick all

Examples of some of these follow. In all cases I made these actual bets. More detail on them with charts, etc are in Ziemba (2019).

Investing in traditional financial markets has many parallels with racetrack and lottery betting and much of the analysis is similar. Behavioral anomalies such as the favorite-longshot bias are pervasive and also exist and are exploitable in the S&P500 and FTSE100 futures and equity puts and calls options markets. This is not discussed in this paper but I use this in personal and private managed accounts and in an offshore hedge fund. Biases there favor buying high probability favorites and selling low probability longshots just like the high probability low payoff racing wagers. But in complex low probability high payoff exotic wagers such as the Pick 6, the bias reverses to overbet the favorite so one must include other value wagers in the betting program. Fundamental information such as breeding is important and is especially useful for the Kentucky Derby and Belmont Stakes where horses have never run that far before. This is the dosage theory discussed in Chapter 17.

Kelly and fractional Kelly betting is used extensively in racetrack betting. Full Kelly is the maximization of the expected logarithm of final wealth subject to constraints, see some specific formulations below. That means: take an expected utility approach with $u(w) = logw$. Log with very low Arrow-Pratt risk aversion $-u''(w)/u'(w) = 1/w \cong 0$ is very risky short term despite wonderful long term growth properties; see MacLean, Thorp and Ziemba (2011) for an extensive treatment of the key ideas and major papers. Fractional Kelly is simply the idea to blend cash with the Kelly strategy. This under lognormal asset assumptions amounts to a less risky negative power utility function rather than log which is the most risky utility function one would ever want to use.

Fractional Kelly leads usually to less growth and more security and a less violent wealth path. Half Kelly is a frequently used strategy. It has 75% of the full Kelly growth but the security, measured by the probability of breaking even rising from 87% with full Kelly to 95.4% with half Kelly. For lognormal assets this is $u(w) = -1/w$ and this is approximate otherwise. To show this visually, see Figure 19.1(a) for the Kentucky Derby from 1934 to 2005 and Figure 19.1(b) with the dosage filter to eliminate horses that cannot run $1\frac{1}{4}$ miles on the first Saturday in May of their three year old career. These use the Dr Z system discussed in Section 19.4. The system that bets on the favorite turns \$2500 into \$480 so is a loser; while the full and half Kelly Dr Z systems have gains.

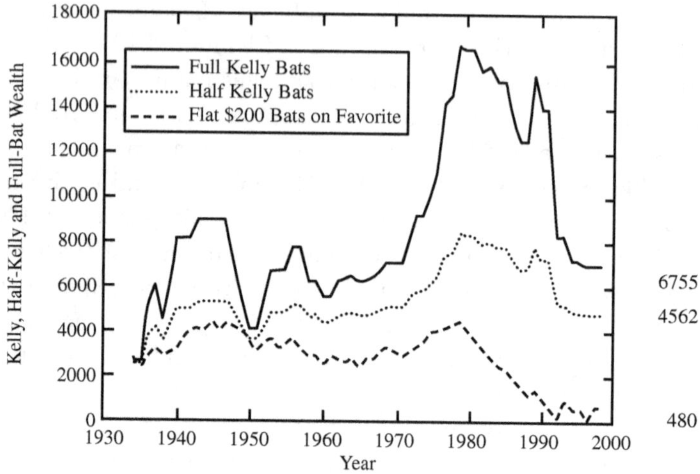

(a) Kelly, half Kelly and betting on the favorite

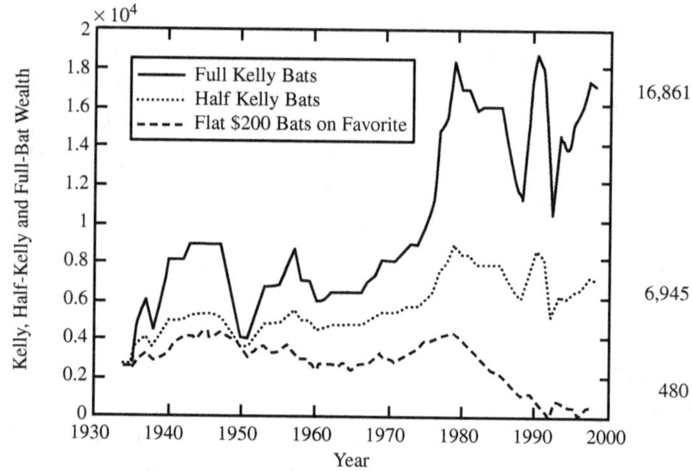

(b) same as (a) with dosage filter

Figure 19.1. Wealth history of some Kentucky Derby bets (1934–2005).

In all cases the strategy to win is the same as in the financial markets:

1. get the mean right: thus one must have accurate probabilities of various outcomes;
2. use the actual odds and a betting model such as the Kelly criterion to optimize the bet sizes, that is the allocations.

For situations with not many wagers, the Kelly capital growth maximize expected logarithm or, its safer version, fractional Kelly, is useful as a decision tool especially with many repeated bets. Then one has a stochastic program to maximize the expected utility using a logarithmic utility function of final wealth subject to various constraints. The Kelly strategy bets more on the attractive situations. In wagers where one makes hundreds of bets, it is often better to use a tree approach where many of the bets are of equal value. Besides being more convenient to make these multiple bets, this gets around integer problems as the wagers will be integers that can easily be bet. Whereas the Kelly optimization needs modifications to produce integer wagers. Also this approach can be computerized to print out the tickets — see the examples later in the paper, and the higher probability wagers can be bet more to approximate a Kelly strategy.

19.2. The Importance of Getting the Mean Right

Table 19.2 and Figure 19.2 show that getting the mean right is the most important aspect of any portfolio decision problem. Chopra and Ziemba (1993) discuss that and look at the effect of errors in means, variances and covariances using the cash equivalent of the approximate vs. exact optimal solutions. Basically it is in the ratio 20:2:1 for errors in means, variances and covariances in terms of error impact. We measure risk aversion by the Arrow-Pratt risk aversion index $R_A(w) = -u''(w)/u'(w)$, where primes denote differentiation of the utility of wealth function u. In investment practice, risk tolerance $t = 100/(1/2R_A)$ is typically used.

Referring to Table 19.2, we see that low risk aversion utility functions such as log with $R_A = 1/w \cong 0$, the effect of the errors is more like 100:3:1 so getting the mean right is even more important. And for horse racing, that is the probabilities for horses coming first, second, third, etc.

Table 19.2. Average Ratio of CEL for Errors in Means, Variances and Covariances.

t Risk Tolerance	Errors in Means vs. Covariances	Errors in Means vs. Variances	Errors in Variances vs. Covariances
25	5.38	3.22	1.67
50	22.50	10.98	2.05
75	56.84	21.42	2.68
	↓	↓	↓
	Error Mean	Error Var	Error Covar
	20	2	1

Source: Chopra and Ziemba (1993).

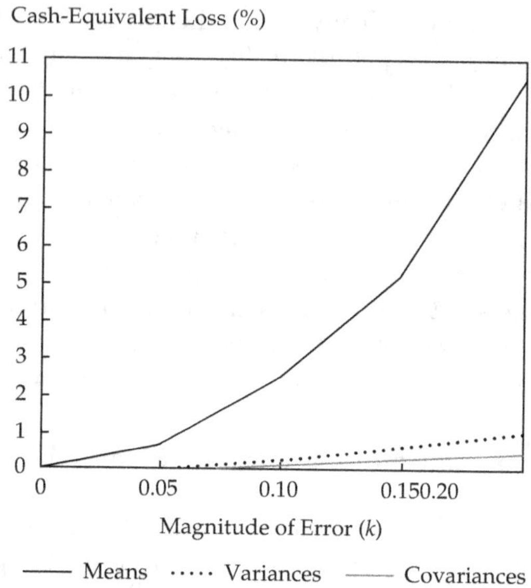

Figure 19.2. Typical relative importance of errors in means, variances and covariances in terms of certainty equivalent.

Source: Chopra and Ziemba (1993).

19.3. The Favorite-Longshot Bias

The favorite-longshot bias is the tendency in horseracing, sports betting, and financial options for the most likely outcome to be underbet and the less likely outcomes overbet. So people tend to like junk and dislike the best possibilities. This bias has been well known to Irish and other bookmakers who actually create the bias with the bets they offer for the last 100+ years. Figure 19.3 shows the 1949 study by Griffin for 1386 races in 1947 for races at Churchill Downs, Belmont and Hialeah. In this graph, there are the number of entries, winners and winners times odds for every odds group. The axes show the odds, the subjective probabilities, vs. the actual number of inners, the objective probabilities.

Figure 19.4 shows the effective track payback less breakage for various odds levels in California and New York, more than 300,000 races over various years and tracks, as of 1986 as reported in Ziemba and Hausch (1986).

There actually was a small profit, about 3%, in betting horses to win at US odds of 3–10 (UK odds of 1.30 or less) and that at odds of 100–1, the fair odds are about 700–1 so that such bets were worth about 13.7

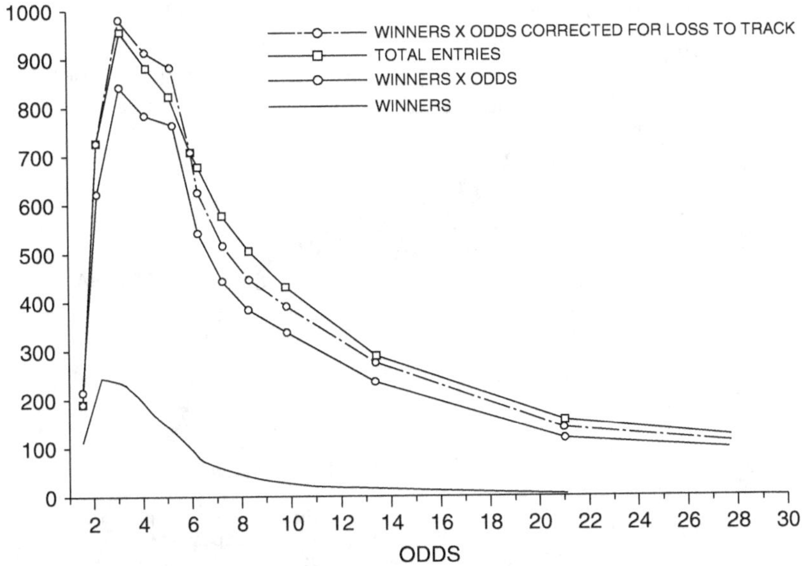

Figure 19.3. Griffith's 1949 study on the favorite-longshot bias; see Hausch, Lo and Ziemba (2008) for the reprinted paper.

cents per dollar bet. The California and New York graphs differ slightly because of different track takes. There are approximately three piecewise linear segments, small profits on extreme favorites with favorites underbet and longshots overbet, more and more losses as the odds lengthen and extremely poor returns at high odds levels like lotto tickets.

Since 1986 there have been a number of developments that have tended to influence the betting and have shifted these graphs such as:

1. There are no longer separate pools for individual races at different racetracks. All the races now have pooled betting which now comes in late with about half the bets not recorded in the pools until the race is already running;
2. There are rebates where tracks send a signal with the results and the rebate shops and the track share the track commission between the rebate shop, the tracks and the bettors. So instead of facing 13–30% transaction costs, large bettors are actually charged about 10% net; and
3. Betting shops such as Betfair, offer long and short bets on racing and many other events such as political campaigns, etc. Online internet

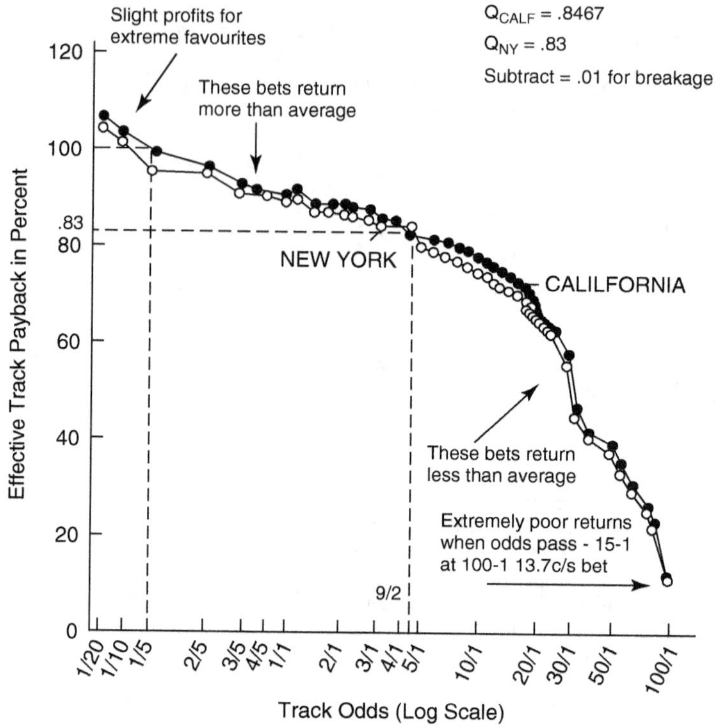

Figure 19.4. The effective track payback less breakage for various odds levels in California and New York (more than 300,000 races over various years and racetracks).
Source: Ziemba and Hausch (1986).

betting of this sort is legal in Canada, the UK and many other countries but it is not legal in the US.

Figure 19.5(a–c) look more closely at the extreme favorites in the US and the UK. Figure 19.5(c) shows that in Britain, bookies construct odds, creating the favorite-longshot bias to clear the market and equilibrate bettor demand.

Figure 19.6 shows that the bias curve may be different for different types of races. It shows the bias for the Kentucky Derby for 1903–1986. Other higher quality races like the Derby may well have flatter biases. See also Tompkins, Ziemba and Hodges (2008) who demonstrate similar biases in the S&P500 and FTSE100 index futures options. I use such ideas in an offshore hedge fund and in personal and private investment accounts.

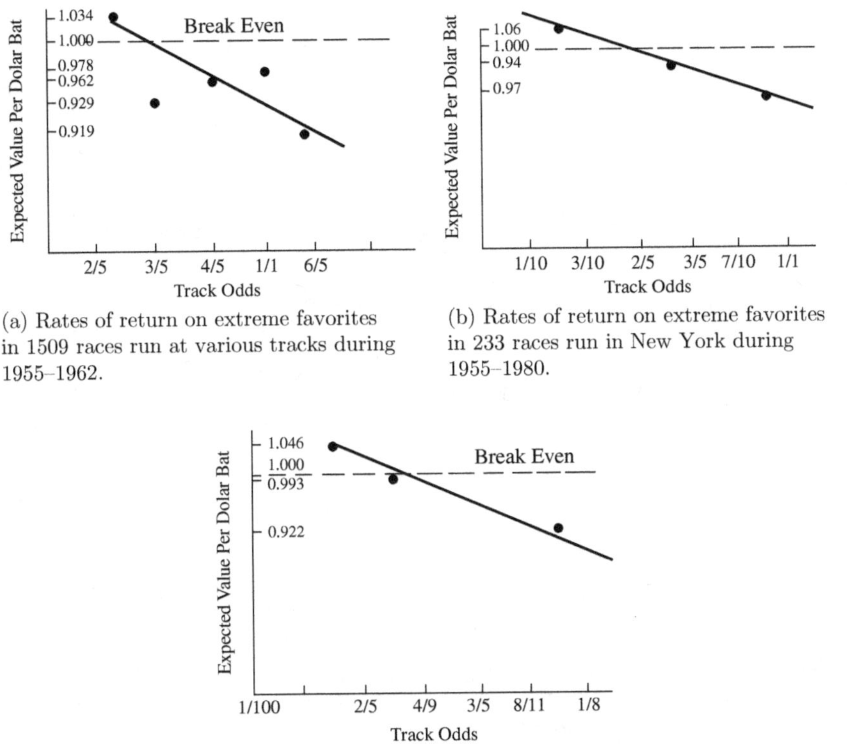

(a) Rates of return on extreme favorites in 1509 races run at various tracks during 1955–1962.

(b) Rates of return on extreme favorites in 233 races run in New York during 1955–1980.

(c) Rates of return on extreme favorites in 1599 races run on British flat racing tracks in 1950, 1965 and 1973.

Figure 19.5. Extreme favorites, small profits: see Ziemba and Hausch (1986) for these references.

Source: (a and b) Fabricand (1965–1979) and (c) Figgis (1974); Lord Rothschild (1978).

Figure 19.7 and its data in Table 19.3 and Figures 19.8(a and b) show the bias based on more recent data. Observe that the favorites are no longer underbet enough to turn a profit betting them and the flatness of the curve until you get to fairly long priced horses. You can still short longshots on Betfair and make a profit if you are careful. Additional discussion and results are in Hausch and Ziemba (2008).

This bias forms part of the Kahneman-Tversky (1979) prospect theory where low probability events are overestimated and high probability events are underestimated. This also forms a part of the behavioral finance

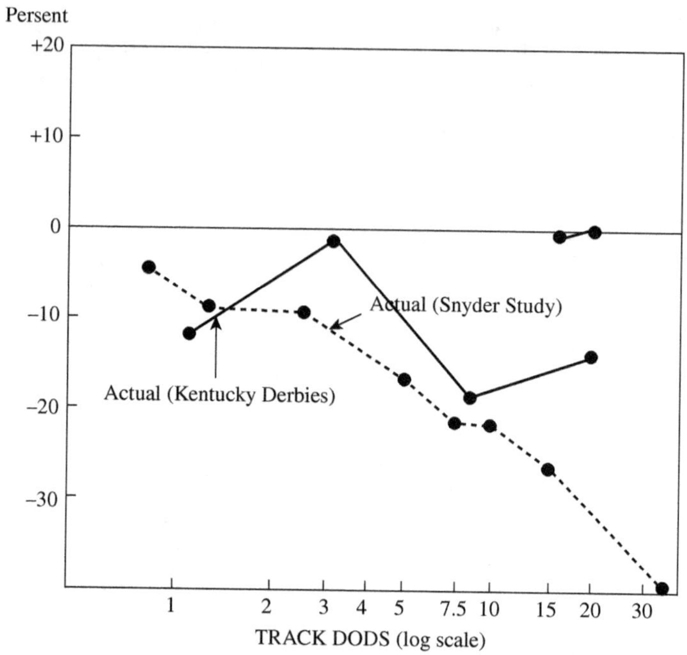

Figure 19.6. Expected return per dollar bet with and without the track take deducted for different odds levels in the Kentucky Derby 1903–1986 and in 35,285 races run during 1947–1975, from data in Snyder (1978).

Source: Ziemba and Hausch (1987).

literature. Thaler and Ziemba (1988) discuss reasons for the bias as do Ziemba and Hausch (1984). These include the fact that there are more bragging rights from picking longshots than from favorites: 50–1, *wow was I smart* while 2–5 is *an easy pick*. Transactions costs are another factor: bet $50 to win $10 is hardly worth the effort.

19.4. Place and Show Optimization with Transactions Costs

The Dr Z system, co-developed with Donald Hausch with some early help from Mark Rubinstein, presents a winning method for betting on underpriced wagers. The idea of the system is simple: use the data from a simple market, in this case the win probabilities to fairly price bets in the more complex markets, such as place and show. For example, with ten horses, there are 720 possible finishes for show. Then one searches for mispriced

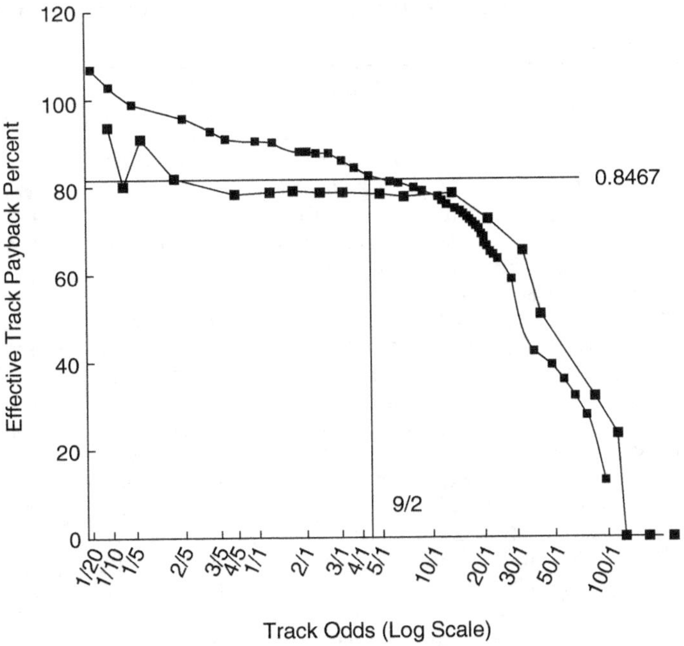

Figure 19.7. Effective track payback less breakage for various odds levels in California. *Source*: Ziemba and Hausch (1986) and Hausch and Ziemba (2008).

place and show opportunities. This is a weak form violation of the efficient market hypothesis based solely on prices. How much to bet depends on how much the wager is out of whack and it is a good application of the Kelly betting system. The formulation below shows such an optimization. There is a lot of data here on all the horses and not much time at the track. So a simplified approach is suggested. Don and I solved thousands of such models with real data and estimated approximation regression equations that only involve four numbers, namely, the amounts bet to win in the total pool and the horse under consideration for a bet. Plus the total place or show pool and the place or show bet on the horse under consideration.

These equations appear below. In our books Ziemba and Hausch (1984, 1986, 1987) and papers Hausch, Ziemba and Rubinstein (1981) and Hausch and Ziemba (1985), we study this in various ways, including different track takes, multiple bets for place and show on the same horse and how many can play the system before the edge is gone. This system revolutionized the way racetrack betting was perceived viewing it as a financial market not

Table 19.3. Data for the effective track payback less breakage for various odds levels in California.

Odds Level	Races	Avg Est Wins	Wins	Total Est Wins	Fav/Longshot	Odds Range
1	9	0.952381	8	8.571429	0.933333287	1/20–1/12
2	54	0.9090909	41	49.0909086	0.835185194	1/12–1/7.4
3	217	0.835003	163	181.195651	0.89958009	1/7.4–1/4.5
4	745	0.7660169	484	570.6825905	0.848107176	1/4.5–1/2.7
5	5990	0.6582732	3197	3943.056468	0.810792345	1/2.7–1/1.65
6	18250	0.5406803	8095	9867.415475	0.820376929	1/1.65–1/1
7	35987	0.4260281	12561	15331.47323	0.819295041	1/1–1.65/1
8	85716	0.3144652	22018	26954.69908	0.816852005	1.65/1–2.72/1
9	120483	0.2219781	21543	26744.58742	0.805508781	2.72/1–4.5/1
10	134990	0.14957	16371	20190.4543	0.810828709	4.5/1–7.4/1
11	136303	0.966803	10827	13177.81493	0.821608139	7.4/1–12/1
12	113285	0.0614053	5504	6956.299411	0.791225287	12/1–20/1
13	89063	0.0380625	2543	3389.960438	0.750156247	20/1–33/1
14	63568	0.023571	976	1498.361328	0.651378264	33/1–54.6/1
15	35808	0.0146932	281	526.1341056	0.534084366	54.6/1–90/1
16	9868	0.009349	28	92.255932	0.303503519	90/1–148.4/1
17	647	0.0059442	1	3.8458974	0.260017337	148.4/1–244.7/1
18	25	0.003213	0	0.080325	0	244.7/1–403.4/1
19	7	0.0020153	0	0.0141071	0	403.4/1–665.1/1
20	3	0.0012285	0	0.0036855	0	665/1–1090.6/1

Source: Ziemba and Hausch (1986) and Hausch and Ziemba (2008).

just a race. This led to pricing of wagers and the explosion of successful betting by syndicates in the US, Hong Kong and elsewhere; see, for example, my joint books referenced here and Hausch, Lo, Ziemba (1994, 2008) and Hausch and Ziemba (2008).

The effect of transactions costs which is called slippage in commodity trading is illustrated with the following place/show horseracing optimization formulation; see Hausch, Ziemba and Rubinstein (1981). Here q_i is the probability that i wins, and the Harville probability of an ij finish is $\frac{q_i q_j}{1-q_i}$, etc. That is $q_j/1-q_j$ is the probability that j wins a race that does not contain i, that is, comes second to i. Q, the track payback, is about 0.82 (but is about 0.90 with professional rebates). The players' bets are to place p_j and show s_k for each of the about ten horses in the race out of the players' wealth w_0. The bets by the crowd are P_i with $\sum_{i=1}^{n} P_i = P$ and S_k with $\sum_{k=1}^{n} S_k = S$. The payoffs are computed so that for place, the first two finishers, say i and j, in either order share the net pool profits once each P_i and p_i bets cost of say \$1 is returned. The show payoffs are computed

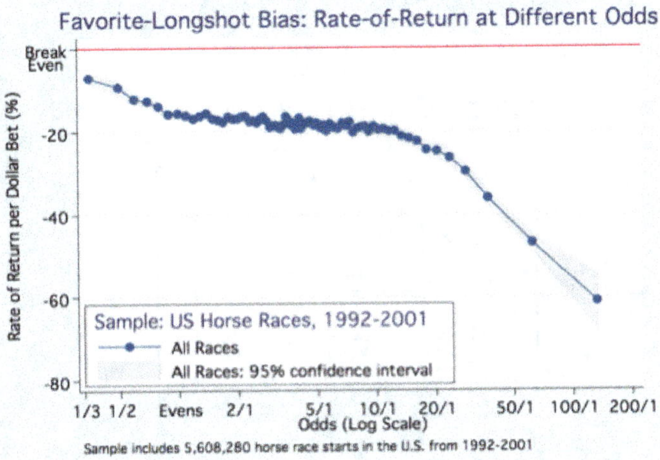

(a) Rates of return

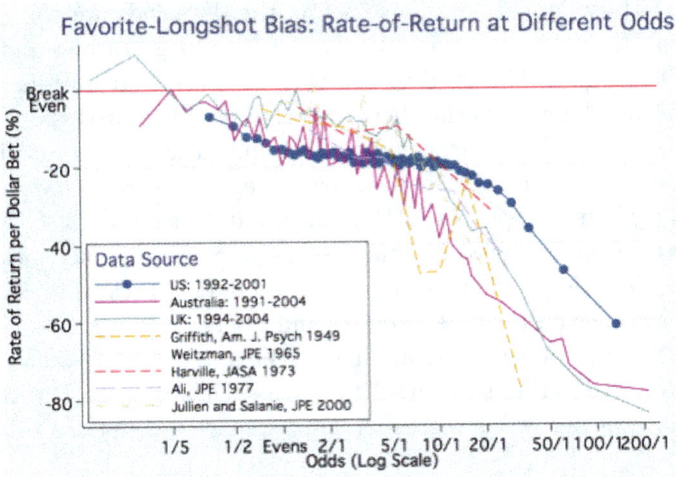

(b) Rates of return

Figure 19.8. Rate of return at different odds.

Source: Snowberg and Wolfers (2008).

similarly. The maximum expected utility model is

$$\max_{p_i, s_i} \sum_{i=1}^{n} \sum_{\substack{j=i \\ j \neq i}}^{n} \sum_{\substack{k=i \\ k \neq i,j}}^{n} \frac{q_i q_j q_k}{(1-q_i)(1-q_i-q_j)}$$

$$\times \log \left[\begin{array}{c} \frac{Q\left(P+\sum_{l=1}^{n} p_l\right)-(p_i+p_j+P_{ij})}{2} \\ \times \left[\frac{p_i}{p_i+P_i} + \frac{p_j}{p_j+P_j}\right] \\ + \frac{Q\left(S+\sum_{l=1}^{n} s_l\right)-(s_i+s_j+s_k+S_{ijk})}{3} \\ \times \left[\frac{s_i}{s_i+S_i} + \frac{s_j}{s_j+S_j} + \frac{s_k}{s_k+S_k}\right] \\ +w_0 - \sum_{\substack{l=i \\ l \neq i,j,k}}^{n} s_l - \sum_{\substack{l=i \\ l \neq i,j}}^{n} p_l \end{array} \right]$$

$$\text{s.t.} \sum_{l=1}^{n} (p_l + s_l) \leqslant w_0, \quad p_l \geqslant 0, \quad s_l \geqslant 0, \quad l = 1, \ldots, n,$$

While the Harville formulas make sense, the data indicate that they are biased. But for place and show, the win favorite-longshot bias and the second and third finish bias tend to cancel so the corrected Harville formulas are not needed here. For other bets to correct for this, professional bettors adjust the Harville formulas, using, for example, discounted Harville formulas,[1] to lower the place and show probabilities for favorites and raise them for the longshots; see papers in Hausch, Lo and Ziemba (1994, 2008) and Hausch and Ziemba (2008) and the discussion below on place pick all.

Rebate is added to final wealth inside the large brackets by adding the rebate rate times all the bets, winners and losers.

This is a non-concave program but it seems to converge when nonlinear programming algorithms are used to solve such problems. But a simpler way is via expected value regression approximation equations using 1000s

[1] The discounted probabilities come from

$$q_i^* = \frac{q_i^\alpha}{\sum_i^n q_i^\alpha}$$

for α about 0.81 then one uses the q_i^* in the second place position. For third one uses α^2 about 0.64. These empirical numbers vary over time and by track. This is more important for exacta pricing than place and show because for the latter the win bias from the favorite-longshot and the second and third biases tends to cancel. The favorite-longshot bias is the empirical observation that favorites are underbet and longshots overbet; see the discussion above.

of sample calculations of the NLP model. These are

$$\text{Ex Place}_i = 0.319 + 0.559\left(\frac{w_i/w}{p_i/p}\right)$$

$$\text{Ex Show}_i = 0.543 + 0.369\left(\frac{w_i/w}{s_i/s}\right).$$

The expected value (and optimal wager) are functions of only four numbers — the totals to win and place for the horse in question and the totals bet. These equations approximate the full optimized optimal growth model. See Hausch and Ziemba (1985) for more on this plus additional features. This is used in Dr Z calculators. See the discussion in Ziemba and Hausch (1986) and Ziemba (2011) for a discussion of typical use at the first Breeders' Cup in 1994.

An example is the 1983 Kentucky Derby.

	Totals	#8 Sunny's Halo	Expected Value Per Dollar Bet	Optimal Bet ($W_0 = 1000$)
Odds		5–2		
Win	3,143,669	745,524		
Show	1,099,990	179,758	1.14	52

Sunny's Halo won the race

Win	Place	Show
7.00	4.80	4.00

$\Pi = 52$

15 second bet!

Watch board in lineup
while everyone is at the TV

Here, Sunny's Halo has about 1/6 of the show pool vs. 1/4 of the win pool so the expected value is 1.14 and the optimal Kelly bet is 5.2% of one's wealth.

You might ask: does the system still work in 2012 and what is changed? The main new features are:

1. these days we bet at rebate shops by phone or electronically. The rebate is a sharing of the track take by the track, the rebater and the bettor. The effect is to take all bets from a track take of 13–30% for various bets to about 10%;
2. betting exchanges in the UK and elsewhere allow for short as well as long wagers; and
3. there is a lot of cross track and last minute betting and this takes time to be sent to the pools at the racetrack. Hence, about 50% of the wagers don't actually appear in the pools until after the horses are running. So one must estimate the final odds (probabilities).

Syndicates exist that break even on their wagers yet make millions on the rebate. Regarding the Dr Z system, John Swetye works with me and we wager with rebate searching for bets at 80 racetracks. Basically the system still works but the task is not easy. One successful six month period in 2004 with a $5000 bankroll, the system lost 7%, received a 9% rebate. The total wagers were $1.5 million giving a 2% or $30,000 profit.

19.5. The Place Pick All

This is a less commonly used and known bet but it is available at Santa Anita, for example. The idea is to create a ticket with I horses over I races where you have either the winner or the second place horse in each race i, $i = 1, \ldots, I$. The number of races I varies from about 7 to 12.

The probability that a ticket with j the chosen horse in race i *wins* that race is the probability that j is first plus the probability that j is second, namely

$$p_{ij} + \sum_{k=1,\ldots,K_i} p_{ik} \frac{q_{ij}}{1 - q_{ik}} \quad \text{for } k \neq j$$

where

$$q_{ik} = \frac{p_{ik}^{\alpha}}{\sum p_{ik}^{\alpha}} \quad \text{and} \quad \alpha \cong 0.81 \text{ and is track dependent.}$$

These are discounted Harville formulas, see papers in Hausch, Lo and Ziemba (1994, 2008) for more on this.

Then the chance that a given ticket with $i = 1, \ldots, I$ is a winner is

$$\hat{p}_{ij} = \prod_{i=1,\ldots,I} \left\{ p_{ij} + \sum_{k=1,\ldots,K_i} p_{ik} \frac{q_{ij}}{1 - q_{ik}} \right\}$$

19.6. Some Stochastic Programming Formulations

There are basically two strategies for the optimization: Kelly expected log optimization and the tree tickets approach that approximates the Kelly strategy. To illustrate a few formulations appear here.

The expected log problems are typically solved using CONOPT which has produced good results even though the problems have non-concavity in them. The bets must be computed very fast as the odds are changing. While this may not be general but because of an epsilon optimality convergence criteria, the Minos-Stanford code may converge to a non-optimal strategy. Hence, CONOPT is safer.

In general, the Kelly Elog optimization given modern computing can be used for essentially all the bets, even possibly Hong Kong's triple trio, namely, getting the 1–2–3 finish in any order in three races with 14 horses in each race of which many horses are 200–1 but they can still finish 3rd. This has 48 million combinations. I focus here on the US bets and suggest that we focus on Elog Kelly optimization for high probability low payoff bets and the tickets approach for the low probability high payoff events which can closely approximate the Kelly strategy and yields easily implemented tickets that are integers.

The simplest bet is the exacta. To win you must get the winner plus the second place finisher. This uses elements of the place pick all formulation except it is just for one race and it is not first **or** second but first **and** second. First is easy, it is just p_i the probability that i wins. Second uses the discounted Harville formula so it $\frac{q_i}{1-q_i}$ where $q_i = \frac{p_i^\alpha}{\sum p_i^\alpha}$, where $\alpha \cong 0.81$ So the probability of an ij finish is $\frac{p_i q_j}{1-q_i}$. Let s_{ij} be our bet on an ij finish. So the Kelly optimization problem is

$$\max_{x \in K} E_w \log W = \sum_{i=1}^{I} \sum_{j \neq i}^{J} p_i \frac{q_j}{1 - q_i} \log \left\{ W_0 + r \sum_{i=1}^{I} \sum_{j \neq i}^{J} x_{ij} \right.$$

$$+Q\frac{\left(E+\sum_{i=1}^{I}\sum_{j\neq i}^{J}x_{ij}\right)}{E_{ij}+x_{ij}}\left(\frac{x_{ij}}{x_{ij}+E_{ij}}\right)$$
$$-\sum_{i=1}^{I}\sum_{j\neq i}^{J}x_{ij}\Bigg\}$$

where r is the rebate percent payable on all bets, losers and winners, E is the total exacta bet by the crowd, with the E_{ij} their bets on ij and Q is the track payback. The constraints can include a maximin bet on any combination ij as well as on each i and on the total bet. The wealth is final wealth plus rebate plus profits minus the bets and Exp is the expected value. Other high probability low payoff bets are similar.

Lets now consider a tickets model as well as an expected log model. I supervised an unpublished MSc thesis on this at the Oxford Math Department, see Assamoi (2010). Some of the theory is there but no calculations. Before we consider this, let us do it for the place pick all. I am not aware of any published research or calculations, real or simulated, on this bet.

Let x_i^l be the bet that the chosen horse i_l wins or comes second in race l, $l = 1, \ldots, L$ for $i_l = 1, \ldots, I_l$ where there are I_l horses in race l. The probability i_l of being first or second is

$$\hat{p}_i^l = p_i^l + \sum_{j=1,\ldots,I_l}\frac{q_j^l}{1-q_i^l} \quad \text{for } i \neq j$$

The expected log Kelly optimization formulation is

$$\max_{x\in K} E\log W = \sum_{l=1}^{L}\sum_{i=1}^{I_l}\hat{p}_i^l \log\Bigg\{w_0 + r\sum_{l=1}^{L}\sum_{i=1}^{I_l}x_i^l$$
$$+Q\frac{\left(\sum_{l=1}^{L}PL^l+\sum_{l=1}^{L}\sum_{i=1}^{I_l}x_i^l\right)}{\sum_{l=1}^{L}x_i^l+\sum_{l=1}^{L}PL_i^l}\left(\frac{\sum_{l=1}^{L}\sum_{i=1}^{I_l}x_i^l}{\sum_{l=1}^{L}(x_i^l+PL_i^l)}\right)$$
$$-\sum_{l=1}^{L}\sum_{i=1}^{I_l}x_i^l\Bigg\}$$

where $PL = \sum_{l=1}^{L} PL^l$ is the place pick all pool with $PL^l = \sum_{i=1}^{I_l} PL_i$ bet on i by the crowd, r is the rebate percent, Q is the track payback percent, and $x \in K$ is the three dimensional list of all the x_i^l and K, the feasibility set.

The ticket formulation breaks the picks, the js, into categories I, II and III for each race j. I's are high value and high probability of winning horses. II's are major contenders and III's are longer odds horses who could upset the favorites. Suppose there are eight races so I=8, where n_{ij} is the number of horses in category ij.

	1	2	3	4	5	6	7	8
I	N_{1I}	N_{2I}						
II	N_{1II}	N_{2II}						
III	N_{1III}	N_{2III}						

Given the probabilities and other factors, the horses are put into I, II or III or not considered in each race i. The score 8 tickets have all I's and they have the most money on them. There are $\prod_{i=1}^{8} N_{iI}$ of these. The score 9 have 7 ones and one II. There are 8 such tickets with lower bets. The score 10 tickets have 6 I's and 2 twos or 7 I's and one III with even lower bets. There are $\binom{8}{2}$ and eight of these with the lowest bets. One might go to score 11 and have bet sizes to approximate a Kelly strategy. As you can see, the number of tickets gets very large here as is the cost. We use a computer program to generate these tickets. For a sample printout, see Section 19.11.

19.7. The Pick3 and Pick 4: Theory of Pricing the Bets

Example: the 9/11 Pick3: don't trust odds from newspaper stories

On September 11, 2011, the tenth anniversary of the attacks on New York and Washington, the first three races at Belmont had winners 9–1–1. The Pick3 paid \$18.60. The parlay on the three track takes vs. one for the Pick3 paid $4.20 * 4.20/2 * 6.20/2 = \$30.5$, which is more than the Pick3 payoff without even factoring in the two extra tack takes. So the 9–1–1 Pick3 was over bet just like popular numbers in lotteries are. The track take for the Pick3 is 26% and for win 16%.

So the fair value of the Pick3 with zero track take is \$18.60/0.74 = \$25.14 and for the parley

$$30.5\left\{\frac{1}{0.84}\right\}^3 = \$51.34,$$

so the numbers 9–1–1 were over bet. A newspaper article said the odds of such an outcome is a million to one. Actually by looking at the final odds on the charts for these three races, we can estimate that. Recall, the probability of winning is

$$\frac{Q + \Delta Q(odds)}{odds + 1}.$$

Referring to a table in Ziemba (2012) for the ΔQs and the payoffs below, the odds of 9–1–1 occurring are about one divided by the probability of this outcome which is

$$\left\{\frac{0.84 - .02315}{2.1}\right\}\left\{\frac{0.84 - .02315}{2.1}\right\}\left\{\frac{0.84 - .0345}{3.45}\right\}$$
$$= 0.3890 * 0.3890 * 0.2335 = 0.0353$$

since the payoffs for win were \$4.20, \$4.20 and \$6.90 for each \$2 bet. The chance of the 9–1–1 outcome then is equal to about $1/.0353 = 28.31$. This means that there was a 1 in 28 chance of the 9–1–1 payoff, not 1 million to 1.

19.8. The Pick 4

This bet has no consolation prize so you need to win all four races to collect. The bet is usually offered twice daily, early and later with the late Pick 4 covering the top races on the card. Like the other multiple race bets, it is hard to win as the probability that you win is $P^4 = P_1P_2P_3P_4$, namely, the product of the probabilities that you win each of the four races. For example, if each P_i is 1/2, so you have a 50% chance of winning each race, then $P^4 = \left\{\frac{1}{2}\right\}^4 = \frac{1}{16} = 6.67\%$ so once every 16 times you would win on average. And getting to 50% in each race is challenging. The bet is \$1 and sometimes 50 cents so you can take many multiple combinations to get P^4 to an acceptable level. As always, try to bet with an advantage so focus on horses of three types: good value and good chance to win and possible bombs to give a large payoff.

When facing the Pick 4, determine a strategy to play the bet. If there are one to three standouts and some wide open races then you can have a simple ticket that singles the standouts and spreads in the contentious races. If the standouts are very strong, then singling make sense otherwise make the standout a I and have some backups as IIs.

I was at Santa Anita on Saturday April 9, 2011 for the Santa Anita Derby, a major prep race for the three year olds before the Kentucky Derby.

There was a standout, Premier Pegasus, who won the San Felipe $1\frac{1}{16}$ (the previous major race) by seven lengths, but in a soft time — he won so easily that his time (1:41:23) was not fast. He towered over the field but unfortunately had a minor injury and was scratched. So was Uncle Mo, another Kentucky Derby hopeful, who disappointed in the Wood Memorial at Aqueduct, finishing third at 1–10 win odds. But he was a dual qualifier and became the favorite. But he too was scratched. The rest of the field looked weak and it was hard to separate them. So spreading was suggested and I took seven horses in that 10th race — all except two very longshots. who were at over 40 to 1 odds. The other three races all had standouts and I singled all three. One was First Dude in race 8 who had never won a race but was second in last years Preakness and third in the Belmont and in the money in many Grade II races. His trainer, Bob Baffert, put him in a \$56k allowance against weaker competition to try to get that first win. He got it at 4–5, winning easily, paying \$3.60 for a \$2 win ticket.

It was good that I spread in the Santa Anita Derby race 10 as Midnight Interlude, trained by Bob Baffert at 13.90 to 1, was the winner, paying \$29.80 for a \$2 win ticket. Baffert has a knack of winning these top races.

Race 9's standout was Cambina, who also won at the essentially even money odds of 1.1 to 1 to pay \$4.20 for a \$2 win ticket.

Race 11's standout, Hey Maria, again at close to even money, won at 1.30 to 1 paying \$4.60 for a \$2 win ticket.

The Pick 4 was a 50 cent bet but I bet \$10 on it costing $7 \cdot 1 \cdot 1 \cdot 1 \cdot \$10 = \$70$. The Pick 4 paid \$99.20 for the 50 cents so I collected \$1995 which was a good gain. Like the Pick6 below, singling top standouts and spreading in tough races often is a very good strategy with low cost that can have a large payoff.

19.9. Example of Pick 4 with embedded Pick3's and Doubles: Travers Day at Saratoga

Saturday, August 27, 2011 was the Travers Stakes at Saratoga. This is the mid summer Derby, the top race for three year old colts between the triple crown races in May and June and the Haskell at Monmouth Park on July 31st and the Breeders' Cup in November. This is a $1\frac{1}{4}$ mile race with a \$1 million purse.

A strategy for the \$1 million guaranteed Pick 4 which was races 9–12 is to accumulate the picks of various handicappers and then cover the bets well. To be a Kelly bettor, you must bet more on the top favorites and less on the longer priced horses. In addition to the handicappers at Saratoga who discuss the races on TV for free and the ones with subscription services, there is betfair.com in London which provides bid-ask spreads on the races to give an idea of the final odds as they allow shorts as well as long bets. A drawback of betfair.com is that the spreads are wide but they close up near race time. Another drawback for US bettors is that you cannot use it in the US but Canadian and British bettors can use it.

The strategy is to establish bets on the Pick 4 races 9–12 and have as backup the races 9–11 and 10–12 Pick 3's and the races 9–10, 10–11 and 11–12 doubles. Thus if you get the P4 right you also win the two P3s and the three P2s. The strategy is to have multiple tickets, they can be through the score 8 system with I's, II's and III's or through straight tickets where you pick several horses in each race and box them all. That means that you win if any one of the horses in each race you selected wins, assuming you win all the races. These boxed tickets put more weight on the weaker horses than the multiple tickets approach. The multiple tickets approach is more complex but fully manageable. For a Pick5 or Pick6 we use a computer program to generate the tickets as there can be many of them. For a Pick 4 there are 17 tickets if you do a score 8 down to II–II–II–II. Examples follow.

Both these approaches are discussed as follows.

Here are the races:

Race 9 was the 9th running of the Victory Ride, a Grade III, $100,000 race for three year old fillies. The past performances follow.

- Saratoga handicapper Mike Watermaker chooses one horse per race and here he chose #6 Hot Summer.
- The TV handicappers Dan Ulman and Mike Beer chose 2,5/6,8,9 and 6/5,8,9. This means double keying 2 and 5 as I's and 6,8,9 as II's. This is set up for the score tickets approach, see below.
- I use three additional services plus two of my colleagues have their picks, but one of them was rained out on that day by the great hurricane Irene. Our handicapper, who selects for superfecta as well so picks the best five horses, liked 2,5,6,8,9. One service ranked them 8–2–9–1–3. The other 2–9–1–8–1–3.

  The third, which are the Equiform pace numbers and final speed figures for the best final time in the last four races, #2 $74\frac{3}{4}$ twice; #5 74; #6 $73\frac{3}{4}$; #8 $71\frac{1}{4}$ and #9 76.

So the suggested picks were 2,5,6,9 because I skipped 8 so the ticket would not be too large. But in the multiple score tickets, 8 must be a II.

The result was 6–1–9. A $16.40 win for a $2 bet was a good start. Watchmaker had it but as we will see that was it for his picks, the other three did not win. An important point - none of the handicappers will get it all right very often so it is important to use several outside handicappers plus your own analysis.

Race 10 was the 33rd running of the Ballerina, a Grade I race with a $250,000 race for three year old fillies. The past performances follow.

- Watermaker picked #7 Sassy's Image who was the favorite but did not win.
- Ulman and Beer chose 6/1,2/3,5,7 and 6,7/2. As we will see, #3 Hilda's Passion won and they basically threw her out because of the last race - a real clunker. But in the previous race to that, she ran a Beyer 107! Ranking her as a III meant that with a score 8 ticket 3 of the 8 spots are used up so one can still win with 2 II's and one I but this score 8 ticket will have the minimum bet $1 or 50 cents depending on the track rules.
- Our handicapper liked 3,6 and 7. One service ranked them 3–6–2–7–5, the other 1–7–5–2–6–4. Equiform's pace service got it right and as we will see, got the next two races correct as well for one third pick and three top ones. A very good performance. But that will not happen all the time. Equiform had #2 $77\frac{1}{4}$ and $77\frac{1}{2}$; #3 $79\frac{3}{4}$; #6 78 and $77\frac{1}{2}$ and #7 $77\frac{1}{2}$.
  So my picks were 2,3,6,7 and #3 Hilda's Passion was a short price and won paying $7.20.

Race 11 was the 27th running of the Foxwoods King Bishop, a 7 furlong Grade I race with a purse of $250,000. The race featured the return to the track of the two year old champion Uncle Mo who had been sidelined since being scratched just prior to the Kentucky Derby where he was favored to win. He had a variety of ailments but had good recent workouts. The big issue was is this the old Uncle Mo? It was a tough challenge.

- Watermaker favored #3 Run Flat Out.
- The TV handicappers favored #1 Flashpoint with one double keying #4 Dominoes, the favorite in the Grade 2 Jim Dandy run on July 30 at $1\frac{1}{8}$ at Saratoga. He lost that race finishing third to Stay Thirsty, ran a Beyer 106 and was in Race 12 at the Travers. So Ulman and Beer had 1/2,5,7

and 1,4/2,6/7. Arguing that the return was too tough for Uncle Mo, they downgraded him to a II and a III, respectively.

- Our handicapper favored 4, 5 and 7. The two services had 1–2–7–4 and 1–7–5–2–6–4. The Equiform pace analysis had #1 76 (but double top); #2 79, #4 75, #5 75, and Uncle Mo #7 $78\frac{3}{4}$ but a long time ago. So this pointed to Caleb's Posse, #2.
  I rather liked Caleb's Posse with the 79 at Saratoga in the Grade II Amsterdam on August 1 with a Beyer of 105 which was higher than Flashpoint's 104 at Monmouth. The 105 for Caleb's was way above his previous high Beyer of 92 so that made it a risk. The only horse to win a Grade I was Uncle Mo who won two as a two year old, the Champaign and Breeders' Cup Juvenile, the latter with a 108 Beyer in the race he got the $78\frac{3}{4}$ speed figure.
  My picks were 1, 2 and 7.

The finish was 2–7–6–4 with Caleb's Posse nipping Uncle Mo at the wire. I had now won the first Pick3 there and the first two of the doubles.

Race 12, the final one in the Pick 4 was the 142nd running of the Travers a Grade I, $1 million purse race. This is the mid summer classic and one of the longest running top races in the US.

- The TV handicappers felt that the winner here would come out of either the Jim Dandy run at Saratoga or the Haskell run at Monmouth. So that favored #7 Coil, #10 Shackleford and #9 Stay Thirsty. They chose 7,9,10/3 and 10/6,9.
- Watermaker liked Shackleford, a front running horse who won the $1\frac{3}{16}$ mile Preakness and was ahead in the Kentucky Derby late in the race, but faded to fifth. His dosage profile was 6–13–9–0–2 for a dosage index of 3.62. This is under the usual Kentucky derby cutoff of 4.00 but is high. Stay Thirsty with 4–6–16–0–0 (2.25), Coil 2–0–9–1–0 (1.18) and Ruler on Ice, the winner of the Grade I Belmont Stakes in the slop with 6–1–9–0–0 (2.56) were more suited for this $1\frac{1}{4}$ mile race. But he still could win going wire to wire.
- Our handicapper favored 7,9,10 with 4 should there be rain and mud which there was not. The two handicapping services had the following rankings: 9–2–7–4–10–6 and 9–2–7–4–6–8–3–10. So they favored Stay Thirsty and did not like Coil much but gave him third and basically threw out Shackleford. They rather liked #2 Rattlesnake Bridge rated

second and the mud runner Ruler on Ice, fourth with two wins on sloppy tracks and the rest mediocre. Rattlesnake did not look competitive to me with three Beyer's of 91, 90 and 91 with one win.
Equiform's top picks were #6 $75\frac{3}{4}$; #7 $74\frac{1}{4}$, 74, 77; #9 $77\frac{1}{4}$ and #10 $76\frac{1}{2}$.
So they suggested #9, Stay Thirsty.
My picks were 6,7,9,10 on the bigger ticket and 7,9,10 on the smaller ticket.

The finish was 9–2–8–4.

My tickets were

2,5,⑥,9/2,③,6,7/1, ②,7/6,7,⑨,10	for $384 less rebate, and
2,5,9/③,6,7/1,②,7/7,⑨,10	for $162 where circles indicate the winners

So the big ticket won the Pick 4, the two Pick 3s and the three daily doubles. I made some win, place and show and superfecta bets. Some won, some lost.

The Pick 4 paid $1453.00, the two Pick 3s $471 and $195 and the three doubles $86.50, $58.00, and $48.80 per $2 bet. So there was a good gain.

The Pick 3 tickets I played were

2,5,⑥,9/2,③,6,7/1,②,7	$96 for $2, to collect $86.50
2,③,6,7/1,②,7/6,7,⑨,10	$96.00 for $2, to collect $195
2,5,9/2,③,6,7/1,②,7	cost $72.00, a loser for $2
③,6,7/1,②,7/7,⑨,10	$54.00, a winner for $2, to collect $195

The doubles were

9/10	2,5,⑥,9/2,③,6,7	winner	$32 for $2 to collect $86.50
	2,5,9/③,6,7	loser	$18 for $2
10/11	2,③,6,7/1,②,7	winner	$24 for $2 to collect $58.00
	③,6,7/1,②,7	winner	$18 for $2 to collect $58.00
11/12	1,②,7/7,⑨,10	winner	$18 for $2 to collect $48.00
			plus rebate on all the bets, winners and losers

I did not play a score ticket approach but it would have had all these winners. It would have cost more but could have returned more since scores 8,7,6,5 and 4 would likely have $20, $10, $5, $3, and $1 tickets. Rather than speculate, I will discuss the tickets approach in other situation where I actually made such bets. Rebate always help.

19.10. The Pick 6: Theory of Pricing the Bets

19.10.1. *2001 Breeders' Cup Insurance bets for SCA*

In 2001, a racing colleague Cary Fotias, creator of the Equiform ratings and I were hired by SCA, a Dallas based sports insurance company, to help insure the Breeders' Cup which was at Belmont near New York City. We insured the $2 to $3 million part. So the insurance company would guarantee a pool of $3 million. For example, if $2.15 million was bet, they would be liable for $850,000. We studied and proposed to bet a random amount if needed. The idea being to get to $3 million and return the insurance company's money by winning Pick 6s and Pick 5/6s. It was risky as September 11 had just occurred and all the Arab owners such as Sheik Mohammed of Dubai were not in attendance. Their horses and trainers were though. It turned out to be a glorious day so the crowd sent the Pick 6 pool well over $4 million. Our client, himself the world's most famous bridge player, Bob Hammond, said you two can just play about $25–30,000 of the tickets. So we had a $2000 ticket twice and what we call a gorilla ticket for $28,000. We had some 5/6's and got most of the money back. The Pick 6 paid $250,000. The race we lost was the sprint. Squirtle Squirt, which my handicapping colleague did not like at 9–1 beat the front running filly, Extra Heat at 14–1, who we had and had led all the way until the finish. So if she had won we would have had three about $450,000 Pick 6s plus more 5/6s. Squirtle Squirt had run at Belmont and had the very top jockey Jerry Bailey and was trained by the recently deceased legendary trainer Broadway Bobby Frankel. I should have over ruled and included Extra Heat on the ticket, adding a bit of extra cost. Too bad. This was another example of a lot of operational risk involved in Pick 6 tickets. It is very easy to have an error leading to a loss. Various models and research yields the horses to include. The optimization creates a good ticket. But it was fun! But the next week we won a similar case at Santa Anita, while guaranteeing a $1 million Pick 6, collecting $240,000 for the client and a nice bonus for us.

19.11. The One That Got Away: The Hitable $2 Million Pick 6 at the 2009 Breeders' Cup

The Breeders' Cup is now up to 14 major races over two days[2] and was held again at Santa Anita on Saturday, November 6 and 7. I went in 2008

[2]In future years there were about 15 Breeders' Cup races.

and it is fun to see it live. This year on wide screen high definition TV it was wonderful to watch. Being at home, the handicapping and betting is a lot easier. There are many opinions. That's what makes a horse race. The spreads on Betfair are fairly tight and it is easy to bet from Canada and you frequently get better odds there than at the track. We don't actually bet at the track but bet through rebate shops that give back part of the track take. That's easy to do on the phone or by email. The rebaters take their cut and the track gets more easy, low expense business to up their revenues.

The big race was as usual the $5 million classic. It is no longer the world's richest race. The $6 million Dubai World Cup has that honor. But it is the most important race in the world and frequently determines the horse of the year. The two candidates for horse of the year are were both female. The 3-year-old Rachel Alexandra won all her 2009 races. She beat the top females in the top female races by 20 lengths. I was at Churchill Downs to see this in the Kentucky Oaks held on the first Friday in May, the day before the Kentucky Derby. In four races against males, she beat them handily. So she would normally be an almost sure bet for horse of the year. But Zenyatta, a five year old mare had won all 13 of her races but always against females. She has a dynamite kick and just cruises by the other horses near the buzzer to win easily. Some of her races were in slow times (76 area on the Equiform scale that I follow) and some in fast times (81 area). To put this scale in perspective, the highest I ever saw was four 84's by Ghostzapper. One of my most treasured but small bets was on Ghostzapper's Breeders' Cup win. There was a top filly in that race, Azeri — I had watched her at Saratoga getting beat by females in a $1\frac{1}{4}$ race so the fact that she had numerous wins at short distances I was pretty sure she would not be in the top 4 in this male dominated $1\frac{1}{4}$ race. So a $20 superfecta bet in 2004 boxing for $5 Ghostzapper (1or 2) with Roses in May (1 or 2) with the two next leading horses, Pleasantly Perfect and Perfect Drift (3 or 4) and (3 or 4) came in to provide a $5000 payoff. The big mistake was not betting more! Ghostzapper ran the $1\frac{1}{4}$ race in 1:59:02, faster than Secretariat's record setting Kentucky Derby 1:59:40. The 5–2 odds were quite generous given Ghostzapper's brilliant record.

The 13/13 of Zenyatta is historic since only Personal Ensign (13/13) in 1988 and Colin in 1907 had undefeated records in the US. Tesio, the great Italian trainer in the 1930s had the other three of the five undefeated horses since 1900, among horses with at least ten major races at major race tracks. Tesio was a great anomaly person looking at many many generations to bread cheap to cheap to get great champions. He did this without computers with a lot of help from his wife.

Currently, the way to check such matings is to go to Steve Roman who does this for ten generations back. See Steve's website, www.chef-de-race.com, for much valuable information.

The Europeans and many other handicappers were pushing for Rip Van Winkle, trained by Irish legend Aidan O'Brien was the pick since he had won his two races on 2009 when he did not face the superstar Sea the Stars. The three times Sea the Stars beat Rip Van Winkle he was close behind and well ahead of the competition. Unfortunately, the Sea the Stars connections preferred to hedge and cash in on this horse reputed to be the best in Europe in ten years by retiring him to stud duties. He had won the Epson Derby, the 2000 Guineas and the ARC. Perhaps they recalled the last "best horse of the decade", Dancing Brave, who "could not lose" but finished fourth in the classic. The polytrack at Santa Anita not dirt or the European's grass could have been a factor too.

Getting back to Zenyatta and Rip Van Winkle. The Betfair and track odds showed the local biases. You could get better odds on Zenyatta in Europe on Betfair and Rip Van Winkle in the US at the track. It was not possible to do an arbitrage here. I just concentrated on better odds on Zenyatta on Betfair. My assumption was despite the fact that her running times were not super outstanding she had the will to win. And indeed she did with Rip Van Winkle finishing out of the money. She could have been retired as the only undefeated mare who beat males in the toughest race in the world.

But let's discuss the Pick 6. In the Pick 6, to win you must have all six winners who share 75% of the net pool with the 5/6 sharing the remaining 25%. The Pick 6 was races 4–9. There were three standouts but they were definitely not certain winners. The other three races seemed wide open. So you could play the Pick 6 in the following very simple way: I thought about doing this but did not — it was a $2 million mistake. You have a single ticket with about 10 horses in the three wide open races and single the three standouts. That would cost about 10*10*10*1*1*1*$2 = $2000, not a large Pick 6 ticket. You only win if all three standouts win and they did.

The payoffs for $2 win tickets were as follows:

Race 4	Dancing in Silks	52.60	
Race 5	Value of York	63.20	
Race 6	Goldikova	4.80	the first standout

Race 7	Furthest Land	44.60	
Race 8	Conduit	3.80	the second standout
Race 9	Zenyatta	7.60	the third standout

Goldikova was the winner of the mile grass race in 2008 and was arguably better this year. Her connections were the same as those of Miesque also a two time winner of this race. The second standout, Conduit, was also the winner last year of the $1\frac{1}{2}$ mile turf.

The Pick 6 paid $1,838,305.20 for one winning 6/6 ticket and the 3*9=27 Pick 5/6 tickets (of the 10 losers in the three wide open races) paid 27*$4822.40 for a total of $130,204.80 plus the 6% rebate on the $2000 of $120 for a grand total of $1,968,630.00. It is not quite $2 million but as Johnnie Hooker played by Robert Redford in the Sting said: "it's not enough but it's close". Of course, taxes would take 25% at the track and be sorted out later when filing and my winning would depress the Pick 6 and Pick 5/6 prizes.

The big question is would I have gotten these three winners from my 10 picks in these races? Of course, more than 10 was possible. So let's look at these three races. I use about 5–6 handicapping services plus my own analysis of the daily racing form and the Equiform pace numbers. So the idea is to handicap the handicappers. In many bets this is computerized.

Race 4. The Sprint, 6 furlongs: Handicapper #1 had 3–1–5–6 (the winner, Dancing in Silks) –8–4 Handicapper #2 had 5–3–8–1–6 So at 12–1 that's one of the 10 for sure especially when you observe that its last race Beyer speed rating at 106 was the highest of any horse in the race and it was right there at Santa Anita. Three of the horses ran higher Beyers than #6 but not in their last race. Actually there were only nine horses in this race so likely I would have taken them all including the 20–1 shot #2 and the 30–1 shot #7, neither of which listed above. #2 had a Beyer of 110 in a Grade I at Santa Anita so must be used. #7 looked greatly outclassed.

Race 5. Juvenile two-year-olds on polytrack with 13 horses: The winner Vale of York (#7) was racing in the UK and in Italy. He always had short odds and had two wins in five races and was close in the other three races. The morning line odds were 20–1. Handicapper #1 had 5–13–4–9–10–8 (so no 7 but he was a foreign shipper so likely not rated by this US service). Handicapper #2 had 13–4–9–5–6. Only handicapper James Quinn with 13–8–11–5–7–6 had 7 anywhere. These are two-year olds so there is a lot of noise. There were four other longshot horses one at 20–1, one at

15–1, one at 30–1 and one at 50–1. So going with all 13 horses called all is suggested.

Race 7. Dirt Mile: #2 Furthest Land won with 10 in the field. #1 had 4–3–7–1–9–2 (the winner). Handicapper #2 had 3–7–2–8. The pace numbers are competitive. So 2 at 20–1 must be used.

Summary: all three of the wide open races had winners that were competitive horses. So they would be on our ticket. But even if we bet on all horses, these three races, the ticket only costs 9*12*10*1*1*1=$2340. This ticket made a lot of sense so I should have played it.[3] It would have had 8+11+9=28 Pick 5/6s. Oh well, there is always next year.

19.12. Professional Racetrack Betting Syndicates

I had a hand with several of the major syndicate hedge fund teams through the *beat the racetrack* books Ziemba and Hausch (1984, 1986, 1987) and Hausch, Lo and Ziemba (1994, 2008) and other contacts. Hausch and I both talked to Bill Benter early in his Hong Kong career. He had started betting but had not put together a successful syndicate yet. So he quizzed us on the Dr Z system and other ideas in phone calls. We did help him a bit but as he said "we were academics spreading knowledge and he was a businessman so could not pay us". He did have other paid consultants on factor models and he pioneered successfully using 80+ factor models of two types:

1. predict the fair odds probabilities of various horses outcomes and compare these to the public's odds, and
2. bet most likely with the Kelly criterion.

I do not know if he picked up the Kelly from Ziemba and Vickson (1975) or from Ed Thorp's blackjack writings. Benter had been a blackjack player and Thorp introduced Kelly betting there as *Fortune's formula* so that may be where he learned it. A key early Thorp paper is in Ziemba and Vickson.

[3]Another way to play this is to have three sets of tickets in which you assume that at least two of the three standouts will win. So you have $N_1^i, N_2^i, N_3^i, N_4^i, 1, 1$ combinations, $i = 1, 2, 3$ all at \$2 each. So depending on the N_j^i you likely have a larger ticket than the three singles approach. You might win more than one Pick 6 and more Pick 5/6s, but you might miss the Pick 6 as well unless the tickets are well spread.

The second type of model is to include the track odds as one of the variables to get even better probability estimates.

Benter pioneered the use of such models. I had a bit of a hand in there as the major paper on this was published while I was the *Management Science* departmental editor for finance and I processed and accepted it for publication. That's the Bolton and Chapman (1986) paper which along with the only paper Benter published are reprinted in Hausch, Lo and Ziemba. Chapman (1994) using Hong Kong data is in our book.

I met Benter in 1993 at the *Informs* meeting in Phoenix where I organized the finance sessions and helped on the racing sessions. I recall correcting Benter's (1994) paper in Hausch, Lo, and Ziemba which had one good new development. As discussed above, in the Dr Z method, the biases to win and being second and third tend to cancel so in the work I did with Donald Hausch, we did not need to make any changes except say that because of approximations, bets should not be made to place or show unless the expected value was significantly above break even. We suggested 1.10 for the best races at the best tracks and 1.14 and 1.18 for lesser races. This worked well for US place and show betting. Benter and others found that the Dr Z system did not really work well in Hong Kong as the biases there were different. Also, he discovered how to correct the second, third, etc biases through the discounted Harville formulations that are discussed above.

Victor Lo did his PhD thesis in Hong Kong, directed by statistician John Bacon-Shone on this problem and much of his research is in Hausch, Lo, Ziemba along with papers by others on this. Bacon-Shone has a joint paper in Hausch and Ziemba (2008) with the late Alan Woods who had his own small team in the Philippines after he left Benter.

Benter's real contribution is shown in Figure 19.9. Namely, he made it all work and in the process became a very rich man with total profits in the one billion area. His paper in Hausch, Lo and Ziemba plus the other papers made our book a cult item with originals selling for $2000 up to $12,000 on EBay and Amazon. Originals are still trading at high prices, about $600. I sold one for $1400 to one of the copycat syndicates in Australia who I was consulting for. Another syndicate wanted to buy up all the Hausch, Lo and Ziemba books and burn them keeping one for their research. I decided to make a second edition which was published with a new preface in 2008 along with the sports and lottos handbook (Hausch and Ziemba, 2008).

The gains in Hong Kong by Benter's team and others were in a market without rebates and high commissions. But they utilized several advantages.

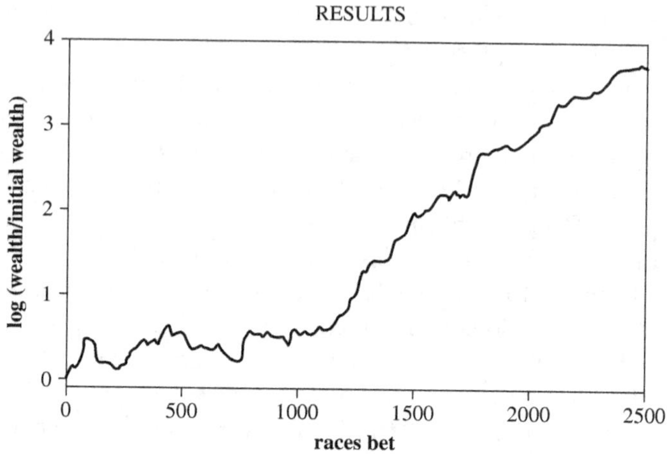

(a) to 1994

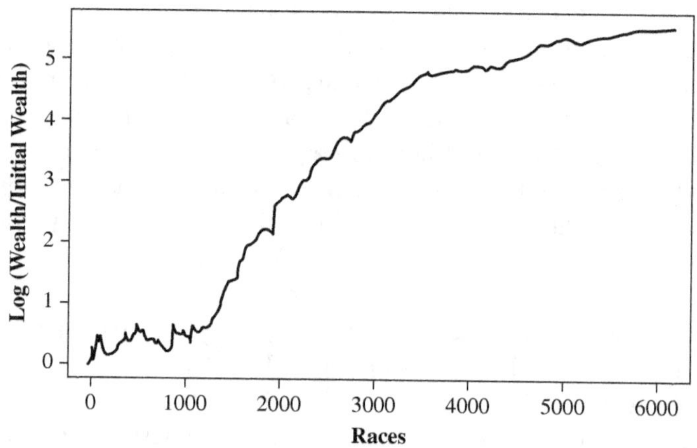

(b) to 2001

Figure 19.9. Benter's Hong Kong Racing Syndicate returns.

1. Hong Kong Chinese betters favor and dislike certain numbers from their culture which makes horses with these numbers differ from the true odds.
2. All the horses are the same ones mostly Australian geldings running in almost all the races on just two racetracks so prediction was easier than in the US.
3. Data feeds were every 12 seconds and later every minute giving access to pool odds which could be successfully used.

4. The market was deep with huge betting so the price impact was low and lastly, they could bet electronically into the pools.

Since the mainland takeover of Hong Kong in 1997, there have been some changes. But the syndicates continue and trade in many markets today in 2012 such as Japan and Korea as well as in the US, Canada and Europe. My personal experience consulting extensively for one other syndicate is that the setup cost for the research and computer implementation is a major time and financial undertaking. Like most markets it was easily earlier and much more difficult now. The syndicate with many workers and good experience have an edge on new ones as I can report from our own activity on this.

19.13. Conclusion

Racetrack betting remains a very active set of markets. The basic betting problems are various versions of portfolio management. The problems are stochastic programs usually one period but with non-concave objective functions because of the fractional functions inside the objective function. But the problems are easily solved and for many situations there are simplified strategies. The objective is usually the Kelly expected log criterion but in cases of low probability high payoff bets there can be hundreds or thousands of separate tickets and the bets must be integers. So a tickets network tree approach is useful and the Kelly strategy to bet more on the higher probability outcomes can be approximated.

The racetrack market is small compared to the financial markets such as currency and stock markets but there's enough there for a number of syndicates in the US, Australia and Hong Kong and elsewhere to make fifty to a hundred million per year. It is not an easy market to enter at a high level as the setup costs are high and the competition fierce. Take a grass race at a mile with seven horses: one has not run in a year but did well then; one has only run on dirt; one has never run past 6 furlongs (three quarters of a mile); one was racing in France long distances $1\frac{1}{2}$ miles plus on grass losing consistently and the others have run similar distances on grass but not on this racetrack. Add in jockey and trainer changes and you see why "it is a supreme intellectual challenge" as argued by Andy Beyer, a noted racetrack writer. The models try to bypass this with probabilities and optimization.

Chapter 20

A Walk into Greatness: June 2017 Visits to Tesio's Horse Stables and the Sassicaia Winery

William T. Ziemba

Frederico Tesio is widely considered to be one of the best, if not the best, horse trainer. He had many great horses that he bred and trained at his various stables in northern Italy. These include Ribot, who ran after Tesio died in 1954, winning the Prix de l'Arc de Triompe twice, and Nearco, whose descendants won the Arc every year from 1985–2010. Also included are three of the four horses that were undefeated with at least ten races at the top level. Such horses are rare as there are only two in the US and only one in Australia. I was fortunate to visit his stables in 2017 and discuss with employees who are taking care of the descendants of Tesio's great horses and visit the stables which are still intact.

Horse breeding, racing and top quality wine production go hand in hand. I was fortunate to visit the stables of Frederico Tesio, an Italian breeder, trainer and co-owner of perhaps the world's greatest collection of race horses ever. Tesio was born in Turin on January 17, 1869 and died at 85 on May 1, 1954. He was orphaned at six and graduated from the University of Florence.

According to my rule on undefeated horses, namely, at least ten races at the highest level with no losses, you have exactly two horses since 1900 in the US, four in Europe and one in Australia. In the US there is only Colin (15–15) in 1907 and Personal Ensign (13–13) in 1988. In Europe, there are three Tesio horses: Ribot (16–16) in 1955–1956, Braque (12–12) in 1956–1957, and Nearco (14–14) in 1937–1938. He had two others with just one dubious defeat. The fourth one is the recent sensational Frankel

(14–14), the leading son of top sire €500,000 stud fee Galileo (now reported at €650,000.[1]

In Australia, with one race at Ascot in the UK, the super sprinter filly Black Cavier (25/25) won almost AUS$8 million in 2010–2012.

In this chapter, I discuss Tesio's racing following visits to three of his eight farms including the two most important. Seven of the farms are at Dormello on the shores of Lake Maggiore where Tesio had his horses and main activities which later moved to Tenuta San Guido, a vast 3000 hectare estate that's 5 kms by 13 kms (65 km^2 or 6500 hectacres) in Bolgheri near Florence. The seven farms formed by Tesio in the 1930s in northern Italy were: Surga, Montaccio, Route, Moretta, Torbeca, Cucchetta, and Molta. Tenuta San Guido, where Sassicaia is also produced, was owned by the Marchese Mario Incisa della Rochetta. Sassicaia was the original super Tuscan wine which Mario started producing for private use in 1945.[2] See the photo of this first wine along with the host of our visit. He felt that the terrain there was similar to Bordeaux and that Cabernet sauvignon would do well there while Sangoviese, the main Tuscan variety, would not. The blend is always 85% Cabernet sauvignon and 15% Cabernet franc. By 1968 the wine was released to the public and not very well received. In 1977 is was first among 33 Cabernets in a blind testing in Paris with French judges and received a perfect 100 by Robert Parker in 1985. The prices vary from 155 euros in their restaurant, 165 in their shop, US$450 in a top restaurant in Indianapolis and US$540 in a top restaurant in Chicago. The secondary wines cost 38 and 18 euros in their shop. Opinions vary and some think

[1]This is tricky as there were undefeated horses in other eras and countries such as in the UK: Eclipse (18/18) born in 1764, Ormonde (16/16) born in 1883, Barcaldine (13/13) born in 1878, High Flyer (14/14) born in 1774, Overdose (12/12) born in 2005; US: Asteroid (12/12) born in 1861, Candy Ride (6/6), Landaluce (5/5), Raise a Native (4/4), Danzig (3/3); Hungary: Kinzsem (54/54) born in 1874; Germany: Nereido (10/10) born in 1933; and Japan: Tokino Minora (10/10) born in 1940 and Kurifuji (also known as Toshifuji) (11/11) also born in 1940.

Some horses such as Peppers Pride (19/19) ran against non top competition.

One defeat greats: Native Dancer (21/22), Man O'War (20/21), Brigadier Gerard (17/18), Ruffian (10/11), Alleged (9/10), Seattle Slew (14/17), Smarty Jones (8/9), Big Brown (7/8), Sea Bird II (7/8), El Gran Senor (7/8), Barbaro (6/7), Lexington (6/7) and Nureyev (2/3).

[2]There is some doubt here as Tignanello, an Antinori wine, is early too but it is made with sangovoise not Cabernet sauvignon. Solaria is the best Tignanello. Ornellaia, made nearby, is now competitive with Sassicaia and even more expensive.

Frederico Tesio

it is overpriced, so I did a test with my wife. We had their three wines on consecutive nights followed by a Far Niente and a Darioush Napa Valley Cabernet. My conclusion was I vote for Napa over Sassicia.[3]

Fini's *Sassicia* is the definitive book covering the wine and family history, a wonderful memoir, somewhat like my own memoir, *Adventures of a modern renaissance academic in investing and gambling* (2017) full of historical stories and pictures.

[3]My wife is also happy to vote for Black Bench Okanagan Bordeaux style blends, which are half or lower in price compared to Napa and lower in price still compared to French Bordeaux.

The Marcuse and Sandra

Our hosts at Tenuta

The Restaurant at Sassicia

French Oak Barrells

The original 1945 Sassaicia

Testing the three wines

In 1892, Tesio and his wife, Lydia, purchased a 19 hectare silkworm farm with thousands of mulberry trees in Dormello. He built stables where mares with foals and stallions were housed. The photos show Tesio's house, Tesio himself, his stables where he preferred stone construction, the guest house and various horses and foals there today and the property and our host along with our most helpful cab driver from Bergamo who drove us to Stresa and the grounds including the original stables, some of the descendants of Tesio's horses and the chestnut wood fencing that held the horses safely in their paddocks and training tracks.

Tesio, with Lydia's help, was a breeding genius mating cheap to cheap to get champions. He, with Lydia keeping the records going back many generations, produced the superior breeding results. Together they were the kind of anomaly researchers that I like to associate with.

Tesio was not rich enough to bankroll this massive operation. The funding came from a very wealthy family led by Mario who became a partner with Tesio in 1932. Mario died in 1983 and his son, the official host of our visit to Tenuta San Guido was the 82 year old Marchese Nicolo Incisa della Rochetta, pictured here with my wife, Sandra Schwartz.

Many of the horses on the property now are descendants of TesioÕs great stallions. Other descendants are at the Tenuta San Guido farm. Seven of these outstanding stallions are listed here. While none of these seven are listed in the top ten horses of all time, it is arguably the top collection of any breeder/owner.

Tesio's house made of stone

Stables at Dormello

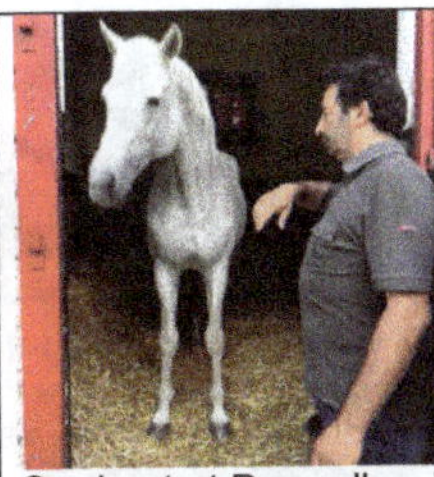
Our host at Dormello with a Tesio horse descendant

Chestnut wood padlocks at Dormello

Bill at the entrance to Dormello

Horses at the Dormello upper farm

Breeding shed at San Guido

A Tesio descendant with our host at Tenuta San Guido

Newspaper in stalls

Hay for the horses

Horse training building

Horse training track

20.1. Seven Top Tesio Horses

(1) Ribot (16–16) undefeated, won the Prix de l'Arc de Triomphe twice in 1955 and 1956. Tesio did not like the looks of Tenerani, the sire of Ribot nor did he like Ribot. But critics argue that Ribot was the horse of the century and thought to be Tesio's breeding masterpiece. In later years he went to Darby Dan Farm in Kentucky on a five year lease but

Ribot's grave

Roberto's grave

the horse refused to return. He was brought there for a high price to be a superior breeding stallion. See his grave, which I saw in May.

(2) Cavaliere dÕArpino (5–5) who Tesio said was his best horse, while Ribot may indeed have been the best horse, he ran after Tesio's death in 1954. Cavaliere sired Bellini, the sire of Tenerani who sired Ribot. He was descended from the great undefeated St Simon (9/9)

(1881) through Rabelais (1900) and the French stallion Havresac (1915).

(3) Nearco (14–14) ran from 1937–1938 and was also undefeated. He sired Neartic (the 1958 Canadian horse of the year) who sired Northern Dancer, who later became the greatest North American sire of the 20th century. Among Nearco's great offspring are Nasrullah, who sired Bold Rules, who sired Secretriat, and Royal Charger, whose offspring include Halo, Sunny's Halo, Roberto and Sunday Silence.
Northern Dancer, Canadian breed, had a vast array of top sons who are very important stallions in their own right.[4] He won the Kentucky Derby in 1964 in exactly 2 minutes flat and in 1985 commanded a US$1,000,000 stud fee (no guarantee). In those days, the top stallions were not breeding very many mares, he was covering 35.
From 1985–2010 every Prix de l'arc de triomphe winner was a descendent of Nearco through his son Nasrullah or his grandson Northern Dancer. Nasrullah sired Bold Ruler whose descendants include Secretariat, Seattle Slew, AP Indy and California Chrome. Nearco sired Royal Charger, who after one more generation, sired Halo and Roberto (see the grave which is at Darby Dan). Halo sired Canadian Kentucky Derby winner SunnyÕs Halo and the legendary Sunday Silence who

Northern Dancer

[4]These include a virtual Breeders Cup set of champions who were bred by Northern Dancer or by one of his sons. The top ones were Chief's Crown, Dancing Brave, Danzig, El Gran Senor, Ferdinand Gate Dancer, Lyphard, Manila, Nijinski II, Nureyev, Sadlers Wells, Shadeed, Storm Cat, and The Minstrel

AP Indy

Donatello II

Blue Peter

not only beat Easy Goer in the Kentucky Derby, Preakness and the Breeders' Cup but was the leading Japanese sire during 1995–2007.[5]

[5]In the Belmont, Sunday Silence's high dosage of 3.80 gave the edge to Easy Goer, who won easily as this theory predicted.

Tesio tried to sell Nearco when he was two years old thinking he did not have enough stamina for the classic distances. However as a three year old, Nearco won all 7 of his races from 1400 to 3000 meters. As a 2 year old he had won all 7 of his races from 1000 to 1400 meters. He was the Italian 2 year old champion and in 1938, Italian horse of the years. When he retired, he was sold for 60,000 GBP in 1938 to Beech House Stud in Newmarket. He was one of the top ten sires in England for 15 years.

Northern Dancer is widely considered the greatest sire in NorthAmerica during the 20th century. Worldwide, Nearco and Phallaris are also in this very top group. All this is debatable, although calculations can be made, such as number of grade I winners in the progeny or money won (this is would need to be adjusted for both inflation and trend in larger purses).

(4) Donatello II (9–10) won the Prax du jockey club and should have been Tesio's fourth undefeated horse except the jockey did not run the horse correctly as he was instructed to and the horse lost that race. He was sired by the legendary Blenheim II, a founding sire of Claiborne Farms in Paris, Kentucky, the top breeding operation in the world in the 1960s to 2000.

(5) Braque (12–12) was the third undefeated Tesio horse by my rule. He was born in 1954 and raced in 1956 and 1957.

(6) Jacopo del Sellaio (x-x) won the 1933 Italian Derby, one of 22 such derby winners Tesio bred, trained and raced.

(7) Botticelli (14–2–2–18) was born in 1951. He won the 1954 Italian Derby and the 1955 Ascot Gold Cup. He was sired by Blue Peter (1936) who was sired by Fairway (1925) who was sired by Phalaris (1913). None of Tesio's horses are listed among the top ten worldwide in the lists that follows. But such lists are a judgment call. Ghostzapper, Frankel and Tesio's top horses and others could be in this list as well. Regarding Arrogate, the 2017 top horse in the world, discussed below, the consensus is that he is not in the top group.

Quoting Steve Roman, 23 July 2017

> In reviewing the PPs of the ten best in The Blood-Horse's Top 100 of the 20th century not one ever threw in a performance like Arrogate did in the San Diego. Dr. Fager lost big in the Woodward but only after setting a 1:09.1 fraction in a 10f race against Damascus and Buckpasser. Forego ran the worst race of his career in the 10f Suburban but it was his 57th and last start

> and he carried 132 pounds. In Secretariat's 1973 Derby he was 4th, beaten by 11 lengths, but it was not a bad performance and, after picking up 6 lengths on the backstretch, he hit the rail on the far turn and lost ground thereafter. Kelso lost a few of his 63 starts by open lengths but never by as much as Arrogate did and almost always carrying 130 pounds or more. One thing to note is that every one of those top ten won not only at 10f or more but also at 6f or less. Arrogate never won a race shorter than a mile-and-a-sixteenth. That may not mean much to many, but to me such versatility is essential when claiming a horse to be among the best ever.
>
> Arrogate is a fine horse and may win again, but talk of him being among the greatest is silly, just as it was for the 2015 Triple Crown winner, American Pharoah.

20.2. The 10 Greatest Racehorses of All Time

(1) Secretariat still holds all the records on dirt from $1\frac{3}{16}$ to $1\frac{5}{8}$ miles and was 0.2 seconds below the $1\frac{1}{8}$ record. He was 16/21 but the five losses were caused by poor health, interference or unfair disqualification and unprepared replacement for another horse in a long distance race. The 16 wins were all by wide margins.

(2) *Man O'War:* In 2006 Big Red, as he was called, was voted the greatest racehorse that ever lived for the 86th year in a row. He won every race except one where Upset beat him by a head. But this was not a real loss as the race had a restart and the horse was not ready when the race started and he was several lengths behind then. At odds of 1–100, he won a race by 100 lengths. He won all his races by wide margins. His stride was longer than those of John Henry and Secretariat as seen at the Kentucky horse museum. In his three year old year, he set track or world records in nearly very race, however, in races where Man O'War and Secretariat ran he same distances, on the same tracks, Secretariat was faster but he didn't get to race such a strong competitor. The great jockey Laffit Pincay, Jr, who rode triple crown winner Affirmed as a four year old, and many other great horses, said that the greatest horse he rode was Sham who broke the record in the Kentucky Derby and the Preakness only to be beaten by Secretariat who still holds the records in these races.

(3) *Seabiscuit:* In his match race with triple crown winner War Admiral at Pimlico, the latter's home track, he won by four lengths.

(4) *Phar Lap:* The Australian horse was 32/2/0 in his last 35 starts at distances of 1400 to 3600 meters. He won the Melbourne Cup and Australia's best race, the Cox Plate, twice. At the end of his career, he won his only North American race, the 2000 meter Aqua Caliente Handicap. Then, tragically, he was poisoned in Menlo Park and died tragically.
(5) *Frankel:* He was undefeated and unchallenged in 11 races winning many by 10+ lengths.
(6) *Ruffian:* She was never behind, even in her match race in 1974 with Kentucky Derby winner Foolish Pleasure. She broke her leg and had to be destroyed at Belmont. I was at Belmont in 1990 when Go for Wand suffered the same fate in the Breeders' Cup Distaff.
(7) *Black Cavier:* She is rated at the top as a sprinter and was undefeated in 25 races in Australia. She was rated the world's number 1 horse in 2013 and Australia's horse of the year in 2011, 2012 and 2013. She had a very high 136 timeform rating though Frankel was higher at 147. She was large at 16.2 hands, like Zenyatta. Black Cavier won a record 15 group 1 races beating Kingston Town's 14.

Royal Academy

Black Cavier was rated only three pounds below the top sprinter of the last 30 years, Dayjur. Despite Dayjur's brilliance, he was defeated in the 1990 Breeders" Cup sprint when he jumped a shadow near the finish line and was beaten by Safely Kept, who was the current sprint champion.

Black Cavier's grandsire was Breeders' Cup mile winner, Royal Academy, shown here. Royal Academy was sired by Nijinsky who was sired by Northern Dancer who is from the Nearco line through Neartic.

On the dam sire side, she was descended from the undefeated supersire Danzig, her great grandsire. Danzig also sired Dayjur.[6]

(8) *Citation:* He won 27 of 29 races as a 3 year old, including the triple crown.

(9) *Zenyatta:* This crowd favorite won easily her first 19 races, mostly on synthetic in California. She was the only mare to win the Breeders' Cup Classic in 2009, a year when she did not win Horse of the Year as Rachel Alexandra won all her races as well including four against males including the Preakness on the east coast. The two great mares never met despite efforts to set up a match race to Oaklawn Park for huge purses.

Zenyatta was Horse of the Year in 2010. That year in her final race, the Breeders' Cup Classic again against an all male field. Jockey Mike Smith more or less agreed with the analysis by former jockey and now painter Nick Martinez and me of why she got beat by Blame by a head in the classic. The race was on dirt at Churchill Downs, only her second dirt race. The other was at Oaklawn Park. She had her usual slow start and the other horses had a fast start. Then around the bend, the horses separated into two groups and Smith could not see how far the lead group was ahead. So once Zenyatta made her run, she was so far behind it was hard to catch up and she faced traffic. Then narrowly beaten by a head. But others, like Steve Roman argue that, at least on that day, Blame was the better horse.

(10) *Seattle Slew:* This $17,000 purchase was undefeated coming into the Kentucky Derby and then won the triple crown.

Steve Roman ranked the top 10 of the horses he actually saw running as follows:

[6] Makybe Diva, a UK female horse who raced in Australia was in the same league with Black Cavier. She beat the males in the Melbourne Cup in 2003, 2004, and 2005 as well as the Cox Plate in 2005. Only four other horses have won the Melbourne Cup more than once. When she could not be sold at a yearling sale, she was taken to Australia with her dam Tugla. She was rated the best long distance performer and top rated filly or mare at 119 four points below the top male. In 36 races, she won 15, placed in four and was third three times. he was descended from Breeders' Cup mile winner Royal Academy pictured here. Her earnings of AUS$14,526,685 is still the Australian record. Her breeding is from the Northern Dancer line through Danzig, Danehill, and the Irish stallion Desert King as well as Nureyev. Her dam sire was River Man with the second sire Roberto who was sired by Hail to Reason who, I recall from my youth, won a Saratoga race by 17 lengths. In the fourth generation, Northern Dancer appears three times. Ribot, Nearco, Princequilla, Nearctic, Nashua, and Vaguely Noble are in the fifth generation.

1. Frankel
2. Sea-Bird
3. Secretariat
4. Spectacular Bid
5. Dr Fager
6. Damascus
7. Kelso
8. Forego
9. Swaps
10. Ghostzapper

Arrogate and American Pharoah would not be in his top 25, Ribot, Man O'War and Citation could be in the top ten but he did not see them so he has no opinion.

I was initially puzzled why Arrogate was not in Steve's top group. Part of the story is distance ability. In the San Diego Handicap, Arrogate finished 4th while Accelerate won the race. Arrogate's four great wins in the 2016 Travers where he set the track record, the 2016 Breeders Cup, the Pegasus and the Dubai world cup were all at races of $1\frac{1}{4}$ miles with one at $1\frac{3}{16}$ In his only short race he was out of the money. The San Diego Handicap was $1\frac{1}{16}$, much shorter. Accelerate had won races at one mile and at $1\frac{1}{8}$. The psr rating service rated Arrogate the highest but Accelerate and the other horses in the race were not much lower.[7] Famed jockey called "Big Money" Mike by his trainer, America's, best Bob Baffert seem to agree with me that the race was too short for Arrogate. Mike also mentioned to me that Baffert felt that the horse was a little off. I spoke to famed jockey Pat Day who also thought the horse did not look good. As we saw, Arrogate finished his career fifth in the $1\frac{1}{4}$ mile Classic. Steve Roman's perceptive analysis was clear — Arrogate was a great horse but is not in the very top group. He did set the US earnings record with more than $17 million.

Steve Roman added the following comparison of Arrogate with Gun Runner, who won all of his grade I races in 2017 after being second, beat by Arrogate in the Dubai World Cup. Steve's PF ratings are evaluated by his model with lower negative values indicating faster times. In Arrogate's three great performances in the US, all at $1\frac{1}{4}$ miles, he was in the -80s and his Dubai World Cup was similar. Then Arrogate regressed for various reasons as discussed above. Gun Runner, who ran all his winning races at

[7]There ratings were 117 and 113.

shorter distances. He had a -79 in the Breeders' Cup Classic when Arrogate, the betting favorite, was fifth out of the money. The previous year, Gun Runner had lost three $1\frac{1}{4}$ mile races while Arrogate had won them, so the betting public was undecided between these to horses. Collected and West Coast had won $1\frac{1}{4}$ mile races and were the secondary choices; they finished second and third.

Steve compares these horses with Ghostzapper who was running in 2003 and 2004. I fondly recall winning the superfecta in the 2004 Breeders' Cup Classic with a \$5 ticket box on Ghostzapper and Roses in May first or second and Pleasantly Perfect and Perfect Drift third or fourth. The \$20 ticket paid \$5000. Steve points out that Ghostzapper was running in the -90s or better which would be 5–10 lengths better than Arrogate over a wide range of distances from $6\frac{1}{2}$ furlongs to $1\frac{1}{4}$ miles.

ARROGATE:

TRACK	DATE	RACE	FINISH	PF (RPR)
DEL MAR	11/04/17	BREEDER'S CUP CLASSIC - GR. 1	5-DH	-57
DEL MAR	08/19/17	PACIFIC CLASSIC STAKES- GR. 1	2	-37
DEL MAR	07/22/17	TVG SAN DIEGO HANDICAP - GR. 2	4	0
MEYDAN RACECOURSE	03/25/17	DUBAI WORLD CUP SPONSORED BY EMIRATES AIRLINE - GR. 1	1	(130) *
GULFSTREAM PARK	01/28/17	PEGASUS WORLD CUP INVITATIONAL STAKES - GR. 1	1	-89
SANTA ANITA	11/05/16	BREEDERS' CUP CLASSIC - GR. 1	1	-84
SARATOGA	08/27/16	TRAVERS STAKES - GR. 1	1	-81
DEL MAR	08/04/16	ALLOWANCE OPTIONAL CLAIMING	1	-13
SANTA ANITA	06/24/16	ALLOWANCE OPTIONAL CLAIMING	1	-39
SANTA ANITA	06/05/16	MAIDEN SPECIAL WEIGHT	1	-13
LOS ALAMITOS	04/17/16	MAIDEN SPECIAL WEIGHT	3	13

GUN RUNNER:

TRACK	DATE	RACE	FINISH	PF (RPR)
DEL MAR	11/04/17	BREEDER'S CUP CLASSIC - GR. 1	1	-79
SARATOGA	09/02/17	WOODWARD STAKES - GR. 1	1	-88
SARATOGA	08/05/17	WHITNEY STAKES - GR. 1	1	-63
CHURCHILL DOWNS	06/17/17	STEPHEN FOSTER HANDICAP - GR.1	1	-86
MEYDAN RACECOURSE	03/25/17	DUBAI WORLD CUP SPONSORED BY EMIRATES AIRLINE - GR. 1	2	(124) *
OAKLAWN PARK	02/20/17	RAZORBACK HANDICAP - GR. 3	1	-66

* DWC COMPARISONS: DUBAI MILLENIUM (139)
CIGAR (135)
INVASOR (132)
CURLIN (131)
ROSES IN MAY (130)
SINGSPIEL (130)

HORSE	PF	FIN	DATE	RACE	GR	AGE/SEX	TRK	DIST	SURF	TRK COND
GHOSTZAPPER	-59	3RD	08/23/03	KING'S BISHOP S	G1	3YO	SAR	7.00	DIRT	FST
GHOSTZAPPER	-105	1ST	09/27/03	VOSBURGH S	G1	3YO&UP	BEL	6.50	DIRT	FST
GHOSTZAPPER	-95	1ST	07/04/04	TOM FOOL H	G2	3YO&UP	BEL	7.00	DIRT	FST
GHOSTZAPPER	-111	1ST	08/21/04	PHILIP H. ISELIN BC H	G3	3YO&UP	MTH	9.00	DIRT	SY
GHOSTZAPPER	-112	1ST	09/11/04	WOODWARD S	G1	3YO&UP	BEL	9.00	DIRT	FST
GHOSTZAPPER	-98	1ST	10/30/04	BC CLASSIC	G1	3YO&UP	LS	10.00	DIRT	FST
GHOSTZAPPER	-124	1ST	05/30/05	METROPOLITAN H	G1	3YO&UP	BEL	8.00	DIRT	FST

Acknowledgment

Thanks to Orley Ashenfelter, Steve Roman, David McKenzie, Mike Smith and my hosts in Dormello and Bolgheri for helpful advise on this chapter.

Chapter 21

Horse Ownership: The Example of Honor Code

William T. Ziemba

I was fortunate to have and still co-own the racehorse Honor Code as part of a syndicate organized by Ben Haggin and Bill Farish of Lane's End stud farm. The group included eight horses of which three like Honor Code had superior breeding. Honor Code was from the last crop of AP Indy out of Storm Cat dam the champion Serena's Cat. AP Indy was the product of Seattle Slew with dam sire Secretariat and became a great racehorse and stallion. I discuss Honor Code's career. In Early 2014 on the strength of a brilliant two year old year he was the morning line favorite for the Kentucky Derby. In 2015 he won two major Grade I races, namely the Met Mile and the Whitney. He was named the champion older dirt horse that year.

21.1. The Setting

Shug McGaughey had been bringing Honor Code along carefully. Comparing Honor Code to Orb, the 2013 Kentucky Derby winner, he said that the reason Orb was so successful in 2013 was that everything went smoothly. "We never missed a work, never missed a race, never had a single setback with Orb all winter."

Things went smoothly for Honor Code in 2013 and his early training in 2014. Then he suffered a minor injury and was out of training for 10 days in January for some bruising of an ankle. That put the schedule behind and the Orb route Fountain of Youth Grade II and Florida Derby Grade I would not work. It was announced that Honor Code would go to the Grade II Rebel stakes at Oaklawn on March 15. Then Shug made a U-turn and entered Honor Code in an allowance at Gulfstream on March 12. That meant no Kentucky Derby points, less money, a $75,000 race rather than the $600,000 Rebel, but no travel. Meanwhile, Shug's other top three year old, Top Billing, did well winning the Fountain of Youth and became one of the Derby favorites. It seemed Shug was not into running the two head to head as trainer Todd Pletcher would do with his 250+ horses. So they would take separate routes with the April 5 Wood Memorial Grade I being a potential target for Honor Code. Then Top Billing suffered a cannon bone injury so was out of the Florida Derby and the Kentucky Derby. So then maybe after the allowance race Honor Code will go back to the Florida Derby plan.

The race arrived and Honor Code was a 3–5 favorite with a top Beyer of 93 as a two year old. The main competition was from Social Inclusion who won his only start by $7\frac{1}{2}$ lengths also with a 93 Beyer. That was in a short six furlong race on February 22 at Gulfstream. Both were rated 104 on the PSR scale and HTR picked Social Inclusion over Honor Code.

The handicappers Mike Beer and Dan Ullman of the *Daily Racing Form* had an analysis close to my thinking. Honor Code was the class of the field, had run long races and had a top trainer and the top jockey J.J. Castellano who won all four of his races on March 12. The allowance was $8\frac{1}{2}$ furlongs. Honor Code gave a weight advantage of five pounds to Social Inclusion and Were all Set and 10 to a Special Night and 15 to Ta Bueno. There was a possibility of a wire to wire by the 3–1 Social Inclusion. The bet on 3–5 shots is usually to place and the Dr Z bets on the exacta are usually the favorite in second place but with a super horse at low odds you also bet the favorite in first position.

The suggested bets were place on #4 and 1–4 and 4–1 exactas. I made those bets at the rebate shop and a win bet at better odds at Betfair plus the place bet there which, with only five horses in the race, only two horses place in the UK system.

An interesting event occurred. In 1990 Donald Hausch and I wrote two racing arbitrage papers (reprinted in my 2012 book *Calendar Anomalies and Arbitrage*, World Scientific). One dealt with creating an arbitrage by betting the horses at different racetracks at different prices. Nowadays all the money for a race is only in the pool at that horse's racetrack. All the money gets shipped there. So that will not work any more. The other paper called *locks at the racetrack* is the situation where one super horse has so much bet on it to place or show that there exists a weighting such that no matter what is the finish you cannot lose.[1]

So if the super horse is in the money the place or show bets on those that collect are the minimum $2.10. And if the super horse is out of the money, the small bets on the so-called weaker horses have huge payoffs. In either case there is a profit and in fact it is equal by construction of the model. Such a lock or arbitrage occurs maybe ten times a year in US racing. Well Honor Code just about made the list in this race. Honor Code opened up at 1–9. The opening pools had Honor Code with 53,170 out of 56,140 for 94.7% in the show pool, well above the level for a lock, namely 91.5%. That's for a five horse field with a 11% track take (the actual track take of 15% with a 4% rebate). By the end of betting, there was was virtually still a lock but not quite.

Track odds for Gulfstream race for the win, place and show tote board from near the start to the close of betting at Gulfstream racetrack were:

---

[1] **The Hausch and Ziemba (1990) condition for a lock** is

$$k > 1 - \frac{Q(n-1)}{21(n-3)} = 1 - \frac{0.98(5-1)}{21(5-3)} = 0.915.$$

Also the bet on $x=$ the favorite must equal

$$\frac{x}{y} = 2 + \frac{Q(n-1)}{1.05(1-k)} = -2 + \frac{0.89(4)}{1.05(0.085)} = 37.89.$$

This formula guarantees a profit of $.05(x+2y)-(n-3)y$ which is positive if a lock exists. So with a bankroll of say $W_0 = \$2500$, $x = \$2,260$ and the four y's $= \$60$ each, and the profit $= -\$1$ as the lock did not quite exist.

In *Dr Z's Beat the Racetrack* (1987), I presented a way to use the Dr Z place and show systems in England. There they only have place which has a different number who collect based on the number of horses in the race. For $4 \leqslant n \leqslant 7$, two collect, for $8 \leqslant n \leqslant 15$, three collect as in the US show, and for larger n, four collect. I saw a flaw in the way they computed these payoffs. Instead of giving back the stake and then sharing the profits, they simply share the proceeds. Hence, with a big favorite, one can get payoffs less than the stake. But the track must pay the minimum. My Dublin colleagues Patrick Waldron and David Jackson saw this independently and used the Hausch-Ziemba locks idea to create an arbitrage. I discussed this with them and said "you will be able to do this once then they will change the rules." Indeed they made 50,000 GBP in one big play and then they changed the rules. See Jackson and Waldron (2003) and on the general concept of arbitrage, see Edelmann and O'Brian (2004).

#	NAME	ODDS	ML	CHG	WIN	PLC	SHW
	$1.00 MIN			TOTALS:	32247	4550	56140
1	Social Inclusion	5	3 ↓	-67%	4365	1344	693
2	We're All Set	46	5 ↓	-820%	564	297	456
3	Specialnightaction	99	10 ↓	-890%	177	16	353
4	Honor Code	1/9	3/5 ↑	81%	26944	2859	53170
5	Ta Bueno	99	8 ↓	-1138%	115	30	261

#	NAME	ODDS	ML	CHG	WIN	PLC	SHW
	$1.00 MIN			TOTALS:	39457	6321	105993
1	Social Inclusion	7/2	3 ↓	-17%	7223	1962	3695
2	We're All Set	33	5 ↓	-560%	943	493	1412
3	Specialnightaction	99	10 ↓	-890%	296	91	666
4	Honor Code	1/9	3/5 ↑	81%	30714	3661	98585
5	Ta Bueno	99	8 ↓	-1138%	254	90	551

#	NAME	ODDS	ML	CHG	WIN	PLC	SHW
	$1.00 MIN			TOTALS:	41958	8082	181027
1	Social Inclusion	3	3	0%	8464	2336	5226
2	We're All Set	25	5 ↓	-400%	1303	663	2646
3	Specialnightaction	92	10 ↓	-820%	371	132	1248
4	Honor Code	1/9	3/5 ↑	81%	31416	4775	170134
5	Ta Bueno	99	8 ↓	-1138%	325	151	1165

#	NAME	ODDS	ML	CHG	WIN	PLC	SHW
	$1.00 MIN			TOTALS:	88480	28655	367625
1	Social Inclusion	2	3 ↑	33%	22387	4998	15134
2	We're All Set	10	5 ↓	-100%	6251	3389	7677
3	Specialnightaction	67	10 ↓	-570%	1061	468	3274
4	Honor Code	1/5	3/5 ↑	67%	56685	18612	335483
5	Ta Bueno	73	8 ↓	-813%	979	558	3212

#	NAME	ODDS	ML	CHG	WIN	PLC	SHW
	$1.00 MIN			TOTALS:	97111	30578	375104
1	Social Inclusion	2	3 ↑	33%	25376	5812	16316
2	We're All Set	10	5 ↓	-100%	6933	3740	8230
3	Specialnightaction	60	10 ↓	-500%	1272	645	3557
4	Honor Code	1/5	3/5 ↑	67%	58828	19503	341210
5	Ta Bueno	64	8 ↓	-700%	1191	688	3486

#	NAME	ODDS	ML	CHG	WIN	PLC	SHW
	$1.00 MIN			TOTALS:	123752	37247	390377
1	Social Inclusion	7/5	3 ↑	53%	41995	9308	21796
2	We're All Set	8	5 ↓	-60%	11057	4890	12087
3	Specialnightaction	51	10 ↓	-410%	1960	1043	4453
4	Honor Code	1/2	3/5 ↑	17%	66989	21046	347778
5	Ta Bueno	57	8 ↓	-613%	1749	959	4261

The Betfair odds for Gulfstream race for win and British place, namely US show. I won the place bet but lost the win bet there. British win odds

Bet view: £2		118.3%	Back	Lay	92.2%	
1. Social Inclusion	3.6 £43	3.7 £2	3.75 £14	4.5 £2	11 £12	17 £3
2. Were All Set	6 £2	6.6 £5	7.6 £4	19 £2	19.5 £3	28 £3
3. Specialnightaction	16 £18	16.5 £16	17 £2	250 £3	300 £3	
4. Honor Code	1.38 £2	1.43 £3	1.5 £5	1.59 £11	1.6 £50	1.63 £20
5. Ta Bueno	16 £18	16.5 £4	17 £2	70 £3	95 £3	300 £3

British place odds

Bet view: £2		209.2%	Back	Lay	187.5%	
1. Social Inclusion	1.2 £16	1.3 £69	1.33 £43	1.36 £8	1.45 £62	1.54 £7
2. Were All Set	2.92 £8	3.2 £4	3.25 £5	3.75 £8	3.8 £60	5.5 £7
3. Specialnightaction	7.2 £2	8 £2	8.6 £4	26 £2	1000 £12	
4. Honor Code £21.70, £-138.00	1.15 £102	1.17 £9	1.18 £2	1.2 £515	1.24 £7	1.25 £366
5. Ta Bueno	8.4 £5	13.5 £2	14.5 £4	1000 £14		

The succeeding pools kept the lock as Honor Code moved to 1–5 then 1–2 and Social Inclusion to 3–1 then 2–1 then 7–5. Social Inclusion got the late money, usually a good sign as that money is usually more informed. At the end there still was close to a lock with Honor Code at 347,778 out of the total 390,377 show pool or 89.1%. This was three times the win pool and more than eleven times the place pool. At 1–2 my place bet was all right with Honor Code having 21,046 of the 37,247 or 56.5% of the place pool vs. 66,989 out of 123,752 or 54.1% in the win pool. Meanwhile the Betfair win and place odds were as shown above. I lost the Betfair win bets and won the smaller place bet.

Social Inclusion ran wire to wire and broke the Gulfstream track record running a Beyer 110. This was quite impressive given that many great horses have run at Gulfstream. It was also the highest Beyer by all three year olds in 2014 including Kentucky Derby and Preakness winner California Chrome who was named horse of the year. Honor Code ran a 93, the same as his Champagne Grade I second and above his 88 in the Grade II Remsen. Honor Code had a decent but not spectacular race but could not keep up and finished second. He added \$13,200 to his earnings which then totaled

$401,200. This is the majority of the $535,990 of the four horses of the nine in this group that have run races.

We have a ways to go to get into profitability given lots of costs off these earnings and 1/8 for Honor Code, Special Agent and Class Leader. Chances are good that with his super pedigree and terrific two year old form and a decent three year old year so far, that eventually Honor Code can be a moderately priced stallion. His only not excellent race saw Social Inclusion breaking the track record at Gulfstream, scoring the third fastest three year old time on chef-de-race scale at 65 and vaulting Social Inclusion into being very valuable.

Despite my place bet being a pretty good one, the place and show payoffs were the minimum $2.10 with the show being a minus pool where the track does not get its full track take. Then they pay the three first finishers the $2.10 payoffs. Social Inclusion paid 4.80 to win, 2.20 to place and 2.10 to show. The 1–4 exacta paid $7 per $2 bet. The superfecta 1–4–2–3 paid $8.20 per $1 bet showing how favored these horses were in a five horse race.

Honor Code at Winstar Farm, May 2014.

Trainer Shug McGaughey was impressed with the winner but also satisfied with Honor Code's effort. He remarked to the Daily Racing Form after the race "I'm disappointed we didn't win but not that disappointed in his race. We got a race into him and Javier obviously didn't beat him up"

The big winners were the trainer Manny Azpura and owner Ron Sanchez of Ronjos Racing Stable of Social Inclusion. By breaking the track record and beating the star Honor Code, there was a lot of interest by others to buy part or all of the horse. He was a $60,000 Keeneland September yearling purchase and now was worth close to $10 million. The top offer was $5 million for 75%. Before the race, the 85 year old trainer said:

> I really like this horse and I like everything he's done since I've got him. I'm so pleased with him and I believe he's going to keep improving, I told my wife before the race, 'You're going to see him break out of the gate and they're never going to catch him. They'll be 10 lengths behind.'

And he was right. There was a possibility that Honor Code and Social Inclusion would meet in the Kentucky Derby. It is hard to wire the field in the Derby but its been done a few times such as by Spend A Buck in 1985 and the filly Winning Colors in 1988.

Honor Code is back.

Unfortunately Honor Code suffered another minor injury showed up and must rest with no training for two months and then restart training and hopefully compete in the fall races. Meanwhile, Social Inclusion ran in the April 5, 2014 Wood Memorial finishing third earning 20 Derby points so he did not have enough points to qualify for the Kentucky Derby. But he was in the Preakness and Belmont Stakes.

As of mid August 2014, Honor Code was essentially ready to be back in training with Shug McGaughey. What we need to complete his dossier to prepare for a top level breeding career is a grade I win. There are not many Grade I's in the late fall so the plan is to run him as a four year old.

Honor Code was doing well and breezed a $\frac{1}{2}$ mile in 29 seconds on the dirt, second best of 14 at the Fair Hill Training Center in Elkton, Maryland. The plan is to ship him to Belmont so Shug can train him over a deeper surface and watch him train daily.

Honor Code finally made it back to racing on Saturday November 22, 2014. That was a $6\frac{1}{2}$ furlong allowance optional claiming race on the dirt with a purse of $69,000 at Aqueduct. Just like in his first race of 7 furlongs, he started slow, was way behind and then had a tremendous finishing kick to win by a length plus. He earned $41,400 but the real gain was getting his reputation back. The NYRA commentators were impressed so the old Honor Code seems to be back. His 106 Beyer was one of the top races by three year olds in 2014. This was an improvement over his previous Beyers which were 89, 93, 88 and 92.

Honor Code charging in the Gulfstream Handicap.

In his two year old races he beat top three year olds Wicked Strong, Ride on Curlin and Cairo Prince. His 2014 second place finish behind Social Inclusion's 110 Beyer is higher but that was higher than than any horse achieved in any of the triple crown races. Wicked Strong was fourth in the Kentucky Derby, third behind Honor Code in the Remsen, won the grade I Wood Memorial beating Social Inclusion and was second in the Travers. Cairo Prince, who is now retired, won the grade II Holy Ball and Nashua Stakes and was fourth in the G1 Florida Derby. Ride on Curlin, who was third behind Honor Code's second in the G1 Champagne, was second in the G1 Arkansas Derby and Preakness, seventh in the Kentucky Derby and 11th in the Belmont Stakes. So Honor Code seems competitive with these and other top three year olds. We will see what the next move is and his four year old year. The current plan is to run him in the G2 $300,000 Gulfstream Handicap on March 7 and hopefully later in the year in some G1 races such as the grade I Met Mile or the grade II Suburban at Belmont Park and later the grade I Whitney at Saratoga in August culminating with the $1\frac{1}{4}$ grade I Breeders' Cup Classic at Keeneland on October 31, 2015.

Honor Code winning the Gulfstream Handicap.

The Gulfstream Handicap had six horses running with #5 Private Zone the favorite. He was rated the best on HTR and at 126 on PSR rating systems. Valid was second in both and at 125. There are very high rankings to put them at the top of the three year olds. In PSR, Honor Code was ranked third and Wicked Strong fourth and in HTR they were reversed. The other two horses, East Hall, a closer like Honor Code and Loverbill. Private zone had won three grade I races and been second in two others. He had a jockey change to a less familiar and top jockey (Carlos Marquez) when his regular riser (Martin Pedrosa) could not get a Florida license. Honor Code had beaten Wicked Strong as a two year old in the G2 Remsen.

So this was tough competition after Honor Code's six month layoff. I was hoping that Honor Code could win and bet him accordingly in all the pools but I had to hedge in case Private Zone beat him and a little bet should Valid win. I assumed that Wicked would not win or be second so downgraded him. The race was vintage Honor Code. He was way at the back. Meanwhile Private Zone and Valid were leading and having a speed dual. One plus for Honor Code was he was ridden by J.J. Castellano, America's top jockey and the pilot of Honor Code's last four races.

According to the *Daily Racing Form*'s Mike Welsh, trainer Shug McGaughey, while watching the Gulfstream Park Handicap on the tv monitors and not seeing Honor Code anywhere near the leading horses said "I was about ready to go home ... I was watching it on tv, and down the back side there wasn't a (1) on there for a long time. Then I saw him swing to the outside. It was the same thing when he broke broke his maiden at Saratoga. I was watching on tv there and he wasn't ever in the picture and I was thinking up excuses already".

Fortunately he stuck around to watch the rest of the race, otherwise he would have missed an incredible performance by Honor Code who rallied down the center of the track from more than a dozen lengths behind to run down the favorite Private Zone and Valid. Honor Code stumbled at the start then dropped far off the early pace set by Private Zone and pressed from the outset by Valid. The leaders posted early splits of 23.51 and 45.96 seconds for the opening quarter and half mile with Honor Code about 15 lengths behind. Jockey Javier Castellano eased Honor Code outside to start his rally from the back stretch as the two leaders continued to battle upfront. But behind them, the rest of the field was hitting them best strides. At the 3/4 mile in 1:10.09, Honor Code had just one horse beat. But a furlong later he had moved into fourth and had the front runners firmly in his sites. Honor Code responded to steady urging while gaining steadily. In the stretch Private Zone and Valid still were ahead but Wicked Strong and Honor Code were gaining. With less than a furlong to run, Wicked Strong's rally stalled and Honor Code swept past him and took aim at the lead. With one final surge he passed the two leaders to win the race. The photos show him gaining ground and then winning. He beat Private Zone by half a length with Valid third, ahead of Wicked Strong for the 1–5–6–2 finish.

Jockey Javier Castellano admitted that their trip was worrying despite his mounts typical running style. "I didn't mind it (being far back), because he is a come from behind horse and the pace set up perfect for him". Private Zone and Valid hooked up together all the way but Castellano was worrying on the back side because Honor Code wasn't picking it up. At the 3/8 pole Honor Code turned around and took off at the top of the stretch. According to Castellano, it was amazing the way he did it.

Honor Code got 60% of the $300,000 purse or $180,000 so he was then four wins and two seconds winning $626,740. I did well in my betting at the rebate shop. Betting Wicked in 3rd and 4th spot and focusing on Honor Code with some Private Zone and less Valid hedging paid off well in all the betting pools. His value is increased and chances to be a good stallion at Land's End now a very good possibility that would turn my investment into a profit.

His seventh race was the G2 $400,000 Alysheba Stakes at Churchill Downs on May 1, 2015 on the Kentucky Oaks undercard. The main competition was the Todd Fletcher trained Protonico. J.J. Castellano chose Honor Code to ride. Somehow it was not Honor Code's day. He apparently did not like the track and finished fifth, although the slow pace was a factor. He had a bit of kick but was not his in his usual form of blazing at the end. A slow pace hurt Honor Code, but still he ran the last $\frac{1}{4}$ mile in 23 seconds. This was a big disappointment. He collected $11,520 for his effort so now has won $638,260. I was there in an owners section of the vast track facility that Churchill has become. Fortunately Honor Code came out of the race in fine shape.

21.1.1. *Back to Honor Code: The Met Mile on the Belmont Stakes undercard, June 6, 2015*

His next race was a tough challenge for Honor Code, especially coming off the disappointing Churchill Downs race, but the $1.25 million 1-mile, 1-turn race was more suitable for him as there would be a fast pace. And is was fast: 1:08.74 for 6 furlongs (good enough to win most 6 furlong races) which compares with the 1:12.4 in the Churchill race. He has done well at Belmont, almost winning the G1 Champagne.

He was the last pick in Betfair as the public viewed him mostly by his last race. So I got 13 to 1 there, plus more later at 9 to 1. At the track he was 7–1 US odds. Almost nobody but me picked him first (and I'll admit to some wishful thinking!). Timeform supplied by Alydar did pick him first as well. In PSR, HTR, Wizard and the odds he was an also ran, so they thought. How could he beat the Breeders' Cup Classic winner Bayern, or Private Zone favored here despite Honor Code beating him in Florida, or last year's Belmont Stakes winner Tonalist? And there were *weaker* horses ridden by hall of fame jockeys Gary Stevens and Mike Smith.

Super Screener and the Wizard had a more positive view. Super Screener in his analysis of the Met Mile rated Honor Code third behind Tonalist and

Bayern and that Honor Code "will be closing fastest of all and a certain board hitter, plus, deadly at one turn miles".

Wizard wrote

> Like Tonalist, this stalker/closer is expected to benefit from a fast pace. He was a G2 winner last year in his third start, and missed in the G1 Champagne over this track and distance by just a neck in his 2nd start. Plagued by layoffs after those first three races, he came back with an impressive win over Private Zone March 7 in a G2 race at today's 1-mile distance. However, when he next raced in the G2 Alysheba on May 1, he was stuck trailing a very slow pace, with no chance to make up appreciable ground in the stretch. Nonetheless, he did past four rivals with an extremely fast final 5/16 of a mile. With a more advantageous pace set up expected today, he could be sitting on a peak performance in this third start off the layoff.

Honor Code winning the Met Mile.

I figured that the fast pace, no matter how good the opposition would set it up for JJ to let him loose and finish strong to beat them all. The race started and Sandra said "where is he"? It looked like he had no chance being 15 lengths behind. Then as the fast pace softened he made his run, a brilliant one, getting a −72 on Steve Roman's score, which was higher than Shared Belief, California Chrome and all the others in his cohort. It was a gem to watch, very similar to his Saratoga fall comeback race and his

Florida race. This was the sixth fastest Met Mile in 120 years. This score compared to mid 60s for the best other top races and a −58 for American Pharoah's Belmont that won him the triple crown. Honor Code's Beyer was 112, the highest of any horse in 2015.

I did fine in my bets making enough on Betfair and two betting shops to cover some nice embroidery and tile bought in Istanbul the previous week.

Honor Code is tied for the 19th best three year old and up in the world in Longine's ratings in June 2015. This was his first time on the list. Shared Belief, who is still injured was tied for second behind American Pharaoh, the leader. Firing Line, who was second in the Kentucky Derby and out of the money in the Preakness, is 9th. California Chrome, who is out for a number of months with a cannon bone injury, is tied for 11th. Dortmund and Main Sequence are tied with Honor Code for 19th.

That puts Honor Code back on top, competitive with the best four year olds and hopefully he runs in the $1.25 million Whitney at Saratoga and the $5 million Breeders' Cup Classic in Keeneland. His status now as a brilliant G1 winner with five wins, two seconds and one fifth with about $1,308,260 in earnings ($680,000 from the Met Mile), makes him a good stallion prospect for Lane's End. Hopefully, Honor Code can meet American Pharoah in the Breeders' Cup Classic on October 31, 2015 at Kneeland. It will be interesting to see who wins and who the competition is. American Pharoah is scheduled for the Grade I Haskell at Monmouth Park in New Jersey and possibly the Travers in Saratoga or the Pennsylvania Derby and then the Classic. From a money point of view all this is a big risk for American Pharoah — he's already reported to be a $200,000 stallion and these fees swamp all but the $5 million purse in the Classic. So retiring him now at the peak of his fame as the number one horse in the world and triple crown winner, might be optimal. Zayat is in a bit of a bind: "I can't win no matter what I do. I am either a greedy owner for running him or I just retired the horse, people would say I deprived the racing public of the horse." It seems that Zayat wants to run him in more races.

That is however a non event because the breeding rights were sold to Coolmore-America for $6 million plus some bonuses when he was the champion two year old. So Zayat gets these purses such as the $1.1 million from winning the August 2, 2015 Haskell. AP is still worldwide #1 with even higher 131 pound rating as of late July 2015. So he should run the horse to collect in the Travers or other one or two races before the October 31, 2015 Breeders' Cup, the natural retirement date. Meanwhile at a reported 175 breeds in Kentucky for about $35 million gross plus possible Australia fees,

Coolmore-America looks like they made a very good deal with a current value about $200 million.

21.1.2. *Honor Code at the Whitney, August 8, 2015*

The talk of all the *Daily Racing Form* analysts was "is Honor Code a one turn horse or can he do two turns?" His two losses were on two turns and all the one turn races were spectacular runs where he looked impressive. Also on the Sunday before the race he did not want to run on the Oklahoma training track and had to be brought to the main track. So there were lots of queries about his ability.

Honor Code was the favorite at 3–1 with Tonalist at 4–1, Noble Bird at 5–1, Liam's Map at 6–1, V.E. Day at 8–1 and Lea at 9–2 with long shots Wicked Strong and Normandy Invasion at 30–1.[2]

We had seats at the 3/8th pole far away from the finish line but with a great view of the two turns (and the large screens) so we could see when Honor Code got moving. It was, as expected, in the middle of the second turn and he moved up fast from his usual last place position. He was blazing fast gaining with each stride on Liam's Map who was five lengths ahead of Honor Code as they passed by us.

One of my colleagues for the syndicate I participate in which owns 1/8th of Honor Code wrote as follows:

[2]Other stats for the Whitney contenders: The chef-de-race ratings from Steve Roman of the main contenders including seven Grade I winners were:

HORSE	PF	FIN	DATE	RACE	GR	AGE/SEX	TRK	DIST	SURF	TRK COND
COACH INGE	-55	1ST	06/06/15	BROOKLYN INVITATIONAL S	G2	4YO&UP	BEL	12.00	DIRT	FST
COACH INGE	-64	3RD	07/04/15	SUBURBAN H	G2	4YO&UP	BEL	10.00	DIRT	FST
HONOR CODE	-53	1ST	03/07/15	GULFSTREAM PARK H	G2	4YO&UP	GP	8.00	DIRT	FST
HONOR CODE	-72	1ST	06/06/15	METROPOLITAN H	G1	3YO&UP	BEL	8.00	DIRT	FST
LEA	-44	1ST	01/10/15	HAL'S HOPE S	G3	4YO&UP	GP	8.00	DIRT	FST
LEA	-76	2ND	02/07/15	DONN H	G1	4YO&UP	GP	9.00	DIRT	FST
LEA	-66	2ND	06/13/15	STEPHEN FOSTER H	G1	3YO&UP	CD	9.00	DIRT	FST
MORENO	-66	2ND	03/07/15	SANTA ANITA H	G1	4YO&UP	SA	10.00	DIRT	FST
MORENO	-54	3RD	03/28/15	NEW ORLEANS H	G2	4YO&UP	FG	9.00	DIRT	FST
MORENO	-65	1ST	04/18/15	CHARLES TOWN CLASSIC S	G2	4YO&UP	CT	9.00	DIRT	FST
MORENO	-46	2ND	05/30/15	CALIFORNIAN S	G2	3YO&UP	SA	9.00	DIRT	FST
NOBLE BIRD	-56	2ND	05/01/15	ALYSHEBA S	G2	4YO&UP	CD	8.50	DIRT	FST
NOBLE BIRD	-67	1ST	06/13/15	STEPHEN FOSTER H	G1	3YO&UP	CD	9.00	DIRT	FST
TONALIST	-73	1ST	05/02/15	WESTCHESTER S	G3	4YO&UP	BEL	8.00	DIRT	FST
TONALIST	-53	2ND	06/06/15	METROPOLITAN H	G1	3YO&UP	BEL	8.00	DIRT	FST
TONALIST	-70	2ND	07/04/15	SUBURBAN H	G2	4YO&UP	BEL	10.00	DIRT	FST
V. E. DAY	-54	2ND	06/06/15	BROOKLYN INVITATIONAL S	G2	4YO&UP	BEL	12.00	DIRT	FST
WICKED STRONG	-39	3RD	04/25/15	EXCELSIOR S	G3	4YO&UP	AQU	10.00	DIRT	FST

Honor Code broke alertly and had a little early foot as he did in the Met Mile but quickly went to the back of the pack around the first turn while racing with Tonalist and V.E. Day. Down the backside Honor Code did what he does and dropped further back even though there was plenty of early pace set by Liam's Map. The first 1/4 mile in 22 3/5 and the 1/2 mile in 46 seconds flat. Honor Code trailed by 19. As the field reached the 1/2 mile pole Honor Code was starting to improve his position but still had plenty to do. Half way around the turn for home he started to gather his momentum but the margin was still 12 lengths. Honor Code approached the top of the stretch while running along the inside but still had much more work to do. With an 1/8th mile to run the deficit was still 4 1/2 lengths as Javier moved Honor Code to the outside of the early pacesetter LiamÕs Map. With a 1/16th to run, Honor Code was all out and gaining. He just managed to get past Liam's Map two jumps from the wire to when by a remarkable neck!!!!

Honor Code winning the Whitney.

Honor Code was actually the morning line favorite at 3-1 with the others odds, PSR, HTR, Wizard as follows:

PP	Horse	ML	PSR	HTR	Wizard
1	Honor Code	3–1	122	3	2
2	Tonalist	4–1	124	1	1
3	Noble Bird	5–1	118	4	
4	Liam's Map	6–1	124	5	
5	Moreno	12–1	107	6	
6	V.E. Day	8–1	102	7	3
7	Lea	9–2	123	2	4
9	Wicked Strong	20–1	107	8	
10	Normandy Invasion	30–1	112	9	

So he won with rather good win, place and show payoffs of 9.50, 5.90 and 3.50. Tonalist at 7–2 was the actual favorite with slightly more bet. A $200 win, place and show bet on Honor Code at one rebate shop returned$1890 plus rebate and at the other rebate shop I had two $50 wps bets plus some small losing exacta bets with Honor Code first or second. He collected $670,000 earnings so now has hit the $2 million mark. The jockey J.J. Castellano did not whip him at all and rode a perfect race. He was sure pleased as the photo shows. The pace was fast at 1:09.72 for six furlongs with Liam's Map 5 lengths ahead of Honor Code. So it set it up for the late running Honor Code.

Only seven horses have won the Met Mile-Whitney double and that includes such greats as Tom Fool (1953), Kelso (1961), Criminal Type (1990), In Excess (1991) and Tizway (2011).

Honor Code's chef-de-race rating for the race was −67. He is now more or less at or near the top of the older male horses in training. California Chrome and Shared Belief are still on the injured list but likely will run in 2016. They are ahead of Firing Line, Dortmund and Main Sequence. Materiality has been retired. Honor Code moved to the top ten worldwide. The next moves for Honor Code were the $400,000 grade II Kelso Mile at Belmont on October 3 and then the $1\frac{1}{4}$ mile Breeders' Cup Classic on October 31. The Whitney was a *you win and you're in* for the Classic. American Pharoah ran in the Travers where he had a speed duel with Frosted and then was narrowly beat by Keen Ice and later scheduled to run in the Breeders' Cup Classic.

Regarding syndications and possible stud fees on retirement, Steve Roman pointed out that Honor Code shapes up well against American Pharoah both in terms of pedigree and performance. The ratings for Honor Code and American Pharoah respectively: BRS 110 vs 109; Equibase 126 vs. 112; Beyer 113 vs. 109 and chef-de-race −72 vs. −70.

Rebecca Ruby Cameron's (2010) honors thesis studies factors affecting stud fees. Breeders prefer stallions that produce winners of stakes and graded stakes races, have high stallion ratings, high comparable stallion ratings and have a pedigree dominated by speed. Location in Kentucky provides an average 55% premium. Fully 90% of the top race horses in North America are from the Northern Dancer line with the remaining 10% from Mr Prospector or Seattle Slew. Important variables are the sire index, comparable sire index, number of foals sold at auction and the running behavior of the foals than the running behavior of the sire. Variables that Cameron found insignificant in her regression equations are the number of crops the stallions have had, the average number of foals per crop, the average earnings per runner and the average auction price of the stallions offspring. The attributes of some of these seemingly important variables which are not important are captured in other significant variables. The stallion's height and best Ragozin number capture the importance of the stallions own importance at the track on his fee. Height is meant to capture physical characteristics that raise fees. Stallions producing a higher percentage of offspring that are stakes winners have higher fees.

Tapit in 2015, with fifteen or more grade 1 winners, was at the top with $300,000 stud fee and a reputed $350,000 in 2016. At the August 2015 Saratoga Select Sale, one Tapit sold for $2 million, another for $950,000 was bought back. In total, seven Tapit's sold for $6.35 million. Fasig Tipton made a big deal that American Pharoah was sold at Saratoga. In reality he was consigned by Zayat and did not make the $300,000 reserve price so was bought back.

At the September Keeneland select sale, a gray/roan Tapit colt out of Silver Colors by Mr Greeley sold for $2.1 million. The colt's second dam was 1988 Kentucky Derby winner Winning Colors. Mandy Pope bought the colt with Bob Baffert (with Kaleem Shah and John Sikura) being the underbidder. Pope bought the colt's full sister for $700,000 at the 2014 Keeneland September sale. The second highest price was for a chestnut colt by Tapit out of the Grade I winner Pure Clan by Pure Prize that sold for $1.65 million to Roy and Gretchen Jackson in partnership with Three Chimneys Farm. Tapit is at the top. Close by are a War Front who had $1.15 million colt out of Grate by AP Indy and Benardini, a son of AP Indy whose colt out of Pilfer by Deputy Minster sold for $1.5 million. My colleagues in group VIII bought two Tapit offspring, one for $850,000 and another for $1.8 million for another partnership.

Cameron (2010) compares why AP Indy was $150,000 and Birdstone $30,000 back in 2009. Each of the variables contributes to the higher fee. AP has a higher percentage of foals that are stakes and graded stakes winners of 8% and 4%, respectively. Also the sire and comparable sire indices are higher and there is more speed in his dosage profile. His is also more popular with more foals sold at auction.

Carpe Diem won the grade I Blue Grass and was the lone dual qualifier for the Belmont until he was scratched with a minor knee chip injury and retired by the Winstar and Stonestreet owners. They bought him as a two year old in training for $1.6 million. He was a $550,000 yearling.

I bought a half share in Carpe Diem joint with my Saratoga colleague. There are 50 shares, the Winstar 25 and the Stonestreet 25, plus 8 to the farm Winstar plus one to the trainer Todd Pletcher and one to another supporter of the stallion, Stonestreet advisor John Moynihan. He was syndicated for $10 million with major owners Winstar and Barbara Banke, the owner of Stonestreet, Curlin and Rachel Alexandra. So it's $200,000 per share. Our share gives us two breeds for each of the next four years plus one in succeeding years, a share of the other stud fees beyond the ones from the other 60 shares, plus possible South America (Brazil, Argentina) breeds in the off season if he is shipped there. Carpe Diem was sired by Giants Causeway who was by Storm Cat with dam Rebridled Dreams and dam sire Unbridled Song. Extra costs are insurance, some interets as we bought with some debt, maintenance fees, etc. Winstar and Stonestreet, like Lanes End are terrific operations so the risk seems worth it. Hopefully, most or all of the investment will be paid back from the proceeds of the breeding before the first horses are running in four years. They if they do well, there would be gains on the investment.

Carpe Diem, like American Pharoah, and Dortmund won grade I races as a two and three year old. Those and Honor Code are likely to be competitors in the new sire superior mare mating game. Dortmund did not run in the Breeders' Cup Classic in 2015 but is still in training. He was rated close to American Pharoah going into the Kentucky Derby. His last race was the Preakness. As a two year old Carpe Diem won the grade I Breeders Futurity also at Keeneland. He retired with 4 wins, one second and the Derby 10th in his six races. He earned $1,519,800.

There is a futures book for the Breeders' Cup on Betfair. For the Classic, Honor code was about 10–1, with the favorites American Pharoah at 2–1 and Beholder at 3–1. My betting strategy is to go long Honor Code, long the brilliant Irish shipper Gleneagles at 18–1, later 12–1, who won a number of group I races and is sired by Galileo, the sire of Frankel and many other top racers. All four of these horses are rated in the top ten worldwide. The other contenders are likely Frosted (who easily won the Pennsylvania Derby), Keen Ice (who beat American Pharaoh in the Travers), Firing Line, Tonalist (whose Betfair odds dropped to 8.8–1 from 16–1 after he easily won the Jockey Club Gold Cup), Dortmund, Bayern (who has had a spotty record lately but won the Classic in 2014), Texas Red (who is now injured and out the rest of 2015) and Palace Malice (who was retired to

3 Chimneys). My strategy was to bet enough on the other possibly winners so if Honor Code and Gleneagles both lose, I at least break even.

California Chrome was a case of good breeding at a cheap price

California Chrome at Dubai.

We saw with Secretariat, his greatest offspring were the sons of his daughters as well as his daughters. A great example of this second generation success is California Chrome who has become the world's highest earning horse by winning the 2016 Dubai $10 million World Cup on March 26, 2016. The $6 million winners share puts California Chrome above $12 million, more than Curlin's $10+ million and all other horses in the US and Europe. Steve Coburn and Perry Martin bred the $8000 claimer Love the Chase to the $2500 stud fee Lucky Pulpit and got the 2014 Kentucky Derby and Preakness winner. When California Chrome lost the Belmont, Coburn complained bitterly that other horses were fresh in the race and California Chrome had to run all three triple crown races. Once that lowpoint passed, they were smart and kept the horse in training. A try at Ascot failed but he was second earning $2 million in the 2015 Dubai World Cup.

Coburn sold his share of California Chrome to Taylor Made for his breeding career. The next step seems to be a try at the 2016 Breeders Cup Classic in the fall. What is interesting is that the low cost worked out well likely because of the pedigree of California Chrome which two generations back includes AP Indy, Cozzene, and Mr Prospector. Three generations back includes Dantzig, Seattle Slew, Northern Dancer and Raise a Native. Secretariat and other greats are in the fourth generation.[3]

This breeding cheap to cheap to get a champion was pioneered in the 1930s to 1950s by Federico Tesio in Italy who bred all three of the undefeated horses in Europe since 1900 in high level competition with at least ten races before the recent Frankel. There have been only two US undefeated horses: Colin in 1907 and Personal Ensign in 1988 (see Chapter 20).

21.1.3. *Honor Code at the Kelso Grade II Mile Race, October 3, 2015*

Honor Code's next race was the \$400,000 Kelso mile to Belmont on October 3 where he was the 3–5 morning line favorite. Trainer Shug had Easy Goer in 1989. He ran in the $1\frac{1}{4}$ Jockey Club Gold Cup and won but lost the Breeders Cup to Sunday Silence. The choice of race is important for success. Sunday Silence's trainer, Charley Whitingham said before the JCGC that, if Easy Goer ran there, then Sunday Silence would beat him in the Classic which was exactly what happened. So Shug sent Honor Code to go the 1 mile Kelso rather than the $1\frac{1}{4}$ mile classic which was on the same day at Belmont.

It had been raining since Friday at Belmont and the track was muddy. This should not be a major factor for Honor Code as he easily won his first race at Saratoga on a muddy track. The competition seemed to be Red Vine, who was 3rd behind Beholder in the Pacific Classic, and Appealing Tale, who won his last race in Santa Anita's Grade II Pat O'Brien at

---

[3] The pedigree of California Chrome

CALIFORNIA CHROME ⓘ (USA) ch. C, 2011 {A4} DP = 7-9-14-0-0 (30) DI = 3.29 CD = 0.77 - 21 Starts, 12 Wins, 3 Places, 1 Shows **Career Earnings:** \$12,532,650

LUCKY PULPIT (USA) ch. 2001	PULPIT (USA) dkb/br. 1994 [IC]	A.P. INDY (USA) dkb/br. 1989 [IC]	SEATTLE SLEW (USA) dkb/br. 1974 [BC]	BOLD REASONING (USA)	dkb/br. 1968
				MY CHARMER (USA)	b. 1969 *
			WEEKEND SURPRISE (USA)* b. 1980	SECRETARIAT (USA)	ch. 1970 [IC]
				LASSIE DEAR (USA)	b. 1974 *
		PREACH (USA) b. 1989	MR. PROSPECTOR (USA) b. 1970 [BC]	RAISE A NATIVE (USA)	ch. 1961 [B]
				GOLD DIGGER (USA)	b. 1962 *
			NARRATE (USA)* dkb/br. 1980	HONEST PLEASURE (USA)	dkb/br. 1973
				STATE (USA)	b. 1974
	LUCKY SOPH (USA) b. 1992	COZZENE (USA) gr. 1980	CARO (IRE) gr. 1967 [IC]	FORTINO (FR)	gr. 1959
				CHAMBORD (GB)	ch. 1955
			RIDE THE TRAILS (USA) b. 1971	PRINCE JOHN (USA)	ch. 1953 [C]
				WILDWOOK (USA)	b. 1965
		LUCKY SPELL (USA) b. 1971	LUCKY MEL (USA) ch. 1954	OLYMPIA (USA)	b. 1946 [B]
				ROYAL MINK (GB)	ch. 1948
			INCANTATION (USA) dkb/br. 1965	PRINCE BLESSED (USA)	b. 1957
				MAGIC SPELL (USA)	b. 1954
LOVE THE CHASE (USA) ch. 2006	NOT FOR LOVE (USA) b. 1990	MR. PROSPECTOR (USA) b. 1970 [BC]	RAISE A NATIVE (USA) ch. 1961 [B]	NATIVE DANCER (USA)	gr. 1950 [IC]
				RAISE YOU (USA)	ch. 1946 *
			GOLD DIGGER (USA)* b. 1962	NASHUA (USA)	b. 1952 [IC]
				SEQUENCE (USA)	b. 1946
		DANCE NUMBER (USA) b. 1979	NORTHERN DANCER (CAN) b. 1961 [BC]	NEARCTIC (CAN)	br. 1954
				NATALMA (USA)	b. 1957 *
			NUMBERED ACCOUNT (USA)* b. 1969	BUCKPASSER (USA)	b. 1963 [C]
				INTRIGUING (USA)	ch. 1964 *
	CHASE IT DOWN (USA) ch. 1997	POLISH NUMBERS (USA) b. 1987	DANZIG (USA) b. 1977 [IC]	NORTHERN DANCER (CAN)	b. 1961 [BC]
				PAS DE NOM (USA)	br. 1968
			NUMBERED ACCOUNT (USA)* b. 1969	BUCKPASSER (USA)	b. 1963 [C]
				INTRIGUING (USA)	ch. 1964 *
		CHASE THE DREAM (USA) b. 1984	SIR IVOR (USA) b. 1965 [IC]	SIR GAYLORD (USA)	br. 1959 [IC]
				ATTICA (USA)	ch. 1953 *
			LA BELLE FLEUR (USA) b. 1977	VAGUELY NOBLE (IRE)	b. 1965 [CP]
				PRINCESS RIBOT (USA)	b. 1964

7 furlongs. PSR, HTR favored Honor Code but the Wizard picked Red Vine and wrote:

PGM #	Horse Name	M/L	Jockey	Trainer
5	**RED VINE**	**5-1**	**ROSARIO J**	**CLEMENT C**

Has a solid chance at an upset today dropping a bit in class and cutting back in distance from a good 3rd in the G1 Pacific Classic behind Beholder, a mare who may be the best horse in the country. Prior to that, Red Vine finished 2nd in his first graded stakes race, beaten by next-out repeater Bradester. Stalker/closer has put in three more works over this track since then and has won 3 of 5 over all on dirt, including 1 for 1 on wet tracks.

PGM #	Horse Name	M/L	Jockey	Trainer
2	**HONOR CODE**	**3-5**	**CASTELLANO J**	**MCGAUGHEY III C**

Honor Code has won back to back G1 races, including the Met Mile over this track and distance, and has proven himself to be one of the best 3 or 4 horses in the country. However, he's coming off a 2-month layoff in what appears to be a 'prep' for the Breeders' Cup, and at expected very short odds today, he may be vulnerable. He comes from far back, and the pace in this race projects to be average, which may compromise his chances a bit. His lone wet track start was a spectacular debut win, so the expected wet weather won't hurt, but he must give from 6 to 11 lbs. to all rivals as well.

PGM #	Horse Name	M/L	Jockey	Trainer
1	**APPEALING TALE**	**6-1**	**TALAMO J**	**MILLER P**

Figures to control the pace, although he may get some pressure from Scarly Charly. 5yo gelding enters in career-best form, having finished first or 2nd in four straight, including his first graded stakes win last time out in the G2 Pat O'Brien at 7F on dirt. He's 1 for 1 on wet tracks and could spring a front-running upset if able to slow down the pace enough at a distance where he's won 4 of 8.

HTR had it Honor Code, Red Vine and Appealing Tale. PSR had Honor Code 121, Appealing Tale 102, Scarley Charley 108, Mylute 102, Matterhorn 104 and Tamarkuz 104. So Honor Code was the pick. At 3–5 Morning Line and 1–5, then 2–5 then 1–2 then 3–5 with Appealing Tale getting the late money. My bet was Honor Code to place.

Well, the Wizard script was right and Appealing Tale won wire to wire with a slow pace with Red Vine second. Honor Code was not too far back and made a run but finished third, beaten by $3\frac{3}{4}$ lengths, Tamarkuz was fourth, Mylute fifth, Scarlay Charly sixth and Matterhorn seventh and last.

21.1.4. *The Breeders Cup Classic, October 31, 2015*

Honor Code came into the race with terrific workouts at Belmont and was shipped to Keeneland a few days before the race. The picture shows him working out there in the rain which does not bother him. The Longines world's best racehorse ratings still have American Pharaoh first at 131 with Arc winner Golden Horn the 4–5 favorite in the turf at 130, two time Arc winner Treve is third at 126, Able Friend is 125, Shared Belief, who was scheduled to race in 2016 has died, was also at 125, Solow who beat Gleneagles (20–1 in the Classic) in the grade I Queen Elizabeth II stakes at Ascot on October 17 is sixth at 129, then there ware eight horses at 123 tied for seventh. The seven include Honor Code,plus the Great Gatsby, Order of St George, Lankan Rupee, Jack Hobbs, Free Eagle, Flintshire (who is not in the Breeders' Cup Turf and I had to hedge out, as best as possible, my Betfair long bet on him) and Designs on Rome. Not there are California Chrome, Beholder the second choice in the Classic above Honor Code, Tonalist, who won the Jockey Club Gold Cup (also 6–1 in the Classic as is Honor Code), Keen Ice (12–1, who beat AP in the Travers), and Frosted (15–1, who won the Pennsylvania Derby). Besides those mentioned Effinex (107) and Smooth Roller (111) have run races with high Beyers.

Honor Code working out at Keeneland.

My feeling in the betting was that at 10–1 on Betfair, Honor Code was my first pick. He had never run $1\frac{1}{4}$ but his sire AP Indy won this race and the $1\frac{1}{2}$ mile Belmont, so his breeding should be ok. My other pick was Gleneagles at prices around 18–1. All his races were on the grass but he won several grade I's.

Then I tried to hedge out the possible winners. I assumed that AP and Beholder would be over bet so I was slightly long Beholder and slightly short AP.

Noted TV handicapper Randy Moss who has created his own pace figures saw it on a webcast: "AP leading followed by Beholder with the late chargers Tonalist, Honor Code, Keen Ice and Smooth Roller making a late run and any of these could win".

The various handicappers favored American Pharaoh for a variety of reasons that he has easily won every race except the Travers second place and his first race fifth. He just ran as fast as he needed to win! His high 4.33

dosage confused me in the Derby and Belmont, but he had plenty of stamina to win those races. He became even more favored when the five year old mare Beholder was scratched. She was thought to be the main competition to AP and was a speed horse who would push him on the lead. I was hoping that Honor Code might win to finish his career. He had great workouts, his regular jockey J.J. Castellano, and looked wonderful. His trainer took the route to run him in the mile race that was a prep instead of tiring him out with a mile and a quarter race. He along with Tonalist were the second or third choice of the handicappers. A worry was his not having run at this distance before, but a bigger worry was that AP was the only speed horse and could easily go wire to wire slowing it down.

The handicapping information is in Table 21.1.

American Pharaoh winning the Classic.

In the end, the race was as expected. AP won easily in a fast time of 2:00.07. Secretariat, Monorchos, Beholder, and a few other have run in the 159s. Steve Roman reminded me that Spectacular Bid holds the world's dirt record for $1\frac{1}{4}$ miles at 1:57.4, about 10–15 lengths better than AP. He retires with the public thinking he is a super star comparable to the greats of the past including Affirmed, Seattle Slew and Secretariat, but some of us feel that he just had a sequence of good pace trips and won some good

Table 21.1. The Handicapping Information for the Classic.

		Odds				Highest'Last		Ranking			
	Horse	ML	Betfair	Track	PA•	Beyer	Roman	SS∓	Alydar	HTR	PSR
1	Tonalist	6–1	9–1	6–1	6–1	111/105	73/72	5–1 B	2	3	120
2	Keen Ice	12–1	14.5–1	8–1	7–1	106/106	62/62	8–1 B	3	5	105
3	Frosted	15–1	23–1	12–1	9–1	106/106	63/63	15–1 C		4	108
4	American Pharaoh	6–5	0.72–1	3–5	5–1	109/105	70/59	3–1 B	1	1	120
5	Gleneagles	20–1	8.4–1	8–1		124/114 RP*	124/114	20–1 X		6	na⋆
6	Effinex	30–1	119–1	33–1		107/92	70/31	20–1 C		7	100
7	Smooth Roller	15–1	**			111/111	73/73	30–1 X			113
8	Hard Aces	50–1	61–1	61–1		103/92	59/27	50–1 X		8	95
9	Honor Code	6–1	9–2	9–2	5–1	113/101	72/50	15–1 C	LP±	2	120
10	Beholder	3–1	**			114/99	66/60	2–1 A			119

Note: •PA = Pace Advantage, ∓SS = Super Screener, A = Must, B = Logical, C = Toss, X = Toss.
*RP = Racing Post, **= Scratched.
±LP = Late Pace, ⋆na = not rated.

races. Except for losing the Travers and the Classic, which he won, he did not face much competition.

Roman's ranking for the Classic was 73, the best of AP's career but that is way below Ghostzapper's 98 and a 124 best. Ghostzapper had four zeros on Ragasin's scale. On Fotias's Equiform he had four 84s. In comparison, Medaglio D'Or's best was an 82. Zenayetta's was an 81. Mineshaft and Candy Ride at Lane's Ends stallions and Invaser at Shadwell, all had 83s. So the evidence points to a very good horse but comparisons with Secretariat, who broke the track record in all three classic races seems not supported by the facts.[4]

AP's stud fee is $200,000+. His sire, Pioneer of the Nile, had his stud fee raised from $60,000 to $125,000 and that was before this final brilliant grand slam. At reputed 175 breeds per year, a gross income of $35 million for the owners of AP. Coolmore America's reputed $6 or $9 million purchase (plus possibly some performance adjustments) of the breeding rights for AP as a two year old sure looks like a jackpot! That's a lot of breeds but it shows the high demand for AP offspring.

Mike Smith with 22 Breeders' Cup wins, many more than any other jockey, guided Effinix, who was 33–1 at the track and a whopping 119–1 on Betfair, to a second place finish. Honor Code made his run but there was just too much ground to make up given the perfect setup for AP but he did get third. The payoffs at the track on AP were 3.40 to win, 3.00 to place (the wise bet), and 2.40. Effinex paid 14.20 and 6.20 to place and show. Honor Code paid 3.40 to show. That was worth $500,000 in earnings

[4]Steve Roman argues that had AP been in a very fast pace with suicidal fractions, he likely would have collapsed and got beat — maybe by Honor Code. Steve points out, as two examples of wire to wire greatness, Spend a Buck's 1985 Jersey Derby run three weeks after his wire to wire Kentucky Derby win (which I recall as I was there and the dosage theory had a perfect 1-2 finish with the exacta paying almost $100 for $2). After fractions of 45.2 and 1.09 for six furlongs keeping up with speed ball Huddle Up, Spend a Buck beat future Belmont winner Creme Fraiche, who was a top quality classic runner, by a neck. The second was Affirmed's 1979 Hollywood Gold Cup. He went wire to wire despite fractions of 45.3, 1.09.3 and the mile in 1:34.1. Affirmed was never more that a head in front of Sirlad, a three time champion in Italy. Sirlad set records at Hollywood Park on the prior and succeeding races at 9 and 12 furlongs. Affirmed was also able to beat Alydar by close margins in all three triple crown races with the two of them close together all the race.

so he now retires having won $2,518,260. The chart for the race is in the footnote.[5]

In the betting, I was able to get AP at 2.0–1 to 2.8–1 US odds on Betfair in the futures and 9–1 on Honor Code. AP was much more favored at the track. I was long mostly Honor Code, some Tonalist, some Gleneagles and Keen Ice and slight net short on AP on all the bets which were some 6 pages on my Betfair account. My goal was to have it such that a group of four or five horses I was long on or neutral would have a net gain so I was hedged like the stock market but the result of short 20 small win bets on AP even at decent odds made me slightly net short.

Just prior to the race, I made a large bet to show at US odds of 1.6 to 1 on Honor Code or $5.20 equivalent. That made up for my slightly short win bet on AP despite those win bets on AP at odds a lot higher than at the track. A mistake was not betting a lot on AP to place, the usual less than even money bet.

So Honor Code goes to a stud career at Lane's End and hopefully I make a gain on my $52,000 investment with some of the net earnings of the nine horses in the group with most of it from Honor Code, plus a share of Honor Code's future stud fees. During the week before the Breeders' Cup, Liam's

---

ELEVENTH RACE
Keeneland
OCTOBER 31, 2015

$1\frac{1}{4}$ MILES. (2.00^{00}) 32ND RUNNING OF THE BREEDERS' CUP CLASSIC. Grade I. Purse $5,000,000 FOR THREE-YEAR-OLDS AND UPWARD. Northern Hemisphere Three-Year-Olds, 122 lbs.; Older, 126 lbs.; Southern Hemisphere Three-Year-Olds, 117 lbs.; Older, 126 lbs. All Fillies and Mares allowed 3 lbs. $50,000 to pre-enter, $50,000 to enter, with guaranteed $5 million purse including travel awards of which 55% to the owner of the winner, 18% to second, 10% to third, 6% to fourth and 3% to fifth; plus travel awards to starters not based in Kentucky.

Value of Race: $4,550,000 Winner $2,750,000; second $900,000; third $500,000; fourth $300,000; fifth $100,000. Mutuel Pool $8,269,736.00 Exacta Pool $4,553,714.00 Superfecta Pool $2,411,198.00 Super High Five Pool $290,125.00 Trifecta Pool $4,070,105.00

Last Raced	Horse	M/Eqt.	A.	Wt	PP	¼	½	¾	1	Str	Fin	Jockey	Odds $1
29Aug15 ^{11}Sar^{2}	American Pharoah	L	3	122	4	1^{1}	1^{1}	1^{2}	$1^{3\frac{1}{2}}$	1^{5}	$1^{6\frac{1}{2}}$	Espinoza V	0.70
3Oct15 ^{10}Bel^{3}	Effinex	L b	4	126	6	$2^{\frac{1}{2}}$	2^{3}	2^{1}	2^{2}	$2^{3\frac{1}{2}}$	$2^{4\frac{1}{2}}$	Smith M E	33.00
3Oct15 ^{5}Bel^{3}	Honor Code	L	4	126	8	8	8	8	$5^{\frac{1}{2}}$	$5^{1\frac{1}{2}}$	$3^{1\frac{1}{2}}$	Castellano J J	4.70
29Aug15 ^{11}Sar^{1}	Keen Ice	L	3	122	2	$5^{1\frac{1}{2}}$	$5^{1\frac{1}{2}}$	$5^{\frac{1}{2}}$	7^{2}	6^{hd}	4no	Ortiz I Jr	9.70
3Oct15 ^{10}Bel^{1}	Tonalist	L f	4	126	1	$3^{1\frac{1}{2}}$	3^{hd}	$4^{6\frac{1}{2}}$	4^{4}	4^{2}	5no	Velazquez J R	6.00
26Sep15 ^{10}SA^{6}	Hard Aces	L b	5	126	7	7^{3}	7^{5}	$6^{\frac{1}{2}}$	6^{1}	7^{4}	6^{hd}	Talamo J	72.80
19Sep15 ^{10}Prx^{1}	Frosted	L b	3	122	3	$4^{1\frac{1}{2}}$	$4^{4\frac{1}{2}}$	3^{hd}	3^{1}	$3^{\frac{1}{2}}$	$7^{12\frac{1}{2}}$	Rosario J	11.30
17Oct15 ^{4}ASC^{6}	Gleneagles-Ire	L	3	122	5	6^{hd}	$6^{\frac{1}{2}}$	$7^{2\frac{1}{2}}$	8	8	8	Moore R L	11.10

OFF AT 5:52 Start Good For All But GLENEAGLES (IRE). Won driving. Track fast.
TIME :23^{4}, :47^{2}, 1:11^{1}, 1:35^{2}, 2:00 (:23.99, :47.50, 1:11.21, 1:35.47, 2:00.07)
(New Track Record)

$2 Mutuel Prices:				
	4 –AMERICAN PHAROAH	3.40	3.00	2.40
	6 –EFFINEX		14.20	6.60
	9 –HONOR CODE			3.40

$2 EXACTA 4–6 PAID $76.40 $2 SUPERFECTA 4–6–9–2 PAID $1,224.00 $1 SUPER HIGH FIVE 4–6–9–2–1 PAID $1,715.10 $2 TRIFECTA 4–6–9 PAID $322.60

[5] **B. c, (Feb), by Pioneerof the Nile – Littleprincessemma, by Yankee Gentleman. Trainer Baffert Bob. Bred by Zayat Stables (Ky).**

Map was sold. As part of the deal our group 8 traded one half share of our four and a half shares of Honor Code for one share of Liam's Map. Honor Code had narrowly beaten Liam's Map in the Whitney with both horses running 113 Beyers. Later Liam's Map ran a 114 in the $1\frac{1}{4}$ mile grade 1 Woodward which he won by 4 lengths. This along with Beholder's 114 in the Pacific Classic, were the fastest races of 2015.

Liam's Map winning the Breeders' Cup Dirt Mile.

Liam's Map was a 1–2 favorite for the Breeders' Cup Las Vegas Dirt Mile run on Friday, October 30. His trainer, Todd Pletcher, and owners wanted a Breeders' Cup win so they put him in an easier race than the Classic. The script was wire to wire like AP but he stumbled at the start, was third behind Bradester and Mr Z who set fractions of 23.10 seconds for the quarter and 46.23 for the half mile. Liam's Map was fighting with JJ Castellano and had a lot of traffic problems but still won easily by $2\frac{1}{2}$ lengths, ably guided by J.J. Castellano, again showing why J.J. is America's top jockey in money earnings.

Lea finished second $3\frac{1}{4}$ lengths ahead of Red Vine who finished $3\frac{1}{4}$ lengths ahead of Wicked Strong. So the top four finished in order of their odds. Valid, Mr Z, Street Strategy, War Story, Bradester, and Tapiture completed the order of finish. He won $550,000 of the $1 million purse and set the track record in 1:34.54 a lot below the previous track of 1:36.23 set by Street Strategy on October 9.

Liam's Map was an $800,000 yearling purchase by Unbridled Song out of Miss Macy Sue by Trippi. He retires to stud with six wins and two seconds in 8 starts with $1,358,940 earnings. Both he and Honor Code are now at Lane's end. Their stud fees are \$25,000 and \$40,000, respectively. Their books with about 150 matings planned, are full and over subscribed. Tonalist is the latest to be retired for stud duty at Lane's End. He won the Belmont beating California Chrome and three other grade I races. In their two meetings, Honor Code prevailed. His stud fee at \$25,000 is the same as Liam's Map and Carpe Diem. Like the others, Carpe Diem is also is great demand and over subscribed. With his better pedigree, more explosive style and, likely, more left to prove in his brief injury plagued career, Honor Code has a certain edge over Liam's Map and Carpe Diem.

21.2. After the Classic

Honor Code, Liam's Map and American Pharoah were retired for stud duty. Honor Code was scheduled to breed to about 140 mares with the best book of mares ever at Lane's End. Our group has four of the forty shares so we receive four breeds which we are selling as seasons in the \$40,000 stud fee area plus we will receive a portion of the funds from the rest of the breeds. But there are considerable costs associated with the breeding including injury or death and fertility insurance. Hopefully the net revenue stream plus the net racing winnings mostly from Honor Code's more than \$2.5 million earnings and Liam's Map's earnings in the Breeders' Cup plus proceeds from our one share of the 50 shares. Our group sold one season for \$30,000, above the standard stud fee with no guarantee plus 2% of the net pooled revenue for mares breed outside the syndicate.

So far Liam's Map has been the more successful sire and his 2021 fee was \$30,000 vs. Honor Code's \$20,000. Both have had excellent offspring. Liam's Map has had Basin, Wicked Whisper and Colonel Liam, all of which have won grade I's. Honor Code has grade I winner and Kentucky Derby top horse Honor AP. He also had Max Player who was in all three triple crown races. Honor AP is now in stud at Lanes End, his 2021 fee was \$15,000.

Both Liam's Map and Honor Code are champions. Honor Code was AP Indy's fifth champion following Mineshaft (Older Male and Horse of the Year), Benardini (Three Year Old Male), Rags to Riches (Three Year Filly), and Tempura (Two Year Old Filly). Tonalist, at \$25,000 fee, was also retired to stud at Lane's End. He, Liam's Map and Honor Code were the three horses nominated for Eclipse Older Male Horse of the Year, with Honor Code the winner as he had beaten both Liam's Map and Tonalist.

Honor Code and Liam's Map arriving at Lane's End.

Investment in horses in training is risky and in most cases is a losing proposition. With a star like Honor Code, we might make a profit. More promising is owning shares in horses that breed. I did that with Carpe Diem who won grade 1 races at two and three years old and was one of the top three year olds. There are 50 shares with a value of $10 million. He sold as a yearling for $600,000 then as a two year old for $1.6 million. The farm gets fees plus some shares plus the original shares that were sold for $200,000. The owners have four years of two breeds per year plus part of the other breeds plus some fees if Carpe Diem is breeding in Brazil or Australia in the off season.

Over the years we sold some seasons and foals, raced some, still have some and I sold back my half share in 2019 with a net gain on the process. Currently I own or co-own two mares: Summer Chant whose pedigree includes two Kentucky Derby and two Belmont Stakes winners and Beginner's Luck sired by Awesome Again who won the Breeders' Cup Classic as did his son Ghostzapper, arguably the fastest horse since Secretariat.

My stable includes one horse running, some horses in training, some breeding and some foals for sale later.

Chapter 22

The Pick 6 and the Rainbow Pick 6

William T. Ziemba

The $2 Pick 6 is too expensive for most bettors to have a decent chance of winning. So it's been more or less replaced by the Rainbow Pick 6 except in Belmont which has a $1 Pick 6. Chapter 23 discusses an interesting Pick 6 at Belmont. In the Rainbow, the tickets cost 20 cents, on tenth of the ordinary Pick 6, and the first prize is a lottery like unique Pick 6 that generates large carryovers. Second prize is the ordinary Pick 6. Splits vary, for example Gulfstream is 60–40 which yields huge carryovers in the millions and Churchill Downs is 10–90 which yields more or less an ordinary Pick 6 at low prices. I discuss some of these and strategies to play ordinary and forced payout days.

The ordinary Pick 6 has been a major bet at racetracks for years. To win the first prize one must get the winner of six separate races with a second prize consolation 5 of 6 paying about 25% of the net pool. At $2 per combination the bet is very expensive. Since it is hard to win the Pick 6 the pool often carries over to create large payoffs. However, since it takes about $3-7,000 to generate a ticket that has a very good chance of winning on a typical day, the bet has dwindled in pool size because of this large outlay. In recent years this ordinary Pick 6, while still offered at most racetracks has been basically replaced by the Rainbow Pick 6 which has ticket cost of 10 or 20 cents per combination. In the Rainbow, the first prize is for the unique Pick 6 which is hard to get since the low priced ticket yields multiple winners on most days. So the carryover gets larger and larger, typically in the millions. Second prize is the shared ordinary Pick 6 which gets a percentage of the net pool. However, at the end of meets and at other times there is mandatory payout of the accumulated carryover pool. So then the Rainbow is really an ordinary Pick 6. In what follows I describe some examples of ordinary and Rainbow Pick 6s.

22.1. Theory of Pricing the Bets

22.1.1. *2001 Breeders' cup insurance bets for SCA*

22.1.1.1. *Insuring the Pick 6*

In 1991, my late racing colleague Cary Fotias and I were hired by the SCA insurance company of Dallas, Texas, to help insure the Breeders' Cup which was at Belmont near New York City. We insured the $2 to $3 million part. So the insurance company would guarantee a pool of $3 million. For example, if $2.15 million was bet, they would be liable for $850,000. We studied and proposed to bet a random amount if needed.

Xtra Heat in Hall of Fame.

The idea being to get to \$3 million and return the insurance company's money by winning Pick 6s and Pick 5/6s. It was risky as September 11 had just occurred and all the Arab owners such as Sheik Mohammed of Dubai were not in attendance. Their horses and trainers were though. It turned out to be a glorious day so the crowd sent the Pick 6 pool well over \$4 million. Our client, Bob Hammond, himself a famous bridge player, said you two can just play about \$25–30,000 of the tickets. So we had a \$2000 ticket twice and what we call a gorilla ticket for \$28,000. We had some 5/6s and got most of the money back. The Pick 6 paid about \$250,000. The race we lost was the sprint. Squirtle Squirt, which my handicapping colleague did not like at 9–1 beat the front running filly, Xtra Heat at 14–1, who we had and had led all the way until the finish. So if she had won we would have had three about \$450,000 Pick 6s plus more 5/6s. Squirtle Squirt had run at Belmont and had the top jockey Jerry Bailey and was trained by the recently deceased legendary trainer Broadway Bobby Frankel. Too bad. But it was fun! But the next week we won a similar case at Santa Anita, while guaranteeing a \$1 million Pick 6, collecting \$240,000 for the client and a nice bonus for us. I learned a lesson: when in doubt about including a horse on the ticket, it usually pays to add it and increase the cost.

22.2. The One That Got Away: The Hitable \$2 Million Pick 6 at the 2009 Breeders Cup

The Breeders' Cup then had 14 major races over two days and was held again at Santa Anita on Saturday, November 6 and 7. I went in 2008 and it is fun to see it live.[1] That year (2009) on wide screen high definition TV it was wonderful to watch. Being at home, the handicapping and betting is a lot easier. There are many opinions. That's what makes a horse race. The spreads on Betfair are fairly tight and it is easy to bet from Canada and you frequently get better odds there than at the track. We don't actually bet at the track but bet through rebate shops that give back part of the track take. That's easy to do on the phone or by email. The rebaters take their cut and the track gets more easy, low expense business to up their revenues.

As usual, the big race was the \$5 million classic. It is no longer the world's richest race. The Pegasus, Dubai World Cup and Saudi Cup have

[1] From subsequent years there have been 13–15 Breeders Cup races.

this honor. Their purses vary from year to year with the Pegasus at $16.3 million in 2018 and the Dubai at $12 million. In 2019, the Pegasus had dirt and grass races with purses of $9 and $7 million, respectively. In 2020 and 2021, the Saudi Cup was $20 million plus all expenses paid.

But the Breeders' Cup Classic is the most important race in the world and frequently determines the horse of the year. The two candidates for horse of the year were both female. The three-year-old Rachel Alexandra won all her 2009 races. She beat the top females in the top female races by 20 lengths. I was at Churchill Downs to see this in the Kentucky Oaks held on the first Friday in May, the day before the Kentucky Derby. In four races against males, she beat all of them handily. So she would normally be an almost sure bet for horse of the year. But Zenyatta, a five year old mare had won all 13 of her races but always against females and mostly in California on polytrack. She had a dynamite kick and just cruises by the other horses near the buzzer to win easily. Some of her races were in slow times (76 area on the Equiform scale that I follow) and some in fast times (81 area). To put this scale in perspective, the highest I ever saw was four 84s by Ghostzapper. These are zero's on the late Len Ragozin's scale.

One of my most treasured but small bets was on Ghostzapper's 2004 Breeders' Cup Classic win. There was a top filly in that race, Azeri — I had watched her at Saratoga getting beat by females in a $1\frac{1}{4}$ race so despite the fact that she had numerous wins at short distances I was pretty sure she would not be in the top 4 in this male dominated $1\frac{1}{4}$ race. So a $20 superfecta bet in 2004 boxing for $5 Ghostzapper (1 or 2) with Roses in May (1 or 2) with the two next leading horses, Pleasantly Perfect and Perfect Drift (3 or 4) and (3 or 4) came in to provide a $5000 payoff. The big mistake was not betting more! Ghostzapper ran the $1\frac{1}{4}$ race in 1:59:02, faster than Secretariat's record setting Kentucky Derby 1:59:40. The 5–2 odds were quite generous given Ghostzapper's brilliant record.

The 13/13 of Zenyatta is historic since only Personal Ensign (13/13) in 1988 and Colin (15/15) in 1907 had undefeated records in the US. Tesio, the great Italian trainer in the 1930s–1950s had three of the four undefeated horses since 1900, among horses with at least ten major races at major race tracks in Europe. Tesio was a great anomaly person looking at many many generations to breed cheap to cheap to get great champions. He did this without computers and with a lot of help from his wife, see chapter 20. Frankel in 2013 retired undefeated running on the grass in the UK beating all opposition there handily to be the fourth undefeated horse. He was never sent to the Breeders Cup or the US. One way to check such matings is to go to Steve Roman who does this for ten generations back. See Roman (2016) for much valuable information.

The Europeans and many other handicappers were pushing for Rip Van Winkle, trained by Irish legend Aidan O'Brien was the pick since he had won his two races on 2009 when he did not face the superstar Sea the Stars. The three times Sea the Stars beat Rip Van Winkle, but he was close behind and well ahead of the competition. Unfortunately, the Sea the Stars' connections preferred to hedge and cash in on this horse reputed to be the best in Europe in ten years by retiring him to stud duties. He had won the Epson Derby, the 2000 Guineas and the ARC. Perhaps they recalled the last "best horse of the decade", Dancing Brave, who "could not lose" but finished fourth in the classic. The polytrack at Santa Anita not dirt or the European's grass could have been a factor too.

Getting back to Zenyatta and Rip Van Winkle. The Betfair and track odds showed the local biases. You could get better odds on Zenyatta in Europe on Betfair and Rip Van Winkle in the US at the track. It was not possible to do an arbitrage here. I just concentrated on better odds on Zenyatta on Betfair. My assumption was despite the fact that her running times were not super outstanding she had the will to win. And indeed she did with Rip Van Winkle finishing out of the money. She could have been retired as the only undefeated mare who beat males in the toughest race in the world.

But let's discuss the Pick 6. In the Pick 6, to win you must have all six winners who share 75% of the net pool with the 5/6 sharing the remaining 25%. The Pick 6 was Races 4–9. There were three standouts but they were definitely not certain winners. The other three races seemed wide open. So you could play the Pick 6 in the following way: I thought about doing this but did not — it was a \$2 million mistake. You have a single ticket with about 10 horses in the three wide open races and single the three standouts. That would cost about 10*10*10*1*1*1*\$2 = \$2000, not a large Pick 6 ticket. You only win if all three standouts win and they did.

The payoffs for \$2 win tickets were as follows:

Race 4	Dancing in Silks	52.60	
Race 5	Value of York	63.20	
Race 6	Goldikova	4.80	the first standout
Race 7	Furthest Land	44.60	
Race 8	Conduit	3.80	the second standout
Race 9	Zenyatta	7.60	the third standout

Goldikova was the winner of the mile grass race in 2008 and was arguably better this year. Her connections were the same as those of Miesque, also a two time winner of this race. The second standout, Conduit, was also the winner last year of the $1\frac{1}{2}$ mile turf.

The Pick 6 paid $1,838,305.20 for one winning 6/6 ticket and the 3*9 = 27 Pick 5/6 tickets (of the 10 losers in the three wide open races) paid 27*$4822.40 for a total of $130,204.80 plus the 6% rebate on the $2000 of $120 for a grand total of $1,968,630.00. It is not quite $2 million but as Johnnie Hooker played by Robert Redford in the Sting said: “it's not enough but it's close”. Of course, taxes would take 25% at the track and be sorted out later when filing and my winning would depress the Pick 6 and Pick 5/6 prizes.

The big question is would I have gotten these three winners from my 10 picks in these races? Of course, more than 10 was possible. So let's look at these three races. I use about 5–6 handicapping services plus my own analysis of the daily racing form and the Equiform pace numbers. So the idea is to handicap the handicappers. In many bets this is computerized.

Race 4. The Sprint, 6 furlongs Handicapper #1 had 3–1–5–6 (the winner, Dancing in Silks) –8–4 Handicapper #2 had 5–3–8–1–6 So at 12–1 that's one of the 10 for sure especially when you observe that its last race Beyer speed rating at 106 was the highest of any horse in the race and it was right there at Santa Anita. Three of the horses ran higher Beyers than #6 but not in their last race. Actually there were only nine horses in this race so likely I would have taken them all including the 20–1 shot #2 and the 30–1 shot #7, neither of which listed above. #2 had a Beyer of 110 in a grade I at Santa Anita so must be used. #7 looked greatly outclassed.

Race 5. Juvenile two-year-olds on polytrack with 13 horses The winner Vale of York (#7) was racing in the UK and in Italy. He always had short odds and had two wins in five races and was close in the other three races. The morning line odds were 20–1. Handicapper #1 had 5–13–4–9–10–8 (so no 7 but he was a foreign shipper so likely not rated by this US service). Handicapper #2 had 13–4–9–5–6. Only handicapper James Quinn with 13–8–11–5–7–6 had 7 anywhere. These are two-year olds so there is a lot of noise. There were four other longshot horses one at 20–1, one at 15–1, one at 30–1 and one at 50–1. So going with all 13 horses called all is suggested.

Race 7. Dirt Mile #2 Furthest Land won with 10 in the field. #1 had 4–3–7–1–9–2 (the winner). Handicapper #2 had 3–7–2–8. The pace numbers are competitive. So 2 at 20–1 must be used.

Summary: All three of the wide open races had winners that were competitive horses. So they would be on our ticket. But even if we bet on all horses in these three races, the ticket only costs 9*13*10*1*1*1 = $2340. This ticket made a lot of sense so I should have played it.[2] It would have had 8+11+9 = 28 Pick 5/6s. Oh well, there is always next year.

22.3. A Big P6 Win

An example of the multiple ticket approach: consider the Pick 6, Santa Anita, March 6, 2002 (Figure 22.1) with $202,790 carryover from Sunday's wagers.

An example: Consider the Pick 6

Santa Anita, March 6, 2002 with $202,790 carryover from Sunday's wagers

Race	3	4	5	6	7	8
Win Payoff	3.60	4.60	12.00	9.20	18.00	7.20

1-5 shot out of the money

Advantage $\equiv \prod_{i=1}^{6}$ (1+edge$_i$)

Pick 6 $86,347.60 - one large transaction cost

Parlay $15,452.40 - six races, six smaller transactions costs

Bet = 1922	1 Pick 6		Score 6	$4
Rebate = 154	11 Pick 5/6	692.00	7	$58
Net bet = 1768	Gross =	93,691.80	8	$376
			9	$1484
				1922

Score 9: you win if the score is 9 or less, here 3 I's, 2 II's, total 9 so we won.

[2] Another way to play this is to have three sets of tickets in which you assume that at least two of the three standouts will win. So you have $N_1^i, N_2^i, N_3^i, N_4^i, 1, 1$ combinations, $i = 1, 2, 3$ all at $2 each. So depending on the N_j^i you likely have a larger ticket than the three singles approach. You might win more than one Pick 6 and more Pick 5/6s, but you might miss the Pick 6 as well unless the tickets are well spread.

Race	3	4	5	6	7	8
I	1, 3	3	7	3	2	2
II	7	1,5	1,2,5,6	4,7,8,10	1,4	5.9
III	5,6	2,4,8		1,2,5		1,6,7,8

8 was scratched

This $1922 ticket was actually 66 separate tickets.

The winning ticket will have one 6/6 winner and multiple 5/6 winners

			Morning Line
Race	1	Madame Pietra	3–1
	2	Love at Noon	3–5
	3	Harvest Girl	8–1
	4	Filigree	4–1
	5	Farah Love	12–1

In Figure 22.2, the behavioral key was that Filigree, the third choice in the morning line in Race 7 went off at 8–1. In the 3rd and 5th races back, he ran faster than the favorite Love at Noon ran in his last two races. So he had a chance to win and he did. So Love at Noon went off at 1–5 and had most of the P6 money so there was a big payoff for the P6 when he lost.

Approximate Kelly with more money on higher probability wagers.

```
$2.00 ;P6; (3) 1 ,3 /(4) 3 /(5) 7 /(6) 3 /(7) 2 /(8) 2
$2.00 ;P6; (3) 7 /(4) 3 /(5) 7 /(6) 3 /(7) 2 /(8) 2
$2.00 ;P6; (3) 1 ,3 /(4) 1 ,5 /(5) 7 /(6) 3 /(7) 2 /(8) 2
$2.00 ;P6; (3) 1 ,3 /(4) 3 /(5) 2 ,3 ,5 ,6 /(6) 3 /(7) 2 /(8) 2
$2.00 ;P6; (3) 1 ,3 /(4) 3 /(5) 7 /(6) 4 ,7 ,8 ,10 /(7) 2 /(8) 2
$2.00 ;P6; (3) 1 ,3 /(4) 3 /(5) 7 /(6) 3 /(7) 1 ,4 /(8) 2
$2.00 ;P6; (3) 1 ,3 /(4) 3 /(5) 7 /(6) 3 /(7) 2 /(8) 5 ,9
$2.00 ;P6; (3) 5 ,6 /(4) 3 /(5) 7 /(6) 3 /(7) 2 /(8) 2
$2.00 ;P6; (3) 1 ,3 /(4) 2 ,4 ,8 /(5) 7 /(6) 3 /(7) 2 /(8) 2
$2.00 ;P6; (3) 1 ,3 /(4) 3 /(5) 7 /(6) 1 ,2 ,5 /(7) 2 /(8) 2
$2.00 ;P6; (3) 1 ,3 /(4) 3 /(5) 7 /(6) 3 /(7) 2 /(8) 1 ,6 ,7 ,8
$2.00 ;P6; (3) 7 /(4) 1 ,5 /(5) 7 /(6) 3 /(7) 2 /(8) 2
$2.00 ;P6; (3) 7 /(4) 3 /(5) 2 ,3 ,5 ,6 /(6) 3 /(7) 2 /(8) 2
$2.00 ;P6; (3) 7 /(4) 3 /(5) 7 /(6) 4 ,7 ,8 ,10 /(7) 2 /(8) 2
$2.00 ;P6; (3) 7 /(4) 3 /(5) 7 /(6) 3 /(7) 1 ,4 /(8) 2
$2.00 ;P6; (3) 7 /(4) 3 /(5) 7 /(6) 3 /(7) 2 /(8) 5 ,9
$2.00 ;P6; (3) 1 ,3 /(4) 1 ,5 /(5) 2 ,3 ,5 ,6 /(6) 3 /(7) 2 /(8) 2
$2.00 ;P6; (3) 1 ,3 /(4) 1 ,5 /(5) 7 /(6) 4 ,7 ,8 ,10 /(7) 2 /(8) 2
$2.00 ;P6; (3) 1 ,3 /(4) 1 ,5 /(5) 7 /(6) 3 /(7) 1 ,4 /(8) 2
$2.00 ;P6; (3) 1 ,3 /(4) 1 ,5 /(5) 7 /(6) 3 /(7) 2 /(8) 5 ,9
$2.00 ;P6; (3) 1 ,3 /(4) 3 /(5) 2 ,3 ,5 ,6 /(6) 4 ,7 ,8 ,10 /(7) 2 /(8) 2
$2.00 ;P6; (3) 1 ,3 /(4) 3 /(5) 2 ,3 ,5 ,6 /(6) 3 /(7) 1 ,4 /(8) 2
$2.00 ;P6; (3) 1 ,3 /(4) 3 /(5) 2 ,3 ,5 ,6 /(6) 3 /(7) 2 /(8) 5 ,9
$2.00 ;P6; (3) 1 ,3 /(4) 3 /(5) 7 /(6) 4 ,7 ,8 ,10 /(7) 1 ,4 /(8) 2
$2.00 ;P6; (3) 1 ,3 /(4) 3 /(5) 7 /(6) 4 ,7 ,8 ,10 /(7) 2 /(8) 5 ,9
$2.00 ;P6; (3) 1 ,3 /(4) 3 /(5) 7 /(6) 3 /(7) 1 ,4 /(8) 5 ,9
$2.00 ;P6; (3) 5 ,6 /(4) 1 ,5 /(5) 7 /(6) 3 /(7) 2 /(8) 2
$2.00 ;P6; (3) 5 ,6 /(4) 3 /(5) 2 ,3 ,5 ,6 /(6) 3 /(7) 2 /(8) 2
$2.00 ;P6; (3) 5 ,6 /(4) 3 /(5) 7 /(6) 4 ,7 ,8 ,10 /(7) 2 /(8) 2
$2.00 ;P6; (3) 5 ,6 /(4) 3 /(5) 7 /(6) 3 /(7) 1 ,4 /(8) 2
$2.00 ;P6; (3) 5 ,6 /(4) 3 /(5) 7 /(6) 3 /(7) 2 /(8) 5 ,9
$2.00 ;P6; (3) 7 /(4) 2 ,4 ,8 /(5) 7 /(6) 3 /(7) 2 /(8) 2
$2.00 ;P6; (3) 1 ,3 /(4) 2 ,4 ,8 /(5) 2 ,3 ,5 ,6 /(6) 3 /(7) 2 /(8) 2
$2.00 ;P6; (3) 1 ,3 /(4) 2 ,4 ,8 /(5) 7 /(6) 4 ,7 ,8 ,10 /(7) 2 /(8) 2
$2.00 ;P6; (3) 1 ,3 /(4) 2 ,4 ,8 /(5) 7 /(6) 3 /(7) 1 ,4 /(8) 2
$2.00 ;P6; (3) 1 ,3 /(4) 2 ,4 ,8 /(5) 7 /(6) 3 /(7) 2 /(8) 5 ,9
$2.00 ;P6; (3) 7 /(4) 3 /(5) 7 /(6) 1 ,2 ,5 /(7) 2 /(8) 2
$2.00 ;P6; (3) 1 ,3 /(4) 1 ,5 /(5) 7 /(6) 1 ,2 ,5 /(7) 2 /(8) 2
```

```
$2.00 ;P6; (3) 1 ,3 /(4) 3 /(5) 2 ,3 ,5 ,6 /(6) 1 ,2 ,5 /(7) 2 /(8) 2
$2.00 ;P6; (3) 1 ,3 /(4) 3 /(5) 7 /(6) 1 ,2 ,5 /(7) 1 ,4 /(8) 2
$2.00 ;P6; (3) 1 ,3 /(4) 3 /(5) 7 /(6) 1 ,2 ,5 /(7) 2 /(8) 5 ,9
$2.00 ;P6; (3) 7 /(4) 3 /(5) 7 /(6) 3 /(7) 2 /(8) 1 ,6 ,7 ,8
$2.00 ;P6; (3) 1 ,3 /(4) 1 ,5 /(5) 7 /(6) 3 /(7) 2 /(8) 1 ,6 ,7 ,8
$2.00 ;P6; (3) 1 ,3 /(4) 3 /(5) 2 ,3 ,5 ,6 /(6) 3 /(7) 2 /(8) 1 ,6 ,7 ,8
$2.00 ;P6; (3) 1 ,3 /(4) 3 /(5) 7 /(6) 4 ,7 ,8 ,10 /(7) 2 /(8) 1 ,6 ,7 ,8
$2.00 ;P6; (3) 1 ,3 /(4) 3 /(5) 7 /(6) 3 /(7) 1 ,4 /(8) 1 ,6 ,7 ,8
$2.00 ;P6; (3) 7 /(4) 1 ,5 /(5) 2 ,3 ,5 ,6 /(6) 3 /(7) 2 /(8) 2
$2.00 ;P6; (3) 7 /(4) 1 ,5 /(5) 7 /(6) 4 ,7 ,8 ,10 /(7) 2 /(8) 2
$2.00 ;P6; (3) 7 /(4) 1 ,5 /(5) 7 /(6) 3 /(7) 1 ,4 /(8) 2
$2.00 ;P6; (3) 7 /(4) 1 ,5 /(5) 7 /(6) 3 /(7) 2 /(8) 5 ,9
$2.00 ;P6; (3) 7 /(4) 3 /(5) 2 ,3 ,5 ,6 /(6) 4 ,7 ,8 ,10 /(7) 2 /(8) 2
$2.00 ;P6; (3) 7 /(4) 3 /(5) 2 ,3 ,5 ,6 /(6) 3 /(7) 1 ,4 /(8) 2
$2.00 ;P6; (3) 7 /(4) 3 /(5) 2 ,3 ,5 ,6 /(6) 3 /(7) 2 /(8) 5 ,9
$2.00 ;P6; (3) 7 /(4) 3 /(5) 7 /(6) 4 ,7 ,8 ,10 /(7) 1 ,4 /(8) 2
$2.00 ;P6; (3) 7 /(4) 3 /(5) 7 /(6) 4 ,7 ,8 ,10 /(7) 2 /(8) 5 ,9
$2.00 ;P6; (3) 7 /(4) 3 /(5) 7 /(6) 3 /(7) 1 ,4 /(8) 5 ,9
$2.00 ;P6; (3) 1 ,3 /(4) 1 ,5 /(5) 2 ,3 ,5 ,6 /(6) 4 ,7 ,8 ,10 /(7) 2 /(8) 2
$2.00 ;P6; (3) 1 ,3 /(4) 1 ,5 /(5) 2 ,3 ,5 ,6 /(6) 3 /(7) 1 ,4 /(8) 2
$2.00 ;P6; (3) 1 ,3 /(4) 1 ,5 /(5) 2 ,3 ,5 ,6 /(6) 3 /(7) 2 /(8) 5 ,9
$2.00 ;P6; (3) 1 ,3 /(4) 1 ,5 /(5) 7 /(6) 4 ,7 ,8 ,10 /(7) 1 ,4 /(8) 2
$2.00 ;P6; (3) 1 ,3 /(4) 1 ,5 /(5) 7 /(6) 4 ,7 ,8 ,10 /(7) 2 /(8) 5 ,9
$2.00 ;P6; (3) 1 ,3 /(4) 1 ,5 /(5) 7 /(6) 3 /(7) 1 ,4 /(8) 5 ,9
$2.00 ;P6; (3) 1 ,3 /(4) 3 /(5) 2 ,3 ,5 ,6 /(6) 4 ,7 ,8 ,10 /(7) 1 ,4 /(8) 2
$2.00 ;P6; (3) 1 ,3 /(4) 3 /(5) 2 ,3 ,5 ,6 /(6) 4 ,7 ,8 ,10 /(7) 2 /(8) 5 ,9
$2.00 ;P6; (3) 1 ,3 /(4) 3 /(5) 2 ,3 ,5 ,6 /(6) 3 /(7) 1 ,4 /(8) 5 ,9
$2.00 ;P6; (3) 1 ,3 /(4) 3 /(5) 7 /(6) 4 ,7 ,8 ,10 /(7) 1 ,4 /(8) 5 ,9
```

	Amount bet	
Score 6	$2	$4
Score 7	$2	$58
Score 8	$2	$376
Score 9	$2	$1,484
Score 10	$2	$0
Score 11	$2	$0
Total 0.54%		$1,922

Figure 22.1. The tickets played for the P6 on March 6, 2002.

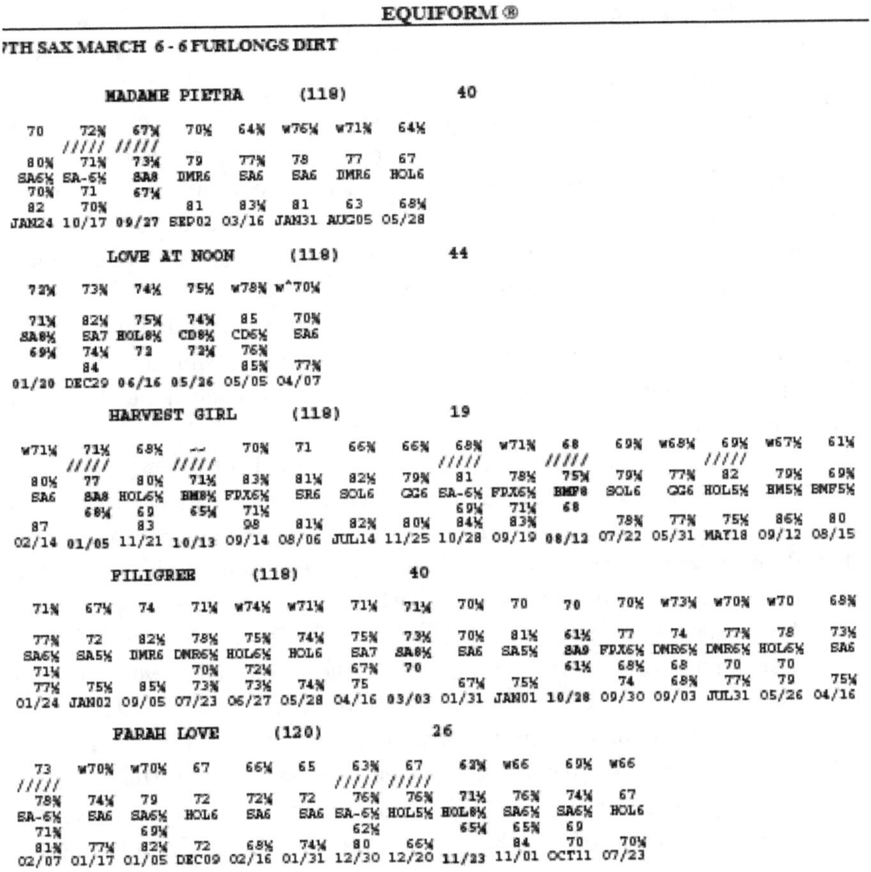

Figure 22.2. Equiform ratings Race 7, Santa Anita, March 6, 2002.

In the Equiform ratings Figure 22.2, the top number is the final speed number and the other numbers are pace numbers within the race.

22.4. The Rainbow Pick 6 at Gulfstream Park

The bet has two prizes. The jackpot is awarded to the holder of the unique Pick 6 ticket. If there is no unique Pick 6 winner but multiple P6 winners, then, after the very large 20% take, the net pool is given 60% to be divided by the multiple P6 winners to share and 40% goes to the carryover. If no one wins the P6 then the entire net pool goes to the carryover. So the expected value of a bet has three parts, namely:

EX = (Prob. you win the unique P6) times (Value of unique P6 which is the carryover plus today's entire net pool) + (Prob. you win a non-unique P6) times (Value of each share of P6) + Rebate.

What makes the bet difficult is that the Rainbow P6 tickets are 10 or 20 cents each rather than the usual \$2 in regular P6s. There is also no 5/6 consolation prize but that shared P6 second prize is awarded if there are two or more P6 winners. So with the cheap 10 cent tickets, \$300 will give you \$6000 worth of \$2 P6 action which frequently wins the P6. So almost for sure the P6 will have multiple winners.

Indeed in January and February 2013, the carryover built up to higher and higher amounts reaching \$3,107,159 by Thursday February 21, 2013. The jackpot was not won on that day so the carryover reached \$3,249,259.28 going into Friday.

It is clear that to have a chance to be the unique P6 winner you usually need 3, 4 or even 5 bombs. That is it is very unlikely to have so many longshots winning. Two bombs will not usually be enough because one can take all the horses in two races for say $10 \times 10 = 100$ combinations but that's only \$10 times the bets made in other races. So the strategy to win the jackpot must be to take some potential bombs in 3, 4, 5 or even 6 races along with some more favored horses in the other races. Observe that using all is not worth much — you can win a shared second prize but it is too expensive so you might win the P6 but lose money on the bet. And taking all in 3, 4, and 5 races becomes very expensive fast. Most of the time this focus on 3–4 potential bombs in 4, 5, or 6 races will lose as more favored horses win some of the time. But let's suppose we take the four longest odds horses in four races and we take two horses in the other two races. Then the cost $= \$0.10 \cdot 2^2 \cdot 4^4 = \$102.40$ less rebate.

But there are $\binom{6}{2}$ ways of doing this, that is 4 bombs and 2 other horses $= \frac{6!}{2!4!} = 15$. So we are up to \$1536 but the question is which of the 2 horses to pick in the other two races. So we might need more money. However we might need only 2 or 3 bomb possibilities in some of the other 4 races. So to do this, the cost is about \$1500 to \$3000 less the rather low rebate of about 3.5% per play. You might need 10 or more such plays to win the jackpot and you may never win. But with a carryover at over \$3 million, such a strategy has positive expectation and might work as the probability of winning can get close to one. In fact it did win on Friday February 22, 2013. The Rainbow P6 was Races 5–10. The payoffs of the winners for a \$2 ticket were:

R5 = \$114; R6 = \$11.40; R7 = \$36.80; R8 = \$17.20; R9 = \$23.60 and R10 = \$23.00.

Aside: playing the regular P6, the second prize requires different types of tickets and basically is not a good bet because of the 40% carryover and the large track take, so I agree with Andy Beyer's (2013) analysis of the part of the bet because going for the second prize has essentially zero chance of getting the jackpot namely the unique P6 win. Of course, rebates bring back about 8% but still the effective payback = 60(−80) + .08=0.56 or a whopping 44% take. Beyer did not mention rebate in his calculation but serious bettors certainly should use rebates.

But the jackpot has a positive expectation. That's hard to estimate as the probability of winning the first prize and the size of the shared second prize are both very hard to determine. While this approach gives a decent chance of eventually winning the first prize, it likely would give some second prizes but not enough to turn a profit unless the jackpot is won.

Let's now compute the parlay versus the actual payoff. The parlay is $0.1(\text{odds}_A+1)(\text{odds}_B+1)\ldots(\text{odds}_F+1) = \$0.1(57)(5.7)(18.4)(8.6)(11.8)(11.5) =$ \$697,663.23 But the parlay has six win track takes versus one P6 take but just on the new money bet on Friday. The carryover is not reduced by any additional track take.

The new money =

$$\frac{\$3,591,245.44 - \$3,240,259.28}{0.8} = \$438,732.70.$$

where we adjust by the 20% win track take on that day's bets.

So if we adjust by the win track take of 17%, we have for the true parlay value

$$0.1\frac{(57)(5.7)(18.4)(8.6)(11.8)(11.5)}{(1-0.17)^6} = \$1,608,904.69.$$

compared to the actual Rainbow P6 payout of \$3,591,245.44 which was the record payout for a single winner on the Rainbow 6 was on February 22, 2013. The record total P6 pool was on July 2, 2007 at Hollywood Park where the pool reached \$10,870,852.60 with 13 winners of \$576,064.40 each.

If the pool is not won, there are mandatory payout days. There was a mandatory payout on April 23, 2011 with a \$1.4 million carryover. The total pool reached \$5.1 million. There were 1,311 winning tickets each worth \$3,279.26. There was another mandatory payout on March 31, 2013, the last day of the meet. The pool had a carryover over \$2 million. So for this, it was optimal to go for second prize, namely, the regular P6 as there was no sense going for the unique P6. The P6 was won that day and paid \$3,932.32 for the \$0.10 ticket with win payoffs of Race 6 \$8.20, Race 7 %16.20, Race 8 \$13.80, Race 9 \$4.20, Race 10 \$22.00 and Race 11 \$9.80. Was the true payday below this payoff? The true parlay is $0.1(4.1)(8.2)(6.90)(2.10)(11.00)(14.90) =$ \$7,984.45.

In 2014, the Rainbow Pick 6 tickets were raised to 20 cents. Going into the May 26 mandatory payout, the carryover pool was \$6,303,426.30. On Sunday the pools was \$6,397.293/35 and Monday's, which was won, was \$6,678,939.12.

On March 31, 2014, one investor playing the \$2,721.60 ticket

1,2,4,5,7,8,9,10,12/1,2,4,5,7,8/1,2,3,6,8,9/1,2,3,4,5,7,8/1,3,4,5,6,7/6

won \$301,933.

Other payoffs were \$791,364, \$414,166.52 and \$327,110.71.

Following the May 26 mandatory payout, the Rainbow 6 was seeded with \$50,000 when racing resumed Friday, May 30. The next mandatory payout was June 29, the end of the fiscal year.

Gulfstream's Memorial Day payout had full fields for a total of 120 horses of which 79 horses (including 9 also eligibles and off the turf only runners) were entered in the Rainbow 6 races — Race 5 through Race 10. These races are:

- Race 5 to be run at $1\frac{1}{16}$ miles on turf with a field 12 of maidens, three-year-olds and up, and an also-eligible.
- Race 6 is at 6.5 furlongs on the main dirt track. The maiden special weight race attracted a field of 11, three-year-olds and up.
- Race 7 is at $1\frac{1}{16}$ miles on turf. The optional claiming allowance has a field of 12 and one also-eligible.
- Race 8 is six-furlongs on the main track. The \$6,250 claiming race has a field of 11 fillies and mares, three-year-olds and up.
- Race 9 is an optional claiming allowance at $1\frac{1}{16}$ miles on turf. A field of 12, along and four also-eligibles entered for a race for three-year-olds and up.
- Race 10 is a $1\frac{1}{16}$-mile race on turf. A field of 12 fillies and mares, plus 3 also-eligibles entered in the race for \$12,500 claimers.

A single bettor, Danny Borislow, won the whole P6 pool on Sunday May 25, 2014, a day before the mandatory payout. The payoffs of Races 3–8 with winning numbers 1–8–6–1–6–5 were \$35.80, \$22.60, \$12.80, \$10.40, \$9.60, and $12.80, respectively. Danny had two tickets each for $7,603.20 with the winning ticket being all-all-all-1,4-all-all as #1 won the 4th leg. The second ticket had the same five "alls" plus two other horses in leg 4.

The P4 for $1 was won for $1,620.80 but the P5 was not won even by the P6 winner. So a consolation 4/5 was paid for the 50 cent winners.

These races have two bombs and four 4–1 or 5–1 horses. Normally two bombs in the $20–30 range and four $10 horses would not yield just one unique P6 winner. The reason this bettor won seems to be low volume in the pool on Sunday as most bettors like me were preparing for Monday's mandatory payout. Also the short fields 6–6–6–10–7–13 allowed Danny to go all in five of the races and four deep in the fourth leg for his 7,603.20 times 2 or $15,206.40 investment.

The net increase in the pool on Sunday was $281,755.77 (total pool of 6,678,939.12 — carryover of 6,397,283.35), dividing by 0.80 gives the total bet of $352,194.71. This was more than Saturday's increase in the carryover of $93,857.05 or the $117,321.31 bet.

The parlay with six win takes of 17% was 0.2(17.9)(11.3)(6.4)(5.2)(4.8)(6.4) = 41,358.62. Then with no track take, the parlay is $4,135,861.62/(1-0.17)^6 = 126,502.02$ which compares to the payoff of 6,678,939.12 which has 20% taken off the total bet.

So bravo to Danny Borislow who seized a good opportunity to win the whole pool. Danny is the owner of the Magic Jack telephone device business. It is extremely unlikely that someone could get the whole pool on mandatory payout day as most likely there would be multiple P6 winners all going after a share of $10+ million pool.

A sad postscript: on Monday July 21, 2004, Danny collapsed and died at age 52 after playing in an indoor soccer game in West Palm Beach, Florida.

Another mandatory payout was on Thursday September 11, 2014. I was consulting in Asia and before I could get the information to construct a bet it was nightfall there and by morning the races were over. But it was very hitable and my strategy of going ***all*** in some races mixing up might have gotten the $48,407.92 payout for a $1000–3000 investment.

The mandatory payout pool had a carryover of $123,063 and on Thursday an additional $572,514 was bet. For the regular days, that is the non-mandatory payouts of the pool, the current payout rates are: 70% to those who pick the most winners, likely all six with 30% carryover. On August 7, a bettor won $40,807.18 with a unique P6. In this case, on September 11, despite the track being sloppy, there was only one bomb, namely a horse named Gameday Spanking ridden by jockey Pedro Monterrey, Jr, paying \$91.20 for a \$2 win ticket in the final Race 10. The other payoffs were:

Race	Horse #	Name	Payout for \$2 win
5	5	Quick Hall	7.80
6	9	R Lovely Lindsay	3.20
7	8	Saturday Special	8.40
8	1	Capriccio Blue	9.20
9	5	USS O'Brien	11.60
10	4	Gameday Spanking	91.20

So the ticket ***all*** in Race 10 (with 10 horses) along with 3–5 the top picks in the other five races got the winner. Than would have cost say $(4)^5 10(0.20) =$ \$512 less rebate. But more tickets would have been bet.

Let's look first at this bomb. Race 10 was a \$15,000 claiming race for 3 year old and upward over 6 furlongs on the dirt with a sloppy track.

HTR rated the horses 1–9–5–2–6–8–7–④–10–3. #4 was 12–1 in the morning line.

Horse	PSR	ML odds	Highest Beyer
1	79	5–2	(72)
2	76	10–1	(67)
3	51	20–1	(60)
④	58	12–1	(60)
5	68	6–1	(60)
6	73	5–1	(77)
7	59	12–1	(46)
8	55	10–1	(48)
9	76	3–1	(66)
10	59	20–1	(45)

#4 was a \$23,000 Keeneland purchase by English Channel out of the Deputy Minister mare Spanked, so the breeding was good. He won a 7 furlong race on February 28, 2014 in a \$10,000 claiming race. He also won a \$12,500 maiden race on December 8, 2013 at Churchill Downs. So #4 was certainly better than a 44-1 shot but was not a top pick so to get him you needed ***all*** or almost all in Race 10. So this is an interesting example with just one bomb. But remember this mandatory payout is a regular Pick 6, not the unique one.

The Rainbow mandatory payout on May 26 was $12,796.04 for a 20 cent ticket. The 50 cent Pick 5 paid $2,598.15 with consolation 4/5 paying $25.85.

There was another mandatory payout on Saturday March 26, 2016. Since being hit for $76,799.38 by one bettor on January 12, 2016, the Rainbow P6 had not been won for 52 racing days. The largest payout of that meet, which opened on December 5, 2015, was $262,634.84 on January 7, 2016. The current record payout was $6.678.939 on May 25, 2014, beating the previous record of $3,591,245 on February 22, 2013. On Wednesday $581,103 was bet with each P6 paying $17,546.64. Some $667,575 was wagered on Thursday which had second prize P6 winners, each receiving $16,248.88. Going into Friday, the carryover was $4,341,678.15. On Friday, $673,828 was wagered with the P6 paying $5,313.56, yielding a carryover going into Saturday from 53 programs with no unique P6 winner of $4,503,332.31.

The Saturday card Rainbow P6 was on Races 7–12. There was one stakes race, namely the $75,000 Sanibel Handicap. All the other races were claiming or maiden of some kind. The fields were big with more than 10 horses in each race. The various handicappers were as follows (winners are circled):

Race 7
HTR: 8,⑩,4,7,~~14~~
PSR: 8,⑩.6,4,1
John Swetye: 8/1,4,⑩/3,7/5,6
David McKenzie: 8
Ron Nicoletti: 8,4,7
Beer Ullman: 8,1,4,⑩,5
Wizard: 8/4,7/⑩
Crist: 8,4,⑩,5, 7
Highest Beyer: 1(63),2(55),4(70), 6(69), 8(83),10(64)

Finish:	10	Mighty Moe	8.60	4.00	3.00
	8	Sir Duddley Digges		2.60	2.40
	1	Ekati Wild Cat			5.00

Race 8
HTR: 2,①,3,7,6
PSR: 2,3,6,7,13,①
John Swetye: 2/3,6/①,4,7,14
David McKenzie: 3–~~11–13~~
Ron Nicoletti: 2,6,3
Beer Ullman: 2,①,5,12,6
Wizard: 6/2,3,11

Crist: 2,3,6,7,12
Highest Beyer: 1(83),2(84),3(94),4(82),5(83),6(85),7(85),8(82),9(75),10(72),11(79), 12(80)

Finish:	1	Derr Dog	15.60	6.40	480
	2	Great Attack		4.00	300
	3	Nobel Prince			3.80

Race 9
HTR: 1,11,13,6,2
PSR: 1,11,13,12,2
John Swetye: 1/2/6,10/③,4,12,13
David McKenzie: 13–1
Ron Nicoletti: 1,11,13
Beer Ullman: 1,③,7,11,12,6
Wizard: 2*,1,11,6
Crist: 1,11,2,6
Highest Beyer: 1(63),3(55),11(61)

Finish:	3	Rose's Dancer	31.80	12.20	6.40
	1	Prime Time Tommy		4.00	3.20
	9	Casino Duke			8.00
	5	Sir Hamoun			5.80

* = best bet

Race 10
HTR: ⑤,8,3,6
PSR: ⑤,11,8,1,6
John Swetye: 1,11/8/3,4,,⑤,/2,6
David McKenzie: 8–⑤
Ron Nicoletti: 11,6,3
Beer Ullman: 6,⑤,8,13,11
Wizard: 3,1,11,8
Crist: 3, 6, 4,11
Highest Beyer: 1(68),3(73),4(74),5(68),6(72),7(68),8(70),9(65),11(72)

Finish:	5	Bibbo	18.80	10.00	6.20
	10	Telling Tony		21.40	11.00
	6	Parmel Landing			4.00

Race 11
HTR: 6,④,5,8,9,11
PSR: 5,④,6,9,8
John Swetye: 5/1,④/2,6,8,9
David McKenzie: 6–11
Ron Nicoletti: 6,④,5,
Beer Ullman: ④,6,5,8,9
Wizard: ④,6,9,5
Crist: ④, 6, 5

Highest Beyer: 4(84),5(83),6(83),8(72),9(73),11(81)

Finish:	4	Harmonize	6.00	3.80	2.40
	9	Shake Down Baby		5.60	3.40
	6	Lira			2.40

Race 12

HTR: 3,5,9,2,⑪

PSR: 3,2,9,8

John Swetye: 6/8/3/2,9

David McKenzie: 8–3

Ron Nicoletti: 3,5,7

Beer Ullman: 5, 1, 3,8,⑪,7

Wizard: ~~1~~5,9,⑪,5,2

Crist: impossible

Highest Beyer: 2(61),3(56),7(48),9(54),11(50)

Finish:	11	Appa	14.20	6.60	4.60
	7	Sir Mogu		7.60	5.80
	8	Giant Inka			5.60

Some $10,782,375 was bet making the pool with the carryover $15,285,707 breaking the $10,870,852 P6 record set at Hollywood Park on July 2, 2007 when there was a three day $3.2 million carryover. The parlay was $221,256 with 147 tickets winning $89,456.54 for each P6. There was not 5/6 payout, which of course we had many times. The total handle for the 12 races was $25.9 million so Gulf Stream cleaned up. This compares to the last two Florida Derby Days which had similar handles of $27.2 million and $26.8 million.

We played two side tickets:

1. Gabby Ticket: $194.40 got 5/6, missed Race 7, won by #10 which Ron had 4,7,8/①,11, 13/③,6,11/⑤,6,10/4,⑤,6/3,5,7,⑪
2. Ron Nicolette Ticket: $172 got 5/6, missed Race 9, won by #3 which Gabby had 7,8,⑩/①,2,3,12/2,11/1,③,6,8/4,⑤,6/3,5,⑪

These tickets had a lot of overlap: some combo in Races 7 and 9 would have won the race.

We also placed two larger tickets. #1 a score 9 for $1784, to win we must get at 3 II's and 3 II's:

	R7	R8	R9	R10	R11	R12
I	8	2,3	1,11	⑤,8	4,⑤,6	3,5
II	1,2,3,4,5,7,⑩	①,6,14	1,2,③,4,6	1,2,3,4,6,11	1	8,9

The second ticket

	R7	R8	R9	R10	R11	R12
I	8	2,3	1,11	1,11	4,5,6	3,5
II	1,4,7,10	1,6,14	1,2,3,4,6	3,4,5,8	1	

We missed the P6 this time, but collected the rebate. Both tickets lost Race 12 when 11 won. There were 53 million tickets, 9 million were live after Race 1, 1,108,951 after 2 races, 44,228 after 3 races and going into the final race 1435 were alive with 147 winning.

22.5. The Pick 6 at the Del Mar Futurity

It was closing day at Del Mar on Wednesday September 5, 2012. There was a large carryover of 194,259 in the Pick 6 pool and there would be a mandatory payout as it was closing day of the meet. Hence if no one won the P6 the 5/6 winners would share the net pool. And if there were no 5/6 winners, then the 4/6 winners would share the payout.

The big race of the day was Race 8, the 65th running of the $300,000 Grade I 7-furlong Del Mar Futurity for two year old fillies. There were 12 runners, 7 of which had had only one race with having a second race. In general, they were expensive purchases. Brad Free, analyzed the race for the *Daily Racing Form* in an audio presentation. His top pick, #5 Know More, ridden by top jockey Garrett Gomez, won a grade II race in her only start with an 82 Beyer, the highest of the ten entrants. A knock was that the second and third finishers in that grade II race did poorly in their next race. So this was a risky favorite. His second pick was #1 Gabriel Charles (Beyer 71) and the third was #10 Rolling Fog (Beyer 62) both winners of their only start. Gabriel was trained by Jeff Mullin who usually does not win with first time starters so her win indicated a strong filly. Rolling Fog's trainer was Bob Baffert, the winning trainer of 3 of the last 4 running of this race and ten of the last 16. Somehow Baffert (31% win rate in 2012) gets them ready and the pilot was Del Mar's leading jockey Rafael Bejarano (24% win rate). Rolling Fog could get the lead and win wire to wire. See the chart in Figure 22.3.

One handicapping system had the following ratings: 5–11–10–2–3–6–1–9–4–12–7–8 with 11 and 12 scratched. Another handicapping service had the following ratings.

EIGHTH RACE **7 FURLONGS. (1.21) 65TH RUNNING OF THE DEL MAR FUTURITY. Grade I. Purse $300,000 FOR TWO-YEAR-OLDS (FOALS OF 2010).**

Del Mar

SEPTEMBER 5, 2012

Value of Race: $300,000 Winner $180,000; second $60,000; third $36,000; fourth $18,000; fifth $6,000. Mutuel Pool $531,639.00 Exacta Pool $301,972.00 Quinella Pool $18,658.00 Trifecta Pool $138,818.00 Superfecta Pool $172,209.00

Last Raced	Horse	M/Eqt.	A.	Wt	PP	St	¼	½	Str	Fin	Jockey	Odds $1
4Aug12 ^{5}Dmr^{1}	Rolling Fog	L b	2	118	9	1	2^{1}	2^{1}	$1\frac{1}{2}$	$1^{1\frac{1}{4}}$	Bejarano R	7.30
5Aug12 ^{8}Dmr^{1}	Know More	L	2	122	4	9	6^{hd}	$7\frac{1}{2}$	5^{hd}	$2^{1\frac{1}{2}}$	Gomez G K	1.70
5Aug12 ^{8}Dmr^{5}	Scherer Magic	L	2	122	10	7	3^{hd}	3^{hd}	4^{1}	3no	Pedroza M A	12.60
4Aug12 ^{7}Dmr^{1}	Capo Bastone	L	2	118	2	4	5^{1}	$4\frac{1}{2}$	3^{hd}	$4\frac{1}{2}$	Velazquez J R	3.10
12Aug12 ^{4}Dmr^{2}	Caballo Del Cielo	L	2	117	8	6	$1\frac{1}{2}$	$1\frac{1}{2}$	2^{1}	$5^{1\frac{1}{4}}$	Smith M E	9.40
21Jly12 ^{6}Dmr^{1}	Gabriel Charles	L b	2	118	1	3	$8\frac{1}{2}$	8^{hd}	7^{1}	$6^{1\frac{1}{4}}$	Talamo J	9.00
8Aug12 ^{7}Dmr^{3}	Switch to the Lead	L b	2	115	3	2	4^{hd}	5^{1}	$6\frac{1}{2}$	$7^{1\frac{1}{4}}$	Leparoux J R	20.60
12Aug12 ^{4}Dmr^{4}	The Whole Deal	L b	2	118	6	8	10^{1}	11	$10\frac{1}{2}$	$8\frac{1}{2}$	Quinonez A	74.60
26Aug12 ^{3}Dmr^{3}	Ive Struck a Nerve	L	2	118	11	10	11	$9\frac{1}{2}$	9^{2}	9^{nk}	Valdivia J Jr	60.10
18Aug12 ^{6}Dmr^{2}	Pure Loyalty	L	2	118	7	11	7^{1}	$6\frac{1}{2}$	8^{1}	$10^{3\frac{1}{4}}$	Flores D R	36.90
5Aug12 ^{8}Dmr^{4}	Heir of Storm	L	2	118	5	5	$9\frac{1}{2}$	10^{1}	11	11	Garcia M	11.50

OFF AT 5:46 Start Good. Won driving. Track fast.

TIME $:22^{4}$, $:45^{4}$, $1:10^{2}$, $1:22^{4}$ (:22.91, :45.89, 1:10.50, 1:22.96)

$2 Mutuel Prices:				
	10 – ROLLING FOG	16.60	7.00	4.80
	5 – KNOW MORE		3.40	2.80
	11 – SCHERER MAGIC			5.80

$1 EXACTA 10–5 PAID $22.80 $2 QUINELLA 5–10 PAID $23.00

$1 TRIFECTA 10–5–11 PAID $199.00 $1 SUPERFECTA 10–5–11–2 PAID $793.70

Gr/ro. c, (Mar), by Posse – Fog Dance , by Unbridled's Song . Trainer Baffert Bob. Bred by British Mist Racing and Breeding (Fla).

ROLLING FOG had good early speed and dueled outside a rival, was floated out a bit into the stretch, gained the lead, kicked away under urging past the eighth pole, drifted in some and held gamely. KNOW MORE chased between horses or off the rail, came out leaving the turn and four wide into the stretch and finished willingly. SCHERER MAGIC close up stalking the pace three deep, came four wide into the stretch, was between horses in deep stretch and edged rivals for the show. CAPO BASTONE stalked inside, inched forward in the stretch, was in tight off heels in midstretch, came out and went between foes late. CABALLO DEL CIELO bumped after the start, had good early speed off the rail, angled in and dueled inside, came a bit off the fence into the stretch, drifted in some in midstretch and weakened late. GABRIEL CHARLES saved ground chasing the pace, waited off heels leaving the turn, came out past midstretch and was outfinished. SWITCH TO THE LEAD stalked between horses to the stretch, was in a bit tight when crowded a sixteenth out and lacked a rally. THE WHOLE DEAL bumped after the start, chased three deep between foes, steadied in tight into the turn, dropped back off the rail, circled five wide into the stretch and could not summon the needed late kick. IVE STRUCK A NERVE veered out at the start, settled four wide chasing the pace, continued outside on the turn and five wide into the stretch and did not rally. PURE LOYALTY bumped between horses just after the start, chased outside, went four wide leaving the turn and five wide into the stretch and weakened. HEIR OF STORM chased between rivals then off the rail, came out into the stretch and also weakened.

Owners– 1, Arnold Zetcher LLC; 2, Reddam Racing LLC; 3, Barber Gary and Cecil; 4, Eclipse Thoroughbred Partners; 5, Durant Jerry; 6, Britt Sam and House Michael; 7, Kona Stable LLC; 8, Ladin Marty; 9, Bryan Matthew W; 10, Norman Robbie; 11, Johnson Ellen and Peter O

Trainers– 1, Baffert Bob; 2, Mora Leandro; 3, Sadler John W; 4, Sadler John W; 5, Bonde Jeff; 6, Mullins Jeff; 7, Biancone Patrick L; 8, Knapp Steve; 9, Desormeaux J Keith; 10, Glatt Mark; 11, Barba Alexis

Scratched– Yankee Rebel (19Jul12 ^{2}Dmr^{1})

$2 Daily Double (11–10) Paid $105.60 ; Daily Double Pool $44,295 .

$1 Pick Three (8–11–10) Paid $198.00 ; Pick Three Pool $106,016 .

$1 Consolation Pick 3 (8–11–4) Paid $26.40 .

$2 Consolation Daily Double (11–4) Paid $8.60 .

Figure 22.3. Chart of Race 8, Del Mar September 5, 2012.

1	Gabriel Charles	87
2	Capo Bastone	87
3	Switch to the lead	84
4	Yankee Rebel	80
5	Know More	93
6	Heir of Storm	83
7	The Whole Deal	73
8	Pure Loyalty	73
9	Caballo Del Clelo	77
10	Rolling Fog	85
11	Scherer Magic	86
12	Ive Struck a Nerve	77

The equiform pace ratings which follow showed a competitive race with the first six having very similar final times and the next four a bit lower, with the last two numbers 11 and 12. So I rated the race as:

I's 5,10 II's none

I had to take Baffert and took 5 over the 11 (among other things 5 beat 11 handily in his only start).

Baffert got it right again and the finish was 10–15–11–2 with the 7–3–1 Rolling Fog paid $16.60 to win.

I decided to double key 5 and 10 to keep the P6 ticket at a lower cost as I had to spend even even more in Races 5 and 6. I show bets I actually made. Racetrack betting is full of potential operational errors. Not betting 10 to win on the exacta or the trifecta was one of them as they made sense and paid well.

Commissioner	**Prior 2 races**	**Distance**	**Running Style**	**1st call**	**2nd call**	**Late Pace**	**Speed Rating**
	Peter Pan Stakes	1 1/8 m	**Mid-Pack Closer**	91	101	100	102
	Ark Derby	1 1/8 m		77	**85**	96	**92**
	This Pletcher charge was trounced by Danza, Ride on Curlin, Chitu, Midnight Hawk, Wildcat Red and General A Rod in his three races prior to the Peter Pan Stakes. Ran a much-improved race in the Peter Pan finishing second to Tonalist on the sealed sloppy surface at Belmont Park that day. Rates well off the Peter Pan Stakes but the figures from that race are coming up a bit suspicious. Though he had trouble in prior races, he was clearly several cuts below the best 3 year-olds in the country. Super Screener says, and pack finish at best.						

22.6. A Pick 6 at Del Mar

On Sunday November 16, 2014, there was a three day $599,482.62 carry-over. The card looked doable as a Pick 6 in Races 4 to 9 with several horses looking like potential standouts so I studied it with help from the PSR, HTR and morning line odds and picks from my colleagues John Swetye, Andrew Dowden and David McKenzie. The various picks were:

Race 4 (40k)
HTR: 1–2–6–8–7–5–3–4
PSR: 2(93), 1(90), 6(26), 8(82), 3(65), 4(62), 5(76), 7(86)
Odds: 1(3–1), 2(5–1), 3(12–1), 4(20–1), 6(6–1), 7(6–1), 8(4–1)
John Swetye: 2,8
David McKenzie: 2,1
Andrew Dowden: 2
Ticket: I(②), II(1,6,7,8)
Finish 2-1-4-8

Race 5
HTR: 10–9–4–8–3–2–7–6–1–5
PSR: 10(85), 2(66), 4(79), 3(74), 8(72), 9(76), 1(69), ~~12~~(66), 5(54), 6(63), 7(52), ~~8~~(72)
Odds: 1(20–1), 2(8–1), 3(6–1), 4(6–1), 5(30–1), 6(10–1), 7(10–1), 8(8–1), 9(3–1), 10(5–2)
John Swetye: 10, 9
David McKenzie: 10, 2
Andrew Dowden:
Ticket: I(⑩), II(2, 4, 9)
Finish 10–9–8–1

Race 6
HTR: 4–3–2–8–5–1–7–9–6
PSR: 2(91), 4(84), 7(87), 3(85), 5(78), 8(83), 9(76), 1(77), 6(79)
Odds: 1(12–1), 2(6–1), 3(5–1), 4(3–1), 5(6–1), 6(15–1), 7(7–2), 8(12–1), 9(5–1)
John Swetye: 2, 8
David McKenzie: 2, 4
Andrew Dowden: 4, 8
Ticket: I(2,8), II(③), 4, 5, 7)
Finish: 3–8–7

Race 7
HTR: 9–3–4–2–~~5~~–7–8–1–6

PSR: 9(83), 3(64), 2(0)[3], 4(77), all others 0
Odds: ~~1~~(20–1), 2(3–1), 3(7–2), 4(6–1), ~~5~~(6–1), 6(20–1), 7(10–1), 8(15–1), 9(5–2)
John Swetye: 9, 4, ~~5~~, 7
David McKenzie: 9, ~~5~~
Andrew Dowden: 9
Ticket: I(9), II(3,4)
Finish: 9–2–4–7

Race 8
HTR: 6–8–~~10~~–~~11~~–1–5–7–4–3–2–9–~~11~~
PSR: 6(103), 5(89), 1(85), 4(81), 7(90), 8(92), 3(83), 2(83), 9(79), ~~10~~(90), ~~11~~(86)
Odds: 1(4–1), 2(12–1), 3(20–1), 4(5–1), 5(7–2), 6(3–1), 7(8–1), 8(5–1), 9(20–1), ~~10~~(4–1), ~~11~~(10–1)
John Swetye: 8, 7
David McKenzie: 6,5
Andrew Dowden: 5,6
Ticket: I(⑥, II(5,7,8)
Finish: 6–1–3–4

Race 9
HTR: ~~7~~–8–3–10–1–6–2–9–4–5
PSR: 4(52), 7(65), 8(64), 10(56), all others 0
Odds: 1(5–2), 2(12–1), 3(5–1), 4(3–1), 5(4–1), 6(15–1), ~~7~~(6–1), 8(7–2), 9(15–1), 10(8–1)
John Swetye: 8, 1, 2
David McKenzie: 1,3
Andrew Dowden: throw darts
Ticket: I(8), II(1, 2,③, 4,5,6,10
Finish: 3–10–5–8–1

I ended up with one large score 9 ticket for $2752 (see Figure 22.4) and a number of smaller side tickets discussed below. The score 9 ticket, with winners circled, was:

	R4	R5	R6	R7	R8	R9
I	②	⑩	2,8	⑨	⑥	8
II	1,6,7,8	2,4,9	③,4,7	3,4	5,7,8	12,③,4,5,6,10

[3] 0 is used for first time starters and horses not rated in the US.

# in Combo	Ticket#	Del Mar, Nov 16 Score 9 Ticket	Cost
	16		$2,736
16	#1	($2) /2,/10,/2,8,/9,/6,/1,2,3,4,5,6,8,10,/	32
64	#2	($2) /1,6,7,8,/10,/2,8,/9,/6,/1,2,3,4,5,6,8,10,/	128
48	#3	($2) /2,/2,4,9,/2,8,/9,/6,/1,2,3,4,5,6,8,10,/	96
24	#4	($2) /2,/10,/3,4,7,/9,/6,/1,2,3,4,5,6,8,10,/	48
32	#5	($2) /2,/10,/2,8,/3,4,/6,/1,2,3,4,5,6,8,10,/	64
48	#6	($2) /2,/10,/2,8,/9,/5,7,8,/1,2,3,4,5,6,8,10,/	96
192	#7	($2) /1,6,7,8,/2,4,9,/2,8,/9,/6,/1,2,3,4,5,6,8,10,/	384
96	#8	($2) /1,6,7,8,/10,/3,4,7,/9,/6,/1,2,3,4,5,6,8,10,/	192
128	#9	($2) /1,6,7,8,/10,/2,8,/3,4,/6,/1,2,3,4,5,6,8,10,/	256
192	#10	($2) /1,6,7,8,/10,/2,8,/9,/5,7,8,/1,2,3,4,5,6,8,10,/	384
72	#11	($2) /2,/2,4,9,/3,4,7,/9,/6,/1,2,3,4,5,6,8,10,/	144
96	#12	($2) /2,/2,4,9,/2,8,/3,4,/6,/1,2,3,4,5,6,8,10,/	192
144	#13	($2) /2,/2,4,9,/2,8,/9,/5,7,8,/1,2,3,4,5,6,8,10,/	288
48	#14	($2) /2,/10,/3,4,7,/3,4,/6,/1,2,3,4,5,6,8,10,/	96
72	#15	($2) /2,/10,/3,4,7,/9,/5,7,8,/1,2,3,4,5,6,8,10,/	144
96	#16	($2) /2,/10,/2,8,/3,4,/5,7,8,/1,2,3,4,5,6,8,10,/	192

Figure 22.4. The 16 tickets bet at Del Mar on November 16, 2014.

So in Race 9 only 9 was out and 7 was scratched. See Figure 22.4 for my tickets.

Our P6 program can display the winning ticket which was #4 and which tickets have Pick 5/6 winners. The P6 paid $3150.40 for each $2 winning ticket. The P5/6 winners are those who lost one race and won the other five races with a I or II. For the race lost, the number of Pick 5 winners equals the number of horses in the category that lost. See Figure 22.5.

Tickets 1, 8, 11, 14, and 15 had 5 winners. The winning ticket had horses rated I–I–II–I–I–II. Only if a race with a I selected was lost is there a Pick 5/6, that is, when any one race was lost there was a Pick 5/6 except for the sixth leg where all the selections were rated II's, the rating of the winning horse.

An explanation: ticket #1 lost the third leg as a I but a II won with 2 I's; for 2 P5s
ticket #8 lost the first leg as a II but a I won with 4 II's for 4 P5s
ticket #11 lost the second leg as a II but a I won with 3 II's for 3 P5s

	Win1	Win2	Win3	Win4	Win5	Win6				
	I	I	II	I	I	II	1.clear form			Del Mar, Nov 16
	1	1	2	1	1	2	2. Enter Win Levels, I, II, etc			
							3. Check for Winners			score 9
	Race 1	Race 2	Race 3	Race 4	Race 5	Race 6	Score		# Combos	Winners
										#4 is a 6/6 winner, check for 5/6s
#1	1	1		1	1	1	5		16	
#2		1		1	1	1	4		64	#1 is a 5/6 winner
#3	1			1	1	1	4		48	#8 is a 5/6 winner
#4	1	1	1	1	1	1	6		24	#11 is a 5/6 winner
#5	1	1			1	1	4		32	#14 is a 5/6 winner
#6	1	1		1		1	4		48	#15 is a 5/6 winner
#7				1	1	1	3		192	
#8		1	1	1	1	1	5		96	
#9		1			1	1	3		128	
#10		1		1		1	3		192	
#11	1		1	1	1	1	5		72	
#12	1				1	1	3		96	
#13	1			1		1	3		144	
#14	1	1	1		1	1	5		48	
#15	1	1	1	1		1	5		72	
#16	1	1				1	3		96	

Figure 22.5. Finding the P6 and 5/6 winners in the P6.

ticket #14 lost the fourth leg as a II but a I won with 2 II's for 2 P5s
ticket #15 lost the fifth leg as a II but a I won with 3 II's for 3 P5s

So there were 14 P5's which paid $53.60 each.
Side Tickets:

#1, $270 this won the P6	1,②,7	⑩	2,③,4,7,8	⑨	⑥	all horses
#2,$648 this ticket lost	1,②,7	⑩	2,4,7 3 won	⑨	1,4,7,8 6 won	all horses
#3, $576 won 2 P5s	②,8	9,⑩	2,8 3 won	4,7,⑨	⑥,7,8	1,③,6,8
#4 won 3 P5s	1,②	2,⑩	2,4,7	~~5~~,⑨	5,⑥	③
#5 lost	②,3,4,5,6,7,8	⑩	2,4	⑨	⑥	1
#6 lost	②	4,⑩	2,4	⑨	5,⑥	1
#7 lost	1	⑩	2	⑨	5,⑥	4
#8 lost	②	⑩	2	⑨	⑥	2

There was $372 in rebate which included the side bets some of the side bets. With the side tickets there was one winner and no 5/6 winners.

The following Pick 3 ticket for Races 4-6 lost: 1,②/2,⑩/2,4,7 and the following Pick 3 ticket on a $5 Pick 3 for Races 7–9: 2,~~5~~,⑨/5,⑥/1,③ which paid $53 for $1. The following $5 double in Races 4 and 5 won: 1,②/2,⑩ and the $2 double in Races 6 and 7 ②,4,7/5,9 lost.

22.7. Rainbow P6 Mandatory Payout, Santa Anita, June 16, 2019

There was a carryover of $1,260,210 for the Rainbow Pick 6 for races 4–9. The total pool bet on the Rainbow was $6,558,165. So there was more than $5 million new money bet. There were some very good horses running highlighted by the Bob Baffert trained Roadster and Mucho Gusto in race 8, the grade III Affirmed Stakes, and, in race 5, Ellie Arroway with a 113 PSR. The handicappers ratings were as follows:

Race 4
HTR: 4,5,2,6,3,7,1
PSR: 1(82),2(90),3(77),4(97),5(100),6(86),7(82)
Odds: 2,3,4,5,6,7 (all with odds less than 10–1)
Timeform: 4,5,7
DJM: 4
Express: 2,3,4,6,7
Finish: 2–5–4–7

Race 5
HTR: 8,4,5,3,1,2,6,7
PSR: 1(90),2(113),3(92),4(86),5(87),6(79),7(83),8(92)
Odds: all 8 have odds less than 10-1
Timeform: 2,1,3
DJM: 2
Express: 3,5,8
Finish: 3–1–7–2

Race 6
HTR: 5–3–7–4–1
PSR: 1(73),2(69),3(89),4(83),5(84),6(77),7(85)
Odds: 1,3,4,5,6,7 (all with odds less than 10–1)
Timeform: 5–6–7
DJM: 5
Express: 1,3,5,7
Finish: 3–5–7–6–1

Race 7
HTR: 4–1–5–8–2
PSR: 1(98),3(89),3(85),4(95),6(96),7(86),8(87)
Odds: 1,2,4,5,6,8 (all with odds less than 10–1)
Timeform: 1–5–2
DJM: 4
Express: 1–2–5
Finish: 8–4–2–6

Race 8
HTR: 5–6–1–4–3–2
PSR: 1(94),2(27), 3(90),4(97),5(99),6(104)
Odds: 1,4,5,6 (all with odds less than 10–1)
Timeform: 6–4–5
DJM: 6
Express: 1–5–6
Finish: 6–5–1–3

Race 9
HTR: 8–10–9–7–1
PSR: 1(81),2(0),3(73),4(65),5(64),6(75),7(80),8(93),9(84),10(74),11(62)
Odds: 1–7–8–9–10 (all with odds less than 10–1)
Timeform: 8–7–10
DJM: 8
Express: 8–10
Finish: 9–8–1–4

P6 payout: $3,187.64

I made the following P6 wagers, ⓪ means the winner. These were simply straight tickets. The tree approach is useful but I just did it this way because it was hard to determine the Is and it did win.

1. ②,3,4,6,7/1,2,③,5,8/1③,5,6,7/1,2,4,5,⑧/5,⑥/7,8,⑨,10
   cost = $1000; this was a P6 winner of $3187.64
2. 4,5/ all /5,6,7/1,2,4,5,⑧/1,4,5,6/1,7,8,⑨,10
   cost = $960, this ticket lost
3. 4/all/5,7/1,2,5,⑧/5,⑥/1,7,8,⑨,10
   cost = $128, this ticket lost
4. = ②,4,5/1,2,③,8/1,③,5,7/all/5,⑥/1,7,8,⑨,10
   cost = $672; this was a P6 winner of $3187.64

So on the P6 I collected $6,375.28 plus $298 of rebate on a bet of $2,760 for a nice gain. The mandatory payout days are the best to play the Rainbow P6 as you then have an edge and you do not have to try get the bombs needed to be the unique P6 winner on regular days.

I also made these side bets:
R4: 4 place; $50, lost
R5: 1 win, place, $20; place collected
R7: 8 win, place, $20, both collected
R10: 8 win, place, $20, both collected plus rebate

Acknowledgment

Thanks to David McKenzie, John Swetye, Constantine Dzhabarov, and Andrew Dowden for data and helpful comments on an earlier draft of this chapter.

Chapter 23

A Pick 6 Tale

William T. Ziemba

This chapter discusses an interesting Pick 6 in the mud at Belmont on May 30, 2021 where I investigate combining the picks of three expert handicappers to try to merge them together to win the Pick 6 and collect a number of Pick 5/6's. It turns out that the merger would have been very successful to get a large Pick 6 and numerous Pick 5/6. Some other Rainbow and ordinary Pick 6's are also studied and suggest that bettors prefer long odds horses in the Pick 6 and not the favorites as widely thought. The results are suggestive of a special type of favorite-longshot bias which is much stronger than the usual bias in the win market.

23.1. Background

It was raining like crazy all day on Sunday May 30, 2021 and the previous few days at the Belmont race track. The track was muddy but sealed. But would the seal be effective? In our *Beat the Racetrack* books, the latest being *Exotic Betting at the Racetrack* which I did myself, the empirical evidence is that the winners have odds that are double normal on muddy days. This means that fewer favorites do well and more longshots do well. In fact a muddy track adds uncertainty. But if the track is sealed properly, this might not be the case and the favorites could do well.

What happened was that the favorites did extremely well and still the Pick 6 payoff was very high compared to the parlay which was much much less largely because bettors, after three days of relentless rain thought that the favorites would not do well so they bet mostly on longshots on the Pick 6.

There was a carryover of $122,783 in the ordinary Pick 6 which was from the previous two days when the rain made it too difficult for anyone to win the Pick 6. The $1 Pick 6 at Belmont gives bettors a better chance of winning than the historical $2 bet.

At many tracks, but not Belmont, there is a Rainbow Pick 6 in addition to the ordinary Pick 6 and it has basically replaced the Pick 6 because of its low price tickets which are usually 20 cents rather than $1 or $2. So the Rainbows have carryovers in the millions not $122,783 like the Pick 6 in Belmont on this day.

I have studied and played Pick 6 's for years including the Rainbow Pick 6 and a primer on these bets discussing strategies and results is in *Exotic Betting at the Racetrack*, Ziemba(2019).

Both the ordinary Pick 6 and the Rainbow which at Saratoga is called the Empire 6 have a first and second prize with the proviso that if the first prize is not won then a portion is carried over to the next day. In the Rainbow, first prize is the *unique* Pick 6 which with 20 cent tickets is very hard to win and prize is the ordinary Pick 6 which is much easier to win with the cheap tickets. Hence, there are huge carryovers. The Rainbows are then cashed out on periodic mandatory payout days. The ordinary Pick 6 has 6/6 as the first prize and 5/6 as the second prize for $2 or $1.

Andy Beyer once said "Racetrack handicapping is the supreme intellectual challenge." Well, we all know it's not easy. Let's see how three expert handicappers do on a tough Pick 6.

For the ordinary Pick 6 at Belmont and the Empire Pick 6 at Saratoga, where each has a first and a second prize, the splits are as follows:

- Belmont for the $1 Pick 6: 75% for the Pick 6, 25% for 5/6 or if there are no 5/6 then 4/6 payoffs; so if the Pick 6 is not won, 75% goes to the carryover
- The 20 cent Empire Pick 6 at Saratoga and the Rainbow Pick 6 at Gulfstream: 100% goes to the first prize if there is a *unique* winner of the Pick 6. If there is no winner or more than one winner then 30% of the prize pool is carried over; and 70% goes to the ordinary Pick 6 winners who share the pot; if there are no winners, the 5/6 winners share the payout.

I characterize racetrack bettors into several groups. They might be amateurs, advanced amateurs who use reasonably sophisticated handicapping methods or they might be professional syndicates that trade huge amounts on all the bets. The amateurs are the stereotypical bettors who bet at the windows at the track or through simulcast sites. The advanced amateurs use their own handicapping, handicapping services and possibly use rebates and are trying to win money at the racetrack. Many are very successful and we can call them superior handicapping bettors. The last group are the professional syndicates. I have consulted for several of them and several of my books and papers are used by them. I discuss them in a recent paper, Ziemba (2021), which is on the economics of racetrack betting and lotteries.

The syndicates bet at many racetracks, possibly in many countries and their goal is very simple. They don't actually want to win as the tracks would not like that so they would earn too much at their large scale. They use rebaters so instead of the track getting, say a 15% take, it gets only 5%. So blended the ordinary bettor is paying more than the 15%, say 18% rather than the 15%. This is split three ways, as an example: the track might get 5% for their signal which are the results; the rebater might get 5% and the syndicates might get the remaining 5%. The goal of the syndicate is not to win betting but to win the rebate with huge turnover. This is not small because betting $800,000 most days yields about $20–40 million in yearly rebates. But it usually takes 1–4 years of research and data collection plus about $1 million to prepare to get a winning system and there is no guarantee they they will actually win consistently.

I guarantee you that this is difficult to pulloff. The top global teams from Sydney, Australia, had 90 people working when I visited them about ten years ago. They now have about 300 people and are in virtually all racing venues worldwide including the US. Other syndicates focus on the US and some other countries like Japan and Korea and the big one with the biggest betting pool, Hong Kong.

In this chapter, I want to focus not on the syndicates but on the advanced amateurs who are trying to win possibly at the track not collecting the rebate, although it is best if they do collect the rebate to add to their returns.

I know from portfolio theory studies as in Figure 23.1, Chopra and Ziemba (1993), that getting the mean right is on average 20 times as important as getting the covariances and 10 times the variances. However, the errors are risk aversion dependent so if one has a risky utility function like log which professional and advanced amateur racetrack bettors use because of the very good long range high wealth outcome usually, it is more like 100:3:1. To win you better get the means right, that's the horse win probabilities or the right horses in the exotic bets. So you better have good handicapping to predict the winners.

Racetrack betting is an example of portfolio theory. The log which is associated with capital growth theory or Kelly criteria has Arrow-Pratt risk

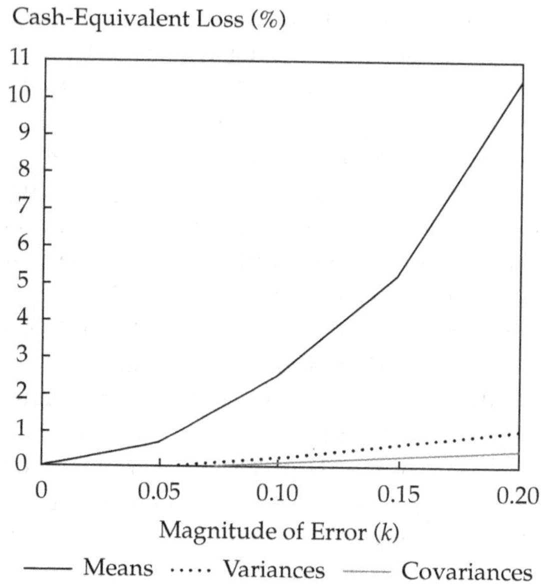

Figure 23.1. Typical relative importance of errors in mens, variances and co-variances in terms of certainty equivalent.
Source: Chopra and Ziemba (1993).

aversion of $1/w$ which is essentially zero for investor wealth w. So log, which has such wonderful long run properties, is risky short term but usually gets the most long run wealth. It is the riskiest utility function you would ever want to use. Betting more has more risk and less mean return so it is best avoided. See my two papers in *Great Investment Ideas*, Ziemba (2017). One is a response to Economics Nobel Laureate Paul Samuelson's objections in three letters he wrote to me before he died. The second has simulations of various fractional Kelly strategies done with Ed Thorp and Len MacLean and one of my students. These show practice related to how to use Kelly strategies well. If you want to see the heavy theory see MacLean, Thorp and Ziemba (2010).

My goal in this chapter is to discuss an interesting Pick 6 that was difficult to win at Belmont and three handicappers who tried to provide good input to actually win it. There are many ways to successfully play the Pick 6 depending on the card. Here is one such example that discusses the way to make good Pick 6 bets. My greatest bet not made but considered was the Pick 6 when Zenyatta won the 2009 Breeders' Cup Classic. There were three standouts: Zenyatta, Goldikova, and Conduit and three races that were wide open. The ticket singling the three standouts and taking all the horses in the other three races with $2 tickets cost $2340 less rebate of about $187.20 at 8%. The three standouts did win and Pick 6 and 28 5/6 consolation prizes returned almost $2 million. I thought about doing this and the cost was not that great; but I did not place the bet. That was a huge mistake.

For those interested, the most likely way that Zenyatta lost to Blame in 2010, based on a conversation that I had with a former jockey, the painter Nick Martinez and confirmed by a conversation with Mike Smith at a Del Mar restaurant: Zenyatta started slow as usual, while the other horses started quite a bit faster. So she got behind quite a bit. The horses broke into two clusters around the first turn. The first group was past the turn so Smith could not see them but he could see the second group which had not gotten to the turn yet. So Smith and Zenyatta got further behind. Then when Zenyatta made her huge run, she had some traffic and Blame won by a small amount. So she was then 19/20 and not undefeated. At Claiborne I was told they had to hide Blame for three months over fears of someone killing him. That was the fame of this great mare and her extreme popularity. Steve Roman has an alternative theory: Blame was simply better that day. I prefer explanation #1 but have deep respect for Steve's racing knowledge.

In the 2009 Breeders' Cup Pick 6, to win you must have all six winners who share 75% of the net pool with the 5/6 sharing the remaining 25%. The Pick 6 was Races 4–9. There were three standouts but they were definitely not certain winners. The other three races seemed wide open. So you could play the Pick 6 in the following way: I thought about doing this but did not — it was a $2 million mistake. You have a single ticket with about 10 horses in the three wide open races and single the three standouts. That would cost about 10*10*10*1*1*$2 = $2000, not a large Pick 6 ticket. You only win if all three standouts win and they did.

The payoffs for $2 win tickets were as follows

Race 4	Dancing in Silks	52.60	
Race 5	Value of York	63.20	
Race 6	Goldikova	4.80	the first standout
Race 7	Furthest Land	44.60	
Race 8	Conduit	3.80	the second standout
Race 9	Zenyatta	7.60	the third standout

Goldikova was the winner of the mile grass race in 2008 and was arguably better this year. Her connections were the same as those of Miesque, also a two time winner of this race. The second standout, Conduit, was also the winner last year of the $1\frac{1}{2}$ mile turf. Zenyatta was undefeated, facing males for the first time in the world's most difficult race.

The Pick 6 paid $1,838,305.20 for one winning 6/6 ticket and the 3*9 = 27 Pick 5/6 tickets (of the 10 losers in the three wide open races) paid 27*$4822.40 for a total of $130,204.80 plus the 6% rebate on the $2000 of $120 for a grand total of $1,968,630.00. It is not quite $2 million but as Johnnie Hooker played by Robert Redford in the Sting said: "it's not enough but it's close". Of course, taxes would take 25% at the track and be sorted out later when filing and my winning would depress the Pick 6 and Pick 5/6 prizes.

23.1.1. *Example 1: An interesting Pick 6*

How do I analyze a Pick 6? My skills are in optimization and finance theory and having worked with top racing syndicates as written in my racing books and the 2021 survey paper, Ziemba (2021). So for handicapping I usually rely on inefficient finance market ideas as in our books along with handicapping services by experts such as HTR, PSR, Time Form, David, Nick, Super Screener and the Wizard.

The *In the Money* racetrack podcast which I highly recommend, expert handicappers JK and PTF are very talented, so is my colleague RD. The question is could these three handicappers get the Pick 6 on a very tough day?

It paid $34,876.50 for 6/6 and $191.50 for 5/6 for the combination: 6/1,2,4,6,7,10/2/9/1,3,6,7/2,12,13.
The parlay (6.4)(2.1)(8.4)(4.3)(2.0)(2.9) paid $2,816.63. This is much less than the Pick 6. Well, some is the carryover, some is the six track takes for each of the races versus one take for the Pick 6 but I think that most of this is the fact that the bettors were going for longshots on a muddy day raining all day after two previous rainy days were the Pick 6 had not been won and generated more carryover. What happened was there was a even money shot, a 1.1–1 favorite, a 1.9–1 favorite, plus a 3.3–1, a 5.4–1 and a 7.4–1. So basically it was what you could call a *chalk Pick 6* but it paid a huge amount because of the circumstances. The parlay also has six track takes for win plus a lower but single Pick 6 takeout. There was also the carryover adding to the Pick 6 payoff.

Some of the horses were scratched, and were replaced by the favorite in those tickets. See the charts in the Appendix.

You also win a number of 5/6 second prizes if you win the if you win the 6/6. It is the number of horses in the lost race. But if you get the Pick 6 you do not have a lost race and construct the 5/6's from the six races taking all the horse in all 6 races since 5/6 in each of the 6 races plus all the horses you had tried to win with.

What happened was that the three handicappers JK, PTF and RD, were pretty good in their picks but none of the three got the actual Pick 6 which was very difficult. What I did was to combine these three handicappers and use a merged larger ticket. PTF had two winners as I's. JK had three winners as I's and two winners as II's so he got some 5/6's. RD also won 5/6's with 3 I's and 2 II's, but he got the race 4 winner as one of the II's which gave the Pick 6 for the combined ticket. JK got the winner #2 in race 6 which the other two handicappers did not get.

The three handicappers picks are in Table 23.1. For now, assume we take A's and B's from the three handicappers as our super ticket. I assume we take all A's and B's from the three handicappers on our combined ticket. My experience is when in doubt add horses. The extra cost is worth it. I use I,II,III's in our Pick 6 program. Carry Fotias and I used this back in about 2000, when my wife made the code which we used for Bob Hammond's insurance plays, see Ziemba (2021). A, B, C is the same but only one of the three handicappers had III's or C's. So I have used them in my combo ticket. The winners are circled.

So what was the smart ticket and how much did it cost and how many 5/6's would have been won?

There will not be the usual 36 tickets for score 9 with only I's and II's and no III's because two races 5 and 7 have no II's. The normal procedure is to bet more on score 6 and less on score 7, score 8 and score 9.

Table 23.1. The three handicappers.

	PTF			**JK**			**RD**		
R	**Top**	**I**	**II**	**Top**	**I**	**II**	**I**	**II**	**III**
4	4	4	5	5	5	4	1,5	⑥,8	3
5	8	3,8,11		8	①,5,8,12		①,8	3,11,12	
6	6	3,6,8	1,8	②	2,4,10	8	4,9,10	8,11	
7	⑨	3,9		⑨	1,9	10	1,3,10	1,⑨	
8	①	1		①	1		①,2	4,5	
9	8	5,8,9		3	3,4,8,9,⑬		6,9,⑬	4,8	

The merged three handicapper ticket if one just adds all the horses as I's and II's is with just one II from handicapper RD. The winners are circled. A second combination ticket below has fewer I's and more II's which is closer to the usual way to play a Pick 6. In race 5, RD had 3,11,12 as II's but PTF had 3,8,11 as I's and JK had 8 as a I. So this first set of combination tickets has them as I's

Race 6 8 was a II for RD and JK but a I for PTF so its a I here.
Race 7 9 and 10 from RD and PTF were I's so I had them as I's on this combo ticket.
Race 8 ① is singled by PTF and JK and RD has 1,2/4,5 so the ticket is 1,2/4,5

The merged ticket is

	R4	R5	R6	R7	R8	R9
I	4,5	①,5,8,11,12	②,3,4,6,8	1,3,⑨,10	①,2	3,4,5,8,9,⑬
II	⑥,8				4,5	
III	3					

Comments: I am going to delete the III's in races 7 and 9 and the II in race 6. In most cases the III's are not worth it unless you have good information.

So the merged ticket has lots of I's, II's in 3 races and a III in race 4. Usually we bet more on score 6 and down the line to score 9. We could bet \$4 on score 6, \$3 on score 7, \$2 on score 8 and \$1 on score 9 and spend more and win over \$100,000. That approximates Kelly capital growth investing and probability weighting where you bet more on the more likely outcomes.

In the Pick 6 there is only one unique ticket that wins betting this way, assuming you bet \$1, but if you bet \$3 you would get three winning ticket.

The Score 6 ticket is:

Ticket 1, Score 6 is: 4,5/①,5,8,11,12/②,3,4,6,8/1,3, ⑨,10/①,2/3,4, 5,8,9,⑬

This has two 5/6's but missed race 4 for the Pick 6. It cost 2*6*5*4*2*6*4 = 2880*\$4 = \$11,520.

That's way too much. We better bet \$1 on all the tickets, it's \$2880 already. You can see that fewer I's and more II's might be better. But let's finish this large combination ticket. The computer program is useful to calculate costs of many combo tickets and if you have probabilities that each horse will win then you can set an overall probability of winning so costs zero in on the best ticket cost probability wise.

There are just 2 score 7 tickets. Normally there are 6 when you have II's in every race but the merged ticket only had II's in races 4 and 8 plus the lone III in race 4.

These two tickets are:

Ticket 2, Score 7: ⑥,8/①,5,8,11,12/②,3,4,6,8/1,3,⑨,10/①,2/3,4,5, 8,9, ⑬

This is the Pick 6 winning ticket. This ticket cost 2*6*5*4*2*6 = $2880 the same as score 6 because there are 2 horses in Race 4 on both tickets. This has the Pick 6 paying the $34,876.50. It also has 2 + 6 + 5 + 4 + 2 + 6 = 25 5/6's worth $191.50 each adding $4787.50 for a return of $39,664.00 plus 0.9% rebate of $90.72 for a total return of $39,754.72 on this ticket. Tax would be taken out but this would be part of the yearly gains and losses of the bettors' tax returns. There is only one unique ticket that wins and this it.

Ticket 3, Score 7 (a loser): 4,5/①,5,8,11,12/②,3,4,6,8/1,3,⑨,10/4,5/3, 4,5,8,9,⑬

The second score 7 ticket uses the II's in race 8, namely 4,5 replacing the 2 horses that were I's

Ticket 4, Score 8 (a loser): For the score 8 ticket, return to the score 7 ticket and replace the horses in race 4 with the III in that race.

3/①,5,8,11,12/②,3,4,6,8/1,3,⑨,10/①,2/3,4,5,8,9,⑬

This ticket has one 5/6.

Ticket 5: Score 9 (a loser) Now to the score 9: these have 4 I's, 1 II and 1 III.

3/①,5,8,11,12/②,3,4,6,8/1,3,⑨,10/4,5/3,4,5,8,9,⑬

This ticket is also a loser. There are no other score 9 tickets because they would have to have 3 II's and 3 III's and there are no 3 races with II's.

This ticket costs half the others with only one horse in race 4, so it cost $1440. So the total cost of the tickets was 3*2880+1440=$10,080. This is quite expensive. But you got the $39,574.72 from ticket 2 and $191.50 * 2 = $383 from ticket 1 for a total of $40,137.72 So you would most likely prefer a possibly cheaper play with some of the I's made into II's. You can still win with 3 I's and 3 II's which you likely would since many I's of the best horses won. We get to that below.

Let's now make another ticket that likely would win the Pick 6.

- First let's delete 3 from the III in race 4. These III's rarely win and at $1440 that's way too much to pay for it.
- In race 5, let's go with RD and make 3,11,12 as II's so the II's are 8, ①,5. We could have dropped the 5 also as only JK has it but he has it as a I so I include it.
- In race 9, the I's are 3,6,⑬,8,9. I can only skip II like I did in the combo ticket.

The second combined ticket is:

	R4	R5	R6	R7	R8	R9
I	4,5	①,5,8	②,4,8,9,10	1,⑨,10,13	①,2	3,5,8,9,⑬
II	⑥,8	3,11,12	1,8,11		4,5	4

Winners: 6/1/2/9/1/13 also some scratches went to the favorite and those won too if favorite won and they did in at least 3 races.

UBC Computer Science Professor Alan Wagner worked with me when I was an expert witness for a Hong Kong Syndicate who were former Bill Benter employees. They hired a statistician to make a full blown Benter-style factor model, It worked but he stole it, making millions. Alan and I were tasked to prove he did which we indeed did show. Alan did the Pick 6 calculations that follow on the second combined Pick 6.

If you bet $3 on score 6, $2 on score 7 and $1 on score 8 this second combined ticket cost $19,344. If you bet $1 on all the tickets the cost is $11,324. Each of these has a rebate of 0.9%. If you bet the 3-2-1 you will get 2 Pick 6's and many 5/6's. We did not do score 9 as it would be prohibitively expensive with so many I's and II's in all the races. Indeed the design decision is either to have more I's and II's or fewer with some III's.

The Pick 6 tickets were as follows:

Score 6
4,5/8,1,5/2,3,4,9,10/9,10,3,1/1,2/3,5,8,9,13

Score 7 and 8
4,5/11,3,12/2,3,4,9,10/9,10,3,1/1,2/3,5,8,9,13
4,5/8,1,5/2,3,4,9,10/9,10,3,1/1,2/4
8,6/8,1,5/2,3,4,9,10/9,10,3,1/1,2/3,5,8,9,13

4,5/8,1,5/8,1,11/9,10,3,1/1,2/3,5,8,9,13
4,5/8,1,5/2,3,4,9,10/9,10,3,1/4,5/3,5,8,9,13
8,6/8,1,5/8,1,11/9,10,3,1/1,2/3,5,8,9,13
8,6/8,1,5/2,3,4,9,10/9,10,3,1/1,2/4
8,6/8,1,5/2,3,4,9,10/9,10,3,1/4,5/3,5,8,9,13
4,5/8,1,5/8,1,11/9,10,3,1/1,2/4
4,5/11,3,12/2,3,4,9,10/9,10,3,1/4,5/3,5,8,9,13
4,5/8,1,5/8,1,11/9,10,3,1/4,5/3,5,8,9,13
4,5/11,3,12/2,3,4,9,10/9,10,3,1/1,2/4
4,5/11,3,12/8,1,11/9,10,3,1/1,2/3,5,8,9,13
8,6/11,3,12/2,3,4,9,10/9,10,3,1/1,2/3,5,8,9,13
4,5/8,1,5/2,3,4,9,10/9,10,3,1/4,5/4

Score 9
8,6/8,1,5/2,3,4,9,10/9,10,3,1/4,5/4
4,5/11,3,12/2,3,4,9,10/9,10,3,1/4,5/4
4,5/8,1,5/8,1,11/9,10,3,1/4,5/4
4,5/11,3,12/8,1,11/9,10,3,1/4,5/3,5,8,9,13
8,6/11,3,12/2,3,4,9,10/9,10,3,1/4,5/3,5,8,9,13
8,6/11,3,12/8,1,11/9,10,3,1/1,2/3,5,8,9,13
4,5/11,3,12/8,1,11/9,10,3,1/1,2/4
8,6/11,3,12/2,3,4,9,10/9,10,3,1/1,2/4
8,6/8,1,5/8,1,11/9,10,3,1/4,5/3,5,8,9,13
8,6/8,1,5/8,1,11/9,10,3,1/1,2/4

The output from the computer program is in Figure 23.2.

23.2. Remarks on How to Win at Racing

There are two parts equally important: good handicapping and good betting. The better you are at one, you can be less good at the other. First you must have an edge so $1 wagered must return more than $1. Here are some ways to win:

Inefficient markets: In our original Hausch–Ziemba books, we used inefficient markets that used probabilities from simple markets like win to price bets in complex markets like place and show and then bet well with

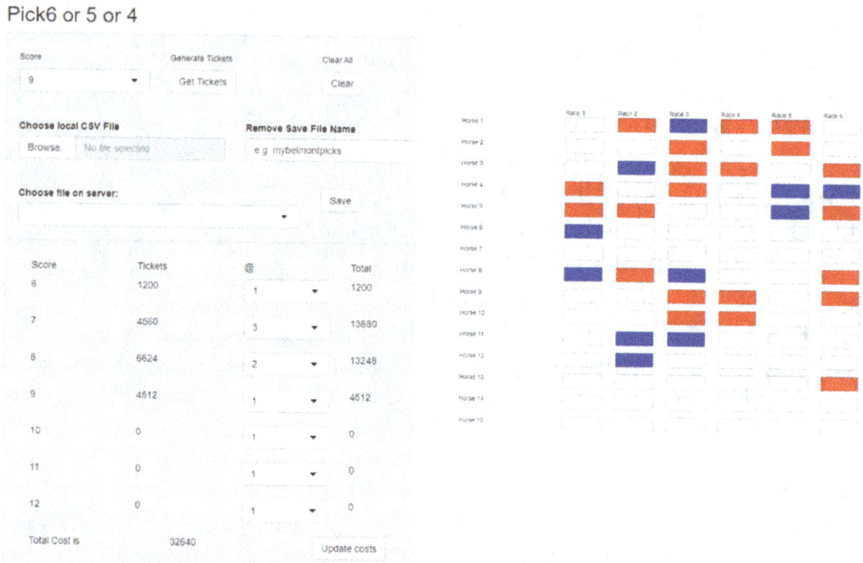

(a) In put template. (b) In 2009–2012.

Figure 23.2. The Pick 6 computer program.

the Kelly criterion (the best). This and the expanded idea for exotics is to price bets then take the best ones and bet well. See *Exotic Betting at the Racetrack*, Ziemba (2019).

Dosage: This was very powerful in the 1970–2000 period because no horses with a dosage index above four won the Kentucky Derby and horses with dosage indices above 3.0 did not do well in the longer Belmont Stakes. For example, the great Sunday Silence won the Kentucky Derby and Belmont but with a 3.8 dosage was crushed by Easy Goer in the Belmont. In recent years the ideas are still useful but not as powerful because the breed has changed more towards speed so some horses with higher dosages have won the Kentucky Derby. However, in the longer Belmont Stakes there have been almost none with a dosage above 3 who have won. See Roman (2016), a masterpiece, Gramm and Ziemba (2008) for the Triple Crown and a tutorial primer in Chapter 19.

Factor models: This is the approach Bill Benter used to make millions in Hong Kong racing and other locales. I had a hand in this because I processed and accepted in the journal *Management Science* where I was the departmental editor for finance, Bolton and Chapman (1992) that showed how to make such models. Chapman did a followup paper on their methods and consulted with Benter who wrote his famous paper in our book *Efficiency of Racetrack Betting*, Hausch, Lo and Ziemba (1994) book. They syndicates use 80-90 variables with two types of models: one includes the track odds which are a good predictor and the other does not include the track odds but compares the model's prediction to the track odds to determine good bets.

Superior handicapping: Approaches inefficient markets and factor models and dosage to some extent tend to augment superior handicapping to improve it with modeling of some kind. But there are many superior handicappers who can win based on their analytic skills in handicapping and betting. There are various books about this and much proprietary analysis.

Conclusion: This chapter is part of the theory and practice of playing the Pick 6 successfully. There are many activities going on that are important such as you need good handicapping, you need good ticket construction, and you need to estimate somehow the behavior of the other bettors to know how they will approach a particular Pick 6. We saw in this example a huge behavioral finance economics effect that the other bettors which was hard to determine in advance.

23.3. Postscript

The concept of merging expert opinion to get better forecasts is valuable for the Pick 6 ticket construction. On Sunday, June 6 there was a mandatory payout of Santa Anita's Rainbow Pick 6 with a carryover of $411,484 with 20 cent tickets. The two handicappers' picks were (winners circled):

RD

	R4	R5	R6	R7	R8	R9
I	2,5	(1),2	3,4	1,3	(4),6	4,5,6
II	(4)	4,8	(2)	2,(4),6	3,7	2
III	6	3	1,5	5	1,2,5	1,3,7

WTZ

	R4	R5	R6	R7	R8	R9
I	2,5	(1),2,3,4	(2),3,4	1,3,(4)	3,6	1,2,4,6
II	(4)	5	7	2,5	1,2,5	(3),5,7,8

23.3.1. *Comments*

RD won the Pick 6 if he used 1,3,7 in race 9. WTZ had a major operational error not including 4 in race 8, a 2-1 with a top jockey he should have been a I not left off. Other than that WTZ had the Pick 6 which paid $4649.36 with a pool of $2,838,921. There was no 5/6 pay out on the mandatory payout day. San Anita's rebates were for win, place and show 3.83%; for doubles 7.51%, for 2 horse exotics like the exacta and quinella 9.83% and for the trifecta, superfecta and Rainbow Pick 6 10.83%.

The score 9 merged ticket eliminating III's did win the Pick 6 with 3 I's and 3 II's.

RD

	R4	R5	R6	R7	R8	R9
I	2,5	①,2	3,4	①,3,4	3,④,6	1,2,4,5,6
II	④	3,4,8	1,②	2,5,6	1,2,6,7	③,7

The race 4 to 9 payoffs were:

R4	R5	R6	R7	R8	R9
$17.20	$4.00	$19.00	$3.60	$7.20	$10

The parlay was $1/10(17.20)(2)(19/2)(1.80)(3.6)(5) = 1058.83$ for a 20 cent ticket which is a little less than 1/4th of the Pick 6 payoff. In this calculation the parlay has 6 tracktakes for win and the Rainbow Pick 6 has one larger tracktake so that slightly depresses the parlay value. I used (1/10) because a 20 cent ticket is (1/10) of the $2 win payoffs.

23.3.2. *Conclusion*

Again, merging the two experts to get a ticket to win the Pick 6 was a good idea. Also, like the mud Pick 6 in this chapter, the Pick 6 paid much more than the parlay, signaling that the bettors are wagering different in the Pick 6 rather than the individual races in the win pools. In this Pick 6, there were two even money or less than even money favorites that won. The other payoffs were $7.20 and $10 with two longer medium odds horses paying $17.20 and $19.

The effect was similar to the mud race with Rainbow Pick 6 bettors preferring longer odds horses. A possible explanation for this comes from the nature of the Rainbow Pick 6 itself. Since the jackpot is the unique Pick 6 in the Rainbow, bettors must get some very long odds horses to be the only winner. However, this is not needed on mandatory payoff days like this example, but the bettors seem to still bet much more on the longshots.

Pick 6 example 3 with some behavioral finance elements: The Pick 6 was Santa Anita, March 6, 2002 with $202,790 carryover from Sunday's wagers. This is included here because it had a behavioral finance element that was crucial to its success.

Race	3	4	5	6	7	8
Win Payoff	3.60	4.60	12.00	9.20	18.00	7.20

1-5 shot out
of the money

$$\text{Advantage} \equiv \prod_{i=1}^{6} (1+\text{edge}_l)$$

Pick 6 $86,347.60 - one large transaction cost

Parlay $15,452.40 - six races, six smaller transactions costs

Bet = 1922	1 Pick 6		Score 6	$4
Rebate = 154	11 Pick 5/6	692.00	7	$58
Net bet = 1768	Gross =	93,691.80	8	$376
			9	$1484
				1922

Score 9: you win if the score is 9 or less, here 3 I's, 2 II's, total 9 so we won.

	R3	R4	R5	R6	R7	R8
I	①,3	③	7	3	2	②
II	7	1,5	1,2,⑤,6	4,7,8,⑩	1,④	5,9
III	5,6	2,4,8				

The $1922 bet had 66 separate tickets. The winning ticket has one 6/6 winner and 11 5/6 winners that follow:

			Morning Line
Race 7	1	Madame Pietra	3–1
	2	Love at Noon	3–5
	3	Harvest Girl	8–1
	4	Filigree	4–1
	5	Farah Love	12–1

The behavioral key is that it is possible that Filigree could run faster than Love at Noon.

- In the 3rd and 5th races back, Filigree had ran faster than the heavy favorite Love at Noon had run in his last two races.
- Filigree, the third choice in the morning line went off at 8–1 and we made him a II.
- Love at Noon went off at 1–5 and had most of the Pick 6 money.

In the following Equiform numbers, the top number is final speed number, and the other two numbers are the pace within the race.

EQUIFORM ®

7TH SAX MARCH 6 - 6 FURLONGS DIRT

```
            MADAME PIETRA        (118)            40

  70    72%    67%    70%    64%  w76%  w71%   64%
       /////  /////
 80%    71%    73%    79     77%   78    77     67
SA6%  SA-6%   SA8    DMR6   SA6   SA6   DMR6   HOL6
 70%    71     67%
 82     70%           81     83%   81    63     68%
JAN24 10/17  09/27  SEP02  03/16 JAN31 AUG05  05/28

            LOVE AT NOON        (118)            44

 72%    73%    74%    75%  w78%  w^70%

 71%    82%    75%    74%   85    70%
SA8%   SA7   HOL8%   CD8%  CD6%  SA6
 69%    74%    72     72%   76%
        84                  85%   77%
01/20 DEC29  06/16  05/26 05/05 04/07

            HARVEST GIRL        (118)            19

w71%   71%   68%    --     70%   71    66%   66%   68%  w71%   68    69%  w68%   69%  w67%   61%
      /////        /////                             /////       /////              /////
 80%   77    80%    71%    83%   81%   82%   79%   81    78%   75%   79%   77%   82    79%   69%
SA6   SA8   HOL6%  BM8%  FPX6%  SR6   SOL6  GG6  SA-6% FPX6%  BMP8  SOL6  GG6  HOL5%  BM5% BMF5%
       68%   69     65%    71%                     69%   71%   68
 87          83            98    81%   82%   80%   84%   83%         78%   77%   75%   86%   80
02/14 01/05 11/21  10/13  09/14 08/06 JUL14 11/25 10/28 09/19 08/12 07/22 05/31 MAY18 09/12 08/15

            FILIGREE        (118)            40

 71%   67%   74     71%  w74%  w71%   71%   71%   70%   70    70    70%  w73%  w70%  w70    68%

 77%   72    82%    78%   75%   74%   75%   73%   70%   81%   61%   77    74    77%   78    73%
SA6%  SA5%  DMR6  DMR6%  HOL6%  HOL6  SA7   SA8%  SA6   SA5%  SA9  FPX6% DMR6% DMR6% HOL6%  SA6
 71%                70%   72%         67%   70                61%   68%   68    70    70
 77%   75%   85%    73%   73%   74%   75          67%   75%         74    68%   77%   79    75%
01/24 JAN02 09/05  07/23 06/27 05/28 04/16 03/03 01/31 JAN01 10/28 09/30 09/03 JUL31 05/26 04/16

            FARAH LOVE        (120)            26

 73   w70%  w70%    67    66%   65    63%   67    62%  w66   69%  w66
/////                                /////  /////
 78%   74%   79     72    72%   72    76%   76%   71%   76%   74%   67
SA-6%  SA6  SA6%   HOL6   SA6   SA6  SA-6% HOL5% HOL8%  SA6%  SA6%  HOL6
 71%         69%                      62%         65%   65%   69
 81%   77%   82%    72    68%   74%   80    66%         84    70    70%
02/07 01/17 01/05  DEC09 02/16 01/31 12/30 12/20 11/23 11/01 OCT11 07/23
```

Normally we approximate Kelly with more money on higher probability wagers, but in the following bets we made equal $2 bets.

```
$2.00 ;P6; (3) 1 ,3 /(4) 3 /(5) 7 /(6) 3 /(7) 2 /(8) 2
$2.00 ;P6; (3) 7 /(4) 3 /(5) 7 /(6) 3 /(7) 2 /(8) 2
$2.00 ;P6; (3) 1 ,3 /(4) 1 ,5 /(5) 7 /(6) 3 /(7) 2 /(8) 2
$2.00 ;P6; (3) 1 ,3 /(4) 3 /(5) 2 ,3 ,5 ,6 /(6) 3 /(7) 2 /(8) 2
$2.00 ;P6; (3) 1 ,3 /(4) 3 /(5) 7 /(6) 4 ,7 ,8 ,10 /(7) 2 /(8) 2
$2.00 ;P6; (3) 1 ,3 /(4) 3 /(5) 7 /(6) 3 /(7) 1 ,4 /(8) 2
$2.00 ;P6; (3) 1 ,3 /(4) 3 /(5) 7 /(6) 3 /(7) 2 /(8) 5 ,9
$2.00 ;P6; (3) 5 ,6 /(4) 3 /(5) 7 /(6) 3 /(7) 2 /(8) 2
$2.00 ;P6; (3) 1 ,3 /(4) 2 ,4 ,8 /(5) 7 /(6) 3 /(7) 2 /(8) 2
$2.00 ;P6; (3) 1 ,3 /(4) 3 /(5) 7 /(6) 1 ,2 ,5 /(7) 2 /(8) 2
$2.00 ;P6; (3) 1 ,3 /(4) 3 /(5) 7 /(6) 3 /(7) 2 /(8) 1 ,6 ,7 ,8
$2.00 ;P6; (3) 7 /(4) 1 ,5 /(5) 7 /(6) 3 /(7) 2 /(8) 2
$2.00 ;P6; (3) 7 /(4) 3 /(5) 2 ,3 ,5 ,6 /(6) 3 /(7) 2 /(8) 2
$2.00 ;P6; (3) 7 /(4) 3 /(5) 7 /(6) 4 ,7 ,8 ,10 /(7) 2 /(8) 2
$2.00 ;P6; (3) 7 /(4) 3 /(5) 7 /(6) 3 /(7) 1 ,4 /(8) 2
$2.00 ;P6; (3) 7 /(4) 3 /(5) 7 /(6) 3 /(7) 2 /(8) 5 ,9
$2.00 ;P6; (3) 1 ,3 /(4) 1 ,5 /(5) 2 ,3 ,5 ,6 /(6) 3 /(7) 2 /(8) 2
$2.00 ;P6; (3) 1 ,3 /(4) 1 ,5 /(5) 7 /(6) 4 ,7 ,8 ,10 /(7) 2 /(8) 2
$2.00 ;P6; (3) 1 ,3 /(4) 1 ,5 /(5) 7 /(6) 3 /(7) 1 ,4 /(8) 2
$2.00 ;P6; (3) 1 ,3 /(4) 1 ,5 /(5) 7 /(6) 3 /(7) 2 /(8) 5 ,9
$2.00 ;P6; (3) 1 ,3 /(4) 3 /(5) 2 ,3 ,5 ,6 /(6) 4 ,7 ,8 ,10 /(7) 2 /(8) 2
$2.00 ;P6; (3) 1 ,3 /(4) 3 /(5) 2 ,3 ,5 ,6 /(6) 3 /(7) 1 ,4 /(8) 2
$2.00 ;P6; (3) 1 ,3 /(4) 3 /(5) 2 ,3 ,5 ,6 /(6) 3 /(7) 2 /(8) 5 ,9
$2.00 ;P6; (3) 1 ,3 /(4) 3 /(5) 7 /(6) 4 ,7 ,8 ,10 /(7) 1 ,4 /(8) 2
$2.00 ;P6; (3) 1 ,3 /(4) 3 /(5) 7 /(6) 4 ,7 ,8 ,10 /(7) 2 /(8) 5 ,9
$2.00 ;P6; (3) 1 ,3 /(4) 3 /(5) 7 /(6) 3 /(7) 1 ,4 /(8) 5 ,9
$2.00 ;P6; (3) 5 ,6 /(4) 1 ,5 /(5) 7 /(6) 3 /(7) 2 /(8) 2
$2.00 ;P6; (3) 5 ,6 /(4) 3 /(5) 2 ,3 ,5 ,6 /(6) 3 /(7) 2 /(8) 2
$2.00 ;P6; (3) 5 ,6 /(4) 3 /(5) 7 /(6) 4 ,7 ,8 ,10 /(7) 2 /(8) 2
$2.00 ;P6; (3) 5 ,6 /(4) 3 /(5) 7 /(6) 3 /(7) 1 ,4 /(8) 2
$2.00 ;P6; (3) 5 ,6 /(4) 3 /(5) 7 /(6) 3 /(7) 2 /(8) 5 ,9
$2.00 ;P6; (3) 7 /(4) 2 ,4 ,8 /(5) 7 /(6) 3 /(7) 2 /(8) 2
$2.00 ;P6; (3) 1 ,3 /(4) 2 ,4 ,8 /(5) 2 ,3 ,5 ,6 /(6) 3 /(7) 2 /(8) 2
$2.00 ;P6; (3) 1 ,3 /(4) 2 ,4 ,8 /(5) 7 /(6) 4 ,7 ,8 ,10 /(7) 2 /(8) 2
$2.00 ;P6; (3) 1 ,3 /(4) 2 ,4 ,8 /(5) 7 /(6) 3 /(7) 1 ,4 /(8) 2
$2.00 ;P6; (3) 1 ,3 /(4) 2 ,4 ,8 /(5) 7 /(6) 3 /(7) 2 /(8) 5 ,9
$2.00 ;P6; (3) 7 /(4) 3 /(5) 7 /(6) 1 ,2 ,5 /(7) 2 /(8) 2
$2.00 ;P6; (3) 1 ,3 /(4) 1 ,5 /(5) 7 /(6) 1 ,2 ,5 /(7) 2 /(8) 2
$2.00 ;P6; (3) 1 ,3 /(4) 3 /(5) 2 ,3 ,5 ,6 /(6) 1 ,2 ,5 /(7) 2 /(8) 2
$2.00 ;P6; (3) 1 ,3 /(4) 3 /(5) 7 /(6) 1 ,2 ,5 /(7) 1 ,4 /(8) 2
$2.00 ;P6; (3) 1 ,3 /(4) 3 /(5) 7 /(6) 1 ,2 ,5 /(7) 2 /(8) 5 ,9
$2.00 ;P6; (3) 7 /(4) 3 /(5) 7 /(6) 3 /(7) 2 /(8) 1 ,6 ,7 ,8
$2.00 ;P6; (3) 1 ,3 /(4) 1 ,5 /(5) 7 /(6) 3 /(7) 2 /(8) 1 ,6 ,7 ,8
$2.00 ;P6; (3) 1 ,3 /(4) 3 /(5) 2 ,3 ,5 ,6 /(6) 3 /(7) 2 /(8) 1 ,6 ,7 ,8
$2.00 ;P6; (3) 1 ,3 /(4) 3 /(5) 7 /(6) 4 ,7 ,8 ,10 /(7) 2 /(8) 1 ,6 ,7 ,8
$2.00 ;P6; (3) 1 ,3 /(4) 3 /(5) 7 /(6) 3 /(7) 1 ,4 /(8) 1 ,6 ,7 ,8
$2.00 ;P6; (3) 7 /(4) 1 ,5 /(5) 2 ,3 ,5 ,6 /(6) 3 /(7) 2 /(8) 2
$2.00 ;P6; (3) 7 /(4) 1 ,5 /(5) 7 /(6) 4 ,7 ,8 ,10 /(7) 2 /(8) 2
$2.00 ;P6; (3) 7 /(4) 1 ,5 /(5) 7 /(6) 3 /(7) 1 ,4 /(8) 2
$2.00 ;P6; (3) 7 /(4) 1 ,5 /(5) 7 /(6) 3 /(7) 2 /(8) 5 ,9
$2.00 ;P6; (3) 7 /(4) 3 /(5) 2 ,3 ,5 ,6 /(6) 4 ,7 ,8 ,10 /(7) 2 /(8) 2
$2.00 ;P6; (3) 7 /(4) 3 /(5) 2 ,3 ,5 ,6 /(6) 3 /(7) 1 ,4 /(8) 2
$2.00 ;P6; (3) 7 /(4) 3 /(5) 2 ,3 ,5 ,6 /(6) 3 /(7) 2 /(8) 5 ,9
$2.00 ;P6; (3) 7 /(4) 3 /(5) 7 /(6) 4 ,7 ,8 ,10 /(7) 1 ,4 /(8) 2
$2.00 ;P6; (3) 7 /(4) 3 /(5) 7 /(6) 4 ,7 ,8 ,10 /(7) 2 /(8) 5 ,9
$2.00 ;P6; (3) 7 /(4) 3 /(5) 7 /(6) 3 /(7) 1 ,4 /(8) 5 ,9
$2.00 ;P6; (3) 1 ,3 /(4) 1 ,5 /(5) 2 ,3 ,5 ,6 /(6) 4 ,7 ,8 ,10 /(7) 2 /(8) 2
$2.00 ;P6; (3) 1 ,3 /(4) 1 ,5 /(5) 2 ,3 ,5 ,6 /(6) 3 /(7) 1 ,4 /(8) 2
$2.00 ;P6; (3) 1 ,3 /(4) 1 ,5 /(5) 2 ,3 ,5 ,6 /(6) 3 /(7) 2 /(8) 5 ,9
$2.00 ;P6; (3) 1 ,3 /(4) 1 ,5 /(5) 7 /(6) 4 ,7 ,8 ,10 /(7) 1 ,4 /(8) 2
$2.00 ;P6; (3) 1 ,3 /(4) 1 ,5 /(5) 7 /(6) 4 ,7 ,8 ,10 /(7) 2 /(8) 5 ,9
$2.00 ;P6; (3) 1 ,3 /(4) 1 ,5 /(5) 7 /(6) 3 /(7) 1 ,4 /(8) 5 ,9
$2.00 ;P6; (3) 1 ,3 /(4) 3 /(5) 2 ,3 ,5 ,6 /(6) 4 ,7 ,8 ,10 /(7) 1 ,4 /(8) 2
$2.00 ;P6; (3) 1 ,3 /(4) 3 /(5) 2 ,3 ,5 ,6 /(6) 4 ,7 ,8 ,10 /(7) 2 /(8) 5 ,9
$2.00 ;P6; (3) 1 ,3 /(4) 3 /(5) 2 ,3 ,5 ,6 /(6) 3 /(7) 1 ,4 /(8) 5 ,9
$2.00 ;P6; (3) 1 ,3 /(4) 3 /(5) 7 /(6) 4 ,7 ,8 ,10 /(7) 1 ,4 /(8) 5 ,9
```

	Amount bet	
Score 6	\$2	\$4
Score 7	\$2	\$58
Score 8	\$2	\$376
Score 9	\$2	\$1,484
Score 10	\$2	\$0
Score 11	\$2	\$0
Total 0.54%		\$1,922

A key behavioral idea was: Consider two overlapping probability distributions. Suppose A is better but B overlaps. So if you choose a point from B it may be better from one chosen from A. And again, the parley is much lower than the Pick 6 payoff on a fast track day.

Pick 6 example 4, the Rainbow Pick 6 on May 25, 2014: In 2014 the Rainbow Pick 6 tickets were raised to 20 cents at Gulfstream racetrack in Florida. Going into the May 26 mandatory payout, the carryover pool was \$6,303,426.30. On Sunday the pool was \$6,397.293.35 and Monday's, which was won, was \$6,678,939.12.

A single bettor, Danny Borislow, won the whole Rainbow Pick 6 pool on Sunday May 25, 2014, a day before the mandatory payout. The payoffs of Races 3-8 with winning numbers 1–8–6–1–6–5 were \$35.80, \$22.60, \$12.80, \$10.40, \$9.60, and \$12.80, respectively. Danny had two tickets each for \$7,603.20 with the winning ticket being all-all-all-1,4-all-all as #1 won the 4th leg. The second ticket had the same five "alls" plus two other horses in leg 4.

These races have two bombs and four 4–1 or 5–1 horses. Normally two bombs in the \$20–30 range and four \$10 horses would not yield just one unique P6 winner. The reason this bettor won was the low volume in the pool on Sunday as most bettors were preparing for Monday's mandatory payout. Also the short fields 6–6–6–10–7–13 allowed Danny to bet all the horses in five of the races and four deep in the fourth leg for his \$7,603.20 times 2 for a total investment of \$15,206.40.

The net increase in the pool on Sunday was \$281,755.77 (total pool of 6,678,939.12 — carryover of 6,397,283.35), dividing by 0.80 gives the total bet of \$352,194.71. This was more than Saturday's increase in the carryover of \$93,857.05 or the \$117,321.31 bet.

The parlay with six win takes of 17% was 0.2(17.9)(11.3)(6.4)(5.2)(4.8)(6.4) = \$41,358.62. Then with no track take, the true parlay was $4,135,861.62/(1-0.17)^6 = \$126,502.02$ which is again below the Rainbow Pick 6 payoff of \$6,678,939.12 which had 20% taken off the total bet.

So bravo to Danny Borislow who seized a good opportunity to win the whole pool. Danny was the owner of the Magic Jack telephone device business. It is extremely unlikely that someone could win the whole pool on mandatory payout day as most likely there would be multiple P6 winners all going after a share of \$10+ million pool. A sad postscript: on Monday July 21, 2014, Danny collapsed and died at age 52 after playing in an indoor soccer game in West Palm Beach, Florida.

Pick 6 example 5, the Zenyatta Breeders' Cup Pick 6 in 2009: The Zenyatta Breeders' Cup Pick 6 discussed in the text. It had no carryover going and the Pick 6 paid \$1,968,630.00 for a \$2 ticket.

The parlay was (52.60)(63.20/2)(2.4)(22.3)(1.9)(3.8)=\$642,282.56 which about one third of the Pick 6 payoff. Again, much less.

Remarks:

- Since the Pick 6 must be bet in advance and the individual races are bet race by race that may be part of the reason why the Pick 6 payoffs are larger.
- We can think of the Pick 6 as a sports lottery where there is skill involved but the complexity of the bet makes it difficult to win.
- I have computed for each of the five examples the actual parlay which is the amount you would actually get after the six track takes if you bet the races in sequence using the proceeds from the previous races.
- What I call the true parlay is the theoretical concept to compare the likelihood of winning the Pick 6 to the likelihoods of winning the individual races.

Appendix

The following are the charts for the Pick 6 races:

BELMONT PARK - May 30, 2021 - Race 4 EQUIBASE
CLAIMING - Thoroughbred
FOR THREE YEAR OLDS AND UPWARD WHICH HAVE NEVER WON TWO RACES. Three Year Olds, 120 lbs.; Older, 126 lbs. Non-winners Of A Race At A Mile Or Over In 2021 Allowed 2 lbs. Claiming Price $16,000 (1.5% Aftercare Assessment due at time of claim otherwise claim will be void). (NW2 L) **Claiming Price:** $16,000
One Mile On The Dirt **Current Track Record:** (Najran - 1:32.24 - May 7, 2003)
Purse: $28,000
Available Money: $28,000
Value of Race: $27,160 1st $15,400, 2nd $5,600, 3rd $3,360, 4th $1,680, 5th $1,120
Weather: Showery **Track:** Sloppy (Sealed)
Off at: 2:34 **Start:** Good for all **Timer:** Electronic

Video Race Replay

Last Raced	Pgm	Horse Name (Jockey)	Wgt	M/E	PP	Start	1/4	1/2	3/4	Str	Fin	Odds	Comments
25Mar21 ^{8}AQU^{1}	6	Beatthatflew (Cancel, Eric)	118	L	4	1	2^{2}	$2^{1\ 1/2}$	$1^{1/2}$	$1^{5\ 1/2}$	$1^{10\ 1/4}$	5.40	dueled 3p, drew off
6May21 ^{5}BEL^{4}	5	Millean (Cardenas, Luis)	120	L	3	2	$4^{1\ 1/2}$	4^{Head}	$3^{1/2}$	$3^{1/2}$	2^{Neck}	1.55*	5w upper, up for 2nd
5Jul20 ^{4}BEL^{6}	4	My Sacred Place (Franco, Manuel)	124	L	2	5	$3^{1/2}$	3^{1}	4^{Head}	5	$3^{1\ 3/4}$	1.80	chased 3-4w, improved
1Apr21 ^{2}AQU^{3}	8	Bellamy Dolce (Carmouche, Kendrick)	120	L f	5	3	5	5	5	$4^{1/2}$	$4^{3\ 1/2}$	3.10	3w upper, weakened
16May21 ^{9}BEL^{10}	3	Quintarelli (Harkie, Heman)	124	L b	1	4	1^{Head}	$1^{1/2}$	$2^{1\ 1/2}$	$2^{1\ 1/2}$	5	21.50	dueled 2p, tired

Fractional Times: 24.16 47.75 1:12.63 **Final Time:** 1:38.85
Split Times: (23:59) (24:88) (26:22)
Run-Up: 80 feet

Winner: Beatthatflew, Dark Bay or Brown Gelding, by Shanghai Bobby out of Dash Dot Dash, by Put It Back. Foaled Mar 10, 2018 in New York.
Breeder: Chester Broman & Mary R. Broman
Owner: GMP Stables LLC, F Bellavia, LLC, JP Racing Stable and Gullo, Gary P.
Trainer: Sciacca, Gary

1 Claimed Horse(s): Beatthatflew New Trainer: Joseph G. Parker New Owner: Rohan Ramdat

Millean(Vet);

Claiming Prices: 6 - Beatthatflew: $16,000; 5 - Millean: $16,000; 4 - My Sacred Place: $16,000; 8 - Bellamy Dolce: $16,000; 3 - Quintarelli: $16,000;

Scratched Horse(s): Patty O'Marc (Veterinarian), Super Silver (Veterinarian), Whichwaytomalibu (Stewards)

Total WPS Pool: $232,762

Pgm	Horse	Win	Place	Show	Wager Type	Winning Numbers	Payoff	Pool
6	Beatthatflew	12.80	5.30	2.90	$1.00 Exacta	6-5	18.20	137,785
5	Millean		3.10	2.30	$1.00 Quinella	5-6	6.60	5,922
4	My Sacred Place			2.50	$0.50 Trifecta	6-5-4	16.62	75,370
					$1.00 Pick 3	3-3-6 (3 correct)	489.50	26,174
					$1.00 Daily Double	3-6	17.70	69,562
					$0.10 Superfecta	6-5-4-8	4.32	37,684

BELMONT PARK - May 30, 2021 - Race 5 EQUIBASE
STARTER ALLOWANCE - Thoroughbred
(UP TO $9,570 NYSBFOA) FOR THREE YEAR OLDS AND UPWARD WHICH HAVE STARTED FOR A CLAIMING PRICE OF $50,000 OR LESS AND WHICH HAVE NEVER WON A RACE OTHER THAN MAIDEN OR CLAIMING. Three Year Olds, 120 lbs.; Older, 126 lbs. Non-winners Of A Race At A Mile Or Over In 2021 Allowed 2 lbs. (If the Stewards consider it inadvisable to run this race on the turf course, this race will be run at One Mile and One Sixteenth on the Main Track.) (Rail at 27 feet). **Claiming Price:** $50,000 - $0
One And One Sixteenth Miles On The Dirt - Originally Scheduled For 1 1/16 Miles On Turf **Current Track Record:** (Transparent - 1:39.22 - September 18, 2014)
Purse: $55,000
Available Money: $55,000
Value of Race: $55,000 1st $30,250, 2nd $11,000, 3rd $6,600, 4th $3,300, 5th $2,200, 6th $413, 7th $413, 8th $413, 9th $411
Weather: Rainy **Track:** Sloppy (Sealed)
Off at: 3:05 **Start:** Good for all **Timer:** Electronic

Video Race Replay

Last Raced	Pgm	Horse Name (Jockey)	Wgt	M/E	PP	Start	1/4	1/2	3/4	Str	Fin	Odds	Comments
25Apr21 ^{2}BEL^{1}	1	First Line (Ortiz, Jr., Irad)	126	- -	6	2	$3^{1/2}$	3^{Head}	$3^{1/2}$	$1^{1/2}$	$1^{3/4}$	1.10*	4w turn,bid1/4,dueled
14May21 ^{5}BEL^{2}	5	Kid Bourbon (Franco, Manuel)	124	L f	2	7	$5^{1\ 1/2}$	4^{Head}	5^{1}	$2^{1\ 1/2}$	$2^{3/4}$	8.10	slw into stride,3w trn
6May21 ^{5}BEL^{2}	13	My First Grammy (Cardenas, Luis)	126	L bf	8	1	$6^{1/2}$	$7^{1/2}$	$6^{1/2}$	$4^{1/2}$	$3^{2\ 1/4}$	35.25	6w trn,ins lead,gained
25Apr21 ^{6}GP^{2}	1A	Mr. Tip (Ortiz, Jose)	126	L b	9	4	8^{4}	6^{Head}	$7^{1/2}$	5^{Head}	4^{1}	1.10*	broke out,4-5wide turn
23May21 ^{8}BEL^{2}	8	Indian Counselor (Cancel, Eric)	126	L b	3	8	7^{Head}	$8^{2\ 1/2}$	$8^{1/2}$	$6^{1\ 1/2}$	$5^{3/4}$	3.65	bmpd after brk,tkn up
29Apr21 ^{7}BEL^{6}	11	Obsessed (Saez, Luis)	126	L b	5	6	2^{1}	2^{1}	$1^{1/2}$	$3^{1/2}$	$6^{5\ 1/2}$	13.70	outside,3-2p turn,wknd
9Apr21 ^{5}AQU^{9}	9	Mr. Kringle (Carmouche, Kendrick)	124	L	4	9	9	9	9	8^{2}	$7^{1\ 3/4}$	23.20	bmpd after brk,tkn up
15May21 ^{9}BEL^{3}	12	Parade Field (Alvarado, Junior)	124	L bf	7	3	4^{Head}	5^{1}	4^{Head}	7^{1}	$8^{3\ 1/4}$	5.20	outside,5w turn,empty
23Apr21 ^{10}KEE^{1}	3	Tallaj (Rosario, Joel)	118	L b	1	5	$1^{1/2}$	1^{Head}	$2^{1/2}$	9	9	9.20	pace,2p3/8,stopped

Fractional Times: 23.61 47.47 1:12.07 1:37.33 **Final Time:** 1:44.01
Split Times: (23:86) (24:60) (25:26) (6:68)
Run-Up: 60 feet

Winner: First Line, Chestnut Gelding, by First Samurai out of Street Line, by Street Cry (IRE). Foaled May 01, 2017 in Kentucky.
Breeder: Sather Family LLC
Owner: Three Diamonds Farm
Trainer: Maker, Michael

Scratched Horse(s): Big Wonder (Off-Turf), Fame to Famous (Off-Turf), Holy Emperor (Off-Turf), Life On Top (Off-Turf), Turn of Events (Off-Turf)

Total WPS Pool: $411,213

Pgm	Horse	Win	Place	Show	Wager Type	Winning Numbers	Payoff	Pool
1	First Line	4.20	2.70	2.10	$1.00 Exacta	1-5	13.80	276,530
5	Kid Bourbon		6.70	4.60	$0.50 Trifecta	1-5-13	87.75	158,257
13	My First Grammy			9.20	$1.00 Pick 3	3-6-1 (3 correct)	32.50	129,044
					$0.50 Pick 4	3-3-6-1/2/4/6/7/10 (4 correct)	1,091.50	150,337
					$0.50 Pick 5	1/2-3-3-6-1/2/4/6/7/10 (5 correct)	2,084.25	505,724
					$1.00 Daily Double	6-1	26.00	46,085
					$0.10 Superfecta	1-5-13-8	85.25	89,410

Past Performance Running Line Preview

BELMONT PARK - May 30, 2021 - Race 6
MAIDEN CLAIMING - Thoroughbred
FOR MAIDENS, THREE YEARS OLD AND UPWARD. Three Year Olds, 118 lbs.; Older, 125 lbs. Claiming Price $20,000 (1.5% Aftercare Assessment Due At Time Of Claim Otherwise Claim Will Be Void). **Claiming Price:** $20,000
One Mile On The Dirt **Current Track Record:** (Najran - 1:32.24 - May 7, 2003)
Purse: $35,000
Available Money: $35,000
Value of Race: $35,000 1st $19,250, 2nd $7,000, 3rd $4,200, 4th $2,100, 5th $1,400, 6th $210, 7th $210, 8th $210, 9th $210, 10th $210
Weather: Showery **Track:** Sloppy (Sealed)
Off at: 3:37 **Start:** Good for all except 2,7 **Timer:** Electronic

EQUIBASE

Video Race Replay

Last Raced	Pgm	Horse Name (Jockey)	Wgt	M/E	PP	Start	1/4	1/2	3/4	Str	Fin	Odds	Comments
7Mar21 ^{3}AQU^{5}	2	Tapit's Flashback (Saez, Luis)	118	L b	1	10	9^{Head}	9^{3}	$3^{1/2}$	$3^{1\ 1/2}$	$1^{2\ 1/4}$	7.40	veer in st, gd courage
5Sep20 ^{7}SAR^{9}	3	Mo Heat (Cancel, Eric)	118	- -	2	6	$1^{1/2}$	1^{1}	1^{Head}	$1^{1/2}$	2^{Head}	6.00	coaxed 3-2w, caught
25Apr21 ^{3}BEL^{5}	11	Tremendous (Rosario, Joel)	118	L	10	1	3^{Head}	$3^{1/2}$	$2^{4\ 1/2}$	$2^{1\ 1/2}$	$3^{1\ 3/4}$	6.50	4-5w upper, ran on
22May21 ^{2}BEL^{7}	5	Our Lucky Man (Harkie, Heman)	118	L b	4	8	$7^{1/2}$	7^{2}	4^{1}	4^{10}	$4^{12\ 1/2}$	14.90	3w upper, kept on
16Apr21 ^{3}AQU^{4}	8	Sinashack (Cardenas, Luis)	118	L bf	7	4	$4^{1/2}$	2^{Head}	$6^{1/2}$	$5^{1/2}$	$5^{5\ 1/2}$	17.70	4-5w, lost whip, tired
24Mar21 ^{10}GP^{6}	10	Core Curriculum (Ortiz, Jr., Irad)	118	L b	9	7	8^{5}	$8^{1\ 1/2}$	$8^{1\ 1/2}$	8^{3}	$6^{2\ 3/4}$	3.05*	bobbled st, overland
7May21 ^{6}BEL^{4}	9	Sixteen Tons (Ortiz, Jose)	125	L b	8	2	$6^{2\ 1/2}$	$6^{1\ 1/2}$	7^{3}	$6^{1/2}$	$7^{15\ 3/4}$	6.50	7w upper tired
23Apr21 ^{9}BEL^{4}	4	Futuro (Alvarado, Junior)	125	L	3	5	2^{1}	$4^{2\ 1/2}$	5^{2}	7^{2}	8^{6}	3.35	4-3w in aim, folded
12Nov20 ^{9}AQU^{6}	7	Tiz Envy (Richards, Gary)	125	L b	6	9	10	10	10	10	$9^{1\ 3/4}$	31.25	leapt, tossed head st
2Apr21 ^{4}AQU^{6}	6	Epona Rising (Lezcano, Jose)	118	L b	5	3	$5^{3\ 1/2}$	5^{3}	9^{10}	9^{12}	10	20.90	chased 3-4w, gave way

Fractional Times: 22.71 46.30 1:11.83 **Final Time:** 1:39.57
Split Times: (23:59) (25:53) (27:74)
Run-Up: 80 feet

Winner: Tapit's Flashback, Gray or Roan Colt, by Flashback out of Inglorious Song, by Broken Vow. Foaled Feb 15, 2018 in Maryland.
Breeder: Barak Farm & Dinos Thoroughbreds LLC
Owner: Gagliano Stables
Trainer: Barrera, III, Oscar

Tremendous(Vet);

Claiming Prices: 2 - Tapit's Flashback: $20,000; 3 - Mo Heat: $20,000; 11 - Tremendous: $20,000; 5 - Our Lucky Man: $20,000; 8 - Sinashack: $20,000; 10 - Core Curriculum: $20,000; 9 - Sixteen Tons: $20,000; 4 - Futuro: $20,000; 7 - Tiz Envy: $20,000; 6 - Epona Rising: $20,000;

Scratched Horse(s): Enroule (Stewards)

Total WPS Pool: $340,229

Pgm	Horse	Win	Place	Show	Wager Type	Winning Numbers	Payoff	Pool
2	Tapit's Flashback	16.80	7.40	5.70	$1.00 Exacta	2-3	64.50	268,607
3	Mo Heat		8.10	5.70	$0.50 Trifecta	2-3-11	246.25	142,358
11	Tremendous			5.50	$1.00 Pick 3	6-1-2 (3 correct)	170.50	63,079
					$1.00 Daily Double	1-2	36.50	48,860
					$0.10 Superfecta	2-3-11-5	320.00	75,623

BELMONT PARK - May 30, 2021 - Race 7
ALLOWANCE OPTIONAL CLAIMING - Thoroughbred
INNER TURF (UP TO $16,356 NYSBFOA) FOR THREE YEAR OLDS AND UPWARD WHICH HAVE NEVER WON $13,000 TWICE OTHER THAN MAIDEN, CLAIMING, STARTER OR STATE BRED ALLOWANCE OR WHICH HAVE NEVER WON THREE RACES OR OPTIONAL CLAIMING PRICE OF $80,000. Three Year Olds, 120 lbs.; Older, 126 lbs. Non-winners Of Two Races Other Than Claiming Or Starter At A Mile Or Over In 2021 Allowed 2 lbs. One Such Race In 2021 Allowed 4 lbs. Claiming Price $80,000 (1.5% Aftercare Assessment Due At Time Of Claim Otherwise Claim Will Be Void). (Rail at 35 feet). (NW2$ X) **Claiming Price:** $80,000
One And One Fourth Miles On The Dirt - Originally Scheduled For 1 3/8 Miles On Inner turf **Current Track Record:** (In Excess (IRE) - 1:58.33 - July 4, 1991)
Purse: $94,000
Available Money: $94,000
Value of Race: $91,180 1st $51,700, 2nd $18,800, 3rd $11,280, 4th $5,640, 5th $3,760
Weather: Showery **Track:** Sloppy (Sealed)
Off at: 4:13 **Start:** Good for all **Timer:** Electronic

EQUIBASE

Video Race Replay

Last Raced	Pgm	Horse Name (Jockey)	Wgt	M/E	PP	1/4	1/2	3/4	1m	Str	Fin	Odds	Comments
3Mar21 ^{6}TP^{2}	9	Burning Bright (Franco, Manuel)	124	L	4	$2^{1\ 1/2}$	1^{Head}	$1^{1\ 1/2}$	1^{1}	$1^{2\ 1/2}$	$1^{7\ 1/4}$	3.30	hit gate,2p2nd,drw off
29Apr21 ^{8}BEL^{4}	1A	Dynadrive (Ortiz, Jr., Irad)	122	L	2	$4^{1\ 1/2}$	$4^{1\ 1/2}$	2^{Head}	2^{2}	$2^{4\ 1/2}$	2^{5}	1.85	shoe repair paddock
15May21 ^{8}BEL^{5}	10	Dark Storm (Lezcano, Jose)	122	L	5	5	5	4^{3}	4^{3}	3^{Head}	$3^{1/2}$	6.50	3w2nd,asked5/16,empty
29Apr21 ^{8}BEL^{7}	8	Malthael (Alvarado, Junior)	122	L	3	$1^{1/2}$	2^{3}	$3^{1\ 1/2}$	3^{1}	4^{3}	4^{7}	7.40	early pace,ins2nd,wknd
1May21 ^{3}BEL^{5}	3	Limonite (Cancel, Eric)	124	L	1	3^{1}	$3^{1/2}$	5	5	5	5	1.75*	shifted 5w1/4,faltered

Fractional Times: 25.95 50.87 1:15.58 1:39.98 **Final Time:** 2:04.50
Split Times: (24:92) (24:71) (24:40) (24:52)
Run-Up: 90 feet

Winner: Burning Bright, Bay Gelding, by Empire Maker out of Forever Together, by Belong to Me. Foaled Apr 02, 2017 in Kentucky.
Breeder: Augustin Stable
Owner: Augustin Stable
Trainer: Thomas, Jonathan

Claiming Prices: 10 - Dark Storm: $80,000; 8 - Malthael: $80,000;

Scratched Horse(s): Basha (Off-Turf), Grumps Little Tots (Veterinarian), Mr. Alec (Off-Turf), Opry (Off-Turf), Price Talk (Off-Turf), Temple (Trainer)

Total WPS Pool: $288,881

Pgm	Horse	Win	Place	Show	Wager Type	Winning Numbers	Payoff	Pool
9	Burning Bright	8.60	4.00	2.50	$1.00 Exacta	9-1	10.20	161,278
1A	Dynadrive		3.30	2.40	$0.50 Trifecta	9-1-10	12.87	68,432
10	Dark Storm			2.80	$1.00 Daily Double	2-9	37.50	32,364
					$1.00 Pick 3	1-2-9 (3 correct)	115.25	65,407
					$0.10 Superfecta	9-1-10-8	6.05	34,656

BELMONT PARK - May 30, 2021 - Race 8 **EQUIBASE**

STAKES Paradise Creek S. Listed - Thoroughbred

FOR THREE YEAR OLDS. Non-Lasix Race pursuant to 4043.2 (7)(e)(5) Lasix not permitted within 48 hours of post time. By subscription of $100 each which should accompany the nomination; $500 to pass the entry box and an additional $500 to start. For horses not originally nominated, a supplemental payment of $1,000 (along with the entry and starting fees) may be made at any time prior to the closing of entries. The purse to be divided 55% to the owner of the winner, 20% to second, 12% to third, 6% to fourth, 4% to fifth and 3% divided equally amongst the remaining finishers. Weight: 123 lbs. Non-winners of a Graded Sweepstakes allowed 3 lbs.; of a Sweepstake other than State-bred or two races other than maiden, claiming, starter or state bred allowance allowed 5 lbs. The New York Racing Association reserves the right to transfer this race to the main track. Starters to be named at the closing time of entries. A presentation will be made to the winning owner. Closed Saturday, May 15, 2021 with 22 Original Nominations and 1 Supplement. (If the Stewards consider it inadvisable to run this race on the turf course, this race will be run at Seven Furlongs on the Main Track.) (Rail at 27 feet).

Seven Furlongs On The Dirt - Originally Scheduled For 7 Furlongs On Turf **Current Track Record:** (Clearly Now - 1:19.96 - July 5, 2014)

Purse: $100,000 Added
Available Money: $100,000
Value of Race: $93,000 1st $55,000, 2nd $20,000, 3rd $12,000, 4th $6,000 Video Race Replay
Weather: Showery **Track:** Sloppy (Sealed)
Off at: 4:41 **Start:** Good for all except 2,4 **Timer:** Electronic

Last Raced	Pgm	Horse Name (Jockey)	Wgt	M/E	PP	Start	1/4	1/2	Str	Fin	Odds	Comments
9May21 ^{8}BEL^{1}	1	Beren (Cancel, Eric)	120	- -	1	1	$1^{1\ 1/2}$	1^{1}	1^{6}	$1^{10\ 3/4}$	1.00*	in hand 3-2w, went clr
1May21 ^{8}CD^{10}	5	Three Two Zone (Carmouche, Kendrick)	118	bf	4	3	2^{4}	$2^{3\ 1/2}$	$2^{1/2}$	2^{Nose}	2.80	chased 4-3w, weakened
24Apr21 ^{3}BEL^{6}	4	Thin White Duke (Rosario, Joel)	120	- -	3	2	$3^{1/2}$	4	$3^{3\ 1/2}$	$3^{7\ 1/2}$	9.50	bumped betw start
2Apr21 ^{7}KEE^{2}	2	Fauci (Castellano, Javier)	118	b	2	4	4	$3^{1/2}$	4	4	2.05	bobbled st, tired

Fractional Times: 22.80 45.64 1:10.03 **Final Time:** 1:23.12
Split Times: (22:84) (24:39) (13:09)
Run-Up: 60 feet

Winner: Beren, Bay Colt, by Weigelia out of Silmaril, by Diamond. Foaled Apr 08, 2018 in Pennsylvania.
Breeder: Susan C Quick & Christopher J Feifarek
Owner: Quick, Susan C. and Feifarek, Christopher J.
Trainer: Reid, Jr., Robert

Scratched Horse(s): Chasing Artie (Off-Turf), Outadore (Off-Turf), Second of July (Off-Turf)

Total WPS Pool: $248,872

Pgm	Horse	Win	Place	Wager Type	Winning Numbers	Payoff	Pool
1	Beren	4.00	2.20	$1.00 Exacta	1-5	3.75	107,286
5	Three Two Zone		2.90	$1.00 Pick 3	2-9-1 (3 correct)	106.00	32,948
4	Thin White Duke			$1.00 Grand Slam	1/5/13-2/3/11-1/9/10-1 (4 correct)	31.75	30,053
				$1.00 Daily Double	9-1	8.60	48,948

BELMONT PARK - May 30, 2021 - Race 9 **EQUIBASE**

MAIDEN CLAIMING - Thoroughbred

FOR MAIDENS, FILLIES AND MARES THREE YEARS OLD AND UPWARD FOALED IN NEW YORK STATE AND APPROVED BY THE NEW YORK STATE-BRED REGISTRY. Three Year Olds, 118 lbs.; Older, 124 lbs. Claiming Price $25,000 (1.5% Aftercare Assessment Due At Time Of Claim Otherwise Claim Will Be Void). (S) **Claiming Price:** $25,000

Six Furlongs On The Dirt **Current Track Record:** (Artax - 1:07.66 - October 16, 1999)

Purse: $37,000
Available Money: $37,000
Value of Race: $37,000 1st $20,350, 2nd $7,400, 3rd $4,440, 4th $2,220, 5th $1,480, 6th $222, 7th $222, 8th $222, 9th $222, 10th $222 Video Race Replay
Weather: Showery **Track:** Sloppy (Sealed)
Off at: 5:15 **Start:** Good for all except 7,8 **Timer:** Electronic

Last Raced	Pgm	Horse Name (Jockey)	Wgt	M/E	PP	Start	1/4	1/2	Str	Fin	Odds	Comments
7May21 ^{5}BEL^{6}	13	Cazilda Fortytales (Ortiz, Jr., Irad)	124	L bf	10	5	2^{1}	1^{Head}	$1^{1/2}$	1^{Neck}	1.90*	3path turn,bumped late
6May21 ^{4}BEL^{4}	11	Tiny Magoo (Franco, Manuel)	124	L b	9	2	3^{1}	3^{4}	3^{5}	$2^{1\ 1/2}$	9.40	4w3/8,bid3/16,bmp late
7May21 ^{9}BEL^{4}	6	Esotica (Saez, Luis)	118	L b	5	1	$1^{1/2}$	$2^{1\ 1/2}$	2^{Head}	3^{1}	4.40	ins-2p,kept on,outkckd
---	3	April Antics (Lezcano, Jose)	118	- -	2	8	$8^{1/2}$	5^{1}	$4^{2\ 1/2}$	$4^{4\ 3/4}$	16.50	off step slw,ins turn
---	8	Danny Deep Cuts (Ortiz, Jose)	118	L	7	10	$9^{8\ 1/2}$	$7^{1/2}$	$5^{2\ 1/2}$	$5^{5\ 1/4}$	6.10	off slow,4-6wide turn
16May21 ^{7}BEL^{5}	1	My Little Lulu (Harkie, Heman)	118	L b	1	3	$5^{1\ 1/2}$	6^{1}	6^{Head}	6^{5}	31.00	ins,4w3/8,drift in3/16
7May21 ^{5}BEL^{4}	9	Decreed (Castellano, Javier)	118	L b	8	6	6^{1}	$9^{15\ 1/2}$	8^{1}	$7^{1/2}$	5.70	off step slw,5-6w turn
11Apr21 ^{9}AQU^{4}	5	Roxen (Luzzi, Michael)	118	- -	4	7	7^{4}	8^{Head}	9^{12}	$8^{3\ 1/4}$	19.70	off step slw,2-3w turn
8May21 ^{3}BEL^{2}	4	Ob La Di (Carmouche, Kendrick)	118	L b	3	4	$4^{1/2}$	4^{2}	7^{1}	$9^{6\ 3/4}$	6.50	4w turn,5w1/4,retreatd
8Dec19 ^{10}AQU^{12}	7	Emerald Banker (Hernandez Moreno, Omar)	114	b	6	9	10	10	10	10	59.00	hit gate brk,checked

Fractional Times: 22.66 45.89 58.67 **Final Time:** 1:12.39
Split Times: (23:23) (12:78) (13:72)
Run-Up: 70 feet

Winner: Cazilda Fortytales, Dark Bay or Brown Filly, by Forty Tales out of Sleek, by Bernardini. Foaled Feb 11, 2017 in New York.
Breeder: Hidden Lake Farm, LLC & Fred Rosen
Owner: Joseph Maroun, Jr.
Trainer: Klesaris, Robert

1 Claimed Horse(s): Decreed New Trainer: Randi Persaud New Owner: Totaram Rampersaud

Danny Deep Cuts(Vet); Esotica(Vet);

Claiming Prices: 13 - Cazilda Fortytales: $25,000; 11 - Tiny Magoo: $25,000; 6 - Esotica: $25,000; 3 - April Antics: $25,000; 8 - Danny Deep Cuts: $25,000; 1 - My Little Lulu: $25,000; 9 - Decreed: $25,000; 5 - Roxen: $25,000; 4 - Ob La Di: $25,000; 7 - Emerald Banker: $25,000;

Scratched Horse(s): Know It All Red (Veterinarian), Ms. Gucci Girl (Stewards), Spun for Lu Lu (Stewards)

Total WPS Pool: $504,313

Pgm	Horse	Win	Place	Show	Wager Type	Winning Numbers	Payoff	Pool
13	Cazilda Fortytales	5.80	4.10	3.00	$1.00 Exacta	13-11	18.60	367,067
11	Tiny Magoo		8.40	4.70	$0.50 Trifecta	13-11-6	33.25	233,625
6	Esotica			3.10	$0.10 Superfecta	13-11-6-3	60.75	153,617
					$1.00 Daily Double	1-13	8.90	122,263
					$1.00 Pick 3	9-1-13 (3 correct)	43.25	155,993
					$0.50 Pick 4	2-9-1/3/6/7-2/10/12/13 (4 correct)	297.50	297,795
					$1.00 Pick 6	6-1-2-9-1-13 (6 correct)	34,876.50	518,845
					$1.00 Pick 6	6-1-2-9-1-13 (5 correct)	191.50	0
					$0.50 Pick 5	1-2-9-1-13 (5 correct)	1,131.00	343,328

Chapter 24

The Triple Crown and Major US Three Year Old Races, 2019

William T. Ziemba

This chapter discusses the 2019 triple crown season beginning with the Florida Derby and some of the major races in the rest of the year. The year 2019 was much more complicated and there were three separate winners of the three Triple Crown races plus a very controversial disqualification in the Kentucky Derby and mixed results in the major summer and fall races with three year olds. War of Will, sired by Warfront, won the Preakness. Sir Winston, sired by Awesome Again, won the Belmont. Code of Honor won the Travers. He was sired by Noble Mission son of the legendary Gallieo, the top sire in Europe and sire of the undefeated Frankel, the top horse worldwide since Secretariat. Gallieo has a reputed stud fee of 650,000€. Vino Rosso by Curlin won the Breeders' Cup Classic.

In 2018, we had another triple crown winner, Justify, the second in three years after a long drought. Justify was a standout and won all six of his races, including the three classics in the triple crown. He was the first Kentucky Derby winner since Apollo in 1888 to have had no two year old races. His career was brief: 6 wins in 6 races in a few months from early 2018 to June 2018. Bought for $500,000 as a yearling, he was sold to Coolmore-Ashford for $70 million and stands for $150,000 per breed in their Ashford stable in Versailles, Kentucky. He and American Pharoah, who is also at Coolmore-Ashford and stands now for $110,000 per breed, went to Australia in the non-US breeding season. Thus Coolmore, masters of the economics of breeding expensive horses, should get their investment back before it is known how good the offspring will be. So far, American Pharoah offspring have sold for very high prices, many over $1 million. They

(a) Justify at Belmont racetrack, June 2018.

(b)American Pharoah at Coolmore-Ashford, June 2019.

Figure 24.1. Justify and American Pharoah.

are running well and one won the Breeders' Cup race for two-year-olds this year. See the pictures of these two stallions in Figure 24.1.

24.1. The 2019 Florida Derby

Leading up to the Kentucky Derby, The Florida Derby winner is often the top choice for the Kentucky Derby as it is the last prep race in Florida before the Kentucky race. On Saturday March 30, 2019, #7 Maximum Security (PSR 110) won the Florida Derby. Going into that race, he was one of the top picks at 9–2 with #1 Hidden Scroll 5–2 (PSR 110) second, #9 Code of Honor third at 3–1(PSR 111) and #4 Bourbon War fourth at 7–2 (PSR 106). Timeform ranked them 1–9–4; David is 1, and HTR 7–1–9–4 (see Table 24.1).

The field and PSRs were: (1) Hidden Scroll (PSR 110), (2) Current (PSR 95), (3) Harvey Wallbanger (PSR 100), (4) Bourbon War (PSR 106), (5) Everfast (PSR 85), (6) Hard Belle (PSR 81), (7) Maximum Security (PSR 110), (8) Bodexpress (PSR 104), (9) Code Of Honor (PSR 111), (10) Union's Destiny (PSR 89), (11) Garter And Tie (PSR 97).

The finish was 7–8–9–4–2. Current was 2.

24.2. The Kentucky Derby

The year 2019 was complicated and there were three separate winners of the three Triple Crown races plus a very controversial disqualification in the

Table 24.1. The HTR ratings for the Florida Derby.

14-GP Sat Mar 30, 2019 05:36 PM 9.0D 3yr GR1 $1000000 111-110 C-C Vi=34 Q6=4 PL-5 14-GP
THREE YEAR OLDS. Nominations close Sunday, March 17. $1,000,000 Guaranteed, plus a $100,000 win-only bonus for registered Florida-bred starters and a $100,000 win-only bonus for Florida Sire Stakes el igible starters. Any horse that has won a graded stakes or has participated in a race at Gulfstream

Pn	PP	Horse	MLO	Ag	Ped-FT		Ch	Lay Wk	Jockey--rtg		TJ%	Trainer--rtg--TPG			Q	R	E	L	PAC-PER--CLASS			(K)	FC	KLine	Pn		SortIndx
7	07	Maximum S	9/2	3c	423	58		038'65	+Saez L	311		Servis	479+	A+	+8	F	3	2	102	110*	107'	111+	85+	1.7>	7		111.2193
1	01	Hidden Sc	*5/2	3c	+532			028'80*	+Castel	348		Mott Wi	260	C-	+6	F	*1	9	*112	105	*108'	109+	81*	2.8	1		108.8870
9	09	Code of H	3/1	3c	437			028'88+	Velazq	354+	22	McGaugh	295	C	2	S	5	6	108	106	108'	100	77	6.4	9		099.9915
4	04	Bourbon W	7/2	3c	+654			028'69	Ortiz,	388+	16	Hennig	263	C-	0	S	6	5	104	106	108'	099	81*	7.0	4		098.5521
11	11	Garter a	15/1	3c	381		bx	056'70	#Sanche	250	06	Nicks R	265	C-	2	P	8	7	101	101	107	079	78	36.7	11	$	078.7305
3	03	Harvey W	15/1	3c	+487			056'86+	Hernan	297	16	McPeek	274	C	0	S	9	4	098	102	103'	076	75	58.8	3	$$	076.3458
2	02	Current	15/1	3c	+862	48		055'82*	+Franco	324	28	Pletche	360	B	0	S	9	1*	096	102	104-	074	71	58.8	2	$	074.3820
8	08	Bodexpre	30/1	3c	392			042'86+	Juarez	247		Delgado	346	B+	+6	E	9	3	101	105	107'	073	77	58.8	8	$$	073.4182
5	05	Everfast	20/1	3c	+624			028'77	Lander	207		Romans	185	C-	5	S	4	8	104	104	106	073	65	58.8	5		072.6345
10	10	Union's	30/1	3c	421			028'93+	#Reyes	208	14	Avila J	300	C+	4	E	7	9	103	101	098'	058	65	99.0	10	$$	058.2700
6	06	Hard Bel	50/1	3c	+513			021 71	#Batist	193		Mejia J	118	D+	+8	E	2	9	101	097	098-	050	65	99.0	6		050.0000

(K) 7-1-9 Price Play 10 MSpot ~ TSpot ~ Scratches ~

Kentucky Derby and mixed results in the major summer and fall races with three year olds. This was the first time that the winner, Maximum Security, was disqualified as he slightly interfered with Country House (65–1). Many observers thought there was not enough interference to cause a disqualification especially since Maximum Security was by far the best horse in the race. Country House was injured and never raced again. Maximum Security came back and won the Haskell and did well in other races as discussed as follows.

There were also other controversies, the most important was the huge number of deaths (over 30) at Santa Anita in the winter and spring of 2019. Changes were made there to try to improve the safety and these did work in the Breeders' Cup on November 1–2, 2019 until the Classic, the very last Breeders' Cup race when Mongolian Groom had a break down and had to be euthanized. Mongolian Groom had won a race at Santa Anita just before the Breeders' Cup with no trouble.

The handicappers ranked the horses as follows: HTR ranked the horses as follows: #7 Maximum Security, #1 War of Will, #13 Code of Honor, #4 Bourbon War with #8 Bodexpress, and #5 Everfast ranked 5th and 6th best.
Timeform ranked them 6–5–8 and David 6
PSR rated them as 1–110, 4–106, 7–110, 8–104 (went off at 70–1), 9–111.
SuperScreener ranked them A: 8-Tacitus, 7-Maximum Security, 16-Game Winner; B+: 17-Roadster, 14-Win Win Win, 2-Tax, 19-Spinoff; B: 3-By My Standards, 5-Improbable, 6-Vekoma; C: 13-Code of Honor, 1-War of Will, 10-Cutting Humor, 20-Country House; X: 18-Long Range Toddy, 21-Bodexpress.

Steve Roman ranked them several ways: (1) PF adjusted speed rating with the more minus preferred: Country House -13; the three Baffert horses were Game Winner −33, Roadster −35, and Improbable −36; Tacitus −37; Maximum Security the best at −52; and (2) using key pace parameters related to the fastest projected 10 furlong, turn time and others relative to finishing velocity and energy distribution and times and the fastest PF for the whole race. This gives the number of times the horse was in the top 5: in order: Maximum Security, Code of Honor, Haikal (not in the race), Game Winner, Win Win Win, Cutting Humor, Long Range Toddy and Omaha Beach (the favorite who was scratched).

Again, like 2018, there was a very muddy track. The track management at Churchill Downs in Louisville, Kentucky seemed not to deal with this before the race. When the horses left their barns and went to the paddock,

Figure 24.2. Country House winner of the Kentucky Derby.

they paraded on the track followed by hundreds of people walking in the mud. It would have been much better to have rollers stabilizing the track and getting rid of the excess water and levelling the mud after all the walkers, but I did not see that. Also there seemed to be a puddle that Maximum Security moved away from and a camera man inside the rail. So the result was that the winner, who had won the Florida Derby and was by most handicappers, including me, the top horse was disqualified. The other major contenders were Tacitus and three Baffert trained horses. Tacitus did finish fourth and was moved to third. The three Baffert horses — Game Winner, Improbable and Roadster did poorly and finished 4th, 5th and 16th. The 65–1 long shot Country House was declared the winner, see him in Figure 24.2. He paid $132.40 to win, $56.60 to place and $24.60 to show for a $2 ticket.

Maximum Security was placed 17th behind the 16th place finisher Bodexpress who was one of the horses interfered with. The others were War of Will and Long Range Toddy. Code of Honor, trained by Shug McGaughey, was moved up to second. He had won the Fountain of Youth, the prep before the Florida Derby. Tacitus, trained by Chad Brown, was moved up to third. Improbable, trained by Baffert, was moved to fourth. These three top horses were active later in the year as discussed below. See Figure 24.3 for the chart of the race.

The controversy continues as the owners of Maximum Security, Gary and Mary West, have sued which the stewards will contest and likely get dismissed. Paulick Report Staff (2019) reported that the West's are appealing

CHURCHILL DOWNS - May 4, 2019 - Race 12
STAKES Kentucky Derby presented by Woodford Reserve Grade 1 - Thoroughbred
FOR THREE-YEAR-OLDS, WITH AN ENTRY FEE OF $25,000 EACH AND A STARTING FEE OF $25,000 EACH.
One And One Fourth Miles On The Dirt **Track Record:** (Secretariat - 1:59.40 - May 5, 1973)
Purse: $3,000,000 Added
Available Money: $3,000,000
Value of Race: $3,000,000 1st $1,860,000, 2nd $600,000, 3rd $300,000, 4th $150,000, 5th $90,000
Weather: Showery **Track:** Sloppy (Sealed)
Off at: 6:51 **Start:** Good for all except 3,15

EQUIBASE

Video Race Replay

Last Raced	Pgm	Horse Name (Jockey)	Wgt	M/E	PP	1/4	1/2	3/4	1m	Str	Fin	Odds	Comments
30Mar19 $^{14}GP^{1}$	7	DQ-Maximum Security (Saez, Luis)	126	L	7	1^{Head}	1^{1}	1^{1}	2^{Head}	1^{1}	$1^{1\,3/4}$	4.50	veer out 5/16p, dug in
13Apr19 $^{11}OP^{3}$	20	Country House (Prat, Flavien)	126	L b	18	$9^{1/2}$	8^{Head}	9^{1}	3^{Head}	2^{Head}	$2^{3/4}$	65.20	brush4wd5/16,outkicked
30Mar19 $^{14}GP^{3}$	13	Code of Honor (Velazquez, John)	126	L	11	$10^{1/2}$	$9^{1/2}$	8^{Head}	1^{Head}	$4^{2\,1/2}$	$3^{3/4}$	14.40	slip thru rail,flttned
6Apr19 $^{10}AQU^{1}$	8	Tacitus (Ortiz, Jose)	126	L	8	$15^{1/2}$	$16^{2\,1/2}$	$14^{1/2}$	$8^{1\,1/2}$	$7^{1/2}$	4^{Head}	5.80	unsettled,good courage
13Apr19 $^{11}OP^{2}$	5	Improbable (Ortiz, Jr., Irad)	126	L	5	8^{2}	$5^{1/2}$	5^{Head}	$6^{1\,1/2}$	$5^{1/2}$	$5^{1/2}$	4.00*	covered up,idled,midly
6Apr19 $^{8}SA^{2}$	16	Game Winner (Rosario, Joel)	126	L	14	18^{4}	$18^{3\,1/2}$	$17^{1\,1/2}$	$9^{1/2}$	$8^{2\,1/2}$	6^{Head}	6.80	wide,bump1/2,brush str
31Mar19 NAK^{2}	15	Master Fencer (JPN) (Leparoux, Julien)	126	--	13	19	19	19	19	12^{Head}	$7^{1/2}$	58.60	veer st,out&in,willing
23Mar19 $^{13}FG^{9}$	1	War of Will (Gaffalione, Tyler)	126	L	1	$6^{1\,1/2}$	4^{1}	$4^{1/2}$	$4^{1\,1/2}$	3^{1}	$8^{3/4}$	16.70	forced out&chckd5/16p
30Mar19 MEY^{1}	9	Plus Que Parfait (Santana, Jr., Ricardo)	126	L b	9	12^{1}	12^{Head}	10^{Head}	$5^{1/2}$	$6^{1\,1/2}$	$9^{3\,1/4}$	57.10	2wd,brief bid,gave way
6Apr19 $^{10}KEE^{2}$	14	Win Win Win (Pimentel, Julian)	126	L	12	17^{5}	$17^{2\,1/2}$	18^{1}	15^{Head}	13^{2}	$10^{3/4}$	16.80	4wd early, no menace
24Mar19 $^{11}SUN^{1}$	10	Cutting Humor (Smith, Mike)	126	L b	10	7^{Head}	$11^{1\,1/2}$	11^{Head}	$7^{1/2}$	11^{1}	11^{2}	24.10	5wd early,fan6wd,wknd
23Mar19 $^{13}FG^{1}$	3	By My Standards (Saez, Gabriel)	126	L	3	13^{Head}	13^{1}	15^{Head}	11^{Head}	10^{Head}	$12^{3\,1/2}$	18.80	squeezed st,bumped1/2m
6Apr19 $^{10}KEE^{1}$	6	Vekoma (Castellano, Javier)	126	L	6	4^{1}	$6^{1\,1/2}$	6^{1}	$16^{1/2}$	17^{1}	13^{Neck}	16.80	close-up 4wd, done 6f
30Mar19 $^{14}GP^{2}$	21	Bodexpress (Landeros, Chris)	126	L	19	2^{Head}	3^{Head}	$3^{1/2}$	$14^{1/2}$	15^{Head}	14^{Head}	71.00	3wd, taken up 5/16p
6Apr19 $^{10}AQU^{2}$	2	Tax (Alvarado, Junior)	126	L	2	$11^{1\,1/2}$	10^{Head}	$12^{1/2}$	12^{Head}	9^{Head}	$15^{1\,1/2}$	35.50	no factor inside
6Apr19 $^{8}SA^{1}$	17	Roadster (Geroux, Florent)	126	L	15	16^{3}	$15^{1/2}$	$13^{1\,1/2}$	18^{1}	18^{1}	$16^{1\,1/2}$	11.60	very wide turns,outrun
13Apr19 $^{11}OP^{6}$	18	Long Range Toddy (Court, Jon)	126	L	16	$3^{1\,1/2}$	$2^{1/2}$	2^{1}	10^{Head}	$16^{1/2}$	17^{Nose}	54.80	vied,checked hard5/16p
23Mar19 $^{13}FG^{2}$	19	Spinoff (Franco, Manuel)	126	L	17	$5^{1/2}$	7^{Head}	7^{Head}	$17^{1/2}$	19	$18^{6\,1/4}$	52.30	wide thruout,empty 1/4
30Mar19 MEY^{2}	4	Gray Magician (Van Dyke, Drayden)	126	L	4	14^{Head}	$14^{1/2}$	16^{Head}	13^{1}	$14^{1/2}$	19	33.80	mild gain2w,tire aft1m

Fractional Times: 22.31 46.62 1:12.50 1:38.63 **Final Time:** 2:03.93
Split Times: (24:31) (25:88) (26:13) (25:30)
Run-Up: 34 feet

Winner: Country House, Chestnut Colt, by Lookin At Lucky out of Quake Lake, by War Chant. Foaled May 08, 2016 in Kentucky.
Breeder: J. V. Shields, Jr..
Winning Owner: Shields, Jr., Mrs. J. V., McFadden, Jr., E. J. M. and LNJ Foxwoods

Disqualification(s): # 7 Maximum Security from 1 to 17

Scratched Horse(s): Haikal (Trainer), Omaha Beach (Trainer)

Total WPS Pool: $65,676,107

Pgm	Horse	Win	Place	Show
20	Country House	132.40	56.60	24.60
13	Code of Honor		15.20	9.80
8	Tacitus			5.60

Wager Type	Winning Numbers	Payoff	Pool	Carryover
$0.50 Pick 3	7-12-20 (3 correct)	638.80	1,512,379	
$0.50 Pick 3	OAKS/FRSTR/DERBY 13-12-20 (3 correct)	2,072.65	686,826	
$0.50 Pick 4	3-7-12-20 (4 correct)	11,325.65	4,091,771	
$0.50 Pick 5	2/8-3-7-12-20 (5 correct)	72,317.60	3,980,809	
$2.00 Pick 6	OAKS/DERBY P6 1-13-3-8-12-20 (5 correct)	67,936.00	479,561	
$0.20 Pick 6 Jackpot	4-2/8-3-7-12-20 (6 correct)	271,869.82	1,066,333	137,594
$1.00 Daily Double	12-20	121.40	1,399,396	
$1.00 Daily Double	OAKS/DERBY 13-20	1,290.50	2,832,209	
$2.00 Exacta	20-13	3,009.60	25,969,517	
$2.00 Future Wager	EXACTA POOL 1 - 24-2	109.40	71,919	
$2.00 Future Wager	EXACTA POOL 2 - 24-18	550.60	134,980	
$2.00 Future Wager	EXACTA POOL 3 - 4-3	1,088.60	103,265	
$2.00 Future Wager	EXACTA POOL 4 - 24-5	792.80	155,989	
$2.00 Future Wager	POOL 1 - 24	4.60	186,470	
$2.00 Future Wager	POOL 2 - 24	7.60	398,997	
$2.00 Future Wager	POOL 3 - 4	61.00	282,199	
$2.00 Future Wager	POOL 4 - 24	40.00	344,418	
$2.00 Future Wager	SIRE EXACTA 24-17	89.20	11,859	
$2.00 Future Wager	SIRE WAGER - 24	13.80	21,065	
$1.00 Superfecta	20-13-8-5	51,400.10	16,581,163	
$1.00 Super High Five	20-13-8-5-16	544,185.90	644,420	
$0.50 Trifecta	20-13-8	5,737.65	34,668,427	

Footnotes
MAXIMUM SECURITY came away in good order to take a short lead through the stretch the first time, edged away up the backstretch slightly off the rail, veered out sharply forcing WAR OF WILL out into LONG RANGE TODDY and BODEXPRESS nearing the five-sixteenths pole, responded when challenged from both flanks by CODE OF HONOR and COUNTRY HOUSE, and edged away from the latter through the final stages. COUNTRY HOUSE settled in the middle of the field three wide off the first turn, advanced four wide into the far turn, was brushed by LONG RANGE TODDY while largely unaffected by the incident five-sixteenths out, loomed boldly outside MAXIMUM SECURITY coming to the eighth-pole, was repelled by that one and held the place. CODE OF HONOR moved closer to the first flight saving ground after a half-mile, was presented with a large opening slipping through to take a short lead after a mile, but flattened out through upper stretch. TACITUS steadied while unsettled behind horses first time through the stretch, found a better rhythm through the middle stages, came five wide off the far turn, exchanged brushes with GAME WINNER late and finished with good courage. IMPROBABLE went along in striking range covered up in the two-path, idled through the far turn in traffic losing some position, shifted out in the drive and offered a mild response. GAME WINNER was well in arrears widest arriving midway up the backstretch, bumped solidly with BY MY STANDARDS near the half-mile pole, continued extremely wide around the far turn and into the stretch, exchanged brushes with TACITUS late and did not have enough. MASTER FENCER (JPN) veered out to get away behind his field, was crowded from heavy outside pressure at the start, went along striding a bit awkwardly far back early inside, moved out up the backstretch, began taking better hold of the track in the two-path into the stretch, moved back inside and finished willingly. WAR OF WILL found a good spot saving ground off the leaders under a firm hold, continued along reserved waiting for room into the far turn, shifted outside MAXIMUM SECURITY leaving the three-eighths pole, was forced out by that rival into LONG RANGE TODDY, checked hard off heels, remained prominent in the three-path to upper stretch and weakened. PLUS QUE PARFAIT was unhurried early two wide, moved through along the rail improving position after the first mile, moved back out to the two-path and could not sustain the bid. WIN WIN WIN raced four wide early, moved inward after that and failed to menace. CUTTING HUMOR entered the backstretch five wide and well back, made a run into the far turn getting fanned six wide in the process, and gave way through the stretch. BY MY STANDARDS was squeezed back at the start to get away slowly, raced three wide around the first turn, moved out wider bumping with GAME WINNER near the half-mile marker, and lacked a serious response. VEKOMA stayed close four wide through the opening half-mile, and began to fade steadily after six furlongs. BODEXPRESS angled inward after breaking alertly, was forwardly placed three wide for six furlongs, was forced to take up sharply between LONG RANGE TODDY and COUNTRY HOUSE near the five-sixteenths, and dropped back. TAX saved ground throughout and was no factor. ROADSTER was six or seven wide off the first turn, continued along extremely wide the rest of the way and was never in contention. LONG RANGE TODDY angled inward after an alert beginning, attended the pace outside MAXIMUM SECURITY, was bumped and forced out into BODEXPRESS while checking sharply approaching the five-sixteenths, and retreated. SPINOFF raced five wide early, moved further out around the far turn and was empty by the quarter-pole. GRAY MAGICIAN gained mildly two wide after six furlongs, but was finished by the quarter-pole. The jockeys of LONG RANGE TODDY and COUNTRY HOUSE lodged an objection against MAXIMUM SECURITY for interference nearing the five-sixteenths marker. Following the Stewards review MAXIMUM SECURITY was disqualified from first and placed seventeenth for veering out and stacking up WAR OF WILL, LONG RANGE TODDY, and BODEXPRESS. Due to the scratches of OMAHA BEACH and HAIKAL, the inside stall of the starting gate was left vacant.

Figure 24.3. Chart of the Kentucky Derby.

the judge's dismissal of their lawsuit against the Kentucky Horse Racing Commission and the stewards who disqualified Maximum Security. Their horse did not run in the Preakness or Belmont Stakes. In addition, they have offered \$5 million to the owners of the four interfered horses if they beat Maximum Security in a future race. It is not clear what they have to put up. The wisdom of this is questionable, but nothing has happened. Meanwhile, Country House got a minor injury and has been out through the fall of 2019 and was retired, never running again.

Noted handicapper Andy Beyer (2019) thought the DQ was not justified. Among other things, he estimated the foul cost Country House about one length so Maximum Security should have remained the winner. When I was in Kentucky in late May 2019, I asked people at major Kentucky horse farms about the DQ and it was about 50–50 for and against it. Maximum Security was clearly the best horse in the race.

Steve Roman's PF rating for the race, which took 2 minutes and 3.93 seconds, was −41 which was not comparable to the best Kentucky Derbys. Roman (2019) agreed with Beyer that the foul was minor. He cited examples such as Bayern in the Breeders' Cup Classic and Codex who mauled Genuine Risk in the Preakness. Neither of these horses were DQ'ed.

Maximum Security returned to Monmouth in the Pegasus Stakes, a \$150,000 race as the 1–2 morning line favorite going off at 1–20 to win. The race was a prep for the Haskell, Travers and Breeders' Cup Classic. In the Pegasus he fought the Uncle Mo sired King for a Day throughout the stretch, narrowly losing to finish second. My book *Beat the Racetrack* recommends betting place on such huge vulnerable favorites, indeed he paid \$2.10 to place and zero to win. See also Ziemba (2018) *Exotic Betting at the Racetrack* In the Haskell, Maximum Security at 4–5 won the race beating the Baffert trained Mucho Gusto. So Maximum Security seemed ready to challenge for top three year old honors, but that was not to be. Though the favorite, he was scratched in the Pennsylvania Derby in September. His late 2019 races and 2020 plans are discussed as follows.

24.3. The Preakness

The Preakness had its own major issue as Bodexpress dropped its jockey J.R. Velasquez (who was not injured) at the gate.

The starters were: (1) War of Will, (2) Bourbon War, (3) Warrior's Charge, (4) Improbable, (5) Owendale, (6) Market King, (7) Alwaysmining,

Figure 24.4. War Front at Claiborne Farm, June 2019.

(8) Signalman, (9) Bodexpress, (10) Everfast, (11) Laughing Fox, (12) Anothertwistafate, and (13) Win Win Win.

The handicappers rated the horses as follows: HTR 4–1–7–12–3; Wizard 5–2–4–1; Timeform 4–12–1; and David 12. Smith had win: 3–6–8–11; place: 1–3–4–6–8–11; and show: 1–3–4–5–6–8–11–13.

War of Will again in post position 1 won the race at generous 6–1 odds. His sire is the highest priced US sire War Front at Claiborne farm in Paris (Figure 24.4), Kentucky, standing for $250,000 per breed. See Figure 24.6 for War Chant who also sired Omaha Beach.

The second place finisher Everfast at 29–1 made no apparent sense. Owendale at nearly 8–1 was third. The supplemented horse, Warrior's Charge, co-owned by my co-author Marshall Gramm, another professor doing racing research, was fourth. Improbable had another poor race and finished sixth.

The finish was 1–10–5–3–11 with the chart in Figure 24.5.

PIMLICO - May 18, 2019 - Race 13 **EQUIBASE**
STAKES Preakness S. Grade 1 - Thoroughbred
FOR THREE-YEAR-OLDS. $15,000 to pass the entry box, starters to pay $15,000 additional. Supplemental nominations may be made in accordance with the rules, upon payment of $150,000. 60% of the purse to the winner, 20% to second, 11% to third, 6% to fourthand 3% to fifth. Weight 126 pounds for Colts and Geldings, 121 pounds for Fillies. A replica of the Woodlawn Vase will be presented to the winning owner to remain his or her personal property.
One And Three Sixteenth Miles On The Dirt **Track Record:** (Farma Way - 1:52.55 - May 11, 1991)
Purse: $1,500,000 Guaranteed
Plus: $150,000 Other Sources
Available Money: $1,650,000
Value of Race: $1,650,000 1st $990,000, 2nd $330,000, 3rd $181,500, 4th $99,000, 5th $49,500
Weather: Cloudy **Track:** Fast
Off at: 7:00 **Start:** Good for all except 9

Video Race Replay

Last Raced	Pgm	Horse Name (Jockey)	Wgt	M/E	PP	Start	1/4	1/2	3/4	Str	Fin	Odds	Comments
4May19 ^{12}CD^{7}	1	War of Will (Gaffalione, Tyler)	126	L	1	1	4^{Head}	$4^{1/2}$	4^{1}	1^{1}	$1^{1\,1/4}$	6.10	rail bid 3/16, driving
4May19 ^{10}CD^{5}	10	Everfast (Rosario, Joel)	126	L	10	11	$11^{2\,1/2}$	11^{2}	$11^{2\,1/2}$	$6^{1/2}$	2^{Nose}	29.30	3wd 3/16,rail 1/8,bid
13Apr19 ^{9}KEE^{1}	5	Owendale (Geroux, Florent)	126	L b	5	10	$9^{1/2}$	9^{2}	$9^{1\,1/2}$	3^{Head}	$3^{1\,1/4}$	7.90	2wd turns,7wd 3/16
12Apr19 ^{8}OP^{1}	3	Warrior's Charge (Castellano, Javier)	126	L	3	2	$1^{1/2}$	1^{1}	1^{1}	$2^{2\,1/2}$	$4^{1\,1/4}$	12.60	rail,2wd 3/16,weaknd
4May19 ^{11}OP^{1}	11	Laughing Fox (Santana, Jr., Ricardo)	126	L	11	12	12	12	12	10^{3}	5^{Nose}	21.60	swung out,closed late
4May19 ^{12}CD^{4}	4	Improbable (Smith, Mike)	126	L	4	7	$7^{1\,1/2}$	$6^{1\,1/2}$	6^{Head}	4^{Head}	$6^{1\,3/4}$	2.50*	unruly,mv btw 4w,flttn
4May19 ^{12}CD^{9}	13	Win Win Win (Pimentel, Julian)	126	L b	13	6	6^{2}	7^{1}	8^{2}	5^{Head}	7^{4}	13.80	3-4wd turns, weakened
30Mar19 ^{14}GP^{4}	2	Bourbon War (Ortiz, Jr., Irad)	126	L b	2	9	$8^{1\,1/2}$	$8^{2\,1/2}$	$10^{1\,1/2}$	$11^{1/2}$	8^{1}	5.60	3wd 1/2,no factor
6Apr19 ^{10}KEE^{3}	8	Signalman (Hernandez, Jr., Brian)	126	L	8	8	10^{12}	10^{7}	7^{1}	9^{Head}	9^{Neck}	20.70	3w first,angld in,fade
13Apr19 ^{9}KEE^{2}	12	Anothertwistafate (Ortiz, Jose)	126	L	12	5	$3^{1\,1/2}$	3^{2}	2^{1}	7^{2}	$10^{2\,3/4}$	14.50	3-4wd,weakened 3/16
20Apr19 ^{10}LRL^{1}	7	Alwaysmining (Centeno, Daniel)	126	L	7	3	5^{2}	$5^{1/2}$	3^{Head}	8^{Head}	$11^{10\,1/4}$	6.60	2-4w,mild bid,tired
6Apr19 ^{10}KEE^{11}	6	Market King (Court, Jon)	126	L	6	4	2^{1}	$2^{1/2}$	$5^{1/2}$	12	12	31.90	chased, gave way
4May19 ^{12}CD^{13}	9	Bodexpress (Velazquez, John)	126	L	9	13	---	---	---	---	---	20.10	reared,unseated jock

Fractional Times: 22.50 46.16 1:10.56 1:35.48 **Final Time:** 1:54.34
Split Times: (23:66) (24:40) (24:92) (18:86)
Run-Up: 30 feet

Winner: War of Will, Bay Colt, by War Front out of Visions of Clarity (IRE), by Sadler's Wells. Foaled Apr 17, 2016 in Kentucky.
Breeder: Flaxman Holdings Limited.
Winning Owner: Gary Barber

Total WPS Pool: $21,755,107

Pgm	Horse	Win	Place	Show
1	War of Will	14.20	7.40	5.40
10	Everfast		32.00	14.40
5	Owendale			6.00

Wager Type	Winning Numbers	Payoff	Pool	Carryover
$0.50 Pick 3	1-1/6/12-1 (3 correct)	256.20	880,691	
$0.50 Pick 4	4/6-1-1/6/12-1 (4 correct)	1,040.90	3,096,722	
$0.50 Pick 5	9-4/6-1-1/6/12-1 (5 correct)	7,353.40	2,360,671	
$0.20 Pick 6 Jackpot	1/8-9-4/6-1-1/6/12-1 (6 correct)	8,622.94	503,057	198,373
$1.00 Daily Double	12-1	19.30	1,062,106	
$2.00 Daily Double	BES-PREAK 8-1	47.40	810,322	
$1.00 Exacta	1-10	473.50	11,814,023	
$1.00 Superfecta	1-10-5-3	51,924.00	6,882,505	
$1.00 Trifecta	1-10-5	4,699.80	13,194,928	
$1.00 X-5 Super High Five	1-10-5-3-11		475,717	404,310

Trainers: 1 - Casse, Mark; 10 - Romans, Dale; 5 - Cox, Brad; 3 - Cox, Brad; 11 - Asmussen, Steven; 4 - Baffert, Bob; 13 - Trombetta, Michael; 2 - Hennig, Mark; 8 - McPeek, Kenneth; 12 - Wright, Blaine; 7 - Rubley, Kelly; 6 - Lukas, D.; 9 - Delgado, Gustavo

Owners: 1 -Gary Barber; 10 - Calumet Farm; 5 - Rupp Racing; 3 - Ten Strike Racing and Madaket Stables LLC; 11 - Lieblong, Alex and JoAnn; 4 - WinStar Farm LLC, China Horse Club International Ltd. and Starlight Racing; 13 - Live Oak Plantation; 2 - Bourbon Lane Stable and Lake Star Stable; 8 - Lewis, Tommie M., Crabtree, Steve, Demaree, Dean, Bernsen, David, Chambers, Jim and Magdalena Racing; 12 - Peter Redekop B. C., Ltd.; 7 - Runnymede Racing LLC; 6 - Baker, Robert C. and Mack, William L.; 9 - Top Racing, LLC, Global Thoroughbred and GDS Racing Stable;

Footnotes
WAR OF WILL broke alertly, was nicely in hand saving ground on the first turn, rated kindly behind the leader down the backstretch, advanced leaving the far turn, had an opening along the inner rail, took command leaving the three sixteenths edged away under brisk urging and held firm. EVERFAST broke inward, was well back entering the first turn, raced along the rail down the backstretch, eased out approaching the stretch, was in the three path in upper stretch, was taken to the inner rail near the eighth pole and rallied gamely. OWENDALE , two wide between horses on the first turn, remained two wide on the turn, swung to the seven path in upper stretch and closed outside horses. WARRIOR'S CHARGE sped to the early lead, set the pace along the rail, drifted to the two path entering the stretch, lost the lead and weakened in the final furlong. LAUGHING FOX lacked speed, was two wide entering the far turn, was caught behind horses in upper stretch, swung to the outside near the sixteenth pole and closed late. IMPROBABLE , fractious in the starting gate, raced between horses the first turn, was well positioned in the three path leaving the backstretch, worked his way to the four path entering the stretch, drifted to the five path in upper stretch then flattened out. WIN WIN WIN , three wide the first turn, stalked the pace down the backstretch, circled the far turn four wide, floated to the six path in upper stretch and faded. BOURBON WAR saved ground the first turn, raced three wide leaving the backstretch, swung very wide in upper stretch and failed to be a factor. SIGNALMAN , three wide well back entering the first turn, angled in near the five eighths pole, saved ground making a mild run around the far turn, remained in touch to upper stretch then succumbed. ANOTHERTWISTAFATE , three wide on the first turn, forced the pace outside WARRIOR'S CHARGE down the backstretch, was three wide turning for home and weakened in upper stretch. ALWAYSMINING , two wide the first turn, stalked the pace down the backstretch, moved up three wide entering the far turn to reach contention, was in the four path in upper stretch and gave way. MARKET KING chased the pace outside WARRIOR'S CHARGE ,failed to keep up on the far turn and dropped back in the stretch. BODEXPRESS reared at the break unseating his rider then galloped around the track far removed from the inner rail.

Figure 24.5. Chart of the Preakness Stakes.

24.4. The Belmont Stakes

The Belmont Stakes had ten runners on a racing card with eight grade I's including the Met Mile which was moved to Belmont for Belmont Stakes day. The entire day was filled with top horses such as Rushing

Falls, Guarana, CeCe Mitole, Serengeti Empress, McKinzie, Thunder Snow, Promise Fulfilled, Firenze, Bricks and Mortar and others in the top races before the Belmont Stakes itself.

The weather was perfect and there were no horse incidents or injuries.

In the Belmont, the ten runners were ranked by the handicappers as follows:

(1) Joevia (PSR 96, ML 30-1), (2) Everfast (PSR 93, ML 12-1), (3) Master Fencer (Jpn) (PSR 102, ML 8-1), (4) Tax (PSR 103, ML 15-1), (5) Bourbon War (PSR 98, ML 12-1), (6) Spinoff (PSR 101, ML 15-1), (7) Sir Winston (PSR 101, ML 12-1), (8) Intrepid Heart (PSR 101, ML 10-1), (9) War Of Will (PSR 109, ML 2-1), and (10) Tacitus (PSR 114, ML 9-5).

Wizard: 10–7–9–8–2–4–3–5–6–1 TimeForm: 9–10–4 David: 9 HTR: 10–9–4–3–6–8–5–2–7–1

Most of the races made a lot of sense so it was a good betting day. I did manage to win the Pick 3 after losing the Pick 4 on Race 8, which had all longshots in the money. In the Belmont, I assumed that one of 4-Tax, 7-Sir Winston, 8- Intrepid Heart, 9-War of Will or 10-Tacitus would win so my exactas, trifectas and superfecta bets focused on them with logical contenders in second, third and fourth position.

Sir Winston at 10-1 won the race. He had the only 100 Beyer which was the fastest previous race just barely above the favorite Tacitus and several others as you can see in the past performances.

Tacitus #10, sired by Tapit, was second which made sense as he was the pick, see Figure 24.6.

Third was the longshot Joevia at 21–1 was not picked by any handicapper. He was rated 96 on PSR above Everfast 93 but below all the others. HSR rated him last just below Sir Winston who they misjudged. Tax at 12–1 was fourth so I did get the exacta but not the trifecta or superfecta. War of Will, the second choice at 7–2, finished 9th beating only Bourbon War. The rest of the field, fourth and 5th to 10th were as follows: Master Fencer, Spinoff, Everfast, Intrepid Heart, War of Will, and Bourbon War. Figure 24.7 is the chart of the race.

24.5. Haskell Invitational, July 17, 2019

The $1 million, $1\frac{1}{8}$ mile, Grade I Haskell Invitational Stakes is the top three year old race in between the Belmont Stakes in June and the Run Happy Travers in August. It is run at Monmouth racetrack on the New Jersey shore.

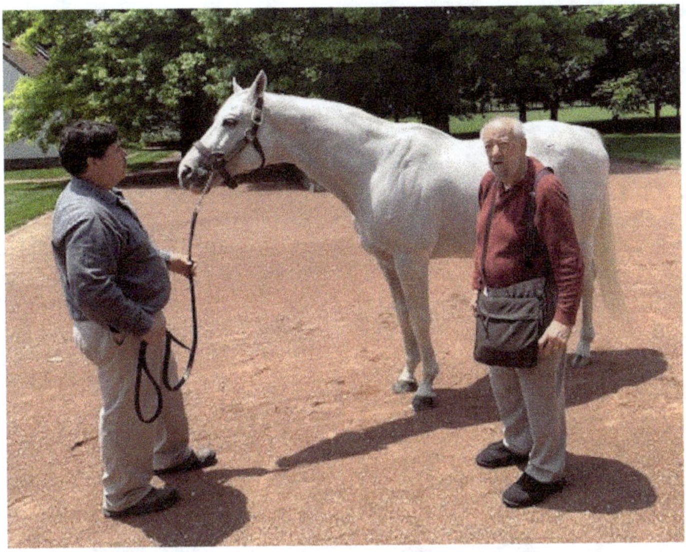

Figure 24.6. Tapit the sire of Tacitus at Gainesway Farm, June 2019.

Maximum Security won beating the Baffert trained Mucho Gusto. Longshot Spun to Run was third. The race was not without controversy as Maximum Security survived a steward's inquiry that he interfered with King for a Day on the far turn. Maximum Security was a 4–5 favorite and paid $3.60 for a $2 win ticket. King for a Day had defeated Maximum Security in the Pegasus on June 16. In the Haskell he was fifth. Figure 24.8 is the chart of the race.

24.6. The Run Happy Travers, August 24, 2019

There were 12 runners for the Run Happy Travers, the summer classic for 3 year old. The horses were ranked as follows:

(1) Owendale (PSR 98, ML 6–1), (2) Code Of Honor (PSR 112, ML 4–1), (3) Highest Honors (PSR 105, ML 10–1), (4) Laughing Fox (PSR 98, ML 30–1), (5) Everfast (PSR 93, ML 30–1), (6) Tacitus (PSR 112, ML 5–2), (7) Mucho Gusto (PSR 113, ML 6–1), (8) Chess Chief (PSR 104, ML 30–1), (9) Looking At Bikinis (PSR 102, ML 10–1), (10) Scars Are Cool (PSR 93, ML 30–1), (11) Endorsed (PSR 96, ML 15–1), (12) Tax (PSR 108, ML 6–1).

Timeform: 6–12–7, David: 6–7 tied, HTR: 7–9–12–6–3–1–2–11–8–10–4–5, Eddie Olczyk (xpressbet): 2.

BELMONT PARK - June 8, 2019 - Race 11
STAKES Belmont S. Grade 1 - Thoroughbred

EQUIBASE

FOR THREE YEAR OLDS. By subscription of $600 each, to accompany the nomination, if made on or before January 26, 2019, or $6,000, if made on or before April 1, 2019. At any time prior to the closing time of entries, horses may be nominated to The BelmontStakes upon payment of a supplementary fee of $50,000 to the New York Racing Association, Inc. $15,000 to pass the entry box and $15,000 additional to start. All entrants will be required to pay entry and starting fees; but no fees, supplemental or otherwise shall be added to the purse. The purse to be divided $800,000 to the winner, $280,000 to second, $150,000 to third, $100,000 to fourth, $60,000 to fifth, $45,000 to sixth, $35,000 to seventh and $30,000 to eighth. Colts and Geldings, 126 lbs.; Fillies, 121 lbs. The winning owner will be presented with the August Belmont Memorial Cup to be retained for one year as well as a trophy for permanent possession and trophies to the winning trainer and jockey.
One And One Half Miles On The Dirt **Track Record:** (Secretariat - 2:24.00 - June 9, 1973)
Purse: $1,500,000 Guaranteed
Available Money: $1,500,000
Value of Race: $1,500,000 1st $800,000, 2nd $280,000, 3rd $150,000, 4th $100,000, 5th $60,000, 6th $45,000, 7th $35,000, 8th $30,000

Video Race Replay

Weather: Clear **Track:** Fast
Off at: 6:38 **Start:** Good for all

Last Raced	Pgm	Horse Name (Jockey)	Wgt	M/E	PP	1/4	1/2	1m	11/4	Str	Fin	Odds	Comments
11May19 ^{4}BEL^{2}	7	Sir Winston (Rosario, Joel)	126	L b	7	8^{1}	8^{1}	7^{1}	3^{1}	2^{1}	1^{1}	10.20	ins,traffic1/4,4w upr
4May19 ^{12}CD^{3}	10	Tacitus (Ortiz, Jose)	126	L	10	$7^{1/2}$	$7^{1\ 1/2}$	8^{1}	$5^{1/2}$	4^{1}	$2^{3/4}$	1.95*	3w1st,5w2nd,bump upr
12May19 ^{9}MTH^{1}	1	Joevia (Lezcano, Jose)	126	L	1	1^{1}	$1^{1/2}$	$1^{1/2}$	1^{Head}	1^{Head}	3^{1}	21.60	ins,ask 1/4,wknd
4May19 ^{12}CD^{14}	4	Tax (Ortiz, Jr., Irad)	126	L	4	2^{2}	$2^{1\ 1/2}$	$2^{1\ 1/2}$	2^{1}	$3^{1/2}$	4^{Head}	11.70	prompt 2w,bid 1/4,flat
4May19 ^{12}CD^{8}	3	Master Fencer (JPN) (Leparoux, Julien)	126	h	3	10	10	9^{1}	9^{1}	9^{2}	5^{Neck}	13.30	ins,3w 3/8,6w lane
4May19 ^{12}CD^{16}	6	Spinoff (Castellano, Javier)	126	L	6	$3^{1/2}$	3^{1}	3^{1}	$6^{1/2}$	$6^{1/2}$	6^{Nose}	10.40	3w both turns, tired
18May19 ^{13}PIM^{2}	2	Everfast (Saez, Luis)	126	L	2	4^{1}	5^{Head}	4^{Head}	$7^{1\ 1/2}$	5^{Head}	$7^{1\ 3/4}$	16.50	ins to 1/2,wedge 2w 2d
11May19 ^{4}BEL^{3}	8	Intrepid Heart (Velazquez, John)	126	L b	8	6^{1}	$6^{1/2}$	6^{Head}	8^{1}	8^{Head}	$8^{2\ 1/4}$	6.90	brush brk,2-3w to 1/4
18May19 ^{13}PIM^{1}	9	War of Will (Gaffalione, Tyler)	126	L	9	5^{1}	4^{1}	$5^{1/2}$	$4^{1/2}$	7^{2}	$9^{4\ 3/4}$	3.65	brsh st,4w,bumped upr
18May19 ^{13}PIM^{8}	5	Bourbon War (Smith, Mike)	126	L	5	$9^{1/2}$	$9^{1/2}$	10	10	10	10	10.00	2w pursuit, no factor

Fractional Times: 23.92 48.79 1:13.54 1:38.27 2:02.72 **Final Time:** 2:28.30
Split Times: (24:87) (24:75) (24:73) (24:45) (25:58)
Run-Up: 78 feet

Winner: Sir Winston, Chestnut Colt, by Awesome Again out of La Gran Bailadora, by Afleet Alex. Foaled Apr 08, 2016 in Kentucky.
Breeder: Tracy Farmer.
Winning Owner: Tracy Farmer

Total WPS Pool: $17,352,418

Pgm	Horse	Win	Place	Show
7	Sir Winston	22.40	8.80	6.10
10	Tacitus		5.90	3.20
1	Joevia			8.70

Wager Type	Winning Numbers	Payoff	Pool
$1.00 Exacta	7-10	48.00	9,914,302
$0.50 Trifecta	7-10-1	622.00	10,567,921
$0.10 Superfecta	7-10-1-4	1,042.80	6,396,259
$1.00 Daily Double	(BEL GC-BEL) 3-7	74.75	455,648
$1.00 Daily Double	8-7	25.75	840,466
$1.00 Pick 3	3-8-7 (3 correct)	147.50	1,336,365
$0.50 Pick 4	8-3-8/9-7 (4 correct)	2,118.00	3,603,840
$0.20 Pick 6	(FESTIVAL P6) 3-3-8-3-8-7 (6 correct)	9,505.90	656,139
$0.20 Pick 6	(FESTIVAL P6) 3-3-8-3-8-7 (5 correct)	63.40	0
$2.00 Pick 6	1/4/8-7-8-3-8/9-7 (5 correct)	180.00	0
$2.00 Pick 6	1/4/8-7-8-3-8/9-7 (6 correct)	35,807.00	1,634,038
$0.50 Pick 5	7-8-3-8/9-7 (5 correct)	10,202.75	480,130

Footnotes
SIR WINSTON made it over to the rail before arriving at the end of the homestretch, tracked the front runners patiently handled, gained sufficient room with which to advance along the inside route after EVERFAST vacated it at the half mile pole, snaked his way into a good striking position, was forced to wait behind some traffic nearing the quarter pole, accelerated when put to some encouragement, out-racing a pair of opponents for position spinning into the lane, straightened away approximately four wide and took off after the ones to catch, ground his way to the front end, wresting away the advantage just inside the furlong marker and edged away. TACITUS brushed with WAR OF WIILL springing from the starting gate, settled into stride and into midpack, raced three wide around the clubhouse bend, was rated proceeding along the backstretch, tipped to the outside coming up to its conclusion, wound up on the overland route making his way on the far turn, got called upon leaving the five-sixteenths marker, bumped with WAR OF WILL as they spun into stretch directly abreast of each other, shifted closer to the rail when rein-ridden traversing through the furlong grounds, was taken hold and maneuvered back into path five at the eighth pole, gained ground in a steadfast manner to garner the place. JOEVIA broke in line with TAX, established the top by the crown of the opening bend, showed the way with the aforementioned rival in attendance to the outside, was put to the test by that opponent nearing the quarter pole and was turned loose, offered resistance before yielding to the winner in midlane, weakened into the show slot. TAX hand urged from the gate, was taken hold once JOEVIA assumed control, prompted the pace two to three wide, bid for the top as the field stepped into the stretch, wandered out four wide during the ensuing furlong, wasn't up to the task at hand and weakened. MASTER FENCER (JPN) rode the rail until the half mile pole, responded when let out a notch, working his way into path three by midpoint, paused at the five-sixteenths pole then proceeded to shift six wide from that station to the three-sixteenths pole, rallied mildly mainly improving position. SPINOFF strung out three wide on both turns, lacked the necessary stretch response. EVERFAST loosely pocketed to the half mile pole, was wedged in between rivals two wide on the second bend, swung into the lane, failed to make the necessary headway and retreated in the last eighth. INTREPID HEART brushed at the start after losing his footing, raced two to three wide to the quarter pole, stepped into the stretch under a ride and had no rally. WAR OF WILL made light contact with TACITUS after losing his footing as the field was sent off and running, was in path four making his way on the first turn, was still in same path in pursuit of the front runners, the widest of all, and without benefit of cover, departed the backstretch once again stationed in the four path, got cued up approaching the quarter pole, turned into the lane in tight quarters with the second place finisher, resulting in a solid bump between them, kept up its pursuit for a little while longer before faltering. BOURBON WAR unhurried during the initial stages sitting at the back of the pack in the two path, failed to reach a contending position.

Figure 24.7. Chart of the Belmont Stakes.

Timeform gave the trifecta and exacta which I had, but I did not get the superfecta. The finish was 2–6–7–11. Figure 24.9 is the chart of this race

24.7. The Pennsylvania Derby at PARX racetrack, September 21, 2019

The $1 million Pennsylvania Derby is the premier race at PARX. The handicappers:

MONMOUTH PARK - July 20, 2019 - Race 12 **EQUIBASE**

STAKES TVG.com Haskell Invitational S. Grade 1 - Thoroughbred
FOR THREE-YEAR-OLDS. By invitation only. No nomination, entry or starting fees. The winning owner to receive $600,000, $200,000 to second, $100,000 to third, $50,000 to fourth, $30,000 to fifth and $10,000 to sixth through last. Weight: 122 lbs. Non-winners of a Triple Crown race allowed 2 lbs.; Non-winners of a Grade I Stake at a mile or over in 2019, 4 lbs. The TVG.com Haskell Invitational has been selected as one of the Breeders' Cup Win and You're In Challenge Races. The nominated winner of the TVG.com Haskell Invitational will be entitled to automatic entry into the 2019 running of the Breeders' Cup Classic Championship race, have pre-entry and entry fees waived for the Championship race and receive a travel award if shipping from a base located outside of California. The winning owner to receive a trophy.
One And One Eighth Miles On The Dirt **Track Record:** (Spend a Buck - 1:46.80 - August 17, 1985)
Purse: $1,000,000 Added
Available Money: $1,000,000
Value of Race: $990,000 1st $600,000, 2nd $200,000, 3rd $100,000, 4th $50,000, 5th $30,000, 6th $10,000 Video Race Replay
Weather: Clear **Track:** Fast
Off at: 8:12 **Start:** Good for all

Last Raced	Pgm	Horse Name (Jockey)	Wgt M/E	PP	Start	1/4	1/2	3/4	Str	Fin	Odds	Comments
16Jun19 ^{10}MTH^{2}	7	Maximum Security (Saez, Luis)	120 L	6	1	3^{Head}	$3^{1/2}$	$2^{1/2}$	1^{Head}	$1^{1\ 1/4}$	0.80*	speed 3w, gamely
16Jun19 ^{8}SA^{1}	5	Mucho Gusto (Talamo, Joseph)	118 L b	4	5	5^{8}	5^{8}	3^{1}	$2^{4\ 1/2}$	2^{8}	3.10	bumped start, 3-4w
23Mar19 ^{8}PRX^{1}	3	Spun to Run (Lopez, Paco)	118 L bf	2	4	4^{1}	4^{Head}	4^{2}	3^{4}	$3^{2\ 1/2}$	34.60	steady 7/8, chased
8Jun19 ^{11}BEL^{7}	6	Everfast (Leparoux, Julien)	118 L	5	6	6	6	6	5^{5}	$4^{1/2}$	8.70	outrun early, belated
16Jun19 ^{10}MTH^{1}	1	King for a Day (Velazquez, John)	118 L	1	3	2^{1}	2^{Head}	1^{Head}	$4^{1/2}$	$5^{14\ 1/2}$	2.90	inside duel, check 1/4
22Jun19 ^{9}TDN^{4}	4	Bethlehem Road (Rodriguez Castro, Luis)	118 L f	3	2	1^{Head}	$1^{1/2}$	5^{7}	6	6	42.30	bumped st, duel btwn

Fractional Times: 22.92 46.71 1:10.17 1:34.96 **Final Time:** 1:47.56
Split Times: (23:79) (23:46) (24:79) (12:60)
Run-Up: 56 feet

Winner: Maximum Security, Bay Colt, by New Year's Day out of Lil Indy, by Anasheed. Foaled May 14, 2016 in Kentucky.
Breeder: Gary & Mary West Stables, Inc..
Winning Owner: West, Gary and Mary

Scratched Horse(s): Joevia (Trainer)

Total WPS Pool: $1,403,416

Pgm	Horse	Win	Place	Show
7	Maximum Security	3.60	2.60	2.20
5	Mucho Gusto		3.40	2.80
3	Spun to Run			5.60

Wager Type	Winning Numbers	Payoff	Pool
$1.00 Exacta	7-5	6.00	666,575
$0.50 Trifecta	7-5-3	22.60	427,597
$0.10 Superfecta	7-5-3-6	18.57	290,030
$0.50 Pick 3	6-2-7 (3 correct)	30.20	132,066
$0.50 Pick 4	7-6-2-2/7 (4 correct)	108.80	439,421
$0.50 Pick 5	1/3/4/5-7-6-2-2/7 (5 correct)	185.80	474,222
$1.00 Daily Double	2-7	8.40	144,695

Trainers: 7 - Servis, Jason; 5 - Baffert, Bob; 3 - Guerrero, Juan; 6 - Romans, Dale; 1 - Pletcher, Todd; 4 - Curry, Dee

Owners: 7 - West, Gary and Mary; 5 -Michael Lund Petersen; 3 -Robert P. Donaldson; 6 - Calumet Farm; 1 - Red Oak Stable (Brunetti); 4 - Ameche, III, Don, Gryphon Investments LLC and Reed, Randall B.;

Footnotes
MAXIMUM SECURITY broke sharply, showed good early speed while three wide, dueled three wide on the backside, put a head in front on the far turn, dueled between rivals, maintained a slight edge turning for home, responded when roused, turned back a bid from MUCHO GUSTO and edged away late for the win. MUCHO GUSTO was bumped at the start, raced four wide early, then stalked while three or four wide, bid three wide on the far turn, dueled outside of MAXIMUM SECURITY in upper stretch, dug in gamely through the final furlong but came up second best. SPUN TO RUN raced two wide early, steadied entering the first turn, chased close up between rivals, came three wide into the lane and finished well for show honors. EVERFAST was outrun early, advanced at the quarter pole and closed belatedly for fourth. KING FOR A DAY moved up along the rail entering the clubhouse turn, contested the pace along the inside, dueled inside on the backstretch, continued to duel inside on the far turn, was dropping back a bit off the top pair, then checked sharply when in tight nearing the quarter pole and weakened after. BETHLEHEM ROAD was bumped at the start, vied two wide for the early lead, dueled between rivals on the backside, chased and gave way on the far turn. After a Stewards' Inquiry into the incident on the far turn, the race was declared official.

Figure 24.8. Chart of the Haskell Invitational, July 17, 2019.

(1) Math Wizard (ML 4–1, PSR 94), (2) Improbable (PSR 115, ML 5–1), (3) Shanghai Superfly (PSR 87, ML 50–1), (4) War Of Will (PSR 100, ML 4–1), (5) Spun To Run PSR 109, ML 8–1), (6) Mr. Money (PSR 111, ML 3–1), (7) Maximum Security (PSR 119, scratched)

Wizard: 6–2–4–5 TimeForm: 2–6–4 David: 2 HTR: 7 (scratch)–2–6–5–4–1–3

Finish: 1–6–4–2

Figure 24.10 is the chart of the race.

24.8. The Jockey Club Gold Cup at Belmont Racetrack, September 28, 2019

This $750,000 grade I race is a fall classic and a prelude to the Breeders' Cup. It is for three year old and older horses. It had five entrants with four standouts.

SARATOGA - August 24, 2019 - Race 11
STAKES Runhappy Travers S. Grade 1 - Thoroughbred

EQUIBASE

FOR THREE YEAR OLDS. By subscription of $1,250 each which should accompany the nomination; $9,000 to pass the entry box and an additional $9,750 to start. For horses not originally nominated, a supplemental payment of $18,750 (along with the entry and starting fees) may be made at any time prior to the closing of entries. The purse for the Runhappy Travers shall be divided as follows: $670,000 to the owner of the winner, $230,000 to second, $125,000 to third, $85,000 to fourth, $50,000 to fifth, $35,000 to sixth, $30,000 to seventh and $25,000 to eighth. Weight 126 lbs. Trophies will be presented to the winning owner, trainer and jockey. Closed August 10,2019 with 17 Nominations.
One And One Fourth Miles On The Dirt **Track Record:** (Arrogate - 1:59.36 - August 27, 2016)
Purse: $1,250,000 Added
Available Money: $1,250,000
Value of Race: $1,250,000 1st $670,000, 2nd $230,000, 3rd $125,000, 4th $85,000, 5th $50,000, 6th $35,000, 7th $30,000, 8th $25,000

Video Race Replay

Weather: Clear **Track:** Fast
Off at: 5:50 **Start:** Good for all except 9

Last Raced	Pgm	Horse Name (Jockey)	Wgt	M/E	PP	1/4	1/2	3/4	1m	Str	Fin	Odds	Comments
6Jul19 ^{6}BEL^{1}	2	Code of Honor (Velazquez, John)	126	L	2	9^{1}	9^{1}	9^{2}	6^{1}	3^{2}	1^{3}	4.40	8w uppr, edged clear
27Jul19 ^{11}SAR^{2}	6	Tacitus (Ortiz, Jose)	126	L b	6	1^{Head}	3^{1}	2^{1}	$2^{1\ 1/2}$	$2^{1/2}$	$2^{1/2}$	2.40*	dueled 3-2w, ran on
20Jul19 ^{12}MTH^{2}	7	Mucho Gusto (Talamo, Joseph)	126	L b	7	$2^{1\ 1/2}$	1^{1}	1^{Head}	1^{Head}	1^{Head}	$3^{1\ 1/4}$	3.45	dueled 4-3w, kept on
26Jul19 ^{9}SAR^{2}	11	Endorsed (Rosario, Joel)	126	L	11	12	12	$10^{1/2}$	$7^{1/2}$	$7^{1\ 1/2}$	4^{Neck}	23.00	brushed st, belatedly
22Jun19 ^{9}TDN^{1}	1	Owendale (Geroux, Florent)	126	L b	1	$4^{1/2}$	6^{1}	$5^{1/2}$	$5^{1/2}$	$4^{1/2}$	$5^{1/2}$	7.40	3w uppr, flattened out
26Jul19 ^{8}SAR^{1}	3	Highest Honors (Saez, Luis)	126	L	3	$5^{1/2}$	$4^{1/2}$	4^{Head}	$4^{1/2}$	$6^{1/2}$	6^{Neck}	13.30	4w uppr, weakened late
27Jul19 ^{11}SAR^{1}	12	Tax (Ortiz, Jr., Irad)	126	L	12	3^{Head}	2^{Head}	$3^{1\ 1/2}$	$3^{1\ 1/2}$	$5^{1/2}$	$7^{2\ 3/4}$	7.90	4-3w 1st trn, wknd lte
3Aug19 ^{6}MNR^{2}	8	Chess Chief (Smith, Mike)	126	L b	8	10^{2}	$10^{1\ 1/2}$	$11^{1/2}$	10^{1}	9^{Head}	$8^{1/2}$	60.25	bumped st, no impact
27Jul19 ^{11}SAR^{4}	4	Laughing Fox (Santana, Jr., Ricardo)	126	L	4	$11^{1/2}$	11^{1}	12	9^{Head}	$8^{1/2}$	$9^{3\ 1/4}$	52.25	bumped st, no rally
21Jul19 ^{5}SAR^{1}	10	Scars Are Cool (Gaffalione, Tyler)	126	L f	10	$8^{1\ 1/2}$	8^{1}	8^{1}	$8^{1\ 1/2}$	10^{7}	$10^{8\ 1/2}$	40.50	3w into 1st, no impact
26Jul19 ^{9}SAR^{3}	9	Looking At Bikinis (Castellano, Javier)	126	L	9	$6^{1\ 1/2}$	5^{Head}	6^{1}	12	$11^{1/2}$	$11^{1\ 1/4}$	11.50	stumbled st, 3w 1st tn
20Jul19 ^{12}MTH^{4}	5	Everfast (Chuan, Martin)	126	L	5	7^{Head}	7^{Head}	7^{Head}	11^{2}	12	12	78.00	5w upper, tired

Fractional Times: 23.11 47.26 1:11.21 1:35.49 **Final Time:** 2:01.05
Split Times: (24:15) (23:95) (24:28) (25:56)
Run-Up: 65 feet

Winner: Code of Honor, Chestnut Colt, by Noble Mission (GB) out of Reunited, by Dixie Union. Foaled May 23, 2016 in Kentucky.
NOBLE MISSION Winner's sire standing at Lane's End
Breeder: W. S. Farish.
Winning Owner: W.S. Farish

Total WPS Pool: $4,896,081

Pgm	Horse	Win	Place	Show
2	Code of Honor	10.80	5.20	3.80
6	Tacitus		3.70	2.80
7	Mucho Gusto			3.80

Wager Type	Winning Numbers	Payoff	Pool	Carryover
$1.00 Pick 3	1-7-2 (3 correct)	63.50	646,548	
$0.50 Pick 4	4-1-7-2 (4 correct)	398.25	1,780,965	
$0.50 Pick 5	6-4-1-7-2 (5 correct)	6,362.00	1,445,980	
$0.20 Pick 6 Jackpot	2/3/6-6-4-1-7-2 (6 correct)	3,991.10	899,588	298,981
$1.00 Daily Double	7-2	21.50	470,139	
$1.00 Exacta	2-6	18.50	2,964,862	
$0.10 Superfecta	2-6-7-11	117.65	1,254,133	
$0.50 Trifecta	2-6-7	35.87	2,091,475	

Trainers: 2 - McGaughey III, Claude; 6 - Mott, William; 7 - Baffert, Bob; 11 - McLaughlin, Kiaran; 1 - Cox, Brad; 3 - Brown, Chad; 12 - Gargan, Danny; 8 - Stewart, Dallas; 4 - Asmussen, Steven; 10 - Hough, Stanley; 9 - Brown, Chad; 5 - Romans, Dale

Owners: 2 -W.S. Farish; 6 - Juddmonte Farms, Inc.; 7 -Michael Lund Petersen; 11 - Godolphin, LLC; 1 - Rupp Racing; 3 -W.S. Farish; 12 - R. A. Hill Stable, Reeves Thoroughbred Racing, Lynch, Hugh and Corms Racing Stable; 8 - Estate of James J. Coleman, Jr.; 4 - Lieblong, Alex and JoAnn; 10 - Sagamore Farm LLC; 9 - Long Lake Stable LLC, Madaket Stables LLC, Coleman, Thomas and Doheny Racing Stable; 5 - Calumet Farm;

Footnotes
CODE OF HONOR just off the inside near the rear in the early stages past the stands and through the opening bend, tipped five paths off the inside once into the backstretch, remained patiently handled among rivals until placed to light coaxing at the half mile pole, remained five wide through the far turn tipping out slightly near the three-eighths as LOOKING AT BIKINIS backed up to the inside, angled eight wide into upper stretch roused for the drive, dug in rallying to confront the top pair straightened away for home, collared the embattled duo inside the eighth pole and edged clear under a drive kept to task to the wire. TACITUS coaxed from the gate, steadily made his way to the inside, the rider peering to the off side as MUCHO GUSTO remained outside going past the stands forwardly placed into the first turn, showed the way into the turn before being displaced on the front midway on the turn, eased off into the backstretch in the three path before advancing once more this time to knock heads with half a mile to run, took over narrow command inside the half mile pole and showed the way given some rein to work with seven-sixteenths from home under pressure from his main pace rival to the outside, got headed near the quarter pole, went four to five wide at that station, dug in under a drive, dueling through the stretch brushing with MUCHO GUSTO nearing the eighth pole and then bumping with that rival head to head inside that station as CODE OF HONOR went on by to the outside, dug in and ran on to best that foe for the place honors. MUCHO GUSTO hustled from the gate, raced forwardly placed three wide into and through the first turn taking command nearing the backstretch, showed the way safely in front four wide early on before TACITUS advanced inside to knock heads nearing the half mile pole, got headed for the front and came under coaxing past the three-eighths in response, took back the front swinging six wide into upper stretch, dug in getting brushed by TACITUS inside the three-sixteenths and then bumped by that rival as the pair came under threat outside from the eventual winner inside the eighth pole, got displaced in tandem at that juncture and continued their battle to the finish keeping on while being bested for the place honors and safe for the show. ENDORSED brushed at the start by TAX who broke inwards, raced just off the inside through the first turn before chasing three to four wide down the backstretch, remained three to four wide through the far turn coming under coaxing at the three-eighths, went nine wide into upper stretch, kicked on belatedly for the last major share. OWENDALE tracked the pace along the inside early on and then just off the inside down the backstretch, came under coaxing tucked inside at the three-eighths, swung three wide into upper stretch, offered up a mild bid to the eighth pole, then flattened out in the late stages. HIGHEST HONORS just off the inside past the stands and through the first turn, chased four then three wide down the backstretch from just off the pace, came under coaxing half a mile from home, angled four wide into upper stretch and weakened in the final furlong. TAX broke in at the start brushing with ENDORSED, raced four then three wide forwardly placed through the opening bend, settled five then four wide in aim of the duel, came under coaxing three furlongs from home, went seven wide into upper stretch and weakened in the final eighth. CHESS CHIEF bumped at the start by LOOKING AT BIKINIS who recovered inwards from a stumble, raced just off the inside early on before taking to the six path six and a half furlongs out, came under taps to the off side five furlongs from home, continued six wide through the far turn urged along from the half mile pole, went nine wide into upper stretch and could not make an impact. LAUGHING FOX bumped at the start by EVERFAST breaking inwards, raced along the rail early on before chasing three wide down the backstretch and through the far turn coming under coaxing at the seven-sixteenths, went eight wide at the head of the stretch and offered no response. SCARS ARE COOL three wide into the first turn, tucked to the two path midway before tipping back out four wide in pursuit down the backstretch, came under coaxing tucked three wide with half a mile remaining, angled six to seven wide at the top of the stretch and made no impact. LOOKING AT BIKINIS stumbled at the start sliding into and then recovering into CHESS CHIEF to his inside, raced three wide through the first turn before chasing five wide down the backstretch just off the pace, tucked four wide under light coaxing into the far turn, faded with seven-sixteenths to go to the rear, swung three wide for home, tired and was not persevered with through the final eighth. EVERFAST broke in at the start bumping LAUGHING FOX, raced inside early on before chasing three then two wide from mid pack, got coaxed along with four furlongs to run, swung five wide into upper stretch and tired and was not persevered with through the final eighth.

Figure 24.9. Chart of the Travers.

Trainers: 1 - Joseph, Jr., Saffie; 6 - Calhoun, W.; 4 - Casse, Mark; 2 - Baffert, Bob; 5 - Guerrero, Juan; 3 - Zulueta, Marcos

Owners: 1 - Fanelli, John, Collarmele Vitelli Stables LLC, Bassett Stables, Zoumas, Ioannis, Wynwood Thoroughbreds and Joseph, Jr., Saffie A.; 6 - Allied Racing Stable, LLC; 4 -Gary Barber; 2 - WinStar Farm LLC, China Horse Club and SF Racing LLC; 5 -Robert P. Donaldson; 3 - Kernan, Jr., Morris E. and M-Z Racing Partnership;

Footnotes
MATH WIZARD reserved inside below slow fractions, trailed at the half, angled out into the turn, continued to advance on the final turn, rallied six wide into the stretch then surged past the leaders late in a blanket finish. MR. MONEY moved inside early under a rating hold, set the pace under constant pressure, moved clear in mid-stretch, continued determinedly but was nailed nearing the wire. WAR OF WILL prompted the pace between rivals under patient handling, loomed a serious threat in the stretch but was outfinished while narrowly holding on for the show award. IMPROBABLE was in motion prior to the start and broke poorly, saved ground without urging, bid with ample room into the stretch but flattened out in the final furlong. SPUN TO RUN under a firm rating hold three wide, continued to pressure the top pair to the stretch where he drifted wider then weakened in the lane while continuing gamely. SHANGHAI SUPERFLY chased outside for half a mile then stopped abruptly.

PARX RACING - September 21, 2019 - Race 11 **EQUIBASE**
STAKES Pennsylvania Derby Grade 1 - Thoroughbred
FOR THREE YEAR OLDS.
One And One Eighth Miles On The Dirt **Track Record:** (Bayern - 1:46.96 - September 20, 2014)
Purse: $1,000,000 Guaranteed
Plus: $15,000 Starters Bonus
Available Money: $1,015,000 Video Race Replay
Value of Race: $1,015,000 1st $600,000, 2nd $200,000, 3rd $100,000, 4th $60,000, 5th $40,000, 6th $15,000
Weather: Clear **Track:** Fast
Off at: 5:50 **Start:** Good for all except 2

Last Raced	Pgm	Horse Name (Jockey)	Wgt M/E	PP	Start	1/4	1/2	3/4	Str	Fin	Odds	Comments
3Aug19 ^{8}MNR^{6}	1	Math Wizard (Ortiz, Jr., Irad)	118 L	1	4	$5^{1/2}$	6	5^{4}	$4^{1/2}$	1^{Neck}	31.10	angled wide,late surge
3Aug19 ^{8}MNR^{1}	6	Mr. Money (Saez, Gabriel)	122 L	6	2	1^{1}	$1^{1/2}$	$1^{1/2}$	1^{1}	2^{1}	1.70	vied, clear, nailed
27Jul19 ^{11}SAR^{5}	4	War of Will (Gaffalione, Tyler)	124 L	4	3	$2^{1/2}$	$2^{1/2}$	2^{Head}	$3^{1/2}$	3^{Nose}	3.30	dueled between, gamely
25Aug19 ^{8}DMR^{1}	2	Improbable (Smith, Mike)	119 L b	2	6	4^{1}	4^{2}	4^{Head}	2^{Head}	4^{Neck}	1.20*	poor start, rail trip
2Sep19 ^{11}PRX^{1}	5	Spun to Run (Lopez, Paco)	122 L bf	5	1	3^{2}	$3^{1\ 1/2}$	$3^{2\ 1/2}$	5^{20}	5^{25}	7.40	rated wide,outfinished
7Sep19 ^{5}MTH^{2}	3	Shanghai Superfly (Pennington, Frankie)	117 L b	3	5	6	5^{Head}	6	6	6	90.40	stopped abruptly

Fractional Times: 24.50 49.60 1:13.44 1:37.98 **Final Time:** 1:50.94
Split Times: (25:10) (23:84) (24:54) (12:96)
Run-Up: 40 feet

Winner: Math Wizard, Chestnut Colt, by Algorithms out of Minister's Baby, by Deputy Minister. Foaled May 04, 2016 in Kentucky.
Breeder: Lucky Seven Stable.
Winning Owner: Fanelli, John, Collarmele Vitelli Stables LLC, Bassett Stables, Zoumas, Ioannis, Wynwood Thoroughbreds and Joseph, Jr., Saffie A.

Scratched Horse(s): Maximum Security (Trainer)

Total WPS Pool: $911,357

Pgm	Horse	Win	Place	Show
1	Math Wizard	64.20	12.00	4.80
6	Mr. Money		3.60	2.60
4	War of Will			4.00

Wager Type	Winning Numbers	Payoff	Pool
$1.00 Pick 3	5/7/8-3-1 (3 correct)	406.50	185,406
$0.50 Pick 4	3/4/6-5/7/8-3-1 (4 correct)	889.40	486,209
$2.00 Daily Double	3-1	578.60	144,386
$2.00 Exacta	1-6	196.00	402,477
$0.10 Superfecta	1-6-4-2	45.44	151,086
$0.50 Trifecta	1-6-4	136.95	241,684

Figure 24.10. Chart of the Pennsylvania Derby.

The handicappers rated the horses as follows. Wizard: 2-Code of Honor (8–5 ML, 113 PSR), jockey Velazquez; 4-Preservationist (9–5 ML, 120 PSR), jockey Alveraz; 1-Tacitus (5–2 ML, 110 PSR), jockey J. Ortiz; 3-Vino Rosso (7–2 ML, 109 PSR), jockey I. Ortiz Jr; 5–Olympic Village (30–1 ML, 98 PSR), jockey J. Castalleno.
TimeForm: 1–2–4
David: 2
HTR: 4–3–1–2

Vino Rosso won the race in a tight duel with Code of Honor but bumped Code of Honor and was disqualified into second position. So the finish was then 2–3–1–4–5. Todd Pletcher, the trainer of Vino Rosso, and others including me thought the DQ was not justified, but Vino Rosso was taken down to second. This win makes Code of Honor the top three year old so far in 2019 since he was second in the Kentucky Derby, won the Fountain

(a) Code of Honor, Fountain of Youth.

(b) Omaha Beach on the right beating Shancelot at the Santa Anita Sprint.

Figure 24.11. Two top three year olds.

of Youth (see Figure 24.11), the Travers and this Jockey Club Gold Cup. Meanwhile, Kentucky Derby favorite and Arkansas Derby winner, the War Front sired Omaha Beach, who was scratched before the Kentucky Derby for a throat problem had a tie back operations so was sidelined from May to October. He then returned to win the 7 furlong Grade I Santa Anita Sprint Championship beating the huge favorite Shancelot.

Maximum Security's Haskell was a Beyer 102, the highest Beyer by a three year old in 2019. His last five Beyers were all 100–102: 101 in the Florida and Kentucky Derbys, 102 in a 7-furlong race at Gulfstream on February 20 and 100 in the Pegasus. Figure 24.12 has the chart of the race.

Maximum Security, Omaha Beach, Tacitus and others might emerge to challenge Code of Honor for top three year old honors. None of them finished the Breeders' Cup with a top record. There are a number of good three year olds but no standouts. Maximum Security skipped the Breeders Cup and instead ran in the $200,000 7 furlong Grade III Bold Ruler Stakes at Belmont on October 26, 2019. As a 3–5 favorite, he led wire to wire in 120.76 minutes (108.37 after 6 furlongs) to win easily paying $3.20 to win, $2.90 to place and $2.60 to show, two Dr Z bets to place and show.

To me, Maximum Security is the best. The market place agrees as his dam, Lil Indy in foal to Quality Road was sold at the Keeneland November Breeding Stock Sale for $1.85 million. The buyer, Jane Lyon owner of Summer Wind Equine Farm said "it was the steal of the century". The future plans for Maximum Security include the $750,000 Grade I Cigar Mile at

BELMONT PARK - September 28, 2019 - Race 10 **EQUIBASE**
STAKES Jockey Club Gold Cup S. Grade 1 - Thoroughbred
FOR THREE YEAR OLDS AND UPWARD.
One And One Fourth Miles On The Dirt **Track Record:** (In Excess (IRE) - 1:58.33 - July 4, 1991)
Purse: $750,000 Guaranteed
Plus: $6,750 Starters Bonus
Available Money: $756,750
Value of Race: $734,250 1st $412,500, 2nd $150,000, 3rd $94,500, 4th $47,250, 5th $30,000
Weather: Clear **Track:** Fast
Off at: 5:49 **Start:** Good for all

Video Race Replay

Last Raced	Pgm	Horse Name (Jockey)	Wgt	M/E	PP	1/4	1/2	3/4	1m	Str	Fin	Odds	Comments
3Aug19 ^{9}SAR^{3}	3	DQ-Vino Rosso (Ortiz, Jr., Irad)	126	L	3	1^{1}	$1^{1/2}$	1^{1}	1^{1}	1^{Head}	1^{Nose}	3.60	ins,out2w1/8,bump 3x
24Aug19 ^{11}SAR^{1}	2	Code of Honor (Velazquez, John)	122	L	2	4^{1}	4^{4}	4^{5}	$3^{1\ 1/2}$	2^{2}	2^{4}	2.00	3w 2nd,ask 3/16,bmp3x
24Aug19 ^{11}SAR^{2}	1	Tacitus (Ortiz, Jose)	122	L b	1	2^{Head}	$2^{1\ 1/2}$	$2^{1\ 1/2}$	2^{1}	$3^{1\ 1/2}$	3^{1}	2.80	2-3w back-1/4,gave way
31Aug19 ^{11}SAR^{1}	4	Preservationist (Alvarado, Junior)	126	L	4	$3^{2\ 1/2}$	$3^{1\ 1/2}$	$3^{1/2}$	4^{6}	$4^{7\ 1/2}$	$4^{18\ 3/4}$	1.80*	3w 1st,2w 2nd,ask5/16
16Aug19 ^{2}SAR^{1}	5	Olympic Village (Castellano, Javier)	122	L	5	5	5	5	5	5	5	37.50	3w 1st,ins 2d,gave way

Fractional Times: 24.02 47.73 1:11.63 1:35.70 **Final Time:** 2:00.30
Split Times: (23:71) (23:90) (24:07) (24:60)
Run-Up: 72 feet

Winner: Code of Honor, Chestnut Colt, by Noble Mission (GB) out of Reunited, by Dixie Union. Foaled May 23, 2016 in Kentucky.
NOBLE MISSION Winner's sire standing at Lane's End
Breeder: W. S. Farish.
Winning Owner: W.S. Farish

Disqualification(s): # 3 Vino Rosso from 1 to 2

Total WPS Pool: $786,456

Pgm	Horse	Win	Place	Show
2	Code of Honor	6.00	3.30	2.20
3	Vino Rosso		4.70	2.80
1	Tacitus			2.30

Wager Type	Winning Numbers	Payoff	Pool
$1.00 Exacta	2-3	11.90	306,341
$0.50 Trifecta	2-3-1	13.25	117,337
$1.00 Daily Double	7-2	12.60	103,183
$1.00 Pick 3	1-7-2 (3 correct)	11.90	92,630
$0.10 Superfecta	2-3-1-4	3.22	71,493
$1.00 Grand Slam	2/3/4-1/5/6-3/6/7-2 (4	25.25	38,437

Trainers: 3 - Pletcher, Todd; 2 - McGaughey III, Claude; 1 - Mott, William; 4 - Jerkens, James; 5 - Hess, Jr., Robert

Owners: 3 - Repole Stable and St. Elias Stable; 2 -W.S. Farish; 1 - Juddmonte Farms, Inc.; 4 - Centennial Farms; 5 - Ron Paolucci Racing, LLC and Lambert, Jeffrey;

Footnotes
VINO ROSSO established the top under a light hand ride on the opening bend, cut over to the inside, got confronted by TACITUS at the top of the backstretch, rated kindly showing the way, attended by the aforementioned foe all the way to the half mile pole, had the pilot revert to a light hand ride departing that station, clung to the top, settled in upper stretch and was put to a drive, came out into path two after some left side stick work at the furlong grounds, bumped thrice with CODE OF HONOR from inside the furlong marker to narrowly beyond the sixteenth pole as the twosome went at it eye to eye, got corrected in the final seventy yards by being yanked off CODE OF HONOR, dug in gamely to be the first to cross the wire. CODE OF HONOR away in good order, was rated two wide early keeping watch on the front runners, shifted into the three path in time for the commencement of the run around the far turn, drafted behind TACITUS, flashed some interest coming up to the quarter pole, swung three wide into the lane, made it to the three-sixteenths pole and was given his cue, drew up on even terms with VINO ROSSO, bumped three times with that opponent for approximately a sixteenth, beginning from a short distance past the eighth pole, with the nemesis having come out each time in varying degrees, fought on with willingness but didn't go by. TACITUS fowardly placed along the inside on the first turn, tipped to the outside during the later stages on it after VINO ROSSO had grabbed the advantage, drew up to apply some pressure on that one by the head of the backstretch, going about the task between paths two and three, kept it up all the way to the quarter pole, got set down spinning onto the top of the lane, failed to keep pace, but stayed on well to secure the show. PRESERVATIONIST strung out three wide on the first turn, was closer to the rail after stepping onto the backstretch, was without benefit of being covered up for the the trip on turn two, got called upon at the five-sixteenths pole, went into the stretch and came up empty. OLYMPIC VILLAGE off one length the tardiest, spun four wide onto the backstretch, brought up the back of the pack, found himself on the inside by the half mile pole, was put to some urging racing around it, cut the corner into the lane and backed away readily. Following a Stewards' Inquiry focusing on the stretch run in addition to a claim of foul lodged by the rider of CODE OF HONOR against the rider of VINO ROSSO, the latter was disqualified from first and placed second for causing interference.

Figure 24.12. Chart of the Jockey Gold Cup at Belmont, September 28, 2019.

Aqueduct on November 29 and the $9 million Pegasus World Cup at Gulfstream in January. He has six wins in eight starts and so far has earned $1,389,400. In the Cigar Mile, Maximum Security led wire to wire running his best race so far with a 111 Beyer speed rating. He beat Breeders' Cup dirt Mile winner Spun to Run by $3\frac{1}{2}$ lengths.

Maximum Security is still in training and may run in the Pegasus in January (now a $3 million race) and possibly the Saudi Cup in February (a $20 million race). Ashford-Coolmore US has purchased a half interest in Maximum Security for his stud career when his racing career is completed.

24.9. The Breeders' Cup, Santa Anita, November 2, 2019

Omaha Beach (Figure 24.11(b) was the favorite, piloted by regular rider Mike Smith in the Grade I Breeders' Cup Big Ass Fans Dirt Mile. He ran well but finished second beaten by the 9–1 shot Spun to Run. Improbable failed again finishing out of the money (5th) as did Mr Money (7th). See the chart in Figure 24.13.

Code of Honor was out of the money in the Breeders' Cup Classic.

It was clear then that none of the three year olds will be horse of the year but which of the older horses will be? Some candidates did not win at the Breeders' Cup so they will most likely not be the top horse. These include Mckinzie (who was second in the Classic), Sister Charley (who was third), and Midnight Bisou (who finished second). So it seems that the top choices to be horse of the year are Bricks and Mortar (who won the $4 million $1\frac{1}{4}$ mile Longines Breeders' Cup Turf to complete an undefeated 6/6 season), Mitole (who won the Breeders' Cup Sprint) and Vino Rosso (who won the $6 million Longines Breeders' Cup Classic). To me it is between Bricks and Mortar and Mitole, grass versus dirt. Bricks and Mortar is the most likely Eclipse winner.

Vino Rosso had a good career with much promise which finally materialized late in his 4th year. He was first in the Jockey Club Gold Cup but was disqualified into second behind Code of Honor. He won the Breeders' Cup Classic by $4\frac{1}{2}$ lengths with a terrific performance that earned him $3.5 million of his $4,813,125 lifetime earnings with 6 wins in 15 starts, 1 second and 3 thirds. He now goes to Spendthrift Farm for a $30,000 stud fee career. Omaha Beach is going the Spendthrift Farm for a $40,000 stud fee and Mitole will be there for $25,000. See Figure 24.14 for the chart of the Classic. According to Ryan (2019), the plans for Omaha Beach are to run in either the Grade I Malibu Stakes at Santa Anita on December 26 or the Grade I Cigar Mile at Aqueduct on December 7 and end his career at the $9 million Pegasus World Cup at Gulfstream on January 25, 2020 and be retired to stud career. So far he is 4–4–1 in nine starts earning $1,471,800.

Vino Rosso's win makes Curlin the second Breeders' Cup Classic winner who sired a Breeders' Cup Classic winner. Previously, Awesome Again who won in 1998 and his son Ghostzapper who won in 2004. Curlin stands at Hill and Dale for a $175,000 stud fee and many of his offspring have sold for over $1 million. Blue Prize, the Argentinian mare who beat the most outstanding Midnight Bisou in the Longines Distaff sold for $5 million at the November 2019 Breeding Stock Sale at Fasig-Tipton. Midnight Bisou

RACE RESULTS

SIXTH RACE
Santa Anita
NOVEMBER 2, 2019

1 MILE. (1.33^{2}) BIG ASS FANS BREEDERS' CUP DIRT MILE Grade I. Purse $1,000,000 FOR THREE-YEAR-OLDS AND UPWARD. Northern Hemisphere Three-Year-Olds, 123 lbs.; Older, 126 lbs. Southern Hemisphere Three-Year-Olds, 120 lbs.; Older, 126 lbs. All Fillies and Mares allowed 3 lbs. $15,000 to pre-enter, $15,000 to enter, with guaranteed $1million purse including travel awards of which 55% to the owner of the winner, 17% to second, 9% to third, 5% to fourth, 3% to fifth, 1% to sixth, 1% to seventh, 1% to eighth; plus travel awards to starters not based in California.

Value of Race: $920,000 Winner $550,000; second $170,000; third $90,000; fourth $50,000; fifth $30,000; sixth $10,000; seventh $10,000; eighth $10,000. Mutuel Pool $3,180,833.00 Exacta Pool $2,093,664.00 Trifecta Pool $1,401,974.00 Superfecta Pool $725,727.00 Super High Five Pool $48,932.00

Last Raced	Horse	M/Eqt.	A.	Wt	PP	St	¼	½	¾	Str	Fin	Jockey	Odds $1
12Oct19 ^{9}Prx^{1}	Spun to Run	L bf	3	123	3	1	$1^{1\frac{1}{2}}$	1^{1}	$1^{1\frac{1}{2}}$	$1^{2\frac{1}{2}}$	$1^{2\frac{3}{4}}$	Ortiz I Jr	9.10
5Oct19 ^{9}SA^{1}	Omaha Beach	L	3	123	5	5	7^{1}	$7^{1\frac{1}{2}}$	$6^{\frac{1}{2}}$	$3^{2\frac{1}{2}}$	$2^{1\frac{1}{4}}$	Smith M E	1.00
8Sep19 ^{7}Seo^{1}	Blue Chipper	f	4	126	8	4	2^{1}	$2^{\frac{1}{2}}$	$2^{4\frac{1}{2}}$	$2^{2\frac{1}{2}}$	$3^{3\frac{1}{4}}$	Prat F	16.10
31Aug19 ^{8}KD^{1}	Snapper Sinclair	L	4	126	10	6	$6^{1\frac{1}{2}}$	6^{2}	$7^{3\frac{1}{2}}$	$5^{\frac{1}{2}}$	$4^{1\frac{3}{4}}$	Santana R Jr	40.70
21Sep19 ^{11}Prx^{4}	Improbable	L b	3	123	2	7	4^{2}	4^{2}	4^{hd}	$4^{1\frac{1}{2}}$	$5^{\frac{1}{2}}$	Bejarano R	4.70
21Sep19 ^{8}Prx^{1}	Coal Front	L	5	126	7	2	$5^{\frac{1}{2}}$	$5^{2\frac{1}{2}}$	5^{1}	7^{2}	$6^{1\frac{1}{4}}$	Castellano J J	16.80
21Sep19 ^{11}Prx^{2}	Mr. Money	L	3	123	4	3	3^{hd}	$3^{\frac{1}{2}}$	$3^{\frac{1}{2}}$	$6^{2\frac{1}{2}}$	7^{1}	Saez G	7.20
5Oct19 ^{10}Kee^{2}	Diamond Oops	L b	4	126	9	8	$8^{\frac{1}{2}}$	8^{1}	9^{2}	9^{1}	8^{nk}	Leparoux J R	11.70
8Oct19 ^{4}CHD^{3}	Ambassadorial	L	5	126	6	9	9^{2}	10	10	10	9^{17}	Spencer J P	82.90
24Aug19 ^{9}Dmr^{2}	Giant Expectations	L bf	6	126	1	10	10	9^{1}	8^{hd}	$8^{\frac{1}{2}}$	10	Ortiz J L	13.90

OFF AT 1:12 Start Good For All But GIANT EXPECTATIONS, DIAMOND OOPS. Won driving. Track fast.

TIME :23, :46^{2}, 1:10^{2}, 1:23^{1}, 1:36^{2} (:23.05, :46.51, 1:10.50, 1:23.31, 1:36.58)

$2 Mutuel Prices:			
3-SPUN TO RUN	20.20	7.00	4.80
5-OMAHA BEACH		3.40	2.40
8-BLUE CHIPPER			6.00

$1 EXACTA 3-5 PAID $27.70 50 CENT TRIFECTA 3-5-8 PAID $176.25 10 CENT SUPERFECTA 3-5-8-10 PAID $570.51 50 CENT SUPER HIGH FIVE 3-5-8-10-2 PAID $3,500.95

Dk. b or br. c, (Mar), by Hard Spun – Yawkey Way, by Grand Slam. Trainer Guerrero Juan Carlos. Bred by Sabana Farm (Ky).

SPUN TO RUN opened clear to dictate terms, widened entering stretch, driftedabout through the final furlong while unchallenged and gamely led throughout. OMAHA BEACH was allowed to settle off of the inside, came under a ride with three furlongs to run, circled five wide through the second turn and into the stretch, failed to menace the winner but churned on to earn the runner up spot. BLUE CHIPPER shadowed the leader three deep, was unable to go on with SPUN TO RUN entering the stretch, weakened slightly during the drive and settled for the minor award. SNAPPER SINCLAIR tucked in to save ground, took closer order through the second turn, was bottled up in traffic near the quarter pole, steadied at the three-sixteenths when MR. MONEY came in, was quickly back into stride and continued on willingly. IMPROBABLE was hustled along on the inside in a forward position, got through every step but toiled fruitlessly through the lane. COAL FRONT settled in hand, advanced between horses, was put in tight and checked when MR. MONEY came out near the three-sixteenths pole, altered course to the outside but lacked a response thereafter. MR. MONEY stalked the pace three deep, was put to pressure midway through the second turn, drifted out stacking up COAL FRONT near the three-sixteenths pole, came back in and tightened up SNAPPER SINCLAIR shortly after and retreated between rivals. DIAMOND OOPS lunged at the start and was away slow, was unhurried into stride, was hung wide throughout and was never a factor. AMBASSADORIAL was unhurried, wheeled out leaving the second turn but failed to make headway. GIANT EXPECTATIONS broke slow, was unhurried along the inside, showed little, was eased to the wire but walked off.

Owners– 1, Donaldson Robert P; 2, Fox Hill Farms Inc; 3, Choi Byungboo; 4, Bloom Racing Stable LLC (Jeffrey Bloom); 5, WinStar Farm LLC China Horse Club International Ltd and Starlight Racing; 6, LaPenta Robert V and Head of Plains Partners LLC; 7, Allied Racing Stable LLC and Spendthrift Farm LLC; 8, Diamond 100 Racing Club LLC Dunne Amy E D P Racing LLC and Patrick L Biancone Ra; 9, Chapple-Hyam Jane; 10, David A Bernsen LLC Exline-Border Racing LLC Gatto Racing LLC and Zubok Garett

Trainers– 1, Guerrero Juan Carlos; 2, Mandella Richard; 3, Young-Kwan Kim; 4, Asmussen Steven M; 5, Baffert Bob; 6, Pletcher Todd A; 7, Calhoun William Bret; 8, Biancone Patrick L; 9, Chapple-Hyam Jane; 10, Eurton Peter

$2 Daily Double (12-3) Paid $394.40; Daily Double Pool $360,237.
50 CENT Pick Three (1-12-3) Paid $205.90; Pick Three Pool $645,762.

Figure 24.13. Chart of the Breeders' Cup Big Ass Fans Dirt Mile.

RACE RESULTS

TWELFTH RACE
Santa Anita
NOVEMBER 2, 2019

$1\frac{1}{4}$ MILES. (1.57^{4}) LONGINES BREEDERS' CUP CLASSIC Grade I. Purse $6,000,000 FOR THREE–YEAR–OLDS AND UPWARD. Northern Hemisphere Three–Year–Olds, 122 lbs.; Older, 126 lbs.; Southern Hemisphere Three–Year–Olds, 117 lbs.; Older, 126 lbs. All Fillies and Mares allowed 3 lbs. $75,000 to pre-enter, $75,000 to enter, with guaranteed $6million purse including travel awards of which 55% to the owner of the winner, 17% to second, 9% to third, 5% to fourth, 3% to fifth, 1% to sixth, 1% to seventh, 1% to eighth; plus travel awards to starters not based in California.

Value of Race: $5,520,000 Winner $3,300,000; second $1,020,000; third $540,000; fourth $300,000; fifth $180,000; sixth $60,000; seventh $60,000; eighth $60,000. Mutuel Pool $7,370,760.00 Exacta Pool $4,250,151.00 Trifecta Pool $3,607,387.00 Superfecta Pool $2,070,398.00 Head2Head Pool $13,424.00 Super High Five Pool $415,627.00

Last Raced	Horse	M/Eqt.	A.	Wt	PP	¼	½	¾	1	Str	Fin	Jockey	Odds $1
28Sep19 ^{10}Bel^{2}	Vino Rosso	L	4	126	10	4^{1}	4^{hd}	$4^{1\frac{1}{2}}$	3^{1}	$2^{4\frac{1}{2}}$	$1^{4\frac{1}{4}}$	Ortiz I Jr	4.60
28Sep19 ^{10}SA^{2}	McKinzie	L	4	126	8	$3^{\frac{1}{2}}$	$3^{2\frac{1}{2}}$	2^{hd}	1^{1}	$1^{\frac{1}{2}}$	$2^{4\frac{1}{4}}$	Rosario J	2.90
28Sep19 ^{10}SA^{3}	Higher Power	L b	4	126	7	$7^{\frac{1}{2}}$	7^{1}	$5^{\frac{1}{2}}$	$5^{\frac{1}{2}}$	3^{2}	$3^{2\frac{1}{4}}$	Prat F	9.80
6Oct19 ^{9}Kee^{2}	Elate	L	5	123	6	$6^{\frac{1}{2}}$	$8^{\frac{1}{2}}$	9^{2}	$10^{\frac{1}{2}}$	$7^{\frac{1}{2}}$	$4^{4\frac{1}{4}}$	Ortiz J L	9.30
21Sep19 ^{11}Prx^{1}	Math Wizard	L	3	122	1	11	11	11	11	9^{1}	5^{nk}	Santana R Jr	39.10
28Sep19 ^{10}SA^{4}	Seeking the Soul	L	6	126	2	8^{2}	$6^{\frac{1}{2}}$	7^{1}	7^{hd}	5^{hd}	6no	Hernandez B J Jr	37.90
28Sep19 ^{10}Bel^{1}	Code of Honor	L	3	122	11	9^{hd}	9^{1}	$8^{1\frac{1}{2}}$	$6^{2\frac{1}{2}}$	4^{hd}	$7^{1\frac{1}{2}}$	Velazquez J R	3.70
31Aug19 ^{11}Sar^{3}	Yoshida-Jpn	L	5	126	5	$10^{3\frac{1}{2}}$	10^{2}	10^{2}	$9^{\frac{1}{2}}$	8^{hd}	8^{3}	Smith M E	7.40
21Sep19 ^{11}Prx^{3}	War of Will	L b	3	122	4	1^{1}	1^{1}	$1^{1\frac{1}{2}}$	4^{2}	6^{2}	$9^{2\frac{3}{4}}$	Gaffalione T	16.00
29Sep19 ^{12}RP^{1}	Owendale	L b	3	122	3	5^{hd}	$5^{1\frac{1}{2}}$	$6^{1\frac{1}{2}}$	8^{1}	10^{2}	10	Castellano J J	14.50
28Sep19 ^{10}SA^{1}	Mongolian Groom	L b	4	126	9	2^{1}	$2^{\frac{1}{2}}$	3^{3}	$2^{\frac{1}{2}}$	11	—	Cedillo A	15.60

OFF AT 5:45 Start Good. Won driving. Track fast.

TIME :23, :47, 1:10^{3}, 1:36^{1}, 2:02^{4} (:23.09, :47.16, 1:10.71, 1:36.35, 2:02.80)

$2 Mutuel Prices:

10 – VINO ROSSO	11.20	5.80	4.00
8 – MCKINZIE		4.80	3.60
7 – HIGHER POWER			6.00

$1 EXACTA 10–8 PAID $23.80 50 CENT TRIFECTA 10–8–7 PAID $98.50 10 CENT SUPERFECTA 10–8–7–6 PAID $121.30 $10 HEAD2HEAD 2–MCKINZIE PAID $16.00 50 CENT SUPER HIGH FIVE 10–8–7–6–1 PAID $7,181.40

Ch. c, (Mar), by Curlin – Mythical Bride, by Street Cry–Ire. Trainer Pletcher Todd A. Bred by John D Gunther (Ky).

VINO ROSSO stalked three wide on the first turn then outside a rival, continued off the inside leaving the backstretch and on the second turn, ranged up three deep into the stretch, bid outside the runner-up in midstretch, gained the advantage past the eighth pole, inched away under left handed urging in deep stretch and drew clear. MCKINZIE tugged some between horses then angled in on the first turn, steadied in tight leaving that turn then came a bit off the fence to stalk the pace, bid between horses to take the lead into the second turn, edged away on that turn, fought back a bit off the rail in midstretch, drifted in and could not match the winner in the final sixteenth while clearly second best. HIGHER POWER broke slowly, went up four wide into and on the first turn, stalked outside on the backstretch and second turn, came three wide into the stretch, drifted in some and bested the others. ELATE chased three deep between horses into and on the first turn, continued off the rail on the backstretch, angled to the inside nearing the stretch, came out in upper stretch and improved position. MATH WIZARD settled off the pace inside, came out some leaving the backstretch and on the second turn, continued three deep into the stretch and lacked a rally. SEEKING THE SOUL chased inside, was bumped and in a bit tight along the rail into the first turn, saved ground chasing the pace, cut the corner into the stretch, altered path around the pulling up rival nearing midstretch, went around a foe in midstretch and could not offer the necessary response inside late. CODE OF HONOR chased three deep then outside a rival, split horses on the second turn, came three wide into the stretch and did not rally. YOSHIDA (JPN) between horses early, settled off the inside chasing the pace, continued outside on the second turn and four wide into the stretch but was not a threat. WAR OF WILL tugged a bit between horses then angled in and set the pace inside, dueled briefly into the second turn, continued along the rail, dropped back in the stretch, was bumped lightly nearing midstretch and weakened. OWENDALE pulled between horses and was bumped when in tight into the first turn, chased between foes then a bit off the rail into and on the second turn, steadied when a bit crowded in upper stretch and also weakened. MONGOLIAN GROOM had speed three deep then stalked outside the runner-up, bid three wide into the second turn, stalked just off the inside leaving that turn, then suffered an injury to the left hind in the stretch, was pulled up and vanned off.

Owners– 1, Repole Stable and St Elias Stable; 2, Watson Karl Pegram Michael E and Weitman Paul; 3, Hronis Racing LLC; 4, Claiborne Farm and Dilschneider Adele B; 5, Fanelli John Mishref Khalid Cash is King LLC LC Racing LLC Collarmele Vitelli St; 6, Fipke Charles E; 7, Farish WS; 8, China Horse Club International Ltd WinStar FarmLLC Head of Plains Partners LLC; 9, Barber Gary; 10, Rupp Racing; 11, Mongolian Stable

Trainers– 1, Pletcher Todd A; 2, Baffert Bob; 3, Sadler John W; 4, Mott William I; 5, Joseph Saffie A Jr; 6, Stewart Dallas; 7, McGaughey III Claude R; 8, Mott William I; 9, Casse Mark; 10, Cox Brad H; 11, Ganbat Enebish

$1 Daily Double (4–10(BCJUV–BCCLASSIC)) Paid $301.00 ; Daily Double Pool $295,988 .
$2 Daily Double (9–10) Paid $25.60 ; Daily Double Pool $1,376,982 .
50 CENT Pick Three (11–9–10) Paid $94.40 ; Pick Three Pool $1,274,855 .
50 CENT Pick Four (11–11–9–10) Paid $440.80 ; Pick Four Pool $3.429.224 .
50 CENT Pick Five (4–11–11–9–10) 5 Correct Paid $1,783.30 ; Pick Five Pool $4,962,568 .
$1 Pick 6 Jackpot (1–4–11–11–9–10) 6 Correct Paid $55,668.80 ;
Pick 6 Jackpot Pool $5,211,517 Carryover Pool $436,837.
$1 Pick 6 Jackpot (1–4–11–11–9–10) Paid $162.30 .

Santa Anita Attendance: Unavailable Mutuel Pool: $.00

Figure 24.14. Chart of the Breeders' Cup Classic.

Figure 24.15. Curlin at Hill and Dale, November 2019.

did not come to the sale and is scheduled to run in the $20 million Saudi Cup in February. Mckinzie is scheduled for a four year old campaign, possibly the Pegasus and Saudi Cups. Irad Ortiz, Jr rode both Bricks and Mortar, Vino Rosso and another Breeders' Cup winner to be the top jockey of the Breeders' Cup.

Curlin, see Figure 24.15, was twice horse of the year and won the Classic in 2007. He started off decent as a stallion and then was moved to Hill and Dale where he went right to the top the world's stallions. He sired Justify as well as Vino Rosso organized by John and Tammy Gunther of Glenwood Farm in Kentucky and Vancouver (like me). Vino Rosso was a $410,000 yearling purchase. Curlin has nine Grade 1 winners with six having multiple Grade 1 wins. His foals have sold for as high as $4.1 million with eight over $1 million as yearlings.

Mitole was purchased as a two year old in Ocala in 2017 for $140,000. He was sired by Eskendereya, The second sire was Giants Causeway son of Storm Cat. The dam sire was Indian Charlie. He had 10 wins, 2 places and 2 shows in 14 starts and career earnings of $3,104,910. In 2019, the only horse to beat him was Imperial Hint in the Grade I Alfred G. Vanderbilt Handicap in track record time. Imperial Hint was not in the Breeders' Cup due to a vet scratch for a tenderness and blister. The vets were very strict in their enforcement of the regulations given all deaths at Santa Anita in 2019 prior to the Breeders Cup. See Figure 24.16 for the chart of the race and a photo of Mitole.

(a) Mitole.

RACE RESULTS

EIGHTH RACE
Santa Anita
NOVEMBER 2, 2019

6 FURLONGS. (1.06[4]) BREEDERS' CUP SPRINT Grade I. Purse $2,000,000 FOR THREE-YEAR-OLDS AND UPWARD. Northern Hemisphere Three-Year-Olds, 124 lbs.; Older, 126 lbs.; Southern Hemisphere Three-Year-Olds, 122 lbs.; Older, 126 lbs. All Fillies and Mares allowed 3 lbs. $30,000 to pre-enter, $30,000 to enter, with guaranteed $2 million purse including travel awards of which 55% to the owner of the winner, 17% to second, 9% to third, 5% to fourth, 3% to fifth, 1% to sixth, 1% to seventh, 1% to eighth; plus travel awards to starters not based in California.

Value of Race: $1,840,000 Winner $1,100,000; second $340,000; third $180,000; fourth $100,000; fifth $60,000; sixth $20,000; seventh $20,000; eighth $20,000. Mutuel Pool $3,562,252.00 Exacta Pool $2,058,167.00 Trifecta Pool $1,257,391.00 Superfecta Pool $592,054.00 Super High Five Pool $59,574.00

Last Raced	Horse	M/Eqt.	A.	Wt	PP	St	¼	½	Str	Fin	Jockey	Odds $1
24Aug19 ^{5}Sar^{1}	Mitole	L	4	126	4	1	4^{2}	$4^{2\frac{1}{2}}$	$2^{1\frac{1}{2}}$	$1^{1\frac{1}{4}}$	Santana R Jr	1.80
5Oct19 ^{9}SA^{2}	Shancelot	L b	3	124	6	5	$1^{1\frac{1}{2}}$	1^{2}	$1^{1\frac{1}{2}}$	$2^{2\frac{1}{4}}$	Ortiz J L	1.50
4Oct19 ^{8}Kee^{2}	Whitmore	L b	6	126	7	8	$7^{3\frac{1}{2}}$	5^{hd}	$4^{\frac{1}{2}}$	$3^{\frac{1}{2}}$	Prat F	19.00
4Oct19 ^{8}Kee^{1}	Engage	L	4	126	5	2	$5^{\frac{1}{2}}$	6^{hd}	5^{hd}	$4^{\frac{1}{2}}$	Velazquez J R	22.50
28Sep19 ^{4}Bel^{2}	Firenze Fire	L	4	126	3	3	$3^{\frac{1}{2}}$	$2^{\frac{1}{2}}$	$3^{1\frac{1}{2}}$	5no	Ortiz I Jr	9.90
4Oct19 ^{8}Kee^{5}	Hog Creek Hustle	L f	3	124	2	7	8	8	8	$6^{\frac{3}{4}}$	Smith M E	22.70
24Aug19 ^{9}Dmr^{1}	Catalina Cruiser	L	5	126	1	6	6^{2}	7^{5}	6^{1}	$7^{4\frac{1}{4}}$	Rosario J	4.20
8Sep19 ^{11}Hsn^{7}	Matera Sky	f	5	126	8	4	$2^{1\frac{1}{2}}$	3^{hd}	7^{2}	8	Take Y	33.00

OFF AT2:38 Start Good For All But HOG CREEK HUSTLE, WHITMORE. Won driving. Track fast.

TIME :21^{2}, :44, :56, 1:09 (:21.47, :44.04, :56.19, 1:09.00)

$2 Mutuel Prices:				
	4 – MITOLE	5.60	3.20	2.60
	6 – SHANCELOT		3.20	2.80
	7 – WHITMORE			5.00

$1 EXACTA 4–6 PAID $7.80 50 CENT TRIFECTA 4–6–7 PAID $29.55 10 CENT SUPERFECTA 4–6–7–5 PAID $40.25 50 CENT SUPER HIGH FIVE 4–6–7–5–3 PAID $473.55

B. c, (Mar), by Eskendereya – Indian Miss, by Indian Charlie. Trainer Asmussen Steven M. Bred by Edward A Cox Jr (Ky).

MITOLE broke sharp, settled off of the pace in hand, tipped out and tracked three deep, commenced his bid leaving the turn, took dead aim on the leader with three-sixteenths to run, was full bore a furlong out, reeled in SHANCELOT and drew clear. SHANCELOT sprinted clear to set a cracking pace along the inside, fought on well but was unable to resist the winner. WHITMORE came away a step slow, was unhurried into stride, responded when roused with three furlongs to run, circled five wide into the stretch and finished willingly for the show spot. ENGAGE was hustled along three deep in mid pack, came four wide, split horses and improved position. FIRENZE FIRE attended the pace along the inside, shifted out and loomed a danger entering the stretch, but wilted in the final furlong and gave way. HOG CREEK HUSTLE broke awkwardly, lagged well back, angled out entering the stretch, finished well but was left with too much to do. CATALINA CRUISER settled saving ground, moved up to make a mild bid, got through but flattened in the drive. MATERA SKY chased three wide through the turn and stopped.

Owners– 1, Heiligbrodt L William and Corinne; 2, Crawford Farms Racing; 3, LaPenta Robert V Southern Springs Stables and Head of Plains Partners LLC; 4, Woodford Racing LLC; 5, Mr Amore Stable; 6, Something Special Racing LLC; 7, Hronis Racing LLC; 8, Tsuyoshi Ono

Trainers– 1, Asmussen Steven M; 2, Navarro Jorge; 3, Moquett Ronald E; 4, Asmussen Steven M; 5, Servis Jason; 6, Foley Vickie L; 7, Sadler John W; 8, Mori Hideyuki

Scratched– Landeskog (21Sep19 ^{9}Prx^{2}), Imperial Hint (28Sep19 ^{4}Bel^{1})

$2 Daily Double (1–4) Paid $88.80 ; Daily Double Pool $363,543 .
50 CENT Pick Three (3–1–4) Paid $181.60 ; Pick Three Pool $529,332 .

(b) Chart of the Breeders' Cup Sprint.

Figure 24.16. Mitole.

RACE RESULTS

TENTH RACE
Santa Anita
NOVEMBER 2, 2019

1⅛ MILES. (1:45^4) LONGINES BREEDERS' CUP DISTAFF Grade I. Purse $2,000,000 FOR FILLIES AND MARES, THREE-YEAR-OLDS AND UPWARD. Northern Hemisphere Three-Year-Olds, 121 lbs.; Older, 124 lbs.; Southern Hemisphere Three-Year-Olds, 116 lbs.; Older, 124 lbs. $30,000 to pre-enter, $30,000 to enter, with guaranteed $2 million purse including travel awards of which 55% to the owner of the winner, 17% to second, 9% to third, 5% to fourth, 3% to fifth, 1% to sixth, 1% to seventh, 1% to eighth; plus travel awards to starters not based in California.

Value of Race: $1,840,000 Winner $1,100,000; second $340,000; third $180,000; fourth $100,000; fifth $60,000; sixth $20,000; seventh $20,000; eighth $20,000. Mutuel Pool $3,580,404.00 Exacta Pool $2,176,832.00 Trifecta Pool $1,531,835.00 Superfecta Pool $765,849.00 Super High Five Pool $71,645.00

Last Raced	Horse	M/Eqt.	A.	Wt	PP	St	¼	½	¾	Str	Fin	Jockey	Odds $1
6Oct19 ^{9}Kee^1	Blue Prize-Arg	L b	6	124	11	8	10^2	$8^{\frac12}$	5^{hd}	$2^{1\frac12}$	$1^{1\frac12}$	Bravo J	8.90
28Sep19 ^{8}Bel^1	Midnight Bisou	L	4	124	4	6	$6^{\frac12}$	$7^{\frac12}$	$8^{1\frac12}$	$3^{\frac12}$	$2^{3\frac14}$	Smith M E	1.00
21Sep19 ^{10}Prx^6	Serengeti Empress	L	3	121	9	2	1^2	1^1	$1^{1\frac12}$	1^{hd}	$3^{1\frac14}$	Prat F	10.40
29Sep19 ^{5}SA^3	Ollie's Candy	L b	4	124	2	7	4^2	$4^{1\frac12}$	2^1	4^3	$4^{1\frac14}$	Rosario J	12.40
6Oct19 ^{9}Kee^3	Dunbar Road	L	3	121	5	5	$9^{\frac12}$	10^2	$10^{\frac12}$	6^1	$5^{6\frac34}$	Ortiz J L	7.10
10Oct19 ^{6}SA^1	Mo See Cal	L	4	124	10	1	$2^{\frac12}$	$3^{\frac12}$	3^2	5^3	6^{hd}	Lopez P	52.40
28Sep19 ^{8}Bel^2	Wow Cat-Chi	L	5	124	6	10	11	11	9^{hd}	9^1	$7^{1\frac14}$	Ortiz I Jr	21.50
21Sep19 ^{10}Prx^1	Street Band	L b	3	121	3	3	$5^{\frac12}$	$5^{1\frac12}$	7^1	$7^{\frac12}$	$8^{1\frac14}$	Doyle S	10.80
29Sep19 ^{5}SA^2	Secret Spice	L	4	124	7	4	7^1	6^1	6^{hd}	$8^{\frac12}$	$9^{6\frac12}$	Velazquez J R	13.00
29Sep19 ^{5}SA^4	La Force-Ger	L	5	124	8	9	$8^{1\frac12}$	9^{hd}	11	10^5	$10^{5\frac12}$	Van Dyke D	100.00
29Sep19 ^{5}SA^1	Paradise Woods	L	5	124	1	11	3^{hd}	2^{hd}	4^2	11	11	Cedillo A	11.70

OFF AT 4:02 Start Good For All But PARADISE WOODS. Won driving. Track fast.

TIME :22^4, :46^3, 1:10^4, 1:37, 1:50^2 (:22.98, :46.68, 1:10.83, 1:37.14, 1:50.50)

$2 Mutuel Prices:

11-BLUE PRIZE-ARG	19.80	5.60	4.20
4-MIDNIGHT BISOU		2.80	2.20
9-SERENGETI EMPRESS			6.00

$1 EXACTA 11-4 PAID $21.10 50 CENT TRIFECTA 11-4-9 PAID $130.75 10 CENT SUPERFECTA 11-4-9-2 PAID $217.12 50 CENT SUPER HIGH FIVE 11-4-9-2-5 PAID $2,577.20

Ch. m, (Aug), by Pure Prize - Blues for Sale-Arg, by Not For Sale-Arg. Trainer Correas Ignacio IV. Bred by Bioart S A (Arg).

BLUE PRIZE (ARG) was unhurried into stride, settled off of the inside, ranged into striking distance on the backstretch, made a swift sweeping move five wide through the second turn, struck the front a furlong out, quickly opened clear and held safely. MIDNIGHT BISOU settled saving ground, advanced between rivals on the second turn, angled out entering the stretch, kicked on well but was unable to reach the winner. SERENGETI EMPRESS sprinted clear to set the pace, controlled the tempo into the stretch, was collared a furlong out, gave way but had enough left to preserve the show spot. OLLIE'S CANDY pulled to contention, shifted out and chased four wide, was still in with a chance entering the stretch, but weakened in the final furlong and faded. DUNBAR ROAD settled toward the inside, came under a ride on the second turn, split horses and angled out entering the stretch, churned on and improved position. MO SEE CAL broke sharp, settled off of the pace along the inside, tipped out entering the stretch, but came up empty in the drive and retreated. WOW CAT (CHI), slow into stride, was unhurried at the tail of the field, wheeled out seven wide entering the stretch and finished with a belated gain. STREET BAND was put in tight and steadied entering the first turn, settled toward the inside but failed to respond thereafter. SECRET SPICE was forced wide into the first turn, hustled along in mid pack, but faltered leaving the second turn and faded. LA FORCE (GER) failed to respond. PARADISE WOODS broke a step slow, rushed to contention between horses, was used up after six furlongs and dropped out.

Owners– 1, Merriebelle Stable LLC; 2, Bloom Racing Stable LLC Madaket Stables LLC and Allen Racing LLC; 3, Politi Joel; 4, Eggert Paul and Eggert Karen; 5, Brant Peter M; 6, Rockingham Ranch and David A Bernsen LLC; 7, Brant Peter M and Stud Vendaval Inc; 8, Francis Ray Jones Cindy Jones J Larry Medallion Racing and MyRaceHorse Stable; 9, Little Red Feather Racing and Flay Bobby; 10, Williford Roberta Williford Ward and Winner Charles N; 11, HS Stable LLC Wygod Martin J and Wygod Pam

Trainers– 1, Correas Ignacio IV; 2, Asmussen Steven M; 3, Amoss Thomas; 4, Sadler John W; 5, Brown Chad C; 6, Miller Peter; 7, Brown Chad C; 8, Jones J Larry; 9, Baltas Richard; 10, Gallagher Patrick; 11, Shirreffs John

$2 Daily Double (11-11) Paid $89.40 ; Daily Double Pool $314,522 .
50 CENT Pick Three (4-11-11) Paid $82.95 ; Pick Three Pool $630,969 .

Figure 24.17. Chart of the Breeders' Cup Longines Distaff Race.

(a) Bricksand Mortar.

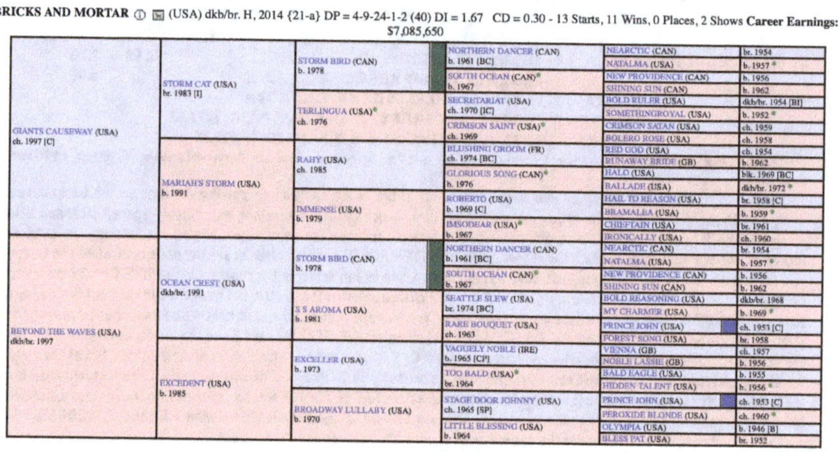

BRICKS AND MORTAR (USA) dkb/br. H, 2014 {21-a} DP = 4-9-24-1-2 (40) DI = 1.67 CD = 0.30 - 13 Starts, 11 Wins, 0 Places, 2 Shows **Career Earnings:** $7,085,650

GIANTS CAUSEWAY (USA) ch. 1997 [C]	STORM CAT (USA) br. 1983 [I]	STORM BIRD (CAN) b. 1978	NORTHERN DANCER (CAN) b. 1961 [BC]	NEARCTIC (CAN)	br. 1954
				NATALMA (USA)	b. 1957 *
			SOUTH OCEAN (CAN)* b. 1967	NEW PROVIDENCE (CAN)	b. 1956
				SHINING SUN (CAN)	b. 1962
		TERLINGUA (USA)* ch. 1976	SECRETARIAT (USA) ch. 1970 [IC]	BOLD RULER (USA)	dkb/br. 1954 [BI]
				SOMETHINGROYAL (USA)	b. 1952 *
			CRIMSON SAINT (USA)* ch. 1969	CRIMSON SATAN (USA)	ch. 1959
				BOLERO ROSE (USA)	ch. 1958
	MARIAH'S STORM (USA) b. 1991	RAHY (USA) ch. 1985	BLUSHING GROOM (FR) ch. 1974 [BC]	RED GOD (USA)	ch. 1954
				RUNAWAY BRIDE (GB)	b. 1962
			GLORIOUS SONG (CAN)* b. 1976	HALO (USA)	blk. 1969 [BC]
				BALLADE (USA)	dkb/br. 1972 *
		IMMENSE (USA) b. 1979	ROBERTO (USA) b. 1969 [C]	HAIL TO REASON (USA)	br. 1958 [C]
				BRAMALEA (USA)	b. 1959 *
			IMSODEAR (USA)* b. 1967	CHIEFTAIN (USA)	br. 1961
				IRONICALLY (USA)	ch. 1960
BEYOND THE WAVES (USA) dkb/br. 1997	OCEAN CREST (USA) dkb/br. 1991	STORM BIRD (CAN) b. 1978	NORTHERN DANCER (CAN) b. 1961 [BC]	NEARCTIC (CAN)	br. 1954
				NATALMA (USA)	b. 1957 *
			SOUTH OCEAN (CAN)* b. 1967	NEW PROVIDENCE (CAN)	b. 1956
				SHINING SUN (CAN)	b. 1962
		S S AROMA (USA) b. 1981	SEATTLE SLEW (USA) br. 1974 [BC]	BOLD REASONING (USA)	dkb/br. 1968
				MY CHARMER (USA)	b. 1969 *
			RARE BOUQUET (USA) ch. 1963	PRINCE JOHN (USA)	ch. 1953 [C]
				FOREST SONG (USA)	br. 1958
	EXCEDENT (USA) b. 1985	EXCELLER (USA) b. 1973	VAGUELY NOBLE (IRE) b. 1965 [CP]	VIENNA (GB)	ch. 1957
				NOBLE LASSIE (GB)	b. 1956
			TOO BALD (USA)* br. 1964	BALD EAGLE (USA)	b. 1955
				HIDDEN TALENT (USA)	b. 1956 *
		BROADWAY LULLABY (USA) b. 1970	STAGE DOOR JOHNNY (USA) ch. 1965 [SP]	PRINCE JOHN (USA)	ch. 1953 [C]
				PEROXIDE BLONDE (USA)	ch. 1960 *
			LITTLE BLESSING (USA) b. 1964	OLYMPIA (USA)	b. 1946 [B]
				BLESS PAT (USA)	br. 1952

(b) Bricks and Mortar Pedigree.

Figure 24.18. Bricks and Mortar.

Midnight Bisou was the favorite for the Grade I Longines Distaff. She was undefeated 7/7 in 2019 with regular rider Mike Smith. Her main competition for top honors was supposed to be Monomy Girl whose colic and muscle strain kept her out of racing in 2019. Midnight Bisou ran a good race but was defeated by the 6 year old Argentinian mare Blue Prize. At the Fastig-Tipton sale in November, Blue Prize sold for $5 million and Midnight Bisou was withdrawn to have a 2020 campaign. See Figure 24.17 for the chart of the race.

RACE RESULTS

ELEVENTH RACE
Santa Anita
NOVEMBER 2, 2019

$1\frac{1}{2}$ MILES. (Turf) (2.22^{3}) LONGINES BREEDERS' CUP TURF Grade I. Purse $4,000,000 DOWNHILL TURF FOR THREE-YEAR-OLDS AND UPWARD. Northern Hemisphere Three-Year-Olds, 122 lbs.; Older, 126 lbs.; Southern Hemisphere Three-Year-Olds, 117 lbs.; Older, 126 lbs. All Fillies and Mares allowed 3 lbs. $50,000 to pre-enter, $50,000 to enter, withguaranteed $4 million purse including travel awards of which 55% to the owner of the winner, 17% to second, 9% to third, 5% to fourth, 3% to fifth, 1% to sixth, 1% to seventh, 1% to eighth; plus travel awards to starters not based in California.

Value of Race: $3,680,000 Winner $2,200,000; second $680,000; third $360,000; fourth $200,000; fifth $120,000; sixth $40,000; seventh $40,000; eighth $40,000. Mutuel Pool $4,142,597.00 Exacta Pool $2,665,766.00 Trifecta Pool $1,987,200.00 Superfecta Pool $1,827,099.00 Super High Five Pool $99,387.00

Last Raced	Horse	M/Eqt.	A.	Wt	PP	¼	½	1	1¼	Str	Fin	Jockey	Odds $1
10Aug19 ^{11}AP^{1}	Bricks and Mortar	L	5	126	9	4^{hd}	7^{1}	$6^{1/2}$	7^{1}	5^{hd}	1^{hd}	Ortiz I Jr	1.00
28Sep19 ^{7}SA^{3}	United	L b	4	126	3	3^{1}	$3^{1/2}$	$4^{1/2}$	$3^{1/2}$	1^{hd}	$2^{1\,1/4}$	Prat F	51.60
14Sep19 ^{4}Leo^{3}	AnthonyVnDyck-Ire	L	3	122	5	6^{hd}	5^{hd}	$8^{1/2}$	6^{hd}	6^{2}	$3^{1/2}$	Moore R L	5.20
5Oct19 ^{9}Bel^{6}	Zulu Alpha	L	6	126	1	1^{2}	1^{2}	1^{2}	1^{2}	11^{hd}	$4^{1/2}$	Ortiz J L	18.90
12Oct19 ^{9}WO^{2}	Alounak-FR	L	4	126	7	$9^{1\,1/2}$	$9^{1/2}$	9^{1}	9^{hd}	4^{hd}	5^{hd}	Lecoeuvre C	50.40
19Oct19 ^{6}Leo^{1}	Mount Everest-Ire	L	3	122	4	$10^{1/2}$	10^{2}	$11^{2\,1/2}$	11^{hd}	8^{hd}	6no	Lordan W M	43.80
5Oct19 ^{9}Bel^{4}	Channel Cat	L	4	126	6	$11^{3\,1/2}$	$11^{2\,1/2}$	10^{hd}	10^{2}	$9^{1/2}$	7^{nk}	Saez L	34.30
5Oct19 ^{9}Bel^{1}	Arklow	L	5	126	11	7^{hd}	6^{hd}	5^{hd}	$5^{1/2}$	7^{1}	$8^{1\,3/4}$	Castellano J J	9.00
28Sep19 ^{7}SA^{2}	Acclimate	L b	5	126	2	1^{2}	$1^{1\,1/2}$	1^{1}	$2^{1\,1/2}$	2^{hd}	9^{nk}	Garcia M	41.30
5Oct19 ^{10}Kee^{8}	Bandua	L	4	126	8	2^{1}	$2^{1/2}$	2^{1}	1^{hd}	3^{1}	$10^{3\,3/4}$	Gaffalione T	45.60
14Sep19 ^{10}WO^{1}	Old Persian-GB	L	4	126	10	$8^{1/2}$	8^{hd}	$7^{1/2}$	$8^{1/2}$	12	11^{nk}	Buick W T	3.80
5Oct19 ^{9}Bel^{2}	Channel Maker	L b	5	126	12	5^{1}	4^{hd}	3^{hd}	4^{hd}	$10^{1/2}$	12	Velazquez J R	22.10

OFF AT 4:41 Start Good. Won driving. Course firm.

TIME $:24^{4}$, $:48^{2}$, $1:13^{1}$, $1:37^{4}$, $2:01^{1}$, $2:24^{3}$ (:24.81, :48.44, 1:13.26, 1:37.91, 2:01.35, 2:24.73)

$2 Mutuel Prices:				
	9 – BRICKS AND MORTAR	4.00	3.20	2.40
	3 – UNITED		25.60	13.00
	5 – ANTHONY VAN DYCK-IRE			4.00

$1 EXACTA 9–3 PAID $68.60 50 CENT TRIFECTA 9–3–5 PAID $219.65 10 CENT SUPERFECTA 9–3–5–1 PAID $274.62 50 CENT SUPER HIGH FIVE 9–3–5–1–7 PAID $11,562.35

Dk. b or br. h, (Mar), by Giant's Causeway – Beyond the Waves, by Ocean Crest. Trainer Brown Chad C. Bred by George Strawbridge Jr (Ky).

BRICKS AND MORTAR stalked the pace between horses, came out some in upper stretch and rallied under moderate urging to collar the runner-up nearing the wire. UNITED saved ground stalking the pace, came out leaving the final turn and three deep into the stretch, bid three wide to gain a slim advantage in midstretch, fought back inside the winner in deep stretch and continued gamely to the end. ANTHONY VAN DYCK (IRE) angled in on the hill and saved ground chasing the pace, came out into the stretch, was in a bit tight off heels in midstretch, rallied outside foes past midstretch then toward the inside late for the show. ZULU ALPHA dropped back and settled inside then off the rail on the backstretch, swung six wide into the stretch and found his best stride late. ALOUNAK (FR) chased between horses, angled to the inside into the stretch, bid along the rail past the eighth pole and was outfinished. MOUNT EVEREST (IRE) broke slowly, angled in and chased inside, came out into the stretch and finished with interest between rivals in the final furlong. CHANNEL CAT settled outside a rival then a bit off the rail, went up three deep into and on the final turn and five wide into the stretch, drifted in some and also finished with some interest between horses. ARKLOW, fractious in the gate, chased four wide to the stretch, angled in some and was outfinished between rivals in the final furlong. ACCLIMATE sped to the early lead, set the pace along the inside, fought back along the rail on the last turn and a bit off the fence in midstretch, was between horses in deep stretch and weakened late. BANDUA stalked outside a rival, bid alongside the pacesetter into and on the final turn, took a short lead then fought back between horses in midstretch and also weakened late. OLD PERSIAN (GB) pulled between horses and steadied on the hill, tugged between foes and steadied again in the stretch the first time, chased between foes then three deep on the final turn and four wide into the stretch and lacked a rally. CHANNEL MAKER tugged his way along five wide on the hill then angled in and stalked three deep to the stretch and lacked a response in the drive. Rail on hill at zero.

Owners– 1, Klaravich Stables Inc and Lawrence William H; 2, LNJ Foxwoods; 3, Magnier Mrs John Tabor Michael B and Smith Derrick; 4, Hui Michael M; 5, Darius Racing; 6, Tabor Michael B Smith Derrick Magnier Mrs John and Flaxman Holdings Ltd; 7, Calumet Farm; 8, Donegal Racing Bulger Joseph and Coneway Peter; 9, The Ellwood Johnston Trust and Timmy Time Racing; 10, Calumet Farm; 11, Godolphin LLC Lessee; 12, Barber Gary Wachtel Stable R A Hill Stable and Reeves Dean

Trainers– 1, Brown Chad C; 2, Mandella Richard; 3, O'Brien Aidan P; 4, Maker Michael J; 5, Hickst Waldemar; 6, O'Brien Aidan P; 7, Pletcher Todd A; 8, Cox Brad H; 9, D'Amato Philip; 10, Sisterson Jack; 11, Appleby Charles; 12, Mott William I

$2 Daily Double (11–9) Paid $56.20 ; Daily Double Pool $408,202 .
$1 Daily Double (2–9(JUVTURF–BCTURF)) Paid $17.70 ; Daily Double Pool $94,447 .
50 CENT Pick Three (11–11–9) Paid $61.70 ; Pick Three Pool $468,597 .

Figure 24.19. Chart of the Longine's Breeders' Cup Turf Race.

Bricks and Mortar, trained by top trainer Chad Brown, is likely to be the first turf and horse of the year champion since Kotashann in 1993. Early on in his career he had a hock injury and was out of racing for 14 months until November 2018. See Figure 24.18 for a photo and his pedigree and Figure 24.19 for the chart of the race. The great Giants Causeway was his sire, see his statute at Ashford-Coolmore America in Figure 24.20.

Figure 24.20. Statue of Giants Causeway at Ashford-Coolmore America.

Interesting and important in the pedigree of Bricks and Mortar is Storm Bird in the third generation in both the sire and dam sides of the pedigree. Bricks and Mortar is now retired to stand at Shadai Farm in Japan.

24.10. A Forecast of the Top Horses of 2019 by Gehrke (2020)

His forecast basically agrees with my assessment.

- Two-Year-Old Filly
  1st: Bast, 2nd: British Idiom, 3rd: Donna Veloce
- Two-Year-Old Male
  1st: Storm the Court, 2nd: Structor, 3rd: Eight Rings
- Three-Year-Old Male
  1st: Maximum Security, 2nd: Code of Honor, 3rd: Omaha Beach
- Three-Year-Old Filly
  1st: Covfefe, 2nd: Serengeti Empress, 3rd: Guarana
- Older Dirt Male
  1st: Mitole, 2nd: Vino Rosso, 3rd: McKinzie
- Older Dirt Female
  1st: Midnight Bisou, 2nd: Blue Prize, 3rd: Come Dancing

- Male Sprinter
  1st: Mitole, 2nd: Imperial Hint, 3rd: World of Trouble
- Female Sprinter
  1st: Covfefe, 2nd: Come Dancing, 3rd: Belvoir Bay
- Male Turf Horse
  1st: Bricks and Mortar, 2nd: Arklow, 3rd: World of Trouble
- Female Turf Horse
  1st: Sistercharlie, 2nd: Uni, 3rd: Got Stormy
- Horse of the Year
  1st: Bricks and Mortar, 2nd: Mitole, 3rd: Midnight Bisou

Acknowledgments

Thanks David McKenzie, Constantine Dzhabarov, Ted Craven, Steve Roman and John Swetye for data and helpful comments on an earlier draft of this chapter and the *Blood Horse Magazine* for useful information.

Chapter 25

The Pegasus World Cup III: Accelerate vs. City of Light

William T. Ziemba

The three year old have their triple crown: the Haskell, the Travers and the Breeders' Cup, where they compete again older horses. The older horses, 4+, have a unique series in the Pegasus (January), the Saudi Cup February, and the Dubai World Cup (March). Dubai has held their big race day for 25 years. The Saudi Cup has been run twice as of 2021 and the Pegasus five times. This chapter discusses the third Pegasus race that featured a duel between Accelerated and City of Light I also discuss the previous two Pegasus races. The Saudi Cup and the Dubai World Cup and Pegasus IV held in 2020 are discussed in Chapter 26.

Pegasus I was a unique concept: a basically self financing race similar to the brilliant John Gaines inspired Breeders' Cup which is financed by breeders giving one season regardless of its price to enable all their offspring to be in the races for a small fee if they qualify. For the Pegasus I, twelve owners put up \$1million each for a \$12 million purse to be split among the 12 runners. So the track, Gulfstream Park in this case, did not have to contribute much and gains a lot in betting revenue from the race. Arrogate won that race en route to record career earnings of \$17,482,600 after he won the Dubai World Cup as well. The idea was for most of the owners to break even or gain. There was a \$250,000 minimum pay out even for 12th finish plus there were TV and other revenues (about \$150–200,000 per horse), so the top four gained, the next four were about even and the bottom four had a partial loss. Of course, these owners also pay typical 10% each to the jockey and trainer plus other costs.

Pegasus II had a competition between Frank Stronach who runs the Pegasus at his Gulfstream Park in Florida and Sheikh Mohammed who runs the Dubai World Cup. The Dubai race was increased from $10 million to 12 million and the Pegasus II was moved to $16,300,000.

In Pegasus II, the owners had to pay $1.25 million. The winner, Gun Runner, received $7 million, en route to lifetime earnings of $15,988,600. The other payouts were $1.6 million for second, $1.3 million for third, $1 million for fourth, $850,000 for fifth and sixth to twelfth received $500,000 each. They also got some fringe benefits including publicity. See *Wilmott* July 2017 and July 2018 for writeups of Pegasus I and II, respectively.

Changes for the Pegasus III: The very high $1.25 million entry fee to run in the Pegasus made it tough to fill out the field for the Pegasus II. That and other considerations resulted in the $16+ million purse being split into a $9 million dirt race and a $7 million grass race in 2019 for Pegasus III which was run on January 26, 2019. The entry fees were still considerable but much lower. For the $7 million grass race the entry fee was $500,000 for each of the 10 runners. The payoffs were: $2,656,250 for first, $796,875 for second, $575,521 for third, $486,975 for fourth, $442,700 for fifth and $350,000 each for sixth to tenth. So the track put up about $2 million of the $7 million with the owners contributing $5 million.

For the $9 million dirt race, the owners also put up $500,000 each. With 12 runners, the owners contributed $6 million of the $9 million purse. The payoffs for the dirt race were $4 million for first, $1.25 million for second, $900,000 for third, $700,000 for fourth, $550,000 for fifth, $250,000 for sixth through ninth and $200,000 for tenth the twelfth. Of course, the owners and horses get publicity and other benefits.

Attendance and betting were down about 15% because of the heavy rain conditions. Still the track did well with much betting on the very good card of races at Gulfstream and on the simulcast sites.

Both these races are very competitive grade I races and the winners are more valuable as stallions.

The big showdown in the dirt race was between Accelerate, who had many grade I wins (5 in 2018) and City of Light, who had beaten Accelerate in a previous race and had top money jockey JJ Castellano. Both of them were runner their final race and were scheduled to begin stud duties at Lane's End where City of Light's sire, Quality Road, stands for $150,000.

City of Light was first of 105 and 104 horses in workouts on January 5, 2019 and 19, respectively. Accelerate was a 3–2 favorite and City of Light was the second choice at 1.90–1. All the other horses were 9–1 or higher.

They included Bravazo who seems to always be in the money but never wins at the top level, Audible who won the Florida Derby on this racetrack, Gunnevera who as a late charger has done well in these top races, Kukalken, a Mexican horse, who had won 14 straight races including a $300,000 race at Gulfstream, Seeking the Soul who was second to City of Light in the Breeders' Cup dirt mile, Tom's d'Etat and four other longshots. The past performances for Race 12 appear at the end of the article (Tables 25.1 and 25.2).

It was assumed to be more or less a match race between the top two horses. The handicappers mostly favored City of Light over Accelerate. Super Screener also favored Seeking the Soul (4) as his second pick. No one liked the Mexican horse.

The picks of the handicappers were:
Wizard: 3, 5, 8, 1, 4
SuperScreener: 3 and 5 are A's, 10 and 6 are B's, 9, 12, 1, 4, 8 are C's and 2, 7, 11 are X.
TimeForm: 5, 3, 6
CJ: 3
HTR: 3, 12, 5, 4, 10, 1, 6, 8, 7, 2, 11, 9
Craven-Sartin: 5, 3, 8, 10, 4, 1
PSR:

1 BRAVAZO	105
2 SOMETHING AWESOME	101
3 CITY OF LIGHT	122
4 SEEKING THE SOUL	105
5 ACCELERATE	114
6 TOM'S D'ETAT	108
7 TRUE TIMBER	122
8 GUNNEVERA	105
9 KUKULKAN (MEX)	86
10 AUDIBLE	105
11 IMPERATIVE	91
12 PATTERNRECOGNITION	126

Some of the handicappers revised their picks do to the heavy rain in the in the days leading up to the race as the track was expected to be muddy and it was.

The Wizard's analysis was:

RACE 12 **Post Time 5:36 1 1/8 Miles I Open I 3 Year Olds And Up I G1**
Pegasus World Cup Invitational S. I Purse: $9,000,000

$1 Exacta / $.50 Trifecta / $.10 Superfecta / $1 Super Hi 5 / $2 HRR (RED 3,5: 4/5. BLK 1,2,4,8,10,12: 6/5. GRN 7,9,6,11: 12/1.)

PGM #	Horse Name	M/L	Jockey	Trainer
3	**CITY OF LIGHT**	**5-2**	**CASTELLANO J**	**MCCARTHY M**

Still fairly lightly-raced, with just ten career starts, this 5-year-old horse is already a 3-time G1 winner. He's been quite versatile, winning G1 races at 7F and a mile, while also winning a G2 race in very fast time in his only prior try at today's 9-furlong distance. City of Light has also won on the lead, pressing, and stalking the pace, which gives jockey Javier Castellano some options in this field that has a lot of other early speed. City of Light's dominant win in exceptional time last out in the G1 Breeders' Cup Dirt Mile was the best race of his career, and he can repeat it today coming off a similar short layoff. He's been working brilliantly for his return, including a best-of-105 workout on January 5, and a best-of-104 drill over this track on January 19, and Hall of Famer Javier Castellano remains aboard after the brilliant Breeders' Cup win.

5	**ACCELERATE**	**9-5**	**ROSARIO J**	**SADLER J**

Won 6 of 7 races last year while earning over $5 million. Five of those six wins were in G1 company, and his only loss on the year was by a neck in the G2 Oaklawn Handicap at today's distance. This will be his last career start before going off to stud, and note that he's coming off a short layoff very similar to the one that preceded his career-best performance when winning the G1 Pacific Classic by 12-1/2 lengths last August 18. He's also proven over a wet track, while some of today's rivals are not. Regular jockey Joel Rosario ships in to retain the mount for trainer John Sadler.

8	**GUNNEVERA**	**8-1**	**ORTIZ, JR. I**	**SANO A**

Late-runner is expected to get a good pace set-up today over his favorite track. He's a G2 winner over this track while winning 4 of 9 lifetime over this surface. He also finished 3rd in last years Pegasus World Cup, and was an outstanding 2nd at 30-1 behind Accelerate when last seen in the G1 Breeders' Cup Classic three months ago. Irad Ortiz rode him for the first time that day and remains aboard, and Gunnevera appears fit and ready off a string of strong 5F and 6F stamina works since the last race.

1	**BRAVAZO**	**12-1**	**SAEZ L**	**LUKAS D**

Steadily-improving 4yo colt has hit the board in six G1 races and is also a G2 winner. He comes off his best race yet, a loss by just a neck at today's 9-furlong distance in the G1 Clark Handicap at Churchill Downs on Nov 23. In that race he rated in 5th and rallied steadily under a long drive, just getting outfinished while nearly 3 lengths clear of 3rd. Today he projects for a similar trip while saving ground from post 1 and switching to leading jockey Luis Saez, who's ridden Bravazo very well in several prior starts.

4	**SEEKING THE SOUL**	**12-1**	**VELAZQUEZ J**	**STEWART D**

Late-runner is a G1 winner at this distance and also finished a strong 2nd to City of Light in the G1 Breeders' Cup Dirt Mile on Nov 3 of last year. He ran well in the G1 Clark at this distance just 20 days later, and has gotten a deserved freshening since. Last year he finished 5th of 12 in this race, but he gets a much better post this time around.

Super Screener commented as follows:

> **#3 City of Light – TOP VALUE/PRESSER** – This horse submitted the best performance over the Breeders' Cup weekend, bar none. He cut absolutely brutal fractions and then went on to win easily while doling out strong energy, late. Can get this distance, especially since horses running on this speed-favoring track can carry their speed further. Working super, offers value and is the one to beat.

and

> **#4 Seeking the Soul – TOP LONG SHOT/CLOSER** – Was clearly 2nd best in the Breeders' Cup Dirt Mile. Came back way too soon after that peak performance, leading to a flat finish in the G1 Clark. Has been working super leading up to this. This is the best candidate of the 20-1+ long shots to make an impact on the Exotics. Will sit the perfect trip mid-pack trip and then continue to grind on.

The finish was: 3, 4, 5, 1, 10.

My bets were:
3 win, place, show: all collected
5 place, show: show collected

I lost the following bets:
3–5 exacta
3,5/3,5/6,9 trifecta
3,5/3,5/1,4,6,8,9,10,12 trifecta

But I won the trifecta 3,5/1,4,6,8,9,10,12/3,5 which paid $103.20 per $1 bet. So a $5 ticket returned $516 plus rebate which was enough to make a gain on the race.

I lost the following two superfectas:
3,5/3,5/1,2,4,6,8,9,10,12/6,8,9,10 and 3,5/3,5/8,10/8,10

Race 11 on grass was run for the first time as the most valuable turf race in the US. The past performances for Race 11 appear at the end of the article.

The picks of the handicappers were:

Wizard: 7, 2, 3, 9
SuperScreener: 2 and 7 are A's, 8 and 9 are B's, 5, 1, 3, 4 are C's, 10 and 6 are X
TimeForm: 9, 2, 7
CJ: 7 and 9
HTR: 7, 9, 2, 4, 1, 3, 5, 8 ,6, 10
Craven-Sartin: 5, 7, 9, 2, 3
PSR:

Table 25.1. Chart race 12.

GULFSTREAM PARK - January 26, 2019 - Race 12 **EQUIBASE**
STAKES Pegasus World Cup Invitational S. Grade 1 - Thoroughbred
THREE YEAR OLDS AND UPWARD. $9,000,000 Guaranteed. $4,000,000 to the winner, $1,250,000 to second, $900,000 to third, $700,000 to fourth, $550,000 to fifth, $250,000 to sixth through ninth, and $200,000 to all horses finishing 10th through 12th. Weight: Three Year Olds, 108 lbs.; Older, 124 lbs. Fillies and Mares allowed 5 lbs; Southern Hemisphere Three Year Olds allowed 3 lbs; horses running without Lasix allowed 7 lbs. Entries close at noon Tuesday, January 22. The first invitational list will be published Sunday, January 6, with a second invitational list to follow on Sunday, January 13. If necessary, an alternate list will be released Sunday, January 20. Any late invitation on entry day will be at the discretion of the racing secretary. All horses that are invited to participate in the Pegasus World Cup Invitational may be subject to out of competition testing prior to the running of the race. Trophy to the winning owner.
One And One Eighth Miles On The Dirt **Track Record:** (Arrogate - 1:46.83 - January 28, 2017)
Purse: $9,000,000 Guaranteed
Available Money: $9,000,000
Value of Race: $9,000,000 1st $4,000,000, 2nd $1,250,000, 3rd $900,000, 4th $700,000, 5th $550,000, 6th $250,000, 7th $250,000, 8th $250,000, 9th $250,000, 10th $200,000, 11th $200,000, 12th $200,000
Video Race Replay
Weather: Rainy **Track:** Sloppy (Sealed)
Off at: 5:42 **Start:** Good for all

Last Raced	Pgm	Horse Name (Jockey)	Wgt	M/E	PP	Start	1/4	1/2	3/4	Str	Fin	Odds	Comments
3Nov18 ^{5}CD^{1}	3	City of Light (Castellano, Javier)	124	L	3	2	2^{Head}	2^{1}	$1^{1\ 1/2}$	$1^{4\ 1/2}$	$1^{5\ 3/4}$	1.90	took over3-4w,rddn out
23Nov18 ^{11}CD^{3}	4	Seeking the Soul (Velazquez, John)	124	L	4	11	12	10^{Head}	10^{Head}	$3^{2\ 1/2}$	$2^{1\ 1/2}$	34.10	bump st,good finish 2p
3Nov18 ^{11}CD^{1}	5	Accelerate (Rosario, Joel)	124	L b	5	6	5^{1}	$5^{1\ 1/2}$	$2^{1/2}$	$2^{1\ 1/2}$	$3^{4\ 3/4}$	1.50*	bmp st,brief4wbid,wknd
23Nov18 ^{11}CD^{2}	1	Bravazo (Saez, Luis)	124	L	1	4	$3^{1/2}$	4^{Head}	4^{Head}	$5^{2\ 1/2}$	4^{Neck}	10.10	well placed,lacked bid
15Dec18 ^{5}GP^{2}	10	Audible (Prat, Flavien)	124	L	10	9	7^{Head}	$8^{1/2}$	9^{Head}	$4^{1/2}$	$5^{3/4}$	9.10	3-5wd turns,no menace
3Nov18 ^{11}CD^{2}	8	Gunnevera (Ortiz, Jr., Irad)	124	L bf	8	12	$11^{1\ 1/2}$	$9^{1/2}$	7^{Head}	$6^{1/2}$	$6^{12\ 1/4}$	9.50	mild advance3w,flttnd
1Dec18 ^{9}AQU^{2}	7	True Timber (Bravo, Joe)	124	L	7	3	$6^{1/2}$	7^{1}	$6^{1/2}$	8^{2}	$7^{3/4}$	73.60	5wd1st,4wd2nd,gave way
7Dec18 ^{8}GP^{9}	11	Imperative (Gaffalione, Tyler)	124	L b	11	10	$10^{1/2}$	$11^{1/2}$	$11^{2\ 1/2}$	$10^{4\ 1/2}$	$8^{1\ 1/4}$	196.00	never prominent 4wd
22Dec18 ^{9}FG^{1}	6	Tom's d'Etat (Bridgmohan, Shaun)	124	L b	6	7	$4^{1/2}$	3^{Head}	3^{1}	$9^{1\ 1/2}$	9^{1}	19.50	4wd turns, faltered 6f
16Nov18 ^{3}LRL^{2}	2	Something Awesome (Prado, Edgar)	124	L bf	2	5	8^{1}	$6^{1/2}$	5^{Head}	$7^{2\ 1/2}$	$10^{3\ 3/4}$	88.50	rail1st, finished3w 6f
8Dec18 ^{11}GP^{1}	9	Kukulkan (MEX) (Dettori, Lanfranco)	124	L	9	8	9^{Head}	12	12	11^{3}	$11^{15\ 1/4}$	26.60	4wd1st,weakened2pth
1Dec18 ^{9}AQU^{1}	12	Patternrecognition (Ortiz, Jose)	124	L	12	1	$1^{1/2}$	1^{Head}	8^{1}	12	12	20.20	hustle,chkd giving way

Fractional Times: 23.23 46.84 1:10.80 1:34.95 **Final Time:** 1:47.71
Split Times: (23:61) (23:96) (24:15) (12:76)
Run-Up: 70 feet

Winner: City of Light, Bay Horse, by Quality Road out of Paris Notion, by Dehere. Foaled May 07, 2014 in Kentucky.
QUALITY ROAD Winner's sire standing at Lane's End
Breeder: Ann Marie Farm.
Winning Owner: Warren, Jr., Mr. and Mrs. William K.

Total WPS Pool: $3,594,544

Pgm	Horse	Win	Place	Show
3	City of Light	5.80	4.20	3.00
4	Seeking the Soul		19.20	8.20
5	Accelerate			2.80

Wager Type	Winning Numbers	Payoff	Pool	Carryover
$1.00 Exacta	3-4	41.10	2,081,010	
$0.50 Trifecta	3-4-5	52.60	1,698,036	
$0.10 Superfecta	3-4-5-1	67.85	1,008,672	
$1.00 Daily Double	7-3	9.30	816,860	
$0.50 Pick 3	1/4/11/13-7-3 (3 correct)	19.80	478,148	
$0.50 Pick 4	6-1/4/11/13-7-3 (4 correct)	83.20	1,669,434	
$2.00 Roulette	RED	2.80	1,538	
$0.50 Pick 5	7-6-1/4/11/13-7-3 (5 correct)	512.65	1,145,342	
$0.50 Pick 5	7-6-1/4/11/13-7-3 (4 correct)	9.15	0	
$0.20 Pick 6 Jackpot	2-7-6-1/4/11/13-7-3 (6 correct)	1,499.58	660,702	764,723
$1.00 Super High Five	3-4-5-1-10	3,218.30	133,468	

1	MAGIC WAND (IRE)	86
2	YOSHIDA (JPN)	99
3	CHANNEL MAKER	85
4	AEROLITHE (JPN)	0
5	NEXT SHARES	99
6	FAHAN MURA	98
7	BRICKS AND MORTAR	104
8	DELTA PRINCE	96
9	CATAPULT	108
10	DUBBY DUBBIE	87

The Wizard's analysis was:

 # 7 BRICKS AND MORTAR (Race 11)
Returned from a 14-month layoff on Dec 22 for Chad Brown with an impressive win in very fast time, earning a career-best figure in the process. He had won his first four career starts, including a G2 race, and also ran extremely well in defeat in two G3 races prior to the long absence. In fact, his narrow defeat behind Yoshida in his last start prior to the layoff was against an extremely strong field that produced 6 next-out winners. Now that Bricks and Mortar has had his 'prep' race, a forward move is expected for Brown, who has won at a 31% rate second start off layoffs of 6 months or more in 2018-19. Bricks and Mortar shows three more excellent turf works since the return race, including a best-of-14 5F stamina drill on the lawn on January 19, and his versatile running style will allow hot jockey Irad Ortiz to stalk the pace or rally from farther back. Lightly-raced 5-year-old horse still has upside potential and could be among the best turf horses in the country this year.

RACE 11 **Post Time 4:51 1 3/16 Miles I Open I 4 Year Olds And Up I G1 Pegasus World Cup Turf Invitational S. I Purse: $7,000,000**

$1 Daily Double / $1 Exacta / $.50 Trifecta / $.10 Superfecta / $1 Super Hi 5 $2 HRR (RED 2,7: 4/5. BLK 1,9,4,8,5: 1/1. GRN 6,10,3: 10/1.)

PGM #	Horse Name	M/L	Jockey	Trainer
7	BRICKS AND MORTAR (Best Bet)	5-1	ORTIZ, JR. I	BROWN C

Gaze into the "Wizard's Crystal Ball" (BEST BET) at the top of the sheet

2	YOSHIDA (JPN)	5-2	ORTIZ J	MOTT W

It's very rare that we see a Grade 1 winner on both turf and dirt, but this 5-year-old horse has accomplished that feat for Hall of Fame trainer Bill Mott. He won the G1 Turf Classic last May 5 over yielding turf, and he may get a lot of 'give' in the ground today. He was also a G1 winner of the Woodward over 13 rivals on Sept 1 of last year. His only start since was a strong rally from too far back in the G1 Breeders' Cup Class on Nov 3 when beaten less than 2 lengths. Mott clearly could have chosen today's Pegasus World Cup Dirt race as well for Yoshida, but feels his runner has a better shot to win top honors in this one. Jose Ortiz, the champion jockey of 2017 in the U.S., elects to stay here over stablemate Channel Maker.

3	CHANNEL MAKER	12-1	CASTELLANO J	MOTT W

Bill Mott's other entrant got really good last summer, winning the G2 Bowling Green, the G1 Turf Classic, and finished a strong 2nd in the G1 Sword Dancer. Those last two were at today's 1-1/2 mile distance, and his two wins were both over 'soft' turf. That's

Page 8 of 10

significant, because there could be a lot of give in the ground today. Mott has freshened Channel Maker for 3 months after the bad fade in the Breeders' Cup and although Jose Ortiz elects to stick with Yoshida, Mott gets Hall of Famer Castellano to ride.

9	CATAPULT	7-2	ROSARIO J	SADLER J

Stalker/closer has hit the exacta in all four starts since the beginning of 2018, including two G2 wins and a game and close 2nd most recently in the G1 Breeders' Cup Mile. He loved the non-firm footing that day, and could get similar footing today. Although he's never raced this far, he did win the G2 Eddie Read at a distance that was just slightly shorter, and he's proven to fire fresh off of similar layoffs.

Super Screener commented as follows:

Chad Brown-trained **#7 Bricks and Mortar** could be undefeated had it not been for troubled trips in those G3 races last year. Injuries forced him to the sidelines for over a year. Connections wanted to run in the BC Turf but couldn't get him ready in time. Come back race was the perfect prep and can move forward off that... added ground is not a concern despite this one erroneously being labeled a "miler".

Table 25.2. Chart race 11.

GULFSTREAM PARK - January 26, 2019 - Race 11 **EQUIBASE**
STAKES Pegasus World Cup Turf Invitational S. Grade 1 - Thoroughbred
THREE YEAR OLDS AND UPWARD. $7,000,000 Estimated. $2,656,250 to the winner, $796,875 to second, $575,521 to third, $486,975 to fourth, $442,708 to fifth, and $350,000 to all horses finishing sixth through 10th. Weight: Three Year Olds, 108 lbs.; Older, 124 lbs. Fillies and Mares allowed 5 lbs; Southern Hemisphere Three Year Olds allowed 3 lbs; horses running without Lasix allowed 7 lbs. Entries close at noon Tuesday, January 22. The first invitational list will be published Sunday, January 6, with a second invitational list to follow on Sunday, January 13. If necessary, an alternate list will be released Sunday, January 20. Any late invitation on entry day will be at the discretion of the racing secretary. All horses that are invited to participate in the Pegasus World Cup Turf Invitational may be subject to out of competition testing prior to the running of the race. Trophy to the winning owner. (If deemed inadvisable to run this race over the turf course, it will be run on the main track at One Mile and Three Sixteenths) (Rail at 96 feet).
One And Three Sixteenth Miles On The Turf **Track Record:** (Suffused (GB) - 1:51.40 - March 4, 2017)
Purse: $7,000,000 Added
Available Money: $6,708,329
Value of Race: $6,708,329 1st $2,656,250, 2nd $796,875, 3rd $575,521, 4th $486,975, 5th $442,708, 6th $350,000, 7th $350,000, 8th $350,000, 9th $350,000, 10th $350,000 Video Race Replay
Weather: Rainy **Track:** Yielding
Off at: 4:57 **Start:** Good for all

Last Raced	Pgm	Horse Name (Jockey)	Wgt	M/E	PP	Start	1/4	1/2	3/4	Str	Fin	Odds	Comments
22Dec18 ^{9}GP^{1}	7	Bricks and Mortar (Ortiz, Jr., Irad)	124	L	7	6	$5^{1\ 1/2}$	$6^{1/2}$	$8^{1/2}$	$2^{1/2}$	$1^{2\ 1/2}$	2.80	rate,ask 3-4wd,sharp
3Nov18 ^{6}CD^{4}	1	Magic Wand (IRE) (Lordan, Wayne)	112	- -	1	1	$4^{1/2}$	5^{1}	5^{Head}	$4^{1\ 1/2}$	2^{Neck}	9.40	move 2w1/4p,kept on
2Nov18 ^{7}AQU^{3}	8	Delta Prince (Dettori, Lanfranco)	124	L	8	8	9^{1}	$7^{1/2}$	6^{1}	1^{1}	$3^{1\ 3/4}$	9.30	prompt 3/8p,vied uppr
3Nov18 ^{8}CD^{2}	9	Catapult (Rosario, Joel)	124	L	9	9	7^{1}	3^{Head}	1^{1}	$3^{1/2}$	4^{2}	6.70	tug to lead,duel uppr
3Nov18 ^{10}CD^{11}	3	Channel Maker (Castellano, Javier)	117	b	3	3	$8^{1\ 1/2}$	9^{Head}	$9^{1\ 1/2}$	5^{1}	5^{Head}	7.50	check late 1st,4-5wd
3Nov18 ^{11}CD^{4}	2	Yoshida (JPN) (Ortiz, Jose)	124	L	2	10	10	10	10	$6^{1/2}$	$6^{5\ 1/4}$	2.00*	off pace,5-6w,no thret
5Jan19 ^{7}SA^{1}	5	Next Shares (Gaffalione, Tyler)	124	L b	5	4	$6^{1/2}$	8^{1}	$7^{1/2}$	7^{1}	7^{Nose}	17.30	steadied 1st,3wd str
23Nov18 ^{7}CD^{1}	10	Dubby Dubbie (Panici, Luca)	124	L b	10	7	$3^{1/2}$	4^{1}	$3^{1/2}$	8^{8}	8^{10}	119.00	3wd in pursuit tn,fade
18Nov18 KYO^{12}	4	Aerolithe (JPN) (Geroux, Florent)	112	- -	4	2	$2^{1\ 1/2}$	$2^{1/2}$	4^{1}	10	$9^{11\ 1/2}$	9.00	stlkd,ask 2w3/8,wknd
29Dec18 ^{4}SA^{1}	6	Fahan Mura (Maldonado, Edwin)	119	L b	6	5	1^{1}	1^{1}	$2^{1/2}$	9^{Head}	10	42.70	forwardly,retreated tn

Fractional Times: 22.94 47.93 1:11.60 1:36.64 **Final Time:** 1:54.59
Split Times: (24:99) (23:67) (25:04) (17:95)
Run-Up: 19 feet **Temporary Rail:** 96 feet

Winner: Bricks and Mortar, Dark Bay or Brown Horse, by Giant's Causeway out of Beyond the Waves, by Ocean Crest. Foaled Mar 02, 2014 in Kentucky.
Breeder: George Strawbridge Jr..
Winning Owner: Klaravich Stables, Inc. and Lawrence, William H.

Total WPS Pool: $1,826,990

Pgm	Horse	Win	Place	Show
7	Bricks and Mortar	7.60	4.20	3.20
1	Magic Wand (IRE)		9.00	6.40
8	Delta Prince			6.60

Wager Type	Winning Numbers	Payoff	Pool
$1.00 Exacta	7-1	30.20	1,104,370
$0.50 Trifecta	7-1-8	101.00	706,986
$0.10 Superfecta	7-1-8-9	119.84	383,888
$1.00 Daily Double	4-7	11.60	185,286
$0.50 Pick 3	6-1/4/11/13-7 (3 correct)	28.40	122,402
$2.00 Roulette	RED	3.00	1,660
$1.00 Super High Five	7-1-8-9-3	4,525.20	22,078

The finish was: 7, 1, 8, 9, 3. The favorite, Yoshida, was never in the race and finished sixth. This was a tougher race to make a gain betting. Bets to win, place, and show on 7 did collect but the focus on Yoshida caused these bets to lose:

2, 7, 8 exacta box; 2, 7, 8, 9 tri box; 2,5,7,9/2,5,7,9/2,5,7,9/2,5,7,9 exacta, trifecta and superfecta; so did win, place and show on Yoshida (2) and win, place and show on Next Shares (5). Fortunately the gain in Race 12 and the rebate were enough to make a small gain on these two races.

Past Performances for Race 12 on Dirt:

12 GULFSTREAM PARK - SATURDAY, JANUARY 26, 2019 — **PURSE $9,000,000**

• Stakes
POST • 1⅛ Miles - Dirt - Ages 3↑
5:36P • CR: 122 (Par of 1:48.29)

Trk Rcrd: (1:46.83) Pegasus World Cup Invitational S. - Grade 1 THREE YEAR OLDS AND UPWARD. $9,000,000 Guaranteed. $4,000,000 to the winner, $1,250,000 to second, $900,000 to third, $700,000 to fourth, $550,000 to fifth, $250,000 to sixth through ninth, and $200,000 to all horses finishing 10th through 12th. Weight: Three Year Olds, 108 lbs.; Older, 124 lbs. Fillies and Mares allowed 5 lbs; Southern Hemisphere Three Year Olds allowed 3 lbs; horses running without Lasix allowed 7 lbs. Entries close at noon Tuesday, January 22. The first invitational list will be published Sunday, January 6, with a second invitational list to follow on Sunday, January 13. If necessary, an alternate list will be released Sunday, January 20. Any late invitation on entry day will be at the discretion of the racing secretary. All horses that are invited to participate in the Pegasus World Cup Invitational may be subject to out of competition testing prior to the running of the race. Trophy to the winning owner.

$1 Exacta / $.50 Trifecta / $.10 Superfecta / $1 Super Hi 5 / $2 HRR (RED 3,5: 4/5. BLK 1,2,4,8,10,12: 6/5. GRN 7,9,6,11: 12/1.)

---

1 Bravazo L124 Dk b c 4
PP-1 Jock: Saez Luis (St 175 W 22% P 15% S 14% ITM 52% ROI +3%)
12/1 Tr: Lukas D Wayne (no starts)

Sire: Awesome Again ($75,000)
Dam: Tiz O' Gold (Cee's Tizzy)
Br: Calumet Farm (KY)(Jan)
Own: Calumet Farm

Lifetime Record	117 (2018)	16 3 4 3	$1,303,528
2019	0 0 0 0 $0	Turf:	0 0 0 0 $0
2018	11 2 3 2 $1,162,600	Mud:	2 0 1 0 $300,000
GP	0 0 0 0 $0	Dist:	4 0 2 0 $317,000

```
23Nov18 11CD ft 1 1/16 :47 1:11 1:36 1:48 3↑Stk 500K G1   117 115 6 7 5½ 4½ 2½ 2nk Rosario J   L118  2.4 -3Leofric Bravazo SeekingTheSoul   Long drv, game effort 8
   Clark H. presented by Norton Healthcare - chased pace early, bid 3wide 1/4, long drive str, game effort
3Nov18 5CD ft 1 :22 :45 1:09 1:33 3↑Stk 1000K G1   115 117 7 4 5½ 5 3 3 3½ Contreras L   L123  14.1 7CityOfLight SeekingTheSl Brvz   ▲Fanned wide,churned on 9
   Breeders' Cup Dirt Mile - hustled along, 3w, fanned 7w, churned on to earn minor award
22Sep18 11PRX ft 1 1/8 :48 1:13 1:39 1:52 3 Stk 1000K G1   108 84 9 2 4½ 3½ 7 7 Saez L   L122  4.8 -2Mckinzie Axelrod TriggerWarning   Close wide, gave way 9
   Pennsylvania Derby - urged close up outside for three quarters then gave way
25Aug18 11Sar ft 1 1/4 :47 1:12 1:36 2:01 3 Stk 1250K G1   110 102 4 5 6½ 7 3 3 Saez L   L126  10.4 -6CatholicBoy Mendelssohn Bravazo   Bulled way out 3w 3/8p 10
   Runhappy Travers S. Presented by NYRA Bets - 2-3w mid pack, tipped out 3w 3/8 bumped foes, 4w uppr, kept on
29Jul18 12Mth ft 1 1/8 :46 1:11 1:37 1:50 3 Stk 1010K G1   109 105 5 4 3 3 2 2 Saez L   L118  5.1 -4GoodMagic Bravazo LoneSailor   3w far turn, rallied 7
   betfair.com Haskell Invitational S. - tracked inside, advanced 3w turn, rallied, finished well
9Jun18 11Bel ft 1 1/2 :48 1:13 2:02 2:28 3 Stk 1500K G1   110 103 3 3 3½ 4 6 6 Saez L   L126  8.0 -4Justify Gronkowski Hofburg   Ins 1st,3w 5/16,empty 10
   Belmont S. Presented by NYRA Bets - to pocket 1st,tip to 3p 5/16,driven 6w to 3/16,no rally
19May18 13Pim sy 1 3/16 :47 1:11 1:36 1:55 3 Stk 1500K G1   108 110 8 7 3 3 5 2½ Saez L   L126  15.3 -4Justify Bravazo Tenfold   4-3wd,alter out,gamely 8
   Preakness S. - 4-3wd stalking dueling leaders,inside rival 5/16,altered out,game
5May18 12CD sy 1 1/4 :45 1:11 1:37 2:04 3 Stk 2000K G1   111 101 13 8 11 11 4 6 Contreras L   L126  66.9 14Justify GoodMagic Audible   ▲Bmp strt,4-5w,flttened 20
   Kentucky Derby presented by Woodford Reserve - bumped start, 4w, decent move passed 3/8, improved, flattened
24Mar18 11FG ft 1 1/8 :46 1:11 1:37 1:50 3 Stk 1000K G2   106 73 1 8 3 4 6 8 Stevens G L   L122  2.9 -3NobleIndy LoneSailor MyBoyJack   ▲Lug out,3-4w1st,6p2nd 10
   Twinspires.com Louisiana Derby
17Feb18 9FG ft 1 1/16 :24 :48 1:12 1:43 3 Stk 400K G2   104 106 7 1 2hd 2hd 2hd 1nk Mena M   L117  21.0 -5Bravazo SnapperSinclair NobleIndy   2-3p turns,4p 1/4,dueld 9
   Risen Star S. presented by Lamarque Ford
13Jan18 5OP ft 1 :22 :46 1:11 1:37 3 Aoc w62.5Knw1x   91 104 2 6 5 2½ 2hd 1nk Stevens G L   L118  2.6 3Bravazo Ezmosh DreamBabyDream   ▲Sqz st,4wbid3/8,duel 8
25Nov17 11CD ft 1 1/16 :23 :47 1:12 1:44 2 Stk 200K G2   96 75 10 7 9 9 10 10 Court J K   L122  30.0 0Enticed TizMischief PromisesFulfilled   Never a threat 14
   Kentucky Jockey Club S.
22Jan19 3f ft GP :37 B 3/4  •17Jan19 3f ft OP :35 B 1/22  •9Jan19 5f ft OP :59 B 1/43  •2Jan19 5f my OP 1:00 B 1/5  •24Dec18 5f ft OP 1:00 B 1/17  10Dec18 4f gd OP :48 B 8/25
•14Nov18 5f ft CD 1:01 B 1/2  •25Oct18 5f ft CD :59 B 1/20  •17Oct18 5f ft CD 1:00 B 1/38  9Oct18 4f ft CD :49 B 15/33  •2Oct18 4f ft CD :48 B 1/24  17Sep18 5f gd CD 1:00 B 2/24
```

---

2 ▲Something Awesome L124 B g 8
PP-2 Jock: Prado Edgar S (St 15 W 7% P 0% S 7% ITM 13% ROI -29%)
20/1 Tr: Corrales Jose (St 20 W 20% P 5% S 5% ITM 30% ROI +30%)

Sire: Awesome Again ($50,000)
Dam: Somethingaboutlaura (Dance Floor)
Br: Adena Springs (ON)(Apr)
Own: Stronach Stables

Lifetime Record	118 (2018)	26 9 3 6	$1,093,601
2019	0 0 0 0 $0	Turf:	1 0 0 0 $322
2018	6 3 1 1 $912,550	Mud:	5 2 1 0 $190,200
GP	2 0 0 2 $8,200	Dist:	2 2 0 0 $741,000

```
16Nov18 3Lrl gd 7f :22 :44 1:09 1:22 3↑Alw 57K   102 106 3 6 6 6 3 2 Prado E S   L122bf  *1.8 3ColonelSharp SomethingAwesm IrshCnl   ▲Bmp,ins mv,angl,useful 6
18May18 9Pim sy 1 3/16 :47 1:11 1:36 1:55 3↑Stk 300K G3   115 79 7 2 6 6 6 8 Prado E S   L124bf  *2.8 3IrishWarCry Untrapped OneLiner   ▲4wd, eased late 8
   Pimlico Special S.
21Apr18 11CT ft 1 1/8 :48 1:13 1:38 1:50 4↑Stk 1200K G2   115 118 4 5 6 5 1hd 1nk Prado E S   L120bf  9.3 2SomethingAwesome WarStory FearTheCwby   Up 3wd,determined drve 7
   Charles Town Classic S.
17Mar18 7Lrl ft 1 1/8 :48 1:12 1:37 1:50 3↑Stk 100K   113 105 1 2 2½ 1hd 1 1 Prado E S   L118bf  2.3 6SomethingAwesome Zanotti DiscreetLover   2wd bid, driving 6
   Harrison E. Johnson Memorial S.
17Feb18 9Lrl sy 7f :22 :45 1:10 1:23 4↑Stk 250K G3   109 109 6 7 7 5 4 1nk Trujillo E   L118bf  *3.1 11SomethingAwesome Fellowship ItsTheJourney   4wd turn,5wd 1/8,up 8
   General George S.
20Jan18 7Lrl ft 6f :22 :45 :56 1:08 4↑Stk 100K   108 113 4 6 5 4 4 3 Trujillo E   L118b  4.4 1AwesomeBanner ItsTheJourney SomethingAwesome   4wd 1/4, rallied 7
   Fire Plug S.
17Dec17 8Lrl ft 6f :23 :47 :58 1:10 3↑Aoc w32Knw3x   102 101 2 3 2 2 1½ 1½ Trujillo E   L122b  *0.7 0SomethingAwesome TwoCharleys HickoryHill   3-4w,bid btw,driving 5
5Nov17 7Lrl sy 6f :22 :45 :57 1:10 3↑Aoc w25Knw2x   97 103 8 3 8 5 2 1 Prado E S   L120b  4.4 8SomethingAwesome HighRoller Warleigh   4-6wd, ridden out 8
   Previously Trained by Daniel J Vella (St 187 W 11% P 14% S 20% ITM 45% ROI -43)
20Aug17 7WO ft 7f :22 :45 1:09 1:21 3↑Aoc w62.5Kc   102 96 5 6 8 6 7 7 Wilson E   L121bf  10.8 -3IkerrinRoad WheresTheWidget LeaveminMalib   ▲Brk inwd,4w,no threat 9
30Jul17 4WO fm 1 1/16 :24 :48 1:11 1:39 3↑Aoc w62.5Kc   101 85 3 1 4 5 6 6 Contreras L   L121bf  10.8 -11EminentForce Shakhimat EthicalFunds   ▲Brk inw,2-3w,no threat (105) 9
2Jul17 2WO ft 7f :23 :45 1:10 1:22 3↑Aoc w62.5Kc   100 96 8 6 4 2 2 2 Da Silva E R   L121bf  *1.4 -4FieldOfCourage SomethingAwesome Oakton   Forced pace,all out 8
10Jun17 10WO ft 1 1/16 :25 :50 1:14 1:45 3↑Aoc w62.5Kc   104 88 2 10 7 3 2 3 Da Silva E R   L121bf  7.4 0GiganticBreeze NevaehsValentine SomethingAwesome   4w,outkicked 12
•20Jan19 5f my GP 1:00 B 1/5  13Jan19 5f my GP 1:02 B 15/34  •6Jan19 8f wf GP 1:42 B 1/2  •15Dec18 9f sy Lrl 2:01 B 1/1  •8Dec18 8f ft Lrl 1:42 B 1/3  •1Dec18 7f ft Lrl 1:28 B 1/1
•24Nov18 7f ft Lrl 1:31 B 1/1  •10Nov18 8f sy Lrl 1:41 B 1/1  •3Nov18 7f my Lrl 1:27 H 1/1  •27Oct18 6f my Lrl 1:13 B 1/2  •29Sep18 6f ft Lrl 1:14 B 1/3  22Sep18 4f ft Lrl :49 B 31/77
10Nov18 1 1/16 gd 9 LRL - Trainer    4Dec16 6f ft 9 GP - Veterinarian    15Jul16 1 gd 9 WO - Main-Track-Only
```

3 City Of Light L124 B h 5
Sire: Quality Road ($25,000)
Dam: Paris Notion (Dehere)
Br: Ann Marie Farm (KY)(May)
Own: Warren, Jr., Mr. and Mrs. William K.
PP-3 Jock: Castellano Javier (St 59 W 24% P 12% S 7% ITM 42% ROI -31%)
5/2 Tr: McCarthy Michael W (St 18 W 22% P 11% S 11% ITM 44% ROI -40%)

Lifetime Record	126 (2018)	10 5 4 1	$1,662,600
2019	0 0 0 0 $0	Turf:	0 0 0 0 $0
2018	5 3 1 1 $1,412,000	Mud:	0 0 0 0 $0
GP	0 0 0 0 $0	Dist:	1 1 0 0 $450,000

KEE SEP YRLG 2015 $710,000

3Nov18 5CD ft 1 :22⁸ :45² 1:09 1:33⁸ 3↑Stk 1000K G1 115 126 1 3 11 12 13 12¾ Castellano J L126 2.6 7 CityOfLight¾SeekingTheSoul¾Bravazo Cracking pace, game 9
Breeders' Cup Dirt Mile - sent to fore, just off rail, crept clear after 1/2, widened, held
25Aug18 9Sar ft 7f :22⁵ :44⁸ 1:08⁷ 1:21⁵ 3↑Stk 600K G1 117 106 8 4 41 41 21 21½ Ortiz Jr I L124 *0.9 -6 Whitmore1½CityOfLightnkLimousineLiberal1¼ 6p trn,7p1/4,willingly 8
Forego S. - tracked outside,6path turn,ask 7p into lane,chased,good courage
26May18 5SA ft 1¼ :47⁴ 1:11⁷ 1:36⁴ 2:01⁴ 3↑Stk 500K G1 120 112 3 2 21 21 3½ 3½ Van Dyke D L121 *1.2 -2 Accelerate¼DrDorr¼CityOfLight¾ Bid,btwn 1/8,best rest 6
Gold Cup at Santa Anita S. - stalked pace, off rail, bid 2 wide 2nd turn,btwn 1/8,best rest
14Apr18 10OP ft 1⅛ :46⁸ 1:11⁵ 1:36¹ 1:48³ 4↑Stk 750K G2 117 117 11 1 43 41 1½ 1nk Van Dyke D L120 4.7 1 CityOfLightnkAccelerate10Untrapped¼ 4p,bid1/2,duel,drvg 11
Oaklawn H.
10Mar18 4SA ft 7f :22³ :44⁶ 1:08⁵ 1:21⁴ 4↑Stk 400K G1 115 116 4 3 2½ 22 2hd 1½ Van Dyke D L124 *1.0 -3 CityOfLight1½BobbyAbuDhabi1½EdwardsGoingLeft5¾ Stalked,bid,clear late 5
Triple Bend S. - stalked pace, btwn foes,2wd,bid 1/4,fanned out,led 1/16,game
26Dec17 8SA ft 7f :22⁵ :44⁸ 1:08⁹ 1:21² 3 Stk 300K G1 113 117 1 7 1hd 11 11 12 Van Dyke D L120 7.5 1 CityOfLight2EdwardsGoingLeft¾FavorableOutcome2¼ Bit off rail str,clear 9
Malibu S. - speed, dueled, inside,inched away,bit off rail lane,clear
3Nov17 3Dmr ft 7f :21⁸ :44³ 1:09⁵ 1:22⁹ 3↑Aoc w40Knw1$x 113 106 2 7 2½ 2½ 12½ 21½ Stevens G L L119 *1.2 12 Dabster1½CityOfLight½MidnightPleasure½ ▲ Bumped, clear, gave in 12
7Oct17 4SA ft 6½f :22² :44⁹ 1:09⁴ 1:16 3↑Aoc w40Knw1$x 110 111 5 1 3½ 1hd 1hd 21 Stevens G L L120 *0.7 14 Americanize1CityOfLight5SirSamson½ 3wd bid,led,outkicked 5
1Sep17 4Dmr ft 6f :21⁶ :44³ :56⁴ 1:09⁴ 3↑Msw 60K 96 115 6 5 1½ 12½ 15 17½ Stevens G L L120 5.2 4 CityOfLight7½CatsBlame½NewDancer2¾ ▲ Drifted in str,handily 10
6Jul17 5LRC ft 6f :21⁶ :44² :57¹ 1:10³ 3↑Msw 45K 96 88 7 5 5¾ 3½ 2½ 21 Stevens G L L120 *1.1 3 ThePartyFactor1CityOfLight1½BelovedHoliday1¼ 4wd into str,bid rail 8

•19Jan19 4f ft GP :47³ B 1/104 11Jan19 5f ft SA 1:00⁸ H 8/101 •5Jan19 5f ft SA 1:00 H 1/105 29Dec18 5f ft SA 1:00 H 2/86 20Dec18 4f ft SA :47⁴ H 2/38 9Dec18 4f ft SA :49⁴ H 54/92
2Dec18 4f ft SA :48⁸ H 29/82 28Oct18 4f ft CD :47⁸ B 3/113 •20Oct18 5f ft SA :59 H 1/40 14Oct18 4f ft SA :50 H 44/56 •7Oct18 5f ft SA :59 H 1/8/ 30Sep18 5f ft SA 1:00 H 4/103

4 Seeking The Soul L124 B h 6
Sire: Perfect Soul (IRE) ($7,500)
Dam: Seeking The Title (Seeking The Gold)
Br: Charles Fipke (KY)(May)
Own: Charles E. Fipke
PP-4 Jock: Velazquez John R (St 62 W 18% P 11% S 11% ITM 40% ROI -26%)
12/1 Tr: Stewart Dallas (St 25 W 20% P 16% S 8% ITM 44% ROI +66%)

Lifetime Record	122 (2018)	23 6 5 6	$1,701,042
2019	0 0 0 0 $0	Turf:	0 0 0 0 $0
2018	6 1 2 1 $1,149,880	Mud:	2 0 0 1 $10,750
GP	1 0 0 0 $850,000	Dist:	8 2 0 4 $1,289,000

23Nov18 11CD ft 1⅛ :47⁶ 1:11⁶ 1:36¹ 1:48⁸ 3↑Stk 500K G1 117 111 3 3 66 5¾ 42 33 Velazquez J R L123 *1.5 -3 LeofricnkBravazo2¾SeekingTheSoul½ Bid str, flattened out 8
Clark H. presented by Norton Healthcare - unhurried early on, 3path far turn, bid stretch, flattened out
3Nov18 5CD ft 1 :22⁶ :45² 1:09 1:33⁸ 3↑Stk 1000K G1 115 122 5 8 8¾ 4¾ 23 2¾ Hernandez B J Jr L126 10.2 7 CityOfLight2¾SeekingTheSoul2¾Brvz5 ▲ Steadied 1/4, kept on 9
Breeders' Cup Dirt Mile - settled, advanced between, in traffic, steadied 1/4, kept on well
29Sep18 8CD ft 1 :24 :47⁶ 1:11⁵ 1:35 3↑Stk 100K G3 117 108 5 1 5½ 3½ 1hd 1½ Hernandez B J Jr L121 3.6 1 SeekingTheSoul½NiceNotNicenkGiantExpectationshd 4path turn, inched clr 6
Ack Ack S.
1Sep18 11Sar ft 1⅛ :47⁷ 1:11⁶ 1:36⁶ 1:48⁹ 3↑Stk 750K G1 115 99 10 11 43 31 125 1312 Castellano J L122 4.5 7 Yoshida2GunneveranoLeofric1 4p1st,2-3p2nd,6p1/4 14
Woodward S. Presented by NYRA Bets - 4p1st turn,settled between,2-3p2nd turn,6p1/4,drop in,empty
14Jul18 5Ind ft 1⅙ :23⁷ :47¹ 1:11⁴ 1:39⁸ 3↑Stk 100K 107 111 2 1 4½ 21 2hd 2hd Hernandez B J Jr L124 *0.5 0 PioneerSpirithdSeekingTheSoul4½GuestSuite2½ 3wd far,duel3/16-wire 5
Michael G. Schaefer Memorial S.
27Jan18 12GP ft 1⅛ :46⁸ 1:10² 1:34³ 1:47⁴ 4↑Stk 16300K G1 130 107 11 7 7½ 7½ 59 514 Velazquez J R L124 41.2 1 GunRunner2½WestCoast10¾Gunnevera½ 3wd bid,flatnd out 12
Pegasus World Cup Invitational S. - 4wd 1st tn, off pace, 3wd 1/8p, flatnd out
24Nov17 11CD ft 1⅛ :47⁴ 1:11⁴ 1:36⁴ 1:48⁹ 3↑Stk 500K G1 117 117 2 5 6¾ 6¾ 2½ 1½ Velazquez J R L116 7.9 -3 SeekingTheSoul½GoodSamaritan1Hoppertunity1¼ Came out 3/16, 1/16 9
Clark H. presented by Norton Healthcare - unhurried early 5path, 3path 1/4, came out 3/16,1/16,held late
21Oct17 3Kee ft 1⅙ :23⁸ :47¹ 1:11³ 1:41⁴ 3↑Aoc w80Knw3$x 109 114 4 2 4½ 42 12½ 15 Hernandez B J Jr L121 2.1 -1 2 SeekingTheSoul5SocietyBeau1ClearTheMinehd Swamped foes, drew off 6
30Sep17 9CD ft 1⅛ :49 1:13⁵ 1:37⁸ 1:49⁴ 3↑Stk 200K G3 111 109 1 3 7¾ 6¾ 3¾ 3½ Geroux F L121 8.4 2 HonorableDuty4½MoneyFlowshdSeekingTheSoul¾ Rallied str,missed plc 7
Lukas Classic S.
23Aug17 2Sar ft 1⅛ :47¹ 1:11⁴ 1:37 1:40⁹ 3↑Aoc w80Knw3$x 105 93 2 4 42 4½ 32 36 Rosario J L122 3.7 -8 DestinnoDonegaMoor5SeekingTheSoul8 3w upper, weakened 5
23Jul17 5Sar ft 1⅛ :49¹ 1:13⁴ 1:38⁸ 1:51⁹ 3↑Aocw62.5Knw2$x 107 103 4 1 5½ 4½ 33 1½ Rosario J L120 9.0 10 SeekingTheSoul½Securitiz¼Thebigfundamental3¼ 5w uppr, up last jumps 8
10Jun17 13Bel ft 7f :22⁷ :45⁸ 1:10¹ 1:23³ 3↑Aocw62.5Knw2$x 115 105 7 11 11 11½ 10½ 68 3½ Geroux F L120 10.8 8 DoShare½RiverEcho1½SeekingTheSoulns 4-5w,8p1/8,late energy 11

19Jan19 5f ft FG :59³ B 2/42 •12Jan19 5f ft FG 1:00 B 1/18 5Jan19 5f ft FG :59⁸ B 2/11 •29Dec18 6f sy FG 1:11 B 1/1 22Dec18 5f ft FG 1:01 B 4/63 15Dec18 5f ft FG 1:01⁸ B 13/66
7Dec18 4f ft FG :51 B 88/11 17Nov18 4f ft CD :48³ B 11/36 26Oct18 4f gd CD :47⁶ B 3/26 19Oct18 5f ft CD 1:01 B 4/42 12Oct18 4f ft CD :51 B 41/51 •22Sep18 4f ft CD :48³ B 1/59
31Dec16 *1 ⓣ fm 6FG - Trainer 29Dec16 1⅛ ft 7FG - Re-entered

5 Accelerate L124 Ch h 6
Sire: Lookin At Lucky ($30,000)
Dam: Issues (Awesome Again)
Br: Mike Abraham (KY)(May)
Own: Hronis Racing LLC
PP-5 Jock: Rosario Joel (St 98 W 17% P 18% S 17% ITM 53% ROI -42%)
9/5 Tr: Sadler John W (St 33 W 12% P 21% S 18% ITM 52% ROI -46%)

Lifetime Record	126 (2017)	22 10 5 5	$5,792,480
2019	0 0 0 0 $0	Turf:	0 0 0 0 $0
2018	7 6 1 0 $5,005,000	Mud:	2 1 1 0 $395,000
GP	0 0 0 0 $0	Dist:	4 3 1 0 $570,000

KEE SEP YRLG 2014 $380,000

3Nov18 11CD ft 1¼ :46⁵ 1:10⁶ 1:35⁹ 2:02⁹ 3↑Stk 6000K G1 122 115 14 5 5¾ 5½ 11 11 Rosario J L126b *2.7 7 Accelerate1Gunnevera½ThunderSnowns Bold bid 4w,clear,held 14
Breeders' Cup Classic - well placed, 3-4w, ranged up after 1/2, drew even 1/4, clear
29Sep18 11SA ft 1⅛ :46² 1:10⁴ 1:36⁷ 1:50⁴ 3↑Stk 300K G1 120 115 6 6 4½ 3hd 1½ 1½ Rosario J L125b *0.3 2 Accelerate2½WestCoast½Isotherm2½ ▲ Hopped start,4wd,3wd 6
Awesome Again S. - bit fractious, hopped bit start,4wd,chased,bid 3wd,led 1/4,game
18Aug18 10Dmr ft 1¼ :46⁷ 1:11² 1:36¹ 2:01⁸ 3↑Stk 1000K G1 120 122 5 3 3½ 3hd 18 113 Rosario J L124b *0.4 2 Accelerate12½Pavel8½PrimeAttraction3¼ ▲ Bobbled start,3w,clear 7
$1 Million TVG Pacific Classic S. - bobbled start, stalked, bid 3wd,led 3/8, drew off under urging
26May18 5SA ft 1¼ :47⁴ 1:11⁷ 1:36⁴ 2:01⁴ 3↑Stk 500K G1 120 120 1 3 3½ 32 1½ 1½ Espinoza V L125b 1.9 -2 Accelerate¼DrDorr¼CityOfLight¾ ▲ 4wd into str,drift in 6
Gold Cup at Santa Anita S. - stalked inside,came out 1/4,4wd into str,led 3wd,drift in,clear
14Apr18 10OP ft 1⅛ :46⁸ 1:11⁵ 1:36¹ 1:48³ 4↑Stk 750K G2 117 116 10 7 32 2½ 2½ 2nk Espinoza V L123b *1.2 1 CityOfLightnkAccelerate10Untrapped¼ 3p,bid1/2,duel,outfnsh 11
Oaklawn H.
10Mar18 10SA wf 1¼ :48 1:12³ 1:36⁹ 2:01⁸ 4↑Stk 600K G1 118 119 6 2 21 2hd 14½ 15½ Espinoza V L123bc *2.5 11 Accelerate5½Mubtaahij7FearTheCowboy1¼ Bid,led btwn,cleared 7
Santa Anita H. Presented by San Manuel Indian Bingo and Casino - stalked pace, 2 wide, bid 2wd,led bwn 1/4,drew off lane
3Feb18 8SA ft 1⅛ :48⁹ 1:12⁸ 1:38² 1:50⁸ 4↑Stk 200K G2 117 120 3 8 5½ 4½ 1½ 1½ Espinoza V L122b 3.7 8 Accelerate½PrimeAttraction2½Mubtaahijnk ▲ Stdied 5-1/2,rail bid 9
San Pasqual S.
26Dec17 3SA ft 1⅙ :24⁷ :49² 1:12⁹ 1:43¹ 3↑Stk 300K G2 127 108 4 2 4½ 3½ 23 2¾ Castellano J L124b 8.9 1 GiantExpectations¾AcceleratenkCollected½ Btwn foes str,held 2nd 5
San Antonio S.
3Nov17 7Dmr ft 1 :22⁹ :47 1:11¹ 1:35² 3↑Stk 1000K G1 126 109 8 6 8½ 9½ 8½ 914 Espinoza V L126b 3.9 12 BattleOfMidway½SharpAzteca¾AwesomeSlew½ ▲ Bmped start, 5w, empty 10
Las Vegas Breeders' Cup Dirt Mile - bumped start, unhurried 5w, lacked a response when called upon
19Aug17 8Dmr ft 1¼ :47² 1:11¹ 1:35³ 2:00⁷ 3↑Stk 1000K G1 128 122 3 2 2½ 2½ 2½ 3½ Espinoza V L124b 3.2 -2 Collected½Arrogate3½Accelerate6½ Pressed pace,best rest 7
$1 Million TVG Pacific Classic S. - pressed pace, btwn foes, 2wd, stalked,3wd into str,best rest
22Jul17 9Dmr ft 1⅙ :23⁵ :47¹ 1:11⁴ 1:42² 3↑Stk 300K G2 122 126 1 1 1½ 11 17 18½ Espinoza V L117b 7.8 10 Accelerate8½Donworth2½CatBurglar4¼ Inside,clear,driving 5
TVG San Diego H.
24Jun17 6SA ft 1⅙ :23⁵ :46⁸ 1:10⁵ 1:41⁵ 3↑Stk 100K G3 114 103 3 5 53 5½ 4½ 316 Baze T L124 2.1 2 Collected14CatBurglar1½Acceleratenk Chased, edged foe 3rd 5
Precisionist S.

•19Jan19 5f ft SA :58³ H 1/45 •11Jan19 7f ft SA 1:27² H 1/4 •5Jan19 6f ft SA 1:13⁴ H 1/20 29Dec18 5f ft SA 1:00⁴ H 5/86 22Dec18 5f ft SA 1:01⁴ H 19/69 15Dec18 4f ft SA :48⁴ H 13/85
8Dec18 4f ft SA :49 H 24/53 •27Oct18 6f ft SA 1:12⁸ H 1/3 20Oct18 5f ft SA :59⁸ H 8/40 14Oct18 4f ft SA :47³ H 11/56 22Sep18 6f ft SA 1:14² H 5/31 15Sep18 5f ft SA 1:00² H 11/79
21Jul18 1⅙ ft 7DMR - Trainer 27May17 1½ ft 8SA - Trainer

Help | TrackMaster.com | 800-334-3800

Access STATSMASTER for GULFSTREAM PARK - SATURDAY, JANUARY 26, 2019 - Race 12 - Page 47 of 51

6 Tom's D'etat

L124 B h 6

Sire: Smart Strike ($85,000)
Dam: Julia Tuttle (Giant's Causeway)
Br: SF Bloodstock Llc (KY)(Mar)
Own: G M B Racing

PP-6 Jock: Bridgmohan Shaun (St 60 W 23% P 12% S 3% ITM 38% ROI -16%)
20/1 Tr: Stall Jr Albert M (St 20 W 20% P 10% S 5% ITM 35% ROI -52%)

Lifetime Record	117 (2017)	9 6 1 0	$278,492			
2019	0 0 0 0	$0	Turf:	1 0 0 0	$292
2018	2 2 0 0	$98,700	Mud:	2 1 0 0	$59,400
GP	0 0 0 0	$0	Dist:	2 2 0 0	$105,600

KEE SEP YRLG 2014 $330,000

22Dec18 9FG ft 1 :23 :47 1:12 1:42 3↑Stk 75K | 112 109 | 5 4 4 3hd 1½ 1¾ Bridgmohan S | L124b | *0.7 10 TomsDetat PhatMan PioneerSpirit | 4p turns,strong urging 7
Tenacious S.
4Nov18 8CD ft 1 :23 :46 1:10 1:34 3↑Aoc w100Kc | 104 112 | 1 1 2½ 1½ 1 3 1 7 Bridgmohan S | L121b | 1.0 3 TomsDetat PioneerSpirit GuestSuite | Drew off, geared down 3
27Jul17 7Sar gd 1⅛ :47 1:12 1:38 1:51 3↑Aoc w80Kc | 110 117 | 2 4 2½ 1 2 1 5½ 1 9 Rosario J | L124b | *0.9 20 TomsDetat FarFromOver Bodhisattva | 2w,bid 3w 2nd,drew off 5
10Jun17 9CD ft 1⅟₁₆ :24 :47 1:12 1:42 3↑Aoc w62.5Knw2x | 102 104 | 1 1 2 1½ 1½ 1 2 1 2 Bridgmohan S | L122b | *1.0-10 TomsDetat TaskForceGlory Archanova | 3pth 1/4,clr,held sway 9
5May17 9CD sy 1⅟₁₆ :23 :48 1:13 1:46 3↑Aoc w62.5Knw2x | 107 91 | 7 6 5 4 2 3 2 4 2 Flores D R | L123b | *2.3 17 TaskForceGlory Langdarma RiverEcho | ▲ In tight, forwardly 11
20Mar17 8FG ft 1 :23 :46 1:11 1:41 3↑Aoc w17.5Knw1x | 95 104 | 7 5 2½ 1hd 1½ 1¾ Flores D R | L119b | 1.5 -8 TomsDetat Philoctetes Handiwork | 3p turns,steady urging 7
5Aug16 6Sar ft 1⅛ :48 1:13 1:37 1:49 3↑Msw 83K | 95 101 | 1 5 1½ 1½ 1 1 1 4 Santana Jr R | L118b | 4.8 -6 TomsDetat TRCrew TaleOfMist | Inside,strong urging 9
30May16 6CD ft 1⅛ :47 1:13 1:38 2:02 3↑Msw 50K | 96 90 | 3 2 2½ 2½ 2 1½ 2 2¾ Santana Jr R | L116b | 9.3 5 HintOfRoses TomsDetat HappyMatch | ▲ Pulled,unable to match 7
6May16 5CD fm 1 :23 :48 1:13 1:37 3↑Msw 62K | 100 64 | 5 12 12 12 12 11 11 Saez L | L116b | 16.4 5 UncleGuy Commend Caribbean | ▲ Broke slow, empty (88) 12

20Jan19 4f ftFG :48 B 8/80 •12Jan19 5f ftFG 1:00 B 1/1/8 6Jan19 4f ftFG :49 B 19/11 15Dec18 4f ftFG :48 B 36/15 7Dec18 4f ftFG :50 B 75/11 29Nov18 4f ftFG :48 B 5/43
22Nov18 4f ftFG :49 B 13/40 23Oct18 5f ftCD 1:01 Bg 9/26 16Oct18 5f ftCD 1:01 B 2/50 5Oct18 5f ftCD 1:00 B 3/27 27Sep18 4f ftCD :47 B 2/68 17Sep18 4f gd CD :51 B 31/32

2Jul16 1½ fm 5 CD - Trainer

7 True Timber

L124 B h 5

Sire: Mineshaft ($30,000)
Dam: Queen's Wood (Tiznow)
Br: Mr. & Mrs. Marc C. Ferrell (KY)(Feb)
Own: Calumet Farm

PP-7 Jock: Bravo Joe (St 29 W 14% P 28% S 7% ITM 48% ROI -17%)
30/1 Tr: McLaughlin Kiaran P (St 23 W 17% P 13% S 30% ITM 61% ROI -23%)

Lifetime Record	113 (2018)	17 4 4 4	$550,550			
2019	0 0 0 0	$0	Turf:	0 0 0 0	$0
2018	7 3 2 2	$347,350	Mud:	3 1 0 2	$65,200
GP	0 0 0 0	$0	Dist:	2 0 0 0	$54,000

KEE NOV BRDG 14 $170,000

1Dec18 9Aqu ft 1 :22 :45 1:09 1:35 3↑Stk 750K G1 | 111 113 | 6 2 4 4½ 2½ 2½ Bravo J | L116 | 31.5-13 Patternrecognition TrueTimber SunnyRidge | 6w upper, mild kick 8
Cigar Mile H. Presented by NYRA Bets - 6w early, to 4p 1/2p, coaxed 3/8, 6w upper, mild kick
2Nov18 7Aqu ft 7f :22 :44 1:10 1:23 3↑Stk 200K G3 | 116 96 | 2 4 5 6 5 5¾ 2¾ Bravo J | L117 | 4.8 3 NoDozing TrueTimber DeltaPrince | Ins,ask3/8,4w into upr 6
Bold Ruler H.
16Sep18 8Bel ft 6f :22 :45 :56 1:08 3↑Aoc w80Kc | 105 110 | 5 1 2 1 2½ 2 1 1nk Bravo J | L123 | 2.3-11 TrueTimber EightTown CelticChaos | 4-3w pursuit, just up 5
10Jun18 5Bel ft 7f :22 :45 1:09 1:21 3↑Aocw62.5Knw2$x | 108 111 | 5 5 2½ 2½ 2hd 1½ Saez L | L122 | 7.6 3 TrueTimber Patternrecognitin PtsPlyCll | ▲ Stumbled st, game 6
5May18 9Bel ft 6f :23 :45 :57 1:09 3↑Aocw62.5Knw2$x | 107 105 | 1 5 3 2½ 3½ 3 3½ 3 4½ Prado E S | L122 | 12.2 9 WonderfulLight PhiBetaExpress TrueTimber | Rail trip,secured show 7
16Mar18 4Aqu ft 6f :23 :48 1:00 1:12 4↑Aocw62.5Knw2$x | 106 97 | 2 2 3 1½ 3 2 3 3 3 5½ Carmouche K | L120 | 2.2 23 KingKranz VeryVeryStella TrueTimber | 3w uppr, wknd late 5
11Feb18 4Aqu sy 6f :22 :46 :58 1:11 4↑Alw 67Knw1$x | 98 102 | 3 4 2½ 3½ 2hd 1 2½ Carmouche K | L121 | 2.8 3 TrueTimber GorgeousCharli PopTheHood | Fog,3w vs duo to 1/8pl 5
25Nov17 9Aqu ft 1⅛ :48 1:13 1:39 1:52 3 Stk 200K G3 | 105 68 | 3 2 2 2½ 2 4 3 8 6 26 Saez L | L116 | 6.0 5 ControlGroup SeniorInvestment BonusPoints | Tracked 3-2w, faltered 6
Discovery S.
13Oct17 3Bel ft 7f :23 :46 1:10 1:22 3↑Alw 77Knw1$x | 100 100 | 4 1 1½ 1½ 2 1½ 2 3 Saez L | L118 | 3.6-15 LastingLegacy TrueTimber BuildToSuit | Coaxed st, ran on 5
8Jul17 6Bel ft 1 :23 :47 1:11 1:35 3 Stk 400K G3 | 103 92 | 4 1 2½ 5 3 5 6½ 5 11 Castellano J | L115 | 20.5 -7 PracticalJoke TaleOfSilence BattalionRunner | 3w betw foes, tired 5
Dwyer S.
20May17 11Pim gd 1⅟₁₆ :23 :48 1:13 1:44 3 Stk 100K | 102 85 | 7 1 1½ 1hd 3½ 3 2½ Rosario J | L116 | 8.9 2 NoMoDough TimeToTravel TrueTimber | Towards ins,duel,game 9
LARC Sir Barton S.
8Apr17 10Aqu ft 1⅛ :47 1:11 1:37 1:50 3 Stk 750K G2 | 104 90 | 5 2 3 2 3 1½ 4 6 4 11 Lopez P | L123 | 21.0 -2 IrishWarCry BattalionRunner CloudComputing | Prompt 2p,to rail 1/2 8
Wood Memorial S. presented by NYRA Bets

18Jan19 4f ftPMM :52 B 36/38 •11Jan19 6f ft Bel 1:14 B 1/1 4Jan19 5f ft Bel 1:00 B 2/4 24Dec18 4f ft Bel :50 B 51/11 19Nov18 4f ft Bel :49 B 14/63 12Nov18 4f ft Bel :50 B 44/60
21Oct18 4f ft Bel :48 B 2/55 14Oct18 5f ft Bel 1:01 B 20/42 5Oct18 4f ft Bel :51 B 20/22 8Sep18 4f ft Bel :49 B 20/79 1Sep18 4f ft Bel :48 B 14/82 25Aug18 4f ft Bel :50 B 44/80

8 ▲Gunnevera

L124 Ch h 5

Sire: Dialed In ($7,500)
Dam: Unbridled Rage (Unbridled)
Br: Brandywine Farm & Stephen Upchurch (KY)
Own: Margoth

PP-8 Jock: Ortiz Jr Irad (St 137 W 20% P 18% S 16% ITM 54% ROI -10%)
8/1 Tr: Sano Antonio (St 62 W 11% P 11% S 3% ITM 26% ROI -11%)

Lifetime Record	121 (2017)	19 6 5 2	$4,111,800			
2019	0 0 0 0	$0	Turf:	0 0 0 0	$0
2018	5 1 2 1	$2,484,600	Mud:	2 0 1 0	$8,400
GP	9 4 2 2	$1,821,800	Dist:	3 0 1 2	$1,535,000

KEE SEP YRLG 2015 $16,000

3Nov18 11CD ft 1¼ :46 1:10 1:35 2:02 3↑Stk 6000K G1 | 122 113 | 4 11 11 11 11 9½ 5 4½ 2 1 Ortiz Jr I | L126bf | 30.8 7 Accelerate Gunnevera ThunderSnow | ▲ Roughed,split,gaining 14
Breeders' Cup Classic - bumped start, settled 3w, advanced between, split, gaining
1Sep18 11Sar ft 1⅛ :47 1:11 1:36 1:48 3↑Stk 750K G1 | 115 113 | 9 5 11 10 4½ 2 2 Zayas E J | L118bf | *3.5 7 Yoshida Gunnevera Leofric | 4-6p trns,swung 10p1/4 14
Woodward S. Presented by NYRA Bets - 5p1st turn,urged along,4-6p2nd turn,10w into lane,good energy
10Aug18 4GP ft 1⅟₁₆ :24 :48 1:11 1:42 3↑Aoc w62.5Kc | 106 115 | 1 5 5 4 2½ 1 4 1 6½ Zayas E J | L122bf | *0.1-15 Gunnevera Leitone MillionaireRunner | 3w,up1/4,clear,wrap up 5
31Mar18 MEY ft 1¼ 2:01 3↑Stk 10000K G1 | 126 117 | Timeform: 104 8 12 Rosario J | 126 | ThunderSnow WestCoast Mubtaahij | Always in rear 10
Emirates Air Dubai World Cup - MEYDAN RACECOURSE (United Arab Emirates) - Alwys in rr
Previously Trained by Antonio Sano (St 658 W 12% P 13% S 15% ITM 40% ROI -11)
27Jan18 12GP ft 1⅛ :46 1:10 1:34 1:47 4↑Stk 16300K G1 | 130 108 | 6 6 9 7½ 9 7 8 10 3 13 Saez L | L124bf | 13.7 1 GunRunner WestCoast Gunnevera | Unhurried,rail,up show 12
Pegasus World Cup Invitational S. - unhurried, rail bid, up for share
4Nov17 12Dmr ft 1¼ :46 1:10 1:35 2:01 3↑Stk 6000K G1 | 128 121 | 9 9 10 14 8 9 5 7 5 9½ Zayas E J | L122bf | 15.0 10 GunRunner Collected WestCoast | 4wd 5/16,rail lane 11
Breeders' Cup Classic - chased, 2 wide, 4 wide 2nd turn,inside into lane,no response
26Aug17 11Sar ft 1¼ :48 1:12 1:36 2:01 3 Stk 1250K G1 | 111 106 | 11 11 11 11 8 5½ 2 1 2 3½ Zayas E J | L126bf | 24.5 -3 WestCoast Gunnevera Irap | ▲ Bmpd hard brk,4-5w2nd 12
Travers S. Presented by NYRA Bets - bmp hard brk,ins-2p1st,mvd out5/8,rally4-5w2nd,6wbid1/4,no match
6Aug17 4GP ft 1⅟₁₆ :25 :51 1:14 1:44 3 Stk 100K | 98 88 | 5 5 4 2 2hd 1 3½ 1 5 Zayas E J | L122bf | *0.2 -5 Gunnevera FrontLoaded Manolete | Drw off,gear down late 5
Tangelo S.
20May17 13Pim ft 1⅟₁₆ :46 1:11 1:36 1:56 3 Stk 1500K G1 | 105 93 | 6 6 6 7½ 6 5½ 3 6 5 9½ Smith M E | L126bf | 11.2 14 CloudComputing ClassicEmpire SeniorInvestment | Urge along ins,flattnd 10
Preakness S. - urged along inside, rail advance under ride 3/16, flattened out
6May17 12CD wf 1¼ :46 1:11 1:37 2:03 3 Stk 2000K G1 | 107 88 | 10 14 15 14 14 12 10 13 7 13 Castellano J | L126bf | 10.0 13 AlwaysDreaming LookinAtLee BattleOfMidway | ▲ Jam up,brush,5w,floatd 20
Kentucky Derby Presented by Yum! Brands - jammed up,bump start,angled 7/8,5wd 3/8,brushed 5/16,floated
1Apr17 14GP ft 1⅛ :47 1:10 1:34 1:47 3 Stk 1000K G1 | 101 95 | 10 10 9 13 8 9 5 8 3 9½ Castellano J | L122bf | *1.1-13 AlwaysDreaming StateOfHonor Gunnevera | Taken back,6w,gain shw 10
Xpressbet Florida Derby - angl rail start, taken back, 6wd, gained show
4Mar17 13GP ft 1⅟₁₆ :23 :47 1:12 1:44 3 Stk 400K G2 | 105 105 | 2 6 7 9 5 4 1½ 1 5½ Castellano J | L122bf | 4.2 12 Gunnevera PracticalJoke ThreeRules | 4w move turn, driving 10
Xpressbet Fountain of Youth S.

•19Jan19 6f ft GPW 1:13 B 1/2 •12Jan19 6f ft GPW 1:15 B 1/2 •5Jan19 6f ft GPW 1:15 B 1/1 29Dec18 5f ft GPW 1:01 B 2/28 22Dec18 5f ft GPW 1:01 B 4/30 15Dec18 5f ft GPW 1:01 B 10/28
8Dec18 4f ft GPW :50 B 32/39 •26Oct18 6f ft GPW 1:15 B 1/1 •20Oct18 5f ft GPW 1:00 B 1/28 13Oct18 5f ft GPW 1:00 B 2/28 7Oct18 5f wf GPW 1:02 B 2/13 •24Aug18 6f ft GPW 1:13 B 1/1

5Jun16 5f fm 7 GP - Main-Track-Only

9 Kukulkan (MEX) L124 Dk b c 4 2nd Time Lasix
PP-9 Jock: Dettori Lanfranco (no starts)
30/1 Tr: Gutierrez Fausto (no starts)
Sire: Point Determined
Dam: The Real Mayo (Bernardini)
Br: Rancho San Jorge (MEX)(Jan)
Own: St. George Stable LLC

Lifetime Record	106 (2018)	14 14 0 0	$326,484
2019	0 0 0 0 $0	Turf:	0 0 0 0 $0
2018	8 8 0 0 $228,810	Mud:	2 2 0 0 $17,795
GP	1 1 0 0 $174,000	Dist:	4 4 0 0 $204,050

8Dec18 11GP ft 1⅛ :49 1:14⁵ 1:40⁹ 1:54⁸ 3 Stk 300K Caribbean Classic S. 102 105 3 2 5³ 1½ 17 1¹⁰ Ortiz Jr I L118 *0.3 46 Kukulkan Bukowski Kandinsky Split foes 3/8,driving 8
27Oct18 HP ft 1⅛ 1:51² 3 Stk 10K Clasico Kremlin (NL) - HIPODROMO DE LAS AMERICAS (Mexico) - 76 81 1¹¹ Rodriguez M A 117 0.1 Kukulkan Literario KiloEcoPapa 4
29Sep18 HP my 1⅛ 1:50⁸ 3 Stk 22K G1 Clasico Criadores Mexicanos (L) - HIPODROMO DE LAS AMERICAS (Mexico) - 96 106 1¹³ Ortega J 117 0.1 Kukulkan Literario KiloEcoPapa 4
7Jul18 HP ft 1⅛ 1:50 3 Stk 17K G1 Derby Mexicano (L) - HIPODROMO DE LAS AMERICAS (Mexico) - 96 100 1⁸½ Ortega J 115 0.1 Kukulkan Kimetz Kublaigo 4
9Jun18 HP ft 1⅛ 1:46² 3 Stk 16K G1 GP Nacional (L) - HIPODROMO DE LAS AMERICAS (Mexico) - 96 105 1⁶¾ Ortega J 115 0.2 Kukulkan Kublaigo Nordico 6
19May18 HP ft 1 1:40 3 Stk 15K G1 Stakes Jockey Club Mexicano (L) - HIPODROMO DE LAS AMERICAS (Mexico) - 96 95 1²¾ Ortega J 117 0.2 Kukulkan Kandinsky RichardRa 5
5May18 HP my 7½f 1:36 3 Stk 7K Clasico Nueva Hipica (NL) - HIPODROMO DE LAS AMERICAS (Mexico) - 76 79 1³¾ Ortega J 117 0.4 Kukulkan Kandinsky RichardRa 7
20Apr18 HP ft 7f 1:25² 3 Alw 3K HIPODROMO DE LAS AMERICAS (Mexico) - 76 83 1³½ Gonzalez G M 117 0.6 Kukulkan Literario RichardRa 6
25Nov17 HP ft 1⅛ 1:48⁸ 2 Stk 51K G1 Futurity Mexicano (L) - HIPODROMO DE LAS AMERICAS (Mexico) - 92 102 1⁷½ Gonzalez G M 118 0.1 Kukulkan Kandinsky KiloEcoPapa 7
4Nov17 HP ft 1 1:41⁸ 2 Stk 81K G1 Cl Roberto A Ruiz (L) - HIPODROMO DE LAS AMERICAS (Mexico) - 92 96 1⁸½ Gonzalez G M 118 0.3 Kukulkan Magno Emporio 5
7Oct17 HP ft 7f 1:28 2 Stk 9K Clasico Dominiciano (NL) - HIPODROMO DE LAS AMERICAS (Mexico) - 72 70 1²½ Gonzalez G M 118 0.5 Kukulkan KiloEcoPapa RichardRa 7
16Sep17 HP ft 6f 1:12⁶ 2 Stk 14K G2 Clasico Carlos Gomez - HIPODROMO DE LAS AMERICAS (Mexico) - 1¹½ Gonzalez G M 118 0.6 Kukulkan RichardRa Magno 8
28Nov18 4f ft GP :50 B 19/31 22Nov18 4f ft GP :48 B 2/12

10 Audible L124 B c 4
PP-10 Jock: Prat Flavien (St 88 W 27% P 18% S 14% ITM 59% ROI -13%)
10/1 Tr: Pletcher Todd A (St 75 W 20% P 20% S 15% ITM 55% ROI -34%)
Sire: Into Mischief ($20,000)
Dam: Blue Devil Bel (Gilded Time)
Br: Oak Bluff Stables, Llc (NY)(Feb)
Own: China Horse Club, Head of Plains Partners LLC

Lifetime Record	109 (2018)	8 5 1 2	$1,220,520
2019	0 0 0 0 $0	Turf:	0 0 0 0 $0
2018	5 3 1 1 $1,141,120	Mud:	2 0 1 1 $219,800
GP	3 2 1 0 $823,320	Dist:	1 1 0 0 $595,200

FTF MAR SEL 2YO TRN 2017 $500,000
15Dec18 5GP sy 1⅛ :25² :49⁸ 1:13⁵ 1:45¹ 3↑Stk 100K G3 Harlan's Holiday S. 102 106 1 6 5⁴ 5¹½ 2hd 2½ Castellano J L116 *0.1 10 SirAnthony Audible Apostle 5w upr,could not reach 6
3Nov18 2CD ft 7f :22⁸ :45⁷ 1:10 1:22⁵ 3 Stk 200K Cherokee Run S. 104 109 2 4 8³½ 7⁵½ 1¹ 1² Castellano J L122 *1.3 7 Audible HonorableTreasure PrincipeGuilherme Bold bid 5w, cleared 10
5May18 12CD sy 1¼ :45⁸ 1:11 1:37⁴ 2:04² 3 Stk 2000K G1 Kentucky Derby presented by Woodford Reserve - between early, advanced, steadied 5/16, altered in, kicked on 111 108 5 12 10⁸½ 12⁸ 3⁵½ 3²½ Castellano J L126 7.0 14 Justify GoodMagic Audible ▲ Std'd5/16,altrd in,bid 20
31Mar18 14GP ft 1⅛ :46⁴ 1:11⁷ 1:37 1:49⁵ 3 Stk 1100K G1 Xpressbet Florida Derby - two-wide first turn, four-wide run to lead, clear, drifted out 109 108 8 3 8⁸½ 5² 1² 1³ Velazquez J R L122 *1.6 1 Audible Hofburg Mississippi ▲ 4wd run1/4p,drift1/16p 9
3Feb18 12GP ft 1⅛ :23⁹ :47¹ 1:12 1:41⁹ 3 Stk 350K G2 Holy Bull S. 99 105 4 4 3² 1½ 1² 1⁵½ Castellano J L116 3.2-26 Audible FreeDropBilly TizMischief Shook free 3/16p,sharp 9
6Dec17 5Aqu ft 1 :23⁵ :46⁴ 1:11⁵ 1:36⁶ 2 Aoc w80Knw1$x 85 90 3 2 2⁴ 2² 1⁴ 1⁹¾ Castellano J L122 *0.4-18 Audible CreasBklynLaw HillsPond 3w upper, went clear 4
15Nov17 6Aqu ft 1 :23⁹ :47⁸ 1:13⁵ 1:40¹ 2 Msw 55K 88 80 3 6 6⁴½ 3² 2½ 1¹¾ Velazquez J R L120 *0.9 8 Audible HonorUp ViolentDelights 3w upper, inched clr 7
27Sep17 5Bel ft 6½f :22⁹ :46 1:11 1:17⁴ 2 Msw 62K 87 82 2 9 8¹⁸ 8²⁰ 6¹² 3⁴½ Velazquez J R L119 2.7 -5 WeShouldTalk SmokinPlatinum Audible ▲ Ins turn,angle,gd kick 9
•19Jan19 4f ft PBD :48 B 1/21 12Jan19 5f ft PBD 1:01 B 5/14 5Jan19 5f ft PBD 1:01 B 4/8 29Dec18 4f ft PBD :49 B 5/10 8Dec18 4f ft PBD :48 B 3/22 •30Nov18 5f ft PBD 1:01 B 1/10
24Nov18 4f ft PBD :49 B 10/16 26Oct18 5f ft Bel 1:01 B 10/18 •19Oct18 5f ft Bel 1:01 B 1/2 13Oct18 5f wf Bel 1:02 B 8/18 7Oct18 4f ft Bel :48 B 13/50 30Sep18 4f ft Bel :49 B 52/14

11 Imperative L124 B g 9
PP-11 Jock: Gaffalione Tyler (St 128 W 12% P 17% S 23% ITM 52% ROI -36%)
30/1 Tr: Quartarolo Anthony T (St 24 W 4% P 12% S 25% ITM 42% ROI -70%)
Sire: Bernardini ($75,000)
Dam: Call Her (Caller I. D.)
Br: Glencrest Farm Llc & Darley (KY)(May)
Own: Ron Paolucci Racing, LLC and Imaginary Stable

Lifetime Record	120 (2016)	44 6 8 4	$2,996,305
2019	0 0 0 0 $0	Turf:	8 0 3 1 $43,270
2018	6 0 0 1 $23,170	Mud:	2 1 0 0 $732,345
GP	2 1 0 0 $238,580	Dist:	14 3 4 0 $2,546,925

KEE SEP YRLG 11 $325,000
7Dec18 8GP ft 1 :23¹ :46¹ 1:10⁸ 1:36⁶ 3↑Aoc w62.5Kc 106 76 9 7 9⁶½ 8⁷½ 9¹¹ 9²⁰ Hernandez B J Jr L121b 7.3 8 BreakingLucky MrAtila EyeOfAJedi Outrun throughout 11
11Nov18 7Lrl ft 1⅛ :23⁶ :46⁷ 1:10⁸ 1:42² 3↑Aoc 50Knw3x 105 104 5 6 6¹⁸ 4¹¹ 5³½ 3¹¾ Pino M G L122b 9.3 -7 BonusPoints SaratogaJack Imperative ▲ Gamely thru traffic 7
6Oct18 10Kee gd 1 :23⁴ :47¹ 1:12² 1:37 3↑Stk 1000K G1 Shadwell Turf Mile S. - through early 118 87 3 3 6⁶½ 11⁹½ 13¹⁴ 13²⁰ Jimenez A L126 117.1 18 NextShares GreatWideOpen Qurbaan Through early (111) 13
1Sep18 11Sar ft 1⅛ :47⁷ 1:11⁶ 1:36⁶ 1:48⁹ 3↑Stk 750K G1 Woodward S. Presented by NYRA Bets - ins-2p 1st turn,settled,empty rail 2nd turn,faltered,eased,walked 115 37 2 4 7⁴½ 12⁷½ 14²² 14⁵³ Cohen D L118 70.8 7 Yoshida Gunnevera Leofric ▲ Near ins,easd,wlkd off 14
Previously Trained by Jeffrey A Radosevich (St 768 W 23% P 15% S 14% ITM 52% ROI -17)
4Aug18 7Mnr ft 1⅛ :24² :48¹ 1:11⁶ 1:42⁷ 3↑Stk 200K G3 West Virginia Governor's S. 110 99 3 3 3² 3¹ 4²½ 4⁵ Spieth S L119 8.0-21 Leofric TermOfArt Matrooh Well placed,no punch 5
Previously Trained by Robert B Hess (St 257 W 12% P 15% S 12% ITM 39% ROI -27)
30Jun18 8Mth ft 1⅛ :24⁹ :48⁸ 1:12⁵ 1:44⁵ 3↑Stk 100K G3 Philip H. Iselin S. 113 92 3 3 4²½ 4⁴ 4⁷½ 4¹⁵ Gallardo A A L116 4.0 14 HarlanPunch PageMckenney Backsidfthmn ▲ Stumbled start, bumped 4
22Apr17 11CT sy 1⅛ :47⁴ 1:12⁶ 1:39 1:53 4↑Stk 1250K G2 Charles Town Classic S. 114 108 5 7 6³ 5²½ 4²½ 1nk Castellano J L118 5.0 -1 Imperative MattKingCoal WarStory Determined,final strds 8
11Mar17 10SA ft 1¼ :47⁵ 1:11⁹ 1:36² 2:01⁶ 4↑Stk 750K G1 Santa Anita H. Presented by San Manuel Indian Bingo and Casino - stalked pace, 3 wide, 4wd backstretch, off rail 2nd turn,wkened 121 91 9 7 7²½ 7⁴½ 8¹⁴ 9²² Gallardo A A L119 9.9 -4 ShamanGhost MidnightStorm FollowMeCrev 4wd,off rail,weakened 9
28Jan17 5GP ft 1⅛ :48¹ 1:12³ 1:36¹ 1:49 4↑Stk 400K Poseidon H. 110 114 3 5 4³ 1hd 2½ 1hd Gallardo A A L118 7.2 3 Imperative Stanford Madefromlucky 4w move, long drive 9
Previously Trained by Richard Baltas (St 447 W 17% P 17% S 13% ITM 47% ROI -16)
27Nov16 8Dmr gd 1⅛ :48⁴ 1:13⁵ 1:39 1:51⁶ 3↑Stk 100K G3 Native Diver S. 124 105 4 1 3¹½ 3¹½ 5⁹ 6¹³ Desormeaux K J L121 2.1 34 MidnightStorm PointPiper HardAces Btwn,inside 1/4,wkened 7
3Nov16 6SA ft 1 :23² :46⁸ 1:11³ 1:36 3↑Stk 80K Big Bear S. 112 116 7 6 8⁵½ 7⁴½ 3²½ 1¹½ Desormeaux K J L120 *1.4 20 Imperative ConquestCobra MagicMark 4wd into lane,rallied 8
20Aug16 9Dmr ft 1¼ :47³ 1:11² 1:35⁷ 2:00¹ 3↑Stk 1000K G1 $1 Million TVG Pacific Classic S. - 3 wide 7/8, chased, btwn foes,2wd 2nd turn,3wd lane,wkened 123 93 6 6 7⁵½ 6⁵½ 7¹³ 6²³ Arroyo N Jr L124b 57.4 6 CaliforniaChrome Beholder Dortmund Chased, weakened 9
18Jan19 5f ft GP 1:01 B 3/13 •6Jan19 4f wf GP :46 B 1/84 29Dec18 4f ft GP :48 B 4/85 3Nov18 5f ft CD 1:01 B 6/24 26Oct18 5f gd CD 1:01 B 24/38 19Oct18 6f ft CD 1:16 B 2/2
27Sep18 5f ft CD 1:01 B 7/18 24Aug18 5f ft Sar 1:00 B 3/20 •18Aug18 5f ft Tdn 1:02 B 1/3 25Jul18 4f ft Tdn :51 B 16/19 •23Jun18 6f ft Kee 1:12 B 1/1 •17Jun18 6f ft SA 1:15 H 1/1
2Nov18 1⅛ ft 10 CD - Trainer 8Jan16 1 ft 3 SA - Re-entered 25Oct13 1⅛ fm 7 SA - Also-Eligible 11Oct13 1 fm 6 SA - Trainer 31Aug13 1⅛ fm 10 DMR - Also-Eligible

12 Patternrecognition L124 B h 6
PP-12 Jock: Ortiz Jose L (St 130 W 18% P 18% S 10% ITM 46% ROI -1%)
10/1 Tr: Brown Chad C (St 43 W 26% P 21% S 2% ITM 49% ROI -22%)
Sire: Adios Charlie ($3,500)
Dam: Almost A Valentine (High Cotton)
Br: Ocala Stud (FL)(Mar)
Own: Klaravich Stables, Inc. and Lawrence, William

Lifetime Record	115 (2018)	11 5 5 0	$812,325
2019	0 0 0 0 $0	Turf:	0 0 0 0 $0
2018	5 3 1 0 $668,725	Mud:	2 2 0 0 $86,600
GP	0 0 0 0 $0	Dist:	0 0 0 0 $0

OBS SPR 2YO 2015 $420,000
1Dec18 9Aqu ft 1 :22⁹ :45⁷ 1:09⁷ 1:35 3↑Stk 750K G1 Cigar Mile H. Presented by NYRA Bets - away well, in hand 3-2w, set down 3-2w uppr, dug in, held well 111 115 8 1 1¹ 1¹ 1¹½ 1½ Ortiz J L L118 5.4-13 Patternrecognition TrueTimber SunnyRidge In hand 3-2w,held well 8
22Sep18 8Bel ft 1 :23⁸ :46⁸ 1:10³ 1:34² 3↑Stk 300K G2 Kelso H. 114 109 6 1 1¹ 1¹ 1¹½ 1¹ Gaffalione T L116 5.6 -5 Patternrecognition SunnyRidge Timeline Ins trn,ask 1/4,dug in 7
11Aug18 9Sar gd 7f :22⁶ :45¹ 1:09⁶ 1:22⁷ 3↑Aocw62.5Knw2$x 109 114 1 4 1hd 1hd 1½ 1½ Saez L L122 *2.3 20 Pttrnrcgntn PhBtExprss AlwysASspct ▲ Lunged st, held gamely 7
10Jun18 5Bel ft 7f :22⁵ :45⁶ 1:09⁵ 1:21⁹ 3↑Aocw62.5Knw2$x 108 109 3 2 1½ 1½ 1hd 2¹½ Castellano J L120 *1.2 3 TrueTimber Patternrecognition PetesPlayCall Coaxed 2p, ran on 6
5May18 9Bel ft 6f :23 :45⁸ :57⁵ 1:09⁵ 3↑Aocw62.5Knw2$x 107 102 3 2 4⁴½ 4⁵ 4⁵½ 4⁵¾ Gaffalione T L120 *1.8 9 WonderfulLight PhiBetaExpress TrueTimber 3w,drive 5/16,5w upper 7
4Nov17 7Aqu ft 1 :23⁹ :46⁹ 1:11⁶ 1:36² 3↑Alw 67Knw1$x 99 97 2 1 2¹½ 1½ 1³ 1⁶½ Gaffalione T L121 *0.7-21 Patternrecognition Spieth HammerinAamer 3w upper, drew clear 6
7Oct17 2Bel ft 1⅛ :23⁵ :46 1:09⁵ 1:41¹ 3↑Alw 77Knw1$x 99 93 4 2 2¹ 2¹ 2⁴½ 2⁶½ Ortiz J L L121 *1.1-16 CopperTown Patternrecognition StarshipZeus 3w,prompted winner 5
30Aug17 8Sar ft 7f :22⁷ :45⁷ 1:09⁵ 1:22¹ 3↑Alw 85Knw1$x 109 98 2 3 3² 4²½ 3⁴½ 2⁶½ Castellano J L124 2.1 -3 MrCrow Patternrecognition Foreset 2w,3w upper,no match 6
21Jul17 4Sar ft 6f :22¹ :45⁸ :57⁷ 1:09⁹ 3↑Alw 85Knw1$x 102 111 3 7 5⁶½ 5⁴ 4⁵½ 2⁶½ Castellano J L124 *1.1 17 Takaful Patternrecognition HardScramble 4w 3/8,7w 1/8,rallied 9
8Jun17 7Bel ft 6½f :22¹ :45² 1:09⁸ 1:16² 3↑Alw 90Knw1$x 100 98 5 4 3¹½ 4² 2³½ 2³½ Ortiz J L L124 1.4 -7 CoalFront Patternrecognition DivineIntervention Chase 2p,drive by 5/16 9
5Apr17 2Aqu gd 6f :22⁵ :45⁵ :57⁷ 1:10⁴ 3↑Msw 60K 92 96 4 2 1hd 2¹ 1¹½ 1⁴½ Ortiz J L L124 *1.2 -8 Patternrecognition BlessedHalo Javelin 3w upper, edged clear 6
19Jan19 4f ft PMM :49 B 17/70 13Jan19 5f ft PMM 1:02 B 8/12 6Jan19 5f ft PMM 1:02 B 4/11 •30Dec18 5f ft PMM 1:00 B 1/18 22Dec18 4f ft PMM :48 B 12/76 25Nov18 4f my Bel :50 B 11/32
18Nov18 4f ft Bel :49 B 44/15 •11Nov18 5f ft Bel 1:00 B 1/5 •4Nov18 4f ft Bel :47 B 1/33 27Oct18 4f ft Sar :50 B 6/9 •21Oct18 4f ft Sar :47 B 1/46 15Oct18 4f ft Sar :48 B 5/42

Past Performances for Race 11 on Dirt:

11 **GULFSTREAM PARK - SATURDAY, JANUARY 26, 2019** — **PURSE $7,000,000**

• Stakes
POST • 1 3/16 Miles - Turf - Ages 4↑
4:51P • CR: 120 (Par of 1:51.94)

Trk Rcrd: (1:51.40) Pegasus World Cup Turf Invitational S. - Grade 1 (Rail at 96 feet). THREE YEAR OLDS AND UPWARD. $7,000,000 Estimated. $2,656,250 to the winner. $796,875 to second. $575,521 to third. $486,975 to fourth. $442,708 to fifth. and $350,000 to all horses finishing sixth through 10th. Weight: Three Year Olds, 108 lbs.; Older, 124 lbs. Fillies and Mares allowed 5 lbs; Southern Hemisphere Three Year Olds allowed 3 lbs; horses running without Lasix allowed 7 lbs. Entries close at noon Tuesday, January 22. The first invitational list will be published Sunday, January 6, with a second invitational list to follow on Sunday, January 13. If necessary, an alternate list will be released Sunday, January 20. Any late invitation on entry day will be at the discretion of the racing secretary. All horses that are invited to participate in the Pegasus World Cup Turf Invitational may be subject to out of competition testing prior to the running of the race. Trophy to the winning owner. (If deemed inadvisable to run this race over the turf course, it will be run on the main track at One Mile and Three Sixteenths)

$1 Daily Double / $1 Exacta / $.50 Trifecta / $.10 Superfecta / $1 Super Hi 5 $2 HRR (RED 2,7: 4/5. BLK 1,9,4,8,5: 1/1. GRN 6,10,3: 10/1.)

1 Magic Wand (IRE) 112 B f 4 — Off Lasix
PP-1 Jock: Lordan Wayne (no starts)
9/2 Tr: O'Brien Aidan P (no starts)
Sire: Galileo (IRE)
Dam: Prudenzia (IRE) (Dansili (GB))
Br: Ecurie Des Monceaux & Skymarc Farm (IRE)
Own: Tabor, Michael, Smith, Derrick, Magnier, Mrs.

Lifetime Record	126 (2018)	10 2 2 1	$657,101
2019	0 0 0 0	$0	Turf: 10 2 2 1 $657,101
2018	9 2 2 1	$657,101	Soft: 6 1 0 1 $204,419
GP	0 0 0 0	$0	Dist: 0 0 0 0 $0

ARAUG 2016 $1,562,820

3Nov18 6CD gd 1⅛ :51 1:18 1:44 2:21 3↑Stk 2000K G1 118 113 10 2 2 1 2 1 3 1½ 4 2¾ Moore R L L120 5.5 58 Sistercharlie Wildillusion ARavingBeauty — 5path 1/4, weakened (133) 14
Maker's Mark Breeders' Cup Filly and Mare Turf - tracked pace early, 5path final turn, weakened late stretch
Previously Trained by Aidan O'Brien
7Oct18 LCH fm *1½ 2:04 3↑Stk 576K G1 121 117 2 1 Moore R L 123 5.0 Wildillusion MagicWand Homerique — No gain on winner 15
P de l'Opera Longines - LONGCHAMP (France) -
16Sep18 LCH fm *1½ 2:26 3↑Stk 697K G1 121 126 2 hd Lordan W M 121 5.0 Kitesurf MagicWand Zarkamiya — Led, driven, headed 8
Qatar P Vermeille - LONGCHAMP (France) -
23Aug18 YOR gf *1½ 2:30 3↑Stk 452K G1 120 117 Timeform: 114 5¾ Moore R L 124 7.0 SeaOfClass Coronet Eziyra — Gradually weakened 8
Darley Yorkshire Oaks - YORK (England) - led: pushed along 3f out: rdn wl over 1f out: drvn and hdd ins fn
21Jul18 CUR gd 1½ 2:32 3 Stk 469K G1 113 101 Timeform: 100 5 9½ Moore R L 126 0.9 SeaOfClass ForeverTogether MaryTudor — No extra, eased 7
Darley Irish Oaks - CURRAGH (Ireland) -
21Jun18 ASC gf *1½ 2:28 3 Stk 263K G2 111 119 Timeform: 113 1 4 Moore R L 126 3.3 MagicWand Wildillusion SunMaiden — Ran on strongly, easy 10
Ribblesdale S. - ASCOT (England) - led for 3f: trckd ldr tl led again travelling strly over 2f out:
1Jun18 EPS sf *1½ 2:40 3 Stk 665K G1 117 107 Timeform: 97 4 11 Moore R L 126 4.0 ForeverTogether Wildillusion ByeByeBaby — No threat to leaders 9
Investec Oaks - EPSOM (England) - chsd ldrs: 3rd st: sn rdn and switching rt to stands' rail: strug
9May18 CHE gd *1⅝ 2:28 3 Stk 103K 96 96 Timeform: 100 1 3½ Moore R L 126 3.0 MagicWand ForeverTogether PrincessYaiza — Always in command 10
Arkle Finance Cheshire Oaks - CHESTER (England) - mde all: kicked on 2f out: abt 4 l clr 1f out: r.o wl and a in co
16Apr18 LEO hy 1¼ 2:26 3 Msw 20K 93 93 Timeform: 83 3 6½ Heffernan J A 126 3.5 Jaega Samasthiti MagicWand — Lost 2nd on line 8
Irish Stallion Farms EBF - LEOPARDSTOWN (Ireland) -
22Oct17 LEO sf 1 1:49 2 Msw 21K 89 68 Timeform: 59 7 14 Heffernan J A 126 3.3 Contingent Alghabrah ForeverTogether — Never nearer 18
ISF EBF - LEOPARDSTOWN (Ireland) -

2 ▲Yoshida (Jpn) L124 B h 5
PP-2 Jock: Ortiz Jose L (St 130 W 18% P 18% S 10% ITM 46% ROI -1%)
5/2 Tr: Mott William I (St 40 W 28% P 15% S 8% ITM 50% ROI -34%)
Sire: Heart's Cry (JPN) ($46,120)
Dam: Hilda's Passion (Canadian Frontier)
Br: Northern Farm (JPN)(Feb)
Own: China Horse Club International Ltd., WinStar

Lifetime Record	120 (2018)	12 5 3 0	$1,589,770
2019	0 0 0 0	$0	Turf: 10 4 3 0 $889,770
2018	5 2 0 0	$1,040,670	Soft: 4 2 1 0 $389,600
GP	0 0 0 0	$0	Dist: 0 0 0 0 $0

JRHA WEAN YRLG 15 $765,160

3Nov18 11CD ft 1¼ :46 1:10 1:35 2:02 3↑Stk 6000K G1 122 112 10 12 12 14 13 11 4 4 4 1½ Ortiz J L L126 14.5 7 Accelerate Gunnevera ThunderSnow — ▲ Bobbled, 6 w run, hung 14
Breeders' Cup Classic - bobbled start, unhurried 4w, advanced, swung 6w, loomed, hung
1Sep18 11Sar ft 1⅛ :47 1:11 1:36 1:48 3↑Stk 750K G1 115 116 1 7 10 5½ 9 5½ 3½ 1 2 Rosario J L122 6.2 7 Yoshida Gunnevera Leofric — Ins1st,3-5p2nd,9p1/4 14
Woodward S. Presented by NYRA Bets - ins 1st,reserved,mvd out 1/2,3-5p2nd,swung9w 1/4,rallied,going away
11Aug18 8Sar gd 1 :23 :46 1:11 1:36 3↑Stk 500K G1 118 112 6 6 4 8½ 6 2½ 5 3 5 3¾ Franco M L122 *1.8 27 VoodooSong DeltaPrince Divisidero — 3p 1st,ins-2p2nd,3p1/4 (134) 6
Fourstardave H. - broke out,3p 1st,settled outside,mvd in 5/8,ins-2p2nd,3p 1/4,evenly
Previously Trained by William Mott
19Jun18 ASC gf 1 1:38 4↑Stk 858K G1 122 120 Timeform: 119 5 1½ Ortiz J 126 11.0 AccidentalAgent LordGlitters LightningSpear — Not much room 15
Queen Anne S. - ASCOT (England) - ponied to s: hld up wl in tch in midfield: swtchd lft and effrt e
Previously Trained by William I Mott (St 657 W 13% P 14% S 13% ITM 40% ROI -30)
5May18 11CD yl 1⅛ :50 1:16 1:41 1:54 4↑Stk 500K G1 120 109 8 4 4 6 3 3½ 1½ 1¾ Ortiz J L L120 9.9 61 Yoshida BeachPatrol Synchrony — Rate,3-4w,duel,drvng (133) 9
Old Forester Turf Classic S. - rate in clear,bid 3-deep 5/16,took over 3/16,duel,driving
7Oct17 9Bel fm 1⅛ :49 1:13 1:35 1:47 3 Stk 500K G3 106 106 2 7 3 2½ 3 2½ 3 1½ 1 nk Franco M L116 4.2 0 Yoshida Luculan BricksAndMrtr — ▲ 3w 1/4, tight betw, up (125) 9
Hill Prince S.
2Sep17 9Sar fm 1⅛ 1:46 3 Stk 300K G3 110 93 2 4 5 3 5 3 3 2½ 2 nk Ortiz Jr I L121 3.1 5 VoodooSong Yoshida BricksAndMrtr — ▲ Waitd held up2nd,5w1/4 8
Saranac S.
4Aug17 9Sar fm 1⅙ :23 :48 1:11 1:39 3 Stk 200K G2 110 98 3 3 4 3½ 3 1½ 2½ 2¾ Ortiz Jr I L121 *2.2 -7 BricksAndMrtr Yshd BgHndsm — ▲ Bobbled st, battled on (119) 9
National Museum of Racing Hall of Fame S.
8Jul17 10Bel fm 1¼ :49 1:14 1:37 2:00 3 Stk 1200K G1 109 111 7 3 4 2 3 2 3 3 5 4½ Velazquez J R L122 *3.0 -2 OscarPerformance CalledToTheBar Homesman — 4w upper, wknd late (127) 11
Belmont Derby Invitational S. - bumped early, just off pace 2-3w, 4w upper, bid, weakened late
20May17 8Pim gd 1 :23 :46 1:11 1:36 3 Stk 100K 100 101 6 12 11 21 8 8 2½ 1 4 Rosario J L116 2.8 15 Yoshida ChubbyStar MoMaverick — ▲ Pnchd start,rddn out (123) 12
James W. Murphy S.
9Apr17 4Kee fm 1⅛ :47 1:13 1:37 1:49 3 Msw 70K 98 102 3 1 1 2 1 1 1 3½ 1 4 Ortiz J L L120 2.6 -15 Yoshida ImTheCaptainNow Sakonnet — Speed, widened, held (117) 11
19Nov16 4Aqu gd 1 :24 :50 1:16 1:40 2 Msw 60K 90 81 7 9 7 5 6 5½ 3 3 2¾ Ortiz J L 120 9.7 19 ColemanRocky Yoshida AdonisCreed — ▲ Shift into foe,in hand (101) 10

20Jan19 4f ft Pay :51 B 9/12 13Jan19 4f ft Pay :49 B 4/40 •6Jan19 5f ft Pay 1:02 B 1/2 30Dec18 4f ft Pay :49 B 4/13 23Dec18 4f ft Pay :50 B 4/5 16Dec18 3f ft Pay :38 B 5/5
29Oct18 4f ft CD :49 B 19/37 22Oct18 5f ft CD 1:00 B 7/37 •15Oct18 5f ft Sar 1:02 B 1/4 8Oct18 5f ft Sar 1:02 B 2/3 1Oct18 4f ft Sar :50 B 24/62 24Sep18 4f ft Sar :51 B 28/33

3 Channel Maker 117 Off Lasix Ch g 5
Sire: English Channel ($25,000)
Dam: In Return (Horse Chestnut (SAF))
Br: Tall Oaks Farm (ON)(Feb)
Own: Wachtel Stable, Barber, Gary, R. A. Hill Stab
PP-3 Jock: Castellano Javier (St 59 W 24% P 12% S 7% ITM 42% ROI -31%)
12/1 Tr: Mott William I (St 40 W 28% P 15% S 8% ITM 50% ROI -34%)

Lifetime Record	117 (2017)	21 4 4 3	$1,090,000		
2019	0 0 0 0	$0	Turf:	19 4 3 3	$1,029,124
2018	8 2 1 1	$644,880	Soft:	5 3 0 0	$452,621
GP	2 0 0 0	$9,730	Dist:	0 0 0 0	$0

3Nov18 10CD gd 1½ :49 1:14 2:07 2:32 3↑Stk 4000K G1 | 122 86 | 3 2 2 2 10 11 Ortiz J L | L126b 7.5 58 Enable Magical SadlersJoy | Prompt 3w, faltered (94) 13
Longines Breeders' Cup Turf - prompted pace 3wd, retreated past 5/16, eased late
29Sep18 8Bel sf 1½ :50 1:16 2:06 2:30 3↑Stk 500K G1 | 118 117 | 7 1 1 1hd 1 1 Ortiz J L | L126b 5.0 55 ChannelMaker RobertBruce SadlersJoy | At/near ins,ask upper (141) 7
Joe Hirsch Turf Classic S. - vie at/near ins,shook free 5/16,asked into lane,drew off
25Aug18 10Sar fm 1½ :48 1:13 2:01 2:24 3↑Stk 1000K G1 | 118 115 | 7 2 2 2 2 2 Rosario J | L120b 7.2-13 GloriousEmpire ChannelMaker SpringQuality | 2w,pull to 1/4,2d best (136) 10
Sword Dancer S. - 2w,stalked winner pulling on bit, bid 1/4,staved off,2nd best
28Jul18 9Sar sf 1⅜ :51 1:17 1:41 2:10 4↑Stk 250K G2 | 117 117 | 2 3 4 4 2 1 Rosario J | L122b 5.8 0 ChannelMaker GloriousEmpire SadlersJy | Pull to 1/2,3w 3rd,gme (141) 8
Bowling Green S.
9Jun18 10Bel fm 1⅜ :48 1:12 1:35 1:58 4↑Stk 1000K G1 | 114 116 | 9 12 12 13 12 8 Ortiz J L | L122b 17.6 10 SpringQuality SadlersJoy HiHappy | 3w upper, not enough (137) 13
Woodford Reserve Manhattan S. - broke in st, saved grd near rear, 3w upper, closed, not enough
5May18 11CD yl 1⅛ :50 1:16 1:41 1:54 4↑Stk 500K G1 | 120 101 | 4 7 5 8 6 5 Castellano J | L118b 9.4 61 Yoshida BeachPatrol Synchrony | ▲ Stdy upper and late (127) 9
Old Forester Turf Classic S. - settled inside,move up 5/16,steadied upper,angled,steady late
10Mar18 5SA fm 1 :22 :45 1:09 1:33 4↑Stk 400K G1 | 118 114 | 8 8 8 8 5 3 Castellano J | L120b 7.1 7 BowiesHero NextShares ChannelMaker | 6wd into str,3wd wire (137) 8
Frank E. Kilroe Mile S. - unhurried early, bit off rail,6wd into lane,drift in,bid 3wd,game
10Feb18 9GP fm 1⅛ :48 1:12 1:35 1:47 4↑Stk 300K G1 | 118 111 | 8 7 8 8 8 5 Juarez N | L121b 6.4 3 HeartToHeart Kurilov HiHappy | Lack room uppr,too lte (137) 8
Gulfstream Park Turf S. - in back, lacked room uppr, too late
25Nov17 7Dmr fm 1⅛ :47 1:11 1:34 1:46 3 Stk 300K G1 | 114 117 | 3 5 7 8 4 2 Castellano J | L122b 9.2 4 MoTown ChannelMaker BigScore | Split foes,rail bid (137) 9
Hollywood Derby - pulled, chased, inside, split horses 1/8,rail run for 2nd
28Oct17 9SA fm 1⅛ :47 1:10 1:33 1:45 3 Stk 200K G2 | 110 109 | 7 9 8 7 8 4 Van Dyke D | L120b 7.3 0 SharpSamurai BigScore BowiesHero | 4wd,3wd,edged 3rd (130) 9
Twilight Derby
30Sep17 10Bel fm 1½ :48 1:13 2:03 2:26 3↑Stk 500K G1 | 117 110 | 7 7 7 9 7 6 Franco M | L121b 58.5 3 BeachPatrol FancifulAngel OscarPerformance | 3w turns, no impact (130) 11
Joe Hirsch Turf Classic S. - 3w both turns, commenced stretch 5w, no impact
20Aug17 8WO fm 1½ :51 1:16 2:05 2:29 3 [illegible]Stk 400K | 95 97 | 2 9 8 9 1 1ns Hernandez R M | L126b *1.8 13 ChannelMaker FinalCpy KngAndHsCrt | ▲ Rank,3-7w,bmp,drift in (111) 10
Breeders' S.

20Jan19 4f ft Pay :51 B 9/12 13Jan19 4f ft Pay :50 B 33/40 6Jan19 4f ft Pay :50 B 8/15 30Dec18 4f ft Pay :50 B 7/13 23Dec18 4f ft Pay :50 B 4/5 16Dec18 3f ft Pay :37 B 2/5
9Dec18 3f ft Pay :39 B 8/8 28Oct18 4f ft CD :49 B 46/11. 21Oct18 4f ft CD :49 B 12/42 13Oct18 4f [illegible]ft Sar :49 B 4/47 24Sep18 4f [illegible]ft Sar :50 B 17/33 15Sep18 4f [illegible]ft Sar :50 B 57/66

4 Aerolithe (JPN) 112 Gr/ro m 5
Sire: Kurofune ($34,590)
Dam: Asterix (JPN) (Neo Universe (JPN))
Br: Northern Racing (JPN)(May)
Own: Sunday Racing Co. Ltd.
PP-4 Jock: Geroux Florent (St 70 W 21% P 21% S 13% ITM 56% ROI -14%)
8/1 Tr: Kikuzawa Takanori (no starts)

Lifetime Record	124 (2018)	13 4 5 0	$3,032,293		
2019	0 0 0 0	$0	Turf:	13 4 5 0	$3,032,293
2018	5 1 2 0	$1,389,854	Soft:	3 0 0 0	$229,040
GP	0 0 0 0	$0	Dist:	0 0 0 0	$0

18Nov18 KYOfm *1 1:33 3↑Stk 1861K G1 | 124 118 | 12 Moore R L | 121 4.1 Stelvio PersianKnight AlAin | 18
Mile Championship - KYOTO (Japan) -
7Oct18 TOKfm *1⅛ 1:44 3↑Stk 1122K G2 | 118 119 | 1 Moreira J | 121 1.3 Aerolithe Stelvio Kiseki | 13
Mainichi Okan - TOKYO (Japan) -
3Jun18 TOKfm *1 1:31 3↑Stk 1917K G1 | 124 124 | 2nk Tosaki K | 123 9.7 MozuAscot Aerolithe SuaveRichard | 16
Yasuda Kinen - TOKYO (Japan) -
13May18 TOKgd *1 1:32 4↑Stk 1823K G1 | 123 122 | 4 Tosaki K | 121 4.3 JourPolaire LysGracieux RedAvancer | 18
Victoria Mile - TOKYO (Japan) -
25Feb18 NAKfm *1⅛ 1:47 4↑Stk 1109K G2 | 118 118 | 2nk Yokoyama N | 121 6.4 WinBright Aerolithe MalteseApogee | 10
Nakayama Kinen - NAKAYAMA (Japan) -
15Oct17 KYOyl *1¼ 2:00 3 Stk 1566K G1 | 118 109 | 7 Yokoyama N | 121 2.6 Deirdre LysGracieux MozuKatchan | 18
Shuka Sho - KYOTO (Japan) -
30Jul17 SAPfm *1⅛ 1:45 3↑Stk 614K G3 | 110 112 | 1 Yokoyama N | 115 2.2 Aerolithe TosenVictory QueensMilagro | 13
Hokkaido Shimbn Hai Queen S. - SAPPORO (Japan) -
7May17 TOKfm *1 1:32 3 Stk 1601K G1 | 120 121 | 1 Yokoyama N | 121 4.8 Aerolithe RienoTesoro BomServico | 18
NHK Mile Cup - TOKYO (Japan) -
9Apr17 HSNgd *1 1:34 3 Stk 1577K G1 | 118 116 | 5 Yokoyama N | 121 22.6 ReineMinoru LysGracieux SoulStirring | 17
Oka Sho Japanese 1000 Gns - HANSHIN (Japan) -
11Feb17 TOKfm *1 1:33 3 Stk 588K G3 | 107 106 | 2 Yokoyama N | 119 7.8 AdmireMiyabi Aerolithe FlawlessMagic | 16
Daily Hai Queen Cup - TOKYO (Japan) -
8Jan17 NAKfm 1 1:34 3 Stk 569K G3 | | 2 Yokoyama N | 119 1.6 | 16
Fairy S. - NAKAYAMA (Japan) -
2Oct16 NAKfm 1 1:34 2 Stk 188K | | 2ns Yokoyama N | 119 1.2 | 12
Saffron Sho - NAKAYAMA (Japan) -

23Jan19 4f ft GP :51 B 15/19

5 Next Shares

L124 Dk b g 6

PP-5 Jock: Gaffalione Tyler (St 128 W 12% P 17% S 23% ITM 52% ROI -36%)
15/1 Tr: Baltas Richard (St 52 W 19% P 27% S 12% ITM 58% ROI -33%)

Sire: Archarcharch ($10,000)
Dam: Two Dot Slew (Evansville Slew)
Br: Buck Pond Farm, Inc. (KY)(Apr)
Own: Iavarone, Michael, Iavarone, Jules, McClanaha

Lifetime Record	120 (2018)	22 6 4 2	$1,187,697
2019 1 1 0 0	$120,000	Turf: 21 6 4 2	$1,187,487
2018 10 2 2 2	$903,890	Soft: 3 1 0 0	$601,125
GP T 1 1 0 0	$24,000	Dist: 0 0 0 0	$0

KEE NOV BRDG 17 $190,000

5Jan19 7SA fm 11/8 T :4841:125 1:3641:486 4↑Stk 200K G2 | 116 119 | 7 8 87½ 84½ 41½ 1nk Franco G L124b *1.6 21NextShares CleopatrasStrike LiamTheCharmer 4wd into str,up wire (138) 9
San Gabriel S.
3Nov18 8CD gd 1 T :247 :498 1:15 1:398 3↑Stk 2000K G1 | 122 112 | 2 7 63½ 72½ 95½ 136 Gaffalione T L126b 7.3 58ExpertEye Catapult Analyzeit Contended, faded (135) 14
Breeders' Cup Mile - hustled along, between horses, empty entering stretch, faded
6Oct18 10Kee gd 1 T :234 :471 1:122 1:37 3↑Stk 1000K G1 | 118 120 | 1 1 63½ 31½ 12½ 13½ Gaffalione T L126b 23.4 18NextShares GreatWideOpen Qurbaan Inside trip, drew away (140) 13
Shadwell Turf Mile S. - chased pace off rail, inside 1/4, took over str, drew away late
6Sep18 9KD fm 1 T :242 :485 1:131 1:418 3↑Stk 250Kc | 112 111 | 4 7 711 52½ 11 1½ Van Dyke D L121b *2.9 -8NextShares SiemRiep Parlor Drove pst 3wd, cleared (130) 11
Old Friends S.
19Aug18 8Dmr fm 1 T :232 :467 1:101 1:334 3↑Stk 200K G2 | 118 100 | 12 12 55 64 106 128½ Pereira T J L118b 17.9 1Catapult FlyToMars SharpSamurai 3wd,4wd,weakened (122) 13
Del Mar Mile H.
22Jul18 8Dmr fm 11/8 T :476 1:11 1:343 1:461 3↑Stk 250K G2 | 117 116 | 2 10 98½ 96 86½ 62½ Bejarano R L120b 12.4 4Catapult SharpSamurai PrimeAttraction 4wd into str,outkicked (139) 10
Eddie Read S.
28May18 7SA fm 1 T :232 :467 1:102 1:341 3↑Stk 400K G1 | 116 112 | 7 7 813 87 64½ 3½ Bejarano R L121b 8.6 9Hunt HeartToHeart NextShares 4wd into str,rallied (137) 8
Shoemaker Mile S. - unhurried early, inside, off rail, 4 wide into lane,rallied
13Apr18 9Kee fm 1 T :241 :479 1:118 1:347 4↑Stk 300K G1 | 117 111 | 7 8 73½ 75 63½ 74½ Nakatani C S L120b 7.1 -5HeartToHeart BallaghRocks Forge Back 5pth, 6path 1/4 (134) 9
Maker's 46 Mile S. - back early on 5path, 6path far turn, lacked needed rally stretch
10Mar18 5SA fm 1 T :228 :456 1:091 1:335 4↑Stk 400K G1 | 118 115 | 3 7 67½ 65 41½ 2½ Maragh R L120b 16.6 7BowiesHero NextShares ChannelMaker 5wd into str,bid btwn (137) 8
Frank E. Kilroe Mile S. - saved ground, chased, came out 2nd turn,5wd into str,bid btwn
10Feb18 5SA fm 1 T :226 :458 1:101 1:335 4↑Stk 100K G3 | 119 114 | 1 6 614 65 34 3½ Bejarano R L120b 5.6 8Om BowiesHero NextShares 4wd into str,3wd wire (139) 6
Thunder Road S.
1Jan18 7SA fm *6½f T :22 :446 1:068 1:124 4↑Stk 75K | 118 110 | 10 9 108 96½ 76½ 22½ Bejarano R L122b 10.0 15PeeWeeReese NextShares RichardsBoy 4wd into str,rallied (118) 10
Joe Hernandez S.
Previously Trained by William I Mott (St 718 W 15% P 14% S 11% ITM 40% ROI -26)
10Nov17 8Aqu fm 6f T :222 :453 :573 1:092 3↑Aocw62.5Knw2$x | 110 103 | 3 8 89½ 85½ 64 1½ Rosario J L122b *1.7 7NextShares CleverRoyal Blackout 5w upper, good finish (110) 8

•20Jan19 4f T gd SA :49 H 1/1 29Dec18 5f T ft SA 1:03 H 14/15 •22Dec18 6f T ft SA 1:14 H 1/1 16Dec18 6f T ft SA 1:14 H 3/9 10Dec18 5f T ft SA 1:02 H 7/9 4Dec18 4f T ft SA :50 H 9/14
28Oct18 4f T sf Kee :53 Bd 5/5 21Oct18 5f T gd Kee 1:04 Bd 2/4 30Sep18 5f ft Kee 1:02 B 22/31 22Sep18 4f T sf Kee :52 Bd 4/9 12Aug18 5f T fm Dmr 1:00 Hd 2/17 6Aug18 4f ft Dmr :52 H 65/65
30Aug15 11/16 T fm 7 SAR - Also-Eligible

6 Fahan Mura

L119 Ch m 5

PP-6 Jock: Maldonado Edwin A (St 30 W 13% P 13% S 3% ITM 30% ROI -47%)
30/1 Tr: Cerin Vladimir (St 23 W 13% P 13% S 9% ITM 35% ROI -30%)

Sire: English Channel ($25,000)
Dam: Celtic Cross (Giant's Causeway)
Br: Michael J. Moran (PA)(Mar)
Own: Bran Jam Stables and Clark, David W.

Lifetime Record	117 (2018)	23 9 2 4	$431,815
2019 0 0 0 0	$0	Turf: 22 9 2 4	$430,555
2018 11 7 1 1	$365,665	Soft: 1 1 0 0	$15,600
GP T 3 1 1 0	$21,740	Dist: 0 0 0 0	$0

KEE SEP YRLG 2015 $90,000

29Dec18 4SA fm 11/8 T :474 1:112 1:348 1:466 3↑F Stk 150K G3 | 112 115 | 4 4 12½ 12½ 12 1¾ Maldonado E A L122b *1.7 2FahanMura ExcellentSunset Quebec Inside,held gamely (131) 8
Robert J. Frankel S.
2Dec18 7Dmr fm 1 T :228 :463 1:106 1:344 3↑F Stk 300K G1 | 114 105 | 3 2 14 11½ 4¾ 129½ Maldonado E A L123b 12.1 16Uni DaddyIsALegend Quidura Speed,inside,wkened (117) 13
Matriarch S. - speed, angled in, set pace, inside, fought back 1/8,wkened
4Nov18 4SA fm 1 T :227 :462 1:097 1:335 3↑F Stk 200K G2 | 115 111 | 8 1 11½ 11 11½ 21½ Maldonado E A L121b 6.2 3Vasilika FahanMura MadameStripes Inside,held 2nd (127) 8
Goldikova S.
7Oct18 10SA fm 1 T :221 :448 1:082 1:326 3↑F S Stk 70K | 110 117 | 10 1 12 12 12 1¾ Maldonado E A L123b *2.8 12FahanMura Quebec WayToVersailles Speed,inside,held game (133) 11
Swingtime S.
1Sep18 10Dmr fm 11/8 T :472 1:119 1:354 1:472 3↑F Stk 200K G2 | 114 108 | 4 1 13½ 11½ 11½ 31¼ Maldonado E A L119b 7.9 10Vasilika Cambodia FahanMura Off rail str,edged 2nd (125) 11
John C. Mabee S.
20Jul18 7Dmr fm 11/16 T :234 :474 1:111 1:411 3↑F S Stk 75Kc | 110 114 | 10 3 12½ 12 12½ 1¼ Maldonado E A L121b 6.7 13FahanMura Achira MidnightCrossing Speed,inside,held game (131) 10
Osunitas S.
8Jun18 9Bel fm 11/4 T :464 1:104 1:349 1:592 4↑F Stk 600K G2 | 111 93 | 1 1 18½ 16½ 1½ 65 Maldonado E A L118b 16.4 -5FourstarCrook Sistercharlie DaddysLilDarling Spurted inside, wknd (113) 9
New York S. Presented by NYRA Bets
5May18 6SA fm 1 T :229 :46 1:098 1:339 3↑F Aocw62.5Knw2$x | 105 110 | 3 1 16 11½ 13 12½ Maldonado E A L121b *1.1 1FahanMura TheTulip FizzyFriday Inside,clear,held (125) 7
25Mar18 4SA fm 1 T :23 :465 1:098 1:343 4↑F Aoc w40Knw1$x | 101 101 | 5 1 11 14 15 17½ Maldonado E A L120b 7.3 -7FahanMura SiberianIris TammysWindow Inside, drew off (121) 9
19Feb18 4SA fm 1 T :235 :48 1:119 1:362 4↑F Clm 32K | 98 94 | 5 1 2½ 11 11 1½ Maragh R L123b 5.9 15FahanMura MissBoomBoom PeachCove Stalked,bid,led,held (111) 7
26Jan18 5SA fm 1 T :237 :472 1:109 1:351 4↑F Clm 32Knw3l | 93 95 | 5 1 2½ 2hd 1½ 1nk Desormeaux K J L123b 3.5 5FahanMura QuinnMurphy Scattering Inside duel,led,held (110) 7
Previously Trained by John T Toscano (St 284 W 13% P 15% S 13% ITM 41% ROI -15)
10Dec17 2Aqu gd 1 :237 :472 1:136 1:408 3↑F Clm 35Kc | 87 46 | 3 1 2½ 43½ 513 522 Carmouche K L121b 8.9 9ChristmasSky Andesine WinnersDream 3w upper, tired 6

20Jan19 5f T ft SA 1:02 H 21/29 10Jan19 4f T ft SA :50 H 6/9 23Dec18 5f T ft SA 1:01 H 10/19 16Dec18 4f ft SA :49 H 23/74 26Nov18 5f ft SA 1:03 H 39/44 19Nov18 5f ft SA 1:02 H 27/36
13Nov18 4f ft SA :48 H 6/29 28Oct18 5f ft SA 1:01 H 20/71 21Oct18 5f ft SA 1:02 H 44/45 30Sep18 5f ft SA 1:02 H 63/10 23Sep18 4f ft SA :50 H 76/96 25Aug18 6f ft Dmr 1:14 H 4/4
15Aug18 11/8 T fm 5 DMR - Veterinarian 4Aug18 11/16 T fm 8 DMR - Trainer 27Jul17 11/8 my 10 SAR - Off-Turf 21Apr17 11/16 T fm 1 AQU - Veterinarian 16Nov16 1 gd 4 AQU - Off-Turf

7 Bricks And Mortar

L124 Dk b h 5

PP-7 Jock: Ortiz Jr Irad (St 137 W 20% P 18% S 16% ITM 54% ROI -10%)
5/1 Tr: Brown Chad C (St 43 W 26% P 21% S 2% ITM 49% ROI -22%)

Sire: Giant's Causeway ($85,000)
Dam: Beyond The Waves (Ocean Crest)
Br: George Strawbridge Jr. (KY)(Mar)
Own: Klarovich Stables, Inc. and Lawrence, William

Lifetime Record	116 (2018)	7 5 0 2	$362,000
2019 0 0 0 0	$0	Turf: 7 5 0 2	$362,000
2018 1 1 0 0	$25,200	Soft: 0 0 0 0	$0
GP T 2 2 0 0	$48,000	Dist: 0 0 0 0	$0

KEE SEP YRLG 2015 $200,000

22Dec18 9GP fm 1 T :234 :472 1:109 1:343 3↑Aoc w75Kc | 110 116 | 8 6 63½ 43 21½ 1½ Ortiz Jr I L121 *1.8 12BricksAndMortar MrCub Krampus 3wd, forged past late (134) 10
7Oct17 9Bel fm 11/8 T :491 1:131 1:358 1:471 3 Stk 500K G3 | 106 105 | 6 4 75 54 52 3½ Rosario J L120 *1.5 0Yoshida Lucln BrcksAndMrtr ▲ Tight betw, gd courage (124) 9
Hill Prince S.
2Sep17 9Sar fm 11/8 T 1:462 3 Stk 300K G3 | 110 92 | 4 6 610 2½ 22 3½ Rosario J L123 *2.0 5VoodooSong Yoshida BricksAndMortar ▲ Shut-off brk,4-3p2nd 8
Saranac S.
4Aug17 9Sar fm 11/16 T :239 :481 1:115 1:395 3 Stk 200K G2 | 110 99 | 1 4 32½ 41½ 32 1¾ Rosario J L121 4.1 -7BricksAndMortar Yoshida BigHandsome Rated ins, good kick (124) 9
National Museum of Racing Hall of Fame S.
4Jul17 8Bel fm 1 T :24 :479 1:11 1:331 3 Stk 100K | 103 100 | 1 3 75½ 75 52½ 1nk Rosario J L118 3.3-13BricksAndMortar BigHandsome SecretryAtWr Ins,alt 4w 1/16pl,up (121) 7
Manila S.
9Jun17 7Bel fm 1 T :247 :494 1:125 1:345 3 Aoc w80Knw1$x | 103 101 | 3 3 22 31 1½ 1¾ Rosario J L122 2.7 3BricksAndMortar SnapDecision HelloHoliday 3w upper, inched away (118) 9
18Feb17 7GP fm 11/16 T :241 :495 1:136 1:43 3 Msw 46K | 93 101 | 7 10 64½ 63 21 1¼ Rosario J L120 6.0 4BricksAndMortar BrooklynBobby SecretryAtWr 4w rally, drove clear (117) 12

•19Jan19 5f T fm PMM :59 B 1/14 12Jan19 5f T fm PMM 1:01 Bd 9/24 5Jan19 4f T fm PMM :48 B 3/36 15Dec18 5f T fm PMM 1:02 Bd 20/25 8Dec18 5f T fm PMM 1:00 B 7/28 1Dec18 4f ft PMM :49 B 5/41
24Nov18 4f ft PMM :49 B 18/47 11Nov18 4f ft Bel :48 B 16/54 4Nov18 4f T ft Bel :50 B 43/65 26Oct18 4f T ft Sar :49 B 23/39 21Oct18 4f T ft Sar :49 B 7/46 14Oct18 4f T ft Sar :49 B 16/45
10Nov18 1 gd 8 AQU - Off-Turf

8 Delta Prince L124 Dk b h 6 Sire: Street Cry (IRE) ($150,000) Dam: Delta Princess (A.p. Indy) Br: Adena Springs (KY)(Apr) Own: Stronach Stables Blinkers - OFF

PP-8 Jock: Dettori Lanfranco (no starts)
15/1 Tr: Jerkens James A (St 15 W 20% P 27% S 27% ITM 73% ROI -18%)

Lifetime Record	118 (2018)	11 4 3 3	$418,298
2019 0 0 0 0	$0	Turf: 8 4 2 1	$374,798
2018 4 1 1 1	$234,598	Soft: 2 0 1 1	$125,000
GP 3 2 1 0	$85,200	Dist: 0 0 0 0	$0

2Nov18 7Aqu ft 7f :221 :449 1:102 1:238 3↑Stk 200K G3 Bold Ruler H. 116 94 6 6 64 43 37 311 Cohen D L119b 3.5 3NoDozing TrueTimber DeltaPrince Climb bit,3w1/2,5w upr 6

15Sep18 8WO fm 1 :248 :488 1:115 1:331 3↑Stk 800K G1 Ricoh Woodbine Mile S. - stalked inside, saved ground, in contention, chased 120 101 2 6 3½ 3½ 4½ 4¾ Castellano J L123 *2.2 2OscarPerformance MrHavercamp StormyAntarctic Stalk ins, chased str (125) 8

11Aug18 8Sar gd 1 :235 :469 1:112 1:36 3↑Stk 500K G1 Fourstardave H. - ins 1st,settled,roused 4p2nd,rallied,bid 1/16,determinedly,denied 118 118 1 5 6½ 42 2½ 2nk Castellano J L118 2.7 27 VoodooSong DeltaPrince Divisidero Ins1st,4p2nd,bid 1/16 (140) 6

30Jun18 6WO fm 1 :238 :466 1:091 1:324 3↑Stk 175K G2 King Edward S. 115 107 8 4 4½ 21 2½ 1½ Castellano J L117 *2.2 -4DeltaPrince Shakhimat ConquestPanthr ▲ Brk out,2-3w,drv clr (131) 8

4Sep17 7Sar yl 1⅛ :243 :48 1:12 1:424 3↑Stk 250K G2 Bernard Baruch H. 116 112 3 3 42 4½ 23 3½ Velazquez J R L115 3.2 40HeartToHeart Forge DeltaPrince ▲ 2-3w turns,bmpd 3/16 (134) 7

5Aug17 5Sar fm 1 :238 :473 1:111 1:348 3↑Aocw62.5Knw2$x 110 115 5 3 3½ 31 1½ 1¾ Velazquez J R L122 *1.0 11DeltaPrince DerbyChampagne Mutazen 5-4w uppr, edged clear (134) 12

1Apr17 4GP fm 1 :234 :463 1:097 1:331 4↑Stk 200K G3 Appleton S. 114 116 6 4 3½ 3½ 1½ 2½ Ortiz J L L117 2.9 -8AllIncluded DeltaPrince OurWay Game,late lead,outkick (133) 6

18Feb17 12GP fm 1 :232 :472 1:109 1:342 4↑Alw 48Knw1x 106 110 5 6 5½ 4½ 3½ 1nk Velazquez J R L121 *1.2 4DeltaPrince Alasaal GalleonMast Rated,drvng4w,in time (128) 11

26Dec16 8GP fm 1 :233 :485 1:121 1:35 3↑Msw 42K 96 106 12 5 2hd 2hd 1½ 14 Gallardo A A L122 3.6 -7DeltaPrince NotionSonet Mutazen Press pace, drew off (121) 12

12Nov16 6Aqu ft 1 :233 :462 1:118 1:38 3↑Msw 60K 97 95 2 8 42 41 2hd 23 Rosario J 121 *1.8 6TRCrew DeltaPrince ImAmazing ▲ Bmp st,3w,shy bit 1/8 8

2Oct16 4Bel gd 6½f :229 :459 1:098 1:162 3↑Msw 75K 90 82 1 4 3½ 33 36 37½ Rosario J 119 1.7 2MightyMoses Imasuperstar DeltaPrince ▲ Bumped st, greenly 5

•19Jan19 6f fm PMM 1:101 B 1/3 •12Jan19 8f fm PMM 1:43 Bd 1/1 5Jan19 5f ft PMM 1:01 B 8/26 •27Dec18 5f ft PMM 1:01² B 1/6 18Dec18 4f ft PMM :483 B 3/44 4Dec18 4f ft Bel :526 B 59/59

•22Oct18 4f ft Bel :475 B 1/40 •15Oct18 5f ft Bel 1:00 B 1/7 6Oct18 4f ft Bel :485 B 2/75 6Sep18 4f ft Bel :486 B 13/95 •1Sep18 5f fm Sar :592 B 1/10 24Aug18 4f ft Sar :509 B 22/30

18Nov17 1 fm 8 AQU - Trainer 9Oct17 1⅛ gd 8 BEL - Trainer 19Oct16 7f fm 6 BEL - Veterinarian

9 Catapult L124 Dk b h 6 Sire: Kitten's Joy ($50,000) Dam: Gata Bella (Storm Cat) Br: Breffni Farm (KY)(Apr) Own: Woodford Racing, LLC

PP-9 Jock: Rosario Joel (St 98 W 17% P 18% S 17% ITM 53% ROI -42%)
7/2 Tr: Sadler John W (St 33 W 12% P 21% S 18% ITM 52% ROI -46%)

Lifetime Record	121 (2018)	16 6 4 1	$961,384
2019 0 0 0 0	$0	Turf: 15 5 4 1	$910,384
2018 4 2 2 0	$623,800	Soft: 7 1 2 1	$478,000
GP 0 0 0 0	$0	Dist: 0 0 0 0	$0

KEE SEP YRLG 2014 $350,000

3Nov18 8CD gd 1 :247 :498 1:15 1:398 3↑Stk 2000K G1 Breeders' Cup Mile - tugged between horses, bold bid 4w, fought on, grudgingly 122 121 8 4 5½ 21 21 2½ Van Dyke D L126 7.5 58ExpertEye Catapult Analyzelt Tugged, loomed,denied (142) 14

19Aug18 8Dmr fm 1 :232 :467 1:101 1:334 3↑Stk 200K G2 Del Mar Mile H. 118 114 1 4 8¾ 7½ 4½ 1½ Van Dyke D L121 5.1 1Catapult FlyToMars SharpSamurai ▲ Waited 1/4,3w into str (138) 13

22Jul18 8Dmr fm 1⅛ :476 1:11 1:343 1:461 3↑Stk 250K G2 Eddie Read S. 117 120 5 5 75 7½ 6¾ 1nk Van Dyke D L120 21.0 4Catapult SharpSamurai PrimeAttraction Came out str,up 3wd (143) 10

17Jun18 6SA fm 1 :239 :477 1:113 1:352 3↑Aoc w75Kc Previously Trained by Chad C Brown (St 766 W 26% P 18% S 15% ITM 59% ROI -15) 109 110 1 3 6½ 6½ 4½ 2½ Van Dyke D L124 3.3 23SharpSamurai Catapult Isotherm ▲ Steadied 3/4,bid btwn (127) 6

30Sep17 8Lrl fm 1 :236 :462 1:103 1:342 3↑Stk 200K G2 Baltimore/Washington International Turf Cup S. 113 100 4 5 412 37 3½ 2½ Lynch F L118 2.2 1Projected Catapult RingWeekend ▲ Alterd 1/8,run bw,game (125) 6

4Aug17 5Sar fm 1 :242 :484 1:121 1:353 3↑Aoc w80Knw3$x 110 115 6 4 38 3½ 25 1½ Castellano J L120 3.1 18Catapult Changewildoyagood NightProwler 2w,ask 5/16,late surge (139) 8

18Jun17 8Bel yl 1 :23 :461 1:104 1:35 4↑Stk 300K G3 Poker S. 113 105 5 2 1½ 2½ 33 45 Ortiz J L L120b 3.5 25BallaghRocks Projected NightProwler Work to rail turn,tird (125) 5

20May17 12Pim gd 1⅛ :241 :494 1:139 1:432 3↑Stk 250K G2 Longines Dixie S. 112 108 8 7 53 5½ 34 4¾ Castellano J L118b 6.5 15WorldApproval Projected Blacktype ▲ Steadied,checked,tired (124) 10

9Apr17 8Aqu yl 1 :234 :468 1:106 1:361 4↑Stk 100K Danger's Hour S. 112 110 2 3 4½ 3½ 2½ 2½ Ortiz Jr I L115b *1.1 8Macagone Catapult CageFighter 2-3w upper, mild kick (132) 7

11Feb17 9Tam fm 1⅛ :234 :478 1:11 1:406 4↑Stk 150K G3 Tampa Bay S. 110 112 6 8 32 31 4½ 43 Ortiz J L L116b *2.8 3InspectorLynley Kasaqui IrishStrait Bid 3w, outkicked (127) 9

24Nov16 3Aqu gd 1⅛ :246 :507 1:15 1:446 3 Stk 125K Gio Ponti S. 107 101 5 2 2½ 21 1½ 1½ Castellano J L119b *1.6 17Catapult StrikeMidnight HunterOrley 2-3w,bit errant lane (121) 6

23Oct16 7Bel sf 1 :233 :482 1:138 1:377 3 Stk 100K English Channel S. 107 106 5 6 4½ 1hd 2hd 3½ Castellano J L119b 3.8 46DragonBay StrikeMidnight Catapult Ins,keen 1/2,nail 1/16 (124) 11

19Jan19 5f ft SA 1:00 H 8/45 11Jan19 6f ft SA 1:142 H 4/22 5Jan19 6f ft SA 1:14 H 4/20 30Dec18 6f ft SA 1:148 H 6/17 23Dec18 5f ft SA 1:014 H 17/70 16Dec18 5f ft SA 1:01 H 22/70

9Dec18 4f ft SA :478 H 4/92 2Dec18 4f ft SA :50 H 58/82 •28Oct18 5f ft SA 1:002 H 1/71 •22Oct18 6f ft SA 1:122 H 1/9 16Oct18 6f ft SA 1:142 H 3/8 7Oct18 5f ft SA :594 H 2/87

10 Dubby Dubbie L124 Dk b g 4 Sire: Ice Box ($7,500) Dam: I'm Cozy (Grand Slam) Br: Al Horton (KY)(Feb) Own: Ron Paolucci Racing, LLC

PP-10 Jock: Panici Luca (St 62 W 11% P 0% S 13% ITM 24% ROI -11%)
30/1 Tr: Hess Jr Robert B (St 35 W 11% P 17% S 17% ITM 46% ROI -35%)

Lifetime Record	106 (2018)	16 4 4 1	$191,700
2019 0 0 0 0	$0	Turf: 11 3 4 1	$170,950
2018 12 3 4 1	$174,600	Soft: 6 2 1 0	$103,580
GP 0 0 0 0	$0	Dist: 0 0 0 0	$0

Previously Trained by Michelle Lovell (St 126 W 10% P 15% S 10% ITM 35% ROI -36)

23Nov18 7CD yl 1⅛ :489 1:15 1:407 1:539 3↑Aoc 62.5Knw2x 108 104 8 4 2½ 22 1½ 1½ Geroux F L118b 15.1 49DubbyDubbie Markitoff SouperTapit Drew clear,geared down (124) 11

14Oct18 2Kee sy *1⅛ :239 :479 1:129 1:439 3 Alw 73Kc 106 86 3 2 32 42 45 410 Gilligan J L120b 5.5 0RoamingUnion Reride ZeroGravity 5path 3/16, faded 4

29Sep18 7CD gd 1⅛ :496 1:154 1:409 1:542 3 Stk 100K Jefferson Cup S. 106 86 9 1 75 7½ 57 5½ Gilligan J L118 8.4 42HotSprings Discovered CaptivatingMoon 3path 1/4, belatedly (113) 9

11Aug18 9AP gd 1½ :473 1:116 1:365 2:01 3 Stk 400K G1 Secretariat S. - towards rear, 2wide, lacked response 109 92 11 7 89 11½ 127 11½ Gilligan J L119 104.7 0Carrick Analyzelt Bandua 2w, lacked response (115) 13

7Jul18 5AP fm 1⅛ :474 1:114 1:355 1:478 3 Stk 100K G3 American Derby 103 106 4 2 45 57 5½ 32 Gilligan J L119 5.3 -7RealStory CaptivatingMoon DubbyDubbie 2w to 1/4,rail rally (128) 8

24Jun18 5CD gd 1 :244 :483 1:133 1:388 3 Aoc w100Knw3l 98 106 4 1 5½ 34 3½ 1½ Gilligan J L120 5.9 32DubbyDubbie MadisonsLuna SmartRemark Drove past 3wide str (124) 6

20May18 8CD fm 1⅛ :475 1:122 1:373 1:495 3 Alw 55Knw1x 93 93 3 5 53 5½ 1½ 1nk Gilligan J L118 6.6 -1DubbyDubbie EgoTrip Pickford Long drv late, held (107) 11

22Apr18 6Kee fm 1⅛ :489 1:15 1:393 1:509 3 Str 50Kc 91 84 5 3 21 2½ 2hd 2½ Beschizza A L118b 4.1 -4CullumRoad DubbyDubbie Messiah Bid btw late,not enuff (100) 9

25Mar18 8FG fm *1⅛ :234 :488 1:142 1:45 3 Aoc w50Knw1x 88 93 4 1 2½ 2hd 2hd 21 Hernandez C J L120b 11.2 0Ezmosh DubbyDubbie CaymansCobra 2-3p turns,outfinished (105) 10

25Feb18 6FG gd *1⅛ :248 :512 1:162 1:481 3 Aoc w50Knw1x 85 88 7 2 2hd 21 21 21 Beschizza A L120b 9.4 25TigersRule DubbyDubbie ShadowSphinx Ins 1st,2p2nd,re-bid 1/4 (101) 7

3Feb18 9FG gd *1 :245 :494 1:144 1:398 3 Aoc w50Knw1x 85 80 6 2 5½ 5½ 5½ 41 Beschizza A L120b 3.2 4PotentialDanger GsTurn ShadowSphinx 2-3wide turns,gaining (99) 6

6Jan18 7FG fm *1 :252 :502 1:16 1:401 3 Aoc 50Knw1x 88 78 3 3 32 42 33 2¾ Cannon D L120b 36.7 12RideAComet DubbyDubbie SharedValue Inside turns,no match (95) 9

19Jan19 5f fm GP 1:028 B 4/4 •13Jan19 5f fm GP 1:04 B 1/1 15Dec18 4f ft FG :522 B 145/1 7Dec18 4f ft FG :489 B 8/115 13Nov18 5f gd CD 1:01 B 5/50 4Nov18 4f ft CD :479 B 6/63

22Sep18 5f ft CD 1:022 B 26/44 15Sep18 4f ft CD :496 B 51/78 5Aug18 5f ft CD 1:016 B 9/32 29Jul18 4f ft CD :48 B 6/86 22Jul18 4f ft CD :534 B 11/11 16Jun18 4f ft CD :494 B 50/70

29Dec18 1 sy 7 FG - Trainer 23Jun18 1 fm 5 CBY - Stewards

Acknowledgment

Thanks to Ted Craven, Constantine Dzhabarov, Ben Haggin and David McKenzie for helpful data and discussions.

Chapter 26

The Big Money Older Horse Races: Pegasus, Saudi Cup and Dubai World Cup in 2020

William T. Ziemba

The Saudi Cup, worth $20 million with $10 million to the winner, is now the world's richest horse race. It's part of the big money races for older (4+ years) horse races including the Pegasus and the Dubai World Cup. Top horses enter these races. The Saudi Cup winner was Maximum Security, who was disqualified in the Kentucky Derby in a controversial decision discussed in Chapter 24. As of June 2021, the Saudi Cup purse has yet to be paid as Jason Servis, trainer of Maximum Security, has been accused of administering illegal performance enhancing drugs to his horses. The case continues.

26.1. The Pegasus

I begin with the Pegasus which was held for the fourth time at Gulfstream racetrack in Florida. The three previous Pegasus races are in *Wilmott* columns with a summary in chapter 25. The Stronach group which owns Gulfstream, Santa Anita and other tracks set up this series as a competitor and preclude to the Dubai World Cup. The first year the race had 12 entrants each putting up $1 million each for a $12 million purse. Then it went to $16 million, again with the horse owners putting up the purse. Then in 2019, the third year, there were two parts: a $9 million dirt race and a $7 million grass race and higher entry fees of $500,000 for each race. This year's races have been cut back to $3 million for the dirt race and $1 million for the grass race.

Table 26.1. The handicappers rated the Pegasus Turf Race, winners circled.

#	Horse	PSR
①	Zulu Alpha	96
2	Arklow	98
3	Without Parole (Gb)	105
4	Sadler's Joy	105
5	Channel Cat	99
6	Instilled Regard	106
7	Admission Office	101
8	Henley's Joy	95
9	Next Shares	102
10	Mo Forza	103
11	Sacred Life	(Fr) 104
12	Magic Wand (Ire)	0
13	Tusk	109

Timeline: 2–4–①
David: ①
DJM: none
Jeremy Plonk: 11,12,2
Johnny D: 10, 12, 3
Tyler Frausto: 6,10,12

```
   11-GP    Sat Jan 25, 2020   04:49 PM   9.5T   4up GR1  $1000000  108-111   F-D   Vi=27!  Q6=0   PL-5   11-GP
     FOUR YEAR OLDS AND UPWARD WITH NO RACE DAY MEDICATION.
--------------------------------------------------------------------------------------------------------------------
Pn    PP Horse       MLO  Ag  Ped-St Ch  Lay Wk    Jockey--rtg   TJ%  Trainer--rtg--TPG   Q R  E L   PAC-PER--CLASS  (K)  FC  KLine Pn
SortIndx
--------------------------------------------------------------------------------------------------------------------
3     03 Without P  4/1   5h +576 GB LO  084'78   #Dettor  215        Brown C  423+  A     1 P  4 5   103 108*  111+  105  61   2.7>|3 |
105.4291
6     06 Instille  10/1   5h +470 KY LO  042'79    Ortiz,  403+  26   Brown C  449+  A     2 P  9 3   098 106   108   098  81*  5.5>|6 |$$
097.8033
12    12 Magic Wan *7/2   5m +990 IR L2 F048 00   #Moore   215        O'Brien  135   F-                         *112+  098+       6.0 |12|
097.6805
5     05 Channel   10/1   5h +599 KY LO  042'80*   Velazq  319   24   Pletche  374   B     2 S  9 1*  095 106   108   096  81*  7.3>|5 |$
096.3358
4     04 Sadler's   8/1   7h +611 KY LO  063'65    Castel  374+       Albertr  224   C-    3 S  9 6   098 103   109   091  78   12.5 |4 |
091.1108
11    11 Sacred L  12/1   5h +566 FR LO  056'78   +Ortiz   337   19   Brown C  442+  A     3 S  6 4   101 106   109   090  75   12.5 |11|$
090.1514
10    10 Mo Forza   5/1   4c +458 KY LO  028'79    Rosari  404+  28   Miller   341   B     5 E  2 9   103 105   106   087  71   18.4 |10|
086.9997
2     02 Arklow     6/1   6h +498 KY LO  084'83*  +Saez L  306   28   Cox Bra  430+  B     4 S  3 9   101 105   108   087  69   18.4 |2 |$
086.5910
1     01 Zulu Alp  12/1   7g +466 KY LO  084'85+  #Gaffal  292   14   Maker M  302   B     3 S  9 8   096 102   107   081  65   34.0 |1 |$$
080.7034
7     07 Admissio  30/1   5h  345 KY LO  042'78   +Prat F  385+       Lynch B  250   C+    0 R  8 2   099 107   109   076+ 82*  57.3 |7 |
076.4150
9     09 Next Sha  30/1   7g +460 KY LO  056'93+   Valdiv  391+       Baltas   317   B+    0 S  5 7   102 107   108   068  83*  99.0 |9 |$$
067.5489
13(A)13 Tusk       30/1   7g +538 KY LO  014 76   +Lopez   401+  53+  Joseph,  447+  A+    5 E *1 9  *106 106   107   066  65   99.0 |13|$$
066.1399
8     08 Henley's  30/1   4c +558 KY LO  056'80*  #Leparo  267   17   Maker M  305   B     2 P  7 9   097 102   107   052  65   99.0 |8 |$
051.8885

          (K) 3-6-12     Price Play 13      MSpot ~       TSpot 13      Scratches ~
```

See Tables 26.1 and 26.3 for the major handicappers ratings of the Pegasus Turf and Dirt races and Tables 26.2 and 26.4 for Super Screener ratings.

Zulu Alpha ridden by Tyler Gaffalione won the grass race, see Figure 26.1 for the chart. Given that the $20 million Saudi Cup was coming

Table 26.2. Super screener for the Pegasus grass.

Gulfstream Park R11: Pegasus Turf (G1)

Post Time: 4:49 PM ET // Playability Score = 7 (High Payoff Potential)

Headliner:

MAGIC WAND

KEY SCREENING CRITERIA

- Advantaged by pace set up
- Proven ability at this distance
- Superior Super Screener Energy Reserve Index ™
- Projected progression in form cycle
- Strong turn of foot
- Success in G1 races
- 7 other Super Screener criteria

PACE SET UP

PACE PAR — First Call = **93**; 2nd Call = **101**
PROJECTED — First Call = 86; 2nd Call = 94

PACE LEADER(S): #5 Channel Cat
PRESSERS: #12 Magic Wand, #6 Instilled Regard, #10 Mo Forza

WIN CONTENDERS

Without history, had to use G1 turf stakes races run at GP to inform screening criteria. The pace here will be quite modest with no need-the-lead types in the field. Connections of **#5 Channel Cat** are likely to send here as his best races came carving out or sitting near the pace. **#12 Magic Wand** is a Top Win pick here by virtue of how advantaged this mare will be by the pace set up and how she has competed well against saltier company. She finished 2nd twice to potential horse-of-the-year Bricks and Mortar in both the inaugural running of this race last year and later in the Arlington Million. She is certainly one to beat here but offers little in the way of value. **#3 Without Parole** is our Top Win pick and offers enticing value. This horse got his career off to a fast start winning 4 straight including a Group 1 affair. Showed nothing in his next 5 starts. Was put away in May and sent to Chad Brown in October. After the 6-month break finished a solid 3rd behind Uni and Got Stormy showing a good turn of foot. Really needed that race and will relish more ground. Will sit closer here and look for a huge move forward. Very live value play. His stablemate, **#6 Instilled Regard** is a viable win contender in his own right and another that is ready to pop a new lifetime top in his 3rd race off the 6-month layoff. Secures a great trip here pressing in the clear and continues on with abundant energy release in the final stages.

VALUE PLAYERS AND LONG SHOTS

#3 Without Parole and **#6 Instilled Regard** are by far the best value plays in this race and that pair should be used in 1st and 2nd in wagers as your primary wagering strategy. As if Chad Brown wasn't loaded enough with that pair, Sacred Life is projected to be sitting on really big race 2nd off the layoff despite facing tougher and going longer. Certainly a viable "under" player at a price.

When it comes to the bottom of the Superfecta, anything can happen in this relatively open affair so don't hesitate to hit the ALL button in the 4th place spot.

Race Insights

Pace: Soft/Modest Pressure

Track Bias: Inside

Race Shape: Slow/Fast

Tough Trips: None

Key Preps

BC Turf (G1)

BC Mile (G1)

Ft. Lauderdale (G2)

Seabiscuit (G2)

2020 Super Screener| superscreener.com | @Super_Screener |

Gulfstream Park R11: Pegasus Turf (G1)

Post Time: 4:49 PM ET // Playability Score = 7 (High Payoff Potential)

Horse	Comments	Odds	Rank	Multi-race
#3 Without Parole	**OFF PACE** Chad Brown has had this horse pointed to this race since coming to his barn back in October. Got his career off to a brilliant start as 2017 ended and 2018 began culminating into a really brilliant Group 1 win in June 2018. Went off form after that and after two poor starts in 2019 was put away from May until when Brown entered him in the Breeders' Cup Mile where that good form returned showing that great turn of foot he displayed at the start of his career finishing a close-up third to the elite pair of Uni and Got Stormy. He really needed that race and it was the perfect prep for this one laying out energy in that ideal balanced way. Will be positioned closer here and will unleash that lethal turn of foot to run big here. Added ground poses no concern. A lot of value to be had.	4-1	A	must
#12 Magic Wand	**PRESSER** Finished 2nd to the immortal Bricks and Mortar in the G1 Arlington Million. Pace sets up perfectly for this presser as it will be modest allowing this Aidan O'Brien charge to reserve ample energy for that sprint to the wire. No Bricks and Mortar here. Value will be hard to come by.	7-2	A	must
#6 Instilled Regard	**TOP VALUE/PRESSER** Stablemate to Without Parole is getting good at the right time. Started on dirt but is a much better horse on grass and has finished in the Trifecta in all 4 turf starts. Form cycle and Chad Brown trainer analysis indicates that this horse is getting good at the right time and is sitting on a huge new lifetime top 3rd race off the 6-month layoff. Without much pace signed on, this one will sit the ideal, clean trip either pressing or sitting just off the pace with plenty of reserve energy in the tank for that final critical furlong. A top win contender to be sure.	10-1	A	must
#2 Arklow	**TOP BOARD HITTER/CLOSER** Tough to know when this horse will get into the race early or dawdle in the back but once they turn for home, he always comes on like a freight train. In the Breeders' Cup Turf he was 3rd best behind Bricks and Mortar and United as he covered far more ground than any other horse in the race with that very wide trip. Will run another big one here but would prefer more ground. Use some for the win; more under.	6-1	B	if spreading
#11 Sacred Life	**TOP LONG SHOT/CLOSER** What this horse may lack in credentials he more than makes up for it with that devastatingly keen turn of foot. Stablemate to Without Parole and Instilled Regard has hit the Exacta in his 4 US starts. Was clearly much better than Next Shares last out as he we stymied behind horses getting shuffled back some but swung to the outside to burst down the lane and easily defeat that foe. His best race to date is coming here.	12-1	B	if spreading
#7 Admission Office	**TOP LONG SHOT/DEEP CLOSER** Looks like this one is finally rounding into form and ready for a peak effort at the right time. Is pace dependent so the modest pace here along with quick-footed presser/off-the-pace types will make it tough for this one who faces his stiffest test to date. Working in his favor is that this distance should be ideal while others would prefer longer and his quick turn of foot is a key asset give the softer pace.	30-1	B	if spreading
#4 Sadler's Joy	**DEEP CLOSER** Another year older now this productive turf stakes veteran has been sparingly raced in 2019. With a campaign that commenced in late July. Progressed in every race after that up to his next short layoff. While he is one that prefers more ground, form cycle analysis says...watch out... as he'll be advancing off that last effort to pop an effort similar to his prior two G1 efforts. Solid player to use "under".	8-1	B	if spreading
#1 Zulu Alpha	**CLOSER** Found his best races once landing in the Mike Maker barn and moving to his preferred 1 1/2 miles distance. Connections know it is a long shot for this one to win but they would be happy with a piece of the big money and he is certainly capable of catching the bottom of the Superfecta on a turf course he relishes despite having to shorten up here.	12-1	C	toss
#5 Channel Cat	**PACE/PRESSER** His best efforts have come when he is on or just off the lead. Without a lot of pace competition, connections might just send him as they did in that victorious G2 Bowling Green outcome. Is another that would prefer more ground and the top ranked horses in here will be tough to hold off even with the pace advantage.	10-1	C	toss
#10 Mo Forza	**PRESSER** Is clearly the best 3 yr-old turf horse on the West Coast. Picked a tough spot to face older for the first time and has had a long campaign without a break. The goal was to win the G1 Hollywood Derby. He has peaked and the goal is to just pick up a check here.	12-1	C	toss
#9 Next Shares	**OFF PACE/CLOSER** Won last out via the perfect trip against much easier. Got dusted by Without Parole in the BC Mile...pass	30-1	X	toss
#8 Henley's Joy	**OFF PACE** Has had a long campaign without a break. Was no match for Mo Forza. G1 Belmont Derby win was flucky...toss	30-1	X	toss

A/A, A/B and B/A Wagering Strategy	Ticket Cost	Top Long Shots 3rd and 4th Wagering Strategy	Ticket Cost
$10 Exacta Box 3,6,12	$60	$.40 Superfecta 3,6,12 with 2,3,6,7,11,12 with 7,11 with ALL (no 8,9)	$50.40
$10 Exacta 3,6,12 with 2,11	$60	$.40 Superfecta 3,6,12 with 2,3,6,7,11,12 with ALL (no 8,9) with 7,11	$50.40
$1 Trifecta 2,11 with 3,6,12 with ALL (no 8,9)	$48	$.10 Superfecta 2,3,6,7,11,12 with 3,6,12 with 7,11 with ALL (no 8,9)	$16.80
		$.10 Superfecta 2,3,6,7,11,12 with 3,6,12 with ALL (no 8,9) with 7,11	$16.80

Table 26.3. The handicappers rated the Pegasus dirt race.

#	Horse	PSR
1	True Timber	107
2	Tax	115
3	Diamond Oops	118
4	Seeking The Soul	99
5	Omaha Beach	121
6	Higher Power	106
7	War Story	108
8	Mr Freeze	107
10	Mucho Gusto	105
11	Tenfold	98
12	Bodexpress	107

Timeline: 2–10–3
David: tied 2 and 3
DJM: none but 11 is the best closer
Jeremy Plonk: 2, 6, 10
Johnny D: 10, 6, 7
Tyler Frausto: 6, 10,12

12-GP Sat Jan 25, 2020 05:34 PM 9.0D 4up GR1 $3000000 112-113 B-D Vi=32 Q6=4 PL-5 12-GP
FOUR YEAR OLDS AND UPWARD WITH NO RACE DAY MEDICATION.

Pn	PP Horse	SortIndx	MLO	Ag	Ped-St	Ch	Lay Wk	Jockey	--rtg	TJ%	Trainer	--rtg	--TPG	Q	R	E	L	PAC	-PER	--CLASS	(K)	FC	KLine	Pn
5	05 Omaha Bea	109.9282	*1/1	4c	+612	KY LO	028'86+	Smith	374+	29	Mandell	346	B	5	P	8	2	107	109	114+	110+	82*	1.6	|5 |
2	02 Tax	100.5886	8/1	4g	+524	KY LO	056'75	+Ortiz	337		Gargan	358	B+	5	E	7	1*	*110	113*	112+	101+	75	4.2>	|2 |$$
3	03 Diamond	095.6856	15/1	5g	+644	KY LO	035'84*	Leparo	287	10	Biancon	268	C	4	P	4	3	108	112	112+	096	77	6.4>	|3 |$$
10	09 Mucho Gus	093.6076	9/2	4c	+482	KY LO	118'92+	+Ortiz,	378+		Baffert	418+	A	+6	E	9	4	102	106	112+	094	69	9.0	|10|
6	06 Higher Po	088.9305	6/1	5h	+594	KY LO	084'91+	Prat F	402+	25	Sadler	365	B+	4	P	9	6	104	106	109	089	71	14.2	|6 |$$
1	01 True Tim	087.1879	15/1	6h	+506	KY LO	049'75	Bravo	259	09	McLaugh	287	C-	+6	E	*1	9	*110	111	*115+	087	91+	17.4	|1 |$$
8	08 Mr Freez	072.4243	20/1	5h	426	KY LO	057'80*	+Saez L	306	07	Romans	179	C-	+7	F	6	7	107	110	114+	072	84*	50.0	|8 |$
12	11 Bodexpre	070.6063	30/1	4c	390	KY LO	042'78	Jarami	372+	37+	Delgado	339	B	+8	F	2	8	109	111	109	071	69	50.0	|12|$
7	07 War Stor	066.0082	30/1	8g	450	KY LO	042'65	+Rosari	354+		Dobles	246	C	4	P	3	9	108	111	112+	066	65	99.0	|7 |
11	10 Tenfold	061.5078	30/1	5h	+832	KY LO	035'67	#Gaffal	292	14	Asmusse	334	B	0	S	5	9	104	108	110	062	65	99.0	|11|$
4	04 Seeking	053.6787	30/1	7h	442	KY LO	057'91+	+Velazq	332		Stewart	211	C	2	S	9	5	103	107	112+	054	76	99.0	|4 |$$

(K) 5-2-3 Price Play 6 MSpot ~ TSpot ~ Scratches ~

up, many top horses skipped to $3 million dirt race. Mucho Gusto ridden by Irad Oritz, Jr won the race beating Mr Freeze ridden by Luis Saez, see Figure 26.2. The morning line favorite, Omaha Beach, was scratched. The handicappers pretty much had the race figured out, so the betting went well.

Table 26.4. Super screener for the Pegasus dirt.

Gulfstream Park R12: Pegasus World Cup (G1)

Post Time: 5:30 PM ET // Playability Score = 7 (High Payoff Potential)

KEY SCREENING CRITERIA

- Superior Super Screener Energy Reserve Index
- Advantaged by the pace set up
- Balanced Energy Distribution Profile
- Projected progression in form cycle
- Favor pressers and up-close off pace horses
- Last race was a Breeder's Cup Race
- 5 other Super Screener criteria

PACE SET UP

PACE PAR — First Call = **95**; 2nd Call = **106**
PROJECTED — First Call = **95**; 2nd Call = **104**

PACE LEADER(S): #12 Bodexpress, #1 Diamond Oops
PRESSERS: #2 Tax, #8 Mr Freeze, #10 Mucho Gusto

Headliner:

HIGHER POWER

WIN CONTENDERS

Half the field will be running within 2 lengths of one another applying heavy pressure throughout. Pressers or up-close off the pace types have won this race in every one of the previous editions regardless of the pace set up. This will really benefit our top pick **#6 Higher Power.** He exploded for a field best running line in winning the G1 Pacific Classic. He understandably regressed off that huge top and encountered trouble at the gate in his last two starts. Finished a distant 3rd behind Vino Rosso and McKinzie in the BC Classic...a key race that accounted for the last 2 winners of the Pegasus.

With both Omaha Beach and Spun to Run scratched, **#2 Tax** moves up here and becomes an "A" horse. He will benefit from that inside trip tracking a more modest pace now and will have plenty of reserve energy as this one is sitting on a big race off the layoff. Form cycle analysis indicates a significant advancement forward.

VALUE PLAYERS AND LONG SHOTS

#7 War Story is coming into this race the right way and gets plenty of pace pressure to close into. In his best races he lays out energy so evenly and at an elevated level posting nearly 100+ BRIS 2nd Call, Late Call, Speed Rating figures. Looked good prepping last out on this surface and form cycle analysis indicates he will move forward off that last effort. There is no question about his ability to handle this distance as it is right in his wheelhouse. Faces tougher but the set up is favorable.

#11 Tenfold is a little sneaky here as he is another benefactor of the pace set up and he certainly gets this distance. His best race to date was that win the G2 Jim Dandy but after the G3 Pimlico Special win he went off form. However, did show some life in that race off the layoff last out traveling wide but showing a good turn off foot for trainer Steve Asmussen. Could improve off that and make an impact on the Exotics here at a big price.

Race Insights		Key Preps	
Pace: Swift/Strong Pressure	Track Bias: Pressers/Off Pace	Malibu (G1)	Cigar Mile (G1)
Race Shape: Fast/Moderate	Tough Trips: 4,6	BC Classic (G1)	Harlan's Holiday (G3)

2020 Super Screener| superscreener.com

Gulfstream Park R12: Pegasus World Cup (G1)

Post Time: 5:30 PM ET // Playability Score = 7 (High Payoff Potential)

Horse	Comments	Odds	Rank	Multi-race
#6 Higher Power	**TOP VALUE/OFF PACE** That Pacific Classic running line is the best of any horse in this race. Encountered trouble leaving the gate in his two follow up efforts costing him a few lengths. Was distanced by Vino Rosso and McKinzie in the BC Classic but finished a solid 3rd. With a clean break will secure a great stalking trip. Speed comes back to him.	3-1	A	must
#5 Om[illegible] Scratch	**PRESSER/OFF PACE** No horse is coming into this race better than this one. He is training brilliantly and poised to pop a new [illegible] his swan song race. Added ground will be [illegible] Scratch [illegible] pace/pressers 3 lengths back and [illegible] this fighter with a lot of heart will lay down the gauntlet [illegible] very tough to catch. Top win contender.	Scratch		must
#2 Tax	**PRESSER/OFF PACE** Really needed that break after the G1 Travers. Showed a different dimension in the come back race which will serve him well here given all the speed that has signed on. Will really pop forward with a big race 2nd off the layoff.	5-1	A	must
#7 War Story	**TOP LONG SHOT/TOP BOARD HITTER/CLOSER** Likely to get overlooked in the wagering to our benefit as this race couldn't set up any better for this horse who won his prep on this track in good order nearly laying out BRIS 2nd Call, Late Pace and Speed Rating of 100+. Moves forward 2nd off the layoff. Offers tremendous value.	20-1	B	if spreading
#9 Spu[illegible] Scratch	**PRESSER** Has been brilliant as of late and deadly at 1 mile. He's had a long campaign and form cycle analysis indicates no [illegible] here. This distance remains a question Scratch [illegible] further on this surface and he own superior pace figures over his other rivals. Pace set up works against him so while there is a slight win chance, better used under.	Scratch		if spreading
#10 Mucho Gusto	**PRESSER** Baffert was debating to send this one and with good reason as the swift pressured pace and 1 1/8 miles works against him. He was clearly Baffert's "C" horse on the Ky Derby trail last spring and is now a "B" horse going shorter.	4-1	B	if spreading
#8 Mr Freeze	**PRESSER** Will certainly be part of the pace mix. He can get this distance but has yet to come close to that break out performance in the West Virginia Derby a year and a half ago. Last 3 races were solid but all about the same. Use under.	15-1	B	toss
#3 Diamond Oops	**PACE** Has been crushing it going sprint distances but has yet to make an impact going a route of ground let alone 1 1/8 miles against tougher. Will be on or near the lead with plenty of other speed types so that pace set up does not work in his favor.	10-1	B	if spreading
#11 Tenfold	**TOP LONG SHOT/CLOSER** This Asmussen-trained horse went off form after that Pimlico Special win but returned last out to finish well against easier. Pace sets up for this horse that doles out sustained energy over 1 1/8+ distances. Gets a piece at a price.	30-1	C	toss
#4 Seeking the Soul	**CLOSER** Finished 2nd in the slop in this race last year passing horses that were tiring trying to chase down the winner, City of Light. Gets a similar pace set up here but just not coming into this race like he was last year. Could clunk up for 3rd or 4th.	20-1	C	toss
#1 True Timber	**OFF PACE** Was the Super Screener Top Long Shot pick last out playing into a previous pattern and he hit the Trifecta at 32-1 finishing behind Maximum Security. Typically regresses off those tops and the added ground will cause a problem for him.	20-1	X	toss
#12 Bodexpress	**PACE** Will strike to the front but will be hounded throughout by other pace/presser types. Runs fast early then fades late.	20-1	X	toss

A/A, A/B and B/A Wagering Strategy	Ticket Cost	Top Long Shots 3rd and 4th Wagering Strategy	Ticket Cost
$20 Exacta Box 2,6	$40	$5 Trifecta 2,6 with 2,3,6,8,10 with 7	$40
$15 Exacta 2,6 with 7	$30	$2 Trifecta 2,3,6,8,10 with 2,6 with 7	$35
$6 Exacta 2,6 with 3,8,10	$36	$.50 Superfecta 2,6 with 2,6,7,10 with ALL with 7,11	$35
$10 Exacta 7 with 2,6	$20		
$1 Trifecta 3,8,10 with 2,6 with ALL (no1,12)	$36	**BONUS:** $1 High Five 2,6 with 2,3,6,7 with 2,3,6,7,10 with ALL with 11	$108

Saturday, January 25, 2020

11 Gulfstream Park
1 3/16 Miles Turf
Stakes Grade 1 4yo+

Pegasus World Cup Turf Invitational S. presented by Runhappy
FOUR YEAR OLDS AND UPWARD WITH NO RACE DAY MEDICATION.

Purse : $1,000,000 Available Money : $1,000,000 Distributed Money : $1,000,000
Off at 5:00 firm / clear Run Up : 19 ft Rails : 96 ft
Par Time : 1:52.21 3 Year Best Time : 1:51.40 Projected Winning Time : 1:50.34
Fractions : 24.06 48.45 1:11.94 1:34.82 Final Time : 1:51.60
Splits : (24.39) (23.49) (22.88) (16.78)

SC	Horse	Earnings	Foal	A/S	Med	Wt	Eq	H Wt	Claim $	F1	F2	F3	Final	PP	St	1/4	1/2	3/4	Str	Fin	Comment	Odds
1	Zulu Alpha	$531,000	KY	7/m		124		1225		24.68	49.23	1:12.73	1:51.60	1	4	103¼	94¼	104¼	3½	12	settled,rail bid,clear	11.80
12	Magic Wand (IRE)	$177,000	IRE	5/f		119		1040		24.06	48.45	1:11.94	1:51.96	12	8	1½	1hd	11	1hd	22	pressured pace,outkikd	3.70
6	Instilled Regard	$88,500	KY	5/m		124		1116		24.43	48.76	1:12.32	1:52.00	6	1	52	51¾	52	4¾	32¼	in range,ins1/4,3-4wd	10.10
11	Sacred Life (FR)	$44,250	FR	5/m		124		1065		24.15	48.86	1:12.43	1:52.54	11	7	2½	62¼	72¾	73¾	45¼	swung wide,imprved	12.10
2	Arklow	$26,550	KY	6/m		124		1206		24.58	49.33	1:12.53	1:52.56	2	5	92¾	104¾	83¼	63¾	55¼	bump st,steady early	9.50
4	Sadler's Joy	$25,000	KY	7/m		124		1133		25.47	49.71	1:12.92	1:52.58	4	12	127¼	126¾	115¼	94	65½	bump back st,wide str	10.90
8	Henley's Joy	$25,000	KY	4/m		124	b	1066		24.24	48.47	1:12.14	1:52.59	8	2	31	2hd	31	2hd	75½	stalk,duel tn,gaveway	29.60
7	Admission Office	$15,000	KY	5/m		124	b	1152		24.56	49.04	1:12.71	1:52.77	7	3	82¾	83¼	94¼	114½	86½	2wd 1/4p,trafic,no kik	22.00
10	Mo Forza	$25,000	KY	4/m		124	b	1196		24.45	48.95	1:12.23	1:52.82	10	11	62	72¾	41½	52¼	96¾	6w 1st,midpack,bid,wkn	4.50
5	Channel Cat	$25,000	KY	5/m		124		1038		25.07	49.62	1:13.01	1:53.04	5	10	115¼	116¼	125¾	104½	108	bump start,no rally	12.80
3	Without Parole (GB)	$0	GB	5/m		124		1049		24.47	48.67	1:12.42	1:53.06	3	9	72¼	41¼	62½	84	118	in range,urgd tn,wknd	3.40
9	Next Shares	$0	KY	7/m		124	b	1189		24.34	48.49	1:12.12	1:53.80	9	6	41½	3nk	21	125	1212	track pace,faded str	54.60

1	**Zulu Alpha**	**$25.60**	**$11.40**	**$7.60**
12	**Magic Wand (IRE)**		**$5.40**	**$3.80**
6	**Instilled Regard**			**$6.60**

WPS Pool : $1,798,565

$1.00	**Daily Double**	**11-1**	**$573.90**	**$184,678**
$1.00	**Exacta**	**1-12**	**$88.30**	**$1,171,448**
$0.50	**Pick 3 (3 right)**	**11-11-1**	**$2,692.35**	**$118,086**
$2.00	**Quinella**	**1-12**	**$85.60**	**$25,976**
$0.10	**Superfecta**	**1-12-6-11**	**$765.42**	**$389,405**
$0.50	**Trifecta**	**1-12-6**	**$420.40**	**$729,691**
$1.00	**X-5 Super Hi 5**	**1-12-6-11-2**		**$28,923**

Scratches.... 13 Tusk (AE) - Trained by Saffie A. Joseph, Jr.

SC	Horse	Jockey	Trainer	Owner	Last Raced		Fin
1	Zulu Alpha	Tyler Gaffalione	Michael J. Maker	Michael M. Hui	02Nov 19	SA 11	4
12	Magic Wand (IRE)	Ryan L. Moore	Aidan P. O'Brien	Tabor, Michael B., Magnier, Mrs. John, and Smith, Derrick	08Dec 19	ST	2
6	Instilled Regard	Irad Ortiz, Jr.	Chad C. Brown	OXO Equine LLC	14Dec 19	GP 9	1
11	Sacred Life (FR)	Jose L. Ortiz	Chad C. Brown	Dubb, Michael, Madaket Stables LLC, Wonder Stables and Bethlehem Stables LLC	30Nov 19	DMR 6	2
2	Arklow	Luis Saez	Brad H. Cox	Donegal Racing, Bulger, Joseph and Coneway, Peter	02Nov 19	SA 11	8
4	Sadler's Joy	Javier Castellano	Thomas Albertrani	Woodslane Farm	23Nov 19	AQU 9	1
8	Henley's Joy	Julien R. Leparoux	Michael J. Maker	Bloom Racing Stable LLC (Jeffrey Bloom)	30Nov 19	DMR 8	8
7	Admission Office	Flavien Prat	Brian A. Lynch	Amerman Racing LLC	14Dec 19	GP 9	2
10	Mo Forza	Joel Rosario	Peter Miller	Bardy Farm and OG Boss	28Dec 19	SA 10	1
5	Channel Cat	John R. Velazquez	Todd A. Pletcher	Calumet Farm	14Dec 19	GP 9	3
3	Without Parole (GB)	Lanfranco Dettori	Chad C. Brown	Gunther, John D. and Gunther, Tanya	02Nov 19	SA 9	3
9	Next Shares	Jose Valdivia, Jr.	Richard Baltas	Baltas, Debby, Baltas, Richard, Dunn, Christopher T., Iavarone, Jules, Iavarone,	30Nov 19	DMR 6	1

ZULU ALPHA was allowed to settle out of the gate then steadied along inside nearing the first turn, secured inside position and settled nicely off the early pace, was patiently handled entering the far turn then hustled up near the quarter pole, cut the corner entering the lane, came under right handed pressure along the rail upper stretch, kicked in gamely up the inside, seized command

Chart for Jan 25 2020 GP Race 11 Page 19 Data as of 01/28/2020 17:26:05 R2

from MAGIC WAND near the furlong marker and drew clear. MAGIC WAND (IRE) cleared on top out of the gate and crossed over to the inside, secured inside position and set a pressured pace down the backstretch, vied for the lead racing inside of HANLEY'S JOY around the final turn, dug in gamely and held a slim lead upper stretch, got collared by the winner near the furlong marker but stayed on game to hold place. INSTILLED REGARD was forwardly placed out of the gate then settled and raced in range through middle stages, positioned as a sharp factor while patiently handled along the inside around the far turn, tipped out turning for home, put to a drive three to our wide and stayed on with response to clear share. SACRED LIFE (FR) raced near midpack between foes going by the half mile marker, lodged a bid moving through the far turn then swung out wider into upper stretch, remained in pursuit under steady pressure along the outside and improved position. ARKLOW got bumped a step out of the gate then steadied racing two wide nearing the first turn, settled off the early pace then launched an outside bid entering the far turn, coaxed five to six wide in stretch run and needed more for late impact. SADLER'S JOY got bumped back between foes and lost ground at the start, continued unhurried down the backstretch, picked up the pace along the outside around the far turn, raced extremely wide and lost ground entering upper stretch then gained a few spots. HENLEY'S JOY was forwardly placed and stalked the pacesetter down the backstretch, prompted and advanced to duel for the lead with MAGIC WAND around the far turn, remained up close upper stretch then gave way in the final furlong. ADMISSION OFFICE raced three wide entering the first turn then settled off the early pace, moved through the far turn two wide, hit some traffic top stretch then switched out wider and failed to kick on. MO FORZA fanned out six wide entering the first turn, rated along the outside near midpack down the backstretch, was ridden along four wide positioned in range around the far turn then failed to sustain bid in the lane. CHANNEL CAT got bumped steps out of the gate, was unhurried racing two to three wide down the backstretch, saved ground and urged for response along the rail in the far turn but failed to threaten. WITHOUT PAROLE (GB) got bumped a step out of the gate, moved up to race in range mid-pack at the half mile marker then launched a bid entering the far turn, failed to gain closer contention then gave way. NEXT SHARES raced five wide entering the first turn, tracked the pace to the far turn, remained in close contention entering the turn then put to a drive but had no response when called upon.

Figure 26.1. Chart for the Pegasus grass.

26.2. The Saudi Cup

The inaugural Saudi Cup was held at King Abdulaziz racetrack in Riyadh, Saudi Arabia on February 29, 2020. The top older US horses were invited and the terms were very generous with all expenses paid and a US$20+ million purse with no entry fees. Given the large amount of money involved, many of the top US horses skipped the Pegasus — now $3 million down from $7, $16 and $12 million in previous years plus high entry fees to come here. So Maximum Security, Tacitus, the mare Midnight Bisou and McKinzie went to Saudi Arabia. Also Mucho Gusto who won the Pegasus was there. It was thought that he beat a weak Pegasus field but he won and he, like

Saturday, January 25, 2020

12 **Gulfstream Park**
1 1/8 Miles Dirt
Stakes Grade 1 4yo+

Pegasus World Cup Invitational S. presented by Runhappy
FOUR YEAR OLDS AND UPWARD WITH NO RACE DAY MEDICATION.

Purse : $3,000,000 Available Money : $3,000,000 Distributed Money : $3,000,000
Off at 5:47 fast / clear Run Up : 70 ft
Par Time : 1:47.95 3 Year Best Time : 1:47.41 Projected Winning Time : 1:46.69
Fractions : 23.77 47.78 1:11.84 1:35.83 Final Time : 1:48.85
Splits : (24.01) (24.06) (23.99) (13.02)

SC	Horse	Earnings	Foal	A/S	Med	Wt	Eq	H Wt	Claim $
10	Mucho Gusto	$1,662,000	KY	4/m		124	b	1201	
8	Mr Freeze	$554,000	KY	5/m		124		1051	
7	War Story	$277,000	KY	8/m		124		1127	
3	Diamond Oops	$138,500	KY	5/m		124	b	1155	
12	Bodexpress	$83,100	KY	4/m		124		1111	
11	Tenfold	$50,000	KY	5/m		124		1169	
4	Seeking the Soul	$50,000	KY	7/m		124		1076	
1	True Timber	$30,000	KY	6/m		124		1153	
2	Tax	$50,000	KY	4/m		124		1206	
6	Higher Power	$50,000	KY	5/m		124	b	1217	

SC	Horse	F1	F2	F3	Final	PP	St	1/4	1/2	3/4	Str	Fin	Comment	Odds
10	Mucho Gusto	23.97	48.16	1:12.30	1:48.85	8	1	31	42	32½	12½	14½	led early,rebid3wd,drv	3.40
8	Mr Freeze	23.77	47.78	1:11.84	1:49.68	7	8	11	11	1½	22½	24½	pressured,dug in place	7.30
7	War Story	25.78	50.10	1:14.03	1:49.82	6	10	1010¼	1012¼	1011¾	58	35¼	slow st, angled widest	15.60
3	Diamond Oops	24.17	48.35	1:12.67	1:49.96	3	2	52¼	53	54½	46	46	advncd ins 1/4, evenly	5.70
12	Bodexpress	23.95	47.96	1:11.93	1:50.10	10	3	21	21	2½	33½	56¾	keyed up,2wdbid, faded	12.40
11	Tenfold	25.06	49.22	1:12.89	1:50.81	9	4	96¾	97¾	85¾	69½	610½	mild advance,flttn out	38.00
4	Seeking the Soul	24.67	49.20	1:13.08	1:50.95	4	5	84¾	87½	96¾	710½	711¼	jostled erly,no factor	17.90
1	True Timber	24.65	48.72	1:12.87	1:51.19	1	6	74¾	75	75½	810½	812½	early bumps, tired 6f	18.50
2	Tax	24.27	48.44	1:12.68	1:51.72	2	7	62¾	63½	64½	912½	915¼	stumbled st,3-5w,tired	4.30
6	Higher Power	23.99	48.15	1:12.39	1:52.50	5	9	41¼	32	43	1014½	1019¼	driven4wd, no response	2.80

		Win	Place	Show
10	**Mucho Gusto**	**$8.80**	**$5.00**	**$3.80**
8	**Mr Freeze**		**$7.60**	**$5.20**
7	**War Story**			**$6.80**

WPS Pool : $2,678,927

$1.00	**Daily Double**	**1-10**	**$84.40**	**$832,151**
$1.00	**Exacta**	**10-8**	**$39.10**	**$1,723,120**
$0.50	**Pick 3 (3 right)**	**11-1-10**	**$1,528.85**	**$541,687**
$0.50	**Pick 4 (4 right)**	**11-11-1-10**	**$12,082.85**	**$1,357,438**
$0.50	**Pick 5 (4 right)**	**4-11-11-1-10**	**$217.85**	
$0.50	**Pick 5 (5 right)**	**4-11-11-1-10**	**$74,735.90**	**$1,289,664**
$0.20	**Pick 6 Jackpot (6 right)**	**5-4-11-11-1-10**	**$394,349.13**	**$1,408,825**
$2.00	**Quinella**	**8-10**	**$48.80**	**$34,310**
$1.00	**Super High 5**	**10-8-7-3-12**	**$47,509.00**	**$168,386**
$0.10	**Superfecta**	**10-8-7-3**	**$334.98**	**$680,254**
$0.50	**Trifecta**	**10-8-7**	**$222.40**	**$1,229,822**

Scratches.... 5 Omaha Beach (Trainer) - Trained by Richard E. Mandella
Spun to Run (Trainer)

SC	Horse	Jockey	Trainer	Owner	Last Raced	Fin
10	Mucho Gusto	Irad Ortiz, Jr.	Bob Baffert	HRH Prince Faisal Bin Khaled	29Sep 19 RP 12	4
8	Mr Freeze	Luis Saez	Dale L. Romans	Bakke, Jim and Isbister, Gerald	29Nov 19 CD 11	3
7	War Story	Joel Rosario	Elizabeth L. Dobles	Imaginary Stables and Ellis, Glenn	14Dec 19 GP 10	1
3	Diamond Oops	Julien R. Leparoux	Patrick L. Biancone	Diamond 100 Racing Club, LLC, Dunne, Amy E., D P Racing LLC and Patrick L. Bianc	21Dec 19 GP 10	1
12	Bodexpress	Emisael Jaramillo	Gustavo Delgado	Top Racing, LLC, Global Thoroughbred and GDS Racing Stable	14Dec 19 GP 10	3
11	Tenfold	Tyler Gaffalione	Steven M. Asmussen	Winchell Thoroughbreds LLC	21Dec 19 FG 12	4
4	Seeking the Soul	John R. Velazquez	Dallas Stewart	Charles E. Fipke	29Nov 19 CD 11	6
1	True Timber	Joe Bravo	Kiaran P. McLaughlin	Calumet Farm	07Dec 19 AQU 10	3
2	Tax	Jose L. Ortiz	Danny Gargan	R. A. Hill Stable, Reeves Thoroughbred Racing, Lynch, Hugh and Corms Racing Stab	30Nov 19 AQU 8	2
6	Higher Power	Flavien Prat	John W. Sadler	Hronis Racing LLC	02Nov 19 SA 12	3

MUCHO GUSTO broke to the lead and moved inward, deferred around the first turn content to follow along from close range, was guided out three wide midway on the far turn, responded readily

Chart for Jan 25 2020 GP Race 12 Page 21 Data as of 01/28/2020 17:26:05 R2

to overtake MR FREEZE and BODEXPRESS from outside at the top of the stretch, and drew well clear under a drive. MR FREEZE was crowded a bit by MUCHO GUSTO at the break, went into the first turn in the six-path before moving inward and coming away with the lead before completing the first quarter-mile, moved inside cutting an even pace through the middle stages, fended off a challenge from BODEXPRESS around the far turn, could not cope with the winner into the lane and dug in to save the place. WAR STORY was slow into stride and taken over to the rail after the start, trailed for six furlongs saving ground, angled to the far outside leaving the far turn and rallied steadily to get up for third. DIAMOND OOPS saved ground early under a firm hold, moved off the rail entering the backstretch, advanced mildly in the two-path after six furlongs, moved further out in the stretch and finished evenly. BODEXPRESS became keyed up vying up front into th first turn between horses, tugged along pressing MR FREEZE up the backstretch, challenged sternly after six furlongs, but weakened at the top of the stretch and faded late. TENFOLD was six wide going to the first turn before moving inward, advanced mildly after six furlongs two then three wide on the far turn, and flattened out. SEEKING THE SOUL got jostled around between horses four then three wide into the first turn, and never became a factor. TRUE TIMBER exchanged light bumps and brushes with TAX into the first turn, lagged in the second flight two wide, moved inside and dropped back after six furlongs. TAX stumbled at the start, bumped and brushed lightly with TRUE TIMBER into the first turn, settled in the middle of the field three wide for six furlongs, and faded steadily in the five-path into the stretch. HIGHER POWER was forwardly placed four then three wide on the first turn, came under a ride past the half-mile pole attempting to keep pace with the leaders, but had little to offer and began dropping back steadily between horses outside the quarter-pole.

Figure 26.2. Chart for the Pegasus dirt.

McKinzie, is a Baffert horse, so a contender. The full day had purses of US$29 million, similar to the Breeders' Cup and the Dubai World Cup.

I was betting at the RGS rebate shop plus on Betfair UK. RGS has live stream video. Races like this can be seen also on TVG, Fox Sports 1, and for those without access to that, inexpensive monthly packages are available from flowsports.tv. I had access to Super Screener and horseracingnation.com's analysis and picks, past performances and plus my own analysis (Figures 26.3 and 26.4). Twinspires.com is a good user friendly site with good video plus easy to bet software. There are no rebates but there are some betting bonuses.

A number of the horses were European or Japanese, and basically unknown except for their records. See the Appendix for the past performances.

Super Screener had As: 10 Mucho Gusto, 12 Tacitus and 13 Midnight Bisou Bs: 8 McKinzie, 7 Maximum Security and the Japanese horse 3 Chysoberyl

I did like these horses but felt Maximum Security, the track favorite, was the best, followed by McKinzie. After the Derby DQ that really was not justified, Maximum Security has won a number of top races and McKinzie has been first or second in 13 of 14 starts at the top level.

I also liked Benbatl, a UK based horse who was 7–1 in the Morning Line, 13–1 track odds and 26–1 area on Betfair and horseracingnation.com's top pick.

So on Betfair, to be simple, I just went long all these horses to win in such a way that if any of them won, there would be a net gain. It is actually optimal in most cases to short all the horses to win that are unfavorable as only one can win. These Betfair and track odds shown here in Figures 26.5 and 26.6 were those near the end of the betting period. Remember that Betfair odds are locked in prices when you wager as a match against another bettor and the track odds are parimutuel so change until the end of betting. So you could bet Maximum Security at 4–1 UK odds, 3–1 US on Betfair versus about even money or 6–5 at the track odds.

It is interesting how much risk arbitrage was in these prices. I just did a little. When Maximum Security won I had a small gain in Betfair. It is small because I lost the other wagers.

The finish of the $1\frac{1}{8}$ mile race in 1:50.59 was Maximum Security at 6–5, Midnight Bisou at 8–1, Benbatl at 13–1, and Mucho Gusto at 6–1. Tacitus failed again at fifth place and McKinzie at 7–2 was eighth, see Figure 26.7

The track payoffs were

7	4.40	3.40	2.80
14		8.00	4.00
1			9.00

Exacta 7–14 paid 22.40 for $1
Trifecta 7–14–1 paid 241.90 for $1
Superfecta 7–14–1–10 paid 1217.70 for $1

My on-track bets were:
⑦–8–10/7–8–10–12–⑭/①–6–7–8–10–12–14
this $3 exacta cost $36 and the $1 trifecta cost $60 and won the exacta and trifecta

King Abdulaziz Racecourse R8: The Saudi Cup

Post Time: 12:40 PM ET // Playability Score = 7 (High Payoff Potential)

KEY SCREENING CRITERIA

- Superior Super Screener Energy Reserve Index
- Advantaged by the pace set up
- **Balanced Energy Distribution Profile**
- Anticipated move forward in form cycle
- Strong record the the local track
- Speed dropping from longer races
- 5 other Super Screener criteria

PACE SET UP

PACE PAR — First Call = ? 2nd Call = ?
PROJECTED — First Call = 98; 2nd Call = 109

PACE LEADER(S): #7 Maximum Security, #11 North America
PRESSERS: #1 Bentbatl, #2 Capezzano, #4 Gold Dream, #5 Great Scot, #8 McKinzie, #13 Magic Wand

Headliner:

Mucho Gusto

WIN CONTENDERS

With no race history, we're using screening criteria from top G1 US dirt races. Pace projects to be quite hot here and that is bad news for the forwardly placed types because unlike US dirt tracks in which you can expect up to 70% of winners to be on the lead or stalking, on this dirt course, horses coming from off the pace win about half the time according to Bob Turman, King Abdulaziz **Racecourse's Track Superintendent. Since this surface plays more than fair and** we have a ferociously pressured pace set up with 8 runners pushing each other through brisk and pressured fractions, give more consideration to runners that can close from off the pace. #10 Mucho Gusto is just getting good at the right **time and has really filled out now. His last race was his best as he laid out 100+** BRIS Pace/Speed Ratings in the last 3 slots with a crushing 117 in the Late Pace category. Traveled well and has been working super since the Pegasus win. Like **how he is finally able to relax off the pace now...the perfect tactic to deploy** here to get the win. #12 Tacitus is sort of the forgotten horse now as he always came up just short against other G1 company after the impressive Wood **Memorial win. He's a much bigger and stronger horse now and is just gliding** over this race surface. He is ready for a peak effort right off the bench. Will take back and run 4 to 5 lengths off the heated battle up front and then proceed with vigorous energy to the wire as he gets back to the distance he prefers. Watch out for #14 Midnight Bisou for she is working up a storm in preparation for this and is ready for another peak effort off her good BC distaff effort. No horse will be more advantaged by the pace set up than this one.

VALUE PLAYERS AND LONG SHOTS

We have extolled the virtues of our Top Long Shot pick, #12 Tacitus and our Top Value selections #10 Mucho Gusto and #14 Midnight Bisou **...with all three horses earning the Super Screener "A" designation. Now, for the** bottom of those Trifecta tickets and, even more so, your Superfecta wagers. Give #6 Gronkowski a look especially if M/L odds hold around 30-1. This **distance is a bit too short for him but we are not thinking he'll crack the** Exacta, however, this closer has run primarily on speed favoring surfaces (especially true for the Meydan dirt course in Dubai). In addition, he has been the victim of slow pace set ups for the vast majority of his starts. Gets the desired hot and pressured pace here on a surface that does not penalize his late engine.

#9 Mjjack is a local star having won his last 5 races including the Group 1 **affair on this surface earlier this month. He faces infinitely tougher here but these "horse for course" types can often hit the bottom of the Superfecta at** monster odds. Will sit off the pace and continue on with interest and one of the few in here who avoided overseas travel.

Race Insights

Pace Swift/Heavy Pressure Track Bias: Off pace

Race Shape: Fast/Slow Tough Trips: 2,4,5,6

Key Preps

Pegasus World Cup (G1) Cigar Mile (G1)

BC Distaff (G1) Jockey Club Gold Cup (G1)

2020 Super Screener| superscreener.com

King Abdulaziz Racecourse R8: The Saudi Cup

Post Time: 12:40 PM ET // Playability Score = 7 (High Payoff Potential)

Horse	Comments	Odds	Rank	Multi-race use
#10 Mucho Gusto	TOP VALUE/PRESSER **Is the "now" horse getting really good at the right time. Runaway winner of a weak edition of the G1** Pegasus World Cup but he did it the right way sitting patiently off the pace and then exploded down the lane in very fast time.	6-1	A	must
#12 Tacitus	TOP LONG SHOT/CLOSER **Will love this very neutral dirt course and this closer couldn't ask for a better pace set up as a ton of** speed up front will start coming back to him late. This is his ideal distance. Pressed in the last two but will sit back some here.	15-1	A	must
#14 Midnight Bisou	TOP VALUE/TOP BOARD HITTER/OFF PACE Talented mare has yet to miss the Trifecta in 19 starts and 6 tries as this distance. Will be patiently ridden by Mike Smith with plenty of pace to close into on a surface that plays very fair. Runs well off a layoff.	8-1	A	must
#8 McKinzie	PRESSER Is 13 for 14 in the Exacta competing against the best dirt runners in the world. Will appreciate the cut back in **distance and runs well off these breaks. Seems like he was better at Saratoga and Churchill Downs so he'll like this surface.**	3-1	B	logical
#3 Chrysoberyl	OFF PACE Japan-based, 4 yr-old colt is undefeated in 6 starts with most of those victories coming as blow away wins. The most impressive score was the one notched in the Japan Dirt Derby back in July. Bigger now and very powerful. Pace advantaged.	10-1	B	if spreading
#7 Maximum Security	VULNERABLE FAVE/PACE Hard to argue with that nearly perfect record in 9 starts. His last race, the G1 Cigar Mile, was clearly his best. However, #10 Mucho Gusto is a much better horse than when he faced him last and those ranked above are very tough.Target on back.	5-2	B	if spreading
#6 Gronkowsky	TOP LONG SHOT/CLOSER Needs longer but should relish this dirt course and the swift and pressured pace really works to his favor as he has raced primarily on speed-favoring surfaces which is especially true for the Meydan dirt surface. Use under.	30-1	C	toss
#9 Mjjack	TOP LONG SHOT/PRESSER/OFF PACE This horse for course has won his last 5 including the Group 1 affair last out. Faces a whole **other kind here but don't underestimate the value of strong performances on the local course and no travel required. Use!**	60-1	C	toss
#13 Magic Wand	PRESSER Wow! Talk about a work horse! This sturdy mare has raced an incredible 10 times in the past 6 months and sometimes **twice a month as she just did in January. Really tough spot to now try dirt for the first time and her pressing style doesn't help.**	30-1	C	toss
#4 Gold Dream	PRESSER Very consistent 7 yr-old based in Japan has not missed the Superfecta in his last 10 starts and while he narrowly missed to #3 Chrysoberyl two back it was clear the latter horse was much the best. Will make a good showing of himself.	30-1	C	toss
#1 Benbatl	PRESSER Several wins are surrounded by real duds with most of his running coming on the turf. Took advantage of the speed-favoring Meydan dirt course last out when dusting #6 Gronkowski and 8 others. Faces a whole different surface and set up.	7-1	C	toss
#2 Capezzano	PACE/PRESSER **Loves the speedy Meydan surface and will win when facing much easier. Super tall order here...pass.**	10-1	X	toss
#11 North America	PACE This Dubai-based 8 yr-old gelding still can deliver against easier but he is at his best when on the lone lead and he **certainly won't get that advantage here. Adds to the already contentious pace. Will not like the "fairer" dirt surface.**	30-1	X	toss

A/A, A/B, B/A Wagering Strategy	Ticket Cost	Top Long Shot 1st, 2nd, 3rd Wagering Strategy	Ticket Cost
$10 Exacta Box 10,12,14	$60	$12 Exacta 12 with 3,7,8,10,14	$60
$1 Trifecta 10,12,14 with 3,7,8 with 3,6,7,8,9,10,12,14	$54	$8 Exacta 3,7,8,10,14 with 12	$40
.50 Trifecta 3,7,8 with 10,12,14 with 3,6,7,8,9,10,12,14	$27	$2 Trifecta 3,7,8,10,14 with 3,7,8,10,14 with 12	$40
SAVER: $5 Exacta Box 3,7,8	$30	BONUS: $.20 Superfecta 10,12,14 with 3,7,8,10,12,14 with ALL (no 2,5,11) with 6,9	$48

Figure 26.3. Super screener analysis, Saudi Cup.

Pgm	PP	Horse	Sex/Age	Equip	Wgt	Jockey	Trainer	Odds	Earnings	Last 3 Fin
Race 8 PT 12:40pm ET Purse $20,781,500.				Win, Place, Swinger, Exacta, Trifecta, Quartet						
										One And One Eighth Miles
1		BENBATL (GB)	B.h.6		126	O Murphy	Saeed bin Suroor	7-1		1-1-16
2		CAPEZZANO (USA)	B.g.6		126	M Barzalona	S Bin Ghadayer	10-1		1-12-1
3		CHRYSOBERYL (JPN)	B.c.4		126	C Soumillon	H Otonashi	10-1		1-1-1
4		GOLD DREAM (JPN)	B.h.7		126	C Lemaire	O Hirata	30-1		4-2-3
5		GREAT SCOT (GB)	B.g.4		126	A Moreno	Mishrif	60-1		1-4-11
6		GRONKOWSKI (USA)	B.h.5		126	L Dettori	S Bin Ghadayer	30-1		3-3-2
7		MAXIMUM SECURITY (USA)	B.c.4		126	Luis Saez	Jason Servis	5-2		1-1-1
8		MCKINZIE (USA)	B.h.5		126	J Rosario	Bob Baffert	3-1		2-2-1
9		MJJACK (IRE)	Gr.h.6		126	A Aloufi	S Al Harabi	60-1		1-3-6
10		MUCHO GUSTO (USA)	Ch.c.4		126	I Ortiz Jr	Bob Baffert	6-1		1-4-3
11		NORTH AMERICA (GB)	B.g.8		126	R Mullen	S Seemar	30-1		3-7-1
12		TACITUS (USA)	Gr/ro.c.4		126	J Lezcano	William Mott	15-1		3-2-2
13		MAGIC WAND (IRE)	B.m.5		121	R L Moore	Aidan O'Brien	30-1		2-4-2
14		MIDNIGHT BISOU (USA)	Dk b/br.m.5		121	M Smith	Steven Asmussen	8-1		2-1-1
15		STAUNCH (GB)	B.h.7		126	Reserve	Naif Almandeel			2-3-2
						SELECTIONS: 1- 12- 2				

Figure 26.4. horseracingnation.com analysis for the Saudi Cup.

17:40 Riyadh
Sat 29 Feb | 1m1f Grd1

Live Stream Radio Tote Multiples

Win Place

Going In-Play i Rules Pin Betfair SP [?] Matched: GBP 33,642 Refresh

15 selections	105.2%		Back all	Lay all		98.4%
7 (7) Maximum Security Luis Saez £130.00	3.7 £114	3.75 £3	3.8 £424	3.85 £26	3.9 £85	3.95 £303
8 (9) Mckinzie Joel Rosario £25.00	6 £178	6.2 £116	6.4 £15	6.8 £4	7 £7	8 £2
1 (3) Benbatl Oisin Murphy £58.48	7.8 £38	8 £147	8.2 £10	8.4 £61	8.6 £67	8.8 £9
10 (8) Mucho Gusto Irad Ortiz, Jr -£30.00	8.8 £26	9 £111	9.2 £37	9.8 £14	10 £27	10.5 £24
3 (10) Chrysoberyl Christophe Soumillon -£270.00	10 £9	10.5 £212	11 £64	11.5 £109	12 £79	12.5 £48
12 (2) Tacitus Jose Lezcano £30.00	11 £24	11.5 £47	12 £22	13 £24	13.5 £4	14 £50
2 (13) Capezzano Mickael Barzalona -£270.00	17.5 £47	18.5 £13	19 £20	20 £3	21 £5	26 £6
14 (6) Midnight Bisou Mike E. Smith £105.00	25 £2	28 £42	29 £3	34 £7	80 £2	
6 (5) Gronkowski Frankie Dettori -£270.00	1.06 £2	14.5 £6	22 £10	27 £45	29 £4	30 £18
13 (12) Magic Wand Ryan Moore -£270.00	32 £23	34 £4	36 £2	42 £4	44 £8	46 £9
11 (4) North America Richard Mullen -£270.00	50 £24	55 £17	60 £6	70 £3	75 £7	80 £2
4 (1) Gold Dream Christophe-Patrice Lemaire -£270.00	40 £13	42 £5	44 £5	50 £5	60 £24	75 £2
9 (14) Mjjack Abdullah Aloufi -£270.00	75 £3	90 £7	100 £11	140 £2	150 £3	180 £7
5 (11) Great Scot Alexis Moreno -£270.00	100 £19	110 £4	120 £4	160 £2	180 £2	
15 Staunch Reserve -£270.00	1.05 £2	1.21 £2	100 £10	230 £2	240 £2	470 £3

Figure 26.5. Betfair odds for the Saudi Cup.

1 1/8 MILE STAKES DIRT AGE: 4 YEAR OLDS AND UP PURSE: 20781500.00 Ref

	#	Name	Odds	ML	Rank	WIN PRICE	WIN	PLC	SHW
L1		Total Wagered This Race: $0.00					$178,092	$49,649	$23,117
1	1	BENBATL (GB)	33	7		$34.30	4,150	1,076	547
2	2	CAPEZZANO (USA)	112	10		$113.10	1,259	333	442
3	3	CHRYSOBERYL (JPN)	30	10		$31.80	4,475	1,533	800
4	4	GOLD DREAM (JPN)	137	30		$138.00	1,032	383	243
5	5	GREAT SCOT (GB)	236	60		$237.70	599	216	214
6	6	GRONKOWSKI (USA)	22	30		$23.50	6,062	2,871	2,186
7	7	MAXIMUM SECURITY (	4/5	5/2	1	$1.80	75,635	14,133	3,962
8	8	MCKINZIE (USA)	5	3	3	$6.20	22,729	4,599	2,936
9	9	MJJACK (IRE)	166	60		$167.80	849	517	237
10	10	MUCHO GUSTO (USA)	5	6	2	$6.10	23,033	7,203	3,147
11	11	NORTH AMERICA (GB)	161	30		$162.50	876	321	241
12	12	TACITUS (USA)	5	15	4	$6.90	20,487	9,727	3,992
13	13	MAGIC WAND (IRE)	42	30		$43.00	3,308	1,644	1,033
14	14	MIDNIGHT BISOU (US	9	8		$10.40	13,597	5,094	3,138
15	15	~~STAUNCH (GB)~~	~~SCR~~			~~$0.00~~	~~0~~	~~0~~	~~0~~

Figure 26.6. Track odds for the Saudi Cup.

⑦–8–10–12–⑭/①–6–8–10–12–14/1–6–8–⑩–12–14
the $5 exacta cost $20, the $1 trifecta cost $20 and the $1 superfecta cost $80 and won the exacta, trifecta and superfecta

These two bets plus the rebate paid enough to cover my losses. The other bets were:

7–8 exacta for $25
8–7 exacta for $10

Figure 26.7. The finish for the Saudi Cup.

(a) (b)

Figure 26.8. Maximum Security at the Saudi Cup.

7–8/7–8/1–6–10–13–14 trifecta cost $80 and superfecta cost $80
10/7–8/1–6–7–8–12–14/1–6–7–8–12–14 a $5 exacta for $10, a $1 trifecta for $10, a $1 superfecta for $40
3/7–8/7–8/3 two $5 exactas for $10 each
3 for win-place-show $10 for $30
3–10/10–3 $3 each for $3

Gary and Mary West, the owners of Maximum Security, also gained a lot from the 4 year old son of Breeders' Cup winner New Year's Day as the horse started as an $18 thousand claimer and was first in all but one race. Coolmore always so smart and bold purchased part of the breeding rights for Maximum Security who now is much more valuable. His owners,

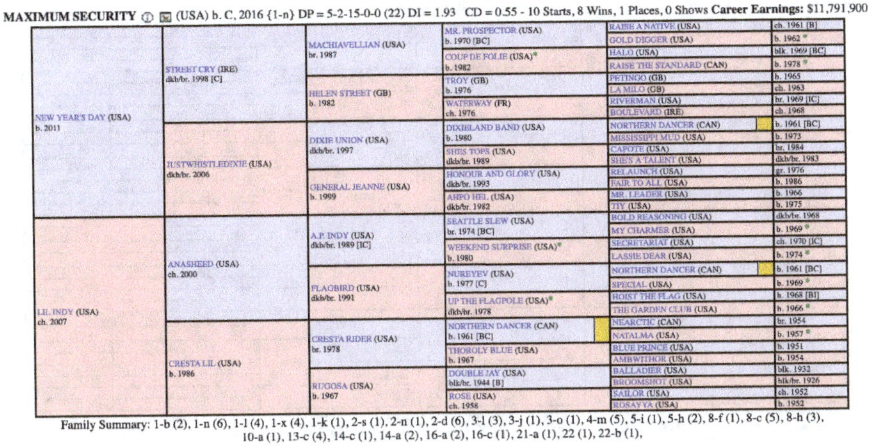

MAXIMUM SECURITY (USA) b. C, 2016 {1-n} DP = 5-2-15-0-0 (22) DI = 1.93 CD = 0.55 - 10 Starts, 8 Wins, 1 Places, 0 Shows Career Earnings: $11,791,900
NEW YEAR'S DAY (USA) b. 2011
STREET CRY (IRE) dkb/br. 1998 [C]
MACHIAVELLIAN (USA) br. 1987
MR. PROSPECTOR (USA) b. 1970 [BC]
RAISE A NATIVE (USA) ch. 1961 [B]
GOLD DIGGER (USA) b. 1962
COUP DE FOLIE (USA) b. 1982
HALO (USA) blk. 1969 [BC]
RAISE THE STANDARD (CAN) b. 1978
HELEN STREET (GB) b. 1982
TROY (GB) b. 1976
PETINGO (GB) b. 1965
LA MILO (GB) ch. 1963
WATERWAY (FR) ch. 1976
RIVERMAN (USA) br. 1969 [IC]
BOULEVARD (IRE) ch. 1968
JUSTWHISTLEDIXIE (USA) dkb/br. 2006
DIXIE UNION (USA) dkb/br. 1997
DIXIELAND BAND (USA) b. 1980
NORTHERN DANCER (CAN) b. 1961 [BC]
MISSISSIPPI MUD (USA) b. 1973
SHES TOPS (USA) dkb/br. 1989
CAPOTE (USA) br. 1984
SHE'S A TALENT (USA) dkb/br. 1983
GENERAL JEANNE (USA) b. 1999
HONOUR AND GLORY (USA) dkb/br. 1993
RELAUNCH (USA) gr. 1976
FAIR TO ALL (USA) b. 1986
AHPO HEL (USA) dkb/br. 1982
MR. LEADER (USA) b. 1966
TIY (USA) b. 1975
LIL INDY (USA) ch. 2007
ANASHEED (USA) ch. 2000
A.P. INDY (USA) dkb/br. 1989 [IC]
SEATTLE SLEW (USA) br. 1974 [BC]
BOLD REASONING (USA) dkb/br. 1968
MY CHARMER (USA) b. 1969
WEEKEND SURPRISE (USA) b. 1980
SECRETARIAT (USA) ch. 1970 [IC]
LASSIE DEAR (USA) b. 1974
FLAGBIRD (USA) dkb/br. 1991
NUREYEV (USA) b. 1977 [C]
NORTHERN DANCER (CAN) b. 1961 [BC]
SPECIAL (USA) b. 1969
UP THE FLAGPOLE (USA) dkb/br. 1978
HOIST THE FLAG (USA) b. 1968 [BI]
THE GARDEN CLUB (USA) b. 1966
CRESTA LIL (USA) b. 1986
CRESTA RIDER (USA) br. 1978
NORTHERN DANCER (CAN) b. 1961 [BC]
NEARCTIC (CAN) br. 1954
NATALMA (USA) b. 1957
THOROLY BLUE (USA) b. 1967
BLUE PRINCE (USA) b. 1951
AMBWITHOR (USA) b. 1954
RUGOSA (USA) b. 1967
DOUBLE JAY (USA) blk/br. 1944 [B]
BALLADIER (USA) blk. 1932
BROOMSHOT (USA) blk/br. 1926
ROSE (USA) ch. 1958
SAILOR (USA) ch. 1952
ROSAYYA (USA) b. 1952
Family Summary: 1-b (2), 1-n (6), 1-l (4), 1-x (4), 1-k (1), 2-s (1), 2-n (1), 2-d (6), 3-l (3), 3-j (1), 3-o (1), 4-m (5), 5-i (1), 5-h (2), 8-f (1), 8-c (5), 8-h (3), 10-a (1), 13-c (4), 14-c (1), 14-a (2), 16-a (2), 16-c (1), 21-a (1), 22 (1), 22-b (1),

Figure 26.9. Pedigree for Maximum Security.

the Wests and Coolmore, pick up a huge payoff from this win. Maximum Security is skipping the Dubai World Cup and returning to the US and will eventually be a breeding stallion at Ashford-Coolmore America. The horse ran in Coolmore's colors (Figure 26.8).

The pedigree of Maximum Security is in Figure 26.9. Why is he so good? You can attribute it to Street Cry who sired Zenatta, the winner of 19 straight races beating males in the Breeders' Cup Classic; the Aussie great Winx who beat males at the top level for many years and won all of her last 32 races, a truly remarkable feat; AP Indy who sired countless champions; Mr. Prospector, the top speed sire of the 20th century; and Northern Dancer, the top sire of the 20th century plus other greats such as Seattle Slew and Nurevyev. Maximum Security's dosage of 1.93 is perfect for long races. Of course, another angle is the reputed drug charge against Maximum Security's trainer, Jason Servis. An investigation is on going, so we will need to wait till this is settled.

The pedigree of Midnight Bisou is in Figure 26.10. She is from the Mr. Prospector-Fappiano line through Quiet American, Real Quiet and Midnight Lute on her sire side and Northern Dancer on her dam sire. Her dosage of 11.00 is high, suggesting speed but that was enough in the $1\frac{1}{8}$ mile Saudi Cup. There are few chefs in her pedigree so her stamina possibly comes from Fappiano, Deputy Minister, Northern Dancer, and Sea Bird. Real Quiet won the Kentucky Derby and Preakness and almost won the Belmont, but he only sired one graded stakes winner over nine furlongs.

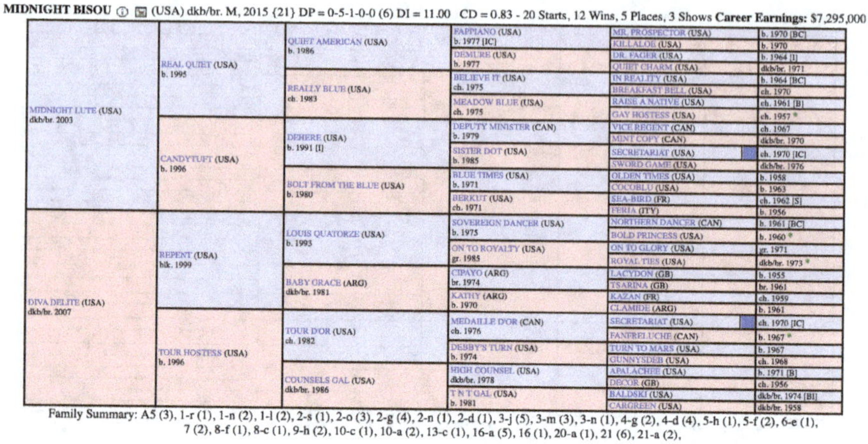

MIDNIGHT BISOU (USA) dkb/br. M, 2015 {21} DP = 0-5-1-0-0 (6) DI = 11.00 CD = 0.83 - 20 Starts, 12 Wins, 5 Places, 3 Shows Career Earnings: $7,295,000
MIDNIGHT LUTE (USA) dkb/br. 2003
REAL QUIET (USA) b. 1995
QUIET AMERICAN (USA) b. 1986
FAPPIANO (USA) b. 1977 [IC]
MR. PROSPECTOR (USA) b. 1970 [BC]
KILLALOE (USA) b. 1970
DEMURE (USA) b. 1977
DR. FAGER (USA) b. 1964 [I]
QUIET CHARM (USA) dkb/br. 1971
REALLY BLUE (USA) ch. 1983
BELIEVE IT (USA) ch. 1975
IN REALITY (USA) b. 1964 [BC]
BREAKFAST BELL (USA) ch. 1970
MEADOW BLUE (USA) ch. 1975
RAISE A NATIVE (USA) ch. 1961 [B]
GAY HOSTESS (USA) ch. 1957
CANDYTUFT (USA) b. 1996
DEHERE (USA) b. 1991 [I]
DEPUTY MINISTER (CAN) b. 1979
VICE REGENT (CAN) ch. 1967
MINT COPY (CAN) dkb/br. 1970
SISTER DOT (USA) b. 1985
SECRETARIAT (USA) ch. 1970 [IC]
SWORD GAME (USA) dkb/br. 1976
BOLT FROM THE BLUE (USA) b. 1980
BLUE TIMES (USA) b. 1971
OLDEN TIMES (USA) b. 1958
COCOBLU (USA) b. 1963
BERKUT (USA) ch. 1971
SEA-BIRD (FR) ch. 1962 [S]
FERIA (ITY) b. 1956
DIVA DELITE (USA) dkb/br. 2007
REPENT (USA) blk. 1999
LOUIS QUATORZE (USA) b. 1993
SOVEREIGN DANCER (USA) b. 1975
NORTHERN DANCER (CAN) b. 1961 [BC]
BOLD PRINCESS (USA) b. 1960
ON TO ROYALTY (USA) gr. 1985
ON TO GLORY (USA) gr. 1971
ROYAL TIES (USA) dkb/br. 1973
BABY GRACE (ARG) dkb/br. 1981
CIPAYO (ARG) br. 1974
LACYDON (GB) b. 1955
TSARINA (GB) br. 1961
KATHY (ARG) b. 1970
KAZAN (FR) ch. 1959
CLAMIDE (ARG) b. 1961
TOUR HOSTESS (USA) b. 1996
TOUR D'OR (USA) ch. 1982
MEDAILLE D'OR (CAN) ch. 1976
SECRETARIAT (USA) ch. 1970 [IC]
FANFRELUCHE (CAN) b. 1967
DEBBY'S TURN (USA) b. 1974
TURN TO MARS (USA) b. 1967
GUNNYSDEB (USA) ch. 1968
COUNSELS GAL (USA) dkb/br. 1986
HIGH COUNSEL (USA) dkb/br. 1978
APALACHEE (USA) b. 1971 [B]
DECOR (GB) ch. 1956
T N T GAL (USA) b. 1981
BALDSKI (USA) dkb/br. 1974 [BI]
CARGREEN (USA) dkb/br. 1958
Family Summary: A5 (3), 1-r (1), 1-n (2), 1-l (2), 2-s (1), 2-o (3), 2-g (4), 2-n (1), 2-d (1), 3-j (5), 3-m (3), 3-n (1), 4-g (2), 4-d (4), 5-h (1), 5-f (2), 6-e (1), 7 (2), 8-f (1), 8-c (1), 9-h (2), 10-c (1), 10-a (2), 13-c (1), 16-a (5), 16 (1), 20-a (1), 21 (6), 21-a (2),

Figure 26.10. Pedigree for Midnight Bisou.

Midnight Bisou's sire Midnight Lute, was a champion sprinter consistent with a high dosage, so again the story is fuzzy.

There is an interesting story about Real Quiet. John Swetye and I have a colleague who was a big time construction magnet from Ohio. He once owned the Vinery Farm and a huge estate in Paris, Kentucky, three miles past Claiborne. The property is a square with houses on the four corners and on the middle on both sides for employees who take care of the property. The main home is 10,000 square feet on each of the three floors plus a guest house. On the property are Scottish cattle, Nelson Bunker Hunt mares and other horses.

Our colleague had many ups and downs including owning the magic field, a quarter section of his property on which five Kentucky Derby winners grew up. With his three-year old year, Real Quiet, the second string horse in Bob Baffert's barn, behind Indian Charlie, had won a grade I and then finished last in a race. After this disappointing performance our colleague made a superior wager: he purchased for $1.1 million, the breeding rights of Real Quiet. Then when Real Quiet was a great success in the Triple Crown races he sold 2/3rds of the breeding rights for $16.5 million and kept 1/3rd. Another great example of financial mean reversion.

26.3. The Dubai World Cup

A number of the horses that were shipped to Saudi Arabia for the Saudi Cup were moved over to Dubai for the World Cup. They included Sir Winston and Tacitus who were 1,2 in the 2019 Belmont, Mucho Gusto who won the Pegasus and was 4th in the Saudi Cup, Math Wizard and War Story. However, because of the worldwide COVID-19 pandemic, the 2020 race was postponed. It was to be the 25th edition of the race with $35 million total purses on the day and $12 million for the World Cup. Thundersnow won the Dubai World Cup race in 2018 and 2019.

26.3.1. *Racing is in trouble*

The years 2019 and 2020 have had a number of problems for the racing industry.

Maximum Security was moved to the barn of America's top trainer Bob Baffert. Whoops, another trainer with drug trouble with his horses. Most of Baffert's horses are clean and win an extraordinary number of important races. However, there have been 30 horses in 40 years, including Justify, the 2018 Triple Crown winner who failed a drug test. Mostly the authorities have overlooked these violations possibly because of Baffert's terrific training record. The 2021 Kentucky Derby winner Medina Spirit had a violation so Baffert has been banned, at least temporarily, from Churchill Downs, the New York NYRA and some others but not all tracks. The Derby finish has not been settled yet regarding possible disqualification of Medina Spirit. One wonders why the greatest trainer has so many clean horses but also so many tainted. Illegal drugs can come from a variety of sources such as the wrong type of hay. So this situation is very confusing. Baffert also has a large number of horses that were destroyed after breaking a leg.

1. There were many horses destroyed from injuries sustained at Santa Anita early in 2019. These number more than 30 and were on the dirt track, on the grass and in training. The reason for this is unclear. Lots of rain and the atmosphere is possibly involved. Steps have been taken to fix the problems and the November 2019 Breeders' Cup had only one incident. Mongolian Green who had won a race there broke down in the Classic and was destroyed.
2. In May Maximum Security won the Kentucky Derby but was disqualified for interference in a very controversial call, especially when it was clear he was the best horse in the race. After that Maximum Security has done well, winning all his races except one second. Meanwhile the longshot Country House who was given the win at 65–1 has not run since and retired.

3. There were many cancellations of races because of the Covid-19 world wide crisis. The 2020 Kentucky Derby was moved to September. Many racetracks were closed and others including Gulfstream are racing with no track audience but large off-track betting.
4. Twenty-seven trainers and veterinarians were charged with illegal drugs including PED and doping in the US. These include Jason Servis who trained Maximum Security. They are appealing the charges, however these trainers won a much higher percentage than other top trainers. So how did they do it?
   The owners Gary and Mary West have moved the horse to trainer Bob Baffert. Now there is the issue of whether Maximum Security will be disqualified from the Saudi Cup win and Midnight Bison declared the winner. At best it is a mess. Baffert is now in favor of a national standards board to oversee the racing industry. Keeneland, NYRA, the Stronach group and others have revoked the licenses of these trainers and veterinarians. This has caused a reshuffling of the top rated US horses. Maximum Security who was first is now fourth, Midnight Bisou is now rated first, followed by Mucho Gusto and Zulu Alpha. Mr Freeze is fifth and Firenze Fire is eighth. The \$10 million of the \$11,791,000 that Maximum Security received from the Saudi Cup might be in jeopardy and given to Midnight Bisou who got \$3.5 million of her \$7,250,000 lifetime earnings.
5. Sheik Mohammed, one of the world's top owners and promotors of the sport, was convicted in the UK of trouble with his estranged wife and daughters who escaped Dubai. Since he supports UK racing as well as worldwide, there will be problems from this.

Appendix: Past Performances for the Saudi Cup

King Abdulaziz Racecourse(KSA) Stk 20781500K 1⅛ Mile 4&up Saturday, February 29, 2020 **Race 8** — **brisnet.com** *the handicapper's edge*

8

WIN; PLACE; SWINGER; EXACTA; TRIFECTA; QUARTET

1⅛ Mile. Stk 20781500K **THE SAUDI CUP - DIRT For 4 year olds and upwards Stake**
Post Time: (12:40)/11:40/10:40/ 9:40

---

1 pp3 **Benbati (NA 0)**
Own: Godolphin
7/1 Royal Blue
Murphy O

B. h. 6
Sire: Dubawi (IRE) (Dubai Millennium (GB)) $331,467
Dam: Nahrain (GB) (Selkirk)
Brdr: (GB)
Trnr: bin Suroor Saeed

126

Life:	20	10 - 3 - 1	$5,141,002		Fst	1	1 - 0 - 0	$270,000
2020	2	2 - 0 - 0	$406,826		Off	0	0 - 0 - 0	$0
2019	2	1 - 0 - 0	$75,424		Dis	0	0 - 0 - 0	$0
KAR	0	0 - 0 - 0	$0		Trf	19	9 - 3 - 1	$5,445,702
					AW	0	0 - 0 - 0	$0

Sire Stats: AWD 8.9 22%Mud 124MudSts 2.98spi
Dam'sSire: AWD 8.8 12%Mud 34MudSts 2.24spi

DATE	TRK	DIST	RR	RACETYPE	CR	Fin	JOCKEY	ODDS	Top Finishers	Comment
06Feb20	Dubai - Meydan(Uae)	*1 3/16 ft 1:56⁴ 3↑		Stk 450000 Al Maktoum Challenge Round 2 Sponsored by Mubadala-G2		1^{2}	SoumillonC126		Bnbatl^{2}MltryLw^{6¾}**Grnkwsk**^{3½}	Dubai - Meydan(Uae) 10
09Jan20	Dubai - Meydan(Uae)	Ⓣ *1⅛ gd 1:52 3↑		Stk 245000 Singspiel S. Presented by Longines Master Collection-G2		$1^{4¾}$	SoumillonC130		*Bnbtl*^{4¾}ForthTop^{hd}MajstcMamb^{hd}	Dubai - Meydan(Uae) 5
19Oct19	Ascot(GB)	Ⓣ 1m hy 1:44⁴ 3↑	120	Stk 1403993 Queen Elizabeth II S. Sponsored by Qipco-G1	114	16^{43}	MurphyO130	3.50	KingofChange^{1¼}ThRvnant^{1½}SafVoyag^{1½} *10-19-19 Chased leaders; lost place over 2f out; eased*	Ascot(GB) 16
27Sep19	Newmarket(GB)	Ⓣ 1m gd 1:35³ 3↑	119	Stk 120871 Shadwell Joel S.-G2	123	1^{5}	MurphyO130	4.00	Benbati^{5}King of Comedy^{1¼}Zaak^{nk} *09-27-19 Made all; quickened clear entering final furlong; unchallenged*	Newmarket(GB) 6
27Oct18	Moonee Valley(Aus)	Ⓣ *1¼ gd 2:03² 3↑		Stk 3544500 Ladbrokes Cox Plate-G1		2^{2}	MurphyO130	9.00	Winx^{2}*Benbati*^{2¾}Humidor^{3}	Moonee Valley(Aus) 8
13Oct18	Caulfield(Aus)	Ⓣ *1¼ gd 2:00⁴ 3↑		Stk 711500 Ladbrokes Caulfield S.-G1		1no	CosgraveP130	8.00	Benbati^{no}Blair House^{2¼}Humidor^{hd}	Caulfield(Aus) 11
22Aug18	York(GB)	Ⓣ *1 5/16 gd 2:07³ 3↑	122	Stk 1347602 Juddmonte International S.-G1	122	$5^{5¾}$	CrowleyJ132	10.00	*Roaring Lion*^{3¼}Poet's Word^{½}*Thundering Blue*^{1¼} *08-22-18 Tracked leader; led over 2f out; soon ridden; headed over 1f o*	York(GB) 8
29Jly18	Munchen(Ger)	Ⓣ *1¼ gd 2:06³ 3↑		Stk 180670 Grosser Dallmayr-Preis - Bayerisches Zuchtrennen-G1		$1^{2¾}$	MurphyO132		Benbati^{2¾}Stormy Antarctic^{2}Va Bank^{¾}	Munchen(Ger) 9
19Jun18	Ascot(GB)	Ⓣ 1m gd 1:38⁴ 4↑	120	Stk 839175 Queen Anne S.-G1	120	$10^{5¼}$	SoumillonC126	2.75	AcidentalAgent^{½}LordGliters^{nk}*LightningSpar*^{no} *06-19-18 Tracked leader; led 2f out; headed over 1f out; no extra insid*	Ascot(GB) 15
31Mar18	Dubai - Meydan(Uae)	Ⓣ *1⅛ gd 1:46 3↑		Stk 6000000 Dubai Turf Sponsored by Dp World-G1		$1^{3¼}$	MurphyO126		Benbati^{3¼}Vivlos^{nk}Real Steel^{dh}	Dubai - Meydan(Uae) 15

---

2 pp13 **Capezzano (NA 0)**
Own: Sultan Ali
10/1 Dark Blue, Orange Star And Star On Cap
Barzalona M

B. g. 6
Sire: Bernardini (A.P. Indy) $40,000
Dam: Cableknit (Unbridled's Song)
Brdr: ()
Trnr: Ghadeyer S Bin

Blnkr On
126

Life:	16	6 - 1 - 2	$743,828		Fst	14	6 - 2 - 2	$831,839
2020	1	1 - 0 - 0	$114,420		Off	0	0 - 0 - 0	$0
2019	4	3 - 0 - 0	$471,334		Dis	0	0 - 0 - 0	$0
KAR	0	0 - 0 - 0	$0		Trf	3	0 - 0 - 0	$0
					AW	0	0 - 0 - 0	$0

Sire Stats: AWD 7.5 19%Mud 1045MudSts 2.01spi
Dam'sSire: AWD 7.2 18%Mud 1788MudSts 3.15spi

DATE	TRK	DIST	RR	RACETYPE	CR	Fin	JOCKEY	ODDS	Top Finishers	Comment
13Feb20	Dubai - Meydan(Uae)	*1m ft 1:36¹ 3↑		Stk 200000 Firebreak Stakes Sponsored by Gulfnews.Com-G3		1^{7}	BarzalonaM126		Capzano^{7}ScrtAmbition^{¾}Matrhorn^{3½}	Dubai - Meydan(Uae) 8
30Mar19	Dubai - Meydan(Uae)	*1¼ ft 2:03⁴ 3↑		Stk 12000000 Dubai World Cup Sponsored by Emirates Airline-G1		12^{32}	BarzalonaM126		ThndrSnw^{no}**Grnksk**^{2¾}Gnvra^{½}	Dubai - Meydan(Uae) 12
09Mar19	Dubai - Meydan(Uae)	*1¼ ft 2:05 3↑		Stk 600000 Al Maktoum Challenge Round 3 Sponsored by Emirates Airline-G1		$1^{9½}$	BarzalonaM126		Capzano^{9½}*ThndrSnow*^{nk}Dlkng^{1¼}	Dubai - Meydan(Uae) 10
31Jan19	Dubai - Meydan(Uae)	*1m ft 1:36⁴ 3↑		Hcp 175000 Mina Rashid		1^{14}	BarzalonaM126		*Capzan*^{14}Thgratclctn^{3}*AfrcnRd*^{2½}	Dubai - Meydan(Uae) 14
17Jan19	Dubai - Meydan(Uae)	*1m ft 1:38 3↑		Hcp 135000 Azizi Aliyah		$1^{2¼}$	FfrenchR122		*Capzano*^{2¼}Thgratcolction^{¾}Glvnz^{5}	Dubai - Meydan(Uae) 11
20Dec18	Dubai - Meydan(Uae)	*1m ft 1:38⁴ 3↑		Hcp 72158 Dubai Creek Mile Sponsored by Azizi		7^{40}	FfrenchR126		Stned^{hd}OnMnBnd^{5½}Thgratcolcton^{¾}	Dubai - Meydan(Uae) 7
31Mar18	Dubai - Meydan(Uae)	*1m ft 1:36¹ 3↑		Stk 1000000 Godolphin Mile Sponsored by Mohammed Bin Rashid Al Maktoum City - District One-G2		13^{22}	SmithME126		Heavy Metal^{2}Muntazah^{½}Adirato^{2½}	Dubai - Meydan(Uae) 14
10Mar18	Dubai - Meydan(Uae)	*1¼ ft 2:01³ 3↑		Stk 400000 Al Maktoum Challenge Round 3 Sponsored by Emirates Airline-G1		7^{47}	BarzalonaM126		**NrthArc**^{5¼}*ThndrSn*^{9¾}FrCrzd^{9}	Dubai - Meydan(Uae) 12
22Feb18	Dubai - Meydan(Uae)	*1m ft 1:38³ 3↑		Hcp 125000 District One Mediterranean		$1^{1¼}$	BarzalonaM123		Capzano^{1¼}Ftbrdg^{½}ClaimthRoss^{5¼}	Dubai - Meydan(Uae) 8
18Jan18	Dubai - Meydan(Uae)	Ⓣ *1¼ gd 2:01⁴ 3↑		Hcp 60000 Yahsat Satellite Cup		15^{74}	BuickW130		Janszoon^{5}*Rio Tigre*^{1}Mustahdaf^{3}	Dubai - Meydan(Uae) 16

---

3 pp10 **Chrysoberyl (NA 0)**
Own: U Carrot Farm
10/1 Emerald Green, White Hoops, White Sleeves, Red Armlets,
Soumillon C

B. c. 4
Sire: Gold Allure (JPN) (Sunday Silence) $27,498
Dam: () (El Condor Pasa)
Brdr: (JPN)
Trnr: Otonashi H

126

Life:	4	4 - 0 - 0	$700,311		Fst	0	0 - 0 - 0	$0
2019	4	4 - 0 - 0	$700,311		Off	4	4 - 0 - 0	$1,043,751
2018	0	0 - 0 - 0	$0		Dis	0	0 - 0 - 0	$0
KAR	0	0 - 0 - 0	$0		Trf	0	0 - 0 - 0	$0
					AW	0	0 - 0 - 0	$0

Sire Stats: AWD 7.9 10%Mud 3851MudSts spi
Dam'sSire: AWD 8.8 10%Mud 1591MudSts spi

DATE	TRK	DIST	RR	RACETYPE	CR	Fin	JOCKEY	ODDS	Top Finishers	Comment
01Dec19	Chukyo(Jpn)	*1⅛ ft 1:48² 3↑		Stk 1735508 Champions Cup-G1		1^{nk}	KawadaY121	3.40	Chrysoberyl^{nk}**Gold Dream**^{1¼}Inti^{½}	Chukyo(Jpn) 16
23Sep19	Funabashi(Jpn)	*1⅛ gd 1:52 3↑		Hcp 503936 Nippon Tv Hai		1^{4}	KawadaY121	*0.10	*Chrysobryl*^{4}LndnTwn^{4}NonkonoYme^{25}	Funabashi(Jpn) 8
10Jly19	Ooi(Jpn)	*1¼ gd 2:06		Hcp 703035 Japan Dirt Derby		1^{3}	KawadaY123	*0.20	*Chrysoberyl*^{3}Derma Louvre^{hd}Mutually^{hd}	Ooi(Jpn) 14
02May19	Sonoda(Jpn)	*1 3/16 my 1:57¹		Hcp 431040 Hyogo Championship		1^{5}	LemaireC123	*0.10	*Chrysoberyl*^{5}Weltblick^{2½}Ban Rose Kings^{1}	Sonoda(Jpn) 12
02Mar19	Hanshin(Jpn)	*1⅛ gd 1:52¹		Alw 122657		1^{7}	KawadaY123	*0.60	*Chrysoberyl*^{7}Avance^{hd}Salt Ibuki^{2½}	Hanshin(Jpn) 11
17Sep18	Hanshin(Jpn)	*1⅛ ft 1:55¹		Stk 119528		1^{7}	KawadaY119	*0.20	*Chrysoberyl*^{7}*Hagino Homme Ideal*^{1}^{16}	Hanshin(Jpn) 11

International King Abdulaziz Racecourse(KSA) Stk 20781500K 1⅛ Mile 4&up Saturday, February 29, 2020 **Race 8** brisnet.com *the handicapper's edge*

4 PP1 **Gold Dream (NA 0)**
Own: Katsumi Yoshida
30/1 Red, Yellow Stripes, Black Sleeves, Yellow And Red Striped
Lemaire C

B. h. 7
Sire: Gold Allure (JPN) (Sunday Silence) $27,498
Dam: 0 (French Deputy)
Brdr: (JPN)
Trnr: Hirata O

Blnkr On 126

Life:	21	7 - 7 - 2	$3,384,541	Fst	1	0 - 0 - 0	$0
2019	5	1 - 2 - 1	$0	Off	7	3 - 1 - 0	$995,764
2018	5	2 - 3 - 0	$1,162,733	Dis	0	0 - 0 - 0	$0
KAR	0	0 - 0 - 0	$0	Trf	0	0 - 0 - 0	$0
				AW	0	0 - 0 - 0	$0

Sire Stats: AWD 7.9 10%Mud 3851MudSts spi
Dam'sSire: AWD 7.3 11%Mud 4210MudSts 2.05spi

DATE	TRK	DIST	RR	RACETYPE	CR	Fin	JOCKEY	ODDS	Top Finishers	Comment
29Dec19	Ooi(Jpn)	*1¼ gd 2:04^4 3↑		Stk 1242530 Tokyo Daishoten-G1		4$^{3\frac{1}{2}}$	LemaireC^{126}	*1.30	OmegaPerfme^{1}NonkonoYume^{2}MoganiaFlavor$^{\frac{1}{2}}$	Ooi(Jpn) 13
01Dec19	Chukyo(Jpn)	*1⅛ ft 1:48^2 3↑		Stk 1735508 Champions Cup-G1		2^{nk}	LemaireC^{126}	*2.50	**Chrysoberyl**^{nk}Gold Dream$^{1\frac{1}{2}}$Inti$^{\frac{1}{2}}$	Chukyo(Jpn) 16
14Oct19	Morioka(Jpn)	*1m ft 1:34^1 3↑		Hcp 643732 Mile Championship Nambu Hai		3^3	LemaireC^{126}	*0.30	Sunrise Nova$^{1\frac{1}{2}}$Arctos$^{1\frac{1}{2}}$Gold Dream^{nk}	Morioka(Jpn) 16
06May19	Funabashi(Jpn)	*1m gd 1:40^1 4↑		Hcp 918000 Kashiwa Kinen		1$^{1\frac{1}{2}}$	LemaireC^{126}	0.90	Gold Dream$^{1\frac{1}{2}}$Inti^{2}Apollo Kentucky$^{1\frac{1}{2}}$	Funabashi(Jpn) 11
17Feb19	Tokyo(Jpn)	*1m ft 1:35^3 4↑		Stk 1719500 February S.-G1		2^{nk}	LemaireC^{126}	2.00	Inti^{nk}*Gold Dream*^{4}Yuranoto$^{1\frac{1}{4}}$	Tokyo(Jpn) 14
29Dec18	Ooi(Jpn)	*1¼ ft 2:05^4 3↑		Stk 1233520 Tokyo Daishoten-G1		2$^{\frac{3}{4}}$	LemaireC^{126}	*1.20	Omega Perfume$^{\frac{3}{4}}$Gold Dream$^{1\frac{1}{2}}$K T Brave$^{1\frac{1}{2}}$	Ooi(Jpn) 16
08Oct18	Morioka(Jpn)	*1m ft 1:35^1 3↑		Hcp 593325 Mile Championship Nambu Hai		2$^{1\frac{1}{2}}$	LemaireC^{126}	*0.60	*LeVentSeLeve*$^{1\frac{1}{2}}$GoldDram^{3}MishoUtag^4	Morioka(Jpn) 14
27Jun18	Ooi(Jpn)	*1¼ ft 2:04^1 4↑		Hcp 927180 Teio Sho		1^{nk}	LemaireC^{126}	2.40	Gold Dream^{nk}*K T Brave*$^{1\frac{1}{2}}$Sound True^3	Ooi(Jpn) 15
02May18	Funabashi(Jpn)	*1m ft 1:39^1 4↑		Hcp 928200 Kashiwa Kinen		1^1	LemaireC^{126}	2.20	*Gold Dream*^{1}All Blush^{hd}Incantation$^{\frac{3}{4}}$	Funabashi(Jpn) 12
18Feb18	Tokyo(Jpn)	*1m ft 1:36 4↑		Stk 1787900 February S.-G1		2^{nk}	MooreR^{126}	*1.10	Nonkono Yume^{nk}*Gold Dream*^{nk}Incantation^3	Tokyo(Jpn) 16

5 PP11 **Great Scot (NA 0)**
Own: Prince Faisal Bin Khaled Bin A/aziz
60/1 Red, White Epaulettes, Black Cuffs
A Moreno

B. g. 4
Sire: Requinto (IRE) (Dansili (GB)) $4,000
Dam: La Rosiere (Mr. Greeley)
Brdr: (GB)
Trnr: Mishrif

126

Life:	11	4 - 1 - 2	$150,745	Fst	0	0 - 0 - 0	$0
2019	6	1 - 1 - 1	$92,410	Off	0	0 - 0 - 0	$0
2018	5	3 - 0 - 1	$58,335	Dis	0	0 - 0 - 0	$0
KAR	0	0 - 0 - 0	$0	Trf	11	4 - 1 - 2	$146,553
				AW	0	0 - 0 - 0	$0

Sire Stats: AWD 6.5 Mud 0MudSts 0.71spi
Dam'sSire: AWD 6.9 14%Mud 1985MudSts 1.56spi

DATE	TRK	DIST	RR	RACETYPE	CR	Fin	JOCKEY	ODDS	Top Finishers	Comment
07Sep19	Haydock Park(GB)	Ⓣ *1m sf 1:44 3↑	119	Stk 76159 Bet in Play on the Betfair Exchange Superior Mile S.-G3	122	1$^{3\frac{3}{4}}$	KingscoteR^{124}	3.50	GreatScot$^{3\frac{3}{4}}$Materhorn$^{\frac{1}{2}}$RaisingSand$^{\frac{3}{4}}$	Haydock Park(GB) 6 *09-07-19 Made all; quickened 3f out; ridden and ran on; unchallenged*
15Aug19	Salisbury(GB)	Ⓣ 1m sf 1:45^4 3↑	119	Stk 85045 Tattersalls Sovereign S.-G3	119	4^1	KingscoteR^{122}	3.50	Kick On^{no}Accidental Agent$^{\frac{1}{2}}$Flashcard$^{\frac{1}{2}}$	Salisbury(GB) 6 *08-15-19 Led; ridden over 1f out; headed inside final furlong; no extra*
20Jun19	Ascot(GB)	Ⓣ 1¼ sf 2:08^1	118	Stk 112593 Hampton Court S.-G3	117	11^9	CrowleyJ^{126}	14.00	Sangarius$^{2\frac{1}{4}}$*Fox Chairman*^{nk}King Ottokar^1	Ascot(GB) 13 *06-20-19 Tracked leaders; pulled hard; edged right over 2f out; soon bu*
19May19	Koln(Ger)	Ⓣ *1m gd 1:37^4		Stk 170869 Mehl-Mulhens-Rennen German Two Thousand Guineas-G2		3$^{\frac{1}{2}}$	KingscoteR^{128}		Fox Champion^{nk}Arctic Sound^{nk}Great Scot$^{2\frac{1}{4}}$	Koln(Ger) 11
04May19	Newmarket(GB)	Ⓣ 1m gd 1:36^4	119	Stk 678690 Qipco Two Thousand Guineas-G1	120	9$^{6\frac{3}{4}}$	KingscoteR^{126}	25.00	MagnaGrcia$^{2\frac{1}{2}}$*KingofChange*$^{1\frac{3}{4}}$Skard^{hd}	Newmarket(GB) 19 *05-04-19 Mid-division; ridden and headway over 1f out; kept on same pace*
13Apr19	Newbury(GB)	Ⓣ 7f sf 1:26^4	118	Stk 90012 Watership Down Stud Greenham S.-G3	121	2$^{\frac{3}{4}}$	KingscoteR^{126}	4.00	Mohaather$^{\frac{3}{4}}$Great Scot$^{2\frac{1}{4}}$Urban Icon$^{1\frac{3}{4}}$	Newbury(GB) 8 *04-13-19 Held up in 6th; headway far side of group chasing leaders 2f o*
27Oct18	Doncaster(GB)	Ⓣ 1m sf 1:37^3	118	Stk 291506 Vertem Futurity Trophy-G1	120	5$^{1\frac{1}{4}}$	KingscoteR^{127}	14.00	*MgnGrc*^{hd}*PhnxSpan*$^{\frac{3}{4}}$WstrnAstralia^{hd}	Doncaster(GB) 11 *10-27-18 In rear; headway over 2f out; ridden and every chance inside f*
08Sep18	Haydock Park(GB)	Ⓣ *1m hy 1:49^4	116	Hcp 31970 32red Casino Ascendant S.	116	1^{dh}	KingscoteR^{128}	1.62	GratScot^{dh}FloatngArtst^{dh}*CrtainLad*^{dh}	Haydock Park(GB) 5 *09-08-18 Pulled hard early; tracked leaders; every chance over 1f out;*
18Aug18	Deauville(Fr)	Ⓣ *1m sf 1:47^1	117	Hcp 139379 Criterium Du Fonds Europeen De L'elevage	118	3^{nk}	KingscoteR^{128}		Al Hilalee^{hd}Duke of Hazzard^{hd}*Great Scot*$^{\frac{3}{4}}$	Deauville(Fr) 7
21Jly18	Haydock Park(GB)	Ⓣ 7f gd 1:27^3	115	Alw 12924 Smarkets British E.B.F. Novice Stakes (Class 4) (Plus 10 Race)	119	1^1	KingscoteR^{131}	5.00	Great Scot^1*Line of Duty*^{4}Massam$^{2\frac{1}{4}}$	Haydock Park(GB) 6 *07-21-18 Held up in touch in rear; driven 2f out; headway under pressur*

6 PP5 **Gronkowski (NA 0)**
Own: Phoenix Thoroughbred III & Khalid Bin Mishr
30/1 White, Green Epaulettes, Green, White Hooped Sleeves,
Dettori L

B. h. 5 TATAPR 2017 $404.1k
Sire: Lonhro (AUS) (Octagonal (NZ)) $30,000
Dam: Four Sugars (Lookin At Lucky)
Brdr: 0
Trnr: Ghadayer S Bin

Blnkr On 126

Life:	14	4 - 3 - 3	$3,230,869	Fst	8	0 - 2 - 3	$2,806,716
2020	1	0 - 0 - 1	$48,375	Off	0	0 - 0 - 0	$0
2019	3	0 - 1 - 1	$2,721,230	Dis	1	0 - 0 - 1	$24,000
KAR	0	0 - 0 - 0	$0	Trf	2	0 - 1 - 0	$1,761
				AW	4	4 - 0 - 0	$133,980

Sire Stats: AWD 7.1 10%Mud 117MudSts 1.28spi
Dam'sSire: AWD 7.6 14%Mud 590MudSts 1.94spi
SoldAt: TATAPR 2017 $404.1k (1/8) SireAvg: $131.9k StudFee: $30k

DATE	TRK	DIST	RR	RACETYPE	CR	Fin	JOCKEY	ODDS	Top Finishers	Comment
06Feb20	Dubai - Meydan(Uae)	*1$\frac{3}{16}$ ft 1:56^4 3↑		Stk 450000 Al Maktoum Challenge Round 2 Sponsored by Mubadala-G2		3$^{6\frac{3}{4}}$	BarzalonaM^{126}		**Bnbatl**^{2}MltaryLaw$^{6\frac{3}{4}}$Grnkwsk$^{3\frac{1}{2}}$	Dubai - Meydan(Uae) 10
05Dec19	Dubai - Meydan(Uae)	*1¼ ft 2:07 3↑		Hcp 72158 The Entisar Sponsored by Dp World Uae Region		3^4	FfrenchR^{131}		MilitaryLaw^{3}SaltaVan^{1}Gronkowsk^3	Dubai - Meydan(Uae) 7
30Mar19	Dubai - Meydan(Uae)	*1¼ ft 2:03^4 3↑		Stk 12000000 Dubai World Cup Sponsored by Emirates Airline-G1		2no	MurphyO^{126}		ThndrSnow^{no}Grnkwsk$^{2\frac{3}{4}}$Gnevera$^{\frac{1}{2}}$	Dubai - Meydan(Uae) 12
09Mar19	Dubai - Meydan(Uae)	*1¼ ft 2:05 3↑		Stk 600000 Al Maktoum Challenge Round 3 Sponsored by Emirates Airline-G1		5^{12}	FfrenchR^{126}		**Capzan**$^{9\frac{1}{2}}$*ThndrSnw*^{nk}Dlkng$^{1\frac{1}{4}}$	Dubai - Meydan(Uae) 10

DATE/TRK	DIST						RR	RACETYPE	CR												Fin	JOCKEY		ODDS	Top Finishers	Comment
24Nov18Aqu^6	1⅛	ft	:50	1:14^1	1:38^4	1:52	119	Discovry-G3	120	77	80/	101	-11	-11	**92**	4	4$^{5\frac{1}{2}}$	4^1	4^2	3$^{4\frac{1}{2}}$	3$^{2\frac{1}{4}}$	OrtizJL^{120}	Lb	1.30	Plainsman$^{1\frac{3}{4}}$*Title Ready*$^{\frac{1}{2}}$Gronkowski$^{14\frac{1}{4}}$	Ran on 4
29Sep18Bel^{10}	1¼	ft	:45^3	1:09	1:33^4	1:59^4 3↑	121	JkClbGC-G1	120	73	90/	100	+13	+10	**99**	2	7^{16}	7^{17}	6^{13}	6$^{8\frac{1}{2}}$	6$^{6\frac{3}{4}}$	OrtizJL^{122}	Lb	5.70	Discreet Lover^{nk}Thunder Snow$^{1\frac{3}{4}}$Mendelssohn$^{2\frac{1}{2}}$	3w into 8
25Aug18Sar^{11}	1¼	ft	:47^4	1:11^4	1:36^1	2:01^4	120	Travrs-G1	118	73	97/	81	-14	+5	**93**	3	9^6	8$^{4\frac{3}{4}}$	8$^{7\frac{3}{4}}$	8^{11}	8^{13}	RosarioJ^{126}	Lb	3.45	Catholic Boy^{4}Mendelssohn^{1}Bravazo$^{1\frac{1}{2}}$	No impact 10
09Jun18Bel^{11}	1½	ft	:48	1:13^1	2:02^4	2:28	119	Belmnt-G1	124	92	110/	98	-9	+6	**107**	6	10^{14}	9$^{8\frac{1}{2}}$	3$^{2\frac{1}{2}}$	2^2	2$^{1\frac{3}{4}}$	OrtizJL^{126}	Lb	24.75	Justify$^{1\frac{3}{4}}$Gronkowski$^{1\frac{3}{4}}$*Hofburg*^{nk}	Rail run3/8 10

DATE	TRK	DIST	RR	RACETYPE	CR	Fin	JOCKEY	ODDS	Top Finishers	Comment
30Mar18	Newcastle(GB)	Ⓐ 1m ft 1:37^2	117	Hcp 138200 32red Burradon S.	121	1$^{1\frac{1}{4}}$	SpencerJP^{128}	1.62	Grnkwsk$^{1\frac{1}{4}}$IconicSnset^{hd}DarkAclaim^{hd}	Newcastle(GB) 10 *03-30-18 In rear; ridden and headway over 1f out; soon led; held on wel*
07Mar18	Kempton Park(GB)	Ⓐ 1m ft 1:37^3	116	Alw 68196 'road to the Kentucky Derby' Conditions Stakes (Class 2) (Plus 10 Race)	118	1$^{\frac{3}{4}}$	SpencerJP^{131}	1.50	*Grnkwsk*$^{\frac{3}{4}}$CortHose$^{1\frac{1}{4}}$FortnsParl$^{1\frac{1}{2}}$	Kempton Park(GB) 7 *03-07-18 Took keen hold; held up; rapid headway to press leader over 3f*

brisnet.com *the handicapper's edge*

InternKingpAbdulaziz Racecourse(KSA) Stk 20781500K 1⅛ Mile 4&up Saturday, February 29, 2020 **Race 8**

7 Maximum Security (NA 0)

Own: West, Gary And Mary
5/2 Blue, Orange Spot, Orange Stripes On Sleeves, Orange
Luis Saez

B. c. 4
Sire : New Year's Day (Street Cry (IRE)) $27,498
Dam: Lil Indy (Anasheed)
Brdr: 0
Trnr: Servis Jason

126

Life:	9	7 - 1 - 0	$1,871,705		Fst	7	6 - 1 - 0	$1,782,100
2019	8	6 - 1 - 0	$1,861,065		Off	2	1 - 0 - 0	$19,800
2018	1	1 - 0 - 0	$10,640		Dis	2	2 - 0 - 0	$1,182,800
KAR	0	0 - 0 - 0	$0		Trf	0	0 - 0 - 0	$0
					AW	0	0 - 0 - 0	$0

Sire Stats: AWD 6.9 15%Mud 170MudSts 1.58spi
Dam'sSire: AWD 7.7 13%Mud 335MudSts 0.52spi

DATE TRK	DIST							RR	RACETYPE	CR												Fin	JOCKEY		ODDS	Top Finishers	Comment
07Dec19Aqu^{10}	1m	ft	:22^4	:46	1:11	1:36^2	3↑	120	CigarMiH-G1	124	104	113/	99	+8	+5	**108**	5	1^{hd}	1½	1^1	1^3	1^{3½}	SaezL^{122}	L	*1.30	MaximmSecrity^{3½}SpuntoRun^{2}TrueTimber½	Edged clear 11
26Oct19Bel^6	7f	ft	:22^4	:45^1	1:08^1	1:20^3	3↑	120	BoldRlrH-G3	123	89	98/	98	-8	-7	**99**	1	1	1½	1½	1^2	1^{1¾}	SaezL^{121}	L	*0.60	*Maximum Security*^{1¾}Tale of Silence^{2½}True Timber¾	Drve 6
20Jly19Mth^{12}	1⅛	ft	:46^3	1:10	1:34^4	1:47^2		118	Hskllnv-G1	122	85	101/	101	-99	-99	**104**	6	3^1	3½	2^{hd}	1^{hd}	1^{1¼}	SaezL^{120}	L	*0.80	*MaximmSecrity*^{1¼}**MchoGsto**^{8}*SpntoRn*^{2½}	Gamely 6
16Jun19Mth^{10}	1$\frac{1}{16}$	ft	:23^2	:46^4	1:10^2	1:42^3		117	PegasusL 150k	120	103	112/	91	+8	+7	**103**	2	1½	1½	1^{hd}	1½	2^1	SaezL^{123}	L	*0.05	KngforaDay^1*MaximmSecrity*^{5½}DirctOrdr^6	Stumbled start 6
04May19CD^{12}	1¼	sy^s	:46^3	1:12^2	1:38^3	2:03^4		118	KyDerby-G1	122	97	83/	104	+5	-16	**99**	7	1^{hd}	1^1	2^{hd}	1^1	1^{1¾}	SaezL^{126}	L	4.50	MaximmSecrity^{1¾}CountryHouse¾*CodeofHonor*¾	Dug in 19
									Kentucky Derby presented by Woodford Reserve-G1																	*(Placed 17th through disqualification)*	
30Mar19GP^{14}	1⅛	ft	:48^4	1:12^4	1:36^1	1:48^4		116	FlaDerby-G1	121	71	77/	123	-22	-25	**102**	7	1^1	1½	1^1	1^3	1^{3½}	SaezL^{122}	L	4.80	MaximmSecrity^{3½}Bodxprs^{3½}CodofHonor¾	Drv to 70yd 11
20Feb19GP^2	7f	ft	:22^3	:45^3	1:09^3	1:21^3		113	OC50k-N	121	90	92/	105	-7	-13	**100**	1	5	1½	1½	1^{11}	1^{18}	OrtizIJ^{124}	L	*0.10	*MaximmSecrity*^{18}FirstandThree^{1}WarBridle½	Clearly best 6
24Jan19GP^9	6f	my^s	:22	:45^1	:57	1:09^4		114	OC50k-N	119	89	100/	91	0	-3	**96**	2	3	3^{3½}	2^{hd}	1^3	1^{6½}	MaraghRR^{115*}	L	*0.30	*MaximmSecrity*^{6½}RBoyBode^{3½}StadyEarn^{nk}	Wrap up 5
20Dec18GP^{10}	6½	ft	:23^1	:46^1	1:10^1	1:16^4		108	MC16000	116	89	91/	97	-6	-11	**94**	5	1	1½	1½	1^5	1^{9¾}	MaraghRR^{115*}	L	2.70	*MaximmSecrity*^{9¾}Guereron^1*MathWizard*^{12½}	Ridden out 11

8pp9 McKinzie (NA 0)

Own: Watson, Karl, Pegram, Michael E And Weitm,
3/1 Red, Yellow Disc, Red Sleeves, Yellow Stripes, Quartered
Rosario J

B. h. 5 KEESEP 2016 $170k
Sire : Street Sense (Street Cry (IRE)) $75,000
Dam: Runway Model (Petionville)
Brdr: 0
Trnr: Baffert Bob

126

Life:	14	7 - 6 - 0	$5,667,130		Fst	12	6 - 5 - 0	$3,038,000
2019	7	2 - 5 - 0	$4,771,957		Off	2	1 - 1 - 0	$280,560
2018	5	4 - 0 - 0	$797,856		Dis	4	2 - 2 - 0	$1,191,000
KAR	0	0 - 0 - 0	$0		Trf	0	0 - 0 - 0	$0
					AW	0	0 - 0 - 0	$0

Sire Stats: AWD 7.3 16%Mud 1280MudSts 1.90spi
Dam'sSire: AWD 6.8 14%Mud 2117MudSts 1.16spi
SoldAt: KEESEP 2016 $170.0k (6/47) SireAvg: $81.1k StudFee: $40k

DATE TRK	DIST							RR	RACETYPE	CR												Fin	JOCKEY		ODDS	Top Finishers	Comment
02Nov19SA^{12}	1¼	ft	:47	1:10^3	1:36^1	2:02^4	3↑	121	BCClasic-G1	123	98	126/	78	+3	+15	**106**	8	3^2	3^{1½}	1^1	1½	2^{4¼}	RosarioJ^{126}	L	*2.90	Vino Rosso^{4¼}McKinzie^{4¼}Higher Power^{2½}	2d best 11
28Sep19SA^{10}	1⅛	ft	:48^1	1:12	1:36^4	1:49^1	3↑	120	AwsmAgn-G1	122	87	96/	104	-6	-5	**102**	4	3^{1½}	3^1	3^2	2½	2^{2¼}	SmithME^{125}	L	*0.30	Mongolian Groom^{2¼}McKinzie^{5½}Higher Power^1	2nd best 6
03Aug19Sar^9	1⅛	ft	:47^2	1:11^1	1:35	1:47	3↑	120	Whitney-G1	124	93	101/	111	-2	-6	**109**	5	2^{hd}	2^1	2^1	1^1	1^{1¾}	SmithME^{124}	L	*0.85	McKinzie^{1¾}Yoshida^{4¾}Vino Rosso^{1¼}	Hand ride 7
08Jun19Bel^9	1m	ft	:22	:44^1	1:08^1	1:32^3	3↑	121	MtropltH-G1	123	94	104/	98	+10	+6	**103**	2	8^6	8^5	5^{2½}	5^{2½}	2¾	SmithME^{124}	L	*1.65	Mitole¾*McKinzie*^{nk}Thunder Snow^{3¼}	Stdy 2x 9
03May19CD^7	1$\frac{1}{16}$	gd	:23^4	:47^3	1:11^3	1:41	4↑	120	Alysheba-G2	124	93	100/	117	-5	-9	**112**	1	1½	2½	2^{1½}	1^2	1^{4¾}	SmithME^{118}	L	*0.70	McKinzie^{4¾}Tom's d'Etat^{3¾}*Seeking the Soul*½	Drew off 8
06Apr19SA^{10}	1¼	ft	:49^1	1:13^3	1:38^1	2:03	4↑	119	SAH-G1	121	73	95/	104	-18	-8	**105**	1	3^{1½}	3^2	3^1	1^{hd}	2no	SmithME^{123}	L	*0.40	Gift Box^{no}*McKinzie*^{3¾}Mongolian Groom^{1¾}	Gamely 6
02Feb19SA^9	1⅛	sy^s	:46	1:09^1	1:33^4	1:46^4	4↑	120	SnPsqal-G2	123	99	111/	97	+4	+5	**107**	4	3^{1½}	2½	2½	2^{hd}	2½	SmithME^{124}	L	*0.50	BattleofMidway½McKinzi^{4½}GiantExpctations^{5½}	Outgamed 5
26Dec18SA^9	7f	ft	:22^1	:44^4	1:09^4	1:22^2		119	Malibu-G1	122	83	91/	108	-6	-7	**102**	13	12	10^5	8^{4½}	2½	1^{4¾}	SmithME^{124}	L	*1.20	McKinzi^{4¾}IdentityPolitics^{hd}StillHavingFun^{nk}	Ridden out 14
03Nov18CD^{11}	1¼	ft	:46^2	1:10^3	1:35^4	2:02^4	3↑	122	BCClasic-G1	117	93	107/	34	0	+6	**73**	6	2^1	2^1	6^{2¾}	11^{10}	12^{31}	SmithME^{122}	L	3.90	Accelerate^{1}Gunnevera¾Thunder Snow^{no}	Faltered 14
22Sep18Prx^{11}	1⅛	ft	:48^4	1:13^2	1:39^2	1:52		119	PaDrby-G1	124	99	111/	108	0	-1	**112**	7	3^{1½}	2^{hd}	1^{hd}	1^1	1^{1¾}	SmithME^{122}	L	*2.00	McKinzi^{1¾}Axdrod^{7½}TrigerWarning^1	Vied; led;repelled foe 9

9pp14 Mijack (NA 0)

Own: Prince Faisal Bin Khaled Bin A/aziz
60/1 Red, White Epaulettes, Black Cuffs
Aloufi A

Gr. h. 6 TATHIT 2018 $346.5k
Sire : Elzaam (AUS) (Redoute's Choice (AUS)) $4,000
Dam: Docklands Grace (Honour and Glory)
Brdr: (IRE)
Trnr: Al Harabi S

126

Life:	18	6 - 2 - 2	$304,671		Fst	9	5 - 1 - 1	$210,531
2020	1	1 - 0 - 0	$153,097		Off	0	0 - 0 - 0	$0
2018	6	2 - 0 - 1	$69,321		Dis	0	0 - 0 - 0	$0
KAR	9	5 - 1 - 1	$210,531		Trf	17	5 - 2 - 2	$151,260
					AW	0	0 - 0 - 0	$0

Sire Stats: AWD 7.2 0%Mud 1MudSts 0.67spi
Dam'sSire: AWD 6.8 14%Mud 2191MudSts 1.15spi
SoldAt: TATHIT 2018 $348.5k (1/6) SireAvg: $49.1k StudFee: $ 0k

DATE	TRK	DIST				RR	RACETYPE	CR	Fin	JOCKEY	ODDS	Top Finishers	Comment
08Feb20	King Abdulaziz Racecourse(Ksa)	*1⅛	ft	2:06^1	4↑		Stk 266667		1½	AlawfiA^{126}		Mijck½**Stanch**¾Hibo^1	King Abdulaziz Racecourse(Ksa) 18
							Custodian of the Two Holy Mosques Cup-G1						
25Jan20	King Abdulaziz Racecourse(Ksa)	*1m	ft	1:38^2	4↑		Stk 40000		1^{1¾}	AlawfiA^{126}		*Mijc*^{1¾}**Stnch**^{2}Mypl^{5¾}	King Abdulaziz Racecourse(Ksa) 9
							Ministry of Foreign Affairs Cup-G3						
11Jan20	King Abdulaziz Racecourse(Ksa)	*1⅛	ft	1:52^2	4↑		Hcp 32000		1^{2¼}	AlawfiA^{127}		*Mijc*^{2¼}Crbinc¾**Stnch**^{3}	King Abdulaziz Racecourse(Ksa) 16
							Europe Cup						
14Dec19	King Abdulaziz Racecourse(Ksa)	*1⅛	ft	1:52^4	3↑		Alw 26667		1^{3¾}	AlawfiA^{137}		*Mij*^{3¾}GdsSpd½Alkhtb^{3¼}	King Abdulaziz Racecourse(Ksa) 10
08Nov19	King Abdulaziz Racecourse(Ksa)	*1m	ft	1:38^2	3↑		Hcp 33333		1^{7¾}	AlawfiA^{137}		*Mij*^{7¾}GdsSpd^{4}Mhtr^{1¼}	King Abdulaziz Racecourse(Ksa) 13
							Equestrian Club Award						
26Oct19	King Abdulaziz Racecourse(Ksa)	*1m	ft	1:39^3	3↑		Hcp 32000		3^{6½}	AlaudeebAS^{127}		LAnOrr^{1¾}StrnGls^{4¾}*Mij*^{2¼}	King Abdulaziz Racecourse(Ksa) 12
							General Intelligence Presidency Cup						
23Mar19	King Abdulaziz Racecourse(Ksa)	*7f	ft	1:24	3↑		Alw 26640		17	AlawfiA^{132}		Maypl^{2¼}Adly½Vjay^{nk}	King Abdulaziz Racecourse(Ksa) 18
02Mar19	King Abdulaziz Racecourse(Ksa)	*1¼	ft	2:04^2	4↑		Stk 266600		8^{11}	AlawfiA^{126}		Igider^{2½}*Jorvick*¾Hibou^{no}	King Abdulaziz Racecourse(Ksa) 18
							Custodian of the Two Holy Mosques Cup-G1						
23Feb19	King Abdulaziz Racecourse(Ksa)	*1m	ft	1:36^1	4↑		Hcp 31992		2^1	AltoairshR^{126}		*Maypl*^{1}Mijc^{3}¾Indibiink^{2½}	King Abdulaziz Racecourse(Ksa) 18
							North and South America Cup						
20Oct18	Ascot(GB)	Ⓣ 1m	sf	1:43^2	3↑	118	Hcp 321499	121	3^{1¼}	LeeC^{132}	20.00	*Sharja Bridge*¾Escobar½Mijack^{nk}	Ascot(GB) 20
							Balmoral Handicap Stakes (Class 2) (Sponsored by Qipco)					*10-20-18 Chased leaders; led over 2f out until 2f out; stayed on inside*	

10pp8 Mucho Gusto (NA 0)

Own: Hrh Prince Faisal Bin Khaled
6/1 Red, White Epaulettes, Black Cuffs
Ortiz Jr I

Ch. c. 4 FTMMAY 2018 $625k
Sire : Mucho Macho Man (Macho Uno) $10,000
Dam: Itsagiantcauseway (Giant's Causeway)
Brdr: 0
Trnr: Baffert Bob

Blnkr On
126

Life:	11	6 - 2 - 2	$2,464,503		Fst	10	5 - 2 - 2	$2,351,800
2020	1	1 - 0 - 0	$1,662,000		Off	1	1 - 0 - 0	$90,000
2019	7	3 - 1 - 2	$660,636		Dis	4	1 - 1 - 1	$1,962,800
KAR	0	0 - 0 - 0	$0		Trf	0	0 - 0 - 0	$0
					AW	0	0 - 0 - 0	$0

Sire Stats: AWD 6.9 15%Mud 79MudSts 2.02spi
Dam'sSire: AWD 8.1 14%Mud 1813MudSts 2.48spi
SoldAt: FTMMAY 2018 $625.0k (1/13) SireAvg: $171.2k StudFee: $15k

DATE TRK	DIST							RR	RACETYPE	CR												Fin	JOCKEY		ODDS	Top Finishers	Comment
25Jan20GP^{12}	1⅛	ft	:47^3	1:11^4	1:35^4	1:48^4	4↑	120	PWCInvit-G1	124	90	100/	117	-4	-6	**111**	8	3^1	4^2	3^{2½}	1^{2½}	1^{4½}	OrtizIJ^{124}	b	3.40	Mucho Gusto^{4½}Mr Freeze¾War Story¾	Drv 10
									Pegasus World Cup Invitational S. presented by Runhappy-G1																	*01-25-20 Led early;rebid3wd;drv*	
29Sep19RP^{12}	1⅛	ft	:48	1:12^1	1:36^1	1:49^1		116	OkDrby-G3	118	87	97/	100	-2	-5	**101**	9	2^1	2^{2½}	2^{hd}	3^{nk}	4^2	TalamoJ^{124}	Lb	*0.90	Owendale^{1¾}*Sleepy Eyes Todd*^{nk}Chess Chief^{hd}	Hung 10
24Aug19Sar^{11}	1¼	ft	:47^1	1:11^1	1:35^2	2:01		118	Travers-G1	120	97	118/	82	+1	+10	**104**	7	2^{hd}	1^1	1^{hd}	1^{hd}	3^{3½}	TalamoJ^{126}	Lb	3.45	*Code of Honor*^{3}**Tacitus**½Mucho Gusto^{1¼}	Kept on 12
20Jly19Mth^{12}	1⅛	ft	:46^3	1:10	1:34^4	1:47^2		118	Hskllnv-G1	121	84	100/	100	-99	-99	**102**	4	5^{2¼}	5^{1¼}	3½	2^{hd}	2^{1¼}	TalamoJ^{118}	Lb	3.10	***MaximmSecrity***^{1¼}MchoGsto^8*SpuntoRun*^{2½}	3-4w 6
16Jun19SA^6	1$\frac{1}{16}$	ft	:24	:48^4	1:13^1	1:45		116	Affirmed-G3	119	77	86/	100	-11	-8	**95**	6	4^{1½}	4¾	3^{nk}	1^2	1^{2¼}	TalamoJ^{124}	Lb	1.90	Mucho Gusto^{2¼}Roadster^{1}Visitant^1	Clear 6
18May19SA^6	7f	ft	:22^2	:45^2	1:10^2	1:22^4		115	LBrrera-G3	118	91	92/	100	-5	-11	**96**	1	3	1½	1½	1^{1½}	1^{3¼}	TalamoJ^{124}	Lb	*0.50	*Mucho Gusto*^{3¼}Manhattan Up^{hd}Vantastic^{3½}	Cleared 6
24Mar19Sun^{11}	1⅛	ft	:45^3	1:09^3	1:34^3	1:46^4		113	SunDrby-G3	115	89	95/	86	-3	-4	**92**	1	1½	1^{hd}	1½	2½	3^6	TalamoJ^{122}	Lb	*0.90	CuttingHumor^{nk}Anothrtwistafat^{5¾}*MuchoGusto*^{1½}	Wknd 9
02Feb19SA^6	1$\frac{1}{16}$	sy^s	:23^3	:46^2	1:10^2	1:41^4		115	RBLewis-G3	117	82	92/	95	-3	-3	**95**	5	3^{1½}	2^{2½}	2^{hd}	1^2	1^{4¾}	TalamoJ^{122}	Lb	*0.60	Mucho Gusto^{4¾}Gunmetal Gray¾Easy Shot^{2¼}	Cleared 5
08Dec18Lrc^5	1$\frac{1}{16}$	ft	:23^1	:47^1	1:10^4	1:41		116	LosAlFt-G1	117	91	94/	93	-1	-6	**95**	6	1½	1½	1^{hd}	2^1	2^5	TalamoJ^{120}	Lb	4.20	Improbable^5*Mucho Gusto*^{3}*Extra Hope*^{3}	2nd best 6
17Nov18Dmr^6	7f	ft	:22^1	:45^1	1:10^1	1:23^2		114	BobHpe-G3	116	92	94/	91	-3	-6	**92**	2	2	1½	1^1	1½	1^{1½}	TalamoJ^{118}	Lb	*0.80	Mucho Gusto^{1½}Savagery^{hd}Sparky Ville¾	Rail 5

International King Abdulaziz Racecourse(KSA) Stk 20781500K 1⅛ Mile 4&up Saturday, February 29, 2020 **Race 8** **brisnet.com** *the handicapper's edge*

11 PP4 **North America (NA 0)**
Own: Ramzan Kadyrov
30/1 Red, White And Emerald Green Striped Sleeves, White
Mullen R

B. g. 8 TATDEC 2012 $168.4k
Sire: Dubawi (IRE) (Dubai Millennium (GB)) $331,467
Dam: Northern Mischief (Yankee Victor)
Brdr: (GB)
Trnr: Seemar S

126

Life:	19	7 - 3 - 3	$754,883	Fst	13	7 - 1 - 2	$1,077,275
2020	1	0 - 0 - 1	$39,095	Off	0	0 - 0 - 0	$0
2019	3	2 - 0 - 0	$323,812	Dis	0	0 - 0 - 0	$0
KAR	0	0 - 0 - 0	$0	Trf	5	0 - 1 - 1	$3,303
				AW	1	0 - 1 - 0	$1,431

Sire Stats: AWD 8.9 22%Mud 124MudSts 2.98spi
Dam'sSire: AWD 6.6 14%Mud 574MudSts 1.20spi
SoldAt: TATDEC 2012 $168.4k (4/6) SireAvg: $229.5k StudFee: $ 0k

DATE	TRK	DIST				RR	RACETYPE CR	Fin	JOCKEY	ODDS	Top Finishers	Comment	
09Jan20	Dubai - Meydan(Uae)	*1m	ft	1:37^{2}	3↑		Stk 350000 Al Maktoum Challenge Round 1 Presented by Longines Conquest V H P-G2	3^{nk}	MullenR^{126}		Kmbr^{hd}ScrtAmbton^{hd}NrthAmrca^{9}	Dubai - Meydan(Uae)	7
30Mar19	Dubai - Meydan(Uae)	*1¼	ft	2:03^{4}	3↑		Stk 12000000 Dubai World Cup Sponsored by Emirates Airline-G1	7$^{7\frac{3}{4}}$	MullenR^{126}		ThndrSnw^{no}**Grnksk**$^{2\frac{3}{4}}$Gnvra½	Dubai - Meydan(Uae)	12
07Feb19	Dubai - Meydan(Uae)	*1$\frac{3}{16}$	ft	1:58^{3}	3↑		Stk 450000 Al Maktoum Challenge Round 2 Sponsored by Al Naboodah Allied Products Division-G2	1$^{2\frac{1}{4}}$	MullenR^{126}		NrthAmrc$^{2\frac{1}{4}}$NwTrls$^{4\frac{3}{4}}$CsmCharl$^{1\frac{1}{4}}$	Dubai - Meydan(Uae)	6
10Jan19	Dubai - Meydan(Uae)	*1m	ft	1:35^{4}	3↑		Stk 350000 Al Maktoum Challenge Round 1 Sponsored by Mubadala-G2	1^{9}	MullenR^{126}		*NorthAmrica*^{9}Kimbar$^{1\frac{3}{4}}$*Mntazah*$^{1\frac{3}{4}}$	Dubai - Meydan(Uae)	9
31Mar18	Dubai - Meydan(Uae)	*1¼	ft	2:01^{1}	3↑		Stk 10000000 Dubai World Cup Sponsored by Emirates Airline-G1	10^{51}	MullenR^{126}		ThndrSnow$^{5\frac{3}{4}}$WstCast^{nk}Mbthj$^{1\frac{3}{4}}$	Dubai - Meydan(Uae)	10
10Mar18	Dubai - Meydan(Uae)	*1¼	ft	2:01^{3}	3↑		Stk 400000 Al Maktoum Challenge Round 3 Sponsored by Emirates Airline-G1	1$^{5\frac{1}{4}}$	MullenR^{126}		NrthAmrc$^{5\frac{1}{4}}$*ThndrSn*$^{3\frac{3}{4}}$FrCrzd^{9}	Dubai - Meydan(Uae)	12
08Feb18	Dubai - Meydan(Uae)	*1$\frac{3}{16}$	ft	1:57^{4}	3↑		Stk 250000 Al Maktoum Challenge Round 2 Sponsored by Gulf News-G2	2^{nk}	MullenR^{126}		ThndrSnw^{nk}*NrthAmrc*^{4}*HvyMtl*$^{1\frac{1}{2}}$	Dubai - Meydan(Uae)	6
11Jan18	Dubai - Meydan(Uae)	*1m	ft	1:37^{4}	3↑		Stk 250000 Al Maktoum Challenge Round 1 Presented by Longines Gents Master Collection-G2	3^{12}	MullenR^{126}		HvyMtl$^{4\frac{1}{2}}$*ThndrSn*$^{7\frac{1}{2}}$NrthAmrc$^{3\frac{3}{4}}$	Dubai - Meydan(Uae)	8
25Mar17	Dubai - Meydan(Uae)	*1m	ft	1:35^{3}	3↑		Stk 1000000 Godolphin Mile Sponsored by Meydan Sobha-G2	10^{26}	MullenR^{126}		ScondSmmr^{nk}*Ros*$^{\frac{3}{4}}$ShrpAztc$^{4\frac{1}{4}}$	Dubai - Meydan(Uae)	13
11Feb17	Dubai - Meydan(Uae)	*1m	ft	1:36^{2}	3↑		Stk 200000 Firebreak S. Sponsored by Meydan One Mall-G3	1^{7}	MullenR^{126}		NrthAmrc^{7}EnobldFrnd$^{3\frac{1}{4}}$LndAmr$^{1\frac{1}{2}}$	Dubai - Meydan(Uae)	8

12 PP2 **Tacitus (NA 0)**
Own: Juddmonte Farms, Inc
15/1 Green, Pink Sash, White Sleeves, Pink Cap
Lezcano J

Gr/ro. c. 4
Sire: Tapit (Pulpit) $200,000
Dam: Close Hatches (First Defence)
Brdr: 0
Trnr: Mott William

126

Life:	9	3 - 3 - 2	$2,436,883	Fst	7	2 - 3 - 1	$1,339,000
2019	7	2 - 3 - 2	$2,394,520	Off	2	1 - 0 - 1	$338,500
2018	2	1 - 0 - 0	$42,363	Dis	2	1 - 1 - 0	$520,000
KAR	0	0 - 0 - 0	$0	Trf	0	0 - 0 - 0	$0
				AW	0	0 - 0 - 0	$0

Sire Stats: AWD 7.6 18%Mud 1758MudSts 2.92spi
Dam'sSire: AWD 6.8 19%Mud 404MudSts 1.82spi

DATE TRK	DIST							RR	RACETYPE	CR													Fin	JOCKEY		ODDS	Top Finishers	Comment	
28Sep19Bel^{10}	1¼	ft	:47^{3}	1:11^{3}	1:35^{3}	2:00^{1}	3↑	120	JkyClbGC-G1	120	95	108/	92	0	+1	**104**	1	2^{1}	2½	2^{1}	3^{2}		3^{4}	OrtizJL^{122}	Lb	2.80	*Vino Rosso*^{no}Code of Honor^{4}Tacitus^{1}	Gave way	5
24Aug19Sar^{11}	1¼	ft	:47^{1}	1:11^{1}	1:35^{2}	2:01		118	Travers-G1	120	95	118/	83	+1	+10	**105**	6	1^{hd}	3^{1}	2^{hd}	2^{hd}		2^{3}	OrtizJL^{126}	Lb	*2.40	*Code of Honor*^{3}Tacitus½**Mucho Gusto**$^{1\frac{1}{4}}$	Ran on	12
27Jly19Sar^{11}	1⅛	ft	:48^{4}	1:12^{2}	1:36^{3}	1:49^{1}		118	JimDandy-G2	119	73	89/	104	-10	-6	**98**	5	6^{5}	6$^{4\frac{1}{2}}$	4^{2}	2$^{1\frac{1}{2}}$		2$^{\frac{3}{4}}$	OrtizJL^{122}	L	*1.60	Tax$^{\frac{3}{4}}$Tacitus$^{3\frac{3}{4}}$Global Campaign½	Ins trns	6
08Jun19Bel^{11}	1½	ft	:48^{3}	1:13^{2}	2:02^{3}	2:28^{1}		117	Belmont-G1	119	86	94/	95	-15	-1	**100**	10	7$^{4\frac{1}{2}}$	8$^{4\frac{3}{4}}$	5$^{2\frac{1}{2}}$	4$^{1\frac{1}{2}}$		2^{1}	OrtizJL^{126}	L	*1.95	Sir Winston^{1}Tacitus$^{\frac{3}{4}}$*Joevia*^{1}	Bump upr	10
04May19CD^{12}	1¼	sy^{s}	:46^{3}	1:12^{2}	1:38^{3}	2:03^{4}		118	KyDerby-G1	120	79	74/	106	+5	-16	**96**	8	15^{10}	16^{9}	8$^{4\frac{1}{4}}$	7$^{6\frac{1}{2}}$		4$^{3\frac{1}{4}}$	OrtizJL^{126}	L	5.80	**MaxmmScrty**$^{1\frac{3}{4}}$ContryHos$^{\frac{3}{4}}$*CdfHnr*$^{\frac{3}{4}}$	Good courage	19
									Kentucky Derby presented by Woodford Reserve-G1																		*(Placed 3rd through disqualification)*		
06Apr19Aqu^{10}	1⅛	ft	:46^{4}	1:11^{2}	1:37^{4}	1:51^{1}		116	WoodMem-G2	121	91	100/	101	+13	+12	**103**	2	4^{6}	4^{8}	4$^{7\frac{1}{2}}$	1^{hd}		1$^{1\frac{1}{4}}$	OrtizJL^{123}	L	*2.60	Tacitus$^{1\frac{1}{4}}$Tax$^{2\frac{3}{4}}$Haikal½	2wto1/4	11
09Mar19Tam^{11}	1$\frac{1}{16}$	ft	:22^{3}	:45^{4}	1:09^{2}	1:41^{4}		115	TamDby-G2	117	78	87/	100	+9	+8	**95**	10	6^{8}	6^{10}	7^{8}	3^{2}		1$^{1\frac{1}{4}}$	OrtizJL^{117}	L	8.90	*Tacitus*$^{1\frac{1}{4}}$Outshine$^{1\frac{1}{4}}$Win Win Win½	Driving	11
10Nov18Aqu^{5}	1m	gd	:23^{2}	:46^{4}	1:12^{4}	1:38^{3}		111	Mdn 70k	115	79	79/	93	-2	-5	**85**	6	6$^{1\frac{3}{4}}$	5^{2}	3½	1^{hd}		1^{nk}	OrtizJL^{119}		*0.65	*Tacitus*^{nk}Erlich^{3}Motagally^{1}	Gamely	7
04Oct18Bel^{8}	1$\frac{1}{16}$	ft	:22^{4}	:45^{3}	1:09^{4}	1:41^{3}		111	Mdn 75k	113	96	100/	84	+8	+5	**93**	5	3½	3^{1}	2½	3$^{1\frac{1}{2}}$		4$^{2\frac{1}{2}}$	OrtizJL^{119}		8.00	KingforaDay$^{2\frac{1}{4}}$FelixtheFox^{nk}*KentckyWildcat*^{hd}	Wknd late	8

13 PP12 **Magic Wand (NA 0)**
Own: Tabor, Michael B , Magnier, Mrs John, And Sl
30/1 Blue, Orange Ball, Orange Stripe On Sleeves, Blue And
Moore R L

B. m. 5 ARQAUG 2016 $1563.5k
Sire: Galileo (IRE) (Sadler's Wells)
Dam: Prudenzia (IRE) (Dansili (GB))
Brdr: (IRE)
Trnr: O'Brien Aidan

121

Life:	30	3 - 9 - 3	$2,882,947	Fst	0	0 - 0 - 0	$0
2020	2	0 - 1 - 0	$49,341	Off	0	0 - 0 - 0	$0
2019	18	1 - 6 - 2	$2,172,409	Dis	0	0 - 0 - 0	$0
KAR	0	0 - 0 - 0	$0	Trf	23	3 - 9 - 2	$4,323,240
				AW	0	0 - 0 - 0	$0

Sire Stats: AWD 10.4 4%Mud 80MudSts 6.08spi
Dam'sSire: AWD 9.2 5%Mud 41MudSts 2.74spi
SoldAt: ARQAUG 2016 $1563.5k (3/34) SireAvg: $586.1k StudFee: $ 0k

DATE	TRK	DIST				RR	RACETYPE CR	Fin	JOCKEY	ODDS	Top Finishers	Comment	
25Jan20GP^{11}		Ⓣ 1$\frac{3}{16}$ fm :48^{2} 1:11^{4}1:34^{4}		1:51^{3}	4↑	119	PWCTfInv-G1 120 98 111/ 101 0 0 **109** 12 1½ 1^{hd} 1^{1} 1^{hd}	2^{2}	MooreRL^{119}	3.70	Zulu Alpha^{2}Magic Wand^{nk}Instilled Regard^{3}	Outkkd	12
17Jan20	Kranji(Sng)	Ⓣ 6f	gd	1:09^{4}	4↑		Hcp 72500 Class 3	4$^{1\frac{3}{4}}$	CcW^{130}	b	Ironside^{1}Pax Animi$^{\frac{3}{4}}$Baffert^{hd}	Sin(Sng)	7
08Dec19	Sha Tin(HK)	Ⓣ *1¼	gd	2:00^{2}	3↑		Stk 3576871 Longines Hong Kong Cup-G1	2no	MooreR^{122}	5.00	Win Bright^{no}Magic Wand½Landfall$^{1\frac{1}{4}}$	Sha Tin(HK)	8
09Nov19	Flemington(Aus)	Ⓣ *1¼	gd	2:01^{4}	3↑		Stk 1371754 Seppelt Mackinnon S.-G1	1^{1}	MooreRL^{126}	4.00	Magic Wand^{1}Melody Belle^{no}Hartnell^{hd}	Flemington(Aus)	16
05Nov19	Flemington(Aus)	Ⓣ *2m	sf	3:24^{3}	3↑		Stk 5336250 Lexus Melbourne Cup-G1	10$^{3\frac{1}{4}}$	MooreRL^{118}	25.00	VwAndDclr^{hd}MastrfRalty^{no}PrncfAran^{no}	Flemington(Aus)	24
26Oct19	Moonee Valley(Aus)	Ⓣ *1¼	gd	2:04^{1}	3↑		Stk 3410514 Ladbrokes Cox Plate-G1	4$^{3\frac{3}{4}}$	MooreRL^{126}	8.00	*LysGracx*$^{1\frac{1}{2}}$Castlvchio^{2}TAkShrk^{nk}	Moonee Valley(Aus)	14
20Oct19	Kranji(Sng)	Ⓣ 7f	gd	1:22	4↑		Hcp 72500 Class 3	11$^{5\frac{1}{4}}$	LernerM^{129}		Salamnc^{hd}SiamVipasiri^{nk}Threeandforpence^{hd}	Sin(Sng)	13
22Sep19	Kranji(Sng)	Ⓣ 1m	gd	1:34^{1}	4↑		Hcp 88500 Class 2	4$^{2\frac{1}{4}}$	CcW^{116}	b	Black Jade½Real Success$^{1\frac{1}{4}}$Yabadabadoo½	Sin(Sng)	9
14Sep19	Leopardstown(Ire)	Ⓣ 1¼	gd	2:06^{2}	3↑	121	Stk 1273528 122 Qipco Irish Champion S.-G1	2$^{2\frac{1}{4}}$	HeffernanJA^{130}	20.00	Mgcl$^{2\frac{1}{4}}$MgcWnd^{hd}AnthnyVanDyck½ *09-14-19 Soon raced in 5th; closed travelling smoothly between horses s*	Leopardstown(Ire)	8
25Aug19	Kranji(Sng)	Ⓣ 7f	gd	1:21^{4}	4↑		Hcp 88500 Class 2	3^{3}	CcW^{116}	b	Top Knight^{2}Nepean^{1}Magic Wand½	Sin(Sng)	10

brisnet.com *the handicapper's edge*

Intern **King Abdulaziz Racecourse(KSA)** Stk 20781500K 1⅛ Mile 4&up Saturday, February 29, 2020 **Race 8**

14 pp6 **Midnight Bisou (NA 0)**
Own: Bloom Racing Stable, Llc, Madaket Stables L
8/1 Red, Black Star, Red Dots On White Sleeves, Red Cap
Smith M

Dkbbr. m. 5 OBSAPR 2017 $80k
Sire : Midnight Lute (Real Quiet) $15,000
Dam: Diva Delite (Repent)
Brdr: ()
Trnr: Asmussen Steven

121

Life:	19	11 - 5 - 3	$2,286,848	**Fst**	17	10 - 4 - 3 $3,240,000
2019	8	7 - 1 - 0	$1,486,898	**Off**	2	2 - 0 - 0 $510,000
2018	9	4 - 2 - 3	$767,511	**Dis**	6	2 - 2 - 2 $1,211,000
KAR	0	0 - 0 - 0	$0	**Trf**	0	0 - 0 - 0 $0
				AW	0	0 - 0 - 0 $0

Sire Stats: AWD 7.0 16%Mud 826MudSts 1.56spi
Dam'sSire: AWD 7.3 14%Mud 1219MudSts 0.89spi
SoldAt: OBSAPR 2017 $80.0k (5/16) SireAvg: $84.3k StudFee: $25k

DATE TRK	DIST						RR	RACETYPE	CR												Fin	JOCKEY		ODDS	Top Finishers	Comment	
02Nov19SA 10	1⅛ ft	:46 3	1:10 4	1:37	1:50 2	3↑	120	ⒻBCDistaf-G1	124	102	109/	99	+17	+16	**106**	4	6 5	7 5½	8 7¾	3 1½	2 1½	SmithME 124	L	*1.00	BlePrize 1½ MidnightBiso 3¼ SrngtlEmprs 1¼	Kept at bay	11
28Sep19Bel 8	1⅛ ft	:48	1:11 4	1:36 1	1:48 4	3↑	119	ⒻBldmInv-G2	123	84	92/	95	-4	-3	**96**	1	2 1	2 1	1 hd	1½	1 3¼	VelazquezJR 123	L	*0.15	Midnight Bisou 3¼ Wow Cat 6¼ Crimson Frost 1	3w&bmp upr	5
24Aug19Sar 9	1⅛ ft	:47 4	1:11 2	1:35 3	1:47 4	3↑	121	ⒻPrsnlEns-G1	124	80	87/	104	-4	-6	**98**	1	6 4½	6 3½	5 2½	2 hd	1 no	SmithME 124	L	1.70	*Midnight Bisou* no Elate 8½ She's a Julie 1¼	Dueld	6
20Jly19Mth 8	1 1/16 ft	:24 3	:49	1:13 2	1:43 2	3↑	119	ⒻMPtchr-G3	121	71	69/	110	-99	-99	**90**	2	3 1½	3 1½	4 2	2 1	1 1	SmithME 123	L	*0.05	*Midnight Bisou* 1 Coach Rocks 5¼ Cosmic Burst ½	Willingly	5
08Jun19Bel 5	1 1/16 ft	:23 2	:45 4	1:09 1	1:39 3	4↑	122	ⒻOPhipps-G1	124	88	102/	99	-1	+3	**102**	2	4 1½	4 2	2 1½	1 1½	1 3½	SmithME 123	L	1.70	*Midnight Bisou* 3½ *Come Dancing* ¾ Mopotism 6¾	Light drve	5
14Apr19OP 6	1 1/16 gd	:23	:47	1:12	1:43 4	4↑	120	ⒻApIBlsmH-G1	123	89	103/	100	+6	0	**104**	6	5 7½	5 5½	2½	2½	1 no	SmithME 122	L	*0.90	*Midnight Bisou* no Escape Clause 2¾ *Elate* 9	Held foe	6
16Mar19OP 7	1 1/16 ft	:24 2	:48 4	1:12 4	1:42 3	4↑	120	ⒻAzeri-G2	122	67	78/	111	-18	-14	**96**	2	3 1½	4 2½	4 2	2 1	1 1	SmithME 119	L	1.20	*Midnight Bisou* 1 Elate 1 Shamrock Rose 4¾	Drvg	5
27Jan19Hou 9	1 1/16 ft	:24 3	:49 1	1:13 1	1:44 2	4↑	119	ⒻHouLdyCl-G3	121	75	89/	103	-9	-5	**98**	6	5 2½	6 2¾	4 1¼	3 2	1¾	SmithME 123	L	*0.20	*MidnightBiso* ¾ MoonlitGardn nk *Havnhasmynikki* 3¼	Up late	6
03Nov18CD 9	1⅛ ft	:47 2	1:12	1:36 3	1:49 3	3↑	121	ⒻBCDistaf-G1	123	101	111/	98	+12	+7	**107**	7	7 4½	7 4	4 2½	3 3½	3 1½	VelazquezJR 121	L	5.90	Monomoy Girl 1 Wow Cat ½ *Midnight Bisou* hd	Gaining	11
22Sep18Prx 10	1 1/16 ft	:24	:48 3	1:13	1:45 4		118	ⒻCotilln-G1	123	87	98/	106	-3	-1	**104**	7	5 2½	5 2¼	3 3	2 1½	2 nk	SmithME 124	L	4.20	*MnmyGrl* nk MdnghtBs 10½ WndrGadt nk	Steered out; drifted	8
								Cotillion S.-G1																		*(Placed 1st through disqualification)*	

15 **Staunch (NA 0)**
Own: Prince A/aziz Bin Fahd Bin A/aziz
Green, Black Epaulettes, Black Cuffs
Reserve

B. h. 7 TATHIT 2016 $70.5k
Sire : Pivotal (GB) (Polar Falcon) $53,035
Dam: Striving (IRE) (Danehill Dancer (IRE))
Brdr: (GB)
Trnr: Almandeel Naif

126

Life:	6	1 - 2 - 1	$65,813	**Fst**	19	4 - 6 - 3 $158,786
2020	1	0 - 1 - 0	$57,910	**Off**	0	0 - 0 - 0 $0
2016	5	1 - 1 - 1	$7,903	**Dis**	0	0 - 0 - 0 $0
KAR	17	4 - 5 - 2	$149,453	**Trf**	5	1 - 1 - 1 $8,195
				AW	0	0 - 0 - 0 $0

Sire Stats: AWD 7.9 14%Mud 103MudSts 2.34spi
Dam'sSire: AWD 8.1 7%Mud 72MudSts 2.21spi
SoldAt: TATHIT 2016 $70.5k (4/23) SireAvg: $30.6k StudFee: $85k

DATE	TRK	DIST				RR	RACETYPE	CR	Fin	JOCKEY	ODDS	Top Finishers	Comment	
08Feb20	King Abdulaziz Racecourse(Ksa)	*1⅛	ft	2:06 1	4↑		Stk 266667		2½	AlfouraidiA 126		**Mjjck** ½ Stanch ¾ Hibo 1	King Abdulaziz Racecourse(Ksa)	18
							Custodian of the Two Holy Mosques Cup-G1							
25Jan20	King Abdulaziz Racecourse(Ksa)	*1m	ft	1:38 2	4↑		Stk 40000		2 1¾	AlfouraidiA 127		***MJjc*** 1¾ Stnch 2 Maypl 5¾	King Abdulaziz Racecourse(Ksa)	9
							Ministry of Foreign Affairs Cup-G3							
11Jan20	King Abdulaziz Racecourse(Ksa)	*1⅛	ft	1:52 2	4↑		Hcp 32000		3 3	AlfouraidiA 127		***MJjc*** 2¼ Crblnc ¾ Stnch 3	King Abdulaziz Racecourse(Ksa)	16
							Europe Cup							
28Dec19	King Abdulaziz Racecourse(Ksa)	*1½	ft	2:33	3↑		Stk 240000		6 13	AlfouraidiA 130		Cntng 9 Mhtm ½ GsSp 2¼	King Abdulaziz Racecourse(Ksa)	18
							Crown Prince Cup-G1							
29Nov19	King Abdulaziz Racecourse(Ksa)	*1⅛	ft	1:51 1	3↑		Hcp 33333		1 9	AlfouraidiA 137		Stnch 9 Hwk nk Crblnc nk	King Abdulaziz Racecourse(Ksa)	14
							Equestrian Club Award							
23Mar19	King Abdulaziz Racecourse(Ksa)	*1¼	ft	2:03 4	4↑		Stk 66600		4 3½	MorenoA 132		Jrvck 1½ Alnfr 1½ Igidr ¾	King Abdulaziz Racecourse(Ksa)	13
							King Abdulaziz Racetrack Champion Cup-G1							
08Mar19	King Abdulaziz Racecourse(Ksa)	*1⅛	ft	1:50 2	4↑		Hcp 29326		1 3¼	MorenoA 137		Stnc 3¼ FntstcFr 1¾ Brcfl 2	King Abdulaziz Racecourse(Ksa)	13
							Equestrian Club Award							
02Mar19	King Abdulaziz Racecourse(Ksa)	*1¼	ft	2:04 2	4↑		Stk 266600		6 6½	MorenoA 126		Igider 2½ *Jorvick* ½ Hibou no	King Abdulaziz Racecourse(Ksa)	18
							Custodian of the Two Holy Mosques Cup-G1							
09Nov18	King Abdulaziz Racecourse(Ksa)	*1⅛	ft	1:51 3	3↑		Alw 26660		2 1	MorenoA 134		Hibo 1 Stnch 3 EvningHll 4	King Abdulaziz Racecourse(Ksa)	13
17Mar18	King Abdulaziz Racecourse(Ksa)	*1m	ft	1:37	4↑		Hcp 32004		2 2¼	AldahamM 126		LAnOrr 2¼ Stn hd BlOnBl 2¼	King Abdulaziz Racecourse(Ksa)	16
							North and South America Cup							

Acknowledgment

Thanks go to Constantine Dzhabarov, David McKenzie, Steve Roman and Mick Thomason for data and helpful comments on this chapter.

Chapter 27

The COVID-19 Triple Crown, 2020

William T. Ziemba

This chapter discusses the Triple Crown races in 2020 during the COVID-19 period. The order of the races and dates run were changed, there were no fans at the tracks and there were scandals. Yet the season ended reasonably well.

The 2020 triple crown and three year old races were unusual to say the least. Normally the Kentucky Derby at $1\frac{1}{4}$ miles is run on the first Saturday in May, often in the mud, at Churchill Downs in Louisville Kentucky. The race has about twenty horses and is possibly the toughest race of their careers early in their three year old year. This is basically equivalent to twelve year olds running a tough race. It is an extreme test of speed and stamina and some horses never recover from it.

Two weeks later, they run the $1\frac{3}{16}$ mile Preakness at Pimlico in Baltimore. That's usually an easier race and often the Derby 1–2 finishers are favored and do well in this race. Then the $1\frac{1}{2}$ mile Belmont is three weeks later early in June. Later in the season the top horses run in the ($1\frac{1}{8}$ mile Haskell at Monmouth, New Jersey and the $1\frac{1}{4}$ mile Travers at Saratoga in August. The season culminates at the Breeders' Cup in November.

This year because of the worldwide COVID-19 cases and deaths and the poor US response, the tracks were closed. They slowly opened with no fans. Jockeys, trainers, owners and others were there with masks and fairly safe social distancing. Still many jockeys and racing personnel got the virus.

This year the races were all mixed up and took place over a much longer time frame. Gulfstream was open early during the first phase of the virus when most tracks were closed. They held the $1\frac{1}{4}$ mile Florida Derby on March 28.

After the preps, the Belmont Stakes was held on June 20. Besides the change of date, it was run at the shorter distance of $1\frac{1}{8}$ miles. Then the Haskell on July 18 which was followed by the Travers at $1\frac{1}{4}$ miles on August 8. Then the $1\frac{1}{4}$ mile Kentucky Derby was run on September 5. Finally, the Preakness at its usual distance of $1\frac{3}{16}$ was run on October 3 at Pimlico in Baltimore. Later the horses ran in the Breeders' Cup in Lexington at Keeneland on November 6 and 7.

We begin the analysis with the Florida prep races. Tiz the Law easily won the grade III Holy Bull at Gulfstream on February 1 and then he won the grade I Curlin Florida Derby at $1\frac{1}{4}$ mile by just under 3 lengths. Tiz the Law was sired by Constitution, the winner of four races out of eight run winning $1,031,596. Constitution was sired by Tapit and dam sire Distorted Humor who is often rated the top US broodmare sire. Tiz the Law's superb breeding shown in Figure 27.1 includes the two time Breeders' Cup Classic winner Tiznow.

27.1. The Belmont Stakes

Table 27.1 show the Belmont Stakes field with the morning line odds and Table 27.2 gives the handicappers picks. Table 27.3 shows the betfair odds. Tiz the Law was a deserving big favorite and did win at 4–5 odds. His pedigree is in Figure 27.1 and he is shown in Fgure 27.2. Dr. Post at 7.9–1 by Curlin was second and Max Player by Honor Code which I own a part of at 14.2–1. Honor Code also sired Honor AP who won the Santa Anita Derby and was the second choice for the Kentucky Derby. He later was retired to stud at Lanes End where Honor Code and AP Indy were.

Figure 27.4 shows the chart of the race. Steve Roman's PF adjusted speed ratings, −61 in Figure 27.3 shows that Tiz the Law's dosage index of 4.33, is not far off the predicted value of 3.97.

27.2. The 146th Kentucky Derby

The Derby at $1\frac{1}{4}$ miles was held on the September 5th, the first Saturday in September not May as usual. The last time the Derby was not run in May was in 1945. Racing had been suspended from December 1944 till war conditions permitted. After VE day, the Derby was scheduled for June 9 when Hoop Jr won. The Preakness and Belmont Stakes were run on June 16 and 23 respectively.

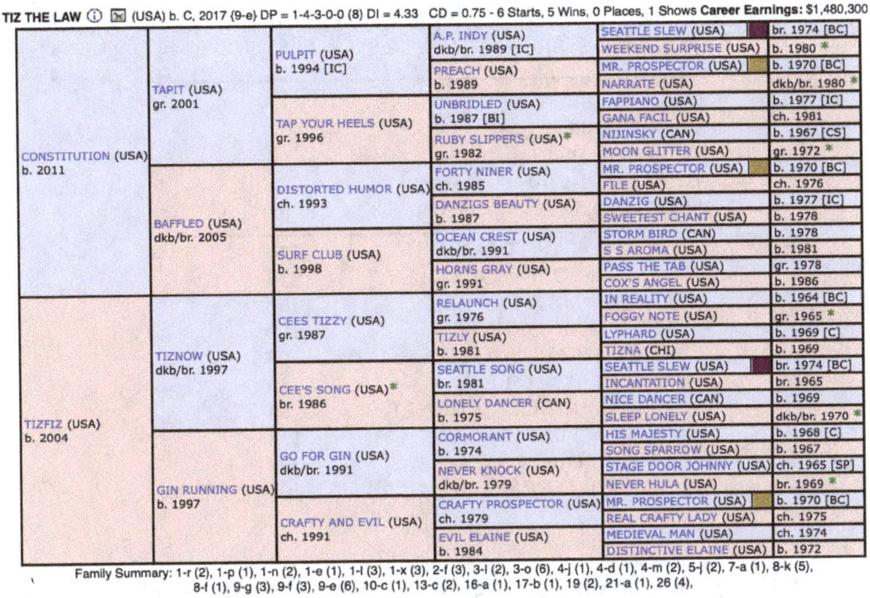

TIZ THE LAW (USA) b. C, 2017 {9-e} DP = 1-4-3-0-0 (8) DI = 4.33 CD = 0.75 - 6 Starts, 5 Wins, 0 Places, 1 Shows **Career Earnings:** $1,480,300
CONSTITUTION (USA) b. 2011
TAPIT (USA) gr. 2001
PULPIT (USA) b. 1994 [IC]
A.P. INDY (USA) dkb/br. 1989 [IC]
SEATTLE SLEW (USA) br. 1974 [BC]
WEEKEND SURPRISE (USA) b. 1980 *
PREACH (USA) b. 1989
MR. PROSPECTOR (USA) b. 1970 [BC]
NARRATE (USA) dkb/br. 1980 *
TAP YOUR HEELS (USA) gr. 1996
UNBRIDLED (USA) b. 1987 [BI]
FAPPIANO (USA) b. 1977 [IC]
GANA FACIL (USA) ch. 1981
RUBY SLIPPERS (USA)* gr. 1982
NIJINSKY (CAN) b. 1967 [CS]
MOON GLITTER (USA) gr. 1972 *
BAFFLED (USA) dkb/br. 2005
DISTORTED HUMOR (USA) ch. 1993
FORTY NINER (USA) ch. 1985
MR. PROSPECTOR (USA) b. 1970 [BC]
FILE (USA) ch. 1976
DANZIGS BEAUTY (USA) b. 1987
DANZIG (USA) b. 1977 [IC]
SWEETEST CHANT (USA) b. 1978
SURF CLUB (USA) b. 1998
OCEAN CREST (USA) dkb/br. 1991
STORM BIRD (CAN) b. 1978
S S AROMA (USA) b. 1981
HORNS GRAY (USA) gr. 1991
PASS THE TAB (USA) gr. 1978
COX'S ANGEL (USA) b. 1986
TIZFIZ (USA) b. 2004
TIZNOW (USA) dkb/br. 1997
CEES TIZZY (USA) gr. 1987
RELAUNCH (USA) gr. 1976
IN REALITY (USA) b. 1964 [BC]
FOGGY NOTE (USA) gr. 1965 *
TIZLY (USA) b. 1981
LYPHARD (USA) b. 1969 [C]
TIZNA (CHI) b. 1969
CEE'S SONG (USA)* br. 1986
SEATTLE SONG (USA) br. 1981
SEATTLE SLEW (USA) br. 1974 [BC]
INCANTATION (USA) br. 1965
LONELY DANCER (CAN) b. 1975
NICE DANCER (CAN) b. 1969
SLEEP LONELY (USA) dkb/br. 1970 *
GIN RUNNING (USA) b. 1997
GO FOR GIN (USA) dkb/br. 1991
CORMORANT (USA) b. 1974
HIS MAJESTY (USA) b. 1968 [C]
SONG SPARROW (USA) b. 1967
NEVER KNOCK (USA) dkb/br. 1979
STAGE DOOR JOHNNY (USA) ch. 1965 [SP]
NEVER HULA (USA) br. 1969 *
CRAFTY AND EVIL (USA) ch. 1991
CRAFTY PROSPECTOR (USA) ch. 1979
MR. PROSPECTOR (USA) b. 1970 [BC]
REAL CRAFTY LADY (USA) ch. 1975
EVIL ELAINE (USA) b. 1984
MEDIEVAL MAN (USA) ch. 1974
DISTINCTIVE ELAINE (USA) b. 1972
Family Summary: 1-r (2), 1-p (1), 1-n (2), 1-e (1), 1-l (3), 1-x (3), 2-f (3), 3-l (2), 3-o (6), 4-j (1), 4-d (1), 4-m (2), 5-j (2), 7-a (1), 8-k (5), 8-f (1), 9-g (3), 9-f (3), 9-e (6), 10-c (1), 13-c (2), 16-a (1), 17-b (1), 19 (2), 21-a (1), 26 (4),

Figure 27.1. Pedigree for Tiz the Law.

Table 27.1. Field for the Belmont.

POST	HORSE	ML ODDS
1	Tap It to Win	6-1
2	Sole Volante	9-2
3	Max Player	15-1
4	Modernist	15-1
5	Farmington Road	15-1
6	Fore Left	30-1
7	Jungle Runner	50-1
8	Tiz the Law	6-5
9	Dr. Post	5-1
10	Pneumatic	8-1

Table 27.2. The handicappers rated the Belmont, winner circled.

Timeform:⑧-2-10
David: ⑧- Tied 1 & 2
DJM: none, but 5 is the best closer
HTR: 1-⑧-1-9-10
Super Screener: A: ⑧, 9; B:1, 2,3,; C: 4, 10, 5; X: 7, 6

1 TAP IT TO WIN	110
2 SOLE VOLANTE	110
3 MAX PLAYER	101
4 MODERNIST	100
5 FARMINGTON ROAD	98
6 FORE LEFT	89
7 JUNGLE RUNNER	83
8 TIZ THE LAW	112
9 DR POST	102
10 PNEUMATIC	109

The Derby was run on a drying out but not muddy track. There were no fans and considerable COVID-19 precautions but it was on TV and betting sites. Since RGS and Betfair were blocked, I bet on Twin Spires, the very nice Churchill Downs site. It does not have rebates, at least at my level, but it did have a lot of bonus betting. It is very user friendly plus has a lot of good information including a video.

Tiz the Law easily won the Florida Derby, the shortened Belmont Stakes and the Travers by multiple lengths (Table 27.4). Hence he was a legimate less than even money favorite. Indeed, on one site with about 12 handicappers, all had him picked first. But others, particularly 10-Thousand Words, 15-Ny Traffic, 16-Honor AP and 18-Authentic were close behind.

Table 27.5 shows the Derby field with the morning line odds and Table 27.6 gives the handicappers picks.

Number 1-Finick the Fierce who has just one eye, was vet scratched for security reasons. Also 6-King Guillermo was scratched for health reasons.

Because of COVID-19 restrictions, many of the top jockeys like the Ortiz's were in Saratoga but Javier Castelano, Florent Gerout, Mike Smith and John Velazquez and Manny Franco (Tiz the Law's jockey) were there.

The pedigree for Authentic who won beating Tiz the Law is in Figure 27.4.

My bets were as follows. I focused on 17 first, second or third or out with 18, 16, 15, 10 in first and second position and 2, 4, 7, 9, 10, 13, 15, 16,

Table 27.3. Betfair odds for the Belmont.

22:42 Belmont Park (USA)

Sat 20 Jun | R10 1m1f Grd1

Live Stream Radio Tote Form & Results Multiples

Win 3 Places AvB

Going In-Play Rules Pin BSP [?] Timeform Matched: **GBP 3,239** Refresh

10 selections	105.4%		Back all	Lay all		92.4%
1 **Tap It To Win** John R. Velazquez £339.00	**6** £4	**8** £22	**9.4** £52	**9.8** £77	**12** £40	**16** £40
2 **Sole Volante** Luca Panici -£45.00	**8.4** £58	**8.6** £11	**8.8** £6	**9.4** £33	**17** £2	**18** £7
3 **Max Player** Joel Rosario £82.38	**10** £28	**10.5** £3	**14** £2	**22** £2	**80** £3	**140** £4
4 **Modernist** Junior Alvarado -£45.00	**12.5** £3	**30** £3	**44** £7	**55** £8	**60** £42	**160** £3
5 **Farmington Road** Javier Castellano -£45.00	**13** £4	**30** £5	**50** £4			
6 **Fore Left** Jose L. Ortiz -£45.00	**50** £8	**60** £10	**80** £7	**240** £7		
7 **Jungle Runner** Reylu Gutierrez -£45.00	**13** £5	**50** £2	**100** £8	**390** £20	**990** £2	
8 **Tiz The Law** Manuel Franco -£45.00	**1.85** £65	**1.86** £5	**1.9** £5	**1.92** £2	**1.94** £25	**2** £36
9 **Dr Post** Irad Ortiz, Jr. -£45.00	**8.8** £2	**9** £11	**9.2** £5	**14.5** £4	**15** £7	**17** £2
10 **Pneumatic** Ricardo Santana, Jr. -£45.00	**15** £14	**15.5** £2	**16** £4	**18** £20	**18.5** £10	**19** £7

18 in 3rd and 4th positions for trifectas and supfectas plus some exacta, win, place and show.

Comments on the race: Steve Roman rated the winner, Authentic, at -54PF on his scale. The time for the ten furlong race was 2:00:61 versus Secretariat's record of 1:59:2. But as Steve pointed out, this was a very fast track all day and the race was run in September not May (4 months later). He said that the par value for a September race should be about 12PF units better then May because the horses have matured but indeed they have raced less and differently than usual so older but did not necessarily have more actual racing experience. Steve suggests instead of a par of -56 it should be -68.

Figure 27.2. Tiz the Law.

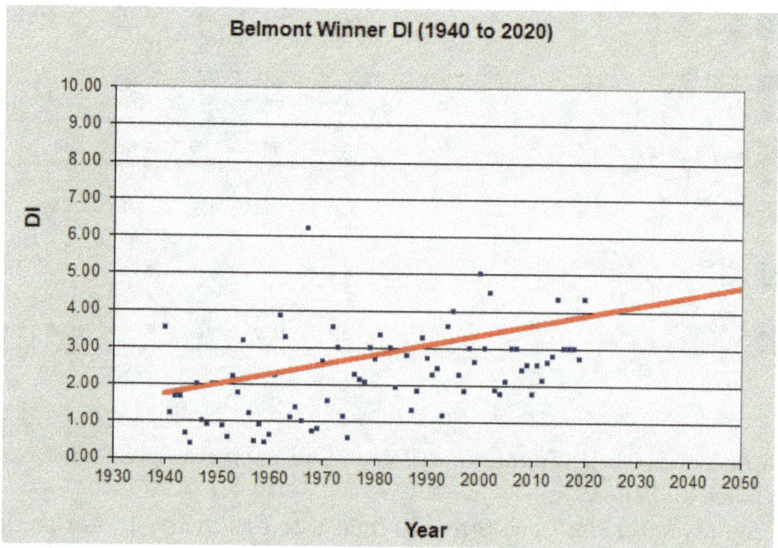

Figure 27.3. Steve Roman's PF adjusted speed ratings.
Source: Steve Roman (2016).

The finish was 18-Authentic at 8–1, 17-Tiz the Law at 3–5, 9-Mr Big News at 46–1 and 16-Honor AP at 7–1. My bets did fine with the $2000 account ending up at $5799. A minor error in the superfecta ticket gave an extra ticket rather than the superfecta. Otherwise the Twin Spires betting

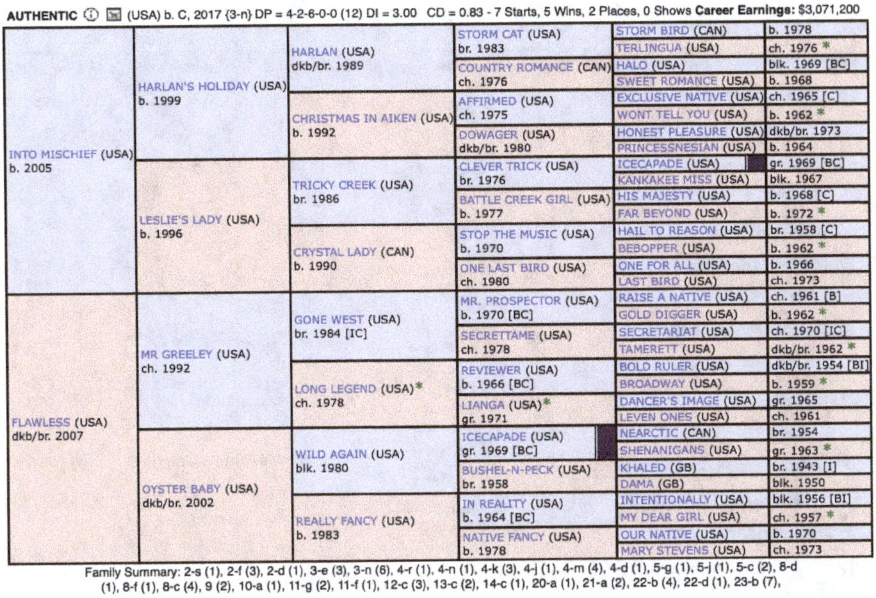

AUTHENTIC (USA) b. C, 2017 {3-n} DP = 4-2-6-0-0 (12) DI = 3.00 CD = 0.83 - 7 Starts, 5 Wins, 2 Places, 0 Shows Career Earnings: $3,071,200
INTO MISCHIEF (USA) b. 2005
HARLAN'S HOLIDAY (USA) b. 1999
HARLAN (USA) dkb/br. 1989
STORM CAT (USA) br. 1983
STORM BIRD (CAN) b. 1978
TERLINGUA (USA) ch. 1976 *
COUNTRY ROMANCE (CAN) ch. 1976
HALO (USA) blk. 1969 [BC]
SWEET ROMANCE (USA) b. 1968
CHRISTMAS IN AIKEN (USA) b. 1992
AFFIRMED (USA) ch. 1975
EXCLUSIVE NATIVE (USA) ch. 1965 [C]
WONT TELL YOU (USA) b. 1962 *
DOWAGER (USA) dkb/br. 1980
HONEST PLEASURE (USA) dkb/br. 1973
PRINCESSNESIAN (USA) b. 1964
LESLIE'S LADY (USA) b. 1996
TRICKY CREEK (USA) br. 1986
CLEVER TRICK (USA) br. 1976
ICECAPADE (USA) gr. 1969 [BC]
KANKAKEE MISS (USA) blk. 1967
BATTLE CREEK GIRL (USA) b. 1977
HIS MAJESTY (USA) b. 1968 [C]
FAR BEYOND (USA) b. 1972 *
CRYSTAL LADY (CAN) b. 1990
STOP THE MUSIC (USA) b. 1970
HAIL TO REASON (USA) br. 1958 [C]
BEBOPPER (USA) b. 1962 *
ONE LAST BIRD (USA) ch. 1980
ONE FOR ALL (USA) b. 1966
LAST BIRD (USA) ch. 1973
FLAWLESS (USA) dkb/br. 2007
MR GREELEY (USA) ch. 1992
GONE WEST (USA) br. 1984 [IC]
MR. PROSPECTOR (USA) b. 1970 [BC]
RAISE A NATIVE (USA) ch. 1961 [B]
GOLD DIGGER (USA) b. 1962 *
SECRETTAME (USA) ch. 1978
SECRETARIAT (USA) ch. 1970 [IC]
TAMERETT (USA) dkb/br. 1962 *
LONG LEGEND (USA)* ch. 1978
REVIEWER (USA) b. 1966 [BC]
BOLD RULER (USA) dkb/br. 1954 [BI]
BROADWAY (USA) b. 1959 *
LIANGA (USA)* gr. 1971
DANCER'S IMAGE (USA) gr. 1965
LEVEN ONES (USA) ch. 1961
OYSTER BABY (USA) dkb/br. 2002
WILD AGAIN (USA) blk. 1980
ICECAPADE (USA) gr. 1969 [BC]
NEARCTIC (CAN) br. 1954
SHENANIGANS (USA) gr. 1963 *
BUSHEL-N-PECK (USA) br. 1958
KHALED (GB) br. 1943 [I]
DAMA (GB) blk. 1950
REALLY FANCY (USA) b. 1983
IN REALITY (USA) b. 1964 [BC]
INTENTIONALLY (USA) blk. 1956 [BI]
MY DEAR GIRL (USA) ch. 1957 *
NATIVE FANCY (USA) b. 1978
OUR NATIVE (USA) b. 1970
MARY STEVENS (USA) ch. 1973
Family Summary: 2-s (1), 2-f (3), 2-d (1), 3-e (3), 3-n (6), 4-r (1), 4-n (1), 4-k (3), 4-j (1), 4-m (4), 4-d (1), 5-g (1), 5-j (1), 5-c (2), 8-d (1), 8-f (1), 8-c (4), 9 (2), 10-a (1), 11-g (2), 11-f (1), 12-c (3), 13-c (2), 14-c (1), 20-a (1), 21-a (2), 22-b (4), 22-d (1), 23-b (7),

Figure 27.4. Pedigree for authentic.

Table 27.4. The chart of the Belmont Stakes.

BELMONT PARK - June 20, 2020 - Race 10 **EQUIBASE**
STAKES Belmont S. Presented by NYRA Bets Grade 1 - Thoroughbred
FOR THREE YEAR OLDS.
One And One Eighth Miles On The Dirt **Track Record:** (Secretariat - 1:45.40 - September 15, 1973)
Purse: $1,000,000 Guaranteed
Available Money: $1,000,000
Value of Race: $1,000,000 1st $535,000, 2nd $185,000, 3rd $100,000, 4th $65,000, 5th $40,000, 6th $30,000, 7th $25,000, 8th $20,000
Video Race Replay
Weather: Clear **Track:** Fast
Off at: 5:46 **Start:** Good for all

Last Raced	Pgm	Horse Name (Jockey)	Wgt	M/E	PP	Start	1/4	1/2	3/4	Str	Fin	Odds	Comments
28Mar20 ^{14}GP^{1}	8	Tiz the Law (Franco, Manuel)	126	L	8	5	3^{1}	$3^{1/2}$	$3^{1\ 1/2}$	$1^{4\ 1/2}$	$1^{3\ 3/4}$	0.80*	3w,ask 3/16,kick away
25Apr20 ^{9}GP^{1}	9	Dr Post (Ortiz, Jr., Irad)	126	L	9	9	6^{3}	6^{Head}	$6^{1\ 1/2}$	$2^{1/2}$	$2^{1\ 1/2}$	7.90	4w turn,6w upr,rally
1Feb20 ^{8}AQU^{1}	3	Max Player (Rosario, Joel)	126	L b	3	7	$9^{2\ 1/2}$	9^{3}	8^{2}	$5^{3\ 1/2}$	$3^{2\ 1/2}$	14.20	2w turn,fan 7w upper
23May20 ^{10}CD^{3}	10	Pneumatic (Santana, Jr., Ricardo)	126	L	10	1	5^{1}	5^{Head}	4^{1}	$3^{1\ 1/2}$	$4^{6\ 1/4}$	17.80	3-4w turn,5w upr,tired
4Jun20 ^{8}BEL^{1}	1	Tap It to Win (Velazquez, John)	126	L	1	4	1^{1}	1^{1}	1^{1}	$4^{1/2}$	$5^{1\ 3/4}$	5.20	ins turn,3w upper,tird
10Jun20 ^{9}GP^{1}	2	Sole Volante (Panici, Luca)	126	L f	2	8	10	10	9^{2}	$7^{1\ 1/2}$	$6^{4\ 3/4}$	11.20	2w1/2,wander 7w lane
21Mar20 ^{12}FG^{3}	4	Modernist (Alvarado, Junior)	126	L	4	6	$7^{1/2}$	$7^{1\ 1/2}$	5^{1}	$6^{1/2}$	$7^{3/4}$	23.40	brush st,ins1/2,4w
2May20 ^{13}OP^{4}	5	Farmington Road (Castellano, Javier)	126	L b	5	10	$8^{2\ 1/2}$	8^{1}	$7^{1/2}$	9^{14}	$8^{1\ 1/2}$	17.60	brush start,4w1/2pl
6Feb20 MEY^{1}	6	Fore Left (Ortiz, Jose)	126	L	6	2	2^{1}	2^{1}	$2^{1/2}$	8^{1}	$9^{16\ 1/2}$	25.25	2w1/2,allow fade away
2May20 ^{11}OP^{8}	7	Jungle Runner (Gutierrez, Reylu)	126	L	7	3	4^{Head}	4^{1}	10	10	10	29.50	inside turn, gave out

Fractional Times: 23.11 46.16 1:09.94 1:34.46 **Final Time:** 1:46.53
Split Times: (23:05) (23:78) (24:52) (12:07)
Run-Up: 44 feet

Winner: Tiz the Law, Bay Colt, by Constitution out of Tizfiz, by Tiznow. Foaled Mar 19, 2017 in New York.
Breeder: Twin Creeks Farm.
Winning Owner: Sackatoga Stable

Total WPS Pool: $12,033,521

Pgm	Horse	Win	Place	Show
8	Tiz the Law	3.60	2.90	2.60
9	Dr Post		5.80	4.20
3	Max Player			5.20

Wager Type	Winning Numbers	Payoff	Pool	Carryover
$1.00 Exacta	8-9	9.80	6,454,317	
$0.50 Trifecta	8-9-3	49.75	6,520,042	
$0.10 Superfecta	8-9-3-10	55.65	3,665,491	
$1.00 Daily Double	2-8	6.50	504,910	
$1.00 Pick 3	1-2-8 (3 correct)	13.90	574,235	
$0.50 Pick 4	12-1-2-8 (4 correct)	70.12	1,164,073	
$1.00 Pick 5	1-2-1-2-8(2 DAY PICK 5) (5 correct)	780.50	352,547	
$0.50 Pick 5	2-12-1-2-8 (5 correct)	204.25	2,134,162	
$0.20 Pick 6 Jackpot	8-2-12-1-2-8 (6 correct)	291.00	685,177	328,126

Table 27.5. Field for the Derby.

*Rating is based on HRN fan votes, which rank the Top Active Horses in training.

#	Silks	Horse / Sire	Rating	Trainer / Jockey	Last Start	HRN
2		**Max Player** Honor Code	6.57	S. Asmussen R. Santana, Jr.	3rd, 2020 Travers Stakes (G1)	30-1
3		**Enforceable** Tapit	6.74	M. Casse A. Beschizza	4th, 2020 Blue Grass Stakes (G2)	30-1
4		**Storm The Court** Court Vision	6.56	P. Eurton J. Leparoux	2nd, 2020 La Jolla Handicap (G3)	50-1
5		**Major Fed** Ghostzapper	6.19	G. Foley J. Graham	2nd, 2020 Indiana Derby (G3)	50-1
7		**Money Moves** Candy Ride	4.88	T. Pletcher J. Castellano	2nd, Sar AlwOC (7/25/2020-R8)	30-1
8		**South Bend** Algorithms	5.74	W. Mott T. Gaffalione	4th, 2020 Travers Stakes (G1)	50-1
9		**Mr. Big News** Giant's Causeway	6.31	W. Calhoun G. Saez	6th, 2020 Blue Grass Stakes (G2)	50-1
10		**Thousand Words** Pioneerof the Nile	6.05	B. Baffert F. Geroux	1st, 2020 Shared Belief Stakes (LS)	15-1
11		**Necker Island** Hard Spun	6.17	S. Hough M. Mena	3rd, 2020 Ellis Park Derby (LS)	50-1
12		**Sole Volante** Karakontie	6.93	P. Biancone L. Panici	6th, 2020 Belmont Stakes (G1)	30-1
13		**Attachment Rate** Hard Spun	6.03	D. Romans J. Talamo	2nd, 2020 Ellis Park Derby (LS)	50-1
14		**Winning Impression** Paynter	4.09	D. Stewart J. Rocco, Jr.	7th, 2020 Ellis Park Derby (LS)	50-1
15		**Ny Traffic** Cross Traffic	6.53	S. Joseph, Jr. P. Lopez	2nd, 2020 Haskell Stakes (G1)	20-1
16		**Honor A. P.** Honor Code	7.28	J. Shirreffs M. Smith	2nd, 2020 Shared Belief Stakes (LS)	5-1
17		**Tiz the Law** Constitution	8.01	B. Tagg M. Franco	1st, 2020 Travers Stakes (G1)	3-5
18		**Authentic** Into Mischief	6.79	B. Baffert J. Velazquez	1st, 2020 Haskell Stakes (G1)	8-1

site worked well, is user friendly and is to be recommended. Some bonuses for new bettors gave two \$100 bonuses which was sort of a rebate. With no fans or on track betting, fewer horses entered and nine favorites who did not win during the day, wagering was a lot less in 2020 versus 2019 or \$79.4 million versus \$165.5 million on the Derby and \$126.0 million versus \$250.9 million on the whole card. But high rollers still bought \$2500 mint juleps.

Table 27.6. The handicappers rated the Derby, winner circled.

Timeform: 17–16–⑱
HTR: ⑱–17–16–15–10
David: 17
DJM: none
Diamond: A: 17, ⑱; B: 10, 15, 16, C: 2, 4, 9, X: 3 & 5 and 7 & 8, 11, 12, 13 14

---

1 FINNICK THE FIERCE	89
2 MAX PLAYER	100
3 ENFORCEABLE	89
4 STORM THE COURT	97
5 MAJOR FED	88
6 KING GUILLERMO	98
7 MONEY MOVES	92
8 SOUTH BEND	92
9 MR. BIG NEWS	88
10 THOUSAND WORDS	104
11 NECKER ISLAND	93
12 SOLE VOLANTE	91
13 ATTACHMENT RATE	98
14 WINNING IMPRESSION	84
15 NY TRAFFIC	112
16 HONOR A. P.	105
17 TIZ THE LAW	112
18 AUTHENTIC	116

```
   14-CD    Sat Sep 05, 2020   06:01 PM   10.0D  3yr GR1  $3000000  112-112   C-D   Vi=31   Q6=6   PL-5   14-CD
    FOR THREE-YEAR-OLDS, WITH AN ENTRY FEE OF $25,000 EACH AND A STARTING FEE OF $25,000 EACH.
--------------------------------------------------------------------------------------------------------------------
----------------------
Pn   PP Horse       MLO  Ag  Ped-St Ch  Lay Wk    Jockey--rtg   TJ%  Trainer--rtg--TPG   Q R  E L   PAC-PER--CLASS  (K)  FC  KLine Pn
SortIndx
--------------------------------------------------------------------------------------------------------------------
----------------------
18   18 Authentic  8/1  3c +576 KY     049'84*  #Velazq  294    45+  Baffert  475+  A   +8 F  2 8  *111 110*  109'  107+ 82*  1.9>|18|$$
107.1175
17   17 Tiz the L *3/5  3c +544 NY     028'94+   Franco  320    31+  Tagg Ba  286   C-  +7 E  9 2   105 110* *110   104+ 86+  2.9 |17|
103.6142
16   16 Honor A.   5/1  3r  450 KY     035'81*   Smith   336    33+  Shirref  402+  B+   5 E  7 6   105 109   109'  097  75   5.8 |16|
097.3134
15   15 Ny Traff  20/1  3c +564 NY     049'87+   Lopez   362+  41+  Joseph,  406+  B   +7 E  4 7   110 109   106-  090  81* 11.5>|15|$$
090.2502
10   10 Thousand  15/1  3c +599 FL     035'84*  +Geroux  305         Baffert  430+  A    3 P  6 5   106 109   107-  089  81* 14.0>|10|$
088.8010
6    06 King Gui  20/1  3c +652 KY     126'84*   Camach  327    15   Avila J  262   C+  +6 E  5 9   106 104   105'  080  72  36.5 |6 |$$
080.0674
2    02 Max Play  30/1  3c +503 KY     028'87+  #Santan  290    19  #Asmusse  326   B-   2 S  9 1*  101 107   103'  059  71  99.0 |2 |$$
058.5942
12   12 Sole Vol  30/1  3g +489 KY     077'90+   Panici  235    19   Biancon  273   C    0 R  8 9   102 104   107-  056  68  99.0 |12|$$
056.3541
9    09 Mr. Big   50/1  3c +455 KY     056'93+  +Saez G  261    21   Calhoun  341   B    0 S  9 9   100 100   103-  050  65  99.0 |9 |$$
050.0000
3    03 Enforcea  30/1  3c +718 KY     056'87+  #Beschi  227    04   Casse M  265   C    0 R  9 9   098 101   105-  050  65  99.0 |3 |$$
050.0000
11   11 Necker I  50/1  3c +510 KY bx  027'82*  #Mena M  183         Hartman  278   C-   5 P  9 9   097 101   105-  050  65  99.0 |11|$
050.0000
4    04 Storm th  50/1  3c  326 KY     027'91+  #Leparo  268         Eurton   270   C+  +6 E *1 9   107 104   107-  050  80* 99.0 |4 |$$
050.0000
13   13 Attachme  50/1  3c +546 VA     027'80*   Talamo  248    16   Romans   206   C-   3 P  3 9   108 109   108   050  75  99.0 |13|$
050.0000
14   14 Winning   50/1  3g +464 KY     027'94+   Rocco,  179         Stewart  188   C-   0 S  9 9   099 101   101-  050  65  99.0 |14|$$
050.0000
5    05 Major Fe  50/1  3c +558 KY     059'84*   Graham  270    45+  Foley G  315   B    2 S  9 9   094 100   103-  050  65  99.0 |5 |$
050.0000
1    01 Finnick   50/1  3g +489 KY     056'84*  +Garcia  274         Hernand  244   C+   3 P  9 9   099 100   106-  050  65  99.0 |1 |$$
050.0000
7    07 Money Mo  30/1  3c +676 KY     042'80*  +Castel  325    28   Pletche  369   B-  +6 E  9 4   098 103   102'  050  65  99.0 |7 |$
050.0000
8    08 South Be  50/1  3c +462 KY     028'77   +Gaffal  318    27   Mott Wi  306   C    0 S  9 3   102 105   102-  050  65  99.0 |8 |
050.0000

        (K) 18-17-16    Price Play 18       MSpot ~        TSpot ~        Scratches ~
```

The Beyer and Equibase ratings agreed that the race was below standard. The Beyer was 105 versus an historical 108 and the Equibase 109 versus 111. The super fast track had 13 of 14 favorites not winning. John Velasquez won his 100th GI race, a major feat. Bob Baffart won his 6th Kentucky Derby tying Ben Jones's record. Baffart's other horse, Thousand Words, jumped up in his stall flipped over and injured assistant trainer Jimmy Barnes, so was scratched. Authentic's −54 PF is about 4 lengths below par. Mr Big News, who was 3rd, got a −41 PF, was beaten by only $3\frac{1}{4}$ lengths despite never earning a Beyer speed figure above 96.

The $2 win, place, show payoffs were as follows:

18	18.80	6	5
	17	3.40	3.20
	9		16.80
$2	eacta	18–17	$41
50 cents	trifecta	18–17–9	$655.90
$1	superfecta	18–17–9–16	$7925.80

27.3. Preakness

The final triple crown extended three year old racing season ended with the Preakness (Table 27.7). There were 11 starters in race 11, these are listed in Table 27.8 along with the morning line odds. Table 27.6 gives the handicappers picks. The favorite at 9–5 was 9-Authentic who won the

Table 27.7. Ragason Sheets (lower ratings are better), last race on left.

Horse	Rating	Comment
17	3,5,7,5	legimate favorite
16	4, 5,8	
15	4,8, 9	
18	5, 5, 5, 8, 9	front runner, Baffart
2	7, 8, 9	
3	10, 10, 10, 8	
10	7, 9, 26, 15, 10	other Baffart
7	6, 9, 17	trending lower
13	6, 12, 8, 12	
9	12, 11, 15,14	Giant's Causway/Galilleo
4	9, 7, 12, 10	

Table 27.8. Field for the preakness.

PROBABLES	HORSE	ML ODDS
1	Excession	30-1
2	Mr. Big News	12-1
3	Art Collector	5-2
4	Swiss Skydiver	6-1
5	Thousand Words	6-1
6	Jesus' Team	30-1
7	Ny Traffic	15-1
8	Max Player	15-1
9	Authentic	9-5
10	Pneumatic	20-1
11	Liveyourbeastlife	30-1

Kentucky Derby. He and 5-Thousand Words were trained by Bob Baffert who has won the Preakness 7 times.

The race in good weather looked ideal for Authentic's front running style. But there was lots of tough competition. 3-Art Collector at 5–2 was the second choice. Art Collector had won the Blue Grass and the Ellis Park Derby and was undefeated in four races in 2020. 4-Swiss Skydiver at 6–1 was a top filly, running against the males. Six times the Preakness had been won by a filly including Rachel Alexandra in 2009. Other contenders included 5-Thousand Words at 6-1who had been scratched from the Kentucky Derby after flipping over in his stall. 2-Mr Big News at 12–1 was third in the Kentucky Derby at 46–1. He had super breeding being sired by Giant's Causeway with dam sire the great Galilleo. 7-New York Traffic and 8-Max Player were jointly bumped in the Derby and had finished out of the money. They were both 15–1 in the Preakness morningline. Some handicappers including Horseracenation rated 10-Pneunmatic (20–1) close to the top (Table 27.9).

The pedigree for Swiss Skydiver is in Figure 27.5 and Figure 27.6 shows the photo finish. We now discuss the results and payoffs which are in Table 27.10.

Jockey Bobby Alvarado made a dramatic move that allowed Swiss Skydiver to gain and pass Authentic in the stretch. Then the two had a match

Table 27.9. The handicappers rated the Preakness, winner circled.

Timeform: 9–④–3
HTR: 9–3–5
David: 9–3–15
DJM: none but 8 is the best closer
Highest Beyer: 9–105, 5–104, 3–103, ④102, 2–101, 7–101, 8–99, 10–98
Eddie Olczyk: 3–9–11–8
John White: 9–3–④–10

1 EXCESSION	91
2 MR. BIG NEWS	96
3 ART COLLECTOR	111
4 SWISS SKYDIVER	102
5 THOUSAND WORDS	104
6 JESUS' TEAM	91
7 NY TRAFFIC	94
8 MAX PLAYER	95
9 AUTHENTIC	119
10 PNEUMATIC	105
11 LIVEYOURBEASTLIFE	88

```
11-PIM   Sat Oct 03, 2020   04:36 PM   9.5D   3yr GR1  $1000000  112-113   B-C   Vi=35   Q6=5   PL-5   11-PIM
  FOR THREE-YEAR-OLDS. $10,000 to pass the entry box, starters to pay $10,000 additional. Supplemental
   nominations may be made in accordance with the rules, upon payment of $25,000, 60% of the purse to
  the winner, 20% to second, 11% to third, 6% to fourth and 3% to fifth. Weight 126 pounds for Colts a
------------------------------------------------------------------------------------------------------------
Pn   PP Horse       MLO  Ag  Ped-St Ch  Lay Wk     Jockey--rtg   TJ%  Trainer--rtg--TPG   Q R  E L   PAC-PER--CLASS  (K)  FC  KLine Pn
SortIndx
------------------------------------------------------------------------------------------------------------
9    09 Authentic *9/5  3c +600 KY      028'88+    Velazq  331        Baffert  423+  A    +8 F *1 9  *110 110*  111    112+ 78    1.7>|9 |PSF
111.9131
3    03 Art Colle  5/2  3c +620 KY      055'91+    Hernan  302   38+  Drury,   350   B-   +7 E  2 8   108 110* *112+  109+ 86+   3.1 |3 |
109.4300
5    05 Thousand   6/1  3c +600 FL bo   063'89+   +Geroux  300        Baffert  423+  A     3 P  4 5   107 110*  108    102  76    6.1 |5 |$$
101.8391
7    07 Ny Traff  15/1  3c +533 NY      028'90+   +Karama  317        Joseph,  369   B    +8 E  3 9  *110 110*  107-   097  81*   9.3>|7 |$$
096.6273
4    04 Swiss Sky  6/1  3f +990 KY      029'86+   #Albara  145        McPeek   251   C    +8 E  6 6   101 107   110    090  82*  15.5 |4 |$$
090.2867
2    02 Mr. Big   12/1  3c +464 KY      028'77     Saez G  252   26   Calhoun  358   B+    0 S  8 3   103 105   105-   084  75   28.9 |2 |
084.4186
10   10 Pneumati  20/1  3c +676 KY      049'83*    Bravo   352+       Asmusse  305   B-    5 E  5 4   106 109   110'   080  80*  40.0 |10|$
080.3185
8    08 Max Play  15/1  3c +482 KY      028'74    +Lopez   348        Asmusse  305   B-    0 S  9 1*  099 102   106-   073  68   64.1 |8 |$
073.2685
6    06 Jesus' T  30/1  3c  354 KY      028'81*   +Toledo  315        D'Angel  297   B-    5 P  7 7   103 106   108    065  65   99.0 |6 |$
064.6149
1    01 Excessio  30/1  3c +454 KY      203'81*   +Russel  332        Asmusse  305   B-    0 S  9 9   095 099   106-   061       99.0 |1 |$
061.3205
11   11 Liveyour  30/1  3c +524 KY      028'85+   +McCart  335        Abreu J  236   C    +6 P  9 2   099 104   105-   057  65   99.0 |11|$$
056.8012

       (K) 9-3-5      Price Play 11      MSpot ~      TSpot ~      Scratches ~
```

race with Swiss Skydiver winning by a head. The longshot Jesus' Team was third followed by Art Collector and Max Player was fifth.

Swiss Skydiver had won the Gulfstream Park Oaks (G2), Fantasy (G3), and Santa Anita Oaks (G2) and then finished second against males in the Blue Grass (G2) at Keeneland in July. She won the Alabama (G1) at Saratoga. In the Kentucky Oaks she had an unfavorable inside run from post 1 and finished second to Shedaresthedevil.

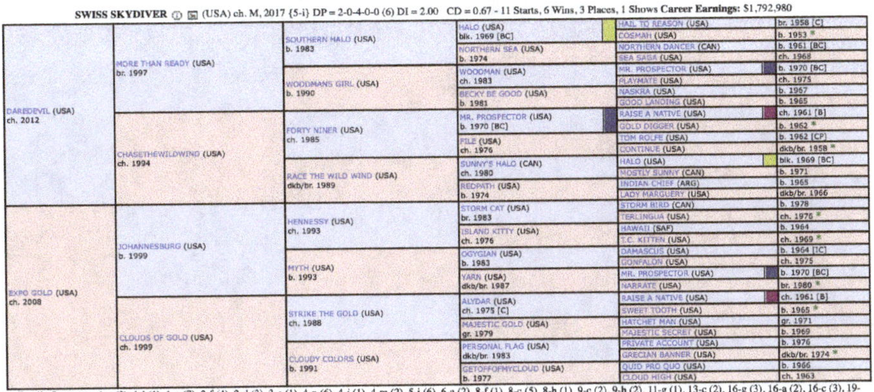

SWISS SKYDIVER (USA) ch. M, 2017 {5-i} DP = 2-0-4-0-0 (6) DI = 2.00 CD = 0.67 - 11 Starts, 6 Wins, 3 Places, 1 Shows **Career Earnings:** $1,792,980

DAREDEVIL (USA) ch. 2012	MORE THAN READY (USA) br. 1997	SOUTHERN HALO (USA) b. 1983	HALO (USA) blk. 1969 [BC]	HAIL TO REASON (USA)	br. 1958 [C]
				COSMAH (USA)	b. 1953 *
			NORTHERN SEA (USA) b. 1974	NORTHERN DANCER (CAN)	b. 1961 [BC]
				SEA SAGA (USA)	ch. 1968
		WOODMANS GIRL (USA) b. 1990	WOODMAN (USA) ch. 1983	MR. PROSPECTOR (USA)	b. 1970 [BC]
				PLAYMATE (USA)	ch. 1975
			BECKY BE GOOD (USA) b. 1981	NASKRA (USA)	b. 1967
				GOOD LANDING (USA)	b. 1965
	CHASETHEWILDWIND (USA) ch. 1994	FORTY NINER (USA) ch. 1985	MR. PROSPECTOR (USA) b. 1970 [BC]	RAISE A NATIVE (USA)	ch. 1961 [B]
				GOLD DIGGER (USA)	b. 1962 *
			FILE (USA) ch. 1976	TOM ROLFE (USA)	b. 1962 [CP]
				CONTINUE (USA)	dkb/br. 1958 *
		RACE THE WILD WIND (USA) dkb/br. 1989	SUNNY'S HALO (CAN) ch. 1980	HALO (USA)	blk. 1969 [BC]
				MOSTLY SUNNY (CAN)	b. 1971
			REDPATH (USA) b. 1974	INDIAN CHIEF (ARG)	b. 1965
				LADY MARGUERY (USA)	dkb/br. 1966
EXPO GOLD (USA) ch. 2008	JOHANNESBURG (USA) b. 1999	HENNESSY (USA) ch. 1993	STORM CAT (USA) br. 1983	STORM BIRD (CAN)	b. 1978
				TERLINGUA (USA)	ch. 1976 *
			ISLAND KITTY (USA) ch. 1976	HAWAII (SAF)	b. 1964
				T.C. KITTEN (USA)	ch. 1969 *
		MYTH (USA) b. 1993	OGYGIAN (USA) b. 1983	DAMASCUS (USA)	b. 1964 [IC]
				GONFALON (USA)	ch. 1975
			YARN (USA) dkb/br. 1987	MR. PROSPECTOR (USA)	b. 1970 [BC]
				NARRATE (USA)	br. 1980 *
	CLOUDS OF GOLD (USA) ch. 1999	STRIKE THE GOLD (USA) ch. 1988	ALYDAR (USA) ch. 1975 [C]	RAISE A NATIVE (USA)	ch. 1961 [B]
				SWEET TOOTH (USA)	b. 1965 *
			MAJESTIC GOLD (USA) gr. 1979	HATCHET MAN (USA)	gr. 1971
				MAJESTIC SECRET (USA)	b. 1969
		CLOUDY COLORS (USA) b. 1991	PERSONAL FLAG (USA) dkb/br. 1983	PRIVATE ACCOUNT (USA)	b. 1976
				GRECIAN BANNER (USA)	dkb/br. 1974 *
			GETOFFOFMYCLOUD (USA) b. 1977	QUID PRO QUO (USA)	b. 1966
				CLOUD HIGH (USA)	ch. 1963

Family Summary: 1-n (3), 1-l (1), 1-x (7), 2-f (4), 2-d (3), 3-e (1), 4-n (6), 4-j (1), 4-m (2), 5-i (6), 6-a (2), 8-f (1), 8-c (5), 8-h (1), 9-c (2), 9-h (2), 11-g (1), 13-c (2), 16-g (3), 16-a (2), 16-c (3), 19-c (1),

Figure 27.5. Pedigree for Swiss skydiver.

Figure 27.6. Swiss skydiver and authentic at the preakness.

I won the win, place, show bet on Swiss Skydiver, the place and show on Authentic and the $4 exacta. But with Jesus' Team third, I lots the trifecta and superfecta bets.

The race was fast with Swiss Skydiver running the second fastest Preakness ever at 1:53:28, beaten only by Secretariat's 1975 record of 1:53. Steve Roman rated the winner as a -64, one length above par.

Table 27.10. Payoffs for the preakness.

RACE 11

#	RUNNER	MIN	WIN	PLC	SHW
4	Swiss Skydiver	$1	$12.70	$4.20	$2.90
9	Authentic	$1		$1.80	$1.60
6	Jesus' Team	$1			$6.10
3	Art Collector				
8	Max Player				

$1 EXACTA (4/9) Paid: 37.80
$1 TRIFECTA (4/9/6) Paid: 1,205.70
$1 DOUBLE (9/4) Paid: 150.60
$0.5 PICK FOUR (7/3,10,11/9/4) Paid: 4,574.00
$1 SUPERFECTA (4/9/6/3) Paid: 5,053.00
$0.2 PICK SIX (7/4/7/3,10,11/9/4) Paid: 28,428.20
$0.5 PICK THREE (3,10,11/9/4) Paid: 369.20
$0.5 PICK FIVE (4/7/3,10,11/9/4) Paid: 64,423.60
$1 PENTAFECTA (4/9/6/3/8) Paid: 64,812.60

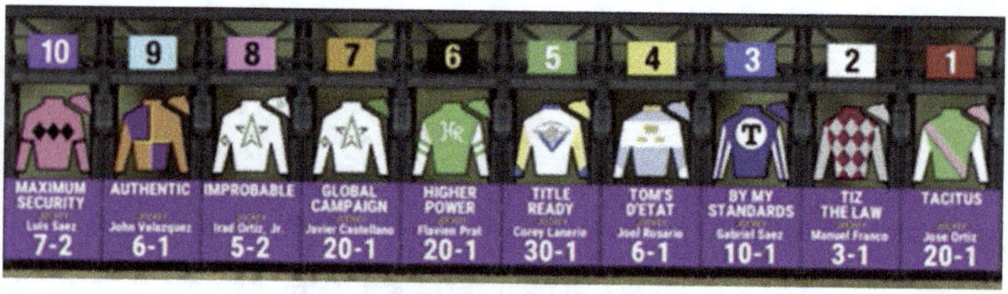

Figure 27.7. Field for the Breeders' Cup Classic.

27.4. Breeders' Cup

Several of the top three year old horses plus top four year olds ran in the Breeders' Cup Classic (Figure 27.7). Preakness winner Swiss Skydiver went to the Distaff and was beaten by Monomy Girl who now has 8 wins in 8 GI races. Swiss Skydiver stumbled at the start and finished out of the money.

Tiz the Law, Authentic and Improbable were in the Classic. Maximum Security who was so strong in 2019 but had several missteps like being disqualified from winning the Kentucky Derby and winning the $20 million Saudi Cup only to be tainted by his trainer's charges for illegal drugs. Tacitus, who ran an under two minute $1\frac{1}{4}$ mile race but consistently failed in most races despite being the top choice, was there at 20–1.

Table 27.11 gives the handicappers picks. Table 27.12 shows the betfair odds.

Table 27.11. The handicappers rated the Breeders Cup Classic, winner circled.

Timeform: ⑨–2–10
HTR: 8, 10, ⑨, 2, 4
Mick: 8, 10 , ⑨ / 12,4, 3

1 TACITUS	103
2 TIZ THE LAW	116
3 BY MY STANDARDS	104
4 TOM'S D'ETAT	114
5 TITLE READY	103
6 HIGHER POWER	96
7 GLOBAL CAMPAIGN	104
8 IMPROBABLE	117
9 AUTHENTIC	123
10 MAXIMUM SECURITY	119

12-KEE Sat Nov 07, 2020 05:18 PM 10.0D 3up GR1 $6000000 111-112 C-C Vi=32 Q6=4 PL-5 12-KEE
FOR THREE-YEAR-OLDS AND UPWARD. Northern Hemisphere Three-Year-Olds, 122 lbs.; Older, 126 lbs.; Sout hern Hemisphere Three-Year-Olds, 118 lbs.; Older, 126 lbs. All Fillies and Mares allowed 3 lbs. $75, 000 to pre-enter, $75,000 to enter, with guaranteed $6 million purse including travel awards of whi

Pn SortIndx	PP Horse	MLO	Ag	Ped-St Ch	Lay Wk	Jockey--rtg	TJ%	Trainer--rtg--TPG	Q R E L	PAC-PER--CLASS	(K)	FC	KLine Pn
8 112.8798	08 Improbabl	*5/2	4c	+532 KY	042'91+	+Ortiz, 420+		Baffert 444+ A	5 E 3 8	*110 109 111+	113+	75	1.9>|8 |PSF
10 109.6289	10 Maximum S	7/2	4c	+825 KY	042'90+	Saez L 362+	23	Baffert 467+ A	+7 E *1 9	108 109 111+	110+	86+	3.4>|10|
9 107.3748	09 Authentic	6/1	3c	+580 KY	035'93+	Velazq 307		Baffert 444+ A	+8 F 2 7	107 111* 112+	107	76	5.2>|9 |$$
2 101.0394	02 Tiz the L	3/1	3c	+550 NY	063'87+	Franco 304	20	Tagg Ba 282 C	+6 E 4 6	106 109 112+	101	69	8.3 |2 |
4 090.3616	04 Tom's d'E	6/1	7h	+525 KY	098'84*	Rosari 386+	27	Stall, 288 B-	3 P 9 1*	095 109 *115+	090+	82*	17.8 |4 |$$
3 089.2722	03 By My St	10/1	4c	+790 KY	064'95+	Saez G 273	23	Calhoun 366 B+	5 E 9 2	098 109 113+	089	79	21.1 |3 |$$
7 081.1214	07 Global C	20/1	4c	+824 KY	063'88+	+Castel 319		Hough S 342 B	+6 E 7 3	104 108 110	081	71	44.7 |7 |$$
1 075.0934	01 Tacitus	20/1	4c	+964 KY	028'84*	Ortiz 344	19	Mott Wi 302 B	5 E 8 4	101 107 110	075	76	70.1 |1 |$
6 074.3140	06 Higher P	20/1	5h	+600 KY	077'87+	Prat F 410+	12	Sadler 320 C+	5 P 5 9	102 107 109	074	65	70.1 |6 |$$
5 059.8717	05 Title Re	30/1	5h	329 KY	028'85+	Laneri 264	07	Stewart 201 C	2 S 6 5	098 107 109	060	81*	99.0 |5 |$$

The race had five horses that seemed best, namely, 2, 4, 8, 9 and 10, see the PSR and HTR in Table 27.11. It was a speed favoring track with Jerry Bailey pointed out how fast the track was all day with the advantage going to early speed. So I favored 9-Authentic who had the best early speed. The finish was 9–8–7–1. Tom's D'Etat and Tiz the Law failed, perhaps worn out from previous races. The payoffs of the Breeders' Cup Classic are in the chart of the race in Table 27.13.

My bets on Betfair are shown in Table 27.12. The win gain was 221£ and 40£ on a 2–1 show bet.

I also bet on RGS $25 WPS on Authentic and $5 exacta on 8–9 and lost $1 trifecta and superfecta $1 bets with 2, 8, 9, 10 and 9/1,8,10/2,8,10/2,8,10. For a gain in total in the terrific $6 million Classic.

So the 3 year old horse of the year will be Authentic.

Table 27.12. Betfair Odds for the Breeders' Cup Classic and My Betfair Bets.

10 selections		102.5%		Back all	Lay all		99.7%
1 Tacitus, Jose L. Ortiz	-£220.00	28 £6	29 £10	30 £68	32 £72	34 £134	36 £9
2 Tiz The Law, Manuel Franco	£47.50	4.3 £260	4.4 £538	4.5 £423	4.6 £1590	4.7 £133	4.8 £126
3 By My Standards, Gabriel Saez	-£220.00	28 £52	29 £15	30 £90	32 £52	34 £114	36 £5
4 Toms Detat, Joel Rosario	-£220.00	4.5 £58	4.6 £144	4.7 £582	4.8 £32	4.9 £1014	5 £424
5 Title Ready, Corey J. Lanerie	-£220.00	150 £12	170 £4	180 £5	220 £2	320 £2	330 £5
6 Higher Power, Flavien Prat	-£220.00	55 £9	60 £28	65 £17	70 £2	75 £4	80 £9
7 Global Campaign, Javier Castellano	-£220.00	30 £20	32 £29	34 £133	36 £59	38 £141	40 £30
8 Improbable, Irad Ortiz, Jr.	£15.00	4.6 £263	4.7 £408	4.8 £281	4.9 £175	5 £354	5.1 £159
9 Authentic, John R. Velazquez	£211.00	6 £181	6.2 £244	6.4 £227	6.6 £185	6.8 £525	7 £299
10 Maximum Security, Luis Saez	£98.48	8.8 £74	9 £91	9.2 £12	9.4 £45	9.6 £9	9.8 £32

Table 27.13. The chart of the Breeders' Cup.

KEENELAND - November 7, 2020 - Race 12 EQUIBASE

STAKES Longines Breeders' Cup Classic Grade 1 - Thoroughbred

FOR THREE-YEAR-OLDS AND UPWARD. Northern Hemisphere Three-Year-Olds, 122 lbs.; Older, 126 lbs.; Southern Hemisphere Three-Year-Olds, 118 lbs.; Older, 126 lbs. All Fillies and Mares allowed 3 lbs. $75,000 to pre-enter, $75,000 to enter, with guaranteed $6 million purse including travel awards of which 52% to the owner of the winner, 17% to second, 9% to third, 5% to fourth, 3% to fifth, 2% to sixth, 1% to seventh, 1% to eighth, 1% to ninth, 1% to tenth; plus travel awards to starters not based in Kentucky.

One And One Fourth Miles On The Dirt **Track Record:** (Authentic - 1:59.19 - November 7, 2020)

Purse: $6,000,000 Guaranteed

Available Money: $6,000,000

Value of Race: $5,520,000 1st $3,120,000, 2nd $1,020,000, 3rd $540,000, 4th $300,000, 5th $180,000, 6th $120,000, 7th $60,000, 8th $60,000, 9th $60,000, 10th $60,000 Video Race Replay

Weather: Clear **Track:** Fast

Off at: 5:19 **Start:** Good for all except 6

Last Raced	Pgm	Horse Name (Jockey)	Wgt	M/E	PP	1/4	1/2	3/4	1m	Str	Fin	Odds	Comments
3Oct20 ^{11}PIM^{2}	9	Authentic (Velazquez, John)	122	L	9	$1^{1\ 1/2}$	$1^{2\ 1/2}$	1^{1}	1^{1}	$1^{1\ 1/2}$	$1^{2\ 1/4}$	4.20	loose lead, kicked clr
26Sep20 ^{10}SA^{1}	8	Improbable (Ortiz, Jr., Irad)	126	L b	8	$5^{1/2}$	6^{4}	4^{Head}	$2^{1/2}$	2^{Head}	2^{1}	3.70	bmp early,bid,no match
5Sep20 ^{11}SAR^{1}	7	Global Campaign (Castellano, Javier)	126	L f	7	$4^{1/2}$	4^{1}	$3^{1/2}$	3^{1}	3^{1}	3^{2}	25.20	bmpd,bothered early
10Oct20 ^{9}BEL^{3}	1	Tacitus (Ortiz, Jose)	126	L b	1	$9^{2\ 1/2}$	9^{3}	8^{2}	$7^{1\ 1/2}$	$5^{1/2}$	4^{Nose}	21.20	bid str, leveled off
26Sep20 ^{10}SA^{2}	10	Maximum Security (Saez, Luis)	126	L	10	2^{Head}	$2^{1/2}$	2^{Head}	$4^{1/2}$	$4^{1/2}$	5^{Head}	4.40	ins into lane,weakened
5Sep20 ^{14}CD^{2}	2	Tiz the Law (Franco, Manuel)	122	L	2	3^{Head}	$3^{1/2}$	5^{1}	5^{1}	$6^{2\ 1/2}$	$6^{7\ 1/4}$	3.20*	restrained ins,4p 1/4
10Oct20 ^{8}KEE^{3}	5	Title Ready (Lanerie, Corey)	126	L b	5	$8^{1\ 1/2}$	8^{Head}	9^{1}	$9^{1\ 1/2}$	$7^{1/2}$	$7^{1\ 1/4}$	66.40	botherd,squeezed early
4Sep20 ^{10}CD^{1}	3	By My Standards (Saez, Gabriel)	126	L	3	6^{4}	5^{Head}	$6^{2\ 1/2}$	$8^{2\ 1/2}$	$9^{2\ 1/2}$	$8^{1\ 3/4}$	16.30	wandered out,bmp early
1Aug20 ^{9}SAR^{3}	4	Tom's d'Etat (Rosario, Joel)	126	L b	4	7^{1}	$7^{1\ 1/2}$	7^{Head}	6^{Head}	8^{1}	$9^{14\ 1/4}$	4.20	in tight,jostled early
22Aug20 ^{10}DMR^{4}	6	Higher Power (Prat, Flavien)	126	L b	6	10	10	10	10	10	10	43.40	unprepared at start

Fractional Times: N/A N/A N/A N/A **Final Time:** 1:59.19

Run-Up: 50 feet

Winner: Authentic, Bay Colt, by Into Mischief out of Flawless, by Mr. Greeley. Foaled May 05, 2017 in Kentucky.

INTO MISCHIEF Winner's sire standing at Spendthrift Farm

Breeder: Peter E. Blum Thoroughbreds, LLC.

Winning Owner: Spendthrift Farm LLC, MyRaceHorse Stable, Madaket Stables LLC and Starlight Racing

Total WPS Pool: $8,740,648

Pgm	Horse	Win	Place	Show
9	Authentic	10.40	5.40	4.20
8	Improbable		4.80	3.20
7	Global Campaign			8.80

Wager Type	Winning Numbers	Payoff	Pool
$0.50 Pick 3	10-3-9 (3 correct)	47.20	1,942,290
$0.50 Pick 4	15-10-3-9 (4 correct)	4,556.15	4,278,680
$0.50 Pick 5	7-15-10-3-9 (4 correct)	238.70	0
$0.50 Pick 5	7-15-10-3-9 (5 correct)	81,406.70	5,098,469
$1.00 Pick 6	11-7-15-10-3-9 (5 correct)	33,393.70	3,285,407
$1.00 Daily Double	3-9	29.60	1,367,217
$1.00 Daily Double	BCJUV/BCCLASSIC 5-9	49.10	366,920
$1.00 Exacta	9-8	22.70	4,664,737
$0.50 Super High Five Jackpot	9-8-7-1-10	8,791.45	387,827
$0.10 Superfecta	9-8-7-1	335.55	2,322,035
$0.50 Trifecta	9-8-7	167.95	3,959,601

Comments: Authentic broke the track record with a 1.59:.19 time on the fast track. He now has won 6 of 8 races and $6,371,200. He was a $350,000 Keeneland yearling purchase. He was sired by super star Into Mischief who stands at Gainesway. Since he produced star sprinter Gamine as well as Practical Joke and Cofefe among other good runners, his stud fee was raised to $200,000 from $175,000 for the 2020 breeding season. His sire, Harlan's Holiday won 3 with 3 places in his 6 starts. Authentic's ownership includes Starlight Racing Stables, Spendthrift Farm LLC, Madaket Stables LLC and the syndicate Myracehorsestable which includes some 5,214 micro share owners.

Steve Roman calculated Authentic's speed as −86 PF which is two lengths better than par and the same as two times horse of the year and top stallion Curlin. This is consistent with Beyer's 109 speed rating. So it was a super performance. Authentic is now retired to Gainesway Farm for stud duties.

Acknowledgment

Thanks to Richard Diamond, David McKenzie, Steve Roman and Mick Thomason for helpful data and discussions.

Chapter 28

Dr Z's Place & Show Racetrack Betting System at the First Breeders' Cup

William T. Ziemba

In 1984 our *Beat the Racetrack* book came out and Ed Thorp did the cover quote saying "this is one of the only gambling systems that actually works." We went to the first Breeders' Cup to test the place and show system with Ed and my late UBC colleague Bruce Fauman. It was a glorious day, the first Breeders' Cup was held in Los Angeles at Hollywood Park. This chapter describes our betting and social day and some of the Hollywood stars who were there.[1]

This chapter recalls a memorable day on November 10, 1984 when Ed Thorp and I attended, with my late Vancouver colleague Bruce Fauman, the first Breeders' Cup day at Hollywood Park. The purpose of the day in addition to fun, was to test my Dr Z system co-developed with Donald Hausch with some early help from Mark Rubinstein. The idea of the system is simple: use the data from a simple market, in this case the win probabilities to fairly price bets in the more complex markets, such as place and show. For example, with ten horses, there are 720 possible finishes for show. Then one searches for mispriced place and show opportunities. This is a weak form violation of the efficient market hypothesis based solely on prices. How much to bet depends on how much the wager is out of whack and it is a good application of the Kelly betting system. The formulation below shows such an optimization. There is a lot of data here on all the horses

[1]Adapted from a column in *Wilmott* magazine.

and not much time at the track. So a simplified approach is suggested. Don and I solved thousands of such models with real data and estimated approximation regression equations that only involve four numbers, namely, the amounts bet to win in the total pool and the horse under consideration for a bet. Plus the total place or show pool and the place or show bet on the horse under consideration.

These equations appear below. In our books Ziemba and Hausch (1984, 1986, 1987) we study this in various ways, including different track takes, multiple bets for place and show on the same horse and how many can plan the system before the edge is gone. This is described in Fauman's report in Section 28.2 and there is more technical detail in Ziemba and Hausch (1986). This system revolutionized the way racetrack betting was perceived viewing it as a financial market not just a race. This led to pricing of wagers and the explosion of successful betting by syndicates in the US, Hong Kong and elsewhere; see, for example, my joint books referenced here.

28.1. Transactions Costs

The effect of transactions costs which is called slippage in commodity trading is illustrated with the following place/show horseracing formulation; see Hausch, Ziemba and Rubinstein (1981). Here q_i is the probability that i wins, and the Harville probability of an ij finish is $\frac{q_i q_j}{1-q_i}$, etc. That is $q_j/1 - q_j$ is the probability that j wins a race that does not contain i, that is, comes second. Q, the track payback, is about 0.82 (but is about 0.90 with professional rebates). The players' bets are to place p_j and show s_k for each of the about ten horses in the race out of the players' wealth w_0. The bets by the crowd are P_i with $\sum_{i=1}^{n} P_i = P$ and S_k with $\sum_{k=1}^{n} S_k = S$. The payoffs are computed so that for place, the first two finishers, say i and j, in either order share the net pool profits once each P_i and p_i bets cost of say \$1 is returned. The show payoffs are computed similarly. The model is

$$\max_{p_i, s_i} \sum_{i=1}^{n} \sum_{\substack{j=i \\ j\neq i}}^{n} \sum_{\substack{k=i \\ k\neq i,j}}^{n} \frac{q_i q_j q_k}{(1-q_i)(1-q_i-q_j)}$$

$$\times \log \left[\begin{array}{l} \dfrac{Q\left(P+\sum_{l=1}^{n} p_l\right)-(p_i+p_j+P_{ij})}{2} \\ \qquad \times \left[\dfrac{p_i}{p_i+P_i}+\dfrac{p_j}{p_j+P_j}\right] \\ +\dfrac{Q\left(S+\sum_{l=1}^{n} s_l\right)-(s_i+s_j+s_k+S_{ijk})}{3} \\ \qquad \times \left[\dfrac{s_i}{s_i+S_i}+\dfrac{s_j}{s_j+S_j}+\dfrac{s_k}{s_k+S_k}\right] \\ +w_0-\sum_{\substack{l=i \\ l\neq i,j,k}}^{n} s_l-\sum_{\substack{l=i \\ l\neq i,j}}^{n} p_l \end{array} \right]$$

$$\text{s.t.} \sum_{l=1}^{n}(p_l + s_l) \leqslant w_0, \quad p_l \geqslant 0, \quad s_l \geqslant 0, \quad l = 1, \ldots, n,$$

While the Harville formulas make sense, the data indicate that they are biased. To correct for this, professional bettors adjust the Harville formulas, using, for example, discounted Harville formulas,[2] to lower the place and show probabilities for favorites and raise them for the longshots; see papers in Hausch, Lo and Ziemba (1994, 2008) and Hausch and Ziemba (2008).

This is a non-concave program but it seems to converge when nonlinear programming algorithms are used to solve such problems. But a simpler way is via expected value regression approximation equations using 1000s of sample calculations of the NLP model. These are

$$\begin{aligned} \text{Ex Place}_i &= 0.319 + 0.559\left(\frac{w_i/w}{p_i/p}\right) \\ \text{Ex Show}_i &= 0.543 + 0.369\left(\frac{w_i/w}{s_i/s}\right). \end{aligned}$$

The expected value (and optimal wager) are functions of only four numbers — the totals to win and place for the horse in question and the totals bet. These equations approximate the full optimized optimal growth model. See Hausch and Ziemba (1985). This is used in Dr Z calculators. See the discussion in Fauman's accompanying paper for a description of a typical day's betting and, for more, technical detail see Ziemba and Hausch (1986).

An example is the 1983 Kentucky Derby.

---

[2]The discounted probabilities come from

$$q_i^* = \frac{q_i^\alpha}{\sum_i^n q_i^\alpha}$$

for α about 0.81 then one uses the q_i^* in the second place position. For third one uses α^2 about 0.64. These empirical numbers vary over time and by track. This is more important for exacta pricing than place and show because for the latter the win bias from the favorite-longshot and the second and third biases tends to cancel. The favorite-longshot bias is the empirical observation that favorites are underbet and longshots overbet; see the figures in Chapter 19. I use these ideas in futures options trading where there is a similar bias.

	Totals	#8 Sunny's Halo	Expected Value Per Dollar Bet	Optimal Bet ($W_0 = 1000$)
Odds		5-2		
Win	3,143,669	745,524		
Show	1,099,990	179,758	1.14	52

Sunny's Halo won the race

Win	Place	Show
7.00	4.80	4.00

$$\Pi = \$52$$

15 second bet!

Watch board in lineup
while everyone is at the TV

Here, Sunny's Halo has about 1/6 of the show pool versus 1/4 of the win pool so the expected value is 1.14 and the optimal Kelly bet is 5.2% of one's wealth.

A race by race analysis of that Breeders' Cup day, plus the previous day when I went by myself, with racing charts, optimal wagers, etc is in Ziemba and Hausch (1986). Fauman wrote his own version which is attached, and was written in 1995 but never published. So I have edited it slightly and updated it in a few places. A few comments appear as a postscript after his paper from Ziemba and Hausch (1986). I did not alter his comments about me which on the whole are correct. It is a colorful account so I bring it to your attention.

Before that begins, you might ask: does the system still work in 2021 and what is changed? The main new features are:

1. these days we bet at rebate shops by phone or electronically. The rebate is a sharing of the track take by the track, the rebater and the bettor. The effect is to take all bets from a track take of 13–30% for various bets to about 10%;
2. betting exchanges in the UK and elsewhere allow for short as well as long wagers; and

3. there is a lot of cross track and last minute betting and this takes time to be sent to the pools at the racetrack. Hence, about 50% of the wagers don't actually appear in the pools until after the horses are running. So one must estimate the final odds (probabilities).

Syndicates exist that break even on their wagers yet make millions on the rebate. Regarding the Dr Z system, John Swetye works with me and we wager with rebate searching for bets at 80 racetrack. Basically the system still works but the task is not easy. One successful six month period with a $5000 bankroll, the system lost 7%, received a 9% rebate. The total wagers were $1.5 million giving a 2% or $30,000 profit.

28.2. Three to Beat the Breeders' Cup by Bruce C. Fauman

[A]t the first Breeders' Cup in 1984, three ordinary jamokes in their forties, among whom one could count a total of three wives, six kids, nine degrees, about 500 IQ points, and a system to beat the track, set out for Hollywood Park to test their theories and equations on horseracing's biggest day ever.

Bruce Fauman

28.2.1. *First Race: The Juvenile, one mile, for two year old colts and geldings, purse $1,00,000*

The ground growls as I stand at the rail beside the sixteenth pole. The vibrations travel faster through earth than through air, so I feel the horses before I hear them. The front runners reach the head of the stretch, three wide, a length behind one another. Their hooves sound not a distinct clip clop beat but a series of overlapping thuds upon the fast track surface.

Number 5, a bay with white stockinged forelegs, has gained steadily on the early leader throughout the back stretch. As they pass me, he pulls even and tries to fend off another bay's late charge between horses. At 35 miles an hour, the horses spew fragments of track soil with each hoofs raising. The warm November morning accentuates the aromas of rich soil, fresh manure, damp straw, saddle leather and horse sweat, which in a more subtle form are often invoked as barnyard bouquet when complimenting a well balanced mature Burgundy.

Watching a horse race from the stands is as different from watching at track side as it is from watching on television. I left our box to see the first race from the rail and became so engrossed in the pre race ritual that I forgot to make the first system bet of the day. The possible opportunity appeared early on the tote, but by the time I remembered to ignore the horses and recheck the odds, the horses were loading, and I was too late to get to the betting window. Some say the first things to go in an ex athlete are the knees. Not true; it's the short term memory. The grandson of both Northern Dancer and Secretariat holds on to win by nearly a length. Remembering our day's real purpose, I will no longer be so cavalier as to watch a race for pleasure. We're not here to enjoy the races, but to beat the track on what promises to be horseracing's biggest day in history

28.2.2. *Second Race: The Juvenile Fillies, one mile, for two year old fillies, purse $1,000,000*

Dr Z introduces Ed, Jeff and me to the occupants of the box to our right, Lindsay a local newspaper reporter and an English author of handicapping books who mumbles his name, Foofraw or Frew faw, in upper class Brit speak.

Bill Ziemba, is my colleague, sometime coauthor, and seminal mind behind the system. I am the creator of his Dr Z nom de plume, the reality checker of his mathematical manipulations, and one of the few people willing to tolerate his bustling, blustering and occasional boorishness in return for access to the treasures of a polymath's mind.

Our third adventurer is Ed Thorp, who developed the original card counting system for beating blackjack in the 1960s, and since no casino will let him near a 21 table anymore, he has gone on to other things. But Ed is always interested in any system that can actually beat the house, and is here to see for himself whether the system will beat the racetrack.

Ed wears a cocoa heather herringbone jacket and beige slacks. I'm in my I can go anywhere uniform of a navy blazer, gray flannels, button down shirt and sincere necktie. Ed and I remove our ties, which we believed were required in the clubhouse. Jeff's is unchanged from half mast. Bill is in a conservative glen plaid suit adorned with a most un conservative floral tie.

Foofraw asks me which filly I like in the race, but before I can answer, he tells me, "The 3 if she runs true to form, with the 9 right after that. Unless the 6 filly has been laying in the weeds and I'm quite taken with number 8's works, so she could upset."

Bill and Ed made. the system bets on Chief's Crown in the first. Dr Z tells me at $2.40 to show his $100 wager puts him $20 ahead. Ed doesn't say how much he bet. In addition to disappointment in my forgetfulness, I'm also a little disappointed in the small payoff, while Dr Z is pleased that the horses are running true to form, which means the system should run true to form as well.

We check the tote board with each flash. The favored filly, number 4, has offered a likely system bet since early in the wagering. The show bet underlay fluctuates around 35%, which ought to give me an expected payback of 1.17, or $1.17 for every dollar bet. My usual cutoff is 1.15, which means I'll make a bet only when I have at least a 15% advantage. However, for an event like the Breeders' Cup, with great horses and ideal conditions, I reduce the cutoff to 1.10. Throwing darts at the racing program gives an expectation of about 85 cents per dollar wagered, since the track take is 15 cents of each dollar wagered. A fair bet is like tossing a coin, where the expectation is 1.00. Unless a bet is for small sums between friends, fair is for fools.

Just like Wall Street, the racetrack is a financial market, in which people invest money in ventures with uncertain outcomes. The stock market is said to be "efficient," because neither knowing how a stock has performed in the past, nor having public information about the company's activities, provides any prediction about the stock's future price. The current price reflects all available information and is the best predictor of the future. The racetrack is also a financial market, a turf market, and efficient as well. The odds offered are the best predictor of any given horse's probability of winning. The tote board odds reflect all available information about each horse's relative speed, stamina, breeding or other factors that predict performance. Some handicappers rely directly on such historical information about a horse to make betting decisions, while others eyeball the animals being saddled or parading to the post. However, the tote odds already reflect the handicappers' varying opinions. Forty years of research confirm that horses whose post time odds predict a 25% probability of winning do win 25%, of the time. There is a tendency for the turf market investors to underbet heavy favorites and significantly overbet longshots.[3]

While the win betting market may be efficient, often the market for place or show is not, giving a profitable opportunity to those who can recognize the inefficiency and take a risk arbitrage position in the turf market.

I am not a gambler. However, I have been known to invest money in events with uncertain outcomes, but only if I can expect to take out somewhat more than I put in. When the efficient win pool indicates a horse is two to one, but the show pool offers me a payoff equivalent to that of three to one, I invest.

The system is based on similar reasoning and much more exactitude.[4] Dr Z developed the nonlinear estimation and optimization routines to calibrate the equations which tell us whether and how much to bet. Dr Z and Donald Hausch wrote a book on the system titled Beat the Racetrack. Originally they used the terms "Hausch Ziemba algorithm" and "H Z method" to describe the system. When I reviewed the draft of the 1981 working paper[5] and suggested Dr Z as a better name for title system and a nom de plume for Bill's non academic writing. Their manuscript now refers to it as the "Dr Z System." Bill wrote a column for Gambling Times on lotteries and horseracing for some time under the Dr Z byline before noticing another sports writer for Sports Illustrated, who I don't think is a real doctor of anything, use the same Dr Z moniker. I guess that's what happens when you choose, such a common name; there are 273 John Smiths or J. Smiths in my local white pages, but not even one Pocahontas. Later Bill told me a lawyer checked and he has the rights to the name.

The system has been tested a number of times at our local racetrack. It's a small track with a. small crowd, in a climate that makes. for an iffy track surface, which offers only two or three system bet opportunities

[3]See the graphs in Ziemba's chapter 19. More graphs are in Ziemba (2019).

[4]The 1984 book Beat the Racetrack, which was revised in 1987 into the book with the title *Dr Z's Beat the Racetrack*, has simulated results from Exhibition Park, Aqueduct and Santa Anita plus calculations on how the Dr Z bets affect the odds, how many can play the system, etc.

[5]This was the paper Bill and Don along with Mark Rubinstein of portfolio insurance infamy published in *Management Science in 1981.*

in a, typical day's. ten race, card. Furthermore, a wager of $200 or so is big enough to influence the odds in the parimutuel betting pool in which the bets of the losers are divided among the winners. We needed better controlled conditions to validate the system. Today Hollywood Park has become our laboratory. The Breeders' Cup is the biggest day, in racing history, offering $10,000,000 in purses for the horse owners. The dirt track is fast' so each horse should run true to form; the purses are huge, so no trainer or jockey will hold back; and another ten million should pass through the betting windows, making the pools big enough in which we will always be small fish whose wagers won't alter the payoff odds.

The tote board flash at one minute to post indicates an acceptable 25%,underlay. Dr Z and I each bet $100 on number 4. Again Ed doesn't say how much he bet. The horses are off to a start of thumping and bumping. Our filly breaks stride early and finishes well back.

I feel my chest drop into my stomach as the race ends. I know you can't win them all; nevertheless, I'd like to. The system delivers cashable tickets only 75% of the time. I sure hope that Lindsay and Foofraw hadn't bet the 22-1 or 75-1 fillies that finished one-two. They hadn't. A loser loves company, even if they are I time losers. Foofraw tells Dr Z that an exacta bet on the longshots would have paid $8,000, ignoring the fact that this race has no exacta betting. Bill and Don developed an exacta variant of the system, which would almost never consider a bet that includes even one such long odds horse, in their 1986 book Betting at the Racetrack, since it would not price out to have an advantage.[6]

28.2.3. *Third Race: The Sprint, six furlongs, for three year olds and up, purse $1,000,000*

En route to the track I picked up Ed Thorp, who lives in a gated community on a Newport Beach hilltop. After passing muster with the gatehouse guard, I drove up to Ed's brand new, old California mansion. He greeted me and offered coffee, pointing to a bigger than a breadbox, brass plated, Italian gizmo, and said he'd be ready to go in five. Ed is about as average looking as a rocket scientist can be pushing fifty, gray shot walnut hair, but all still there, tortoise shell glasses over blue eyes, an inch or so less than six feet, medium build, probably within five pounds of his graduation weight because of the marathons he still runs. I too am within five pounds of my

[6] More on this is in Ziemba (2019).

graduation avoirdupois of 230, but some of it must have migrated South from my chest and shoulders, since my waistline has grown an inch or four. I no longer run the long distances of my high school and college days, which were seldom more than a furlong on a track and forty yards on a football or rugby field. I've also lost half an inch of my six three, which my daughter attributes to my hair having been blown away from driving too fast in my convertible. My counter reminds her that until I had children I had a full head of thick black hair; post hoc ergo propter hoc.

Mug of world class coffee in hand, I roamed the main floor and could understand how there was several million in the place at least 10,000 square feet of house, twelve foot ceilings, Architectural Digest kitchen, a view out to China a, sunken tennis court, indoor outdoor pool. The kind of house fit for one of the greatest hedge fund traders of all time.

As I salivated at the stereo and video components in the den, a face Killroyed over the eight foot oatmeal leather sofa. Once standing, he introduced himself as Ed's son Jeff, and said he was coming to Hollywood Park with us. Jeff was 19 or 20, five ten, with rust brown hair and a few freckles. He wore a dress shirt, a neck tie pulled halfway down, pressed khakis and polished Weejuns.

Ed descended and sent Jeff upstairs to fetch something. When I asked about the curious slot in the kitchen ceiling, Ed said that his wife didn't like to carry packages in from her car. The slot was an industrial conveyor track, leading from the garage, through double hinged doors and into the kitchen. He demonstrated, hanging one of a dozen yellow plastic baskets from a concealed hook and pressed buttons that smoothly carried the basket around the loop. I guess an ex nerd with imagination and money can indulge himself in creative gadgetry, for Ed exuded an inventor's pride in the device. Judging from the house, the gadgets, and the cars, Ed spilled more before breakfast than Dr Z or I earned in a year.

In my Hertz hippopotamus on wheels, I told Ed, "I became a decent skier thanks to you. Your book paid for four winters of skiing at Tahoe." Ed is the math professor who developed the card counting technique for beating blackjack. After the casinos banned him from play he wrote Beat the Dealer, a book describing the technique. I mastered his method, and before the casinos changed their rules for everyone, I could play blackjack for an hour or two before, dinner at a North Shore casino and pick up the $100 or so that would pay for a week end of skiing, at Squaw Valley 15 years ago.[7] While a grad student, I skied 20 days a winter courtesy of Ed Thorp, and now might have a chance to repay him.

I think Ed's accustomed to such occasional acknowledgements, for he just shrugged. He's now into bigger things. After being banned from blackjack, he worked out the techniques for stock warrant hedging, the precursor of options theory, portfolio insurance and methods of valuing various derivative securities. Ed now runs a hedge fund of seven figures from each of a few dozen investors. His fund searches for small discrepancies among the prices of equivalent securities, such as convertibles, warrants, options and the underlying stock, then risk arbitrages that discrepancy.

Ed played navigator, reaching into the satchel at his feet for an inch thick road atlas of the L.A. area, and directed me through the back streets of Inglewood, avoiding the heavy track bound traffic.

As the horses begin the parade to the post for the third, with ten minutes to go, I scan the tote board and see possible place and show system bets on the three horse Ellio. Every minute or so Dr Z keys data from the tote board into his gozinto. The calculator Bill holds in the palm of his hand contains a custom chip on which he programmed the system. It has more computing power than the M.I.T. mainframe Ed used for his original blackjack analysis in 1959. At three minutes to post time I estimate underlays of about 50% to place and 55% to show. Dr Z confirms my approximation and indicates the optimal bet size. He bets $110 to place and $215 to show; I do $100 and $250, because I'm lazy. Ed buys tickets on both, but still isn't saying how much he bet.

Our choice leads wire to wire, with just enough stamina to hold off a late closing 35–1 bay, and wins by a nose.

The average margin of victory in a Class I stakes race is only one length, or 20 feet in a mile and a quarter race, which makes the second best horse 99.7% as fast as the winner. There aren't many second place finishers in business, sports, school, or the arts, who the public perceives to be 99.7% as good as the person who finishes first. The winner is remembered but not the runner up. How many of us can name the world's second best cellist or high jumper?

I go to the window to cash my tickets. Ed just hands his to Jeff. While I'm delighted at the $3.80 place and $2.80 show payoffs on a 6–5 horse, when I return I see Dr Z is unhappy. With both place and show bets on the

[7]in the 1970s.

same horse, the system should adjust the optimal wager amount to reflect the joint probabilities. Bill hadn't had time to complete the additional calculations with only one minute to post. Afterward he computed that the optimal bets should have been $84 to place and $351 to show, which would have netted him another $31.

28.2.4. *Fourth Race: The Mile, one mile on the grass, for three year olds and up, purse $1,000,000*

I scan the crowd through Jeff's field glasses. Inside the glass walled V.I.P. dining pavilion to my right, where neckties definitely are required, I see Cary Grant at a table directly in line with the finishing pole. He's on the Hollywood Park board of directors and deserves a prime table. I focus the 10 × 50s on him and think I'd like to look that good when I get to be his age. Actually, I expect that by the time I get to be Cary Grant's age, I'll have been dead for ten years.

Dr Z hasn't eaten in more than, two hours, probably a daylight personal best. He has only two paces fast and even faster and needs to refuel every hundred ideas or so. Nevertheless, Bill is finicky about his diet and won't ever eat junk food like most of us. Before the tote odds firm up, he canters to the V.I.P. dining pavilion, where he's able to procure a take out order a club sandwich on whole wheat toast, with no butter, no mayo and no bacon for $18.00, plus tax and tip.

Dr Z is a fortyish dervish with curly graying red hair and a beard to match. Even while wearing a suit that a banker might buy, he frequently sports the bright blue tam o'shanter knit by his wife. He's written a dozen books in as many years on everything from stochastic optimization in corporate finance, to Turkish tapestries, the mathematics of lotteries, and now his system for beating the racetrack. Bill flits around the world, often towing his wife and a beardless five year old minature of himself, to give invited talks at universities and conferences before audiences who bob their heads in understanding. Back home, most of his UBC colleagues are of two types the majority, who cannot understand the depth and range of his work, and therefore resent him, and the few who can understand but not match it, and with quiet envy, resent him even more.

A conversation with Dr Z is like taking a drink of water from a fire hydrant. If I could bottle and sell injections of that energy and intellect, I'd have even more money than Ed and a conveyor track system with a spur line to my wine cellar.

Bill once told me that I was probably his best friend, and appeared somewhat miffed when I didn't reciprocate. But throughout life I've had only one very good friend at a time, and in the 14 years since she was naive enough to marry me, my wife has been that friend. Besides, having Dr Z for a friend isn't all that easy. You've got to accept his occasional grating idiosyncrasies with his brilliant insights, as indivisible as a quark. He talks nearly full time at full speed, even more so than I, and frequently while his mouth is filled with one of the six meals a day it takes to fuel his mega metabolism. He changes topics in mid sentence, because even at 200 words a minute his mouth is three lengths behind his mind. Yet he's unnecessarily generous with his coauthors, listing each alphabetically. But I think that Bill Ziemba is hoping to find a new protege named Zollen or Zufiuyden.

Having me for a friend or colleague isn't that easy either. I don't suffer fools gladly. I know a bad idea when I see one, and am outspoken enough to say so, believing that keeping silent does no one a service. My outspokenness extends to carrying on my part of an insulting dialogue with the TV news anchor, shouting expletives about his half truths and omissions at the man in the $50 haircut on Channel Two, who doesn't seem to respond to my compelling debating points.

Back in our box, Dr Z alternately punches tote board data into the gozinto and chomps the portion of his $18.00 sandwich that doesn't slop on his tie. "Elizabeth Taylor is eating lunch over there," he mumbles through the turkey and toast in his teeth, and gestures at the dining pavilion, flinging half a tomato slice on my shoe. I'm skeptical, since Dr Z probably hasn't had the patience to sit through a two hour movie since Liz was on her third husband.

Dr Z and I each handle the tote information differently. I do approximations in my head. He keys in the data about every third flash and gets precise results. The system's algorithm calculates how much to bet, based upon the advantage offered and the bettor's risk capital. He shouts the exact amount to bet, based on a bankroll updated for the day's income or outgo from earlier races, and even the $18.00 club sandwich. Bill gives numbers like $366.47, which means I'll. bet either $350 or $400. Given Ed's bankroll, he ought to bet ten times as much, but, doesn't say. The earlier computer simulations used exact whole dollar amounts, a technical nicety that isn't practical in the real world. Imagine the patience of a typical bettor behind you in the queue should you request exactly 183 $2.00 show tickets with half a minute to post time.

At each flash the tote's been bouncing on either side of the cutoff point for a system bet on number 1, the only filly in the field. I want to make a bet, but only if I have a healthy edge. Remember, fair is for fools.

We move from the box and stand at our key vantage point, as close to the $100 betting window as we can yet still see the tote board. With one minute to post the show bet crosses the 1.10 threshold and Dr Z and I each bet $100. Ed is taciturn as usual, but I see that he keeps a half inch thick stack of $100 bills in the inside left breast pocket of his jacket, fastened shut with a two inch safety pin.

On the backstretch our filly is steadily overtaking horses. She wins the race by more than a length, sets a new American record for a mile on turf, and pays $2.80 to show. A veteran winner now, I eschew walking up to the payoff window and nonchalantly hand my ticket to Jeff to cash.

28.2.5. *Fifth Race: The Distaff, 1 1/4 miles, for fillies and mares, three year olds and up, purse $1,000,000*

I'm getting the bettor's blues. When you lose, you regret losing the money you bet. But when you win, you regret not making a bigger bet. Damon Runyon said that all life was eight to five against. Runyon was optimist.

After returning with our pelf, Jeff goes to find lunch for the two of us, foraging passable corned beef sandwiches, packets of regular and hot mustard, a bag of Fritos and a couple of Pepsis. Ed pulls a container of yogurt from his satchel.

I open my wallet to give Jeff money for the sandwiches. "Ed, look at this," I say, and pull the Thorp card from between my birth certificate and medical insurance card. It's a chart of Ed's high low blackjack counting system. I've carried it in my wallet since 1964, in case I happen to stumble upon a casino, like on a cruise ship, a Caribbean island or Anytown Nevada.

As I said, I don't gamble, and don't go places just to gamble, but I will invest in opportunities with uncertain outcomes, so long as I am in the neighborhood anyway, and most importantly, have advantage. When we go to Palm Springs each winter, I play in a modest stakes poker game that gives me such an edge. Leo Durocher is a semi regular in the game. The winter before last, when I told him that Elston Howard had died earlier in the day, Leo reminisced fondly about the Yankee catcher and said, "Ellie was a winner in a loser's game." "You too, kid," he added "that's how you stay at this table." Since he's twice my age with half my hair, Leo can call me kid; and he's right about how I play. At our level, poker is a loser's game, in which money is lost by those players who make big mistakes, and then divided up among the other players who don't make the mistakes. Conversely, big money poker is a winner's game, in which the money is made by the players who make brilliant decisions and collected from the other players who don't make such plays. The racetrack is a major loser's game, since the house cuts 15% or more off the top. To win at the races you have to identify enough big mistakes by the crowd to offset that track take. The system can do so for those who have the knowledge, patience and discipline.

Ed focuses thoroughly on one major endeavor at a tune, gets seriously rich by practicing it. Dr Z has several projects underway at a time, each getting his best for several hours or days at a time, but few earning him anything but professional accolades. I am merely a dilettante, a dabbler in many things, few in depth or with passion. I like academic research, and keep up with the literature in several fields, but have little interest in doing much myself. My few publications in big league academic journals aren't sufficient for tenure, and my published recipes and satirical columns on business mid economics don't count. Because I'm an omnivorous reader, and the more meaningless the information, the more likely I retain it, I've amassed at least twice the amount of useless knowledge about more subjects than the two of them combined. I ought to make a good Jeopardy! contestant since I can't get anyone to play Trivial Pursuit against me anymore.

An odds on favorite offers the only possible system bet in the fifth. I check each flash of the tote board. In the last five minutes Foofraw has touted four different horses as possible winners in a seven horse field. Should one of them prevail, he'll say, "See, I gave you that winner," or the Brit mumble equivalent. I suspect that Dr Z may be a closet handicapper, because he says he thinks highly of the four year old favorite. Foofraw jumps on the bandwagon and cites dosage index numbers, workout times and the filly's recent races. Ed doesn't care about horse lingo, for he knows that the value of dosage is already imputed in the tote odds. Didactically, he explains to Foofraw that since none of us owns a horse in the race, we cannot win any part of the $1,000,000 purse, only a return on our bets. "Buying a hundred shares of General Motors stock isn't the same as buying a Buick."

With three minutes to post time, the possible system bet on number I still hasn't materialized. We're here to test the system, but without a horse whose odds meet our criterion we won't wager. Dr Z and I check the tote board at each flash, as if our encouragement will cause the numbers to change and give us the opportunity to bet. I can understand a little of how a compulsive gambler must feel, ever eager to place a bet. At one minute to go I guesstimate that the expected payout has across our threshold. Dr Z's computer confirms it. We buy our tickets as the horses are loading at the gate. Ed and I walk down the stairs as the horses break from the gate. Hearing the track announcer calling the race over the P.A., Ed asks, "What's the horse we bet on?"

"What's on second," I respond, on automatic shtick, in a pretty fair Bud Abbott voice. "I think it's Princess something?"

"Bruce, I only hope she has four legs."

Princess Rooney, all four legs intact, romps to win by half a dozen lengths. She pays a disappointing $2.20, which is why this odds on favorite was nevertheless only borderline as a system bet. Foofraw and Lindsay hold an exacta, wheel with her and each of the other six entrants. So they win their exacta but the bet actually loses money doing so, spending $30.00 for each six ticket wheel on which they'll collect only $28.00.

28.2.6. *Sixth Race: The Turf, 1 1/2 miles on the grass, for three year olds and up, purse 1,000,000*

The Turf attracts several European horses. Foofraw is holding forth beside us, rating the imports against the locals, although all are American bred. He and the newspaper guy are serious handicappers. They pore over past performance charts in the Daily Racing Form, and talk speed ratings and bloodlines. Foofraw mumbles overmuch. Were a Henry Higgins present, I'd offer two to one he'd pronounce Foofraw a non U fraud.

Lindsay and Foofraw favor the low probability, high payoff exotic bets. Foofraw calls ours, "ladies' bets," saying that wagering on a favorite to show for a $2.60 payoff, isn't really wagering at all. Except for the pyhrric exacta in the fifth, those two haven't cashed a ticket yet, while after each race Jeff returns and deals out $100 bills to Ed, Dr Z and me like it was a card game. It takes a lot more real testosterone to maintain the self discipline to bet our way than his. I don't mind if Foofraw insults my manhood; keep those hundreds coming.

The starting gate is now at the head of the grass turf course. There are eleven horses in the field, but only All Along, the crowd's second choice at 7–2, is a decent Dr Z system bet. She's a 30% underlay.

In addition to keying data into the computer, Dr Z also scrawls information about the win, place and show pools at five, three and one minutes before post time. A month earlier I'd hypothesized that a late drop in the win pool odds might be so called smart money, a predictor that a horse would win. If true, the anomaly would violate our assumptions of an efficient turf market, yet provide us new higher payoff betting opportunities. He was collecting information to test my conjecture. Dr Z isn't really sure the, stock market is efficient either, citing anomalies. Ed, knows it isn't, and has made his fortune arbitraging many small inefficiencies.

The zoom lens on Jeff's camera can't shoot the tote board in a single frame. Ed says we could capture the data quite easily by mounting a camera with a 20mm wide angle lens and motor winder, focussing on the tote board and snapping the shutter every minute. I one up him suggesting a video camera cabled to a digitizer which would not only capture the image but also convert it to numerical data and directly input it to the computer. Ed tops me with a scheme to transmit the computer's betting instructions by radio signal to one of us at the $100 window. That's not too fanciful, for five years ago a group of Ed's fans in Silicon Valley constructed a toe operated computer built into a sneaker and programmed to at roulette.[8]

Ed has never been to Hollywood Park before, and I'm not sure he's even been to any racetrack in twenty years. He's here to see the system in action, in the real world, in real time, with real money. When Bill first explained the reasoning behind the system and the basis of the complex optimization calculations, Ed took all of five minutes to concur, probably performing the pages of calculus equations in his head as Dr Z spouted them. Ed's experience in the financial markets has made him question any theory's applicability in practice. He's seen what happens to the bid ask spread when he tries to take a big position in a stock. He thinks that in a paramutuel betting system, the payoff offered when we make a decision won't be the same as when we go to cash our tickets if we get cash them at all. Ed also doesn't care for the idea of putting money on humans or animals, because there's too much random error in a one performance of one jockey on one horse in one race. Furthermore, he's discomfited knowing the turf market offers only ten races a day, and a top horse will typically run in a

[8]Ed Thorp wrote a column about this in Gambling Times. A power function is estimated based on what numbers cross the start and the time of one revolution. One then forecasts where the ball might land. This leads to the winning system.

dozen races a year for two or three years. A small number of investment opportunities, high transaction costs and a fat tailed distribution are an anathema to a man who makes hundreds of individual trades a day in the Wall Street and Chicago financial markets. The few thousand dollars he'll bet today are merely to test whether Dr Z system is valid in practice.[9]

Hearing I too would be in Los Angeles that weekend, Dr Z invited me to join the expedition. The box he'd borrowed had empty seats and, since I was in the neighborhood anyway, why not. When I was Jeff's age, my uncle entered one of his horses in the Kentucky Derby. Since then I've enjoyed horseracing, but in moderation. At home my trips to the track with Dr Z are purely for research purposes, although on a sunny afternoon we'll each bring a daughter along to enjoy the event and to log a twofer of betting and father bonding. Once or twice a year I go to the track with friends for dinner, and as long as I'm there and I have an advantage, I'll make a few system bets to pay for the wine, and sometimes for the dinner too.

Dr Z is here for all of it. He wants to validate his system on horseracing's biggest day in history. He also wants Ed Thorp to watch him do it, in real time for real money. But Bill really does like horses and racing. He's trying to get a release to use a picture of himself with Secretariat on the dust jacket of Beat the Racetrack, the book he and Don Hausch have in press. If he makes any money on the securities market anomalies project he is beginning, I think he'd like to squander it on owning a racehorse. I do believe Dr Z is a closet handicapper.

The field breaks cleanly from the gate and. Willy Shoemaker rides his roan out to an early lead along the rail. The field is tightly bunched as they cross the patch of dirt track and back onto the grass. On the backstretch All Along steadily gains on the leaders and pulls into the lead before the stretch run. She's nipped by a neck and finishes second to a 50–1 longshot. Since a 12–1 horse finishes third, this should be a big pavoff on our system bet. At $4.40 to show, it's huge. Hooray for Hollywood Park!

28.2.7. *Seventh Race: The Classic, 1 1/4 miles, for three year olds and up, purse $3,000,000*

This is a tough race for most other bettors to get excited about. The standout, a son of Seattle Slew, should go off odds on. While the payoff will likely be modest, there'll almost certainly be a system bet available, because the

[9]Which he confirmed in the preface to Beat the Racetrack.

crowd does agree with Foofraw. Back at the office on Monday, there will be no bragging rights in telling how you cashed a $2.20 ticket, so the crowd won't wager heavily on the favorite in the place or show pools.

Super favorites often provide outstanding returns if you bet them with enough conviction. While the system is new and quantitatively sophisticated, some people had been doing the no brainer equivalent for years. There's a likely apocryphal bettor in Kentucky called the Bridge Jumper. Whenever offered a one to five or shorter odds on favorite, the Jumper would bet $20,000 to show, buying several different tickets so he needn't fill out IRS forms when he cashes them in separately. While California requires a payout of $2.10 on a $2.00 bet, the Kentucky minimum is $2.20. At one to five, assuming an efficient turf market and independent sub races, the probability of the favorite finishing out of the money is only one-half of one per cent but the track has to pay off as if it were nine per cent, a huge underlay. Looming above is the one half of one per cent risk he's a Joe Bltsftk that day, and the $20K goes kaput; hence the bridge.

If you owned a thousand inch color TV, it would be the Diamond Vision screen in Hollywood Park's infield that displays close ups and replays of each race. Following each winning system bet, I watch the Diamond Vision replay of the finish line through Jeff's field glasses and zoom in on the efficient market equine benefactor who favored us by running true to form.

Dr Z returns from fetching another $18.00 plus club sandwich, without mentioning anyone famous. There are system bet possibilities for both place and show on Slew O'Gold. Dr Z likes the horse as well as the tote, citing data from the Daily Racing Form. I Groucho my eyebrows and flick an imaginary cigar, letting him know my doubts about his piety toward the system.

The 30% underlay is enough for me to make both bets three minutes before post time. Returning to the box I see the tote board flash a big change. In the last minute someone has bet another $50,000 to win, making the respective place and show underlays 40% and 50%. Dr Z punches in the new numbers. The optimization genie in the gozinto still says our $250 place bets are in line, but the show bets should have been $927, not the $500 we'd each bet. I push Jeff aside,mount the stairs in threes and sprint toward the $100 window. I shout to the clerk from 20 feet, $100 Show, Number One, four times." Midway through my plea, the bell rings. I'm shut out at the window.

Even though the race action isn't supposed to matter, I thrill in watching this outstanding finish. The horses bump and shove on the long Hollywood

Park stretch run. Three horses are in contention. Slew O'Gold with Angel Cordero, Jr., up is getting sandwiched between number 2, Wild Again, on the rail and number 5, Gate Dancer with his muffed ear covers, veering in from the outside. The horses finish 2, 5 and 1, no more than an armspan separating first from third,, some five lengths ahead of the also rans. Wild Again won at 30-1. He was supplemented at considerable cost by his owners and the win was one of the starting points for the career of the great jockey Pat Day.

The inquiry sign, on the tote board lights, indicating either the stewards' or a jockey's claim, of foul. Dr Z keys in the final betting pool data, and tells us his last pre race estimates were within three per cent of the algorithm's optimum bet. Right now I don't care about the algorithm. Will the race result hold up? Will the stewards, take down Slew O'Gold? As the horses finished, we lose our place bets, and don't make enough on the show bets to offset that loss, but if I'd gotten the additional $400 down, it would have. However if the stewards completely disqualify Slew O'Gold my loss will be that much greater. I ruminate on all the woulda coulda shoulda combinations. The stewards take four or five minutes, which is geological time for the tenterhooked ticket holders of the maybe in the money horses. The Diamond Vision screen replays the stretch run at full speed, then in slow motion. The inquiry light turns off and the tote displays the official results. The finish order is now 2, 1 and 5; the stewards took Gate Dancer down. Our place and show system bets both pay off, at $3.00 and $2.20.

Dr Z too likes to invest in other uncertain situations, so long has he has an advantage, and we have a few followers who will join us when we spot one. A year ago we each independently found a one shot., one day lottery opportunity which offered an expected payout of $2.38 for each $1.00 ticket. We rounded up the usual suspects from the department. The six of us each descended on a different local retailer at 7:00 am on a Friday, politely asked to commandeer the lottery terminal, and then spent the morning hours making it spit out 1,000 or 2,000 tickets. All day Sunday we sorted through grocery bags led with lottery tickets gleaning our winners, and collected our predicted payoff.

While my confidence in Dr Z is high, it's less than perfect. He sometimes needs my reality-checking skepticism. Last winter Bill calculated a way to regularly play the lottery that had a payback with an expected value of almost $11,00 for each $1.00 ticket bought. We have each consulted for government lotteries, he on the mathematics of game design and I on marketing and strategy, so once we discussed the logic behind it, I trusted his estimate. Our departmental syndicate bought 100 tickets on each lotto draw. When after five months we were so far behind, I asked Dr Z to recheck his calculation of the expectation, and also to look at the higher moments of the probability distribution. The next day we lunched at the Faculty Club, and when he treated me to a Heineken, I knew there was bad news coming. Yes, at 10.7267 the long run expected payout was as he'd previously calculated. Since such a huge chunk of the lottery prize pool goes to a winner who hits all six numbers of the 6/49, a 13.9 million to one shot, it might take some time to achieve that expected value. Even if we bought 1,000 tickets a week, it would be more than 15 years before we could be 90% certain of being ahead of buying government bonds instead. John Maynard Keynes said, "In the long run, we're all dead."

28.2.8. *Eighth Race: Fleet Nasrullah Stakes, six furlongs, for two year olds, purse $60,000 added*

Much of the crowd was leaving. Cary Grant's table was empty. Elizabeth Taylor had left, if she'd even been there. The seven Breeders' Cup races were at the start of the day to reach East coast TV audiences, so Hollywood Park slated two more races to fill out the program. The tote board isn't leaving with Cary and the illusory Liz, even though only about one third as much is being bet on this race as on the Classic. None of the entrants are important to Dr Z and Ed still doesn't care to know the horses' names., There are five contenders and two long shots, in the seven horse field. The tote has been pretty steady, offering a show bet on only the fourth favorite, number 3. We make the bet.

Naturally, who was the catcher on Bud Abbotts baseball team, our pick Teddy Naturally, leads the field throughout and wins by nearly ten lengths, to pay $3.40 to show. While Ed still isn't talking about how much he's bet, I see his other inside. breast pocket now holds a second stack of hundreds as thick as the first, without a protective safety pin.

28.2.9. *Ninth Race: Seabiscuit Claiming Stakes, 1 1/2 miles on the grass, for three year olds and up, purse $100,000 added*

Even though this is a claimer, with claiming prices of $500,000 and $1,000,000, there are no ringers in the race.

An early scan of the tote board gives me possible place and show bets on the favorite, number 10. Five minutes before post time I make the underlays

35% to place and 50% to show. Maybe he's another double dipper? Bill's tracking the tote on his gozinto. As the horses are milling before the starting gate, we walk up to bet both to place and to show. I'm approaching the window, when Dr Z shouts to me to come back. Starting at the vantage point, he tells me the system bet to place has disappeared, and the optimum show bet is $219. I put the extra bills back in my pocket and bet $200 to show. This is the day's final race, so Dr Z bets exactly $219.

Our horse starts from the outside post position, runs at the back of the pack for the first half of the race, and then begins to chip away at the field to finish second by a length. He pays $3.00 to show, and $4.00 to place, had we made the place bet.

We cash the last tickets on our way to the parking lot. Dr Z is going North. Ed, Jeff and I are headed South. Ed and his street atlas route us through a new set of one way Inglewood alleys, getting us to the freeway at least two times faster than by driving the rhumb line.

Two days later, before going to the airport, I stopped in to be tested for Jeopardy! and got a passing grade. When the contestant coordinator said they received a late cancellation for the next day's taping, I postponed my flight and stayed over. I postponed it again each of the following days. Just to show that there are some payoffs for being a dilettante, I became an undefeated five-day champion. For me it was that once in a lifetime experience, winning a year's salary ($43,398) on a TV game show. Assuming he had a typical ho hum time at the office, Ed made more money those few days than I.

Bruce Fauman August, 1995

28.3. Postscript by Ziemba

My bankroll was $1500 and the track payback at Hollywood Park was 0.8467. I used my calculator and a 1.10 cutoff with the proviso that for bets with expected values above 1.02 (pretty well the breakeven point) but below 1.10 I would bet $100 for the fun of it, if I liked the horse.

The last race of the day often has a Dr Z system bet, since by then most bettors are looking for a good way to get even, not for a favorite to show. Lady's Secret was such a bet on November 9 and the pools evolved as follows:

With three minutes to go the pools were

	Totals	#8 Lady's Secret	Expected Value Per Dollar Bet	Optimal Kelly Bet
Odds	2-1			
Win	93,141	25,816		
Place	26,987	5,214	1.15	104
Show	11,842	1,571	1.37	118
With two minutes to go				
Odds	2-1			
Win	100,043	27,436		
Place	29,216	5,526	1.16	110
Show	12,587	1,845	1.29	99
With one minute to go				
Odds	9-5			
Win	137,631	39,482		
Place	38,322	9,557	0.99	0
Show	17,644	3,250	1.17	129

The place bet completely fizzled in the last minute. A reminder not to bet too early! I bet the $129 to show. On November 9, Lady's Secret won the race and paid $3.00 to show so I made $64.50 profit. My final bankroll was $1939.50 for a profit on the day of $439.50.

At post time the toteboard was

Odds	9–5			
Win	140,271	40,533		
Place	39,764	10,388	0.97	0
Show	18,699	3,983	1.10	54

The Breeders' Cup was conceived by John Gaines of Gainesway farm on the Paris Pike near Lexington, Kentucky. Its purpose is to promote racing at the highest level both through bonus additions to purses at various race tracks across North America and through a major culmination day of racing. Breeders' Cup Day features seven races of which five have purses of $1 million and the others have purses of $2 and $3 million. The day is meant to bring together a tremendous collection of the top horses. With a four hour TV special it's like a World Series of racing. The Breeders' Cup program is paid for by stallion season donations. For a horse to be eligible for Breeders' Cup races, the owner of the horse's sire must donate the equivalent of one breeding season that year, be it worth $500,000 or $1,000. Thus to have a chance to collect the large purses and fame, breeders have to donate. It's a brilliant idea for breeding and racing and so far it has been quite successful. In 1984 the purses were $1 million for each of the first races with the $1\frac{1}{2}$ mile grass race for $2 million and $3 million for the classic in 1984 a total of $10 million. In 2011 there are now 15 races over two days with the classic at $5 million and some $2 and $1 million purses.

The inaugural Breeders' Cup Day was held on November 10, 1984 at Hollywood Park. Ed Thorp and Bruce Fauman joined me. I pocketed my earlier winnings and again started with a bankroll of $1500. Again I would bet $100 on horses with expected values above 1.02 but below 1.10 and use 1.10 as my cutoff for Dr. Z system bets. The first race was the Breeders' Cup Juvenile and featured the top two year old colts and geldings running over a mile. The favorite was Chief's Crown. Near post time the toteboard was as follows:

	Totals	#5 Chief's Crown	Expected Value Per Dollar Bet	Optimal Kelly Bet
Odds	3–5			
Win	382,370	188,217		
Place	200,081	88,147	0.97	0
Show	127,999	51,579	1.04	0

I bet $100 to show on Chief's Crown. He won the race and paid $2.40 so I made $20 profit and my bankroll was $1520.

The third race was the Breeders' Cup sprint over six furlongs. The feeling was that Eillo would dominate if he did not break down. This son of Mr. Prospector had bandages on all four legs and ran in a very dangerous style. He was a Dr Z system bet both to place and show.

With three minutes to go

	Totals	#5 Eillo	Expected Value Per Dollar Bet	Optimal Kelly Bet
Odds		6–5		
Win	310,679	114,405		
Place	123,682	30,439	1.19	263
Show	87,548	20,666	1.18	413

With one minute to go

	Totals	#5 Eillo	Expected Value Per Dollar Bet	Optimal Kelly Bet
Odds		7–5		
Win	415,309	146,279		
Place	162,447	40,278	1.14	223
Show	113,462	25,230	1.18	423

The optimal bets of \$223 to place and \$423 to show were each based on making only one bet. Since both wagers were Dr Z system bets.it would be too risky and overbetting to make both these wagers at these levels. There are formulas in Ziemba and Hausch (1987) that allow you to compute the optimal full Kelly bets which were \$351 to show and \$84 to place.[10] However, I did not have time to make these calculations, keep track of the mutuel pools for the Ziemba and Hausch (1986) book and still make the bet. So as a conservative approximation I simply halved the suggested wagers and bet \$110 to place and \$215 to show.

Eillo won the race leading wire to wire just nipping the charging Commemorate at the finish. He paid \$4.60 to win, an excellent \$3.80 to place and a respectable \$2.80 to show. I made \$99 on my place bet and \$86 on my show bet for a profit of \$185 on the race. My bankroll was now \$1605. The final tote board was as follows:

	Totals	#5 Eillo	Expected Value Per Dollar Bet	Optimal Kelly Bets (both Wagers)
Odds		6–5		
Win	457,470	163,868		
Place	180,253	46,216	1.13	215 $\to$ 48
Show	125,282	27,584	1.19	460 $\to$ 388

The final Breeders' Cup race was for a purse of \$3 million. The classic was for three year olds and upwards over 1 1/4 miles. The choice was Slew O'Gold. A win here would probably have sewed up horse of the year honors over John Henry. Slew O'Gold was part of an entry with Mugatea. With one minute to go the toteboard was:

[10]The place bet is minimum $(p^*, 1.59p^*-0.639s^*)$ = minimum $[223, 1.59(223) - 0.639(423)]$ = minimum $(223, 84.20)$ = \$84.20. Here $p^* = 223$ and $s^* = 423$. The show bet is $0.907s^* - 0.134p^* = 0.907(423) - 0.134(223)$ = \$351. So the optimal bets at one minute to post were \$84 to place and \$351 to show.

	Totals	#1,1a Slew O'Gold and Mugatea	Expected Value Per Dollar Bet	Optimal Kelly Bet
Odds	3–5			
Win	716,354	367,710		
Place	255,600	99,846	1.19	613 → 367
Show	128,746	50,090	1.19	951 → 780

Clearly it was time to load up! The edge for place and show is good but the safety of a 3–5 place horse and even more so a 3–5 show horse plus having an entry leads to a very big Kelly bet. With the huge pools you do not influence the odds much at all. Betting for place by itself indicated a bet of \$613 and for show \$951. When you consider the effect of both bets using the formulas, the optimal bets become \$367 for place and \$780 for show. These are gigantic bets with my fortune of \$1785; but recall that is a Kelly property when the chance of losing is small. I bet \$250 to place and \$500 to show — roughly the 1/2, 1/2 idea I used before.

The race was a classic with Wild Again at the rail, Gate Dancer charging on the outside and Slew O'Gold sandwiched in the middle with Angel Cordero Jr. attempting to bring him in. There was a tremendous amount of bumping among these three horses. In the end Wild Again won the race followed by Gate Dancer and Slew O'Gold. Fortunately for us the stewards took Gate Dancer down and awarded Slew O'Gold second place. Mugatea finished last. Slew O'Gold paid \$3.00 to place and only \$2.20 to show (breakage cut deeply into this payoff.) I made \$125 on my place bet and \$50 on my show bet so my bankroll was now \$1960. The final toteboard and chart were as follows: so the Dr Z bets on Slew O'Gold to place and show were even better at post time than when I bet.

	Totals	#1,1a Slew O'Gold and Mugatea	Expected Value Per Dollar Bet	Optimal Optimal Kelly Bet
Odds	3–5			
Win	809,920	423,222		
Place	269,107	102,480	1.24	694 → 386
Show	151,289	52,467	1.30	1135 → 957

The eighth race was the Fleet Nasrullah Stakes, a \$60,000 added event. A bit of a comedown after the Breeders' Cup races but still a high class race. The feature and late races are prime candidates for Dr Z system bets. Late in the day most bettors are behind and do not want to consider low paying bets to place or show. These races also feature excellent horses. The 9th race ws the Seabiscuit Claiming stakes, at $500,000 and up, this was no ordinary claiming race. I bet $35 on Teddy Naturally who won the 8th race (for a profit of $29.50) and I bet $219 to show on Late Act in the 9th. Late Act finished second and paid $3.00. My profit was $109.50. That gave me a final bankroll of $2094 for a nice profit of $594 on the day.

My colleagues Ed Thorp and Bruce Fauman did well also. Ed was betting heavier than I was, using a $10,000 initial fortune that led to bets in the range $500–750. He made $1851 on the day. He did not feel that he needed to look at the Daily Racing Form or a program. This made a great impression on the handicappers in the next box. Here a talented student of betting was able to win big without knowing much about the horses while they, the experts on handicapping, were having a rough go of it. The odds board told the story. Bruce who made bets similar to mine made a tidy $345.

We all had a fun time at the Breeders' Cup and it was very profitable. Except for the mishap on Bessarabian, we had excellent luck that helped us. On average Dr Z system bets win about 60% of the time. The bets with expected values between 1.02 and 1.09 on favorites have similar outcomes. However, these bets will not on average have payoffs as good as the Dr Z system bets. To gain our edge of 10–20% we will have our ups and downs, winning and losing streaks. However, if played properly, the Dr Z system should provide you with an upward drift in your bankroll at a rate of about 10% of the value of your wagers. I wound up losing $143 the day after Breeders' Cup.

28.4. Off Track and Other Track Betting

In the past few years the racing industry has experimented with ways to increase the attendance and wagering at tracks. Certainly the growth of state lotteries has been one of the pressures on the tracks to cater more and more to the wishes of the public. One approach has been the continued increase in the use of exotic wagering, a form of wagering that is very popular with the public, even when a higher track take is imposed. A second approach has been the Breeders' Cup Races. The publicity surrounding these races and the four hours of national television coverage have certainly attracted new bettors to racing.

A third approach, and the focus here, has been to add to the locations where bettors can wager. Examples of these are from home with phone betting, and from Nevada casino and betting parlors in several states with off-track betting. The Dr Z pricing systems cannot be used with the phone betting unless you have access to the public's odds. The intertrack and off-track betting can however, offer overlays of the type studied in this book. Their special circumstances, though, can mean that slight variations of the system as presented are needed to best determine when and how much to wager. These variations are described here.

Off-track Betting Bettors have long been able to wager in OTB (off-track betting) shops in New York. The advantage they offer to New York bettors is, of course, ease — rather than make the long trip to the track, they just step into the OTB and then go on with their day. There are disadvantages, though. First, on-track bettors have access to more information. New OTB facilities provide good simulcasts and betting pool information, but this difficulty is not eliminated. Second, an additional 5% surcharge is taken off OTB winnings. Although I feel that the serious bettor should bet at the track as winning is difficult enough without adding the OTB's disadvantages, it is becoming much more common, and some off-track betting facilities offer better conditions than New York's OTB.[11] Connecticut has long had off-track betting, an example of which will be considered below. Illinois also has OTB. Each Illinois track is allowed two OTB parlors, at sites of their choosing. The first two facilities have been built in Peoria and Rockford. Plans for at least one parlor in Chicago are complicated by the OTB bill's restriction that any registered voter within 500 feet of the proposed site can veto the plan. Louisiana also has OTB parlors.

28.4.1. *Teletrack in New Haven, Connecticut*

The Teletrack facility in New Haven, Connecticut, near Yale University, takes wagers on thoroughbred races run at Aqueduct, Belmont, and Saratoga, and harness races from Roosevelt and Yonkers. Prior to each race, the Teletrack public's betting is displayed on a screen, and as the race is run, it is televised live. The Teletrack's odds are established independent of the track's odds, but they do include the bets from a number of off-track betting shops in Connecticut.

The Dr Z system can be directly employed with no variations in this setting. As an example consider the seventh race at Aqueduct on November 12, 1981, a day when I was at Teletrack, having given a racing investment

[11]Professional syndicate betting, of course, is different with computers and TV screens in an office atmosphere. See Chapter 19 and Ziemba (2019) for a discussion on this.

talk at Yale. The morning-line favorite was Come Rain or Shine, ridden by Angel Cordero, Jr. The pools, as usual, were quite small, but the Cordero mount was a good Dr Z bet throughout the betting period. At two minutes till the end of betting, the pools were:

#3		
Totals	Come Rain or Shine	
Odds	5–2	
Win	10,463	2,313
Show	837	115

The expected value was 1.14, but the susceptibility of small pools to dramatic changes, even in the last minute of betting, led me to make a cautious wager of $20. With the final bets, including mine, the expected return had dropped to 1.12. Come Rain or Shine did win with the following final mutuels and payoffs at Teletrack:

Totals	Come Rain or Shine	
Odds	3–1	
Win	12,032	2,471
Show	1,312	174

3	8.00	3.80	3.40
2	3.20	2.60	
4	3.40		

The $20 bet produced a profit of $14. The payoffs at Aqueduct, which follow, were very different than Teletrack's payoffs. Notice that Come Rain or Shine was not a Dr Z bet on-track. In fact he only paid $2.40 to show compared to the $3.40 at Teletrack.

3	6.20	3.00	2.40
	2	2.80	2.20
		4	5.80

Nevada Sports Books in Las Vegas, Nevada

The wife of David Cross, trainer of Sunny's Halo, won $20,000 on a $200 bet when Sunny's Halo won the 1983 Kentucky Derby. How did she get 100–1 odds when his odds were 5–2 at Churchill Downs? She had made the wager several months before the Derby in the Las Vegas winter book. With 405 nominations for the race and several months to worry about Sunny's Halo's fitness, these were perhaps reasonable odds. These Las Vegas future books are quite common on the classic races and the Breeder's Cup races. A very knowledgeable handicapper or a good student of pedigrees can probably find bargains in the future book odds but the takes tend to be quite high so one must be careful.

While the Dr Z system does not have much to say about future odds betting, it can point to overlays in another form of betting on Nevada Sports books — namely bets on races that are piped into the casinos as they are being run at a track elsewhere in the country. If the on-track pools are flashed onto the casino screens, as they sometimes are, then you can do the Dr Z place and show calculations just as you would if you were on-track. There's even an advantage to betting in the sports book — your wagers do not influence the odds. This means your optimal bets are even greater than those indicated in Figures 24–29 and 33–38 in Chapter 11 in Ziemba and Hausch (1986) because these figures have taken into account your effect on the odds in parimutuel betting.

As an illustration of the Dr Z system in this setting, we use a race that was run at Golden Gate Fields on April 27, 1986 and simulcast at Caesar's Palace. Is She Coming had been first or second in her first three races of 1986 and was now the consensus bets bet of the day. At post time the mutuels were:

	#1 Is She Coming		
Totals		Expected Value Per Dollar Bet	Optimal Kelly Bet
Odds	4–5		
Win	49,313	21,820	
Place	35,350	10,740	1.16
Show	14,450	4,482	1.12

If one chooses to determine amounts to wager using the graphs in Ziemba and Hausch (1986), there are two complications: one's bets do not effect the odds and, with a cutoff of 1.10, there are Dr Z bets both to place and to show. My recommendation throughout this book has been if there is uncertainty or if the situation is less than ideal, then bet less. This recommendation suggests an easy solution to the first complication: Just use Figures 25 and 29. These figures deal with large place and show pools and, therefore, they recommend wagers for situations where our bets have only a minor influence on the odds. Our bets actually have no effect on the odds so the recommended wagers from these figures will actually be a little low. They will be close, though, and conservative at worst.

Returning to our example, assume a bankroll of \$500. Now q1 = W1/W = 21820/49313 = 0.44. Then, from Figure 24, the recommended place wager is about $90. The multiple wager complication must be solved. The recommended wagers from these figures suppose that one and only one wager will be made. So with two or more bets, betting the recommended amounts would likely be overbetting and quite risky. One method that accounts for this double betting on one horse is given in Ziemba and Hausch (1986, footnote 6). It leads to suggested bets of $34 to place and $142 to show. As is apparent from the footnote, though, the necessary calculations for this method can take time — something lacking in the last two minutes of the betting period. Therefore, one must have this method programmed into a calculator or another simple method must be used. The former, if possible, is certainly the better alternative but an ad hoc simple method might be to just halve the wagers from those given in the figures. Then, rather than betting $90 to place and $170 to show, more appropriate bets would be $45 to place and $85 to show.

It the $34 place bet and the $142 show bet had been made, then the return would have been $228.80 for a profit of $52.80 when Is She Coming finished first and paid $3.80 to win, $2.60 to place and $2.60 to show.

Intertrack Betting: Ferdinand's victory in the 1986 Kentucky Derby was worth $37.40 to those Churchill Downs' bettors who backed him to win. However, there were 56 sites other than Churchill Downs where a Kentucky Derby wager was possible: the OTBs in both New York and Connecticut, and 54 tracks across the US and Canada. These sites operated pools separate from Churchill Downs' pools and, therefore, a variety of odds on a horse was possible. In fact, the odds varied considerably. For example, Ferdinand paid as low as $13.20 at Fairplex and $16.80 at Hollywood to as high as $90.00 at Evangeline Downs and $79.60 at Woodbine. At Churchill Downs, $6,165,119 was wagered on the Derby. The other sites wagered $19,776,332 for a grand total of $25,941,451. Each track's incentives for offering betting on the Derby and for providing a simulcast were, of course, the revenue from the betting and its carry over effects on attendance and betting on other races at the site that day. The incentive for Churchill Downs was a fee (about 5% of the handle) from each site.

Intertrack betting is available on more than just a few major races like the Triple Crown events. There are many tracks that now simulcast another track's whole season of racing. This allows a track to have its racing season, and then, rather than close down for several months, it can pipe in races and continue to accept wagers. For instance, Bay Meadows in San Mateo, California had its races simulcast to county fairs and Golden Gate Fields (25 miles away) and then, after its racing season ends, it received simulcasts from other local tracks such as Golden Gates (until it closed down to have the site developed into other uses), and Santa Anita. The negative effect on the on-track (the track where the decline in attendance due to the other sites taking some of its spectators. On the positive side, though, it receives a portion of each site's handle and it can more than make up the lost spectators when it received other tracks' simulcasts later. Intertrack arrangements have each site operating a common pool. This is the same as with off-track betting.

Intertrack wagering also exists among many of the tracks in Southern California. There, a restriction against simulcasting within a 45 mile radius of existing tracks means that Santa Anita and Hollywood cannot simulcast the other's race and, therefore, neither will lose many on-track bettors. Maryland's Racing Commission has approved intertrack wagering between Pimlico and Laurel Race Courses. Nebraska has intertrack arrangements among Ak-Sar-Ben, Fonner Park, and Lincoln Park, and Louisiana Downs accepts simulcasts from Fair Grounds. Illinois also has intertrack wagering among its tracks. The Kentucky Derby example and arrangements between New York and other stakes indicate that the wagering need not be just within a state, either.

As far as betting in an intertrack setting, one must be able to view the wagering pools, have an eye on the simulcast (shown on either on infield screen or on television screens throughout the track) to learn when the end-of-betting will occur, and know the track take being offered. With this information, the Dr Z system can be applied exactly as presented in earlier chapters.

The Belmont Stakes is the third and final jewel in the Triple Crown. In 1982, for the first time, betting on both the Preakness and the Belmont Stakes was allowed at several other tracks, including two California tracks — Golden Gate Fields in Albany, and Los Alamitos Race Course. Each of these tracks had separate betting pools and betting closed just before the actual race at the home track. The race was then viewed on closed-circuit television or on the infield screen if there was one. With separate betting pools, all the tracks paid different amounts to win, place, and show for the horses in the money. The idea of other-track betting is gaining popularity, and in the future we will probably see more and more such races.

The Belmont field included the highly touted Linkage, as well as the Kentucky Derby and Preakness winners, Gato Del Sol and Aloma's Ruler. These three horses were all ridden by their regular jockeys, Bill Shoemaker,

Eddie Delahoussaye, and Jack Kaenel, respectively. The other leading contender was Conquistador Cielo, who had impressive Eastern wins but was running on only four days' rest. His regular jockey, Eddie Maple, was unable to ride because of an injury and had been replaced by Laffit Pincay, Jr. Delahoussaye, Pincay, and Shoemaker flew in from California to ride the race. It is common for top jockeys such as these to fly across the country to ride in an important race. They usually return immediately to their home track so they miss only one day's races there.

The final tote board betting amounts at Golden Gate were

	#1	#2	#3	#4	#5	#6
Odds	4–1	80–1	60–1	9–1	30–1	10–1
Win	28,027	1,717	2,371	13,755	4,234	13,303
Place	9,311	721	1,040	6,851	2,529	7,185
Show	5,034	703	962 2,931	1,729	3,356	

	#7	#8	#9	#10	#11	Totals
Odds	8–5	20–1	40–1	8–1	7–2	
Win	56,629	5,917	3,565	15,759	30,301	175,578
Place	24,353	2,598	2,035	6,512	8,653	71,788
Show	11,491	1,639	1,339	3,051	3,658	35,893

A quick scan of the tote board pointed to a possible show bet on #11, Conquistador Cielo. The expected return on a dollar bet to show was 1.24. For different wealth levels, the optimal bets were

Wealth Level	100	500	1,000	2,500	5,000	10,000
Optimal Bet	5	25	38	76	99	145

Conquistador Cielo won the race by an impressive 14 lengths, breaking the track record at Belmont for 1.5 miles on an off track. He was followed by Gato Del Sol and Illuminate, who finished third.

The mutuel payoffs at Golden Gate were as follows:

11	9.80	6.80	5.60
	1	6.60	4.60
		8	10.20

Compare these mutuel payoffs with those in the chart of the race at Belmont:

Los Alamitos Race Course also had other track betting on the Belmont Stakes. Their final tote board figures and payoffs help show the large differences in the public opinions in different locations.

At Los Alamitos they were as follows:

	#1	#2	#3	#4	#5	#6
Odds	5–2	99–1	99–1	11–1	40–1	8–1
Win	10,877	217	342	3,350	955	4,565
Place	4,340	116	140	1,701	438	2,507
Show	1,725	108	103	702	323	1,493

	#7	#8	#9	#10	#11	Totals
Odds	1–1	40–1	99–1	12–1	6–1	
Win	19,388	862	394	3,197	5,428	49,575
Place	7,238	263	221	1,362	1,986	20,312
Show	3,222	234	194	653	877	9,634

11	15.40	7.40	6.00
1	4.40	4.00	
8	17.20		

There was no Dr Z system bet at Los Alamitos.

Bibliography

Abdellaoui, M. (2000). Parameter-free elicitation of utility and probability weighting functions. *Management Science 46*(11), 1497–1512.

Abdellaoui, M., H. Bleichrodt, and C. Paraschiv (2007). Loss aversion under prospect theory: A parameter-free measurement. *Management Science 53*(10), 1659–1674.

Albert, J. (2012). Hitting with runners in scoring position. *Chance 15*(4), 8–16.

Allais, M. (1953). Le comportement de l'homme rationnel devant le risque: critique des postulats et axiomes de l'école Américaine. *Econometrica 21*(4), 503–546.

Allais, M. and O. Hagen (1979). *Expected Utility Hypotheses and the Allias Paradox.* Dordrecht, Holland: Reidel.

Arrow, K. J. (1965). The theory of risk aversion. In Y. J. Saatio (Ed.), *Aspects of the Theory of Risk Bearing.* Helsinki. Reprinted in: *Essays in the Theory of Risk Bearing*, Markham Publ. Co., Chicago, 1971, pp. 90–109.

Assamoi, K. V. (2010). Optimal investment strategies with Kelly capital growth criterion. Thesis: M.Sc in Mathematical Finance, Christ Church, University of Oxford.

Bacon-Shone, J. and A. Woods (2008). Modeling money bet on horse races in Hong Kong. In D. B. Hausch and W. T. Ziemba (Eds.), *Handbook of Sports and Lottery Markets*, pp. 17–25, North Holland.

Baltussen, G., T. Post, and P. van Vliet (2006). Violations of cumulative prospect theory in mixed gambles with moderate probabilities. *Management Science 52*(8), 1288–1290.

Barra, A. (2003). *Clearing the Bases: The Greatest Baseball Debates of the Last Century.* MacMillan Press, New York, NY.

Benoit, A. (2017). SI's MMQB top 400 NFL players. *Sports Illustrated* (September 4).

Benter, W. (1994). Computer based horse race handicapping. In D. B. Hausch, V. Lo, and W. T. Ziemba (Eds.), *Efficiency of Racetrack Betting Markets*, pp. 173–182, Academic Press, San Diego, CA.

Berri, D. J. (1999). Who is "most valuable"? Measuring the player's production of wins in the National Basketball Association. *Managerial and decision economics 20*, 411–427.

Beyer, A. (2019). The kentucky derby decision was a bad one. Washington Post, May 11.

Bolton, R. N. and R. G. Chapman (1986). Searching for positive returns at the track: a multinomial logit for handicapping horse races. *Management Science 32*, 1040–1–59.

Bordley, R. and C. Kirkwood (2004). Preference analysis with multiattribute performance targets. *Operations Research 52*, 823–835.

Bordley, R. and M. LiCalzi (2000). Decision analysis using targets instead of utility functions. *Decisions in Economics and Finance 23*(1), 53–74.

Bornn, L., D. Cervone, A. Franks, and M. A. (2017). Studying basketball through the lens of player tracking data. In J. Albert, M. E. Glickman, T. B. Swartz, and R. H. Koning (Eds.), *Handbook of Statistical Methods and Analyses in Sports*. Chapman and Hall, London, U.K.

Bradley, R. and M. Terry (1952). Rank analysis of incomplete block designs: I. The method of paired comparisons. *Biometrika 39*(3/4), 324–345.

Buhlmann, H. and P. J. Huber (1963). Pairwise comparison and ranking in tournaments. *Annals of Mathematical Statistics 34*(2), 501–510.

Burke, B. (2008). Expected Points. Advanced Football Analytics http://archive.advancedfootballanalytics.com/2008/08/expected-points.html.

Byrne, K. (2011). Qbr: Espn's deeply flawed made-for-tv stat. *Cold Hard Football Facts*, Football Nation LLC.

Cameron, R. R. (2018). Determinants of thoroughbred racehorse stud fees. PhD Honors Economics Thesis, Emory University. Unpublished thesis.

Carroll, B., P. Palmer, and J. Thorn (1988). *The Hidden Game of Football*. Warner Books.

Carter, V. and R. E. Machol (1970). Operations research on football. Technical report, Northwestern University.

Carter, V. and R. E. Machol (1978). Optimal strategies in football. *Management Science 24*(6), 1758–1762.

Castagnoli, E. and M. LiCalzi (1996). Expected utility without utility. *Theory and Decision 41*, 281–301.

Chapman, R. G. (1994). Still searching for positive returns at the track: Empirical results from 2000 Hong Kong races. In D. B. Hausch, V. Lo, and W. T. Ziemba (Eds.), *Efficiency of Racetrack Betting Markets*, pp. 173–181. Academic Press, San Diego, CA.

Chopra, V. K. and W. T. Ziemba (1993). The effect of errors in mean, variance and co-variance estimates on optimal portfolio choice. *Journal of Portfolio Management 19*, 6–11.

Cover, T. M. and C. W. Keilers (1977). An offensive earned-run average for baseball. *Operations Research 25*(5), 729–740.

Cox, L. A. (2008). What's wrong with risk matrices? *Risk Analysis 28*(2), 497–512.

Deshpande, S. K. and S. T. Jensen (2016). Estimating an NBA player's impact on his team's chances of winning. *Journal of Quantitative Analysis in Sports 12*, 2–51.

DiFilippo, M., K. Krieger, J. Davis, and A. Fodor (2014). Early season NFL over/under bias. *Journal of Sports Economics 15*(2), 201–211.

Edelman, D. C. and N. R. O'Brian (2004). Tote arbitrage and lock opportunities in racetrack betting. *European Journal of Finance 10*, 370–378.

Ellsberg, D. (1961). Risk, ambiguity, and the Savage axioms. *Quarterly Journal of Economic 75*(4), 643–669.

Elo, A. (1986). *The Rating of Chess Players, Past and Present.* Arco Pub, New York, NY.

Elo, A. E. (2008). *Logistic Probability as a Rating Basis: The Rating of Chess-players, Past & Present.* ISHI Press International.

Epstein, L. and S. E. Zin (1989). Substitution, risk aversion and the temporal behavior of consumption and asset returns: A theoretical framework. *Econometrica 57*(4), 937–969.

Ericsson, K. A. (1996). The acquisition of expert performance: An introduction to some of the issues. In K. A. Ericsson (Ed.), *The Road to Excellence: The Acquisition of Expert Performance in the Arts and Sciences, Sports, and Games.* Lawrence Erlbaum Associates, Inc., New Jersey, NJ.

Fama, E. F. (1965a). The behavior of stock market prices. *Journal of Business 64*, 34–105.

Fama, E. F. (1965b). Random walks in stock market prices. *Financial Analysts Journal 21*(5), 55–59.

Fama, E. F. and K. R. French (1992). The cross-section of expected stock returns. *The Journal of Finance 47*(2), 427–465.

Ferrari, V. (2009). Possession is everything. http://vhockey.blogspot.com/2009/05/possession-is-everything.html.

Fini, M. (2017). *Sassicaia: The Original Super Tuscan.* Te Neves Press, Germany.

Fishburn, F. (1969). A general theory of subjective probabilities and expected utilities. *Annuals of Mathematical Statistics 40*(4), 1419–1429.

Franks, A., A. Miller, L. Bornn, K. Goldsberry, *et al.* (2015). Characterizing the spatial structure of defensive skill in professional basketball. *Annals of Applied Statistics 9*, 94–121.

Friedman, M. and L. J. Savage (1948). Utility analysis of choices involving risk. *Journal of Political Economy 56*(4), 279–304.

Gehrke, G. Division rankings: My final eclipse awards ballot. Horse Racing Nation, January 1.

Gergaud, O. and W. T. Ziemba (2012). Great investors: Their methods, results and evaluation. *Journal of Portfolio Management 28*(4), 128–147.

Gramacy, R., S. Jensen, and M. Taddy (2013). Estimating player contribution in hockey with regularized logistic regression. *JQAS 9*(1), 97–111.

Gramm, M. and W. T. Ziemba (2008). The dosage breeding theory for horse racing predictions. In D. B. Hausch and W. T. Ziemba (Eds.), *Handbook of Sports and Lottery Markets*, pp. 307–340, North Holland, Amsterdam.

Hanoch, G. and H. Levy (1969). The efficiency analysis of choices involving risk. *Review of Economic Studies 36*, 335–346.

Hardegree, G. M. (2014). Base-advance average. Retrosheet.org.

Hausch, D. B., R. Bain, and W. T. Ziemba (2006). An application of expert information to win betting on the Kentucky Derby, 1981–2001. *European Journal of Finance 12*(4), 283–302.

Hausch, D. B., V. Lo, and W. T. Ziemba (Eds.) (1994). *Efficiency of Racetrack Betting Markets.* Academic Press, San Diego, CA.

Hausch, D. B., V. Lo, and W. T. Ziemba (Eds.) (2008). *Efficiency of Racetrack Betting Markets* (2 ed.), World Scientific, Singapore.

Hausch, D. B. and W. T. Ziemba (1985). Transactons costs, extent of inefficiencies, entries and multiple wagers in a racetrack betting model. *Management Science 31*, 381–394.

Hausch, D. B. and W. T. Ziemba (1990). Locks in racetrack minus pools. *Interfaces* (May–June), 41–48.

Hausch, D. B. and W. T. Ziemba (Eds.) (2008). *Handbook of Sports and Lottery Markets.* North Holland, Amsterdam.

Hausch, D. B., W. T. Ziemba, and M. E. Rubinstein (1981). Efficiency of the market for racetrack betting. *Management Science XXVII*, 1435–1452.

Jackson, D. and P. Waldron (2003). Parimutuel place betting in Great Britain and Ireland. In L. V. Williams (Ed.), *The Economics of Gambling*, Cambridge Unviersity Press, Cambridge, pp. 18–29.

James, B. (1994). *The Bill James Player Ratings Book 1994.* Collier Books, New Jersey, NJ.

Janacek, K. (1999). Optimal growth in gambling and investing. Thesis: Charles University, Prague.

Kahneman, D. and A. Tversky (1979). Prospect theory: an analysis of decisions under risk. *Econometrica 47*(2), 263–92.

Kahneman, D. and A. Tversky (1984). Choices, values, and frames. *American Psychologist 39*(4), 314–350.

Kelly, Jr., J. R. (1956). A new interpretation of the information rate. *Bell System Technical Journal 35*, 917–926.

Lane, D. and W. T. Ziemba (2004). Arbitrage and risk arbitrage in team Jai Alai. *European Journal of Finance*, 353–369.

Lane, D. and W. T. Ziemba (2008). Arbitrage and risk arbitrage in team jai alai. In D. Hausch and W. T. Ziemba (Eds.), *Handbook of Sports and Lottery Markets*, pp. 253–271, North Holland, Amsterdam.

Levy, H. (1973). Stochastic dominance, efficiency criteria, and efficient portfolios: The multi-period case. *American Economic Review 63*(5), 986–994.

Levy, H. (2001). *Stochastic Dominance: Investment Decision Making under Uncertainty.* Springer.

Levy, M. and H. Levy (2002). Prospect theory: Much ado about nothing. *Management Science 48*(10), 1334–1349.

Levy, M. and H. Levy (2004). Prospect theory and mean–variance analysis. *Review of Financial Studies 17*(4), 1015–1041.

Lewis, M. (2003). *Moneyball: The Art Of Winning An Unfair Game Paperback.* Norton, New York, NY.

Likens, J. (2011). Shots, Fenwick and Corsi. http://objectivenhl.blogspot.com/2011/02/shots-fenwick-and-corsi.html.

Lock, D. and D. Nettleton (2014). Using random forests to estimate win probability before each play of an NFL game. *Journal of quantitative analysis in sports 10*(2), 197–205.

Lorenz, M. (2005). Methods for measuring the concentration of wealth. *Journal of the American Statistical Assoc 44*(9), 209–219.

MacLean, L. and W. Ziemba (2015). A primer on stochastic dominance. *Wilmott* (79), 18–21.

MacLean, L. C. and W. T. Ziemba (2013). The Kelly criterion with games of chance. In L. Vaughn-Williams and D. S. Siegal (Eds.), *Oxford Handbook of Economics of Gambling.* Oxford University Press, Oxford, UK.

MacLean, L. C., W. T. Ziemba, and G. Blazenko (1992). Growth versus security in dynamic investment analysis. *Management Science, Special Issue on Financial Modelling 38*(November), 1562–1585.

MacLean, L. C., E. O. Thorp, Y. Zhao, and W. T. Ziemba (2011). How does the fortune's formula-Kelly capital growth model perform? *Journal of Portfolio Management 37*(4), 96–111.

MacLean, L. C., E. O. Thorp, and W. T. Ziemba (2010). Long term capital growth: The good and bad properties of the Kelly and fractional Kelly capital growth criterion. *Quantitative Finance*, 681–687.

MacLean, L. C., E. O. Thorp, and W. T. Ziemba (2011a). Good and bad Kelly properties. In L. C. MacLean, E. O. Thorp, and W. T. Ziemba (Eds.), *The Kelly Capital Growth Investment Criterion.* World Scientific, Singapore.

MacLean, L. C., E. O. Thorp, and W. T. Ziemba (Eds.) (2011b). *The Kelly Capital Growth Investment Criterion.* World Scientific, Singapore.

MacLean, L. C., Y. Zhao, and W. T. Ziemba (2011). Growth-security models and stochastic dominance. In G. Infanger (Ed.), *Stochastic Programming: the State of the Art in Honor of George B. Dantzig*, pp. 213–258, Springer, Berlin.

MacLean, L. C. and W. Ziemba (2010). The Kelly strategy. Encyclopedia of Quantitative Finance, B. Cont (ed), 5 pages. John Wiley & sons, New York, NY.

MacLean, L. C. and W. T. Ziemba (2018). Player ranking and team performance in american football. *Wilmott.*

MacLean, L. and B. Ziemba (2020). Team composition: are the best players on the best teams? *Wilmott 107*, 34–41.

MacLean, L. C., W. T. Ziemba, and Y. Li (2005). Time to wealth goals in capital accumulation and the optimal trade-off of growth versus security. *Quantitative Finance 5*(4), 343–357.

Malarranha, J., B. Figueira, N. Leite, and J. Sampaio (2013). Dynamic modeling of performance in basketball. *International Journal of Performance Analysis in Sport 13*, 377–387.

Meinert, C. L. (1980). Terminology — a plea for standardization. *Control clin Trials 1*, 97–99.

Melnick, M. J. (2001). Relationship between team assists and win-loss record in the national basketball association. *Perceptual and Motor Skills 92*, 595–602.

Miller, S. (2007). A derivation of the pythagorean win-loss formula in baseball. *Chance 20*, 40–48.

Morris, B. (2015). Kickers are Forever. FiveThirtyEight, https://fivethirtyeight.com/features/kickers-are-forever/.

Myers, D. About box plus/minus (BPM). https://www.basketball-reference.com/about/bpm2.html.

Negahban, S., S. Oh, and D. Shah (2012). Iterative ranking from pair-wise comparisons, *NIPS*.

Page, G. L., G. W. Fellingham, and C. S. Reese (2007). Using box-scores to determine a position's contribution to winning basketball games. *Journal of Quantitative Analysis in Sports 3*, 1–16.

Paine, N. (2015). NFL Elo ratings are back. FiveThirtyEight, September 10.

Paulick Report Staff (2019). An outrageous state of affairs: West's plan to appeal dismissal of Maximum Security Kentucky Derby lawsuit. November 18.

Petersen, A., O. Penner, and H. Stanley (2011). Methods for detrending success metrics to account for inflationary and deflationary factors. *European Physical Journal B 79*(67–78).

Piette, J., L. Pham, and S. Anand (2011). Evaluating basketball player performance via statistical network modeling. MIT Sloan Sports Anal. Conf.

Pratt, J. W. (1964). Risk aversion in the small and in the large. *Econometrica 32*, 122–136.

Quinn, K. (2012). Field position and strategy in american football, In L. H. Kahane and S. Shmanske (Eds.), *The Oxford Handbook of Sports Economics: The Economics of Sports Volume 1.* Oxford University Press, Oxford, UK.

Rabin, M. (2000). Risk aversion and expected utility theory: A calibration theorem. *Econometrica 68*(5), 1281–1292.

Retrosheet. www.retrosheet.org.

Rohrbach, B. (2021). Giannis anteteokounmpo's signature performance secures NBA title for Milwaukee Bucks. Yahoo Sports, July 20.

Roman, S. A. (2016). Pedigree and performance in thoroughbred racing. Report on website: saroman7.winsite.com/dosage.

Roman, S. A. (2019). Private communication.

Rosenbaum, D. (2004). Measuring how NBA players help their teams win. http://www.82games.com/comm30.htm.

Rothschild, M. and J. Stiglitz (1970). Increasing risk: 1. A definition. *Journal of Economic Theory 3*(2), 225–243.

Ryan, R. (2019). Mandella: Omaha Beach now has a choice of two races next. Horse racing nation. November 18.

Sampaio, J., E. J. Drinkwater, and N. M. Leite (2010). Effects of season period, team quality, and playing time on basketball players'. *European Journal of Sport Science 10*, 141–149.

Savage, L. J. (1954). *The Foundations of Statistics.* John Wiley & Sons, Inc., 294 pp.

Schuckers, M. (2010). *Computational Methods in Biometric Authentication: Statistical Methods for Performance Evaluation.* Springer, Berlin.

Shaw, J., E. O. Thorp, and W. T. Ziemba (1995). Convergence to efficiency of the Nikkei put warrant market of 1989-90. *Applied Mathematical Finance 2*, 243–271.

Silver, N. (2015). Introducing NFL Elo ratings. FiveThirtyEight, September 4.

Simpson, E. (1951). The interpretation of interaction in contingency tables. *Journal of the Royal Statistical Society: Series B 13*(238–241).

Skinner, B. and S. J. Guy (2015). A method for using player tracking data in basketball to learn player skills and predict team performance. *PloS one 10:e0136393*.

Snowberg, E. and J. Wolfers (2008). Examining explanations of a market anomaly: Preferences or perceptions? In D. B. Hausch and W. T. Ziemba (Eds.), *Handbook of Sports and Lottery Markets*, pp. 103–136, North Holland, Amsterdam.

Sports Reference. Stathead.com.

Stern, H. (1991). On the probability of winning a football game. *The American Statistican 45*(3), 179–183.

Stutzer, M. (1998). *Mimeo on Investment Strategies.* University of Colorado.

Swann, C., R. Keegan, L. Crust, and D. Piggott (2016). Psychological states underlying excellent performance in professional golfers: "Letting it happen" vs "making it happen". *Psychology of Sport and Exercise 23*, 101–113.

Terner, Z. and A. Franks (2021). Modeling player and team performance in basketball. *Annual Review of Statistics and Its Application 8*, 1–23.

Tesio, F. (1947). *Tesio in His Own Words.* English translation by Mary Burnet in 2005 published by Russell Merdink Co., Ltd. of the Italian Puro Sangue Animale de Esperimento.

Tesio, F. (1958). *Breeding the Racehorse.* J. A. Allen & Co., Ltd., London, UK.

Thaler, R. H. and W. T. Ziemba (1988). Anomalies: Parimutuel betting markets: racetracks and lotteries. *Journal of Economic Perspectives 2*, 161–174.

Thomas, A. C., S. L. Ventura, S. Jensen, and S. Ma (2012). Competing process hazard function models for player ratings in ice hockey. Tech. rep., ArXiv:1208.0799.

Thorp, E. O. (1962). *Beat the Dealer.* Random House, New York, NY.

Thorp, E. O. (2006). The Kelly criterion in blackjack, sports betting and the stock market. In S. A. Zenios and W. T. Ziemba (Eds.), *Handbook of Asset and Liability Management, Volume 1*, pp. 387–428., North Holland, Amsterdam.

Tompkins, R., W. T. Ziemba, and S. Hodges (2008). The favorite-longshot bias in the S&P500 and FTSE100 index futures options: The return to bets and the cost of insurance. In D. B. Hausch and W. T. Ziemba (Eds.), *Handbook of Sports and Lottery Markets*, pp. 161–180, North Holland, Amsterdam.

Tversky, A. and D. Kahneman (1974). Judgment under uncertainty: Heuristics and biases. *Science 185*(4157), 1124–1131.

Vollman, R. (2010). Ten ways to measure defensive contributions. *Hockey Prospectus* (March 4), San Francisco, CA.

Von Neumann, J. and O. Morgenstern (1944). *Theory of Games and Economic Behavior.* Princeton University Press, Princeton, NJ.

Wakker, P. (2002). The data of Levy and Levy (2002) "Prospect Theory: Much ado about nothing?" Actually support prospect theory. *Management Science 49*(7), 979–981.

Walker, J., J. L. Risen, T. Gilovich, and R. H. Thaler (2018). Force overtime? or go for the win? *Journal of Personality and Social Psychology 115*(3), 363–378.

Willett, P. (1986). *Makers of the Modern Thoroughbred.* University Press of Kentucky, Lexington, KY.

Williams, A. M. and P. Ward (2007). Anticipation and decision making: Exploring new horizons. In G. Tenenbaum and R. Eklund (Eds.), *Handbook of sport psychology* (3rd ed.), pp. 203–223, Wiley, New Jersey, NJ.

Winston, W. L. (2009). *Mathletics: How Gamblers, Managers, and Sports Enthusiasts Use Mathematics in Baseball, Basketball, and Football.* Princeton University Press, Princeton, NJ.

Wu, G. and A. Markle (2008). An empirical test of gain-loss separability in prospect theory. *Management Science 54*(7), 1322–1335.

Ziegler, A. and W. T. Ziemba (2014). Returns from investing in S&P500 futures options, 1985-2010. In A. G. Malliaris and W. T. Ziemba (Eds.), *Handbook of Futures*, pp. 643–688., World Scientific, Singapore.

Ziemba, R. E. S. and W. T. Ziemba (2013). *Investing in the Modern Age.* World Scientific, Singapore.

Ziemba, W. T. (2003). *The Stochastic Programming Approach to Asset Liability and Wealth Management.* AIMR, Charlottesville, VA.

Ziemba, W. T. (2005). The symmetric downside-risk sharpe ratio and the evaluation of great investors and speculators. *Journal of Portfolio Management* (Fall): 108–122.

Ziemba, W. T. (2008). Efficiency of racetrack, sports and lottery betting markets? In D. B. Hausch and W. T. Ziemba (Eds.), *Handbook of Sports and Lottery Markets*, pp. 183–222. North Holland, Amsterdam.

Ziemba, W. T. (2010). A tale of five investors: Response to Paul A. Samuelson letters. Working Paper, University of Oxford, New York.

Ziemba, W. T. (2011). Place and show. *Wilmott Magazine* (November), pp. 32–42.

Ziemba, W. T. (2012). *Calendar Anomalies and Arbitrage.* World Scientific, Singapore.

Ziemba, W. T. (Ed.) (2016a). *Great Investment Ideas.* World Scientific, Singapore.

Ziemba, W. T. (2016b). Understanding and using the Kelly capital growth. *Alternative Investment Analyst Review*, 44–55.

Ziemba, W. T. (2017a). *Adventures of a Renaissance Academic in Investing and Gambling.* World Scientific, Singapore.

Ziemba, W. T. (2017b). The road to super bowl 51. *Wilmott*, London, UK.

Ziemba, W. T. (2018). Arbitrage and risk arbitrage in the Nikkei put warrant market. *Wilmott* (May), 42–46, London, UK.

Ziemba, W. T. (2019). *Exotic Betting at the Racetrack.* World Scientific, Singapore.

Ziemba, W. T. (2021). Parimutuel betting markets: racetracks and lotteries revisited. London School of Economics Discussion Paper.

Ziemba, W. T., S. L. Brumelle, A. Gautier, and S. L. Schwartz (1986). *Dr. Z's 6/49 Lotto Guidebook.* Dr. Z Investments, Los Angeles, June.

Ziemba, W. T. and D. B. Hausch (1984). *Beat the Racetrack.* Harcourt, Brace and Jovanovich, San Diego, CA.

Ziemba, W. T. and D. B. Hausch (1986). *Betting at the Racetrack.* Dr Z Investments, San Luis Obispo, CA.

Ziemba, W. T. and D. B. Hausch (1987). *Dr Z's Beat the Racetrack.* William Morrow, New York, NY.

Ziemba, W. T. and L. C. MacLean (2011). Using the Kelly criterion for investment. In M. Bertocchi, G. Consigli, and M. Dempster (Eds.), *Stochastic Optimization Methods in Finance and Energy,* pp. 3–20., Springer, New York, NY.

Ziemba, W. T. and L. C. MacLean (2018). *DR Z's NFL Guidebook.* World Scientific, Singapore.

Ziemba, W. T. and R. G. Vickson (Eds.) (1975). *Stochastic Optimization Models in Finance.* Academic Press, New York, NY.

Ziemba, W. T. and R. G. Vickson (Eds.) (2006). *Stochastic Optimization Models in Finance* (2 ed.). World Scientific, Singapore.

Author Index

Subject Index

C

D

www.ingramcontent.com/pod-product-compliance
Lightning Source LLC
Chambersburg PA
CBHW071352300426
44114CB00016B/2037